The Past Speaks

The Past Speaks

SECOND EDITION

Sources and Problems in British History

VOLUME II: SINCE 1688

Introduced and edited by

Walter L. Arnstein
University of Illinois, Urbana-Champaign

D. C. HEATH AND COMPANY
Lexington, Massachusetts   Toronto

Address editorial correspondence to:
D. C. Heath and Company
125 Spring Street
Lexington, MA 02173

Acquisitions Editor: James Miller

Developmental Editor: Laurie Johnson

Production Editor: Bryan Woodhouse

Designer: Judith Miller

Photo Researchers: Nancy Hale and Mary Stuart Lang

Production Coordinator: Mike O'Dea

Permissions Editor: Margaret Roll

International Standard Book Number: 0–669–24602–6

Library of Congress Catalog Number: 92–73312

10   9   8   7   6

To Peter and Pam

Preface

According to the Book of Ecclesiastes, "Of making many books there is no end; and much study is a weariness of the flesh." The second maxim has been echoed by many a college student. The first may seem an appropriate caution against the publication of yet another "book of readings." Yet if few books of any type may justly lay claim to uniqueness, this anthology, to the best of my knowledge, remains—after a dozen years in print—at least different from every other book of readings devoted to the past three centuries of British history.

Designed for courses in British history, *The Past Speaks* consists solely of primary-source materials organized under thematic headings. As most college teachers are aware, students are not necessarily fascinated by original documents.* Initially, it is the teacher who wishes the student to go beyond the textbook and to taste at least some of the raw historical evidence that is transformed into the carefully prepared, suitably seasoned, multicourse textbook meal. A selection of such documents compels students to work toward generalizations on their own or, at the very least, to test the generalizations in their textbooks.

Experience has shown that students are more likely to be attracted to a document if it is presented not as one of a series of snippets, whose significance is explained in an introductory paragraph, but rather as a piece of a historical jigsaw puzzle. *The Past Speaks* presents us with nineteen such puzzles, and each document helps fill out a portion of the picture.

The author of each document is identified; the chronological and topical context of the document is made clear; and obscure allusions within the document are also explained. No attempt has been made, however, to tell the student where the significance of any given document lies. Instead, questions about each document are raised—important questions but not necessarily the only ones that may be asked. Each chapter, therefore, both invites and deserves classroom discussion.

No collection of historical problems—whether there be nineteen or a hundred—can claim to exhaust the subject. To that degree the selection of topics is necessarily arbitrary, but an attempt has been made at least to touch upon every significant facet of British history since 1688: preindustrial and postindustrial society; the impact of revolutions—"Glorious," American, and French; the status of women; the role of religion;

---

*In some of the selections, the spelling, punctuation, and capitalization have been modernized to make the documents more intelligible to the twentieth-century reader.

democratization; Ireland; imperialism; Britain's connection with the two world wars of the twentieth century; the foundations and evolution of the welfare state; the implications of the "permissive society."

Any one of the topics included might have been dealt with more fully, and often has been treated in greater detail, in one of D. C. Heath's excellent *Problems in European History* series. *The Past Speaks*, however, offers the student, in relatively economical fashion, the opportunity to sample in abbreviated form almost a score of such topics in a single volume.

A volume of documents provides an opportunity for the student to encounter in a more immediate fashion than even the best textbook makes possible the notion that history's "losers" may have had a case worth discussing—whether they were King George III defying the American revolutionaries, Robert Lowe objecting to the advance of political democracy, Joseph Chamberlain espousing the glories of the British Empire, or Eliza Lynn Linton condemning "The Girl of the Period." History truly acquires meaning for many students only when they find it possible to become "present-minded" about the past—indeed, only when they can comprehend that for persons long dead, the future may have seemed as uncertain and the possible alternatives as numerous as the clouded prospects that lie before us in the 1990s.

Finally, college students in our day are not likely to encounter a profusion of courses in Western Civilization. Paradoxically, for many of them a survey of British history may constitute their sole detailed introduction to what was once looked upon as the "Western heritage." For that reason, a deliberate effort has been made to include excerpts from the ideas of some of the giants of the past three centuries. John Locke, Samuel Johnson, Adam Smith, Edmund Burke, Thomas Paine, Thomas Malthus, John Stuart Mill, Thomas Henry Huxley, George Bernard Shaw, and Winston Churchill are all represented in sufficient length to enable students to sample not merely their ideas but also the style and the tone in which those ideas are expressed. In some cases students may even be tempted to utilize the library in order to taste the entire work—or to enroll in another history course during the next semester.

The preparation of this second edition has enabled me to drop some selections and to shorten others. It has also provided me with the opportunity to add new selections by Oliver Goldsmith, John Cartwright, Mary Wollstonecraft, Hannah More, Siegfried Sassoon, William Beveridge, Edward Heath, Neil Kinnock, and Margaret Thatcher, among others. The chapter on the foundations of the welfare state has been subdivided so that one chapter focuses on the pre–World War I period and another on the era of the interwar Great Depression and the challenges of both communism and fascism. The chapters dealing with the post-1945 years have been rearranged so that the first deals with the decline of empire and the lure of the European Community and the second with domestic concerns of the 1960s and 1970s. The third, on the "Thatcher Revolution" of the 1980s, is necessarily brand new.

I have been assisted in the process of revision by a number of reviewers (some of whom remain anonymous to me). Although I have not accepted all their advice, I remain grateful for their suggestions, particularly those of Professor Roger Adelson of Arizona State University. In preparing this edition I have necessarily been guided also by my own experience, now three-and-a-half decades long, in leading classroom discussions and in learning from my students.

W.L.A.

Contents

CHAPTER 17   From Worldwide Empire to European
Community: Necessity or Choice?   379

CHAPTER 18   British Socialism in the 1960s and 1970s:
The Road to Prosperity
or to Stagnation?   401

The Past Speaks

1

The "Glorious Revolution": A Change of Monarchs or a New Political World?

The English Revolution of 1688–1689 has been minimized by some historians as no more than a *coup d'état*, a "palace revolution" involving the substitution of King William III for King James II while confirming the ability of a small elite of land-holding oligarchs to rule British society for the next century or more. Other historians have seen the Revolution of 1688–1689 as the "Glorious Revolution," less dramatic and less bloody than the English Civil War of the 1640s or the French Revolution of 1789 or the Russian Revolution of 1917, but ultimately at least as important because the changes it brought into being endured. It established in Britain a constitutional monarchy in which Parliament had a permanent role to play in the government, in which members of Parliament served as the monarch's ministers, and in which the judiciary was independent of the executive and the legislative branches. Significant rights were assured to all subjects no matter what their social rank (such as freedom from arbitrary arrest, the right to jury trial, the right of petition, and, to a large degree, freedom of speech, press, assembly, and religion) though not necessarily, for the time being, the right to participate in the election of members of the House of Commons. For John Locke the revolution also served as an example of a change of government based on reason and the ultimate right of revolution.

Documents written at the time of an event or a series of events provide an immediate insight into the feelings of contemporary observers and participants. Necessarily they tell us less about the long-range impact of such events. The first document reveals how a diary-keeping contemporary, John Evelyn (1620–1706), saw events as they were happening. He was an interested spectator rather than a participant, though he had held minor government office during the reign of King Charles II (1660–1685). He was also a country gentleman who was an expert on gardens and a founder of the Royal Society. Evelyn is best remembered, however, as the keeper of a diary that began in 1640 and ended only in the year of his death. The diary was first published over a hundred years later (in 1818), but it has been republished on numerous occasions since then because Evelyn was an observant "primary source." What events does

King William III at the Battle of the Boyne (Ireland) in 1690, Where His Forces Defeated Those of King James II

Evelyn suggest were central to the revolution? How ought one to describe Evelyn's own attitude toward the supplanting of King James II by King William III?—delighted? disapproving? reluctantly acceptant?

The second selection provides character sketches of both James II and William III by a Scotsman, Gilbert Burnet (1643–1715), who knew both men personally. It was William rather than James, it is true, whom Burnet advised in Holland during the 1680s and by whom Burnet was appointed Bishop of Salisbury in 1689. In addition to his posthumous *History of My Own Time,* Burnet is remembered for his three-volume *History of the Reformation* (1679–1714). What does he see as the virtues and limitations of each monarch? What do these character sketches reveal about Burnet's own religious beliefs?

The next three selections shed light on different ways in which contemporaries sought to place the events of 1688–1689 in a wider historical, legal, and religious context. The author of *Observations Upon the Late Revolution in England* (1690) is an anonymous Jacobite, an upholder of the claims of James II and his male descendants to the English throne. The author of *A Discourse of God's Ways of Disposing Kingdoms* is William Lloyd (1627–1717), the bishop of St. Asaph, and one of the famous Seven Bishops who refused in May 1688 to read from their pulpits James II's Declaration of Indulgence. John Evelyn describes the event and the bishops' subsequent trial in his diary. The author of the *Second Treatise of Government* (1689) is John Locke (1632–1704), a member of the entourage of the first earl of Shaftesbury, leader of the ultimately unsuccessful movement in the Parliaments of 1679–1681 to bar James II from inheriting the throne. The debates of those years gave rise to a rivalry between Whig and Tory parties, and Shaftesbury was the leader and, in a sense, the founder of the Whigs. In time Locke came to be far better known than his patron, both as a political philosopher and as the author of treatises on religious toleration and human psychology. Locke's two *Treatises on Civil Government* helped make him the philosophical father of modern Anglo-American liberalism. Which of the three authors is most concerned with statute law, which with the workings of Divine Providence, and which with the underlying justification for all human government? On what rather different bases do these authors both explain and either condemn or justify the events of 1688–1689?

"An oral contract," said Hollywood movie mogul Samuel Goldwyn, "is not worth the paper it's written on." No more, might one add, is a written constitution or its equivalent if it does not serve as a description of at least some of the realities as well as the ideals of a society. The Bill of Rights, the sixth selection of this chapter, remains a foundation stone of the "English Constitution" to this day. Is it primarily concerned with the rights and privileges of Members of Parliament, or with all inhabitants of the kingdom, or is it concerned with both? On which rights does the document lay particular stress?

Although King James II proved ultimately unable to recover the throne from which he had been toppled in 1689, the Act of Settlement of 1701, an act passed by Parliament and approved by King William III, reminds us that for a number of years the Revolution of 1688–1689 seemed in grave danger of becoming unsettled. The Act of Settlement was designed to preserve the changes that had been set into motion since 1688. What events made such an Act of Settlement necessary? What light does the act throw on the reign of William III and on the prospect of the Hanoverian succession? In what ways had the powers of the monarchy been limited by the Bill of Rights and the Act of Settlement?

The final document of the chapter, an anonymous poem, reminds us that not all early eighteenth-century Britons were either ideological fanatics or political philosophers. Some, like the fictional "Vicar of Bray," simply adapted to changing circumstances. What kind of adaptation to each of five successive monarchs seems to have been necessary?

JOHN EVELYN **Diary of a Revolution (1688–1689)**

John Evelyn observes a revolution in progress.

[May 1688] 18th. The king[1] enjoining the ministers to read his declaration for giving liberty of conscience (as it was styled) in all the churches of England, this evening, six

SOURCE: From William Bray, ed., *The Diary and Correspondence of John Evelyn*, F.R.S. (London, 1850), Vol. II, pp. 273–293.

[1]*The king:* James II

bishops, Bath and Wells, Peterborough, Ely, Chichester, St. Asaph, and Bristol, in the name of all the rest of the bishops, came to his Majesty to petition him, that he would not impose the reading of it to the several congregations within their dioceses; not that they were averse to the publishing it for want of due tenderness toward dissenters, in relation to whom they should be willing to come to such a temper as should be thought fit, when that matter might be considered and settled in Parliament and Convocation; but that, the declaration being founded on such a dispensing power as might at pleasure set aside all laws ecclesiastical and civil, it appeared to them illegal, as it had done to the Parliament in 1661 and 1672, and that it was a point of such consequence, that they could not so far make themselves parties to it, as the reading of it in church in time of Divine Service amounted to.

The king was so far incensed at this address, that he with threatening expressions commanded them to obey him in reading it at their perils, and so dismissed them. . . .

25th. All the discourse now was about the bishops refusing to read the injunction for the abolition of the Test, etc. It seems the injunction came so crudely from the secretary's office, that it was neither sealed nor signed in form, nor had any lawyer been consulted, so as the bishops, who took all imaginable advice, put the court to great difficulties how to proceed against them. Great were the consults, and a proclamation was expected all this day; but nothing was done. The action of the bishops was universally applauded, and reconciled many adverse parties, Papists only excepted, who were now exceedingly perplexed, and violent courses were every moment expected. Report was, that the Protestant secular Lords and nobility would abet the clergy. . . .

8th June. This day, the archbishop of Canterbury, with the bishops of Ely, Chichester, St. Asaph, Bristol, Peterborough, and Bath and Wells, were sent from the Privy Council prisoners to the Tower, for refusing to give bail for their appearance, on their not reading the declaration for liberty of conscience; they refused to give bail, as it would have prejudiced their peerage. The concern of the people for them was wonderful, infinite crowds on their knees begging their blessing, and praying for them, as they passed out of the barge along the Tower-wharf.

10th. *A young prince* born, which will cause disputes.

About two o'clock, we heard the Tower-ordnance discharged, and the bells ring for the birth of a Prince of Wales. This was very surprising, it having been universally given out that her Majesty did not look till the next month. . . .

15th. Being the first day of term, the bishops were brought to Westminster on habeas corpus, when the indictment was read, and they were called on to plead; their counsel objected that the warrant was illegal; but, after long debate, it was over-ruled, and they pleaded. The court then offered to take bail for their appearance; but this they refused, and at last were dismissed on their own recognizances to appear that day fortnight; the archbishop in £200, the bishops £100 each. . . .

29th. They appeared; the trial lasted from nine in the morning to past six in the evening, when the jury retired to consider of their verdict, and the court adjourned to nine the next morning. The jury were locked up till that time, eleven of them being for an acquittal; but one (Arnold, a brewer) would not consent. At length he agreed with the others. The chief justice, Wright, behaved with great moderation and civility to the bishops. Alibone, a Papist, was strongly against them; but Holloway and Powell being of opinion in their favor, they were acquitted. When this was heard, there was great rejoicing; and there was a lane of people from the King's Bench to the waterside, on their knees, as the bishops passed and repassed, to beg their blessing. Bonfires were made that night, and bells rung, which was taken very ill at court, and an appearance of nearly sixty earls and Lords, etc. were all along full of comfort and cheerful.

Note, they denied to pay the lieutenant of the Tower (Hales, who used them very surlily) any fees, alleging that none were due.

The night was solemnized with bonfires, and other fireworks, etc. . . .

12th July. The camp now began at Hounslow;[2] but the nation was in high discontent.

Colonel Titus, Sir Henry Vane (son of him who was executed for his treason), and some other of the Presbyterians and Independent party, were sworn of the Privy Council, from hopes of thereby diverting that party from going over to the bishops and Church of England, which now they began to do, foreseeing the design of the Papists to descend and take in their most hateful of heretics (as they at other times expressed them to be) to effect their own ends, now evident; the utter extirpation of the Church of England first, and then the rest would follow. . . .

10th August. Dr. Tenison now told me there would suddenly be some great thing discovered. This was the Prince of Orange intending to come over. . . .

23rd. . . . Dr. Sprat, bishop of Rochester, wrote a very honest and handsome letter to the Commissioners Ecclesiastical, excusing himself from sitting any longer among them, he by no means approving of their prosecuting the clergy who refused to read the declaration for liberty of conscience, in prejudice of the Church of England.

The Dutch make extraordinary preparations both at sea and land, which with the no small progress popery makes among us, puts us to many difficulties. The popish Irish soldiers commit many murders and insults; the whole nation disaffected, and in apprehension. . . .

18th September. I went to London, where I found the court in the utmost consternation on report of the Prince of Orange's landing; which put Whitehall into so panic a fear, that I could hardly believe it possible to find such a change.

Writs were issued in order to a Parliament, and a declaration to back the good order of elections, with great professions of maintaining the Church of England, but without giving any sort of satisfaction to the people, who showed their high discontent at several things in the government.

30th. The court in so extraordinary a consternation, on assurance of the Prince of Orange's intention to land, that the writs sent forth for a Parliament were recalled. . . .

7th October. . . . Hourly expectation of the Prince of Orange's invasion heightened to that degree, that his Majesty thought fit to abrogate the commission for the dispensing power (but retaining his own right still to dispense with all laws) and restore the ejected fellows of Magdalen College, Oxford. In the mean time, he called over 5,000 Irish, and 4,000 Scots, and continued to remove Protestants and put in Papists at Portsmouth and other places of trust, and retained the Jesuits about him, increasing the universal discontent. It brought people to so desperate a pass, that they seemed passionately to long for and desire the landing of that prince, whom they looked on to be their deliverer from popish tyranny, praying incessantly for an east wind, which was said to be the only hindrance of his expedition with a numerous army ready to make a descent. To such a strange temper, and unheard-of in former times, was this poor nation reduced, and of which I was an eyewitness. The apprehension was (and with reason) that his Majesty's forces would neither at land nor sea oppose them with that vigor requisite to repel invaders.

The late imprisoned bishops were now called to reconcile matters, and the Jesuits hard at work to foment confusion among the Protestants by their usual tricks. A letter was sent to the archbishop of Canterbury, informing him, from good hands, of what was contriving by them. A paper of what the bishops advised his Majesty was published. The bishops were enjoined to

---

[2]*Hounslow:* the army encampment set up by James outside London, officered by Catholics, to discourage popular demonstrations against his policies

prepare a form of prayer against the feared invasion. A pardon published. Soldiers and mariners daily pressed.

14th. The king's birthday. No guns from the Tower as usual. The sun eclipsed at its rising. This day signal for the victory of William the Conqueror against Harold, near Battel, in Sussex. The wind, which had been hitherto west, was east all this day. Wonderful expectation of the Dutch fleet. Public prayers ordered to be read in the churches against invasion.

28th. A tumult in London on the rabble demolishing a popish chapel that had been set up in the city.

29th. Lady Sunderland acquainted me with his Majesty's taking away the seals from Lord Sunderland, and of her being with the queen to intercede for him. It is conceived that he had of late grown remiss in pursuing the interest of the Jesuitical counsels; some reported one thing, some another; but there was doubtless some secret betrayed, which time may discover.

There was a council called, to which were summoned the archbishop of Canterbury, the judges, the Lord Mayor, etc. The queen dowager, and all the ladies and lords who were present at the queen consort's labor, were to give their testimony upon oath of the Prince of Wales's birth, recorded both at the council-board and at the chancery a day or two after. This procedure was censured by some as below his Majesty to condescend to, on the talk of the people. It was remarkable that on this occasion the archbishop, marquis of Halifax, the earls of Clarendon and Nottingham, refused to sit at the council-table amongst Papists, and their bold telling his Majesty that whatever was done whilst such sat amongst them was unlawful and incurred *praemunire*,[3]— at least, if what I heard be true. . . .

1st November. Dined with Lord Preston, with other company, at Sir Stephen Fox's. Continual alarms of the Prince of Orange, but no certainty. . . .

4th. Fresh reports of the prince being landed somewhere about Portsmouth, or the Isle of Wight, whereas it was thought it would have been northward. The court in great hurry.

5th. I went to London; heard the news of the prince having landed at Torbay, coming with a fleet of near 700 sail, passing through the Channel with so favorable a wind, that our navy could not intercept, or molest them. This put the king and court into great consternation, they were now employed in forming an army to stop their further progress, for they were got into Exeter, and the season and ways very improper for his Majesty's forces to march so great a distance.

The archbishop of Canterbury and some few of the other bishops and Lords in London, were sent for to Whitehall, and required to set forth their abhorrence of this invasion. They assured his Majesty they had never invited any of the prince's party, or were in the least privy to it, and would be ready to show all testimony of their loyalty; but, as to a public declaration, being so few, they desired that his Majesty would call the rest of their brethren and peers, that they might consult what was fit to be done on this occasion, not thinking it right to publish anything without them, and till they had themselves seen the prince's manifesto, in which it was pretended he was invited in by the Lords spiritual and temporal. This did not please the king; so they departed.

A declaration was published, prohibiting all persons to see or read the prince's manifesto, in which was set forth at large the cause of his expedition, as there had been one before from the states.

These are the beginnings of sorrow, unless God in His mercy prevent it by some

---

[3]*praemunire*: the fourteenth-century law against sending legislative and judicial appeals to the papal court at Rome; the council here felt that the mere presence of papists constituted a breach of that law

happy reconciliation of all dissensions among us. This, in all likelihood, nothing can effect except a free Parliament; but this we cannot hope to see, whilst there are any forces on either side. . . .

14th. The prince increases every day in force. Several Lords go in to him. Lord Cornbury carries some regiments, and marches to Honiton, the prince's headquarters. The city of London in disorder; the rabble pulled down the nunnery newly bought by the Papists of Lord Berkeley, at St. John's. The queen prepares to go to Portsmouth for safety, to attend the issue of this commotion, which has a dreadful aspect.

18th. It was now a very hard frost. The king goes to Salisbury to rendezvous the army, and return to London. Lord Delamere appears for the prince in Cheshire. The nobility meet in Yorkshire. The archbishop of Canterbury and some bishops, and such peers as were in London, address his Majesty to call a Parliament. . . .

2nd December. Dr. Tenison preached at St. Martin's on Psalm xxxvi. 5, 6, 7, concerning Providence. I received the blessed Sacrament. Afterwards, visited my Lord Godolphin, then going with the marquis of Halifax and earl of Nottingham as commissioners to the Prince of Orange; he told me they had little power. Plymouth declared for the prince. Bath, York, Hull, Bristol, and all the eminent nobility and persons of quality through England, declare for the Protestant religion and laws, and go to meet the prince, who every day sets forth new declarations against the Papists. The great favorites at court, priests and Jesuits, fly or abscond. Every thing, till now concealed, flies abroad in public print, and is cried about the streets. Expectation of the prince coming to Oxford. The Prince of Wales and great treasure sent privily to Portsmouth, the earl of Dover being governor. Address from the fleet not grateful to his Majesty. The Papists in offices lay down their commissions, and fly. Universal consternation amongst them; it looks like a revolution. . . .

9th. Lord Sunderland meditates flight.

The rabble demolished all popish chapels, and several Papist lords' and gentlemen's houses, especially that of the Spanish Ambassador, which they pillaged, and burnt his library.

13th. The king flies to sea, puts in at Feversham for ballast; is rudely treated by the people; comes back to Whitehall.

The Prince of Orange is advanced to Windsor, is invited by the king to St. James's, the messenger sent was the earl of Feversham, the general of the forces, who going without trumpet, or passport, is detained prisoner by the prince, who accepts the invitation, but requires his Majesty to retire to some distant place, that his own guards may be quartered about the palace and city. This is taken heinously, and the king goes privately to Rochester; is persuaded to come back; comes on the Sunday; goes to mass, and dines in public, a Jesuit saying grace (I was present).

17th. That night was a council; his Majesty refuses to assent to all the proposals; goes away again to Rochester.

18th. I saw the king take barge to Gravesend at twelve o'clock—a sad sight! The prince comes to St. James's, and fills Whitehall with Dutch guards. A council of peers meet about an expedient to call a Parliament; adjourn to the House of Lords. The chancellor, earl of Peterborough, and divers others taken. The earl of Sunderland flies; Sir Edward Hales, Walker, and others, taken and secured.

All the world go to see the prince at St. James's, where there is a great court. There I saw him, and several of my acquaintance who came over with him. He is very stately, serious, and reserved. The English soldiers sent out of town to disband them; not well pleased.

24th. The king passes into France, whither the queen and child were gone a few days before.

26th. The peers and such commoners as were members of the Parliament at Oxford, being the last of Charles II meeting, desire the Prince of Orange to take on him the disposal of the public revenue till a convention of Lords and Commons should meet in full body, appointed by his circular letters to the shires and boroughs, 22nd January. I had now quartered upon me a lieutenant-colonel and eight horses. . . .

1689. 15th January. I visited the archbishop of Canterbury, where I found the bishops of St. Asaph, Ely, Bath and Wells, Peterborough, and Chichester, the earls of Aylesbury and Clarendon, Sir George Mackenzie Lord-Advocate of Scotland, and then came in a Scotch archbishop, etc. After prayers and dinner, divers serious matters were discoursed, concerning the present state of the public, and sorry I was to find there was as yet no accord in the judgments of those of the Lords and Commons who were to convene; some would have the princess made queen without any more dispute, others were for a regency; there was a Tory party (then so called), who were for inviting his Majesty again upon conditions; and there were republicans who would make the Prince of Orange like a stadtholder.[4] The Romanists were busy among these several parties to bring them into confusion: most for ambition or other interest, few for conscience and moderate resolutions. I found nothing of all this in this assembly of bishops, who were pleased to admit me into their discourses; they were all for a regency, thereby to salve their oaths, and so all public matters to proceed in his Majesty's name, by that to facilitate the calling of a Parliament, according to the laws in being. Such was the result of this meeting. . . .

The great convention being assembled the day before, falling upon the question about the government, resolved that King James having by the advice of the Jesuits and other wicked persons endeavoured to subvert the laws of church and state, and deserted the kingdom, carrying away the seals, etc., without any care for the management of the government, had by demise abdicated himself and wholly vacated his right; they did therefore desire the Lords' concurrence to their vote, to place the

crown on the next heir, the Prince of Orange, for his life, then to the princess, his wife, and if she died without issue, to the Princess of Denmark [Anne], and she failing, to the heirs of the prince, excluding forever all possibility of admitting a Roman Catholic. . . .

29th. The votes of the House of Commons being carried up by Mr. Hampden, their chairman, to the Lords, I got a station by the prince's lodgings at the door of the lobby to the House, and heard much of the debate, which lasted very long. Lord Derby was in the chair (for the House was resolved into a grand committee of the whole House); after all had spoken, it came to the question, which was carried by three voices against a regency, which 51 were for, 54 against; the minority alleging the danger of dethroning kings, and scrupling many passages and expressions in the vote of the Commons, too long to set down particularly. Some were for sending to his Majesty with conditions; others that the king could do no wrong, and that the maladministration was chargeable on his ministers. There were not more than eight or nine bishops, and but two against the regency; the archbishop was absent, and the clergy now began to change their note, both in pulpit and discourse, on their old passive obedience, so as people began to talk of the bishops being cast out of the House. In short, things tended to dissatisfaction on both sides; add to this, the morose temper of the Prince of Orange, who showed little countenance to the noblemen and others, who expected a more gracious and cheerful reception when they made their court. The English army also was not so in order, and firm to his interest, nor so weakened but that it might give interruption. Ireland was in an ill posture as well as Scotland. Nothing was yet done towards a settlement. God of His infinite mercy compose these things, that we may be at last a nation and a church under some fixed and sober establishment. . . .

6th February. . . . The Convention of the Lords and Commons now declare the

---

[4]*stadtholder:* elected chief prince

Prince and Princess of Orange King and Queen of England, France, and Ireland (Scotland being an independent kingdom), the prince and princess being to enjoy it jointly during their lives; but the executive authority to be vested in the prince during life, though all proceedings to run in both names, and that it should descend to their issue, and for want of such, to the Princess Anne of Denmark and her issue, and in want of such, to the heirs of the body of the prince, if he survive, and that failing, to devolve to the Parliament, as they should think fit. These produced a conference with the Lords, when also there was presented heads of such new laws as were to be enacted. It is thought on these conditions they will be proclaimed.

There was much contest about the king's abdication, and whether he had vacated the government. The earl of Nottingham and about twenty Lords, and many bishops, entered their protests, but the concurrence was great against them.

The princess hourly expected. Forces sending to Ireland, that kingdom being in great danger by the earl of . Tyrconnel's army, and expectations from France coming to assist them, but that king was busy in invading Flanders, and encountering the German princes. It is likely that this will be the most remarkable summer for action, which has happened in many years.

21st. . . . I saw the *new queen* and *king* proclaimed the very next day after her coming to Whitehall, Wednesday, 13th February, with great acclamation and general good reception. Bonfires, bells, guns, etc. It was believed that both, especially the princess, would have showed some (seeming) reluctance at least, of assuming her father's crown, and made some apology, testifying by her regret that he should by his mismanagement necessitate the nation to so extraordinary a proceeding, which would have showed very handsomely to the world, and according to the character given of her piety; consonant also to her husband's first declaration, that there was no intention of deposing the king, but of succouring the nation; but nothing of all this appeared; she

came into Whitehall laughing and jolly, as to a wedding, so as to seem quite transported. She rose early the next morning, and in her undress, as it was reported, before her women were up, went about from room to room to see the convenience of Whitehall; lay in the same bed and apartment where the late queen lay, and within a night or two sat down to play at basset, as the queen her predecessor used to do. She smiled upon and talked to everybody, so that no change seemed to have taken place at court since her last going away, save that infinite crowds of people thronged to see her, and that she went to our prayers. This carriage was censured by many. She seems to be of good nature, and that she takes nothing to heart: whilst the prince her husband has a thoughtful countenance, is wonderful serious and silent, and seems to treat all persons alike gravely, and to be very intent on affairs: Holland, Ireland, and France calling for his care.

Divers bishops and noblemen are not at all satisfied with this so sudden assumption of the crown, without any previous sending, and offering some conditions to the absent king; or, on his not returning, or not assenting to those conditions, to have proclaimed him regent; but the major part of both Houses prevailed to make them king and queen immediately, and a crown was tempting. . . .

The archbishop of Canterbury and some of the rest, on scruple of conscience and to salve the oaths they had taken, entered their protests and hung off, especially the archbishop, who had not all this while so much as appeared out of Lambeth. This occasioned the wonder of many who observed with what zeal they contributed to the prince's expedition, and all the while also rejecting any proposals of sending again to the absent king; that they should now raise scruples, and such as created much division among the people, greatly rejoicing the old courtiers, and especially the Papists.

Another objection was, the invalidity of what was done by a Convention only, and the as yet unabrogated laws; this drew them on the 22nd [February] new king passing the act own on his head. The lawyers disputed, but necessity prevailed, the government requiring a speedy settlement.

GILBERT BURNET The Character of James II and William III (1701, 1687)

A contemporary who knew both men assesses the personalities of the old king and the new. The description of William was written in 1687 when William was stadtholder of the Dutch Republic but not yet king of England.

King James . . . was a prince that seemed made for greater things than will be found in the course of his life, more particularly of his reign. He was esteemed in the former parts of his life a man of great courage, as he was quite through it a man of great application to business. He had no vivacity of thought, invention or expression; but he had a good judgment where his religion or his education gave him not a bias, which it did very often. He was bred with strange notions of the obedience due to princes, and came to take up as strange ones of the submission due to priests. He was naturally a man of truth, fidelity and justice; but his religion was so infused in him, and he was so managed in it by his priests, that the principles which nature had laid in him had little power over him when the concerns of his church stood in the way.

He was a gentle master, and was very easy to all who came near him; yet he was not so apt to pardon as one ought to be that is the viceregent of that God who is slow to anger and ready to forgive. He had no personal vices but of one sort: he was still wandering from one amour to another. Yet he had a real sense of sin, and was ashamed of it; but priests know how to engage princes more entirely into their interests by making them compound for their sins by a great zeal for holy church, as they call it.

In a word, if it had not been for his popery he would have been, if not a great, yet a good prince. By what I once knew of him, and by what I saw him afterwards carried to, I grew more confirmed in the very bad opinion which I was always apt to have of the intrigues of the popish clergy and of the confessors of kings. He was undone by them, and was their martyr, so that they ought to bear the chief load of all the errors of his inglorious reign and of its fatal catastrophe. . . .

[William] has showed by his conduct and action that notwithstanding all the defects of his education, and his total want of literature, nature is capable of producing great matters, even when she is not at all assisted by art. He has a great application to affairs, and turns them much in his thoughts; and indeed perhaps too much, for his slowness in coming to a resolution is much complained of. But if he is slow in taking up a resolution he is as firm in adhering to it. He has a vast memory, and a true judgment, for he sees presently the critical point of any matter that is proposed to him. He is the closest man in the world, so that it is not possible so much as to guess at his intentions till he declares them. He is extremely calm both in council and actions, and hears very gently things that are said to him, even when he is not pleased with them. But he has the haughtiness of a great mind not to forget too soon injuries done him; but he has never been observed to affect revenges, only he does not easily return to confidences with those that have offended him.

His courage is indeed greater than it ought to be; and though it was very fit for one that had the ambition of arriving at the reputation of his ancestors to hazard his

SOURCES: From M. J. Routh, ed., *History of My Own Time* (London, 1833), Vol. IV, 539–540; H. C. Foxcroft, ed., *Supplement to History of My Own Time* (Oxford, 1902), pp. 190–193.

person sometimes, that so it might appear that he was a soldier as well as a general, yet his great carelessness of all personal danger both in time of peace and war has been censured as excessive, for to see him go about with a footman or two when so much depends on his life has been called rather a tempting of Providence than a trusting to it. This some have ascribed to his belief of predestination, as if that pushed him on headlong in this confidence that all things will be as God will have them. But though he is firmly persuaded of predestination, yet he said to me he never reflected upon it in any of his counsels before things fall out; but he owned to me, when things fall out, the belief that God would have them so quieted his mind much, and has helped him to bear many misfortunes and disappointments very easily. This is his peculiar carriage and the nature of his courage that it does not sink with misfortunes, for when things have miscarried in his hands he has been observed to have the same calm equality that he had upon happier occasions. . . .

He seems to have a real sense of religion, and looks like a man that is in earnest when he is worshipping God. He is a hearty enemy to popery, and in particular to the cruelty of it, for he is a great enemy to persecution on the account of religion. He thinks the Church of England ought to be maintained, but softened a little both with relation to the nonconformists at home and to the foreign churches beyond sea. He has a coldness in his way that damps a modest man extremely, for he hears things with a dry silence that shows too much of distrust of those to whom he speaks. He seems to have made it a maxim to be slow in everything of resolution he takes, and this he carries too far, that he makes those to whom he intends to show favors wait on so long that the grace of giving them is much lost by the slowness; and he does not seem enough to consider the sourness of spirit under which men languish that are perplexed with uncertainty and want.

He has a true notion of government and liberty, and does not think that subjects were made to be slaves; but after the laws and foundations of government are overturned by those who ought to maintain them he thinks the people may assert their freedom. He is a close manager of his affairs, and though he spends much in building yet he is not thought so free-hearted and generous as a great prince ought to be. His martial inclination will naturally carry him, when he comes to the crown of England, to bear down the greatness of France. And if he but hits the nature of the English nation right at first he will be able to give laws to all Europe. . . . But if the prince does not in many things change his way he will hardly gain the hearts of the nation. His coldness will look like contempt, and that the English cannot bear; and they are too impatient to digest that slowness that is almost become natural to him in the most inconsiderable things, and his silent way will pass for superciliousness. But that which is more important, he will be both the king of England and stadtholder. . . .

ANONYMOUS JACOBITE **Observations Upon the Late Revolution in England (1690)**

An unknown Jacobite, fearful of being tried for sedition, denounces the revolution.

If it be true that interest is often mistaken, though it never lie, and that standers-by sometimes see more than gamesters, though they do not understand the game so well, it may not be false that the politic drivers of our late revolution in England

SOURCE: From "Observations Upon the Late Revolution in England," in *A Collection of Scarce and Valuable Tracts* [*Somers Tracts*], Vol. X (London, 1813), pp. 336–348.

(who, 'tis to be feared, have too many of them designed their private interest at least as much as that of the public), have mistaken their way to both, and that one who has been no more than an indifferent looker-on, and who pretends not to be clearer sighted than others, has observed some things which the abler gamesters have not been aware of. Whether it be so or not, who pleases to read the following observations may judge. . . .

First Observation. . . . Though religion was advanced sometimes to lead up the common people, and marched along with liberty and property at the head of parties and pamphlets, when there was occasion to appear in public, it was plain that my lords and gentlemen had no other use of it, than to gull the commonalty; and that the profits and preferments of the government, to which the laws and possession gave them a title, were the things they would never part with, if any other king, or if no king, would preserve them to them.

Second Observation. That their redeemer, the P. of O.,[5] had the same occasion, and made just the same use of religion as his religiously aggrieved inviters and assisters into England; his declaration setting forth the deep sense and concern he had for it . . . ; his unwearied diligence in thwarting every thing K. C. or K. J.[6] had a mind to have done by their own subjects; his great goodness in providing well for all those persons, who, for some goodness or other, had incurred their displeasure, and were banished or proclaimed traitors by those two kings; . . . his constant and firm adherence, after the king's departure, to his declaration (the confidence of which had drawn in all the people to him); first, in his calling a free and legal parliament, than which he declares to have no other design; secondly, in the particular care he took for electing to his parliament, called the Convention, all true churchmen, all such as had been discountenanced, or brow-beaten before, in the way of outlawries, or so, by King Charles the Second, or King James; . . . his transubstantiating (as it has been called) when he was king, the same convention into a parliament, without writs or new elections, lest he should not get the people, who had been deceived by their conventionary members doing what they never dreamed of in making him king, to choose such parliament men as would serve the turns he had to come hereafter; . . . To conclude, upon this whole matter, it is observed, that his Dutch highness, as well as his English factors,[7] consulted his private interest and ambition in the redemption he brought to England, at least as much as he did the good of religion, or the interest of the kingdom. . . .

Fourth Observation. That setting aside the question, whether the proceedings of the people of England have been just or lawful, it is observed that what they have done, is directly against their dearly beloved and espoused interest, and worse for themselves, in the same kind, than any inconveniences King James could have brought them under. . . .

We feared for our laws, not so much I believe for what was done, as for the manner of doing it, for I am persuaded a good part of what King James did might have been done for him in a legal way, and with the consent of the people; but when we saw him assume a dispensing power, not vested in him by law, we were sensible that the same power which overruled one law, might overrule another, and all, and feared the pernicious example: This, I think, was the case and the disease. The antidote now which we have taken against the poison of this bad example, is it not an example as bad, or worse, and our remedy against one illegal power, which we have pulled down, a setting up another altogether as illegal?

For the law acknowledges not for a legal parliament, any number of men, who are strong enough, a legal call; no, though they convene in the parliament-house, and vote themselves a parliament, nor that man for

---

[5] *P. of O.:* Prince of Orange   [6] *K. C. or K. J.:* King Charles or King James   [7] *factors:* supporters

a king, whom the law places not in the throne. Unriddle me now, who can, in what an illegal dispensing power was more dangerous to our laws, than an illegal enactive, or an illegal executive power is; or in what the abdicated example of K. J. to dispense with some laws, was worse than the example set up now, by which any number of men who are strong enough, may assume an absolute power to dispose of all our laws, our religion, our bodies, consciences, and purses as they please, with no more ceremony than the formality of a transubstantiating vote. . . .

In short, illegality is always illegality, and if that were the intolerable pernicious thing before, it is so much the more intolerable now, by how much a legislative illegality is more pernicious than a dispensative one, and an usurped executive power more dangerous than a legal one. . . .

The English government has hitherto stood upon these fundamental maxims, that the king never dies, and that all authority is derived from him. For our wise ancestors were so sensible of the ruinous consequences of interregnums, elections, seditions, and saw so well that nothing could prevent them but a legal king always in being, that they would not allow to death itself, with all its irresistible power over the man, any power over the king, but made the same moment which received the last breath of the man breathe his regal power into the next of blood; and then placing the fountain of all authority in this immortal king, stopped up forever all pretending streams of sedition. By this it was made impossible, for any pretense to cheat or hinder the people from distinguishing the seditious, which they were to avoid, from the just power which they were to obey, there being no more to do, but to ask which flowed from that fountain which they had contrived should always run. Now we have introduced vacant thrones, filling them as pleasure or humor, not as blood directs. . . .

I will not be the melancholy prophet to foretell what will be the consequence, but leave every one to guess, who will reflect what they have seen and felt in one year's time. . . .

Sixth Observation. That though we thought to make our court to our new king by deserting our old, as we are generally an honest, upright people, our consciences possibly, if they were not ashamed to speak, could tell strange stories of the self-denial this compliment cost us, and the hard shifts and pains many of us made, and took to mortify the struggling rebellion of nature against that which we unnaturally hurried ourselves into against our king. . . .

And our reason will tell us we cannot complain, nor expect it ever should be otherwise. For no wise prince will trust a man whom he has cause to suspect will not be true to him; and our K. W.[8] cannot forget that he was not born in England, that he did not inherit the crown, that he cannot reign without wars and taxes: and that therefore he cannot (though he would never so fain) securely count upon those men, whereof every one who presents himself for employment, must of necessity come with this speech in his mouth: You sir, are king *de facto*, and may be sure of me; for I am just come from being false to a king *de facto*, and *de jure* both, who was my countryman, besides, twenty to one, my particular benefactor, and whose reign was a reign of peace and plenty. Our compliment therefore has put an inevitable necessity upon our new king, never to trust us to counsel or fight for ourselves, but under a sure guard, and to furnish himself with store of foreign heads and hands, to carry on the interest of England; at which we are neither to wonder nor complain, for necessity has no law.

Seventh Observation. . . . 'Tis by violence K. W. calls conventions and parliaments; and violence is all the validity of their acts. They have no other authority than the laws which thieves make among themselves to rob the more methodically and safely; and we submit to both, for the same reason, fear of worse. Violence seizes our money and our liberty, and we yield to

---

[8]*K. W.:* King William

it, just as we suffer stronger highwaymen to bind us and take our purses. . . .

Eighth Observation. To conclude: Here we are, and here we must be eternally, till we learn wit of a carter, and set the overturned cart on the wheels again; in plain terms, till we re-settle King James on his throne. The happiness of England depends upon a rightful king, we see it always went out with him, and 'tis in vain to hope it ever will, or can return without him. . . .

WILLIAM LLOYD   A Discourse of God's Ways of Disposing Kingdoms (1691)

The bishop of St. Asaph preaches before King William III and Queen Mary II on November 5, 1689, the first anniversary of William's landing at Torbay.

Psalm LXXV, verses 6, 7

For Promotion cometh neither from the East, nor from the West, nor from the South.
But God is the Judge; He putteth down one, and setteth up another. . . .

It has been proved in all sorts of government, that as the sovereign power in every country or nation is of God, so they that are invested with it, whether one or many, are in the place of God, and have their promotion from him: which was the first part of the doctrine of this text.

The second part is, that the transferring of this power from one to another, is the act of God. And this he does proceeding judicially, as being judge, saith our Psalmist.

Here are two things to be considered. First, that it is God that does this; and secondly, that he does it judicially.

For the first of these, that the transferring of power from one to another is the act of God, this adds much to that which went before in the text. It shows that God has such an interest in the disposing of power, as none can pretend to but himself.

Men have their part in setting up what they cannot put down again. It is a woman's consent makes a man be her husband, the fellows of a college choose one to be their head, a corporation choose one to be their mayor: All these do only choose the person, they do not give him the authority. It is the law that gives that, and that law so binds their hands that they cannot undo what they have done.

No more can a nation undo its own act, in choosing men into sovereign power. I do not say but they may choose men into government, expressly with that condition, that they shall be accountable to the people; and then the government remains in the body of the nation, it is that which we properly call a commonwealth. But for sovereign princes and kings, even where they are chosen by the nation; and much more in hereditary kingdoms; as they have their authority from God, so they are only accountable to him. For he is the only potentate, King of Kings, and Lord of Lords. He alone both makes kings by his sovereign power, and by the same he can unmake them when he pleases. . . .

This can be understood of nothing else but the conquest of one prince over another. For what one resigns by a voluntary act, he is said to lay down, or to give it up to another. But putting down is the act of a superior, by which one's place is taken from him against his will. Now God being the superior that does this by the act of his providence, it must be such an act as gives the power from *one* against his will, to *another* whom God is pleased to set up in

SOURCE: From William Lloyd, *A Discourse of God's Ways of Disposing Kingdoms* (London, 1691), pp. 13–25, 27–28, 61–67.

his stead. Thus in giving one prince a conquest over another, he thereby puts one in possession of the other's dominions, he makes the other's subjects become his subjects. . . .

If a prince will have no law but his will, if he tramples and oppresseth his people, their patience will not hold out always, they will at one time or other show themselves to be but men. At least they will have no heart to fight for their oppressor. So that if a foreign enemy breaks in upon him, he is gone without remedy, unless God interpose. But how can that be, when God is judge himself? Should the judge hinder the doing of justice? It is God's work that foreigner comes to do, howbeit he meaneth not so. He means nothing perhaps, but the satisfying of his own lust. But though he knoweth it not, he is sent in God's message: for which all things being prepared by natural causes, and God not hindering his own work, but rather hastening it, no wonder that it succeeds, and that oftentimes very easily. . . .

In the way of justice, God acts as a judge between two sovereign powers, when they bring their causes before him; that is, when they make war upon one another. And when he seeth his time, that is, when he finds the cause ripe for judgment, if it proceeds so far, then he gives sentence for him that is injured, against him that hath done the injury. The effect of this sentence is a just conquest; and that is the other way in which God, proceeding judicially, puts down one, and sets up another. . . .

It is true according to our doctrine, they [the people] are united to their prince as a wife to her husband; so that they can no more right themselves by arms, than she can sue her husband while the bond of marriage continues. Yet as, when her husband uses her extremely ill, she may complain of him to the judge, who, if he sees cause, may dissolve the marriage by his sentence; and after that she is at liberty to sue him as well as any other man: So a people may cry to the Lord by reason of their oppression, and he may raise them up a deliverer, that shall take the government into his hands; (a foreign prince may lawfully do this, as hath been already shown;) and then they are not only free to defend themselves, but are obliged to join with him, against their oppressor. . . .

JOHN LOCKE **Second Treatise on Government (1689)**

In retrospect, this work by John Locke has become the most famous defense of the "Glorious Revolution," if only because it also helped provide the philosophical basis for the justification of the American Revolution in 1776. Most of Locke's treatise had been written in Holland earlier in the decade, but it was first published in England in 1689.

If man in the state of nature be so free, as has been said, if he be absolute lord of his own person and possessions, equal to the greatest, and subject to nobody, why will he part with his freedom, this empire, and subject himself to the dominion and control of any other power? To which, it is obvious to answer, that though in the state of nature he hath such a right, yet the enjoyment of it is very uncertain, and constantly exposed to the invasions of others. For all being kings as much as he, every man his equal, and the greater part no strict observers of equity and justice, the enjoyment of the property he has in this state is very unsafe, very unsecure. This makes him willing to quit this condition, which, however free, is full of fears and continual dangers; and it is not without reason that he seeks out and is willing to join in society with others, who

SOURCE: The excerpts are taken from Chapter IX, "Of the Ends of Political Society and Government," Chapter XI, "Of the Extent of the Legislative Power," and Chapter XIX, "Of the Dissolution of Government."

are already united, or have a mind to unite, for the mutual preservation of their lives, liberties, and estates, which I call by the general name, property.

The great and chief end, therefore, of men's uniting into commonwealths, and putting themselves under government, is the preservation of their property; to which in the state of nature there are many things wanting. . . .

But though men when they enter into society give up the equality, liberty and executive power they had in the state of nature into the hands of the society, to be so far disposed of by the legislative as the good of the society shall require; yet it being only with an intention in every one the better to preserve himself, his liberty and property (for no rational creature can be supposed to change his condition with an intention to be worse), the power of the society, or legislative constituted by them, can never be supposed to extend farther than the common good, but is obliged to secure every one's property by providing against those . . . defects above-mentioned that made the state of nature so unsafe and uneasy. And so whoever has the legislative or supreme power of any commonwealth is bound to govern by established standing laws, promulgated and known to the people, and not by extemporary degrees; by indifferent[9] and upright judges, who are to decide controversies by those laws; and to employ the force of the community at home only in the execution of such laws, or abroad, to prevent or redress foreign injuries, and secure the community from inroads and invasion. And all this to be directed to no other end but the peace, safety, and public good of the people. . . .

The great end of men's entering into society being the enjoyment of their properties in peace and safety, and the great instrument and means of that being the laws established in that society: the first and fundamental positive law of all commonwealths, is the establishing of the legislative power; as the first and fundamental natural law, which is to govern even the leg-

islative itself, is the preservation of the society, and (as far as will consist with the public good) of every person in it. This legislative is not only the supreme power of the commonwealth, but sacred and unalterable in the hands where the community have once placed it; nor can any edict of anybody else, in what form soever conceived, or by what power soever backed, have the force and obligation of a law, which has not its sanction from that legislative which the public has chosen and appointed. . . .

It is in their legislative that the members of a commonwealth are united and combined together in one coherent living body. This is the soul that gives form, life, and unity to the commonwealth. From hence the several members have their mutual influence, sympathy, and connection. And, therefore, when the legislative is broken or dissolved, dissolution and death follow. For the essence and union of the society consisting in having one will, the legislative, when once established by the majority, has the declaring and, as it were, keeping of, that will. The constitution of the legislative is the first and fundamental act of the society, whereby provision is made for the continuation of their union, under the direction of persons and bonds of laws made by persons authorized thereunto by the consent and appointment of the people, without which no one man or number of men amongst them can have authority of making laws that shall be binding to the rest. . . .

Let us suppose, then, the legislative placed in the concurrence of three distinct persons.

1. A single hereditary person having the constant supreme executive power, and with it the power of convoking and dissolving the other two within certain periods of time.
2. An assembly of hereditary nobility.
3. An assembly of representatives chosen *pro tempore* by the people. Such a form of government supposed, it is evident,

---

[9]*indifferent:* impartial

First, That when such a single person or prince sets up his own arbitrary will in place of the laws which are the will of the society, declared by the legislative, then the legislative is changed. . . .

Secondly, When the prince hinders the legislative from assembling in its due time, or from acting freely, pursuant to those ends for which it was constituted, the legislative is altered. . . .

Thirdly, When, by the arbitrary power of the prince, the electors or ways of elections are altered, without the consent and contrary to the common interest of the people, there also the legislative is altered. . . .

Fourthly, The delivery also of the people into the subjection of foreign power, either by the prince, or by the legislative, is certainly a change of the legislative, and so a dissolution of the government. . . .

Why in such a constitution as this the dissolution of the government in these cases is to be imputed to the prince, is evident; because he, having the force, treasure, and offices of the state to employ, and often persuading himself, or being flattered by others, that, as supreme magistrate he is incapable of control, he alone is in a condition to make great advances toward such changes, under pretense of lawful authority, and has it in his hands to terrify or suppress opposers, as factious, seditious, and enemies to the government. Whereas no other part of the legislative or people is capable by themselves to attempt any alteration of the legislative, without open and visible rebellion, apt enough to be taken notice of, which, when it prevails, produces effects very little different from foreign conquest. . . .

To this perhaps it will be said that, the people being ignorant and always discontented, to lay the foundation of government in the unsteady opinion and uncertain humor of the people is to expose it to certain ruin; and no government will be able long to subsist if the people may set up a new legislative whenever they take offense at the old one. To this I answer: Quite the contrary. People are not so easily got out of their old forms as some are apt to suggest. . . . This slowness and aversion in the people to quit their old constitutions has in the many revolutions which have been seen in this kingdom, in this and former ages, still kept us to, or after some interval of fruitless attempts still brought us back again to, our old legislative of king, lords, and commons. . . .

Such revolutions happen not upon every little mismanagement in public affairs. Great mistakes in the ruling part, many wrong and inconvenient laws, and all the slips of human frailty will be borne by the people without mutiny or murmur. But if a long train of abuses, prevarications, and artifices, all tending the same way, make the design visible to the people, and they cannot but feel what they lie under and see whither they are going, it is not to be wondered that they should then rouse themselves and endeavor to put the rule into such hands which may secure to them the ends for which government was at first erected. . . .

The end of government is the good of mankind. And which is best for mankind? That the people should be always exposed to the boundless will of tyranny, or that the rulers should be sometimes liable to be opposed when they grow exorbitant in the use of their power and employ it for the destruction and not the preservation of the properties of their people?

The Bill of Rights (1689)

This statute was, after long discussion, approved by both Houses of Parliament and King William III in October 1689.

SOURCE: From D. Pickering, ed., *The Statutes at Large* (Cambridge, 1762–1806), Vol. IX, Item 67.

An Act for Declaring the Rights and Liberties of the Subject and Settling the Succession of the Crown.

Whereas the Lords spiritual and temporal, and Commons, assembled at Westminster, lawfully, fully, and freely representing all the estates of the people of this realm, did upon the thirteenth day of February, in the year of our Lord one thousand six hundred eighty-[nine] present unto their Majesties, then called and known by the names and stile of William and Mary, Prince and Princess of Orange, being present in their proper persons, a certain declaration in writing, made by the said Lords and Commons, in the words following: viz.

Whereas the late King James the Second, by the assistance of divers evil counselors, judges, and ministers employed by him, did endeavor to subvert and extirpate the Protestant religion, and the laws and liberties of this kingdom.

By assuming and exercising a power of dispensing with and suspending of laws, and the execution of laws, without consent of Parliament.

By committing and prosecuting divers worthy prelates, for humbly petitioning to be excused concurring to the said assumed power.

By issuing and causing to be executed a commission under the great seal for erecting a court called the Court of Commissioners for ecclesiastical causes.

By levying money for and to the use of the crown, by pretense of prerogative, for other time, and in other manner, than the same was granted by Parliament.

By raising and keeping a standing army within this kingdom in time of peace, without consent of Parliament, and quartering soldiers contrary to law.

By causing several good subjects, being Protestants, to be disarmed, at the same time when Papists were both armed and employed, contrary to law.

By violating the freedom of election of members to serve in Parliament.

By prosecutions in the court of King's Bench, for matters and causes cognizable only in Parliament; and by divers other arbitrary and illegal courses.

And whereas of late years, partial, corrupt, and unqualified persons have been returned and served on juries in trials and particularly divers jurors in trials for high treason, which were not freeholders.

And excessive bail hath been required of persons committed in criminal cases, to elude the benefit of the laws made for the liberty of the subjects.

And excessive fines have been imposed; and illegal and cruel punishments inflicted.

And several grants and promises made of fines and forfeitures, before any conviction or judgment against the persons, upon whom the same were to be levied.

All which are utterly and directly contrary to the known laws and statutes, and freedom of this realm.

And whereas the said late King James the Second having abdicated the government, and the throne being thereby vacant, his Highness the Prince of Orange (whom it hath pleased Almighty God to make the glorious instrument of delivering this kingdom from popery and arbitrary power) did (by the advice of the Lords spiritual and temporal, and divers principal persons of the Commons) cause letters to be written to the Lords spiritual and temporal, being Protestants; and other letters to the several counties, cities, universities, boroughs, and cinque-ports,[10] for the choosing of such persons to represent them, as were of right to be sent to Parliament, to meet and sit at Westminster upon the two and twentieth day of January, in this year one thousand six hundred eighty-[nine], in order to such an establishment, as that their religion, laws,

---

[10]*cinque-ports:* five English Channel ports—Hastings, Sandwich, Dover, Romney, and Hithe—that, during the Middle Ages, had received important privileges from the king in return for providing much of his navy

and liberties might not again be in danger of being subverted: upon which letters, elections have been accordingly made.

And thereupon the said Lords spiritual and temporal, and Commons, pursuant to their respective letters and elections, being now assembled in a full and free representative of this nation, taking into their most serious consideration the best means for attaining the ends aforesaid; do in the first place (as their ancestors in like case have usually done) for the vindicating and asserting their ancient rights and liberties, declare:

That the pretended power of suspending of laws, or the execution of laws, by regal authority, without consent of Parliament, is illegal.

That the pretended power of dispensing with laws, or the execution of laws, by regal authority, as it hath been assumed and exercised of late, is illegal.

That the commission for erecting the late court of commissioners for ecclesiastical causes, and all other commissions and courts of like nature are illegal and pernicious.

That levying money for or to the use of the crown, by pretense of prerogative, without grant of Parliament, for longer time, or in other manner than the same is or shall be granted, is illegal.

That it is the right of the subjects to petition the king, and all commitments and prosecutions for such petitioning are illegal.

That the raising or keeping a standing army within the kingdom in time of peace, unless it be with consent of Parliament, is against law.

That the subjects which are Protestants, may have arms of their defense suitable to their conditions, and as allowed by law.

That election of Members of Parliament ought to be free.

That the freedom of speech, and debates or proceedings in Parliament, ought not to be impeached or questioned in any court or place out of Parliament.

That excessive bail ought not to be required, nor excessive fines imposed; nor cruel and unusual punishments inflicted.

That jurors ought to be duly impaneled and returned, and jurors which pass upon men in trials for high treason ought to be freeholders.

That all grants and promises of fines and forfeitures of particular persons before conviction, are illegal and void.

And that for redress of all grievances, and for the amending, strengthening and preserving of the laws, parliaments ought to be held frequently.

And they do claim, demand, and insist upon all and singular the premises, as their undoubted rights and liberties; and that no declarations, judgments, doings or proceedings, to the prejudice of the people in any of the said premises, ought in any wise to be drawn hereafter into consequence or example.

To which demand for their rights they are particularly encouraged by the declaration of his Highness the Prince of Orange, as being the only means for obtaining a full redress and remedy therein.

Having therefore an entire confidence, That his said Highness the Prince of Orange will perfect the deliverance so far advanced by him, and will still preserve them from the violation of their rights, which they have here asserted, and from all other attempts upon their religion, rights, and liberties.

The said Lords spiritual and temporal, and Commons, assembled at Westminster, do resolve, That William and Mary Prince and Princess of Orange be, and be declared, king and queen of England, France[11] and Ireland, and the dominions thereunto belonging, to hold the crown and royal dignity of the said kingdoms and dominions to them

---

[11]*king . . . France:* Although the Hundred Years' War had been over since 1453 and the city of Calais lost since 1558, the monarchs of England had not yet formally given up their claims to the French throne.

the said prince and princess during their lives, and the life of the survivor of them; and that the sole and full exercise of the regal power be only in, and executed by the said Prince of Orange, in the names of the said prince and princess, during their joint lives; and after their deceases, the said crown and royal dignity of the said kingdoms and dominions to be to the heirs of the body of the said princess; and for default of such issue to the Princess Anne of Denmark and the heirs of her body; and for default of such issue to the heirs of the body of the said prince of Orange. And the Lords spiritual and temporal, and Commons, do pray the said prince and princess to accept the same accordingly. . . .

Upon which their said Majesties did accept the crown and royal dignity of the kingdoms of England, France, and Ireland, and the dominions thereunto belonging, according to the resolution and desire of the said Lords and Commons contained in the said declaration. . . .

And thereunto the said Lords spiritual and temporal, and Commons do, in the name of all the people aforesaid, most humbly and faithfully submit themselves, their heirs and posterities for ever; and do faithfully promise, That they will stand to, maintain, and defend their said Majesties, and also the limitation and succession of the crown herein specified and contained, to the utmost of their powers, with their lives and estates against all persons whatsoever, that shall attempt any thing to the contrary. . . .

The Act of Settlement (1701)

For reasons made clear in the document itself, Parliament found it necessary twelve years after the Revolution of 1688–1689 to make further provisions for the royal succession. In the process, Parliament also set forth specific restrictions upon monarchical authority.

. . . After the making of [the Bill of Rights and settling the succession of the crown in 1689], your Majesty's good subjects, who were restored to the full and free possession and enjoyment of their religion, rights and liberties by the providence of God giving success to your Majesty's just undertakings and unwearied endeavours for that purpose, had no greater temporal felicity to hope or wish for than to see a royal progeny descending from your Majesty, to whom (under God) they owe their tranquility, and whose ancestors have for many years been principal assertors of the reformed religion and the liberties of Europe, and from our said most gracious sovereign lady, whose memory will always be precious to the subjects of these realms; and it having since pleased Almighty God to take away our said sovereign lady and also the most hopeful Prince William, duke of Gloucester (the only surviving issue of her Royal Highness the Princess Anne of Denmark), to the un-speakable grief and sorrow of your Majesty and your said good subjects. . . . Your Majesty's said subjects having daily experience of your royal care and concern for the present and future welfare of these kingdoms, and particularly recommending from your throne a further provision to be made for the succession of the crown in the Protestant line for the happiness of the nation and the security of our religion, and it being absolutely necessary for the safety, peace and quiet of this realm to obviate all doubts and contentions in the same by reason of any pretended titles to the crown, and to maintain a certainty in the succession thereof to which your subjects may safely have recourse for their protection in case the limitations in the said recited act should determine: therefore for a further provision of the succession of the crown in the Protestant line, we . . . do beseech your Majesty that it may be enacted and declared, and be it enacted and declared by the king's most

SOURCE: From *Statutes of the Realm,* 12 and 13 William III, Chapter 2, Vol. VII, pp. 636–638.

excellent Majesty, by and with the advice and consent of the Lords spiritual and temporal and Commons in this present Parliament assembled and by the authority of the same, that the most excellent Princess Sophia, electress and duchess dowager of Hanover, daughter of the most excellent Princess Elizabeth, late queen of Bohemia, daughter of our late Sovereign Lord King James the First of happy memory, be and is hereby declared to be the next in succession in the Protestant line to the imperial crown and dignity of the said realms of England, France and Ireland, with the dominions and territories thereunto belonging, after his Majesty and the Princess Anne of Denmark and in default of issue of the said Princess Anne and of his Majesty respectively, and that from and after the deceases of his said Majesty our now sovereign lord, and of her Royal Highness the Princess Anne of Denmark, and for default of issue of the said Princess Anne and of his Majesty respectively, the crown and regal government of the said kingdoms of England, France and Ireland and of the dominions thereunto belonging, with the royal state and dignity of the said realms, and all honors, styles, titles, regalities, prerogatives, powers, jurisdictions and authorities to the same belonging and appertaining, shall be, remain and continue to the said most excellent Princess Sophia and the heirs of her body being Protestants. . . .

II. Provided always, and it is hereby enacted, that all and every person and persons who shall or may take or inherit the said crown by virtue of the limitation of this present act, and is, are or shall be reconciled to, or shall hold communion with, the see or Church of Rome, or shall profess the popish religion or shall marry a Papist, shall be subject to such incapacities as in such case or cases are by the said recited act provided, enacted and established. . . .

That whosoever shall hereafter come to the possession of this crown shall join in communion with the Church of England as by law established.

That in case the crown and imperial dignity of this realm shall hereafter come to any person not being a native of this kingdom of England this nation be not obliged to engage in any war for the defense of any dominions or territories which do not belong to the crown of England without the consent of Parliament.

That no person who shall hereafter come to the possession of this crown shall go out of the dominions of England, Scotland or Ireland without consent of Parliament.

That from and after the time that the further limitation by this act shall take effect all matters and things relating to the well governing of this kingdom which are properly cognizable in the Privy Council by the laws and customs of this realm shall be transacted there, and all resolutions taken thereupon shall be signed by such of the Privy Council as shall advise and consent to the same.

That after the said limitation shall take effect as aforesaid no person born out of the kingdoms of England, Scotland or Ireland, or the dominions thereunto belonging (although he be naturalized or made a denizen, except such as are born of English parents), shall be capable to be of the Privy Council, or a member of either house of Parliament, or to enjoy any office or place of trust either civil or military, or to have any grant of lands, tenements or hereditaments from the crown to himself or to any other or others in trust for him.

That no person who has an office or place of profit under the king, or receives a pension from the crown, shall be capable of serving as a member of the House of Commons.[12]

That after the said limitation shall take effect as aforesaid judges' commissions be made *quam diu se bene gesserim*,[13] and

---

[12]*no person . . . Commons:* This portion of the act was repealed within four years; otherwise it would have been impossible for ministers of the crown to serve as members of the House of Commons. According to an act of 1705, members of the House of Commons appointed to a crown office that paid a salary first had to be reelected by their constituents.   [13]*quam . . . gesserim:* during good behavior.

their salaries ascertained and established, but upon the address of both houses of Parliament it may be lawful to remove them.

That no pardon under the great seal of England be pleadable to an impeachment by the Commons in Parliament. . . .

The Vicar of Bray (ca. 1725)

This anonymous poem was presumably written during the 1720s.

The Vicar of Bray

In good King *Charles's* golden days,
    When Loyalty no harm meant;
A Furious High-Church Man I was,
    And so I gain'd Preferment.
Unto my Flock I daily Preach'd,
    Kings are by God appointed,
And Damn'd are those who dare resist,
    Or touch the Lord's Anointed.
        And this is Law, I will maintain
            Unto my Dying Day, Sir,
        That whatsoever King shall Reign,
            I will be Vicar of *Bray*, Sir!

When Royal *James* possest the Crown,
    And Popery grew in fashion,
The Penal Law I hooted down,
    And read the Declaration:
The Church of *Rome*, I found would fit,
    Full well my Constitution,
And I had been a Jesuit,
    But for the Revolution.
        And this is Law, etc.

When *William* our Deliverer came,
    To heal the Nation's Grievance,
I turned the Cat in Pan again,
    And swore to him Allegiance;
Old Principles I did revoke,
    Set Conscience at a distance,
Passive Obedience is a Joke,
    A Jest is Non-resistance.
        And this is Law, etc.

When glorious *Ann* became our
        Queen,
    The Church of *England's* Glory,
Another face of things was seen,
    And I became a Tory:
Occasional Conformists base,
    I Damn'd, and Moderation,
And thought the Church in
        danger was,
    From such Prevarication.
        And this is Law, etc.

When *George* in Pudding time[14]
        came o'er,
    And Moderate Men looked big, Sir,
My Principles I chang'd once more,
    And so became a Whig, Sir:
And thus Preferment I procur'd,
    From our Faith's Great Defender,
And almost every day abjur'd
    The Pope, and the Pretender.
        And this is Law, etc.

The Illustrious House of *Hannover*,
    And Protestant Succession,
To these I lustily will swear,
    Whilst they can keep possession:
For in my Faith, and Loyalty,
    I never once will falter,
But *George*, my Lawful King shall be,
    Except the Times shou'd alter,
        And this is Law, etc.

SOURCE: From *The British Musical Miscellany* (London, 1734), Vol. I.

[14]*Pudding time:* a lucky or favorable time

2

Preindustrial England:
A Rural Eden or a
Poor and Troubled Society?

The England of the first half or two-thirds of the eighteenth century is usually seen as the England before the Industrial Revolution, a simple, traditional, and predominantly rural land. Predominantly rural it certainly was—by twentieth-century standards—but the descriptions of contemporaries reveal that neither its economy nor its society was simple. Such descriptions also suggest that while some contemporaries took great pride in their own society and in the direction it seemed to be moving, others were far more aware of the dangers, the uncertainties, and the poverty to be found in that society.

No official census took place in Great Britain before 1801, and although statistics derived from tax returns and parish registers make local and even national estimates possible for the eighteenth and even earlier centuries, they must be seen as good guesses at best. One of the most instructive was produced in the year 1696 by Gregory King (1648–1712), the "secretary to the Commissioners of the Public Accounts." The first selection of this chapter summarizes King's estimates. What do those estimates imply as to the manner in which society was organized? What do they imply as to the way various professions and occupations were ranked? What do they imply as to the division of wealth within the kingdom? What does King presumably mean by stating that certain families were "increasing" and others "decreasing" the wealth of the kingdom?

Eighteenth-century England *was* predominantly rural, and most of the selections that follow are concerned with various aspects of the rural scene. *The Farmer's Tour Through the East of England* (1771) by Arthur Young (1741–1820) provides us with insights into the activities and interests of a man who devoted a lifetime to describing the agricultural practices of his native land and encouraging their improvement. In order to promote greater efficiency in English farm practices, from 1784 to 1809 Young edited and wrote for a monthly publication called the *Annals of*

This fanciful engraving of 1727 illustrates numerous rural activities, sheep and cattle raising, bread making, and dairying among them.

Agriculture; his distinguished contributors included King George III (writing under a pseudonym). In 1793 Prime Minister William Pitt the Younger created a new government office, the board of agriculture, and appointed Young its first secretary. What types of changes does Young propose in this document—improvements involving the use of machinery or alterations in technique and in economic and legal arrangements? In the next selection, *Rural Industry* (1724), Daniel Defoe reminds us that other types of activity besides farming were carried on in the countryside. Defoe (1660–1731) was a prolific journalist, political pamphleteer, and pioneer novelist whose *Robinson Crusoe* (1719) became one of the great best-sellers of the century; it was soon translated into numerous other languages. Late in his career, Defoe wrote the combined travel guide and socioeconomic analysis of Great Britain from which this selection is drawn. What trade does Defoe describe in this document? What types of activities and sources of power does it involve?

The next two documents illuminate other aspects of the eighteenth-century world—sports and games, the diet, and the role of women in society. In 1698 Henri Misson, an obscure Frenchman, visited England. His observations, which included a description of "The Sports and Diversions of England," were subsequently published. Pehr Kalm (1716–1779) was a young Swedish naturalist who spent several months in England in 1748 on his way to North America to make a survey of vegetation there on behalf of the Royal Swedish Academy of Sciences. The *Account of His Visit to England* (1748) is based both on his stay in London and on his travels in the countryside, where presumably he stayed with families in the upper-middle ranks of society. What impressions emerge from Misson's and Kalm's accounts as to the role of sports, the role of women, and the typical diet (in the portion of society with which Kalm became acquainted)?

The extracts from Edmond Williamson's diary (1709–1720) remind us of one universal hazard during the early eighteenth century, the precariousness of human life, while David Davies's selection, *The Case of Labourers in Husbandry* (1795), provides us with insight into the budgets of laboring families in the lower ranks of society. What proportion of income went into food, into rent and fuel, and into clothing? What was the diet like? What light do these accounts throw on the economic roles of men, women, and children in the families of farm laborers?

The city of London constituted the one gigantic exception to the generalization that eighteenth-century Britain was agricultural. As Defoe's description of the city reminds us, London as a geographical entity had long since outgrown its medieval walls, and its population in the 1720s is estimated at 675,000. More than one English man or woman in ten lived there. What characteristics of London impress Defoe most? What types of activities does he believe are most important to the city? What is Defoe's attitude toward construction, innovation, and growth?

The final selection shows us the underside of eighteenth-century big-city life, its poverty and its crime, as described in *An Inquiry Into the Causes of the Late Increase of Robbers* (1751) by Henry Fielding (1707–1754). The career of Fielding was in some respects similar to that of Defoe. He too was a prolific writer, a dramatist as well as a novelist and a journalist. Late in his relatively brief career he was also admitted to the bar, and he became a Justice of the Peace for both Middlesex and Westminster. Many of Fielding's observations are therefore based on his experiences as judge. Although most of Fielding's writings contain a strong vein of irony, the problem of crime was obviously real and serious to him. How does he explain the increase in crime that he discerns in his society? What is his opinion of the criminal law of his day? What is his judgment of the manner in which that law is enforced?

GREGORY KING **A Scheme of the Income and Expense of the Several Families of England (1688)**

A late seventeenth-century statistician estimates the numbers and the incomes of the different ranks of English society at the time of the "Glorious Revolution."

Number of families	Ranks, degrees, titles and qualifications	Heads per family	Number of persons	Yearly income per family £	Total of the estates or income £	Yearly income per head £	Expense per head £	Increase per head £	Total increase per annum £
160	Temporal Lords	40	6,400	2,800	448,000	70	60	10	64,000
26	Spiritual Lords	20	520	1,300	33,800	65	55	10	5,200
800	Baronets	16	12,800	880	704,000	55	51	4	51,000
600	Knights	13	7,800	650	390,000	50	46	4	31,200
3,000	Esquires	10	30,000	450	1,200,000	45	42	3	90,000
12,000	Gentlemen	8	96,000	280	2,880,000	35	$32\frac{1}{2}$	$2\frac{1}{2}$	240,000
5,000	Persons in greater offices	8	40,000	240	1,200,000	30	27	3	120,000
5,000	Persons in lesser offices	6	30,000	120	600,000	20	18	2	60,000
2,000	Merchants and traders by sea	8	16,000	400	800,000	50	40	10	160,000
8,000	Merchants and traders by land	6	48,000	200	1,600,000	33	28	5	240,000
10,000	Persons in the law	7	70,000	140	1,400,000	20	17	3	210,000
2,000	Eminent clergymen	6	12,000	60	120,000	10	9	1	12,000
8,000	Lesser clergymen	5	40,000	45	360,000	9	8	1	40,000
40,000	Freeholders of the better sort	7	280,000	84	3,360,000	12	11	1	280,000
140,000	Freeholders of the lesser sort	5	700,000	50	7,000,000	10	$9\frac{1}{2}$	$\frac{1}{2}$	350,000
150,000	Farmers	5	750,000	44	6,600,000	$8\frac{3}{4}$	$8\frac{1}{2}$	$\frac{1}{4}$	187,000
16,000	Persons in sciences and liberal arts	5	80,000	60	960,000	12	$11\frac{1}{2}$	$\frac{1}{2}$	40,000
40,000	Shopkeepers and tradesmen	$4\frac{1}{2}$	180,000	45	1,800,000	10	$9\frac{1}{2}$	$\frac{1}{2}$	90,000
60,000	Artisans and handicrafters	4	240,000	40	2,400,000	10	$9\frac{1}{2}$	$\frac{1}{2}$	120,000
5,000	Naval officers	4	20,000	80	400,000	20	18	2	40,000
4,000	Military officers	4	16,000	60	240,000	15	14	1	16,000
511,586		$5\frac{1}{4}$	2,675,520	67	34,495,800	$12\frac{9}{10}$	12	$\frac{9}{10}$	2,447,100
50,000	Common seamen	3	150,000	20	1,000,000	7	$7\frac{1}{2}$	$\frac{1}{2}$	75,000
364,000	Laboring people and outservants	$3\frac{1}{2}$	1,275,000	15	5,600,000	$4\frac{1}{2}$	$4\frac{6}{10}$	$\frac{1}{10}$	127,500
400,000	Cottagers and paupers	$3\frac{1}{4}$	1,300,000	$6\frac{1}{2}$	2,000,000	2	$2\frac{1}{4}$	$\frac{1}{4}$	325,000
35,000	Common soldiers	2	70,000	14	490,000	7	$7\frac{1}{2}$	$\frac{1}{2}$	35,000
849,000		$3\frac{1}{4}$	2,795,000	$10\frac{1}{2}$	8,950,000	$3\frac{1}{4}$	$3\frac{9}{20}$	$\frac{1}{5}$	562,000
	Vagrants	—	30,000	—	60,000	2	3	1	60,000
849,000		$3\frac{1}{4}$	2,825,000	$10\frac{1}{2}$	9,010,000	$3\frac{3}{20}$	$3\frac{3}{8}$	$\frac{9}{40}$	622,000
		So the general account is							
511,586	Increasing the wealth of the kingdom	$5\frac{1}{4}$	2,675,520	67	34,495,800	$12\frac{9}{10}$	12	$\frac{9}{10}$	2,447,000
849,000	Decreasing the wealth of the kingdom	$3\frac{1}{4}$	2,825,000	$10\frac{1}{2}$	9,010,000	$3\frac{3}{20}$	$3\frac{3}{8}$	$\frac{9}{40}$	622,000
1,360,586	Net totals	$4\frac{1}{20}$	5,500,520	32	43,505,800	$7\frac{9}{10}$	$7\frac{45}{80}$	$\frac{27}{80}$	1,825,100

SOURCE: From George Chalmers, *An Estimate of the Comparative Strength of Great Britain* (London, 1804), Appendix, pp. 48–49.

ARTHUR YOUNG **The Farmer's Tour Through the East of England (1771)**

Arthur Young, a traveling one-man farm bureau, finds in the agricultural improvements achieved by Norfolk farmers and in the cattle-breeding experiments of Robert Bakewell an example to others.

As I shall presently leave *Norfolk*, it will not be improper to give a slight review of the husbandry which has rendered the name of this county so famous in the farming world. Pointing out the practices which have succeeded so nobly here, may perhaps be of some use to other countries possessed of the same advantages, but unknowing in the art to use them.

From 40 to 60 years ago, all the northern and western, and a part of the eastern tracts of the county, were sheep-walks, let so low as from 6d. to 1s. 6d. and 2s. an acre. Much of it was in this condition only 30 years ago. The great improvements have been made by means of the following circumstances.

FIRST. By inclosing without assistance of parliament.

SECOND. By a spirited use of marle and clay.

THIRD. By the introduction of an excellent course of crops.

FOURTH. By the culture of turnips well hand-hoed.

FIFTH. By the culture of clover and ray-grass.

SIXTH. By landlords granting long leases.

SEVENTH. By the country being divided chiefly into large farms.

In this recapitulation, I have inserted no article that is included in another. Take any one from the seven, and the improvement of *Norfolk* would never had existed. . . .

The Course of Crops

After the best managed inclosure, and the most spirited conduct in marling,[1] still the whole success of the undertaking depends on this point: No fortune will be made in *Norfolk* by farming, unless a judicious course of crops be pursued. That which has been chiefly adopted by the *Norfolk* farmers is,

1. Turnips
2. Barley
3. Clover; or clover and ray-grass
4. Wheat

Some of them, depending on their soils being richer than their neighbors (for instance, all the way from *Holt* by *Aylsham* down through the *Flegg* hundreds) will steal a crop of peas or barley after the wheat; but it is bad husbandry, and has not been followed by those men who have made fortunes. In the above course, the turnips are (if possible) manured for; and much of the wheat the same. This is a noble system, which keeps the soil rich; only one exhausting crop is taken to a cleansing and ameliorating one. The land cannot possibly in such management be either poor or foul.

. . .

Large Farms

If the preceding articles are properly reviewed, it will at once be apparent that no small farmers could effect such great things as have been done in *Norfolk*. Inclosing, marling, and keeping a stock of sheep large enough for folding, belong absolutely and exclusively to great farmers. None of them could be effected by small ones—or such as are called middling ones in other countries.—Nor should it be forgotten, that the best husbandry in *Norfolk* is that of the largest farmers. You must go to a *Curtis*, a *Mallet*, a *Barton*, a *Glover*, a *Carr*, to see

SOURCE: From Arthur Young, *The Farmer's Tour Through the East of England* (London, 1771), Vol. II, pp. 150–151, 156–157, 161–162; Vol. I, pp. 110–114.

[1]*marling:* fertilizing with carbonate of lime

Norfolk husbandry. You will not among them find the stolen crops that are too often met with among the little occupiers of an hundred a year in the eastern part of the county. Great farms have been the soul of the *Norfolk* culture: split them into tenures of an hundred pounds a year, you will find nothing but beggars and weeds in the whole county. The rich man keeps his land rich and clean.

These are the principles of *Norfolk* husbandry, which have advanced the agriculture of the greatest part of that county to a much greater height than is any where to be met with over an equal extent of country. . . .

Mr. *Bakewell* of *Dishley*, one of the most considerable farmers in this country, has in so many instances improved on the husbandry of his neighbors, that he merits particular notice in this journal.

His breed of cattle is famous throughout the kingdom; and he has lately sent many to *Ireland*. He has in this part of his business many ideas which I believe are perfectly new; or that have hitherto been totally neglected. This principle is to gain the beast, whether sheep or cow, that will weigh most in the most valuable joints:— there is a great difference between an ox of 50 stone,[2] carrying 30 in roasting pieces, and 20 in coarse boiling ones—and another carrying 30 in the latter, and 20 in the former. And at the same time that he gains the shape, that is, of the greatest value in the smallest compass; he asserts, from long experience, that he gains a breed much hardier, and easier fed than any others. These ideas he applies equally to sheep and oxen.

In the breed of the latter, the old notion was, that where you had much and large bones, there was plenty of room to lay flesh on; and accordingly the graziers were eager to buy the largest boned cattle. This whole system Mr. *Bakewell* has proved to be an utter mistake. He asserts, the smaller the bones, the truer will be the make of the beast—the quicker she will fat—and her weight, we may easily conceive, will have a larger proportion of valuable meat: *flesh*, not *bone*, is the butcher's object. Mr. *Bakewell* admits that a large boned beast, may be made a large fat beast, and that he may come to a great weight; but justly observes, that this is no part of the profitable enquiry; for stating such a simple proposition, without at the same time shewing [showing] the expense of covering those bones with flesh, is offering no satisfactory argument. The only object of real importance, is the proportion of *grass* to *value*. I have 20 acres; which will pay me for those acres best, large or small boned cattle? The latter fat so much quicker, and more profitably in the joints of value; that the query is answered in their favor from long and attentive experience. . . .

Another particularity is the amazing gentleness in which he brings up these animals. All his bulls stand still in the field to be examined: the way of driving them from one field to another, or home, is by a little swish; he or his men walk by their side, and guide him with the stick where-ever they please; and they are accustomed to this method from being calves. A lad, with a stick three feet long, and as big as his finger, will conduct a bull away from other bulls, and his cows from one end of the farm to the other. All this gentleness is merely the effect of management, and the mischief often done by bulls, is undoubtedly owing to practices very contrary—or else to a total neglect.

The general order in which Mr. *Bakewell* keeps his cattle is pleasing; all are fat as bears; and this is a circumstance which he insists is owing to the excellence of the breed. His land is no better than his neighbors, at the same time that it carries a far greater proportion of stock; as I shall shew by and by. The small quantity, and the inferior quality of food that will keep a beast perfectly well made, in good order, is surprising: such an animal will grow fat in the same pasture that would starve an ill made, great boned one.

---

[2]*stone:* 14 pounds

DANIEL DEFOE **Rural Industry (1724)**

One of early eighteenth-century England's foremost travelers and investigative reporters encounters an unusual example of industry in the countryside near the Yorkshire town of Halifax.

The nearer we came to *Halifax*, we found the houses thicker, and the villages greater in every bottom; and not only so, but the sides of the hills, which were very steep every way, were spread with houses, and that very thick; for the land being divided into small enclosures, that is to say, from two acres to six or seven acres each, seldom more; every three or four pieces of land had a house belonging to it.

Then it was I began to perceive the reason and nature of the thing, and found that this division of the land into small pieces, and scattering of the dwellings, was occasioned by, and done for the convenience of the business which the people were generally employ'd in, and that, as I said before, though we saw no people stirring without doors, yet they were all full within; for, in short, this whole country, however mountainous, and that no sooner we were down one hill but we mounted another, is yet infinitely full of people; those people all full of business; not a beggar, not an idle person to be seen, except here and there an almshouse, where people ancient, decrepid, and past labor, might perhaps be found; for it is observable, that the people here, however laborious, generally live to a great age, a certain testimony to the goodness and wholesomeness of the country, which is, without doubt, as healthy as any part of *England*; nor is the health of the people lessen'd, but help'd and establish'd by their being constantly employ'd, and, as we call it, their working hard; so that they find a double advantage by their being always in business.

This business is the clothing trade, for the convenience of which the houses are thus scattered and spread upon the sides of the hills, as above, even from the bottom to the top; *the reason is this*; such has been the bounty of nature to this otherwise frightful country, that two things essential to the business, as well as to the ease of the people are found here, and that in a situation which I never saw the like of in any part of *England*; and, I believe, the like is not to be seen so contrived in any part of the world; I mean coals and running water upon the tops of the highest hills: This seems to have been directed by the wise hand of Providence for the very purpose which is now served by it, namely, the manufactures, which otherwise could not be carried on; neither indeed could one fifth part of the inhabitants be supported without them, for the land could not maintain them. After we had mounted the third hill, we found the country, in short, one continued village, tho' mountainous every way, as before; hardly a house standing out of a speaking distance from another and (which soon told us their business) the day clearing up, and the sun shining, we could see that almost at every house there was a *tenter*, and almost on every tenter a piece of *cloth*, or *kersie*, or *shalloon*, for they are the three articles of that country's labor; from which the sun glancing, and, as I may say, shining (the white reflecting its rays) to us, I thought it was the most agreeable sight that I ever saw. . . .

Wherever we pass'd any house we found a little rill or gutter of running water, if the house was above the road, it came from it, and cross'd the way to run to another; if the house was below us, it cross'd us from some other distant house above it, and at every considerable house was a *manufactury* or work-house, and as they could not do their business without water, the little streams were so parted and guided by gutters or pipes, and by turning and dividing the

SOURCE: From Daniel Defoe, *A Tour Through the Whole Island of Great Britain* (London, 1724–1727), Vol. III, pp. 97–102.

streams, that none of those houses were without a river, if I may call it so, running into and through their work-houses.

Again, as the dying-houses, scouring-shops and places where they used this water, emitted the water again, ting'd with the dregs of the dying fat, and with the oil, the soap, the tallow, and other ingredients used by the clothiers in dressing and scouring, etc. which then runs away thro' the lands to the next, the grounds are not only universally watered, how dry soever the season, but that water so ting'd and so fatten'd enriches the lands they run through, that 'tis hardly to be imagined how fertile and rich the soil is made by it.

Then, as every clothier must keep a horse, perhaps two, to fetch and carry for the use of his manufacture, (*viz.*) to fetch home his wool and his provisions from the market, to carry his yarn to the spinners, his manufacture to the fulling mill, and when finished, to the market to be sold, *and the like;* so every manufacturer generally keeps a cow or two, or more, for his family, and this employs the two, or three, or four pieces of enclosed land about his

house, for they scarce sow corn enough for their cocks and hens; and this feeding their grounds still adds by the dung of the cattle, to enrich the soil.

But now, to speak of the bounty of nature again, which I but just mentioned; it is to be observed, that these hills are so furnished by nature with springs and mines, that not only on the sides, but even to the very tops, there is scarce a hill but you find, on the highest part of it, a spring of water, and a coal-pit. . . .

Having thus *fire* and *water* at every dwelling, there is no need to enquire why they dwell thus dispers'd upon the highest hills, the convenience of the manufactures requiring it. Among the manufacturers houses are likewise scattered an infinite number of cottages or small dwellings, in which dwell the workmen which are employed, the women and children of whom, are always busy carding, spinning, etc. so that no hands being unemploy'd, all can gain their bread, even from the youngest to the ancient; hardly any thing above four years old, but its hands are sufficient to it self. . . .

Henri Misson   The Sports and Diversions of England (1698)

A visiting Frenchman reminds us that for eighteenth-century Britons, life involved play as well as work.

Besides the sports and diversions common to most other *European* nations, as tennis, billiards, chess, tick-tack, dancing, plays etc., the *English* have some which are particular to them, or at least which they love and use more than any other People. Cock-fighting is a royal pleasure in *England*. Their combats between bulls and dogs, bears and dogs, and sometimes bulls and bears, are not battles to death, as those of cocks: Anything that looks like fighting is delicious to an *Englishman*. If two little boys quarrel in the street, then passengers stop, make a ring round them in a moment,

and set them against one another, that they may come to fisticuffs. When 'tis come to a fight, each pulls off his neckcloth and his waistcoat (some will strip themselves quite naked (their waists), and give them to hold to some of the standers-by; then they begin to brandish their fists in the air; the blows are aim'd all at the face, they kick one another's shins, they tug one another by the hair etc. He that has got the other down, may give him one blow or two before he rises, but no more; and let the boy get up ever so often, the other is oblig'd to box him again as often as he requires it. During the

SOURCE: From Henri Misson, *Memoirs and Observations in His Travels Over England* (London, 1719), pp. 304–306.

fight, the ring of by-standers encourage the combatants with great delight of heart, and never part them while they fight according to the rules: and these by-standers are not only other boys, porters and rabble, but all sorts of men of fashion; some thrusting by the mob that they may see plain, others sitting upon stalls; and all would hire places if scaffolds could be built in a moment. . . . These combats are less frequent among grown men than children, but they are not rare. . . . Wrestling too is one of the diversions of the English, especially in the northern counties. . . . In winter *football* is a useful and charming exercise: it is a leather ball about as big as one's head, fill'd with wind: This is kick'd about from one to t'other in the streets, by him that can get at it, and that is all the art of it. Setting up a cock in some open place, and knocking it down with a stick, at forty or fifty paces distance, is another sport that affords no little pleasure; but this diversion is confin'd to a certain season. . . .

Pehr Kalm Account of His Visit to England (1748)

A Swedish naturalist visits England in 1748 and reports not only on the native flora but also on the eating and other social customs of the English.

Breakfast, which here in England was almost everywhere partaken of by those more comfortably off, consisted in drinking tea, but not as we do in Sweden, when we take a quantity of hot water on an empty stomach, without anything else to it, but the English fashion was somewhat more natural, for they ate at the same time one or more slices of wheat-bread, which they had first toasted at the fire, and when it was very hot, had spread butter on it, and then placed it a little way from the fire on the hearth, so that the butter might melt well into the bread. In the summer they do not toast the bread, but only spread the butter on it before they eat it. The cold rooms here in England in the winter, and because the butter is then hard from the cold, and does not so easily admit of being spread on the bread, have perhaps given them the idea to thus toast the bread, and then spread the butter on it while it is still hot. Most people pour a little cream or sweet milk into the teacup when they are about to drink the tea. The servants in London also commonly get such a breakfast, but in the country they have to content themselves with whatever else they can get.

Dinner did not here consist of one particular kind of food, any more than it does among other peoples: but still the English nation differed somewhat particularly from others in this; that butchers' meat formed with them the greater part of the meal, and the principal dishes. The meat is prepared in various ways; yet generally speaking it is either boiled or roasted. When I say that it was boiled, let no one imagine that it was made into soup. . . . Thus, it is that in England at dinner-time they hardly ever use spoons, for anything but pouring the *sauce* on the "steak," to take turnips, potatoes, carrots, etc. from the dish, and lay them in abundance on their plates. It is indeed true that one sometimes gets a kind of *broth*. . . .

Roast meat is the Englishman's *delice* and principal dish. It is not however always roasted to the same hardness as with us in Sweden. The English roasts are particularly remarkable for two things. 1. All English meat, whether it is of Ox, Calf, Sheep, or Swine, has a fatness and a delicious taste, either because of the excellent pasture, which consist of such nourishing and sweet-scented kinds of hay as there are in this country, where the cultivation of meadows has been brought to such high

SOURCE: From Pehr Kalm, *Account of His Visit to England*, Joseph Lucas, trans. (London: Macmillan & Co., 1892), pp. 13–16, 326–328.

perfection, or some way of fattening the cattle known to the butchers alone, or, for some other reason. 2. The Englishmen understand almost better than any other people the art of properly roasting a joint, which also is not to be wondered at; because the art of cooking as practised by most Englishmen does not extend much beyond roast beef and plum pudding. *Pudding* in the same way is much eaten by Englishmen, yet not so often as butchers' meat, for there are many meals without *pudding*. I do not believe that any Englishman, who is his own master, has ever eaten a dinner without meat. *Puddings* are prepared here in manifold ways, with or without raisins, currants, and such like things in it, but they all deserve the credit of being well prepared. *Potatoes* are now very much used together with the roast meat. They are cooked as we cook turnips, and either put on the same dish as the meat or on a special one. A cup of melted butter stands beside it, to pour on to them. When they have *boiled meat*, whole carrots are laid round the sides of the dish. Cucumbers are much used with their roast meat as before described; also several kinds of green vegetables, as lettuce, salad, sprouts, and other cabbage, prepared mostly like lettuce or spinach, etc. Turnips are here used in exactly the same way as potatoes. There is also eaten much green peas when they can be had; but otherwise than green, beans and peas are very seldom eaten. *Cider* is also much drunk with roast meat. Their *pies*, which are mostly a kind of *tarts* and *pastry*, are also sometimes seen. Cheese nearly always concludes the meal. Commonly, there is set on the table, whole, a large and strong cheese, and each person cuts what he likes from it. . . .

Their drinks are various. Those who can afford it mostly drink wine, others ale, cider, "swag," or small beer, but the favourite drink of all the Englishmen is *Punch*. After meal times one generally sits for an hour at the table, or at least as long as till certain toasts have been drunk by all, such as the king's health, the Prince of Wales, the royal family, absent friends, etc. . . .

When the English women in the country are going out to pay their compliments to each other, they commonly wear a red cloak. They also wear their *pattens*[3] under their ordinary shoes when they go out, to prevent the dirt on the roads and streets from soiling their ordinary shoes. All go laced, and use for everyday a sort of *Manteau*, made commonly of brownish *Camlot*. The same head-dress as in London. Here it is not unusual to see a farmer's or another small personage's wife clad on Sundays like a lady of "quality" at other places in the world, and her every-day attire in proportion. . . . When they go out they always wear straw hats, which they have made themselves from wheat-straw, and are pretty enough. On high days they have on ruffles. One hardly ever sees a woman here trouble herself in the least about outdoor duties, such as *tending*, in the arable[4] and meadows, etc. The duty of the women in this district scarcely consists in anything else but preparing food, which they commonly do very well, though roast beef and *Pudding* forms nearly all an Englishman's eatables.

Besides that, they wash and scour dishes and floors, etc., for about cleanliness they are very careful, and especially in these things, to wash clothes, and to hem one thing and another minutely.

They never take the trouble to bake, because there is a baker in every parish or village, from whom they can always have new bread. Nearly the same can be said about brewing. Weaving and spinning is also in most houses a more than rare thing, because their many *manufacturers* save them from the necessity of such. For the rest, it belongs to the men to tend the cattle, milk the cows, and to perform all the work in the arable fields and meadows, and in the "lodge" and "lathe," etc. I confess that I at

---

[3]*pattens:* wooden clogs   [4]*arable:* cultivated fields

first rubbed my eyes several times to make them clear, because I could not believe I saw aright, when I first came here, out in the country, and saw the farmers' houses full of young women, while the men, on the contrary, went out both morning and evening to where the cattle were, milk-pail in hand, sat down to milk, and afterward carried the milk home. I had found, then, that every land has its customs. In short, when one enters a house and has seen the women cooking, washing floors, plates and dishes, darning a stocking or sewing a chemise, washing and starching linen clothes, he has, in fact, seen all their household economy and all that they do the whole of God's long day, year out and year in, when to these are added some *visitors*. Nearly all the evening occupations which our women in Sweden perform are neglected by them, but, instead, here they sit round the fire without attempting in the very least degree what we call household duties. But they can never be deprived of the credit of being very handsome and very lively in society. In pleasant conversation, agreeable *repartie*, polite sallies, in a word, in all that the public calls *politesse* and *savoir vivre*, they are never wanting.

They are lucky in having turned the greater part of the burden of responsible management on to the men, so that it is very true what both Englishmen and others write, that England is a paradise for ladies and women. It is true that common servant-girls have to have somewhat more work in them, but still this also is moderate, and seldom goes beyond what has been reckoned up above. But the mistresses and their daughters are in particular those who enjoy perfect freedom from work. . . .

EDMOND WILLIAMSON **An Account of the Birth of My Children by My Second Wife (1709–1720)**

Diary entries by an obscure Bedfordshire couple remind us how precarious eighteenth-century life could be.

1709

March 29. My wife fell into labor and a little after 9 in the morning was delivered of a son. Present: aunt Taylor, cousin White, sister Smith, cousin Clarkson, widow Hern, Mrs. Howe, midwife, Mr[s]. Wallis, nurse, Mrs. Holms, Eleanor Hobbs, servants.

April 4. He was baptised by Doctor Battle by the name of John. . . .

[**April**] **16.** The child died about 1 o'clock in the morning.

1711

Sept. 17. My said wife was delivered of a son just before 4 in the morning. Present: Mrs. Thomas Molyneux's lady and maid, Mrs. Mann, midwife, Margaret Williamson, nurse, Susan Nuthall, servant.

Oct. 4. He was baptised by Mr. Trabeck by the name of Talbot after my grandmother's name. Sir John Talbot and John Pulteny esquire were gossips,[5] with my sister Smith godmother. . . .

SOURCE: From F. J. Manning, ed., *Some Bedfordshire Diaries* (Bedford, England: Bedfordshire Historical Record Society [County Record Office], 1960), Vol. XL, pp. 35–37. By permission of the Bedfordshire Historical Record Society.

[5]*gossips:* godfathers

1713

June 9. About 8 at night my said wife began her labor.

[June] 10. Half an hour after 1 in the morning was brought to bed of a son. Present: Mrs. Molyneux, Mrs. Bisset, Mrs. Mann, midwife, Nurse Williamson, Susan Nuthall and Betty Ginger, servants.

[June] 30. Baptised by Mr. Mompesson of Mansfield by the name of Edmond. . . .

1715

March 7. My said wife was brought to bed of a daughter 10 minutes before 6 in the morning. Present: Mrs. Molyneux, Mrs. Mann, midwife, Nurse Williamson, Mary Evans, Mary Cole and Mary Wheeler, servants.

[March] 29. Was baptised by Dr. Mandivel, chancellor of Lincoln, by the name of Christian.

1716

March 9. My wife was delivered of a daughter at 7 at night. Present: aunt Taylor, Mrs. Molyneux, Mrs. Oliver, Mrs. Mann, midwife, Mary Smith, nurse, Jane Kensey, and Mary Wheeler, servants.

[March] 31. Was baptised by Mr. Widmore, the reader of St. Margaret's, by the name of Elizanna. . . . Registered in St. Margaret's, Westminster, as all the rest were.

April 27. Died, was buried in the new chapel yard in the Broadway.

1718

Jan. 21. (C.W.) I was brought to bed of a son about 2 in the morning, Mrs. Mann, midwife, nurse Chatty, dry-nurse, present; Mrs. Taylor, Mrs. White and Mrs. Molyneux, Jane Beadle; servants: Mary Wells, Jane Griffith, Edmond Kinward. He was baptised by Mr. Widmore, reader of St. Margaret's, Westminster, by the name of Francis. . . .

1719

Feb. 21. (C.W.) I was brought to bed of a son between 6 and 7 in the evening, Mrs. Mann, midwife, nurse Chatty, dry-nurse; present: aunt Taylor, Mrs. Molyneux and Jane Beadle; servants: Rebecca Shippy, Betty Hall and Mathew Dowect.

March 7. He was baptised by Mr. Widmore, reader of St. Margaret's, Westminster, by the name of William. . . .

[N.d.] Died and buried at Hadley.

1720

June. (E.W.) My wife brought to bed of a daughter, but the child did not live a minute.

July 21. My wife died and was buried at Isleworth.

Sept. 9. [Francis] died of the smallpox at Nurse Ward's in Hampstead, and was buried at Hadley.

DAVID DAVIES **The Case of Laborers in Husbandry (1795)**

A late eighteenth-century English clergyman collects information on the weekly income and expenses of farm laborer families in his parish.

In visiting the laboring families of my parish, as my duty led me, I could not but observe with concern their mean and distressed condition. I found them in general but indifferently fed; badly clothed; some children without shoes and stockings; very few put to school; and most families in debt to little shopkeepers. In short, there was scarcely any appearance of comfort about their dwellings, except that the children

SOURCE: From David Davies, *The Case of Labourers in Husbandry* (London, 1795), pp. 7–8, 10–11, 110–112.

looked tolerably healthy. Yet I could not impute the wretchedness I saw either to sloth or wastefulness. For I knew that the farmers were careful that the men should not want employment; and had they been given to drinking, I am sure I should have heard enough of it. And I commonly found the women, when not working in the fields, well occupied at home; seldom indeed earning money; but baking their bread, washing and mending their garments, and rocking the cradle. . . .

These accounts of the earnings and expences of laboring families in my own parish, were collected about *Easter* 1787, when affairs relating to the poor were under the consideration of the Parliament and the public. From what loose information I could then gather near home, I saw sufficient reason to believe, that they presented but too faithful a view of the general distress of such families throughout this and the neighboring counties. And the vast increase of the poor-rate, at that time every where a subject of complaint, rendered it very probable that the same misery had overspread the kingdom. . . .

Accounts of the Expenses and Earnings of Six Laboring Families in the Parish of Barkham in the County of Berks, taken at Easter 1787

No. I.

Weekly expenses of a family, consisting of a man and his wife, and five children, the eldest eight years of age, the youngest an infant

	s.	*d.*
Flour, 7½ gallons, at 10*d. per* gallon	6	3
Yeast, to make it into bread, 2½*d.*; and salt 1½*d.*	0	4
Bacon, 1 lb. boiled at two or three times with greens: the pot-liquor, with bread and potatoes, makes a *mess* for the children	0	8
Tea, 1 ounce, 2*d.*; ¾ lb. sugar, 6*d.*; ½ lb. butter or lard, 4*d.*	1	0
Soap, ¼ lb. at 9*d. per* lb	0	2¼
Candles, ⅓ lb. one week with another at a medium, at 9*d.*	0	3
Thread, thrum, and worsted, for mending apparel, etc.	0	3
Total	8	11¼

Weekly earnings of the man and his wife, viz.

	s.	*d.*
The man receives the common weekly wages 8 months in the year	7	0
By task work the remaining 4 months he earns something more: his *extra* earnings, if equally divided among the 52 weeks in the year, would increase the weekly wages about	1	0
The wife's common work is to bake bread for the family, to wash and mend ragged clothes, and to look after the children; but at bean-setting, hay-making, and harvest, she earns as much as comes one week with another to about	0	6
Total	8	6
Weekly expenses of his family	8	11¼
Weekly earnings	8	6
Deficiency of earnings	0	5¼

---

[6]During the eighteenth century—and indeed until 1972—the English monetary system was made up of pounds, shillings, and pence. Each pound (£) consisted of twenty shillings (*s.*), each shilling of twenty pence (*d.*)

Weekly earnings of the same family (Easter, 1787)

	£	s.	d.
The husband receives 8s. per week, throughout the year	0	8	0
The eldest boy...	0	2	6
The next boy	0	1	6
The *wife* was taught by her mother to *read* and *spin*, and she teaches her girls the same. Before she went into service, she used to spin a pair of coarse sheets every winter. When she sits closely to her wheel the whole day, she can spin 2 lbs. of coarse flax for ordinary sheeting and toweling, at 2½d. per lb.; therefore, supposing the business of the family to take up two days in the week, the 8 lbs. spun in the other four days comes to.........................	0	1	8
The *eldest* girl can earn 2d. per day, spinning near 1 lb. of such flax; and supposing her also to lose two days in the week in going of errands, tending the infant, etc. her earnings will be	0	0	8
The *little girl*, aged five, can also spin adroitly; she goes to the wheel when her sister is otherwise employed, but is not kept closely to it, as that might hurt her health.			
This family earns something extraordinary in harvest; and as the *man* does not scruple working over-hours occasionally, and looks after the stock on one of his employer's farms, they are allowed to live rent-free in the farm-house; all which together may be reckoned equal to...	0	1	0
	0	15	4
Amount of *earnings* per annum	39	17	4
Amount of *expenses* per annum..	39	14	4
Surplus of earnings..	0	3	0

Weekly expenses of a family [another case]

Consisting of a Man, and his Wife, and Five Children; the eldest boy aged twelve years; the next a boy aged nine; the third and fourth, girls aged seven and five; the youngest, an infant.

(*This account was taken at Easter* 1787.)

	£	s.	d.
One bushel of flour, on an average, at 10d. per gallon	0	6	8
Yeast and salt	0	0	3½
A *fat hog* bought, weight about fourteen score, at 7s. 6d. per score, 5l. 5s.; And *bacon* bought beside, about six score, at 6½d. per lb. 3l. 5s.; Total 8l. 10s. Per week	0	3	3½
Tea, 1½ oz. 4d.; *Sugar*, ½ lb. 4d.; *Butter*, ½ lb. 4d...	0	1	0
Brews a *peck of malt* once a fortnight, cost 1s. 4d; Buys 1½ gall. of *hopseed*, at 1s. 6d. which serves all the year; a handful of this put into the beer makes it keep well enough for that short time...	0	0	8¼
Soap, Candles, Worsted, etc.	0	0	8
	£.0	12	7¼

The good woman reckons *small beer and bread* a better and cheaper supper, than *bread and cheese and water;* and says, that *cheese* is the dearest article that a poor family can use.

Her general account was this: that the earnings of her husband and the boys maintained the family in food; and that what she herself and the girls earnt by spinning, and in harvest, found them in clothes, linen, and other necessaries: with which the account of particulars agrees.

	£	s.	d.
Twelve shillings and seven-pence per week, is per annum...................................	32	14	4
Add for rent, fuel, clothing, etc.	7	0	0
Amount of *expenses* per annum	£.39	14	4

DANIEL DEFOE **London (1727)**

Daniel Defoe describes the London of the 1720s.

In travelling thro' England, a luxuriance of objects presents it self to our view: . . . New foundations are always laying, new buildings always raising, highways repairing, churches and publick buildings erecting, fires and other calamities happening, fortunes of families taking different turns, new trades are every day erected, new projects enterpris'd, new designs laid; so that as long as England is a trading, improving nation, no perfect description either of the place, the people, or the conditions and state of things can be given. . . .

London, as a city only, and as its walls and liberties line it out, might, indeed, be viewed in a small compass; but, when I speak of London, now in the modern acceptation, you expect I shall take in all that vast mass of buildings, reaching from Black-Wall in the east, to Tot-Hill Fields in the west; and extended in an unequal breadth, from the bridge, or river, in the south, to Islington north; and from Peterburgh House on the bank side in Westminster, to Cavendish Square, and all the new buildings by, and beyond, Hannover Square, by which the city of London, for so it is still to be called, is extended to Hide Park Corner in the Brentford Road, and almost to Maribone in the Acton Road, and how much farther it may spread, who knows? New squares, and new streets rising up every day to such a prodigy of buildings, that nothing in the world does, or ever did, equal it, except old Rome in Trajan's time. . . .

It is the disaster of London, as to the beauty of its figure, that it is thus stretched out in buildings, just at the pleasure of every builder, or undertaker of buildings, and as the convenience of the people directs, whether for trade, or otherwise; and this has spread the face of it in a most straggling, confus'd manner, out of all shape, un-

compact, and unequal; neither long or broad, round or square; whereas the city of Rome, though a monster for its greatness, yet was, in a manner, round, with very few irregularities in its shape. . . .

The extent or circumference of the continued buildings of the cities of London and Westminster, and borough of Southwark, all which, in the common acceptation, is called London, amounts to thirty six miles, two furlongs, thirty nine rods.

It is true, that before the Fire of London [of 1666], the streets were narrow, and publick edifices, as well as private, were more crowded, and built closer to one another; for soon after the Fire, the king, by his proclamation, forbid all persons whatsoever, to go about to re-build for a certain time, viz. till the Parliament (which was soon to sit) might regulate and direct the manner of building, and establish rules for the adjusting every man's property, and yet might take order for a due inlarging of the streets, and appointing the manner of building, as well for the beauty as the convenience of the city, and for safety, in case of any future accident; for though I shall not inquire, whether the city was burnt by accident, or by treachery, yet nothing was more certain, than that as the city stood before, it was strangely exposed to the disaster which happen'd, and the buildings look'd as if they had been form'd to make one general bonfire, whenever any wicked party of incendiaries should think fit.

The streets were not only narrow, and the houses all built of timber, lath and plaster, or, as they were very properly call'd paper work, and one of the finest range of buildings in the Temple, are, to this day, called the Paper Buildings, from that usual expression.

But the manner of the building in those

SOURCE: From Daniel Defoe, *A Tour Through the Whole Island of Great Britain* (London, 1724–1727), 3 vols.: Vol. I, p. iv; Vol. II, pp. v, 95, 106, 110–111, 120–122, 127–129, 132–138, 142–145, 148–150, 153–154, 156–157, 169–172, 176–178, 187–188.

days, one story projecting out beyond another, was such, that in some narrow streets, the houses almost touch'd one another at the top, and it has been known, that men, in case of fire, have escaped on the tops of the houses, by leaping from one side of a street to another. . . .

It should be observed, that the city being now re-built, has occasioned the building of some publick edifices, even in the place which was inhabited, which yet were not before, and the re-building others in a new and more magnificent manner than ever was done before.

That beautiful column, called the Monument, erected at the charge of the city, to perpetuate the fatal burning of the whole, cannot be mentioned but with some due respect to the building itself, as well as to the city; it is two hundred and two feet high, and in its kind, out does all the obelisks and pillars of the ancients, at least that I have seen, having a most stupendous stair-case in the middle to mount up to the balcony, which is about thirty feet short of the top, and whence there are other steps made even to look out at the top of the whole building; the top is fashioned like an urn. . . .

The Royal Exchange, the greatest and finest of the kind in the world, is the next publick work of the citizens, the beauty of which answers for itself, and needs no description here; 'tis observable, that tho' this Exchange cost the citizens an immense sum of money re-building, some authors say, eighty thousand pounds, being finished and embellished in so exquisite a manner, yet it was so appropriated to the grand affair of business, that the rent or income of it for many years, fully answered the interest of the money laid out in building it. . . .

The churches in London are rather convenient than fine, not adorned with pomp and pageantry as in popish countries; but, . . . the beauty of all the churches in the city, and of all the Protestant churches in the world, is the cathedral of St. Paul's; a building exceeding beautiful and magnificent; tho' some authors are pleased to expose their ignorance, by pretending to find fault with it. . . .

Supposing now, the whole body of this vast building to be considered as one city, London, and not concerning myself or the reader with the distinction of its several jurisdictions; we shall then observe it only as divided into three, viz. the city, the court, and the out-parts.

The city is the center of its commerce and wealth.

The court of its gallantry and splendor.

The out-parts of its numbers and mechanicks; and in all these, no city in the world can equal it.

Between the court and city, there is a constant communication of business to that degree, that nothing in the world can come up to it.

As the city is the center of business; there is the custom-house, an article, which, as it brings in an immense revenue to the publick, so it cannot be removed from its place, all the vast import and export of goods being, of necessity, made there; nor can the merchants be removed, the river not admitting the ships to come any farther.

Here, also, is the Excise Office, the Navy Office, the Bank, and almost all the offices where those vast funds are fixed, in which so great a part of the nation are concerned, and on the security of which so many millions are advanced.

Here are the South Sea Company, the East India Company, the Bank, the African Company, etc. whose stocks support that prodigious paper commerce, called stock-jobbing; a trade, which once bewitched the nation almost to its ruin, and which, tho' reduced very much, and recover'd from that terrible infatuation which once overspread the whole body of the people, yet is still a negotiation, which is so vast in its extent, that almost all the men of substance in England are more or less concerned in it, and the property of which is so very often alienated, that even the tax upon the transfers of stock, tho' but five shillings for each transfer, brings many thousand pounds a year to the government; and some have said, that there is not less than a hundred millions of stock transferred forward or backward from one hand to another every year, and this is one thing which makes such a constant daily intercourse between the court part of the town, and the city; and this is given as one of the principal causes of the prodigious conflux of the nobility and gentry from all parts of England to London, more than ever was known in former years. . . .

This is the reason why, notwithstanding the encrease of new buildings, and the addition of new cities, as they may be called, every year to the old, yet a house is no sooner built, but 'tis tenanted and inhabited, and every part is crouded with people, and that not only in the town, but in all the towns and villages round, as shall be taken notice of in its place. . . .

The council, the Parliament, and the courts of justice, are all kept at the same part of the town;[7] but as all suits among the citizens are, by virtue of their privileges, to be try'd within the liberty of the city, so the term is obliged to be (as it were) adjourned from Westminster-Hall to Guild-Hall, to try causes there; also criminal cases are in like manner tried monthly at the Old Baily, where a special commission is granted for that purpose to the judges; but the Lord Mayor always presides, and has the chair.

The equality, however, being thus preserved, and a perfect good understanding between the court and city having so long flourished, this union contributes greatly to the flourishing circumstances of both, and the publick credit is greatly raised by it; for it was never known, that the city, on any occasion, was so assistant to the government, as it has been since this general good agreement. No sum is so great, but the Bank has been able to raise. . . .

[In the city] are several great offices for several societies of ensurers; for here almost all hazards may be ensured; the four principal are called, (1) Royal Exchange Ensurance: (2) The London Ensurers: (3) The Hand in Hand Fire Office: (4) The Sun Fire Office. . . .

The East-India House is in Leadenhall-Street, an old, but spacious building; very convenient, though not beautiful, and I am told, it is under consultation to have it taken down, and rebuilt with additional buildings for warehouses and cellars for their goods, which at present are much wanted. . . .

In the next street (the Old Jury) is the Excise Office, in a very large house, formerly the dwelling of Sir John Fredrick, and afterwards, of Sir Joseph Hern, very considerable merchants. In this one office is managed an immense weight of business, and they have in pay, as I am told, near four thousand officers: The whole kingdom is divided by them into proper districts, and to every district, a collector, a supervisor, and a certain number of gaugers, called, by the vulgar title excise men. . . .

The Post Office, a branch of the revenue formerly not much valued, but now, by the additional penny upon the letters, and by the visible increase of business in the nation, is grown very considerable. This office maintains now, pacquet boats to Spain and Portugal, which never was done before: So the merchants letters for Cadiz or Lisbonne, which were before two and twenty days in going over France and Spain to Lisbonne, oftentimes arrive there now, in nine or ten days from Falmouth. . . .

The penny post, a modern contrivance of a private person, one Mr. William Dockraw, is now made a branch of the general revenue by the Post Office; and though, for a time, it was subject to miscarriages and mistakes, yet now it is come also into so exquisite a management, that nothing can be more exact, and 'tis with the utmost safety and dispatch, that letters are delivered at the remotest corners of the town, almost as soon as they could be sent by a messenger, and that from four, five, six, to eight times a day, according as the distance of the place makes it practicable; and you may send a letter from Ratcliff or Limehouse in the East, to the farthest part of Westminster for a penny, and that several times in the same day.

Nor are you tied up to a single piece of paper, as in the General Post-Office, but any

---

[7]*part of the town:* Westminster

packet under a pound weight, goes at the same price.

I mention this the more particularly, because it is so manifest a testimony to the greatness of this city, and to the great extent of business and commerce in it, that this penny conveyance should raise so many thousand pounds in a year, and employ so many poor people in the diligence of it, as this office employs. . . .

From these publick places, I come next to the markets, which, in such a mass of building, and such a collection of people, and where such business is done, must be great, and very many. To take a view of them in particular;

First, Smithfield market for living cattle, which is, without question, the greatest in the world. . . . [Defoe goes on to describe other markets for meat, fish, herbs, hay, leather, etc.]

There are but two corn[8] markets in the whole city and out parts; but they are monsters for magnitude, and not to be matched in the world. These are Bear Key, and Queen Hith: To the first comes all the vast quantity of corn that is brought into the city by sea, and here corn may be said, not to be sold by cart loads, or horse loads, but by ship loads, and, except the corn chambers and magazines in Holland, when the fleets come in from Dantzick[9] and England, the whole world cannot equal the quantity bought and sold here. . . .

The next market, which is more than ordinary remarkable, is the coal market at Billingsgate. . . . I need not, except for the sake of strangers, take notice, that the city of London, and parts adjacent, as also all the south of England, is supplied with coals, called therefore sea-coal, from Newcastle upon Tyne, and from the coast of Durham, and Northumberland. This trade is so considerable, that it is esteemed the great nursery of our best seamen. . . . The quantity of coals, which it is supposed are, *communibus annis*,[10] burnt and consumed in and about this city, is supposed to be about five

hundred thousand chalder, every chalder containing thirty-six bushels, and generally weighing about thirty hundred weight. . . .

There is one great work yet behind, which, however, seems necessary to a full description of the city of London, and that is the shipping and the pool;[11] but in what manner can any writer go about it, to bring it into any reasonable compass? The thing is a kind of infinite, and the parts to be separated from one another in such a description, are so many, that it is hard to know where to begin.

The whole river, in a word, from London-Bridge to Black Wall, is one great arsenal, nothing in the world can be like it [except Amsterdam]. . . .

I should mention, for the information of strangers, etc. that the buildings of this great city are chiefly of brick, as many ways found to be the safest, the cheapest, and the most commodious of all other materials; by safe, I mean from fire, and as by act of Parliament, every builder is bound to have a partition wall of brick also, one brick and half thick between every house, it is found to be, indeed, very helpful in case of fire.

And as I am speaking of fire and burning of houses, it cannot be omitted, That no where in the world is so good care taken to quench fires as in London; I will not say the like care is taken to prevent them; for I must say, That I think the servants, nay, and masters too in London, are the most careless people in the world about fire, and this, no doubt, is the reason why there are frequently more fires in London and in the out-parts, than there are in all the cities of Europe put them together; nor are they the more careful, as I can learn, either from observation or report, I say, they are not made more cautious, by the innumerable fires which continually happen among them. . . .

There are two great engines for the raising the Thames water, one at the bridge, and the other near Broken Wharf; these raise so great a quantity of water, that, as

---

[8]*corn:* grain   [9]*Dantzick:* Danzig (or Gdansk)   [10]*communibus annis:* by the community annually   [11]*the pool:* port

they tell us, they are able to supply the whole city in its utmost extent, and to supply every house also, with a running pipe of water up to the uppermost story[12]. . . .

The gates of the city are seven, besides posterns, and the posterns that remain are four, besides others that are demolished.

The gates are all remaining, two of them which were demolished at the fire, being beautifully re-built: These are Ludgate and Newgate; the first a prison for debt for freemen of the city only, the other a prison for criminals, both for London and Middlesex, and for debtors also for Middlesex, being the county gaol. . . .

There are in London, and the far extended bounds, which I now call so, notwithstanding we are a nation of liberty, more publick and private prisons, and houses of confinement, than any city in Europe, perhaps as many as in all the capital cities of Europe put together. . . .

To sum up my description of London, take the following heads; There are in this great mass of buildings thus called London,

Two cathedrals.

Four choirs for musick-worship.

One hundred and thirty five parish churches.

Nine new churches unfinished, being part of fifty appointed to be built.

Sixty nine chapels where the Church of England service is perform'd.

Two churches at Deptford, taken into the limits now describ'd.

Twenty eight foreign churches.

Besides Dissenters meetings of all persuasions;

Popish chapels; and

One Jews synagogue.

There are also, thirteen hospitals, besides lesser charities, call'd alms-houses, of which they reckon above a hundred, many of which have chapels for Divine Service.

Three colleges.

Twenty-seven publick prisons.

Eight publick schools, called free schools.

Eighty three charity schools.

Fourteen markets for flesh.

Two for live cattle, besides two herb-markets.

Twenty three other markets, as describ'd.

Fifteen Inns of Court.

Four fairs.

Twenty seven squares, besides those within any single building, as the Temple, Somerset House, &c.

Five publick bridges.

One town-house, or Guild-Hall.

One Royal Exchange.

Two other exchanges only for shops.

One custom-house.

Three artillery grounds.

Four pest-houses.

Two bishops palaces; and

Three royal palaces.

Having dwelt thus long in the city, I mean properly called so, I must be the shorter in my account of other things.

The king's palace, tho' the receptacle of all the pomp and glory of Great Britain, is really mean, in comparison of the rich furniture within, I mean the living furniture, the glorious court of the king of Great Britain: The splendor of the nobility, the wealth and greatness of the attendants, the economy of the house, and the real grandeur of the whole royal family, out-does all the courts of Europe, even that of France itself, as it is now managed since the death of Lewis the Great.

But the palace of St. James's is, I say, too mean. . . .

Even St. Stephen's Chapel, formerly the royal chapel of the palace, but till lately beautify'd for the convenience of the House of Commons, was a very indifferent place, old and decay'd: The House of Lords is a venerable old place, indeed; but how mean, how incoherent, and how straitned are the several avenues to it, and rooms about it? the matted gallery, the lobby, the back ways the king goes to it, how short are they all of

---

[12]*running . . . story:* a possibility not realized during the eighteenth century

the dignity of the place, and the glory of a king of Great Britain, with the Lords and Commons, that so often meet there? . . .

Come we next to Westminster-Hall; 'tis true, it is a very noble Gothick building, ancient, vastly large, and the finest roof of its kind in England, being one hundred feet wide; but what a wretched figure does it make without doors; the front, a vast pinacle or pedement, after the most ancient and almost forgotten part of the Gothick way of working; the building itself, resembles nothing so much as a great barn of three hundred feet long, and really looks like a barn at a distance. . . .

The Abbey, or Collegiate Church of Westminster, stands next to this; a venerable old pile of building, it is indeed, but so old and weak, that had it not been taken in hand some years ago, and great cost bestowed in upholding and repairing it, we might, by this time, have called it a heap, not a pile, and not a church, but the ruins of a church.

But it begins to stand upon new legs now, and as they continue to work upon the repairs of it, the face of the whole building will, in a short while, be entirely new. . . .

It is become such a piece of honor to be buried in Westminster-Abbey, that the body of the church begins to be crowded with the bodies of citizens, poets, seamen, and parsons, nay, even with very mean persons, if they have but any way made themselves known in the world; so that in time, the royal ashes will be thus mingled with common dust, that it will leave no room either for king or common people, or at least not for their monuments, some of which also are rather pompously foolish, than solid and to the purpose.

Near to this church is the Royal Free-School, the best of its kind in England, not out-done either by Winchester or Eaton, for a number of eminent scholars. . . .

From this part of the town, we come into the publick streets, where nothing is more remarkable than the hurries of the people; Charing-Cross is a mixture of court and city; Man's Coffee-house is the Exchange Alley of this part of the town, and 'tis per-petually throng'd with men of business, as the others are with men of play and pleasure. . . .

Advancing thence to the Hay-Market, we see, first, the great new theatre, a very magnificent building, and perfectly accommodated for the end for which it was built, tho' the entertainment there of late, has been chiefly operas and balls.

These meetings are called BALLS, the word *masquerade* not being so well relished by the English, who, tho' at first fond of the novelty, began to be sick of the thing on many accounts; However, as I cannot in justice say any thing to recommend them, and am by no means, to make this work be a satyr[13] upon any thing; I choose to say no more; but go on.

From hence westward and northward, lie those vastly extended buildings, which add so exceedingly to the magnitude of the whole body, and of which I have already said so much: It would be a task too great for this work, to enter into a description of all the fine houses, or rather palaces of the nobility in these parts. . . .

Hospitals like Bedlam and houses of correction like Bridewell indicate that this age has produced some of the most eminent acts of publick charity, and of the greatest value, I mean from private persons, that can be found in any age within the reach of our English history. . . .

These, added to the innumerable number of alms-houses which are to be seen in almost every part of the city, make it certain, that there is no city in the world can shew the like number of charities from private hands, there being, as I am told, not less than twenty thousand people maintained of charity, besides the charities of schooling for children, and besides the collections yearly at the annual feasts of several kinds, where money is given for putting out children apprentices, etc. so that the Papists have no reason to boast, that there were greater benefactions and acts of charity to the poor given in their times, than in our Protestant times. . . .

---

[13]*satyr:* satire

HENRY FIELDING **An Inquiry Into the Causes of the Late Increase of Robbers (1751)**

The eighteenth-century novelist and judge ponders how and why the London of his day has become a crime-ridden city.

The great increase of robberies within these few years is an evil which to me appears to deserve some attention; and the rather as it seems (though already become so flagrant) not yet to have arrived to that height of which it is capable, and which it is likely to attain; for diseases in the political, as in the natural body, seldom fail going on to their crisis, especially when nourished and encouraged by faults in the constitution. In fact, I make no doubt, but that the streets of this town, and the roads leading to it, will shortly be impassable without the utmost hazard; nor are we threatened with seeing less dangerous gangs of rogues among us, than those which the Italians call the banditti.

Should this ever happen to be the case, we shall have sufficient reason to lament that remissness by which this evil was suffered to grow to so great a height. All distempers, if I may once more resume the allusion, the sooner they are opposed, admit of the easier and the safer cure. . . .

For my own part, I cannot help regarding these depredations in a most serious light; nor can I help wondering that a nation so jealous of her liberties, that from the slightest cause, and often without any cause at all, we are always murmuring at our superiors, should tamely and quietly support the invasion of her properties by a few of the lowest and vilest among us: doth not this situation in reality level us with the most enslaved countries? If I am to be assaulted, and pillaged, and plundered; if I can neither sleep in my own house nor walk the streets, nor travel in safety; is not my condition almost equally bad whether a licensed or unlicensed rogue, a dragoon or a robber, be the person who assaults and plunders me? . . .

I cannot help thinking it high time to put some stop to the farther progress of such impudent and audacious insults, not only on the properties of the subject, but on the national justice, and on the laws themselves. The means of accomplishing this (the best which suggest themselves to me) I shall submit to the public consideration, after having first inquired into the causes of the present growth of this evil, and whence we have great reason to apprehend its farther increase. . . .

First then, I think, that the vast torrent of luxury, which of late years hath poured itself into this nation, hath greatly contributed to produce, among many others, the mischief I here complain of. I am not here to satirize the great, among whom luxury is probably rather a moral than a political evil. But vices no more than diseases will stop with them; for bad habits are as infectious by example, as the plague itself by contact. In free countries, at least, it is a branch of liberty claimed by the people to be as wicked and as profligate as their superiors. Thus while the nobleman will emulate the grandeur of a prince, and the gentleman will aspire to the proper state of the nobleman, the tradesman steps from behind his counter into the vacant place of the gentleman. Nor doth the confusion end here; it reaches the very dregs of the people, who aspiring still to a degree beyond that which belongs to them, and not being able by the fruits of honest labor to support the state which they affect, they disdain the wages to which their industry would entitle them;

SOURCE: From Henry Fielding, *An Inquiry Into the Causes of the Late Increase of Robbers* (1751) reprinted in *The Works of Henry Fielding, Esq.* (London: Smith, Elder, 1882), 10 vols.: Vol. VII, pp. 161–164, 171, 176–177, 179–180, 187–188, 218–219, 225, 240–241, 251–252, 256, 263–267, 270.

and abandoning themselves to idleness, the more simple and poor-spirited betake themselves to a state of starving and beggary, while those of more art and courage become thieves, sharpers,[14] and robbers. . . .

But the expense of money, and loss of time, with their certain consequences, are not the only evils which attend the luxury of the vulgar; drunkenness is almost inseparably annexed to the pleasures of such people. A vice by no means to be construed as a spiritual offense alone, since so many temporal mischiefs arise from it; amongst which are very frequently robbery, and murder itself. . . .

The drunkenness I here intend[15] is that acquired by the strongest intoxicating liquors, and particularly by that poison called *Gin*; which I have great reason to think is the principal sustenance (if it may be so called) of more than a hundred thousand people in this metropolis. Many of these wretches there are who swallow pints of this poison within the twenty-four hours; the dreadful effects of which I have the misfortune every day to see, and to smell too. But I have no need to insist on my own credit, or on that of my informers; the great revenue arising from the tax on this liquor (the consumption of which is almost wholly confined to the lowest order of people) will prove the quantity consumed better than any other evidence.

Now, besides the moral ill consequences occasioned by this drunkenness, with which, in this treatise, I profess not to deal; how greatly must this be supposed to contribute to those political mischiefs which this essay proposes to remedy? . . . Many instances of this I see daily; wretches are often brought before me, charged with theft and robbery, whom I am forced to confine before they are in a condition to be examined; and when they have afterwards become sober, I have plainly perceived, from the state of the case, that the *Gin* alone was the cause of the transgression, and have been sometimes sorry that I was obliged to commit them to prison.

But beyond all this there is a political ill consequence of this drunkenness . . . and this is that dreadful consequence which must attend the poisonous quality of this pernicious liquor to the health, the strength, and the very being of numbers of his Majesty's most useful subjects. . . .

I come now to the last great evil which arises from the luxury of the vulgar; and this is gaming; a school in which most highwaymen of great eminence have been bred. This vice is the more dangerous as it is deceitful, and, contrary to every other species of luxury, flatters its votaries with the hopes of increasing their wealth; so that avarice itself is so far from securing us against its temptations, that it often betrays the more thoughtless and giddy part of mankind into them; promising riches without bounds, and those to be acquired by the most sudden as well as easy and indeed pleasant means. . . .

Having now run through the several immediate consequences of a general luxury among the lower people, all which, as they tend to promote their distresses, may be reasonably supposed to put many of them, of the bolder kind, upon unlawful and violent means of relieving the mischief which such vices have brought upon them, I come now to a second cause of the evil, in the improper regulation of what is called the poor in this kingdom, arising, I think, partly from the abuse of some laws, and partly from the total neglect of others; and (if I may presume to say it) somewhat perhaps from a defect in the laws themselves.

It must be matter of astonishment to any man to reflect, that in a country where the poor are, beyond all comparison, more liberally provided for than in any other part of the habitable globe, there should be found more beggars, more distressed and miserable objects, than are to be seen throughout all the states of Europe. . . .

Can a general neglect of the poor be justly charged on a nation in which the poor are provided for by a tax, frequently equal to what is called the land-tax, and where there

---

[14]*sharpers:* swindlers   [15]*intend:* refer to

are such numerous instances of private donations, such numbers of hospitals, almshouses, and charitable provisions of all kinds?

Nor can any such neglect be charged on the legislature; under whose inspection this branch of polity hath been almost continually, from the days of Queen Elizabeth to the present time. . . .

If therefore there be still any deficiency in this respect, it must, I think, arise from one of the three causes above mentioned; that is, from some defect in the laws themselves, or from the perversion of these laws; or, lastly, from the neglect in their execution. . . .

In serious truth, if proper care should be taken to provide for the present poor, and to prevent their increase by laying some effectual restraints on the extravagance of the lower sort of people, the remaining part of this treatise would be rendered of little consequence [but] if we will not remove the temptation, at least we ought to take away all encouragement to robbery. . . .

Now one great encouragement to theft of all kinds is the ease and safety with which stolen goods may be disposed of. It is a very old and vulgar, but a very true saying, "That if there were no receivers there would be no thieves." Indeed could not the thief find a market for his goods, there would be an absolute end of several kinds of theft; such as shoplifting, burglary, etc., the objects of which are generally goods and not money. Nay, robberies on the highway would so seldom answer the purpose of the adventurer, that very few would think it worth their while to risk so much with such small expectations.

But at present, instead of meeting with any such discouragement, the thief disposes of his goods with almost as much safety as the honestest tradesman. . . .

The other great encouragement to robbery, beside the certain means of finding a market for the booty, is the probability of escaping punishment.

First, then, the robber hath great hopes of

being undiscovered; and this is one principal reason why robberies are more frequent in this town, and in its neighborhood, than in the remoter parts of the kingdom.

Whoever indeed considers the cities of London and Westminster, with the late vast addition of their suburbs, the great irregularity of their buildings, the immense number of lanes, alleys, courts, and bye-places; must think, that, had they been intended for the very purpose of concealment, they could scarce have been better contrived. Upon such a view the whole appears as a vast wood or forest, in which a thief may harbor with as great security as wild beasts do in the deserts of Africa or Arabia; for, by *wandering* from one part to another, and often shifting his quarters, he may almost avoid the possibility of being discovered. . . .

Where then is the redress? Is it not *to hinder the poor from wandering*, and this by compelling the parish and peace officers to apprehend such wanderers or vagabonds, and by empowering the magistrate effectually to punish and send them to their habitations? Thus if we cannot discover, or will not encourage any cure for idleness, we shall at least compel the poor to starve or beg at home; for there it will be impossible for them to steal or rob without being presently hanged or transported[16] out of the way.

I come now to a third encouragement which the thief flatters himself with; viz. in his hopes of escaping from being apprehended.

Nor is this hope without foundation: how long have we known highwaymen reign in this kingdom after they have been publicly known for such? Have not some of these committed robberies in open daylight, in the sight of many people, and have afterward rode solemnly and triumphantly through the neighboring towns without any danger or molestation? This happens to every rogue who is become eminent for his audaciousness, and is thought to be desperate; and is, in a more particular manner, the

---

[16]*transported:* permanently exiled to the colonies

case of great and numerous gangs, many of which have, for a long time, committed the most open outrages in defiance of the law. . . .

I now come to a fourth encouragement which greatly holds up the spirit of robbers, and which they often find to afford no deceitful consolation; and this is drawn from the remissness of prosecutors, who are often,

1. Fearful, and to be intimidated by the threats of the gang; or,
2. Delicate, and cannot appear in a public court; or,
3. Indolent, and will not give themselves the trouble of a prosecution; or,
4. Avaricious, and will not undergo the expense of it; nay, perhaps, find their account in compounding the matter; or,
5. Tender-hearted, and cannot take away the life of a man; or,

Lastly, Necessitous, and cannot really afford the cost, however small, together with the loss of time which attends it.

The first and second of these are too absurd, and the third and fourth too infamous, to be reasoned with. But the two last deserve more particular notice, as the fifth is an error springing originally out of a good principle in the mind, and the sixth is a fault in the constitution very easily to be remedied. . . .

But if, notwithstanding all the rubs which we have seen to lie in the way, the indictment is found, and the thief brought to his trial, still he hath sufficient hopes of escaping. . . .

In street-robberies the difficulty of convicting a criminal is extremely great. . . . Street-robberies are generally committed in the dark, the persons on whom they are committed are often in chairs and coaches, and if on foot the attack is usually begun by knocking the party down, and for the time

depriving him of his senses. But if the thief should be less barbarous he is seldom so incautious as to omit taking every method to prevent his being known, by flapping the party's hat over his face, and by every other method which he can invent to avoid discovery. . . .

[According to Lord Hale,[17] the principal purpose of punishment is] "to deter men from the breach of laws. . . . And is not the inflicting of punishment more for example, and to prevent evil, than to punish?" And therefore, says he, presently afterwards, "Death itself is necessary to be annexed to laws in many cases by the prudence of lawgivers, though possibly beyond the single merit of the offense simply considered." No man indeed of common humanity or common sense can think the life of a man and a few shillings to be of an equal consideration, or that the law in punishing theft with death proceeds (as perhaps a private person sometimes may) with any view to vengeance. The terror of the example is the only thing proposed, and one man is sacrificed to the preservation of thousands.

If therefore the terror of this example is removed (as it certainly is by frequent pardons) the design of the law is rendered totally ineffectual; the lives of the persons executed are thrown away, and sacrificed rather to the vengeance than to the good of the public, which receives no other advantage than by getting rid of a thief, whose place will immediately be supplied by another. . . .

But if every hope which I have mentioned fails the thief: if he should be discovered, apprehended, prosecuted, convicted, and refused a pardon; what is his situation then? . . . The design of those who first appointed executions to be public, was to add the punishment of shame to that of death; in order to make the example an object of greater terror. But experience has shown us that the event is directly contrary to this intention. . . . The difficulty here . . . [is] to raise

---

[17]*Lord Hale:* Sir Mathew Hale (1609–1676), Lord Chief Baron of the Exchequer during the reign of King Charles II.

an object of terror, and at the same time, as much as possible, to strip it of all pity and all admiration. . . .

To effect this, it seems that the execution should be as soon as possible after the commission and conviction of the crime; for if this be of an atrocious kind, the resentment of mankind being warm, would pursue the criminal to his last end, and all pity for the offender would be lost in detestation of the offense. Whereas, when executions are delayed so long as they sometimes are, the punishment and not the crime is considered; and no good mind can avoid compassionating a set of wretches who are put to death we know not why, unless, as it almost appears, to make a holiday for, and to entertain, the mob.

Secondly. It should be in some degree private. . . .

If executions therefore were so contrived that few could be present at them, they would be much more shocking and terrible to the crowd without doors than at present, as well as much more dreadful to the criminals themselves, who would thus die in the presence only of their enemies. . . .

Upon the whole, something should be, nay, must be done, or much worse consequences than have hitherto happened are very soon to be apprehended. Nay, as the matter now stands, not only care for the public safety, but common humanity, exacts our concern on this occasion; for that many cart-loads of our fellow-creatures are once in six weeks carried to slaughter is a dreadful consideration; and this is greatly heightened by reflecting, that, with proper care and proper regulations, much the greater part of these wretches might have been made not only happy in themselves, but very useful members of society, which they now so greatly dishonour in the sight of all Christendom.

3

British Thinkers of the Eighteenth Century: Critics of Society or Upholders of the Status Quo?

In the history of European thought, the greater part of the eighteenth century is often summed up as the "Age of Enlightenment," a period during which a host of *philosophes* (scholars, critics, journalists) occupied themselves with substituting reason for superstition, ascertained fact for medieval myth. It is certainly in such a light that most educated persons of Western Europe thought of themselves.

The home of the Enlightenment is generally considered to be the France of Voltaire, of Diderot, of Condorcet, and of Rousseau. French apostles of the Enlightenment tended to be critics of their own society, critics of the French judicial system and of governmental restrictions on civil liberty, critics of the established Roman Catholic Church, and—directly or indirectly—precursors of the French Revolution that began in 1789. But what was the relationship of Britain to the Enlightenment? In many ways it was a peculiar one. On the one hand, two late seventeenth-century figures, Isaac Newton and John Locke, were seen by Frenchmen as well as Englishmen as father figures. It was indeed the aim of the leaders of the Enlightenment to bring to what we today call the social sciences the same sense of certainty that Newton had apparently brought to the world of physics and mathematics. On the other hand, most educated eighteenth-century Britons tended to feel far more satisfied with the society in which they lived and to see it as much superior to that of the continent. Thus Edward Gibbon (1737–1793), the greatest English historian of the century, could take satisfaction in the thought that the continent of Europe had not only recovered from *The Decline and Fall of the Roman Empire* (1776–1788) that he chronicled in six thick volumes, but that Europe had also become a relatively prosperous, civilized, and stable society, "secure from any future irruption of barbarians." Britain in particular had become "perhaps the only powerful and wealthy state which

An Early Eighteenth-Century Coffee House

has ever possessed the inestimable secret of uniting the benefits of order with the blessings of freedom.''[1]

Not all residents of eighteenth-century Britain were persuaded that, in the aftermath of the Revolution of 1688–1689, the ideal had been attained either in government or in the manner in which the kingdom's economy worked. In this chapter we shall first sample three different attitudes toward Britain's government and then two divergent attitudes toward the regulation of the economy.

Although many educated Britons came to see the government of the kingdom as exemplifying a happy mixture of monarchical, aristocratic, and democratic elements, others were less fully convinced. A case in point is Oliver Goldsmith (1731–1774), the Irish-born poet, essayist, playwright, and novelist, who during the 1750s settled in London, where in due course he became a member of Samuel Johnson's Literary Club (see Chapter 4). Like Johnson, Goldsmith defined himself in politics as a Tory, and he used his widely read novel *The Vicar of Wakefield* (1766) as a vehicle to put forward his views. According to Goldsmith's fictional spokesman, which branch of Britain's mixed government had become undesirably weak? In his judgment, what dangers were implicit in the "lib-

---

[1]Cited in Roy Porter, *Edward Gibbon: Making History* (London, 1988), pp. 150–151.

erty" of which many eighteenth-century English people boasted? Writing *Take Your Choice* a few years later in 1776, John Cartwright (1740–1824), a political radical, had come to see his country blessed not with too much liberty but with too little. Cartwright held forth great hopes for the House of Commons, but only if its election procedures first underwent fundamental reform. What forms of corruption afflicted Britain, according to Cartwright? What political reforms did he seek? Because he served for many years as an officer in the Nottinghamshire militia, he was generally known as Major Cartwright, and he was to remain active in Britain's political reform movement for half a century.

Yet other eighteenth-century Englishmen—of whom many were known as Whigs—felt reasonably well satisfied with the fundamentals of their government. A case in point is William Paley (1743–1805), a man who lectured on moral philosophy at Cambridge University during the 1760s and 1770s before being created archdeacon of Carlisle (1782). In his book *The Principles of Moral and Political Philosophy* (1785), Paley sought to provide a summary of what every well-educated university graduate of his day ought to know about the world. In the excerpt published in this chapter, Paley examines the workings of eighteenth-century British government. Does that government, in Paley's eyes, rest on certain simple fundamental principles? Many nineteenth-century reformers were to look back upon the government of Paley's day as a compound of confusion and injustice. How does Paley justify the institutions and customs of that government?

Most of the leaders of England's government during the sixteenth and seventeenth centuries had taken for granted their right to supervise the manner in which the economy operated—even to the extent of setting prices and wages, regulating in detail the process of apprenticeship, and granting monopoly powers to craft guilds at home and to chartered companies that traded with foreign nations. During the eighteenth century, Britain's rulers increasingly lost interest in the detailed supervision of the domestic economy, though laws permitting them this control remained on the statute book. They became more interested than ever, however, in regulating foreign trade, taking it for granted that the kingdom's welfare depended on protecting British merchants against Dutch, French, and Spanish rivals and on maintaining a favorable balance of trade, one in which more gold and silver entered their country than left it. We know as *mercantilism* the laws that embodied such prevalent attitudes. *An Act Banning Imported Persian, Chinese, and Indian Calicoes* (1700) is a typical example of mercantilistic legislation. According to the drafters of the act, what dangers threatened the kingdom if such foreign competition were not to be curbed? What were the sole legal grounds on which the prohibited goods might enter the kingdom? How was the act to be enforced?

Later in the century the assumptions on which such legislation was based were to be subject to close examination by the single best-remembered exemplar of the British (and more specifically the Scottish)

Enlightenment, Adam Smith (1723–1790). A professor of moral philosophy at the University of Glasgow during the 1750s, Smith spent several years in France (1764–1766) as tutor to the duke of Buccleuch and later became Commissioner of Customs for Scotland. He wrote the *Theory of Moral Sentiments* (1759) as well as the *An Inquiry into the Nature and Causes of the Wealth of Nations* (1776), from which the excerpts in the last selection are taken. The *Wealth of Nations* remains *the* pioneer treatise on economics as a separate field of study. The book at the same time constitutes a formidable critique of the attitude and the system of government regulation of both the domestic economy and foreign trade that is known as mercantilism.

Smith clearly sees himself as living in an advanced rather than a primitive state of society and economy. To the working out of what principle does he attribute that advance? What does Smith's description of the details of the economy of eighteenth-century Britain tell us of the nature of what was supposedly a "preindustrial" society? How does Smith explain the relationship between the self-interest of individuals and the well-being of the community? What factors help determine the price of a commodity? What types of regulation on domestic or foreign trade are likely to distort that price? Are such distortions more likely to aid the producer or the consumer? What is, according to Smith, the proper role of government in the economy? Smith has been criticized for assuming in his study that human beings always tend to calculate rationally in seeking to forward their own economic interest. Do these excerpts support such criticism?

OLIVER GOLDSMITH   **The Need for a Powerful King (1766)**

In Chapter 19 of his novel The Vicar of Wakefield, *the Irish-born novelist and poet provides a critique of the English political system of his day.*

The Description of a Person Discontented with the Present Government, and Apprehensive of the Loss of Our Liberties.

The house where we were to be entertained lying at a small distance from the village, our inviter observed that, as the coach was not ready, he would conduct us on foot, and we soon arrived at one of the most magnificent mansions I had seen in that part of the country. The apartment into which we were shown was perfectly elegant and modern. He went to give orders for supper, while the player, with a wink, observed that we were perfectly in luck. Our entertainer[2] soon returned, an elegant supper was brought in, two or three ladies in an easy dishabille were introduced, and the

SOURCE: Oliver Goldsmith, *The Vicar of Wakefield* (New York: Century, 1902), Chapter 19.

[2]*entertainer:* host

conversation began with some sprightliness. Politics, however, were the subject on which our entertainer chiefly expatiated, for he asserted that liberty was at once his boast and his terror. After the cloth was removed, he asked me if I had seen the last *Monitor*, to which replying in the negative, "What! nor the *Auditor*, I suppose?" cried he.

"Neither, sir," returned I.

"That's strange, very strange," replied my entertainer. "Now, I read all the politics that come out—the *Daily*, the *Public*, the *Ledger*, the *Chronicle*, the *London Evening*, the *Whitehall Evening*, the seventeen magazines, and the two reviews, and though they hate each other, I love them all. Liberty, sir, liberty is the Briton's boast, and, by all my coalmines in Cornwall, I reverence its guardians."

"Then it is to be hoped," cried I, "you reverence the king?"

"Yes," returned my entertainer, "when he does what we would have him, but if he goes on as he has done of late, I'll never trouble myself more with his matters. I say nothing; I think only. I could have directed some things better. I don't think there has been a sufficient number of advisers. He should advise with every person willing to give him advice, and then we should have things done in another-guess manner."

"I wish," cried I, "that such intruding advisers were fixed in the pillory. It should be the duty of honest men to assist the weaker side of our Constitution, that sacred power that has for some years been every day declining and losing its due share of influence in the state. But these ignorants still continue the cry of liberty and, if they have any weight, basely throw it into the subsiding scale."

"How," cried one of the ladies, "do I live to see one so base, so sordid, as to be an enemy to liberty and a defender of tyrants? Liberty, that sacred gift of Heaven, that glorious privilege of Britons!"

"Can it be possible," cried our entertainer, "that there should be any found at present advocates for slavery? Any who are for meanly giving up the privileges of Britons? Can any, sir, be so abject?"

"No, sir," replied I, "I am for liberty, that attribute of God's! Glorious liberty! that theme of modern declamation. I would have all men kings. I would be a king myself. We have all naturally an equal right to the throne. We are all originally equal. This is my opinion and was once the opinion of a set of honest men who were called levelers. They tried to erect themselves into a community where all should be equally free. But, alas! it would never answer, for there were some among them stronger and some more cunning than others, and these became masters of the rest, for, as sure as your groom rides your horses because he is a cunninger animal than they, so surely will the animal that is cunninger or stronger than he sit upon his shoulders in turn. Since, then, it is entailed upon humanity to submit, and some are born to command and others to obey, the question is, as there must be tyrants, whether it is better to have them in the same house with us, or in the same village, or still farther off in the metropolis. Now, sir, for my own part, as I naturally hate the face of a tyrant, the farther off he is removed from me, the better pleased am I. The generality of mankind also are of my way of thinking and have unanimously created one king, whose election at once diminishes the number of tyrants and puts tyranny at the greatest distance from the greatest number of people. Now, the great, who were tyrants themselves before the election of one tyrant, are naturally averse to a power raised over them and whose weight must ever lean heaviest on the subordinate orders. It is the interest of the great, therefore, to diminish kingly power as much as possible, because whatever they take from that is naturally restored to themselves, and all they have to do in the state is to undermine the single tyrant, by which they resume their primeval authority. Now, the state may be so circumstanced, or its laws may be so disposed, or its men of opulence so minded as all to conspire in carrying on this business of undermining monarchy. For, in the first place, if the circumstances of our state be such as to favor the accumulation of wealth and make the opulent still more rich, this will increase their ambition. An accumulation of wealth, however, must necessarily be the consequence when, as at present, more riches flow in from external commerce than arise from internal industry, for external commerce can only be managed to advantage by the rich, and they have also, at the same time, all the emoluments arising from internal industry, so that the rich, with us, have two sources of wealth, whereas the poor have but one. For this reason wealth, in all commercial states, is found to accumulate, and all such have hitherto in time become aristocratical. Again, the very laws also of this country may contribute to the accumulation of wealth, as when, by their means, the natural ties that bind the rich and poor together are broken, and it is ordained that the rich shall only marry with the rich, or when the learned are held unqualified to serve their country as counselors merely from a defect of opulence, and wealth is thus made the object of a wise man's ambition. By these means, I say, and such means as these, riches will accumulate. Now, the possessor of accumulated wealth, when furnished with the necessaries and pleasures of life, has no other method to employ the superfluity of his fortune but in purchasing power—that is, differently speaking, in making dependents, by purchasing the liberty of the needy or the venal, of men who are willing to bear the mortification of contiguous tyranny for bread. Thus each very opulent man generally gathers round him a circle of the poorest of the people, and the polity abounding in accumulated wealth may be compared to a Cartesian system, each orb with a vortex of its own. Those, however, who are willing to move in a great man's vortex are only such as must be slaves, the rabble of mankind, whose souls and whose education are adapted to servitude, and who know nothing of liberty except the name. But there must still be a large number of the people without the

sphere of the opulent man's influence, namely, that order of men which subsists between the very rich and the very rabble, those men who are possessed of too large fortunes to submit to the neighboring man in power, and yet are too poor to set up for tyranny themselves. In this middle order of mankind are generally to be found all the arts, wisdom, and virtues of society. This order alone is known to be the true preserver of freedom and may be called the people. Now, it may happen that this middle order of mankind may lose all its influence in a state, and its voice be in a manner drowned in that of the rabble, for, if the fortune sufficient for qualifying a person at present to give his voice in state affairs be ten times less than was judged sufficient upon forming the Constitution, it is evident that great numbers of the rabble will thus be introduced into the political system, and they, ever moving in the vortex of the great, will follow where greatness shall direct. In such a state, therefore, all that the middle order has left is to preserve the prerogative and privileges of the one principal governor with the most sacred circumspection. For he divides the power of the rich and calls off the great from falling with tenfold weight on the middle order placed beneath them. The middle order may be compared to a town, of which the opulent are forming the siege and which the governor from without is hastening the relief. While the besiegers are in dread of an enemy over them, it is but natural to offer the townsmen the most specious terms, to flatter them with sounds and amuse them with privileges. But if they once defeat the governor from behind, the walls of the town will be but a small defense to its inhabitants. What they may then expect may be seen by turning our eyes to Holland, Genoa, or Venice, where the laws govern the poor, and the rich govern the law. I am, then, for, and would die for, monarchy, sacred monarchy, for if there is anything sacred amongst men, it must be the anointed sovereign of his people, and every diminution of his power, in war or in peace, is an infringement upon the real liberties of the subject."

MAJOR JOHN CARTWRIGHT **The Need for Radical Reform (1776)**

A major in the Nottingham militia, Cartwright was one of several late eighteenth-century political reformers who challenged the political status quo in England.

TAKE YOUR CHOICE!

Representation *and* *Respect:* _____	*Imposition* *and* *Contempt.*
Annual Parliaments *and* *Liberty:* _____	*Long Parliaments* *and* *Slavery.*

Introduction

Having proposed to urge upon you, my country men! a reformation, both as to the length, and as to the constituting of your parliaments; it seems but proper, previously to state some of the inconveniences and evils, which I apprehend to be the necessary consequences of, and inseparable from, our present rotten parliamentary system.

All men will grant, that the lower house of Parliament is elected by only a handful of the Commons, instead of the whole; and this, chiefly by bribery and undue influence. Men who will employ such means are villains; and those who dupe their constituents by lying promises, are far from honest men. An assembly of such men is *founded* on *iniquity:* consequently, the fountain of legislation is poisoned. Every stream, how much soever mixed, as it flows with justice and patriotism, will still have poison in its composition.

Nor will it be denied me, that, in consequence of the long duration of a parliament, the members, as soon as seated, feel themselves too independent on the opinion and good will of their constituents, even where their suffrages have not been extorted nor bought; and that, of course, they despise them.

From the first of these data, it will follow, that we are subject to have the House of Commons filled by men of every bad description that can be thought of, and that strict integrity, which ought to be the strongest of all recommendations, amounts to a positive exclusion; except it happen indeed to be united with a capital fortune and great county connections.

From the first and second jointly; our representatives, who are in fact our deputed servants, are taught to assume the carriage and haughtiness of despotic masters; to think themselves unaccountable for their conduct; and to neglect their duty.

Whether, indeed, the House of Commons be in a great measure filled with idle schoolboys, insignificant coxcombs, led-captains and toad-eaters, profligates, gamblers, bankrupts, beggars, contractors, commissaries, public plunderers, ministerial dependents, hirelings, and wretches, that would sell their country, or deny their God for a guinea, let every one judge for himself. And whether the kind of business very often brought before the house, and the usual manner of conducting it, do not bespeak this to be the case; I likewise leave every man to form his own opinion: particularly that independent and noble-minded few, who experience the constant mortification of voting and speaking without even a hope of being able thereby to serve their country.

But without insisting on these things as fact, and only admitting the possibility of

SOURCE: John Cartwright, *Take Your Choice* (London, 1776), pp. ix–xi, xxi–xxv.

them from the combined causes already assigned, of long parliaments, undue influence and bribery, it is natural to expect, as indeed all experience shews it must happen, that a country, whose affairs are *subject to fall* into such hands must be ruined, sooner or later, by those very men who shall be in the office of its guardians and preservers; except it shall make an alteration in this particular. . . .

So ruinous a system needs must, in its progress, grow worse. The chariot of corruption, (if I may be allowed a new metaphor) under the guidance of rotten Whigs would soon enough have arrived, without the whip, at the goal of despotism: but now, that furious Tories have seized the reins, 'tis lashed onward with impetuous haste; nor do they seem sensible to their danger, though its axles are already on fire with its rapidity. The ministers of the present reign have daringly struck at your most sacred rights, have aimed through the sides of America a deadly blow at the life of your Constitution, and have shewn themselves hostile, not only to the being, but to the very name of liberty. The word itself has been proscribed the court; and for any one who dared to utter it, the gentlest appellations have been Wilkite,[3] republican and disturber of the peace. Facts recent in every one's memory I have no need to repeat. I will only therefore just mention the atrocious violation of the first principle of the constitution in the never-to-be-forgotten business of the Middlesex election. An enumeration of all their crimes would shew them to be deserving of the highest punishments. And yet, the sum of all the evils they have brought upon us, added to all those which former ministers had intailed upon the nation, are light and trivial in comparison of the ONE GREAT EVIL OF A LONG PARLIAMENT.[4] Feast the fowls of the air with such ministers, but leave your legislature

unreformed; and you will only add a few inglorious days to the period of your expiring liberties. Succeeding ministers might be more circumspect; but with the aid of a prostitute parliament, they would at last succeed. . . . It is downright quixotism to imagine, that so long as your parliament remains corrupt, you can ever have a patriot minister: and, except Parliament be reformed, 'tis a matter of very great indifference who are *in* and who are *out*. I will not utterly deny the possibility of your having a patriot minister prior to a parliamentary reformation; but I do not myself conceive *how* such a man is to arrive at such a station. One of that stamp could not go through thick and thin, and wade through all the miry paths that lead to it: nor have I any great expectation of a miraculous conversion of anyone, who hath once passed through those ways to the seat of power. Neither do I see the prudence of waiting for so rare a phenomenon as a patriot minister, to do that for you which you can do for yourselves; and thereby put things in such a state, that a patriot minister will no longer be a phenomenon, but a natural and common appearance.

The revolution which expelled the tyrant James from the throne, glorious as it was to the character, and essential to the safety of this nation, was yet a very defective proceeding. It was effected in too anxious a moment, and in too precipitate a manner, to lay a lasting foundation for the security of public freedom and property. *William* the deliverer was but half the friend to liberty which he pretended to be. Had he been a truly patriot prince, his share in the expulsion of a tyrant would have been his smallest merit; and he would have embraced the opportunity afforded him by his own success and the tide of reformation being set in, to have guarded the Constitution against every conceivable danger towards

---

[3]*Wilkite:* refers to the battles waged by another political radical, John Wilkes (1727–1797), between 1763 and 1774 over the limits of freedom of the press and over his right to take the parliamentary seat to which the voters of the county of Middlesex repeatedly elected him (see also Chapter 5) [4]*long Parliament:* refers to the Septennial Act of 1716, which increased the interval between parliamentary elections from three years to a maximum of seven years

which it had any tendency to be exposed in process of time. When the immortal and blessed *Alfred* had overthrown the oppressors of his country, he thought the work of a king only begun; and devoted the rest of his reign to the correcting abuses, the establishing of justice, and laying the broad foundations of liberty and happiness. But history shews *William* to have been a cold-hearted Dutchman, ungrateful to a people who had given him a crown, and more fond of power than of squaring his government with the principles of the Constitution. And this was one of the best of our kings. Then put not your trust in princes: neither have confidence in ministers! Whether they covet inordinate power for its own sake, or for the sake of lucre, they will have it if possible. And when one lusts for gold, the other for dominion, they will be reciprocally the pimps to each others passion. The prince will invade the people's property, in order to enrich his minister; the minister will violate their liberties, in order to render his master absolute. For one *Alfred*, there are a thousand *Charles's;* for one *Falkland*, a thousand *Walpoles.* Trust not, I say, in princes nor in ministers; but trust in YOUR-SELVES, and in representatives chosen by YOURSELVES alone!

WILLIAM PALEY **The Balanced Constitution of England (1785)**

The Cambridge University educator surveys the fundamentals of the government of Great Britain during the eighteenth century. He admits the lack of symmetry, but he argues against radical change.

. . . The Constitution of England, like that of most countries in Europe, hath grown out of occasion and emergency; from the fluctuating policy of different ages; from the contentions, successes, interests, and opportunities of different orders and parties of men in the community. It resembles one of those old mansions, which, instead of being built all at once, after a regular plan, and according to the rules of architecture at present established, has been reared in different ages of the art, has been altered from time to time, and has been continually receiving additions and repairs suited to the taste, fortune, or conveniency of its successive proprietors. In such a building we look in vain for the elegance and proportion, for the just order and correspondence of parts, which we expect in a modern edifice; and which external symmetry, after all, contributes much more perhaps to the amusement of the beholder, than the accommodation of the inhabitant. . . .

The government of England, which has been sometimes called a mixed government, sometimes a limited monarchy, is formed by a combination of the three regular species of government; the monarchy, residing in the king; the aristocracy, in the House of Lords; and the republic being represented by the House of Commons. The perfection intended by such a scheme of government is, to unite the advantages of the several simple forms, and to exclude the inconveniences. To what degree this purpose is attained or attainable in the British Constitution; wherein it is lost sight of or neglected; and by what means it may in any part be promoted with better success, the reader will be enabled to judge, by a separate recollection of these advantages and inconveniences, as enumerated in the preceding chapter, and a distinct application of each to the political condition of this country. We will present our remarks upon the subject in a brief account of the expedients by which the British Constitution provides,

1st, For the interest of its subject.

SOURCE: From William Paley, *The Principles of Moral and Political Philosophy* (London, 1785), pp. 385, 389–392, 394–398.

2dly, For its own preservation.

The contrivances for the first of these purposes are the following:

In order to promote the establishment of salutary public laws, every citizen of the state is capable of becoming a member of the senate; and every senator possesses the right of propounding to the deliberation of the legislature whatever law he pleases.

Every district of the empire enjoys the privilege of choosing representatives, informed of the interests and circumstances and desires of their constituents, and entitled by their situation to communicate that information to the national council. The meanest subject has some one whom he can call upon to bring forward his complaints and requests to public attention.

By annexing the right of voting for members of the House of Commons to different qualifications in different places, each order and profession of men in the community becomes virtually represented; that is, men of all orders and professions, statesmen, courtiers, country gentlemen, lawyers, merchants, manufacturers, soldiers, sailors, interested in the prosperity, and experienced in the occupation of their respective professions, obtain seats in Parliament.

The elections, at the same time, are so connected with the influence of landed property as to afford a certainty that a considerable number of men of great estates will be returned to Parliament; and are also so modified, that men the most eminent and successful in their respective professions, are the most likely, by their riches, or the weight of their stations, to prevail in these competitions.

The number, fortune, and quality of the members; the variety of interests and characters amongst them; above all, the temporary duration of their power, and the change of men which every new election produces, are so many securities to the public, as well against the subjection of their judgments to any external dictation, as against the formation of a junto in their own body, sufficiently powerful to govern their decisions.

The representatives are so intermixed with the constituents, and the constituents with the rest of the people, that they cannot, without a partiality too flagrant to be endured, impose any burden upon the subject, in which they do not share themselves; nor scarcely can they adopt an advantageous regulation, in which their own interests will not participate of the advantage.

The proceedings and debates of Parliament, and the parliamentary conduct of each representative, are known by the people at large.

The representative is so far dependent upon the constituent, and political importance upon public favour, that a Member of Parliament cannot more effectually recommend himself to eminence and advancement in the state, than by contriving and patronizing laws of public utility.

When intelligence of the condition, wants, and occasions of the people, is thus collected from every quarter, when such a variety of invention, and so many understandings are set at work upon the subject, it may be presumed, that the most eligible expedient, remedy or improvement, will occur to some one or other; and when a wise counsel, or beneficial regulation is once suggested, it may be expected, from the disposition of an assembly so constituted as the British House of Commons is, that it cannot fail of receiving the approbation of a majority.

To prevent those destructive contentions for the supreme power, which are sure to take place, where the members of the state do not live under an acknowledged head, and a known rule of succession; to preserve the people in tranquility at home, by a speedy and vigorous execution of the laws; to protect their interest abroad, by strength and energy in military operations, by those advantages of decision, secrecy and dispatch, which belong to the resolutions of monarchical councils;—for these purposes, the Constitution has committed the executive government to the administration and limited authority of an hereditary king.

In the defence of the empire; in the maintenance of its power, dignity, and privileges, with foreign nations; in the advancement of its trade by treaties and conventions; and in the providing for the general administration of municipal justice, by a proper choice and appointment of magistrates, the inclination of the king and of the people usually coincide: in this part, therefore, of the regal office, the constitution entrusts the prerogative with ample powers. . . .

We proceed, in the second place, to inquire in what manner the Constitution has provided for its own preservation; that is, in what manner each part of the legislature is secured in the exercise of the powers assigned to it, from the encroachment of the other parts. This security is sometimes called the *balance of the Constitution;* and the political equilibrium, which this phrase denotes, consists in two contrivances,—a balance of power, and a balance of interest. By a balance of power is meant, that there is no power possessed by one part of the legislature, the abuse, or excess of which is not checked by some antagonist power, residing in another part. Thus the power of the two houses of Parliament to frame laws is checked by the king's negative; that if laws subversive of regal government should obtain the consent of Parliament, the reigning prince, by interposing his prerogative, may save the necessary rights and authority of his station. On the other hand, the arbitrary application of this negative is checked by the privilege which Parliament possesses, of refusing supplies of money to the exigencies of the king's administration. The constitutional maxim, "that the king can do no wrong," is balanced by another maxim, not less constitutional, "that the illegal commands of the king do not justify those who assist, or concur, in carrying them into execution;" and by a second rule, subsidiary to this, "that the acts of the crown acquire not any legal force, until authenticated by the subscription of some of its great officers." The wisdom of this contrivance is worthy of observation. As the king could not be punished, without a civil war, the Constitution exempts his person from trial or account; but, lest this impunity should encourage a licentious exercise of dominion, various obstacles are opposed to the private will of the sovereign, when directed to illegal objects. The pleasure of the crown must be announced with certain solemnities, and attested by certain officers of state. In some cases, the royal order must be signified by a secretary of state; in others, it must pass under the privy seal, and in many, under the great seal. And when the king's command is regularly published, no mischief can be achieved by it, without the ministry and compliance of those to whom it is directed. Now all who either concur in an illegal order, by authenticating its publication with their seal or subscription, or who in any manner assist in carrying it into execution, subject themselves to prosecution and punishment, for the part they have taken, and are not permitted to plead or produce the command of the king, in justification of their obedience. But farther; the power of the crown to direct the military force of the kingdom, is balanced by the annual necessity of resorting to Parliament for the maintenance and government of that force. The power of the king to declare war, is checked by the privilege of the House of Commons, to grant or withhold the supplies by which the war must be carried on. The king's choice of his ministers is controlled by the obligation he is under of appointing those men to offices in the state, who are found capable of managing the affairs of his government, with the two houses of Parliament. Which consideration imposes such a necessity upon the crown, as hath in a great measure subdued the influence of favoritism; insomuch, that it is become no uncommon spectacle in this country, to see men promoted by the king to the highest offices, and richest preferments, which he has in his power to bestow, who have been distinguished by their opposition to his personal inclinations.

By the *balance of interest*, which accompanies and gives efficacy to the *balance of power*, is meant this, that the respective interests of the three estates of the empire are so disposed and adjusted, that whichever of the three shall attempt any encroachment, the other two will unite in resisting it. If the king should endeavor to extend his authority, by contracting the power and privileges of the Commons, the House of Lords would see their own dignity endangered by every advance which the crown made to independency upon the resolutions of Parliament. The admission of arbitrary power is no less formidable to the grandeur of the aristocracy, than it is fatal to the liberty of the republic; that is, it would reduce the nobility from the hereditary share they possess in the national councils, in which their regal greatness consists, to the being made a part of the empty pageantry of a despotic court. On the other hand, if the House of Commons should intrench upon the distinct province, or usurp the established prerogative of the crown, the House of Lords would receive an instant alarm from every new stretch of popular power. In every contest in which the king may be engaged with the representative body, in defense of his established share of authority, he will find a sure ally in the collective power of the nobility. An attachment to the monarchy, from which they derive their own distinction; the allurements of a court, in the habits and with the sentiments of which they have been brought up; their hatred of equality, and of all levelling pretensions, which may ultimately affect the privileges, or even the existence of their order; in short, every principle and every prejudice which are wont to actuate human conduct, will determine their choice, to the side and support of the crown. Lastly, if the nobles themselves should attempt to revive the superiorities, which their ancestors exercised under the feudal constitution, the king and the people would alike remember, how the one had been insulted, and the other enslaved, by that barbarous tyranny. They would forget the natural opposition of their views and inclinations, when they saw themselves threatened with the return of a domination, which was odious and intolerable to both. . . .

There is nothing, in the British Constitution, so remarkable, as the irregularity of the popular representation. The House of Commons consists of five hundred and forty-eight members, of whom, two hundred are elected by seven thousand constituents: so that a majority of these seven thousand, with[out] any reasonable title to superior weight or influence in the state, may, under certain circumstances decide a question against the opinion of as many millions. Or, to place the same object in another point of view: if my estate be situated in one county of the kingdom, I possess the ten thousandth part of a single representative, if in another, the thousandth; if in a particular district, I may be one in twenty who choose two representatives; if in a still more favored spot, I may enjoy the right of appointing two myself. If I have been born, or dwell, or have served an apprenticeship in one town, I am represented in the national assembly by two deputies, in the choice of whom, I exercise an actual and sensible share of power; if accident has thrown my birth or habitation, or service into another town, I have no representative at all, nor more power or concern in the election of those who make the laws, by which I am governed, than if I was a subject of the Grand Signior—and this partiality subsists without any pretense whatever of merit or of propriety to justify the preference of one place to another. Or, thirdly, to describe the state of national representation as it exists in reality, it may be affirmed, I believe, with truth, that about one half of the House of Commons obtains their seats in that assembly by the election of the people, the other half by purchase, or by the nomination of single proprietors of great estates.

This is a flagrant incongruity in the Constitution; but it is one of those objections which strike most forcibly at first sight. The effect of all reasoning upon the subject is to diminish the first impression: on which account it deserves the more attentive examination, that we may be assured, before we adventure upon a reformation, that the magnitude of the evil justifies the danger of the experiment. In the few remarks that follow, we would be understood, in the first place, to decline all conference with those who wish to alter the form of government of these kingdoms. The reformers with whom we have to do, are they, who, whilst they change this part of the system, would retain the rest. If any Englishman expect more happiness to his country under a republic, he may very consistently recommend a new modelling of elections to Parliament; because, if the king and House of Lords were laid aside, the present disproportionate representation would produce nothing but a confused and ill-digested oligarchy. In like manner we have a controversy with those writers who insist upon representation as a *natural* right: we consider it so far only as a right at all, as it conduces to public utility; that is, as it contributes to the establishment of good laws, or as it secures to the people the just administration of these laws. These effects depend upon the disposition and abilities of the national counsellors. Wherefore, if men the most likely by their qualifications to know and to promote the public interest, be actually returned to Parliament, it signifies little who return them. If the properest persons be elected, what matters it by whom they are elected? At least, no prudent statesman would subvert long established or even settled rules of representation, without a prospect of procuring wiser or better representatives. This then being well observed, let us, before we seek to obtain any thing more, consider duly what we already have. We *have* a House of Commons composed of five hundred and forty-eight members, in which number are found, the most considerable landholders and merchants of the kingdom; the heads of the army, the navy, and the law; the occupiers of great offices in the state; together with many private individuals, eminent by their knowledge, eloquence, or activity. Now, if the country be not safe in such hands, in whose may it confide its interests? If such a number of such men be liable to the influence of corrupt motives, what assembly of men will be secure from the same danger? Does any new scheme of representation promise to collect together more wisdom, or to produce firmer integrity? In this view of the subject, and attending not to ideas of order and proportion (of which many minds are much enamored), but to effects alone, we may discover just excuses for those parts of the present representation, which appear to a hasty observer most exceptionable and absurd. It should be remembered as a maxim extremely applicable to this subject, that no order or assembly of men whatever can long maintain their place and authority in a mixed government, of which the members do not individually possess a respectable share of personal importance. Now, whatever may be the defects of the present arrangement, it infallibly secures a great weight of property to the House of Commons, by rendering many seats in that house accessible to men of large fortunes, and to such men alone. By which means those characters are engaged in the defense of the separate rights and interests of this branch of the legislature, that are best able to support its claims. The constitution of most of the small boroughs, especially the burgage[5] tenure, contributes, though undesignedly, to the same effect; for the appointment of the representatives we find commonly annexed to certain great inheritances. Elections purely popular are in this respect uncertain: in times of tranquility, the natural ascendancy of wealth will prevail; but when the minds of men are inflamed by political dissensions, this influence often yields to more impetuous motives.—The variety of tenures and qualifications, upon which the right of voting is founded, appears to me a recommendation of the mode which now subsists, as it tends to introduce into Parliament a corresponding mixture of characters and professions. It has been long observed that conspicuous abilities are most frequently found with the representatives of small boroughs. And this is nothing more than what the laws of human conduct might teach us to expect: when such boroughs are set to sale, those men are likely to become purchasers who are enabled by their talents to make the best of their bargain: when a seat

---

[5]*burgage:* the right to vote granted to men who rent property on a yearly basis from the local "lord of the manor," who owns all or much of the land in the community

is not sold, but given by the opulent proprietor of a burgage tenure, the patron finds his own interest consulted, by the reputation and abilities of the member whom he nominates. If certain of the nobility hold the appointment of some part of the House of Commons, it serves to maintain that alliance between the two branches of the legislature, which no good citizen would wish to see disseuered: it helps to keep the government of the country in the house of commons, in which, it would not perhaps long continue to reside, if so powerful and wealthy a part of the nation as the peerage compose, were excluded from all share and interest in its constitution. If there be a few boroughs so circumstanced as to lie at the disposal of the crown, whilst the number of such is known and small, they may be tolerated with little danger. For where would be the impropriety or the inconveniency, if the king at once should nominate a limited number of his servants to seats in parliament; or, what is the same thing, if seats in parliament were annexed to the possession of certain of the most efficient and responsible offices in the state? The present representation, after all these deductions, and under the confusion in which it confessedly lies, is still in such a degree popular; or rather the representatives are so connected with the mass of the community, by a society of interests and passions, that the will of the people, when it is determined, permanent, and general, almost always at length prevails.

An Act Banning Imported Persian, Chinese, and Indian Calicoes (1700)

In accordance with prevailing ideas that we sum up as mercantilism, Parliament during the late seventeenth century and much of the eighteenth century regarded itself as duty bound to protect Britain's merchants from foreign competition. This measure is one of many "navigation acts" added to the statute book during those years.

Whereas it is most evident, that the continuance of the trade to the East Indies, in the same manner and proportions as it hath been for two years last past, must inevitably be to the great detriment of this kingdom, by exhausting the treasure thereof, and melting down the coin, and taking away the labor of the people, whereby very many of the manufacturers of this nation are become excessively burdensome and chargeable to their respective parishes, and others are thereby compelled to seek for employment in foreign parts: for remedy whereof be it enacted by the King's most excellent Majesty, by and with the advice and consent of the Lords spiritual and temporal, and Commons, in this present Parliament assembled, and by the authority of the same, That from and after the twenty ninth day of September, one thousand seven hundred and one, all wrought silks, bengalls,[6] and stuffs mixed with silk or herba, of the manufacture of Persia, China, or East India, and all calicoes, painted, dyed, printed, or stained there, which are or shall be imported into this kingdom, shall not be worn, or otherwise used within this kingdom of England, dominion of Wales, or town of Berwick upon Tweed, but under such limitations as are herein after mentioned and expressed.

II. And for the better effecting the same, be it enacted by the authority aforesaid, That from and after the said twenty ninth day of September, one thousand seven hundred and one, all such wrought silks, bengalls, and stuffs mixed with silk or herba, of the manufacture of Persia, China, or East India, as aforesaid, and all calicoes, painted, dyed, printed, or stained there, which are or shall be imported into this kingdom of England, dominion of Wales, or town of Ber-

SOURCE: 11 & 12 William III, Chapter 10, *Statutes at Large*, pp. 328–331.

[6]*bengall:* a type of cloth imported from Bengal, India

wick upon Tweed, shall, after entry thereof, be forthwith carried and put into such warehouse or warehouses, as shall be for that purpose approved of by the commissioners of his Majesty's customs for the time being, so as none of them shall be taken or carried out thence upon any account whatsoever, other than in order for exportation, and not until sufficient security be first given to the King's Majesty, his heirs and successors (which the said commissioners are hereby required and impowered to take) that the same and every part thereof shall be exported, and not landed again in any part of this kingdom. . . .

III. And for preventing all clandestine importing or bringing into this kingdom of England, dominion of Wales, or town of Berwick upon Tweed, any of the aforesaid goods hereby prohibited, or intended to be prohibited, from being worn or used in England; be it further enacted by the authority aforesaid, That if any person or persons, or bodies corporate, from and after the said twenty ninth day of September, one thousand seven hundred and one, shall import or bring into any port of or in this kingdom of England, dominion of Wales, or town of Berwick upon Tweed, other than the port of London, any of the aforesaid prohibited goods, or into the port of London, and shall not make due entries of such goods so imported, or brought in, the same shall be, and is hereby adjudged, deemed, accounted, and taken to be clandestine running thereof, and such person or persons, or bodies corporate so offending therein, and their abettors, shall not only forfeit and lose the said goods so clandestinely run, as aforesaid, but also the sum of five hundred pounds. . . .

IV. And be it further enacted, That if any question or doubt shall arise where the said goods were manufactured, the proof shall lie upon the owner or owners thereof, and not upon the prosecutor; any law, usage, or custom to the contrary notwithstanding.

V. And be it further enacted by the authority aforesaid, That if any action, bill, plaint, suit, or information, shall be commenced, or prosecuted against any person or persons, for any seizure, or other thing to be made or done, in pursuance or in execution of any thing before in this act contained, such person or persons, so sued in any court whatsoever, may plead the general issue, and give this act and the special matter in evidence, for their excuse or justification. . . .

VI. And for preventing clandestinely carrying out of the said warehouses any of the said goods hereby prohibited, and by this act intended for exportation, as aforesaid; be it further enacted by the authority aforesaid, That the warehouse-keeper or warehouse-keepers shall keep one or more book or books, wherein he or they shall fairly enter or write down an exact, particular, and true account of all and every chest, bale, and number of pieces therein contained, of such of the aforesaid goods only, which shall be brought into, and carried out of, his or their said warehouse or warehouses, and the days and times when the same shall be so brought in and carried out; and shall every six months in the year transmit in writing an exact account thereof, upon oath, to the said commissioners, together with an exact account how much shall be remaining in his or their said warehouse or warehouses respectively; and the said commissioners are hereby impowered and injoined, within one month after the same shall be transmitted to them, as aforesaid, to appoint one or more persons or persons to inspect the said book or books, warehouse or warehouses, and examine the said accounts, and to lay a true account of the same before the Parliament. . . .

VIII. Provided always, and be it further enacted, That it shall and may be lawful to and for the proprietor or proprietors of the said goods so lodged in any warehouse or warehouses, as aforesaid, to affix one lock to every such warehouse or warehouses, the key of which shall remain in the custody of the said proprietor or proprietors; and that he or they may view, sort, or deliver the said goods, in order for exportation, as aforesaid, in the presence of the said warehouse-keeper or warehouse-keepers, who is and are hereby obliged, at seasonable times, to give attendance for that purpose. . . .

ADAM SMITH   **An Inquiry into the Nature and Causes of the Wealth of Nations (1776)**

The Scottish philosopher outlines both the principles of economics and the costs for Britain of mercantilistic legislation like the act of Parliament reprinted in the previous selection.

Introduction and Plan of the Work

The annual[7] labor of every nation is the fund which originally supplies it with all the necessaries and conveniences of life which it annually consumes, and which consist always either in the immediate produce of that labor, or in what is purchased with that produce from other nations.

According, therefore, as this produce, or what is purchased with it, bears a greater or smaller proportion to the number of those who are to consume it, the nation will be better or worse supplied with all the necessaries and conveniences for which it has occasion.

But this proposition must in every nation be regulated by two different circumstances; first, by the skill, dexterity, and judgment with which its labor is generally applied; and, secondly, by the proportion between the number of those who are employed in useful labor, and that of those who are not so employed. Whatever be the soil, climate, or extent of territory of any particular nation, the abundance or scantiness of its annual supply must, in that particular situation, depend upon those two circumstances. . . .

BOOK I: CHAPTER I

Of the Division of Labor

The greatest improvement in the productive powers of labor, and the greater part of the skill, dexterity, and judgment with which it is any where directed, or applied, seem to have been the effects of the division of labor.

The effects of the division of labor, in the general business of society, will be more easily understood, by considering in what manner it operates in some particular manufactures. . . .

To take an example . . . from a very trifling manufacture; but one in which the division of labor has been very often taken notice of, the trade of the pin-maker; a workman not educated to this business (which the division of labor has rendered a distinct trade), nor acquainted with the use of the machinery employed in it (to the invention of which the same division of labor has probably given occasion), could scarce, perhaps, with his utmost industry, make one pin in a day, and certainly could not make twenty. But in the way in which this business is now carried on, not only the whole work is a peculiar trade, but it is divided into a number of branches, of which the greater part are likewise peculiar trades. One man draws out the wire, another straights it, a third cuts it, a fourth points it, a fifth grinds it at the top for receiving the head; to make the head requires two or three distinct operations; to put it on, is a peculiar business, to whiten the pins is another; it is even a trade by itself to put them into the paper; and the important business of making a pin is, in this manner, divided into about eighteen distinct operations, which, in some manufactories, are all performed by distinct hands, though in others the same man will sometimes perform two or three of them. I have seen a small

SOURCE: From Adam Smith, *An Inquiry into the Nature and Causes of the Wealth of Nations* (Edinburgh, 1863), pp. 1–7, 25–28, 199–204, 290–293, 298, 311.

[7]*annual:* Smith was one of the earliest scholars to look upon the wealth of a nation not as an accumulated fund but as the annual "gross national product."

manufactory of this kind where ten men only were employed, and where some of them consequently performed two or three distinct operations. But though they were very poor, and therefore but indifferently accommodated with the necessary machinery, they could, when they exerted themselves, make among them about twelve pounds of pins in a day. There are in a pound upwards of four thousand pins of a middling size. Those ten persons, therefore, could make among them upwards of forty-eight thousand pins in a day. Each person, therefore, making a tenth part of forty-eight thousand pins, might be considered as making four thousand eight hundred pins in a day. But if they had all wrought separately and independently, and without any of them having been educated to this peculiar business, they certainly could not each of them have made twenty, perhaps not one pin in a day. . . .

In every other art and manufacture, the effects of the division of labor are similar to what they are in this very trifling one; though, in many of them, the labor can neither be so much subdivided, nor reduced to so great a simplicity of operation. The division of labor, however, so far as it can be introduced, occasions, in every art, a proportionable increase of the productive powers of labor. The separation of different trades and employments from one another, seems to have taken place, in consequence of this advantage. This separation too is generally carried furthest in those countries which enjoy the highest degree of industry and improvement. . . .

This great increase of the quantity of work, which, in consequence of the division of labor, the same number of people are capable of performing, is owing to three different circumstances; first, to the increase of dexterity in every particular workman; secondly, to the saving of the time which is commonly lost in passing from one species of work to another; and lastly, to the invention of a great number of machines which facilitate and abridge labor, and enable one man to do the work of many. . . .

It is the great multiplication of the productions of all the different arts, in consequence of the division of labor, which occasions, in a well-governed society, that universal opulence which extends itself to the lowest ranks of the people. Every workman has a great quantity of his own work to dispose of beyond what he himself has occasion for; and every other workman being exactly in the same situation, he is enabled to exchange a great quantity of his own goods for a great quantity, or, what comes to the same thing, for the price of a great quantity of theirs. He supplies them abundantly with what they have occasion for, and they accommodate him as amply with what he has occasion for, and a general plenty diffuses itself through all the different ranks of the society.

Observe the accommodation of the most common artificer or day-laborer in a civilized and thriving country, and you will perceive that the number of people of whose industry a part, though but a small part, has been employed in procuring him this accommodation, exceeds all computation. The woollen coat, for example, which covers the day-laborer, as coarse and rough as it may appear, is the produce of the joint labor of a great multitude of workmen. The shepherd, the sorter of the wool, the wool-comber or carder, the dyer, the scribbler, the spinner, the weaver, the fuller, the dresser, with many others, must all join their different arts in order to complete even this homely production. How many merchants and carriers, besides, must have been employed in transporting the materials from some of those workmen to others who often live in a very distant part of the country! How must commerce and navigation in particular, how many ship-builders, sailors, sail-makers, rope-makers, must have been employed in order to bring together the different drugs made use of by the dyer, which often come from the remotest corners of the world! What a variety of labor too is necessary in order to produce the tools of the meanest of those workmen! To say nothing of such complicated machines as the ship of the sailor, the mill of the fuller, or even the loom of the weaver, let us consider only what a variety of labor is requisite in order to form that very simple machine, the shears with which the shepherd clips the wool. The miner, the builder of the furnace for smelting the ore, the feller of the timber, the burner of the charcoal to be made use of in the smelting-house, the brick-maker, the brick-layer, the workmen who attend the furnace, the mill-wright, the forger, the smith, must all of them join their different arts in order to produce them. Were we to examine, in the same manner, all the different parts of his dress and household furniture, the coarse linen shirt which he wears next his skin, the shoes which cover his feet, the bed which he lies on, and all the different parts which compose it, the kitchen-grate at which he prepares his victuals, the coals which he makes use of for that purpose, dug from the bowels of the earth, and brought to him perhaps by a long sea and a long land carriage, all the other utensils of his kitchen, all the furniture of his table, the knives and forks, the earthen or pewter plates upon which he serves up and divides his victuals, the different hands employed in preparing his bread and his beer, the glass window which lets in the heat and the light, and keeps out the wind and the rain, with all the knowledge and art requisite for preparing that beautiful and happy invention, without which these northern parts of the world could scarce have afforded a very comfortable habitation, together with the tools of all the different workmen employed in producing those different conveniences; if we examine, I say, all these things, and consider what a variety of labor is employed about each of them, we shall be sensible that without the assistance and cooperation of many thousands, the very meanest person in a civilized country could not be provided, even according to, what we very falsely imagine, the easy and simple manner in which he is commonly accommodated. Compared, indeed, with the more extravagant luxury of the great, his accommodation must no doubt appear extremely simple and easy; and yet it may be true, perhaps, that the accommodation of an Eu-

ropean prince does not always so much exceed that of an industrious and frugal peasant, as the accommodation of the latter exceeds that of many an African king, the absolute master of the lives and liberties of ten thousand naked savages.

CHAPTER II

Of the Principle Which Gives Occasion to the Division of Labor

This division of labor, from which so many advantages are derived, is not originally the effect of any human wisdom, which foresees and intends that general opulence to which it gives occasion. It is the necessary, though very slow and gradual, consequence of a certain propensity in human nature which has in view no such extensive utility; the propensity to truck, barter, and exchange one thing for another.

Man has almost constant occasion for the help of his brethren, and it is in vain for him to expect it from their benevolence only. He will be more likely to prevail if he can interest their self-love in his favor, and shew them that it is for their own advantage to do for him what he requires of them. Whoever offers to another a bargain of any kind, proposes to do this. Give me that which I want, and you shall have this which you want, is the meaning of every such offer; and it is in this manner that we obtain from one another the far greater part of those good offices which we stand in need of. It is not from the benevolence of the butcher, the brewer, or the baker, that we expect our dinner, but from their regard to their own interest. We address ourselves, not to their humanity but to their self-love, and never talk to them of our own necessities but of their advantages. Nobody but a beggar chooses to depend chiefly upon the benevolence of his fellow-citizens.

The difference of natural talents in different men is, in reality, much less than we are aware of; and the very different genius which appears to distinguish men of different professions, when grown up to maturity, is not upon many occasions so much the cause, as the effect of the division of labor. The difference between the most dissimilar characters, between a philosopher and a common street porter, for example, seems to arise not so much from nature, as from habit, custom, and education. When they came into the world, and for the first six or eight years of their existence, they were, perhaps, very much alike, and neither their parents nor playfellows could perceive any remarkable difference. About that age, or soon after, they come to be employed in very different occupations. . . . But without the disposition to truck, barter, and exchange, every man must have procured to himself every necessary and conveniency of life which he wanted. . . .

CHAPTER VII

Of the Natural and Market Price of Commodities

There is in every society or neighborhood an ordinary or average rate both of wages and profit in every different employment of labour and stock.[8] This rate is naturally regulated, as I shall show hereafter, partly by the general circumstances of the society, their riches or poverty, their advancing, stationary, or declining condition; and partly by the particular nature of each employment.

There is likewise in every society or neighborhood an ordinary or average rate of rent, which is regulated too, as I shall show hereafter, partly by the general circumstances of the society or neighborhood in which the land is situated, and partly by the natural or improved fertility of the land.

These ordinary or average rates may be called the natural rates of wages, profit, and rent, at the time and place in which they commonly prevail.

When the price of any commodity is neither more nor less than what is sufficient to pay the rent of the land, the wages of the labor, and the profits of the stock employed in raising, preparing, and bringing it to mar-

ket, according to their natural rates, the commodity is then sold for what may be called its natural price.

The commodity is then sold precisely for what it is worth, or for what it really costs the person who brings it to market; for though in common language what is called the prime cost of any commodity does not comprehend the profit of the person who is to sell it again, yet if he sells it at a price which does not allow him the ordinary rate of profit in his neighborhood, he is evidently a loser by the trade; since by employing his stock in some other way he might have made that profit. His profit, besides, is his revenue, the proper fund of his subsistence. As, while he is preparing and bringing the goods to market, he advances to his workmen their wages, or their subsistence; so he advances to himself, in the same manner, his own subsistence, which is generally suitable to the profit which he may reasonably expect from the sale of his goods. Unless they yield him this profit, therefore, they do not repay him what they may very properly be said to have really cost him. . . .

The actual price at which any commodity is commonly sold is called its market price. It may either be above, or below, or exactly the same with its natural price.

The market price of every particular commodity is regulated by the proportion between the quantity which is actually brought to market, and the demand of those who are willing to pay the natural price of the commodity, or the whole value of the rent, labor, and profit, which must be paid in order to bring it thither. Such people may be called the effectual demanders, and their demand the effectual demand; since it may be sufficient to effectuate the bringing of the commodity to market. It is different from the absolute demand. A very poor man may be said, in some sense, to have a demand for a coach and six; he might like to have it; but his demand is not an effectual demand, as the commodity can never be brought to market in order to satisfy it.

When the quantity of any commodity which is brought to market falls short of the effectual demand, all those who are

---

[8]*stock:* capital

willing to pay the whole value of the rent, wages, and profit, which must be paid in order to bring it thither, cannot be supplied with the quantity which they want. Rather than want it altogether, some of them will be willing to give more. A competition will immediately begin among them, and the market price will rise more or less above the natural price, according as either the greatness of the deficiency, or the wealth and wanton luxury of the competitors, happen to animate more or less the eagerness of the competition. Among competitors of equal wealth and luxury the same deficiency will generally occasion a more or less eager competition, according as the acquisition of the commodity happens to be of more or less importance to them. Hence the exorbitant price of the necessaries of life during the blockade of a town or in a famine.

When the quantity brought to market exceeds the effectual demand, it cannot be all sold to those who are willing to pay the whole value of the rent, wages and profit, which must be paid in order to bring it thither. Some part must be sold to those who are willing to pay less, and the low price which they give for it must reduce the price of the whole. The market price will sink more or less below the natural price, according as the greatness of the excess increases more or less the competition of the sellers, or according as it happens to be more or less important to them to get immediately rid of the commodity. The same excess in the importation of perishables, will occasion a much greater competition than in that of durable commodities, in the importation of oranges, for example, than in that of old iron.

When the quantity brought to market is just sufficient to supply the effectual demand and no more, the market price naturally comes to be either exactly, or as nearly as can be judged of, the same with the natural price. The whole quantity upon hand can be disposed of for this price, and cannot be disposed of for more. The competition of the different dealers obliges them all to ac-

cept of this price, but does not oblige them to accept of less.

The quantity of every commodity brought to market naturally suits itself to the effectual demand. It is the interest of all those who employ their land, labor, or stock, in bringing any commodity to market, that the quantity never should exceed the effectual demand; and it is the interest of all other people that it never should fall short of that demand.

If at any time it exceeds the effectual demand, some of the component parts of its price must be paid below their natural rate. If it is rent, the interest of the landlords will immediately prompt them to withdraw a part of their land: and if it is wages or profit, the interest of the laborers in the one case, and of their employers in the other, will prompt them to withdraw a part of their labor or stock from this employment. The quantity brought to market will soon be no more than sufficient to supply the effectual demand. All the different parts of its price will rise to their natural rate, and the whole price to its natural price.

If, on the contrary, the quantity brought to market should at any time fall short of the effectual demand, some of the component parts of its price must rise above their natural rate. If it is rent, the interest of all other landlords will naturally prompt them to prepare more land for the raising of this commodity; if it is wages or profit, the interest of all other laborers and dealers will soon prompt them to employ more labor and stock in preparing and bringing it to market. The quantity brought thither will soon be sufficient to supply the effectual demand. All the different parts of its price will soon sink to their natural rate, and the whole price to its natural price.

The natural price, therefore, is, as it were, the central price, to which the prices of all commodities are continually gravitating. Different accidents may sometimes keep them suspended a good deal above it, and sometimes force them down even somewhat below it. But whatever may be the obstacles which hinder them from settling in this center of repose and continuance, they are constantly tending toward it.

The whole quantity of industry annually employed in order to bring any commodity to market, naturally suits itself in this manner to the effectual demand. It naturally aims at bringing always that precise quantity thither which may be sufficient to supply, and no more than supply, that demand. . . .

A monopoly granted either to an individual or to a trading company has the same effect as a secret in trade or manufactures. The monopolists, by keeping the market constantly under-stocked, by never fully supplying the effectual demand, sell their commodities much above the natural price, and raise their emoluments, whether they consist in wages or profit, greatly above their natural rate.

The price of monopoly is upon every occasion the highest which can be got. The natural price, or the price of free competition, on the contrary, is the lowest which can be taken, not upon every occasion indeed, but for any considerable time together. The one is upon every occasion the highest which can be squeezed out of the buyers, or which, it is supposed, they will consent to give: The other is the lowest which the sellers can commonly afford to take, and at the same time continue their business.

The exclusive privileges of corporations, statutes of apprenticeship, and all those laws which restrain, in particular employments, the competition to a smaller number than might otherwise go into them, have the same tendency, though in a less degree. They are a sort of enlarged monopolies, and may frequently, for ages together, and in whole classes of employments, keep up the market price of particular commodities above the natural price, and maintain both the wages of the labor and the profits of the stock employed about them somewhat above their natural rate.

Such enhancements of the market price may last as long as the regulations of policy which give occasion to them. . . .

BOOK IV: CHAPTER II

Of Restraints Upon the Importation from Foreign Countries of Such Goods as Can Be Produced at Home

As every individual, therefore, endeavors as much as he can both to employ his capital in the support of domestic industry, and so to direct that industry that its produce may be of the greatest value; every individual necessarily labors to render the annual revenue of the society as great as he can. He generally, indeed, neither intends to promote the public interest, nor knows how much he is promoting it. By preferring the support of domestic to that of foreign industry, he intends only his own security; and by directing that industry in such a manner as its produce may be of the greatest value, he intends only his own gain, and he is in this, as in many other cases, led by an invisible hand to promote an end which was no part of his intention. Nor is it always the worse for the society that it was no part of it. By pursuing his own interest he frequently promotes that of the society more effectually than when he really intends to promote it. I have never known much good done by those who affected to trade for the public good. It is an affectation, indeed, not very common among merchants, and very few words need be employed in dissuading them from it.

What is the species of domestic industry which his capital can employ, and of which the produce is likely to be of the greatest value, every individual, it is evident, can, in his local situation, judge much better than any statesman or lawgiver can do for him. The statesman, who should attempt to direct private people in what manner they ought to employ their capitals, would not only load himself with a most unnecessary attention, but assume an authority which could safely be trusted, not only to no single person, but to no council or senate whatever, and which would nowhere be so dangerous as in the hands of a man who had folly and presumption enough to fancy himself fit to exercise it.

To give the monopoly of the home market to the produce of domestic industry, in any particular art or manufacture, is in some measure to direct private people in what manner they ought to employ their capitals, and must, in almost all cases, be either a useless or a hurtful regulation. If the produce of domestic can be brought there as cheap as that of foreign industry, the regulation is evidently useless. If it cannot, it must generally be hurtful. It is the maxim of every prudent master of a family, never to attempt to make at home what it will cost him more to make than to buy. The taylor does not attempt to make his own shoes, but buys them of the shoemaker. The shoemaker does not attempt to make his own clothes, but employs a taylor. The farmer attempts to make neither the one nor the other, but employs those different artificers. All of them find it for their interest to employ their whole industry in a way in which they have some advantage over their neighbors, and to purchase with a part of its produce, or what is the same thing, with the price of a part of it, whatever else they have occasion for.

What is prudence in the conduct of every private family, can scarce be folly in that of a great kingdom. If a foreign country can supply us with a commodity cheaper than we ourselves can make it, better buy it of them with some part of the produce of our own industry, employed in a way in which we have some advantage. The general industry of the country, being always in proportion to the capital which employs it, will not thereby be diminished, no more than that of the above-mentioned artificers; but only left to find out the way in which it can be employed with the greatest advantage. It is certainly not employed to the greatest advantage, when it is thus directed toward an object which it can buy cheaper than it can make. The value of its annual produce is certainly more or less diminished, when it is thus turned away from producing commodities evidently of more value than the commodity which it is directed to produce. According to the supposition, that commodity could be purchased from foreign countries cheaper than it can be made at home. It could, therefore, have been purchased with a part only of the commodities, or, what is the same thing, with a part only of the price of the commodities, which the industry employed by an equal capital would have produced at home, had it been left to follow its natural course. The industry of the country, therefore, is thus turned away from a more, to a less advantageous employment, and the exchangeable value of its annual produce, instead of being increased, according to the intention of the lawgiver, must necessarily be diminished by every such regulation. . . .

. . . Country gentlemen and farmers are, to their great honor, of all people, the least subject to the wretched spirit of monopoly. . . . Dispersed in different parts of the country, [they] cannot so easily combine as merchants and manufacturers, who being collected into towns, and accustomed to that exclusive corporation spirit which prevails in them, naturally endeavor to obtain against all their countrymen, the same exclusive privilege which they generally possess against the inhabitants of their respective towns. . . . It was probably in imitation of them . . . that the country gentlemen and farmers of Great Britain so far forgot the generosity which is natural to their station, as to demand the exclusive privilege of supplying their countrymen with corn[9] and butcher's meat. . . . To prohibit by a perpetual law the importation of foreign corn and cattle, is in reality to enact, that the population and industry of the country shall at no time exceed what the rude produce of its own soil can maintain.

There seem, however, to be two cases in which it will generally be advantageous to lay some burden upon foreign, for the encouragement of domestic industry.

The first is, when some particular sort of industry is necessary for the defense of the country. The defense of Great Britain, for example, depends very much upon the

---

[9]*corn:* grain

number of its sailors and shipping. The act of navigation, therefore, very properly endeavors to give the sailors and shipping of Great Britain the monopoly of the trade of their own country, in some cases, by absolute prohibitions, and in others by heavy burdens upon the shipping of foreign countries. . . . As defense . . . is of much more importance than opulence, the act of navigation is, perhaps, the wisest of all the commercial regulations of England.

The second case, in which it will generally be advantageous to lay some burden upon foreign for the encouragement of domestic industry, is, when some tax is imposed at home upon the produce of the latter. In this case, it seems reasonable that an equal tax should be imposed upon the like produce of the former. This would not give the monopoly of the home market to domestic industry, nor turn toward a particular employment a greater share of the stock and labor of the country, than what would naturally go to it. It would only hinder any part of what would naturally go to it from being turned away by the tax, into a less natural direction, and would leave the competition between foreign and domestic industry, after the tax, as nearly as possible upon the same footing as before it. . . .

CHAPTER VIII

Conclusion of the Mercantile System

. . . The importation of the materials of manufacture has sometimes been encouraged by an exemption from the duties to which other goods are subject, and sometimes by bounties.

The importation of sheep's wool from several different countries, of cotton wool from all countries, of undressed flax, of the greater part of dying drugs, of the greater part of undressed hides from Ireland or the British colonies, of seal skins from the British Greenland fishery, of pig and bar iron from the British colonies, as well as of several other materials of manufacture, has been encouraged by an exemption from all duties, if properly entered at the custom-house. The private interest of our merchants and manufacturers may, perhaps, have extorted from the legislature these exemptions, as well as the greater part of our other commercial regulations. They are, however, perfectly just and reasonable, and if, consistently with the necessities of the state, they could be extended to all the other materials of manufacture, the public would certainly be a gainer.

The avidity of our great manufacturers, however, has in some cases extended these exemptions a good deal beyond what can justly be considered as the rude materials of their work. By the 24 Geo. II. chap. 46. a small duty of only one penny the pound was imposed upon the importation of foreign brown linen yarn, instead of much higher duties to which it had been subjected before, viz. of sixpence the pound upon sail yarn, of one shilling the pound upon all French and Dutch yarn, and of two pounds thirteen shillings and fourpence upon the hundred weight of all spruce of Muscovia yarn. But our manufacturers were not long satisfied with this reduction. By the 29th of the same king, chap. 15. the same law which gave a bounty upon the exportation of British and Irish linen of which the price did not exceed eighteen pence the yard, even this small duty upon the importation of brown linen yarn was taken away. In the different operations, however, which are necessary for the preparation of linen yarn, a good deal more industry is employed, than in the subsequent operation of preparing linen cloth from linen yarn. To say nothing of the industry of the flax-growers and flax-dressers, three or four spinners, at least, are necessary, in order to keep one weaver in constant employment; and more than four-fifths of the whole quantity of labor, necessary for the preparation of linen cloth, is employed in that of linen yarn; but our spinners are poor people, women commonly, scattered about in all different parts of the country, without support or protection. It is not by the sale of their work, but by that of the complete work of the weavers, that our great master manufacturers make their profits. As it is their interest to sell the complete manufacture as dear, so it is to buy the material as cheap as possible. By extorting from the legislature bounties upon the exportation of their own linen, high duties upon the importation of all foreign linen, and a total prohibition of the home consumption of some sorts of French linen, they endeavor to sell their own goods as dear as possible. By encouraging the importation of foreign linen yarn, and thereby bringing it into competition with that which is made by our own people, they endeavor to buy the work of the poor spinners as cheap as possible. They are as intent to keep down the wages of their own weavers, as the earnings of the poor spinners, and it is by no means for the benefit of the workman, that they endeavor either to raise the price of the complete work, or to lower that of the rude materials. It is the industry which is carried on for the benefit of the rich and the powerful, that is principally encouraged by our mercantile system. That which is carried on for the benefit of the poor and the indigent, is too often, either neglected, or oppressed. . . .

The exportation of the materials of manufacture is sometimes discouraged by absolute prohibitions, and sometimes by high duties.

Our woollen manufacturers have been more successful than any other class of workmen, in persuading the legislature that the prosperity of the nation depended upon the success and extension of their particular business. They have not only obtained a monopoly against the consumers by an absolute prohibition of importing woollen cloths from any foreign country; but they have likewise obtained another monopoly against the sheep farmers and growers of wool, by a similar prohibition of the exportation of live sheep and wool. The severity of many of the laws which have been enacted for the security of the revenue is very justly complained of, as imposing heavy penalties upon actions which, antecedent to the statutes that declared them to be crimes, had always been understood to be innocent. But the cruellest of our revenue laws, I will venture to affirm, are mild and gentle, in comparison of some of those which the clamor of our merchants and manufacturers has extorted from the legislature, for the support of their own absurd and oppressive monopolies. Like the laws of Draco, these laws may be said to be all written in blood. . . .

In order to prevent exportation, the whole inland commerce of wool is laid under very burdensome and oppressive restrictions. . . .

It is unnecessary, I imagine, to observe, how contrary such regulations are to the boasted liberty of the subject, of which we affect to be so very jealous; but which, in this case, is so plainly sacrificed to the futile interests of our merchants and manufacturers.

The laudable motive of all these regulations, is to extend our own manufactures, not by their own improvement, but by the depression of those of all our neighbors, and by putting an end, as much as possible, to the troublesome competition of such odious and disagreeable rivals. Our master manufacturers think it reasonable, that they themselves should have the monopoly of the ingenuity of all their countrymen. Though by restraining, in some trades, the number of apprentices which can be employed at one time, and by imposing the necessity of a long apprenticeship in all trades, they endeavor, all of them, to confine the knowledge of their respective employments to as small a number as possible; they are unwilling, however, that any part of this small number should go abroad to instruct foreigners.

Consumption is the sole end and purpose of all production; and the interest of the producer ought to be attended to, only so far as it may be necessary for promoting that of the consumer. The maxim is so perfectly self-evident, that it would be absurd to attempt to prove it. But in the mercantile system, the interest of the consumer is almost constantly sacrificed to that of the producer; and it seems to consider production, and not consumption, as the ultimate end and object of all industry and commerce.

In the restraints upon the importation of all foreign commodities which can come into competition with those of our own growth, or manufacture, the interest of the home-consumer is evidently sacrificed to that of the producer. It is altogether for the benefit of the latter, that the former is obliged to pay that enhancement of price which this monopoly almost always occasions.

It is altogether for the benefit of the producer that bounties are granted upon the exportation of some of his productions. The home-consumer is obliged to pay, first, the tax which is necessary for paying the bounty; and secondly, the still greater tax which necessarily arises from the enhancement of the price of the commodity in the home market.

By the famous treaty of commerce with Portugal,[10] the consumer is prevented by high duties from purchasing of a neighboring country, a commodity which our own climate does not produce, but is obliged to purchase it of a distant country, though it is acknowledged, that the commodity of the distant country is of a worse quality than that of the near one. The home-consumer is obliged to submit to this inconveniency, in order that the producer may import into the distant country some of his productions upon more advantageous terms than he would otherwise have been allowed to do. The consumer, too, is obliged to pay, whatever enhancement in the price of those very productions, this forced exportation may occasion in the home market.

But in the system of laws which has been established for the management of our American and West Indian colonies, the interest of the home-consumer has been sacrificed to that of the producer with a more extravagant profusion than in all our other commercial regulations. A great empire has been established for the sole purpose of raising up a nation of customers who should be obliged to buy from the shops of our different producers, all the goods with which these could supply them. For the sake of that little enhancement of price which this monopoly might afford our producers, the home-consumers have been burdened with the whole expense of maintaining and defending that empire. For this purpose, and for this purpose only, in the two last wars,[11] more than two hundred millions have been spent, and a new debt of more than a hundred and seventy millions has been contracted over and above all that had been expended for the same purpose in former wars. The interest of this debt alone is not only greater than the whole extraordinary profit, which, it ever could be pretended, was made by the monopoly of the colony trade, but than the whole value of that trade, or than the whole value of the goods, which at an average have been annually exported to the colonies.

It cannot be very difficult to determine who have been the contrivers of this whole mercantile system; not the consumers, we may believe, whose interest has been entirely neglected; but the producers, whose interest has been so carefully attended to; and among this latter class our merchants and manufacturers have been by far the principal architects. In the mercantile regulations, which have been taken notice of in this chapter, the interest of our manufacturers has been most peculiarly attended to; and the interest, not so much of the consumers, as that of some other sets of producers, has been sacrificed to it. . . .

Chapter IX

[The Role of Government]

. . . All systems either of preference or of restraint, therefore, being thus completely taken away, the obvious and simple system of natural liberty establishes itself of its own accord. Every man, as long as he does not violate the laws of justice, is left

---

[10]*treaty . . . Portugal:* refers to the Methuen Treaty of 1702, which gave preference to wines from Portugal over those from France. [11]*two last wars:* the war against Spain and France (1739–1748) and the Seven Years' War (1756–1763)

perfectly free to pursue his own interest his own way, and to bring both his industry and capital into competition with those of any other man, or order of men. The sovereign is completely discharged from a duty, in the attempting to perform which he must always be exposed to innumerable delusions, and for the proper performance of which no human wisdom or knowledge could ever be sufficient; the duty of superintending the industry of private people, and of directing it toward the employments most suitable to the interest of the society. According to the system of natural liberty, the sovereign has only three duties to attend to; three duties of great importance, indeed, but plain and intelligible to common understandings: first, the duty of protecting the society from the violence and invasion of other independent societies; secondly, the duty of protecting, as far as possible, every member of the society from the injustice or oppression of every other member of it, or the duty of establishing an exact administration of justice; and, thirdly, the duty of erecting and maintaining certain public works and certain public institutions, which it can never be for the interest of any individual, or small number of individuals, to erect and maintain; because the profit could never repay the expense to any individual or small number of individuals, though it may frequently do much more than repay it to a great society. . . .

4

Religion in Eighteenth-Century England: Reason or Revelation?

One of the more significant preoccupations of educated eighteenth-century people was how to fit religion into a presumed age of reason. The wars of religion were less than a century in the past; in Britain, indeed, the "Glorious Revolution" and the generation of war that followed had provided even more recent echoes.

The first document consists of excerpts from a series of letters written by Philip Stanhope, the fourth earl of Chesterfield (1694–1773). In these letters Lord Chesterfield attempts to set forth a code of manners and ethics for a "man of the world" in the era of the Enlightenment. During the course of his life, Chesterfield served as parliamentarian, as diplomat, and briefly as Lord Lieutenant of Ireland. He was noted as both an orator and a wit, and his letters represented a genuine attempt to educate his illegitimate son in the ways of his own upper-class world. In their immediate purpose they largely failed—the son, who died at age 36, did not become an eminent member of English society—but the *Letters*, published in 1774 after Chesterfield's death, remain a testament to eighteenth-century assumptions and ideals. What is Chesterfield's attitude toward his own time in the context of history? How does he assess the importance of the study of history? What types of learning and behavior does he extol? What is the apparent basis of his own code of ethics? What is his attitude toward the prevalent religions of Europe and the world: hostility, devout belief, or friendly skepticism? What is his attitude toward the lower ranks of society?

Just as in one portion of his book *The Principles of Moral and Political Philosophy* William Paley (1743–1805) justified the political status quo in eighteenth-century England (see Chapter 3), so, in "The Church of England" (1785) drawn from the same work, does Paley justify the religious status quo. On what grounds does Paley defend the existence of an established church like the Church of England? Are those grounds fundamentally "religious" or "rational"?

One of the most extraordinary Englishmen of the century was Dr. Samuel Johnson (1709–1784), journalist, essayist, dictionary-maker, conversationalist, and the subject of one of the most remarkable biographies ever written, James Boswell's *Life of Dr. Samuel Johnson* (1791). Boswell was a faithful diarist with a phenomenal memory who found it possible

William Hogarth's Engraving *The Sleeping Congregation*
(1736)

*The preacher's text is: "Come unto me all ye that Labor and
are heavy laden, and I shall give you rest" (Matthew 11:28).*

to reconstruct long conversations verbatim, conversations that display
Johnson as sage and wit. Johnson looked upon himself as a philosophical
Tory in an age of Whiggery, and the selection that follows, "The Limits
of Liberty of Conscience" (1773), provides a characteristically Johnsonian
appraisal of the proper limits of religious toleration. What are those limits, according to Johnson? How successfully does he deal with the objections raised by Goldsmith and Mayo? What does the very presence of Dr.
Mayo at the same dinner table as Johnson say about the state of religious
toleration in eighteenth-century England?

John Wesley (1703–1791) was a Church of England clergyman who
took issue not so much with the formal teachings of his church as with
its spirit. He was to devote half a lifetime to a campaign of evangelism,
which caused him to travel more than 220,000 miles on horseback

through England, Wales, and Ireland preaching thousands upon thousands of sermons in the open air, often to poor people who did not regularly attend Church of England services. By temperament a paternalistic auto-crat, Wesley remained formally affiliated with the Church of England during his lifetime. The selection, "The Origins, Rules, and the Spirit of Methodism" (1744–1749), provides Wesley's own early account of how his movement began and what type of behavior was expected of believers. What does the selection tell us about the differences in spirit and charac-ter between Methodist religious services and others? What type of life is set forth as the Methodist ideal? How does the cited hymn fit into an "age of reason"?

The next selection, *Observations Upon the Conduct and Behaviour of Methodists,* written and published anonymously by an Anglican prel-ate in 1744, reminds us that a majority of mid-eighteenth-century Church of England clergymen viewed Methodism with suspicion rather than with sympathy. Why were they suspicious? Why were they fearful?

Despite such criticisms, the Methodist movement continued to grow during Wesley's lifetime and during the decades after his death, even as his followers broke away from the Church of England to constitute first one and in due course several distinct Methodist denominations. By the turn of the nineteenth century, the older Nonconformist bodies (like the Congregationalists, the Baptists, the Quakers, and the Unitarians) were also recovering from their mid-eighteenth-century doldrums, and an evangelical revival was stirring as well within the Church of England. For many Britons the assumptions of Enlightenment rationalism were giving way to a spirit of romanticism that could be discerned in religion as well as in literature, in painting, and in architecture.

THE EARL OF CHESTERFIELD **Letters to His Son (1748–1752)**

Philip Stanhope, fourth earl of Chesterfield, instructs his son in "the ways of the world."

. . . What I do, and ever shall regret, is the time which, while young, I lost in mere idleness, and in doing nothing. This is the common effect of the inconsideracy of youth, against which I beg you will be most carefully upon your guard. The value of mo-ments, when cast up, is immense, if well employed; if thrown away, their loss is irre-coverable. Every moment may be put to some use, and that with much more plea-sure, than if unemployed. Do not imagine, that by the employment of time, I mean an uninterrupted application to serious stud-ies. No; pleasures are, at proper times, both as necessary and as useful; they fashion and form you for the world; they teach you char-acters, and show you the human heart in its unguarded minutes. But then remember to make that use of them. I have known many people, from laziness of mind, go through both pleasure and business with equal inat-tention; neither enjoying the one, nor doing the other; thinking themselves men of plea-sure, because they were mingled with those

SOURCE: From Earl of Chesterfield, *Letters to His Son* (New York: Dingwall-Rock, Ltd., 1925), Vol. I, pp. 49–54, 68–72, 106, 159, 160–163, 382. (First published in 1774.)

who were; and men of business, because they had business to do, though they did not do it. Whatever you do, do it to the purpose; do it thoroughly, not superficially. *Approfondissez*: go to the bottom of things. Any thing half done or half known, is, in my mind, neither done nor known at all. Nay worse, it often misleads. There is hardly any place or any company, where you may not gain knowledge, if you please; almost everybody knows some one thing, and is glad to talk upon that one thing. Seek and you will find, in this world as well as in the next. See everything; inquire into everything. . . .

Now that you are in a Lutheran country,[1] go to their churches, and observe the manner of their public worship; attend to their ceremonies, and inquire the meaning and intention of everyone of them. And, as you will soon understand German well enough, attend to their sermons, and observe their manner of preaching. Inform yourself of their church government: whether it resides in the sovereign, or in consistories and synods. Whence arises the maintenance of their clergy; whether from tithes, as in England, or from voluntary contributions, or from pensions from the state. Do the same thing when you are in Roman Catholic countries; go to their churches, see all their ceremonies: ask the meaning of them, get the terms explained to you. As, for instance, Prime, Tierce, Sexte, Nones, Matins, Angelus, High Mass, Vespers, Complines, etc. Inform yourself of their several religious orders, their founders, their rules, their vows, their habits, their revenues, etc. But, when you frequent places of public worship, as I would have you go to all the different ones you meet with, remember, that however erroneous, they are none of them objects of laughter and ridicule. Honest error is to be pitied, not ridiculed. The object of all the public worships in the world is the same; it is that great eternal Being who created everything. The different manners of worship are by no means subjects of ridicule. Each sect thinks its own is the best; and I know no infallible judge in this world, to decide which is the best. . . .

Every excellency, and every virtue, has its kindred vice or weakness; and if carried beyond certain bounds, sinks into one or the other. Generosity often runs into profusion, economy into avarice, courage into rashness, caution into timidity, and so on:—insomuch that, I believe, there is more judgment required, for the proper conduct of our virtues, than for avoiding their opposite vices. . . . I shall apply this reasoning, at present, not to any particular virtue, but to an excellency, which, for want of judgment, is often the cause of ridiculous and blamable effects; I mean, great learning; which, if not accompanied with sound judgment, frequently carries us into error, pride, and pedantry. As, I hope, you will possess that excellency in its utmost extent, and yet without its too common failings, the hints, which my experience can suggest, may probably not be useless to you.

Some learned men, proud of their knowledge, only speak to decide, and give judgment without appeal; the consequence of which is, that mankind, provoked by the insult, and injured by the oppression, revolt; and, in order to shake off the tyranny, even call the lawful authority in question. The more you know, the modester you should be: and (by the bye) that modesty is the surest way of gratifying your vanity. Even where you are sure, seem rather doubtful; represent, but do not pronounce, and, if you would convince others, seem open to conviction yourself.

Others, to show their learning, or often from the prejudices of a school-education, where they hear of nothing else, are always talking of the ancients, as something more than men, and of the moderns, as something less. They are never without a classic

---

[1]*Lutheran country:* refers to the fact that his son and his son's tutor were visiting the German city of Leipzig at the time

or two in their pockets; they stick to the old good sense; they read none of the modern trash; and will show you, plainly, that no improvement has been made, in any one art or science, these last seventeen hundred years. I would by no means have you disown your acquaintance with the ancients: but still less would I have you brag of an exclusive intimacy with them. Speak of the moderns without contempt, and of the ancients without idolatry; judge them all by their merits, but not by their ages. . . . Wear your learning, like your watch, in a private pocket: and do not pull it out and strike it; merely to show that you have one. If you are asked what o'clock it is, tell it; but do not proclaim it hourly and unasked, like the watchman.

Upon the whole, remember that learning (I mean Greek and Roman learning) is a most useful and necessary ornament, which it is shameful not to be master of; but, at the same time most carefully avoid those errors and abuses which I have mentioned, and which too often attend it. Remember, too, that great modern knowledge is still more necessary than ancient; and that you had better know perfectly the present, than the old state of Europe; though I would have you well acquainted with both. . . .

I look with some contempt upon those refining and sagacious historians, who ascribe all, even the most common events, to some deep political cause; whereas mankind is made up of inconsistencies, and no man acts invariably up to his predominant character. The wisest man sometimes acts weakly, and the weakest sometimes wisely. Our jarring passions, our variable humors, nay, our greater or lesser degree of health and spirits, produce such contradictions in our conduct, that, I believe, those are the oftenest mistaken, who ascribe our actions to the most seemingly obvious motives; and I am convinced, that a light supper, a good night's sleep, and a fine morning, have

sometimes made a hero of the same man, who, by an indigestion, a restless night, and rainy morning, would have proved a coward. Our best conjectures, therefore, as to the true springs of actions, are but very uncertain; and the actions themselves are all that we must pretend to know from history. That Caesar was murdered by twenty-three conspirators, I make no doubt: but I very much doubt that their love of liberty, and of their country, was their sole, or even principal motive; and I dare say that, if the truth were known, we should find that many other motives at least concurred, even in the great Brutus himself; such as pride, envy, personal pique, and disappointment. Nay, I cannot help carrying my Pyrrhonism[2] still further, and extending it often to historical facts themselves, at least to most of the circumstances with which they are related; and every day's experience confirms me in this historical incredulity. Do we ever hear the most recent fact related exactly in the same way, by the several people who were at the same time eyewitnesses of it? No. One mistakes, another misrepresents, and others warp it a little to their own turn of mind, or private views. A man who has been concerned in a transaction will not write it fairly; and a man who has not, cannot. But notwithstanding all this uncertainty, history is not the less necessary to be known, as the best histories are taken for granted, and are the frequent subjects both of conversation and writing. . . .

This historical Pyrrhonism, then, proves nothing against the study and knowledge of history; which, of all other studies, is the most necessary for a man who is to live in the world. It only points out to us, not to be too decisive and peremptory; and to be cautious how we draw inferences for our own practice from remote facts, partially or ignorantly related; of which we can, at best, but imperfectly guess, and certainly not know the real motives. The testimonies of ancient history must necessarily be weaker

---

[2]*Pyrrhonism:* skepticism

than those of modern, as all testimony grows weaker and weaker, as it is more and more remote from us. I would therefore advise you to study ancient history, in general, as other people do. . . . But modern history, I mean particularly that of the last three centuries, is what I would have you apply to with the greatest attention and exactness. There the probability of coming at the truth is much greater, as the testimonies are much more recent; besides, anecdotes, memoirs, and original letters, often come to the aid of modern history. . . .

Having mentioned commonplace observations, I will particularly caution you against either using, believing, or approving them. They are the common topics of witlings and coxcombs. . . .

Religion is one of their favorite topics; it is all priest-craft; and an invention contrived and carried on by priests of all religions, for their own power and profit; from this absurd and false principle flow the commonplace, insipid jokes, and insults upon the clergy. With these people, every priest, of every religion, is either a public or a concealed unbeliever, drunkard, and whoremaster; whereas, I conceive, that priests are extremely like other men, and neither the better nor the worse for wearing a gown or a surplice: but if they are different from other people, probably it is rather on the side of religion and morality, or, at least, decency, from their education and manner of life.

Another common topic for false wit, and cool raillery, is matrimony. Every man and his wife hate each other cordially, whatever they may pretend, in public, to the contrary. The husband certainly wishes his wife at the devil, and the wife certainly cuckolds her husband. Whereas, I presume, that men and their wives neither love nor hate each other the more, upon account of the form of matrimony which has been said over them. The cohabitation, indeed, which

is the consequence of matrimony, makes them either love or hate more, accordingly as they respectively deserve it; but that would be exactly the same between any man and woman who lived together without being married.

These and many other commonplace reflections upon nations or professions in general (which are at least as often false as true), are the poor refuge of people who have neither wit nor invention of their own, but endeavor to shine in company by second-hand finery.

La Rochefoucault,[3] is, I know, blamed, but I think without reason, for deriving all our actions from the source of self-love. For my own part, I see a great deal of truth, and no harm at all, in that opinion. It is certain that we seek our own happiness in everything we do; and it is as certain, that we can only find it in doing well, and in conforming all our actions to the rule of right reason, which is the great law of nature. It is only a mistaken self-love that is a blamable motive, when we take the immediate and indiscriminate gratification of a passion, or appetite, for real happiness. But am I blamable if I do a good action, upon account of the happiness which that honest consciousness will give me? Surely not. . . . Give me but virtuous actions, and I will not quibble and chicane about the motives. And I will give anybody their choice of these two truths, which amount to the same thing: He who loves himself best is the honestest man; or, The honestest man loves himself best. . . .

Till sixteen or seventeen I had no reflection; and for many years after that, I made no use of what I had. I adopted the notions of the books I read, or the company I kept, without examining whether they were just or not; and I rather chose to run the risk of easy error, than to take the time and trouble of investigating truth. . . .

But since I have taken the trouble of reasoning for myself, and have had the courage

---

[3]*Francois de la Rochefoucauld (1613–1680):* a French writer famous for his pithy and somewhat cynical observations on human nature and society

to own that I do so, you cannot imagine how much my notions of things are altered, and in how different a light I now see them, from that in which I formerly viewed them, through the deceitful medium of prejudice or authority. Nay, I may possibly still retain many errors, which, from long habit, have perhaps grown into real opinions; for it is very difficult to distinguish habits, early acquired and long entertained, from the result of our reason and reflection.

My first prejudice (for I do not mention the prejudices of boys and women, such as hobgoblins, ghosts, dreams, spilling salt, etc.) was my classical enthusiasm, which I received from the books I read, and the masters who explained them to me. I was convinced there had been no common sense nor common honesty in the world for these last fifteen hundred years; but that they were totally extinguished with the ancient Greek and Roman governments. Homer and Virgil could have no faults, because they were ancient; Milton and Tasso could have no merit, because they were modern. . . . Whereas now, without any extraordinary effort of genius, I have discovered that nature was the same three thousand years ago as it is at present; that men were but men then as well as now; that modes and customs vary often, but that human nature is always the same. And I can no more suppose that men were better, braver, or wiser, fifteen hundred or three thousand years ago, than I can suppose that the animals or vegetables were better then than they are now. . . .

Religious prejudices kept pace with my classical ones; and there was a time when I thought it impossible for the honestest man in the world to be saved out of the pale of the Church of England, not considering that matters of opinion do not depend upon the will; and that it is as natural, and as allowable, that another man should differ in opinion from me, as that I should differ from him; and that if we are both sincere, we are both blameless; and should consequently have mutual indulgence for each other. . . .

Use and assert your own reason; reflect, examine, and analyze everything, in order to form a sound and mature judgment. . . . I do not say that it will always prove an unerring guide; for human reason is not infallible; but it will prove the least erring guide that you can follow. Books and conversation may assist it; but adopt neither blindly and implicitly; try both by that best rule, which God has given to direct us, reason. Of all the troubles, do not decline, as many people do, that of thinking. The herd of mankind can hardly be said to think; their notions are almost all adoptive; and, in general, I believe it is better that it should be so, as such common prejudices contribute more to order and quiet than their own separate reasonings would do, uncultivated and unimproved as they are. We have many of those useful prejudices in this country, which I should be very sorry to see removed. The good Protestant conviction, that the pope is both Antichrist and the Whore of Babylon, is a more effectual preservative in this country against popery, than all the solid and unanswerable arguments of Chillingworth.

The idle story of the pretender's having been introduced in a warming pan into the queen's bed, though as destitute of all probability as of all foundation, has been much more prejudicial to the cause of Jacobitism than all that Mr. Locke and others have written, to show the unreasonableness and absurdity of the doctrines of indefeasible hereditary right, and unlimited passive obedience. And that silly, sanguine notion, which is firmly entertained here, that one Englishman can beat three Frenchmen, encourages, and has sometimes enabled, one Englishman in reality to beat two. . . .

I repeat it, and repeat it again, and shall never cease repeating it to you: air, manners, graces, style, elegance, and all those ornaments, must now be the only objects of your attention; it is now, or never, that you must acquire them. Postpone, therefore, all other considerations; make them now your serious study; you have not one moment to lose.

WILLIAM PALEY   The Church of England (1785)

Paley justifies the position of the Church of England as the established church of the country.

A religious establishment is no part of Christianity, it is only the means of inculcating it. . . . It cannot be proved that any form of church government was laid down in the Christian, as it had been in the Jewish scriptures, with a view of fixing a constitution for succeeding ages; and which constitution, consequently, the disciples of Christianity would, every where, and at all times, by the very law of their religion, be obliged to adopt. Certainly no command for this purpose was delivered by Christ himself. . . .

The authority therefore of a church establishment is founded in its utility: and whenever, upon this principle, we deliberate concerning the form, propriety, or comparative excellency of different establishments, the single view, under which we ought to consider any of them, is that of "a scheme of instruction"; the single end we ought to propose by them is, "the preservation and communication of religious knowledge." Every other idea, and every other end that have been mixed with this, as the making of the church an engine, or even *an ally* of the state; converting it into the means of strengthening or of diffusing influence; or regarding it as a support of regal in opposition to popular forms of government, have served only to debase the institution, and to introduce into it numerous corruptions and abuses.

The notion of a religious establishment comprehends three things; a clergy, or an order of men secluded from other professions to attend upon the offices of religion; a legal provision for the maintenance of the clergy; and the confining of that provision to the teachers of a particular sect of Christianity. If any one of these three things be wanting; if there be no clergy, as amongst the Quakers; or, if the clergy have no other

provision than what they derive from the voluntary contribution of their hearers; or, if the provision which the laws assign to the support of religion be extended to various sects and denominations of Christians, there exists no national religion or established church, according to the sense which these terms are usually made to convey. He, therefore, who would defend ecclesiastical establishments, must show the separate utility of these three essential parts of the constitution.

1. The question first in order upon the subject, as well as the most fundamental in its importance, is, whether the knowledge and profession of Christianity can be maintained in a country, without a class of men set apart by public authority to the study and teaching of religion, and to the conducting of public worship; and for these purposes secluded from other employments. I add this last circumstance, because in it consists, as I take it, the substance of the controversy. Now it must be remembered that Christianity is an historical religion, founded in facts which are related to have passed, upon discourses which were held, and letters which were written, in a remote age, and distant country of the world, as well as under a state of life and manners, and during the prevalency of opinions, customs and institutions, very unlike any which are found amongst mankind at present. Moreover, this religion, having been first published in the country of Judea, and being built upon the more ancient religion of the Jews, is necessarily and intimately connected with the sacred writings, with the history and polity of that singular people: to which must be added, that the records of both revelations are preserved in languages which have long ceased to be spoken in any part of the world. Books which

SOURCE: From William Paley, *Principles of Moral and Political Philosophy* (London, 1785), pp. 456–459, 460–464, 466.

come down to us from times so remote, and under so many causes of unavoidable obscurity, cannot, it is evident, be understood without study and preparation. The languages must be learnt. The various writings which these volumes contain must be carefully compared with one another, and with themselves. What remains of contemporary authors, or of authors connected with the age, the country, or the subject of our scriptures, must be perused and consulted, in order to interpret doubtful forms of speech, and to explain allusions which refer to objects or usages that no longer exist. Above all the modes of expression, the habits of reasoning and argumentation, which were then in use, and to which the discourses even of inspired teachers were necessarily adapted, must be sufficiently known, and can only be known at all, by a due acquaintance with ancient literature. And, lastly, to establish the genuineness and integrity of the canonical scriptures themselves, a series of testimony, recognizing the notoriety and reception of these books, must be deduced from times near to those of their first publication, down the succession of ages through which they have been transmitted to us. The qualifications necessary for such researches demand, it is confessed, a degree of leisure, and a kind of education, inconsistent with the exercise of any other profession; . . . We contend, therefore, that an order of clergy is necessary to perpetuate the evidences of revelation, and to interpret the obscurities of these ancient writings, in which the religion is contained. . . .

2. If then an order of clergy be necessary, if it be necessary also to seclude them from the employments and profits of other professions, it is evident they ought to be enabled to derive a maintenance from their own. Now this maintenance must either depend upon the voluntary contributions of their hearers, or arise from revenues assigned by authority of law. To the scheme of voluntary contribution there exists this insurmountable objection, that few would ultimately contribute any thing at all. However the zeal of a sect, or the novelty of a change, might support such an experiment for a while, no reliance could be placed upon it as a general and permanent provision. It is at all times a bad constitution which presents temptations of interest in opposition to the duties of religion; or which makes the offices of religion expensive to those who attend upon them; or which allows pretenses of conscience to be an excuse for not sharing in a public burthen. If, by declining to frequent religious assemblies, men could save their money, at the same time that they indulged their indolence, and their disinclination to exercises of seriousness and reflection; or if, by dissenting from the national religion, they could be excused from contributing to the support of the ministers of religion, it is to be feared that many would take advantage of the option which was thus imprudently left open to them, and that this liberty might finally operate to the decay of virtue, and an irrecoverable forgetfulness of all religion in the country. Is there not too much reason to fear, that, if it were referred to the discretion of each neighborhood, whether they would maintain amongst them a teacher of religion or not, many districts would remain unprovided with any; that with the difficulties which incumber every measure, requiring the co-operation of numbers, and where each individual of the number has an interest secretly pleading against the success of the measure itself, associations for the support of Christian worship and instruction would neither be numerous nor long continued? The devout and pious might lament in vain the want or the distance of a religious assembly: they could not form or maintain one, without the concurrence of neighbors who felt neither their zeal nor their liberality.

From the difficulty with which congregations would be established and upheld upon the *voluntary* plan, let us carry our thoughts to the condition of those who are to officiate in them. Preaching, in time, would become a mode of begging. With what sincerity, or with what dignity, can a preacher dispense the truths of Christianity, whose thoughts are perpetually solicited to the reflection how he may increase his subscription? His eloquence, if he possess any, resembles rather the exhibition of a player who is computing the profits of his theatre, than the simplicity of a man, who, feeling himself the awful expectations of religion, is seeking to bring others to such a sense and understanding of their duty as may save their souls. Moreover, a little experience of the disposition of the common people will in every country inform us, that it is one thing to edify them in Christian knowledge, and another to gratify their taste for vehement impassioned oratory; that he, not only whose success, but whose subsistence depends upon collecting and pleasing a crowd, must resort to other arts than the acquirement and communication of sober and profitable instruction. For a preacher to be thus at the mercy of his audience, to be obliged to adapt his doctrines to the pleasure of a capricious multitude, to be continually affecting a style and manner neither natural to him, nor agreeable to his judgment, to live in constant bondage to tyrannical and insolent directors, are circumstances so mortifying, not only to the pride of the human heart, but to the virtuous love of independency, that they are rarely submitted to without a sacrifice of principle, and a depravation of character—at least it may be pronounced, that a ministry so degraded would soon fall into the lowest hands; for it would be found impossible to engage men of worth and ability, in so precarious and humiliating a profession.

3. If in deference then to these reasons it be admitted, that a legal provision for the clergy, compulsory upon those who contribute to it, is expedient; the next question will be, whether this provision should be confined to one sect of Christianity, or extended indifferently to all. Now it should be observed, that this question never *can* offer itself where the people are agreed in their religious opinions; and that it never *ought* to arise, where a system may be framed of doctrines and worship wide enough to comprehend their disagreement; and which might satisfy all by uniting all in the articles of their common faith, and in

a mode of divine worship, that omits every subject of controversy or offense. Where such a comprehension is practicable, the comprehending religion ought to be made that of the state. But if this be despaired of; if religious opinions exist, not only so various, but so contradictory, as to render it impossible to reconcile them to each other, or to any one confession of faith, rule of discipline, or form of worship; if consequently, separate congregations and different sects must unavoidably continue in the country: under such circumstances, whether the laws ought to establish one sect in preference to the rest, that is, whether they ought to confer the provision assigned to the maintenance of religion upon the teachers of one system of doctrines alone, becomes a question of necessary discussion and of great importance. And whatever we may determine concerning speculative rights and abstract proprieties, when we set about the framing of an ecclesiastical constitution adapted to real life, and to the actual state of religion in the country, we shall find this question very nearly related to, and principally indeed dependent upon another; namely, "in what way, or by whom ought the ministers of religion to be *appointed?*" If the species of patronage be retained to which we are accustomed in this country, and which allows private individuals to nominate teachers of religion for districts and congregations to which they are absolute strangers; without some test proposed to the persons nominated, the utmost discordancy of religious opinions might arise between the several teachers and their respective congregations. A popish patron might appoint a priest to say Mass to a congregation of Protestants; an Episcopal clergyman be sent to officiate in a parish of Presbyterians; or a Presbyterian divine to inveigh against the errors of popery before an audience of Papists. The requisition then of subscription, or any other test by which the national religion is guarded, may be considered merely as a restriction upon the exercise of private patronage. . . .

The argument, then, by which ecclesiastical establishments are defended, proceeds by these steps. The knowledge and profession of Christianity cannot be upheld without a clergy; a clergy cannot be supported without a legal provision: a legal provision for the clergy cannot be constituted without the preference of one sect of Christians to the rest: and the conclusion will be satisfactory in the degree in which the truth of these several propositions can be made out.

SAMUEL JOHNSON **The Limits of Liberty of Conscience (1773)**

The redoubtable Dr. Johnson defines the proper limits of religious toleration. The setting of the conversation was a dinner on the night of Friday, May 7, 1773, at the home of James Boswell's friends, the booksellers Edward and Charles Dilly. Also present were Dr. Oliver Goldsmith, the playwright and poet, two Anglican clergymen (one of them the Reverend Mr. Toplady), several other men, and Johnson's chief foil on this occasion, Dr. Henry Mayo, a dissenting (non-Anglican Protestant) clergyman. According to Boswell, "Dr. Mayo's calm temper and steady perseverance rendered him an admirable subject for the exercise of Dr. Johnson's powerful abilities."

JOHNSON: Every society has a right to preserve public peace and order, and therefore has a good right to prohibit the propagation of opinions which have a dangerous tendency. To say the *magistrate* has this right is using an inadequate word. It is the *society* for which the magistrate is agent. He may be morally or theologically wrong in restraining the propagation of opinions which he thinks dangerous, but he is politically right.

DR. MAYO: I am of the opinion, sir, that every man is entitled to liberty of conscience in religion, and that the magistrate cannot restrain that right.

JOHNSON: Sir, I agree with you. Every man has a right to liberty of conscience, and with that the magistrate cannot interfere. People confound liberty of thinking with liberty of talking—nay, with liberty of preaching. Every man has a physical right to think as he pleases, for it cannot be discovered how he thinks. He has not a moral right, for he ought to inform himself and think justly. But, sir, no member of a society has a right to *teach* any doctrine contrary to what the society holds to be true. The magistrate, I say, may be wrong in what he thinks, but while he thinks himself right he may and ought to enforce what he thinks.

DR. MAYO: Then, sir, we are to remain always in error, and truth never can prevail, and the magistrate was right in persecuting the first Christians.

JOHNSON: Sir, the only method by which religious truth can be established is by martyrdom. The magistrate has a right to enforce what he thinks, and he who is conscious of the truth has a right to suffer. I am afraid there is no other way of ascertaining the truth but by persecution on the one hand and enduring it on the other.

GOLDSMITH: But how is a man to act, sir? Though firmly convinced of the truth of his doctrine, may he not think it wrong to expose himself to persecution? Has he a right to do so? Is it not, as it were, committing voluntary suicide?

JOHNSON: Sir, as to voluntary suicide, as you call it, there are twenty thousand men in an army who will go without scruple to be shot at and mount a breach for five-pence a day.

GOLDSMITH: But have they a moral right to do this?

JOHNSON: Nay, sir, if you will not take the universal opinion of mankind, I have

SOURCE: From James Boswell, *The Life of Samuel Johnson,* LL.D. (New York, 1880), 4 vols.: Vol. II, pp. 154–158.

nothing to say. If mankind cannot defend their own way of thinking, I cannot defend it. Sir, if a man is in doubt whether it would be better for him to expose himself to martyrdom or not, he should not do it. He must be convinced that he has a delegation from heaven.

GOLDSMITH. I would consider whether there is the greater chance of good or evil upon the whole. If I see a man who has fallen into a well, I would wish to help him out. But if there is a greater probability that he will pull me in than that I shall pull him out, I would not attempt it. So were I to go to Turkey, I might wish to convert the grand Signor to the Christian faith. But when I considered that I should probably be put to death without effectuating my purpose in any degree, I should keep myself quiet.

JOHNSON. Sir, you must consider that we have perfect and imperfect obligations. Perfect obligations, which are generally not to do something, are clear and positive, as, "Thou shalt not kill." But charity, for instance, is not definable by limits. It is a duty to give to the poor, but no man can say how much another should give to the poor or when a man has given too little to save his soul. In the same manner it is a duty to instruct the ignorant, and of consequence to convert infidels to Christianity. But no man in the common course of things is obliged to carry this to such a degree as to incur the danger of martyrdom, as no man is obliged to strip himself to the shirt in order to give charity. I have said that a man must be persuaded that he has a particular delegation from heaven.

GOLDSMITH. How is this to be known? Our first [Protestant] reformers, who were burned for not believing bread and wine to be Christ. . . ?

JOHNSON *(interrupting)*. Sir, they were not burned for not believing bread and wine to be Christ, but for insulting those who did believe it. And, sir, when the first reformers began they did not intend to be martyred. As many of them ran away as could.

BOSWELL. But, sir, there was your countryman Elwal,[4] who you told me challenged King George with his black guards and his red guards.

JOHNSON. My countryman Elwal, sir, should have been put in the stocks—a proper pulpit for him, and he'd have had a numerous audience. A man who preaches in the stocks will always have hearers enough.

BOSWELL. But Elwal thought himself in the right.

JOHNSON. We are not providing for mad people. There are places for them in the neighborhood.[5]

DR. MAYO. But, sir, is it not very hard that I should not be allowed to teach my children what I really believe to be the truth?

JOHNSON. Why, sir, you might contrive to teach your children *extra scandalum*, but, sir, the magistrate, if he knows it, has a right to restrain you. Suppose you teach your children to be thieves?

DR. MAYO. This is making a joke of the subject.

JOHNSON. Nay, sir, take it thus: that you teach them the community of goods, for which there are as many plausible arguments as for most erroneous doctrines. You teach them that all things at first were in common, and that no man had a right to anything but as he laid his hands upon it, and that this still is, or ought to be, the rule amongst mankind. Here, sir, you sap a great principle in society—property. And don't you think the magistrate would have a right to prevent you? Or, suppose you should teach your children the notion of the Adamites and they should run naked into the streets, would not the magistrate have a right to flog 'em into their doublets?

DR. MAYO. I think the magistrate has no right to interfere till there is some overt act.

BOSWELL. So, sir, though he sees an enemy to the state charging a blunderbuss, he is not to interfere till it is fired off!

DR. MAYO. He must be sure of its direction against the state.

JOHNSON. The magistrate is to judge of

---

that. He has no right to restrain your thinking, because the evil centers in yourself. If a man were sitting at this table and chopping off his fingers, the magistrate, as guardian of the community, has no authority to restrain him, however he might do it from kindness as a parent. Though, indeed, upon more consideration, I think he may, as it is probable that he who is chopping off his own fingers may soon proceed to chop off those of other people. If I think it right to steal Mr. Dilly's plate, I am a bad man. But he can say nothing to me. If I make an open declaration that I think so, he will keep me out of his house. If I put forth my hand, I shall be sent to Newgate. This is the gradation of thinking, preaching, and acting. If a man thinks erroneously he may keep his thoughts to himself, and nobody will trouble him. If he preaches erroneous doctrine, society may expel him. If he acts in consequence of it, the law takes place, and he is hanged.

DR. MAYO. But, sir, ought not Christians to have liberty of conscience?

JOHNSON. I have already told you so, sir. You are coming back to where we were.

BOSWELL. Dr. Mayo is always taking a return postchaise, and going the stage over again. He has it at half-price.

JOHNSON. Dr. Mayo, like other champions for unlimited toleration, has got a set of words. Sir, it is no matter, politically, whether the magistrate be right or wrong. Suppose a club were to be formed to drink confusion to King George the Third and a happy restoration to Charles the Third. This would be very bad with respect to the state. But every member of that club must either conform to its rules or be turned out of it. Old Baxter, I remember, maintains that the magistrate should "tolerate all things that are tolerable." This is no good definition of toleration upon any principle, but it shows that he thought some things were not tolerable. . . .

TOPLADY (*to Johnson*). Sir, you have untwisted this difficult subject with great dexterity.

JOHN WESLEY **The Origins, the Rules, and the Spirit of Methodism (1744–1749)**

John Wesley looks back upon the first decade of the Methodist movement, sets forth the rules of Methodist societies, and supplies the words to a Methodist hymn.

I

1. About ten years ago my brother[6] and I were desired to preach in many parts of London. We had no view therein but, so far as we were able (and we knew God could work by whomsoever it pleased Him) to convince those who would hear, what true Christianity was, and to persuade them to embrace it.

2. The points we chiefly insisted upon were four: First, that orthodoxy or right opinions is, at best, but a very slender part of religion, if it can be allowed to be any part of it at all; that neither does religion consist in negatives, in bare harmlessness of any kind, nor merely in externals in doing good or using the means of grace, in works of piety (so called) or of charity: that it is nothing short of or different from the

SOURCES: The first selection is from John Wesley, *A Plain Account of the People Called Methodists* (1749). This pamphlet and the second selection, "Directions Given to the Band Societies, December 25, 1744," are included in *The Words of the Rev. John Wesley* (London: Wesleyan Conference Office, 1872), Vol. VII, pp. 248–250, 273–274. The hymn is included in *A Collection of Hymns for the Use of the People Called Methodists by the Rev. John Wesley, M. A.* (London, 1779).

[6]*my brother:* Charles Wesley (1707–1788), also a Methodist preacher and hymn writer

mind that was in Christ, the image of God stamped upon the heart, inward righteousness attended with the peace of God and joy in the Holy Ghost.

Secondly, that the only way under heaven to this religion is to repent and believe the gospel, or (as the apostle words it) repentance toward God and faith in our Lord Jesus Christ.

Thirdly, that by this faith, he that worketh not, but believeth in Him that justifieth the ungodly, is justified freely by His grace, through the redemption which is in Jesus Christ.

And lastly, that being justified by faith we taste of the heaven to which we are going; we are holy and happy; we tread down sin and fear, and sit in heavenly places with Christ Jesus.

3. Many of those who heard this began to cry out that we brought strange things to their ears, that this was doctrine that they never heard before, or, at least, never regarded. They searched the scriptures whether these things were so, and acknowledged the truth as it is in Jesus. Their hearts also were influenced, as well as their understandings, and they determined to follow Jesus Christ and Him crucified.

4. Immediately they were surrounded with difficulties. All the world rose up against them; neighbors, strangers, acquaintances, relations, friends began to cry out amain, "Be not righteous overmuch: why shouldst thou destroy thyself? Let not much religion make thee mad."

5. One and another and another came to us, asking what they should do, being distressed on every side, as everyone strove to weaken and none to strengthen their hands in God. We advised them, "Strengthen you one another. Talk together as often as you can. And pray earnestly, with and for one another, that you may endure to the end and be saved." Against this advice we presumed there could be no objection, as being grounded on the plainest reason and on so many scriptures, both of the Old Testament

and the New, that it would be tedious to recite them.

6. They said, "But we want you likewise to talk with us often, to direct and quicken us in our way, to give us the advices which you well know we need, and to pray with us, as well as for us." I asked, "Which of you desires this? Let me know your names and places of abode." They did so. But I soon found they were too many for me to talk with severally so often as they wanted it. So I told them, "If you will all of you come together every Thursday in the evening I will gladly spend some time with you in prayer, and give you the best advice I can."

7. Thus arose, without any previous design on either side, what was afterward called a society. . . .

8. There is one only condition previously required in those who desire admission into this society, a desire to flee from the wrath to come, and to be saved from their sins. . . .

You are supposed to have the faith that "overcometh the world." To you, therefore, it is not grievous:

I. Carefully to abstain from doing evil; in particular:

1. Neither to buy nor sell anything at all on the Lord's day.
2. To taste no spiritous liquor, no dram of any kind, unless prescribed by a physician.
3. To be at a word[7] both in buying and selling.
4. To pawn nothing, no, not to save life.
5. Not to mention the fault of any behind his back, and to stop those short that do.
6. To wear no needless ornaments, such as rings, earrings, necklaces, lace, ruffles.
7. To use no needless self-indulgence, such as taking snuff or tobacco, unless prescribed by a physician.

---

[7]*to be at a word:* be as good as one's word

II. Zealously to maintain good works; in particular:

1. To give alms of such things as you possess, and that to the uttermost of your power.
2. To reprove all that sin in your sight, and that in love and meekness of wisdom.
3. To be patterns of diligence and frugality, of self-denial, and taking up the cross daily.

III. Constantly to attend on all the ordinances of God, in particular:

1. To be at church and at the Lord's table every week, and at every public meeting of the bands.
2. To attend the ministry of the word every morning unless distance, business or sickness prevent.
3. To use private prayer every day; and family prayer, if you are at the head of a family.
4. To read the scriptures, and meditate therein, at every vacant hour. And

5. To observe, as days of fasting or abstinence, all Fridays in the year.

1 Author of faith, eternal Word,
    Whose Spirit breathes the active flame;
Faith, like its Finisher and Lord
    To-day, as yesterday the same:
2 To thee our humble hearts aspire,
    And ask the gift unspeakable:
Increase in us the kindled fire,
    In us the work of faith fulfil.
3 By faith we know thee strong to save:
    (Save us, a present Saviour thou!)
Whate'er we hope, by faith we have,
    Future and past subsisting now.
4 To him that in thy name believes,
    Eternal life with thee is given;
Into himself he all receives,
    Pardon, and holiness, and heaven.
5 The things unknown to feeble sense,
    Unseen by reason's glimmering ray,
With strong, commanding evidence,
    Their heavenly origin display,
6 Faith lends its realizing light,
    The clouds disperse, the shadows fly;
Th' Invisible appears in sight,
    And God is seen by mortal eye.

Observations Upon the Conduct and Behavior of Methodists (1744)

An anonymous churchman criticizes the Methodists as unreasonable.

Besides the many irregularities which are justly charged upon these itinerant preachers, as violations of the laws of church and state, it may be proper to inquire whether the doctrines they teach, and those lengths they run, beyond what is practiced among our religious societies or in any other Christian church, be a service or a disservice to religion. To which purpose, the following queries are submitted to consideration.

Query 1. Whether notions in religion may not be heightened to such extremes as to lead some into disregard of religion itself,

through despair of attaining such exalted heights? And whether others, who have imbibed those notions, may not be led by them into a disregard and disesteem of the common duties and offices of life, to such a degree, at least, as is inconsistent with that attention to them, and that diligence in them, which providence has made necessary to the well-being of private families and public societies. . . .

Query 2. Whether the enemy of mankind [i.e., Satan] may not find his account in their carrying Christianity, which was designed for a rule to all stations and all

SOURCE: From *Observations Upon the Conduct and Behaviour of a Certain Sect, Usually Distinguished by the Name of Methodists* (London, 1744), pp. 9–11. The author was probably Bishop Edmund Gibson of London.

conditions, to such heights as make it fairly practicable by a very few in comparison, or rather by none. . . .

Query 4. Whether a due and regular attendance on the public offices of religion, paid by good men in a serious and composed way, does not better answer the true ends of devotion, and is not a better evidence of the cooperation of the Holy Spirit than those sudden agonies, roarings and screamings, tremblings, droppings-down, ravings and madnesses into which their hearers have been cast, according to the relations given of them. . . .

Query 7. Whether a gradual improvement in grace and goodness is not a better foundation of comfort, and of an assurance of a gospel new birth, than that which is founded on the doctrine of a sudden and instantaneous change, which, if there be any such thing, is not easily distinguished from fancy and imagination; the workings whereof we may well suppose to be more strong and powerful while the person considers himself in the state of one who is admitted as a candidate for such a change, and is taught in due time to expect it.

Query 8. Whether, in a Christian nation, where the instruction and edification of the people is provided for by placing ministers in certain districts, to whom the care of the souls within those districts is regularly committed, it can be for the service of religion that itinerant preachers run up and down from place to place and from county to county, drawing after them confused multitudes of people, and leading them into a disesteem of their own pastors, as less willing or less able to instruct them in the way of salvation. . . .

5

King George III and the American Revolution: Tyrant, Enlightened Monarch, or Victim of Circumstances?

The 1760s were marked by vast military triumphs for the British Empire (in the Seven Years' War that ended with the Treaty of Paris of 1763), by the accession of a new king, and by a period of domestic political uncertainty. Not least among the concerns of successive British ministries during that decade as well as the next was the question of how to govern the North American colonies, whose leaders appeared to most British eyes to be unwilling to pay their fair share of the government and defense of the British Empire. The documents in this chapter shed light upon the character of King George III and upon his involvement in both the coming of the American Revolution and the prosecution of the war that followed.

The first document, the debut "Speech from the Throne" that George III delivered in 1760, clarifies the king's intentions shortly after he inherited the throne at the youthful age of twenty-two. What type of personality is revealed in that speech? Although royal "Speeches from the Throne" were drafted by the king's ministers even in George III's day, there is little doubt that, in the two such documents cited in this chapter, the sentiments, and some of the words, are the king's own.

As the second document, "A Letter of 'Junius'" (1769) makes clear, George III's choice of ministers—and his obvious desire to serve as the nation's chief executive in fact as well as in name—helped raise a political storm. The anonymous Junius, a pioneer journalistic muckraker, was probably Sir Philip Francis (1740–1818), a sympathizer with the leaders of the Whig opposition, men who found themselves out of ministerial office when Junius wrote. On what grounds does he criticize the ministers of the day and, by strong implication, the monarch who appointed them? How does Junius's picture of the state of Britain in 1769 compare with George III's description of the state of the kingdom nine years earlier?

One of the matters that troubled Junius was the manner in which successive British ministries were dealing with the claims of the American colonists. The four documents that follow illustrate divergent British

The Horse America, Throwing His Master

A Frenchman is on his way to take over the horse.

approaches during the years (1774 and 1775) that revolution and military conflict were in the air. Edmund Burke (1729–1797) was an Irish-born politician who had served as secretary to the marquis of Rockingham (briefly prime minister, 1765–1766) and who in 1774 had been elected Member of Parliament for the port city of Bristol. The views he expressed in the speech "Conciliation with America" (1775) were representative of those of the parliamentary opposition of the time. Josiah Tucker (1713–1799) was an Anglican clergyman by vocation, and during much of his life he served as dean of the cathedral at Gloucester. By avocation he was a pamphleteer and an economist who held ideas similar to those of Adam Smith. His proposals as outlined in *The True Interest of Great Britain Set Forth in Regard to the Colonies* were exceptional in the Britain of 1774, though they soon came to seem more acceptable. The policy that prevailed in 1774 and 1775, a policy of resistance to colonial demands by King George III and Lord North, is set forth in the Royal Proclamation of August, 1775, and in the "Speech from the Throne" of October, 1775. To what extent do Burke, Tucker, and the king agree in their analyses of the causes of American disaffection? To what extent do they agree in their recommendations as to the best way of dealing with American rebelliousness?

The best remembered of all the documents reprinted in this chapter, *The Declaration of Independence* (1776), combines a relatively brief exposition of a political philosophy with a long, personal indictment of George III. What sorts of charges are levied against the king? What are some of the possible reasons why the declaration concentrates its attention upon the monarch while virtually ignoring his ministers and Parliament? The next document, "A Criticism of *The Declaration of Independence*," published anonymously in the November 1776 issue of the monthly periodical *Gentleman's Magazine*, reminds us that Englishmen of the day did not necessarily find the philosophy of that declaration persuasive. On what grounds does the anonymous Englishman take exception to the American revolutionary manifesto? A *Proclamation for a General Fast* (1776) may be interpreted as King George III's personal reaction to the Declaration of Independence. What is the nature of that reaction? Which of the king's personality traits does the proclamation illustrate?

The final three selections in this chapter throw additional light upon the attitude of George III toward the American Revolution both while the war was going on and after it was over. The first of these is a letter George III wrote to his prime minister in 1778 at a time the war was going badly for the British. The second is John Adams's dramatic account of his initial meeting in 1785 with George III as the first minister of the independent United States to the court of Great Britain. Do the king's remarks to Lord North in 1778 and to John Adams seven years later demonstrate an abrupt change of attitude on the part of George III or do they suggest an underlying consistency? How easily can these documents (and several of the earlier ones) be reconciled with the pen-portrait of the monarch sketched in 1815 by Sir Nathaniel Wraxall (1751–1831)? Wraxall, a Member of Parliament from 1780 to 1794 who knew the king personally, became one of the earliest chroniclers of the king's long and often tumultuous reign.

George III   Speech from the Throne (1760)

On November 25, 1760, the king addressed the assembled Houses of Parliament for the first time.

The king, being seated on the throne, adorned with his crown and regal ornaments, and attended by his officers of state; the Lords being in their robes; the gentleman usher of the black rod received his Majesty's commands, to let the Commons know, "It is his Majesty's pleasure, they attend him immediately, in this House." Who being come, with their speaker; his Majesty was pleased to speak as follows:

My Lords and gentlemen; The just concern which I have felt in my own breast, on the sudden death of the late king my royal grandfather, makes me not doubt but you must all have been deeply affected with so severe a loss: the present critical and difficult conjuncture has made this loss the more sensible, as he was the great support of that system, by which alone the liberties of Europe, and the weight and influence of these kingdoms, can be preserved; and gave life to the measures conducive to those important ends.

I need not tell you the addition of weight which immediately falls upon me, in being

SOURCE: From Cobbett's *Parliamentary History of England*, Vol. XV, cols. 981–985.

called to the government of this free and powerful country at such a time, and under such circumstances: my consolation is in the uprightness of my own intentions; your faithful and united assistance; and the blessing of heaven upon our joint endeavors, which I devoutly implore.

Born and educated in this country, I glory in the name of Briton; and the peculiar happiness of my life will ever consist in promoting the welfare of a people, whose loyalty and warm affection to me, I consider as the greatest and most permanent security of my throne; and I doubt not but their steadiness in these principles will equal the firmness of my invariable resolution, to adhere to and strengthen this excellent constitution in church and state, and to maintain the toleration inviolable. The civil and religious rights of my loving subjects are equally dear to me with the most valuable prerogatives of my crown: and, as the surest foundation of the whole, and the best means to draw down the divine favor on my reign; it is my fixed purpose to countenance and encourage the practice of true religion and virtue.

I reflect with pleasure on the successes with which the British arms have been prospered this last summer. The total reduction of the vast province of Canada, with the city of Montreal, is of the most interesting consequence, and must be as heavy a blow to my enemies, as it is a conquest glorious to us; the more glorious because effected almost without effusion of blood, and with that humanity which makes an amiable part of the character of this nation.

Our advantages gained in the East Indies have been signal; and must greatly diminish the strength and trade of France in those parts, as well as procure the most solid benefits to the commerce and wealth of my subjects.

In Germany, where the whole French force has been employed, and combined army, under the wise and able conduct of my general Prince Ferdinand of Brunswick,

has not only stopt their progress, but has gained advantages over them, notwithstanding their boasted superiority, and their not having hitherto come to a general engagement.

My good brother[1] and ally the king of Prussia, although surrounded with numerous armies of enemies, has, with a magnanimity and perseverance almost beyond example, not only withstood their various attacks, but has obtained very considerable victories over them.

Of these events I shall say no more at this time, because the nature of the war in those parts has kept the campaign there still depending.

As my navy is the principal article of our natural strength, it gives me much satisfaction to receive it in such good condition; whilst the fleet of France is weakened to such a degree, that the small remains of it have continued blocked-up by my ships in their own ports: at that same time, the French trade is reduced to the lowest ebb; and, with joy of heart, I see the commerce of my kingdoms, that great source of our riches, and the fixed object of my never-failing care and protection, flourishing to an extent unknown in any former war.

The valor and intrepidity of my officers and forces both at sea and land have been distinguished so much to the glory of this nation, that I should be wanting in justice to them, if I did not acknowledge it. This is a merit which I shall constantly encourage and reward; and I take this occasion to declare, that the zealous and useful service of the militia, in the present arduous conjuncture, is very acceptable to me.

In this state I have found things at my accession to the throne of my ancestors: happy in viewing the prosperous part of it; happier still should I have been, had I found my kingdoms, whose true interest I have entirely at heart, in full peace: but, since the ambition, injurious encroachments, and dangerous designs of my enemies, rendered the war both just and necessary; and the generous overture made last winter,

---

[1]*brother:* used in the sense of "fellow monarch"

toward a congress for a pacification, has not yet produced a suitable return; I am determined, with your cheerful and powerful assistance, to prosecute this war with vigor, in order to [achieve] that desirable object, a safe and honorable peace: for this purpose, it is absolutely incumbent upon us to be early prepared; and I rely upon your zeal and hearty concurrence to support the king of Prussia and the rest of my allies; and to make ample provision for carrying on the war, as the only means to bring our enemies to equitable terms of accommodation.

Gentleman of the House of Commons, The greatest uneasiness which I feel at this time is, in considering the uncommon burthens necessarily brought upon my faithful subjects: I desire only such supplies as shall be requisite to prosecute the war with advantage, be adequate to the necessary services, and that they may be provided for in the most sure and effectual manner: you may depend upon the faithful and punctual application of what shall be granted.

I have ordered the proper estimates for the ensuing year to be laid before you; and also an account of the extraordinary expenses, which, from the nature of the different and remote operations, have been unavoidably incurred.

It is with peculiar reluctance that I am obliged, at such a time, to mention any thing which personally regards myself; but,

as the grant of the greatest part of the civil list revenues is now determined, I trust in your duty and affection to me, to make the proper provision for supporting my civil government with honor and dignity: on my part, you may be assured of a regular and becoming economy.

My Lords, and gentlemen, The eyes of all Europe are upon you. From your resolutions the Protestant interest hopes for protection; as well as all our friends, for the preservation of their independency; and our enemies fear the final disappointment of their ambitious and destructive views. Let these hopes and fears be confirmed and augmented, by the vigor, unanimity, and dispatch, of your proceedings.

In this expectation I am the more encouraged, by a pleasing circumstance, which I look upon as one of the most auspicious omens of my reign. That happy extinction of divisions, and that union and good harmony which continue to prevail amongst my subjects, afford me the most agreeable prospect: the natural disposition and wish of my heart are to cement and promote them: and I promise myself, that nothing will arise on your part, to interrupt or disturb a situation so essential to the true and lasting felicity of this great people.

Then his Majesty was pleased to retire; and the Commons withdrew.

A Letter of "Junius" (1769)

The anonymous Junius criticizes the manner in which Britain's rulers have acted during the first decade of the reign of King George III. The following public letter was first published in the Public Advertiser *in January 1769.*

21 January, 1769

Sir,

... The situation of this country is alarming enough to rouse the attention of every man, who pretends to a concern for the pub-

lic welfare. Appearances justify suspicion; and, when the safety of a nation is at stake, suspicion is a just ground of inquiry. Let us enter into it with candor and decency. Respect is due to the station of ministers; and, if a resolution must at last be taken, there

SOURCE: C. W. Everett, ed., *The Letters of "Junius."* (London: Faber & Gwyer, 1927), pp. 21–26. This is a reprint of the 1772 edition.

is none so likely to be supported with firmness, as that which has been adopted with moderation.

The ruin or prosperity of a state depends so much upon the administration of its government, that to be acquainted with the merit of a ministry, we need only observe the condition of the people. If we see them obedient to the laws, prosperous in their industry, united at home, and respected abroad, we may reasonably presume that their affairs are conducted by men of experience, abilities and virtue. If, on the contrary, we see an universal spirit of distrust and dissatisfaction, a rapid decay of trade, dissensions in all parts of the empire, and a total loss of respect in the eyes of foreign powers, we may pronounce, without hesitation, that the government of that country is weak, distracted and corrupt. The multitude, in all countries, are patient to a certain point. Ill-usage may rouse their indignation, and hurry them into excesses, but the original fault is in government. Perhaps there never was an instance of a change in the circumstances and temper of a whole nation so sudden and extraordinary as that which the misconduct of ministers has, within these very few years, produced in Great Britain. When our gracious sovereign ascended the throne, we were a flourishing and a contented people. If the personal virtues of a king could have insured the happiness of his subjects, the scene could not have altered so entirely as it has done . . . . Unfortunately, for us, the event has not been answerable to the design. After a rapid succession of changes, we are reduced to that state which hardly any change can mend. Yet there is no extremity of distress, which of itself ought to reduce a great nation to despair. It is not the disorder, but the physician;—it is not a casual concurrence of calamitous circumstances, it is the pernicious hand of government, which alone can make a whole people desperate.

Without much political sagacity, or any extraordinary depth of observation, we need only mark how the principal departments of the state are bestowed, and look no farther for the true cause of every mischief that befalls us.

The finances of a nation, sinking under its debts and expenses are committed to a young nobleman already ruined by play.[2] Introduced to act under the auspices of Lord Chatham, and left at the head of affairs by that nobleman's retreat, he became minister by accident; but, deserting the principles and professions which gave him a moment's popularity, we see him, from every honorable engagement to the public, an apostate by design. As for business, the world yet knows nothing of his talents or resolution; unless a wayward, wavering inconsistency be a mark of genius, and caprice a demonstration of spirit. It may be said, perhaps, that it is his grace's province, as surely it is his passion, rather to distribute than to save the public money, and that while Lord North is Chancellor of the Exchequer, the First Lord of the Treasury may be as thoughtless and as extravagant as he pleases. I hope, however, he will not rely too much on the fertility of Lord North's genius for finance. His lordship is yet to give us the first proof of his abilities: It may be candid to suppose that he has hitherto voluntarily concealed his talents; intending, perhaps, to astonish the world, when we least expect it, with a knowledge of trade, a choice of expedients, and a depth of resources equal to the necessities, and far beyond the hopes, of his country. He must now exert the whole power of his capacity, if he would wish us to forget, that, since he has been in office, no plan has been formed, no system adhered to, nor any one important measure adopted, for the relief of public credit. If his plan for the service of the current year be not irrevocably fixed on, let me warn him to think seriously of consequences before he ventures to increase the public debt. Outraged and oppressed as we are, this nation will not bear, after a six years' peace, to see new millions borrowed,

---

[2]*ruined by play:* because the prime minister, the duke of Grafton, was an inveterate gambler

without an eventual diminution of debt, or reduction of interest. The attempt might rouse a spirit of resentment, which might reach beyond the sacrifice of a minister. . . . The management of the king's affairs in the House of Commons cannot be more disgraced than it has been. A leading minister repeatedly called down for absolute ignorance;—ridiculous motions ridiculously withdrawn;—deliberate plans disconcerted. . . .

A series of inconsistent measures had alienated the colonies from their duty as subjects, and from their natural affection to their common country. When Mr. Grenville was placed at the head of the treasury, he felt the impossibility of Great Britain's supporting such an establishment as her former successes had made indispensable, and at the same time of giving any sensible relief to foreign trade, and to the weight of the public debt. He thought it equitable that those parts of the empire, which had benefited most by the expenses of the war, should contribute something to the expenses of the peace, and he had no doubt of the constitutional right vested in Parliament to raise that contribution. But, unfortunately for this country, Mr. Grenville was at any rate to be distressed, because he was minister, and Mr. Pitt and Lord Camden were to be the patrons of America, because they were in opposition. Their declarations gave spirit and argument to the colonies, and while perhaps they meant no more than the ruin of a minister, they in effect divided one half of the empire from the other.

Under one administration the Stamp Act is made; under the second it is repealed; under the third, in spite of all experience, a new mode of taxing the colonies is invented, and a question revived, which ought to have been buried in oblivion. . . .

It has lately been a fashion to pay a compliment to the bravery and generosity of the commander-in-chief,[3] at the expense of his understanding. They who love him least

make no question of his courage, while his friends dwell chiefly on the facility of his disposition. Admitting him to be as brave as a total absence of all feeling and reflection can make him, let us see what sort of merit he derives from the remainder of his character. If it be generosity to accumulate in his own person and family a number of lucrative employments—to provide, at the public expense, for every creature that bears the name of Manners; and, neglecting the merit and services of the rest of the army, to heap promotions upon his favorities and dependants, the present commander-in-chief is the most generous man alive. Nature has been sparing of her gifts to this noble lord; but, where birth and fortune are united, we expect the noble pride and independence of a man of spirit, not the servile, humiliating complaisance of a courtier. As to the goodness of his heart, if a proof of it be taken from the facility of never refusing, what conclusions shall we draw from the indecency of never performing? And if the discipline of the army be in any degree preserved, what thanks are due to a man, whose cares, notoriously confined to filling up vacancies, have degraded the office of commander-in-chief into a broker of commissions!

With respect to the navy, I shall only say, that this country is so highly indebted to Sir Edward Hawke, that no expense should be spared to secure to him an honorable and affluent retreat. . . .

These principles and proceedings, odious and contemptible as they are, in effect are no less injudicious. A wise and generous people are roused by every appearance of oppressive, unconstitutional measures, whether those measures are supported openly by the power of government, or masked under the forms of a court of justice. Prudence and self-preservation will oblige the most moderate dispositions to make common cause, even with a man whose conduct they censure, if they see him persecuted in a way which the real

---

[3]*commander-in-chief:* John Manners, the Marquis of Granby

spirit of the laws will not justify. The facts, on which these remarks are founded, are too notorious to require an application.[4]

This, Sir, is the detail. In one view, behold a nation overwhelmed with debt; her revenues wasted; her trade declining; the affections of her colonies alienated; the duty of the magistrate transferred to the soldiery; a gallant army, which never fought unwillingly but against their fellow subjects; mouldering away for want of the direction of a man of common abilities and spirit: and, in the last instance, the administration of justice become odious and suspected to the whole body of the people. This deplorable scene admits but one addition—that we are governed by councils, from which a reasonable man can expect no remedy but poison, no relief but death.

JUNIUS

EDMUND BURKE **Conciliation with America (1775)**

A spokesman for the Whig opposition to Lord North's ministry, Burke sought to halt the drift toward military confrontation in North America. The speech was delivered to the House of Commons on March 22, 1775.

In this character of the Americans, a love of freedom is the predominating feature which marks and distinguishes the whole: and as an ardent is always a jealous affection, your colonies become suspicious, restive, and untractable, whenever they see the least attempt to wrest from them by force, or shuffle from them by chicane, what they think the only advantage worth living for. This fierce spirit of liberty is stronger in the English colonies probably than in any other people of the earth; and this from a great variety of powerful causes which, to understand the true temper of their minds, and the direction which this spirit takes, it will not be amiss to lay open somewhat more largely.

First, the people of the colonies are descendants of Englishmen. England, Sir, is a nation, which still I hope respects, and formerly adored, her freedom. The colonists emigrated from you, when this part of your character was most predominant; and they took this bias and direction the moment they parted from your hands. They are therefore not only devoted to liberty, but to liberty according to English ideas, and on English principles. Abstract liberty, like other mere abstractions, is not to be found. Liberty inheres in some sensible object; and every nation has formed to itself some favorite point, which by way of eminence becomes the criterion of their happiness. It happened, you know, Sir, that the great contests for freedom in this country were from the earliest times chiefly upon the question of taxing. . . . The colonies draw from you, as with their life-blood, these ideas and principles. Their love of liberty, as with you, fixed and attached on this specific point of taxing. . . .

They were further confirmed in this . . . by the form of their provincial legislative assemblies. Their governments are popular in an high degree; some are merely popular; in all, the popular representative is the

SOURCE: From *The Works of the Right Honorable Edmund Burke*, 4th ed. (Boston, 1871), Vol. II, pp. 120–127, 136–137, 139, 141–142, 153–154, 170, 179–181.

[4]*facts . . . application:* This refers to the case of John Wilkes, a Member of Parliament who had been charged with "seditious libel" in 1763 and who was eventually found guilty and outlawed. As of 1769 he was back in England, in jail, and seeking reelection and readmission to the House of Commons. After a lengthy controversy, he was allowed to take his seat in 1774.

most weighty; and this share of the people in their ordinary government never fails to inspire them with lofty sentiments, and with a strong aversion from whatever tends to deprive them of their chief importance.

If any thing were wanting to this necessary operation of the form of government, religion would have given it a complete effect. Religion, always a principle of energy, in this new people, is no way worn out or impaired; and their mode of professing it is also one main cause of this free spirit. The people are Protestants; and of that kind, which is the most adverse to all implicit submission of mind and opinion. This is a persuasion not only favorable to liberty, but built upon it. . . . All Protestantism, even the most cold and passive, is a sort of dissent. But the religion most prevalent in our northern colonies is a refinement on the principle of resistance; it is the dissidence of dissent; and the Protestantism of the Protestant religion. . . .

In the southern colonies the Church of England forms a large body, and has a regular establishment. It is certainly true. There is however a circumstance attending these colonies, which, in my opinion, fully counterbalances this difference, and makes the spirit of liberty still more high and haughty than in those to the northward. It is that in Virginia and the Carolinas, they have a vast multitude of slaves. Where this is the case in any part of the world, those who are free, are by far the most proud and jealous of their freedom. Freedom is to them not only an enjoyment, but a kind of rank and privilege. . . .

Permit me, Sir, to add another circumstance in our colonies, which contributes no mean part towards the growth and effect of this untractable spirit. I mean their education. In no country perhaps in the world is the law so general a study. The profession itself is numerous and powerful; and in most provinces it takes the lead. The greater number of the deputies sent to the Congress were lawyers. But all who read, and most do read, endeavor to obtain some smattering in that science. . . . This study renders men acute, inquisitive, dexterous, prompt in attack, ready in defense, full of resources. In other countries, the people, more simple, and of a less mercurial cast, judge of an ill principle in government only by an actual grievance; here they anticipate the evil, and judge of the pressure of the grievance by the badness of the principle. They augur misgovernment at a distance; and snuff the approach of tyranny in every tainted breeze.

The last cause of this disobedient spirit in the colonies is hardly less powerful than the rest, as it is not merely moral, but laid deep in the natural constitution of things. Three thousand miles of ocean lie between you and them. No contrivance can prevent the effect of this distance, in weakening government. . . .

Then, Sir, from these six capital sources; of descent; of form of government; of religion in the northern provinces; of manners in the southern; of education; of the remoteness of situation from the first mover of government; from all these causes a fierce spirit of liberty has grown up. It has grown with the growth of the people in your colonies, and increased with the increase of their wealth; a spirit, that unhappily meeting with an exercise of power in England, which, however lawful, is not reconcileable to any ideas of liberty, much less with theirs, has kindled this flame, that is ready to consume us.

I do not mean to commend either the spirit in this excess, or the moral causes which produce it. . . . But the question is, not whether their spirit deserves praise or blame;—what, in the name of God, shall we do with it? . . .

Perhaps, Sir, I am mistaken in my idea of an empire, as distinguished from a single state or kingdom. But my idea of it is this; that an empire is the aggregate of many states, under one common head; whether this head be a monarch, or a presiding republic. . . . Of course disputes, often too, very bitter disputes, and much ill blood, will arise. . . . Now, in such unfortunate quarrels, among the component parts of a great political union of communities, I can scarcely conceive any thing more completely imprudent, than for the head of the empire to insist, that, if any privilege is pleaded against his will, or his acts, that his whole authority is denied; instantly to proclaim rebellion, to beat to arms, and to put the offending provinces under the ban. . . .

If then the removal of the causes of this spirit of American liberty be, for the greater part, or rather entirely, impracticable; if the ideas of criminal process be inapplicable, or, if applicable, are in the highest degree inexpedient, what way yet remains? No way is open, but the third and last—to comply with the American spirit as necessary; or, if you please to submit to it, as a necessary evil.

If we adopt this mode; if we mean to conciliate and concede; let us see of what nature the concession ought to be. . . .

My idea . . . is *to admit the people of our colonies into an interest in the Constitution;* and, by recording that admission in the journals of Parliament, to give them as strong an assurance as the nature of the thing will admit, that we mean for ever to adhere to that solemn declaration of systematic indulgence. . . .

You will now, Sir, perhaps imagine, that I am on the point of proposing to you a scheme for a representation of the colonies in Parliament. Perhaps I might be inclined to entertain some such thought; but a great flood stops me in my course. *Opposuit natura*—I cannot remove the eternal barriers of the creation. The thing in that mode, I do not know to be possible. As I meddle with no theory, I do not absolutely assert the impracticability of such a representation. But I do not see my way to it. . . .

My resolutions therefore mean to establish the equity, and justice of a taxation of America, by *grant*, and not by *imposition*. To mark the *legal competency* of the colony assemblies for the support of their government in peace, and for public aids in time of war. To acknowledge that this legal competency has had a *dutiful and beneficial exercise;* and that experience has shewn the benefit of their grants, and the

futility of parliamentary taxation as a method of supply. . . .

The Americans will have no interest contrary to the grandeur and glory of England, when they are not oppressed by the weight of it; and they will rather be inclined to respect the acts of a superintending legislature; when they see them the acts of that power, which is itself the security, not the rival, of their secondary importance. . . . My hold of the colonies is in the close affection which grows from common names, from kindred blood, from similar privileges, and equal protection. These are ties, which, though light as air, are as strong as links of iron. . . . As long as you have the wisdom to keep the sovereign authority of this country as the sanctuary of liberty, the sacred temple consecrated to our common faith, wherever the chosen race and sons of England worship freedom, they will turn their faces towards you. . . .

Is it not the same virtue which does every thing for us here in England? Do you imagine then, that it is the land tax act which raises your revenue? that it is the annual vote in the committee of supply, which gives you your army? or that it is the mutiny bill which inspires it with bravery and discipline? No! surely no! It is the love of the people; it is their attachment to their government from the sense of the deep stake they have in such a glorious institution, which gives you your army and your navy, and infuses into both that liberal obedience, without which your army would be a base rabble, and your navy nothing but rotten timber. . . .

Magnanimity in politics is not seldom the truest wisdom; and a great empire and little minds go ill together. . . . Our ancestors have turned a savage wilderness into a glorious empire; and have made the most extensive, and the only honorable conquests; not by destroying, but by promoting, the wealth, the number, the happiness of the human race. Let us get an American revenue as we have got an American empire. English privileges have made it all it is; English privileges alone will make it all it can be.

Josiah Tucker The True Interest of Great Britain Set Forth in Regard to the Colonies (1774)

A disciple of Adam Smith recommends that Britain and its North American colonies should separate in a peaceable manner.

A very strange notion is now industriously spreading, that 'till the late unhappy Stamp-Act, there were no bickerings and discontents, no heart-burnings and jealousies subsisting between the colonies and the mother country. It seems, 'till that fatal period, all was harmony, peace, and love. Now it is scarcely possible even for the most superficial observer, if his knowledge extends beyond the limits of a newspaper, not to know, *That this is entirely false.* And if he is at all conversant in the history of the colonies, and has attended to the accounts of their original plantation, their rise, and progress, he must know, that almost from the very beginning, there were mutual discontents, mutual animosities and reproaches. Indeed, while these colonies were in a mere state of infancy, dependent on their mother-country not only for daily protection, but almost for daily bread, it cannot be supposed that they would give themselves the same airs of self-sufficiency and independence, as they did afterward, in proportion as they grew up to a state of maturity. But that they began very early to shew no other marks of attachment to their antient [ancient] parent, than what arose from views of self-interest and self-love, many convincing proofs might be drawn from the complaints *of*, and the instructions *to* the governors of the respective provinces; from the memorials of our boards of trade, presented from time to time to his Majesty's Privy Council against the behavior of the colonists; from the frequent petitions and remonstrances of our merchants and manufacturers to the same effect; and even from the votes and resolutions of several of their provincial assemblies against the interest, laws, and government of the mother-country; yet I will wave all these at present and content myself with proofs still more authentic and unexceptionable; I mean the public statutes of the realm: For from them it evidently appears, that long before there were any thoughts of the Stamp-Act, the mother-country had the following accusations to bring against the colonies, *viz.* 1st, That they refused to submit to her ordinance and regulations in regard to trade.—2dly, That they attempted to frame laws, and to erect jurisdictions not only independently of her, but even in direct opposition to her authority.—And 3dly, That many of them took unlawful methods to skreen themselves from paying the just debts they owed to the merchants and manufacturers of *Great-Britain.* . . . indeed, and properly speaking, it was not the Stamp-Act which increased or heightened these ill humors in the colonists; rather, it was the reduction of *Canada*, which called forth those dispositions into action which had long been generating before; and which were ready to burst forth at the first opportunity that should offer. For an undoubted fact it is, that from the moment in which *Canada* came into the possession of the *English*, an end was put to the sovereignty of the mother-country over her colonies. They had then nothing to fear from a foreign enemy; and as to their own domestic friends and relations, they had for so many years preceding been accustomed to trespass upon their forbearance and indulgence, even when they most wanted their protection, that it was no wonder they should openly renounce an authority which they never thoroughly approved of, and which now they found to be no longer necessary for their own defense.

SOURCE: Reprinted in R. L. Schuyler, ed., *Josiah Tucker: A Selection from his Economic and Political Writings* (New York: Columbia University Press, 1931), pp. 333–334, 338, 340, 358–359, 362, 364–367. By permission of the publisher.

But here some may be apt to ask, "Had the colonies no provocation on their part? And was all the fault on one side, and none on the other?" Probably not:—Probably there were faults on both sides. But what doth this serve to prove? ... I am far from charging our colonies in particular with being sinners above others; because I believe ... that it is the nature of them all to aspire after independence, and to set up for themselves as soon as ever they find that they are able to subsist, without being beholden to the mother-country. ...

How shall we be able to render these colonies more subservient to the interests, and more obedient to the laws and government of the mother-country, than they *voluntarily chuse to be?* After having pondered and revolved the affair over and over, I confess, there seems to me to be but the five following proposals, which can possibly be made, *viz.*

1st. To suffer things to go on for a while, as they have lately done, in hopes that some favorable opportunity may offer for recovering the jurisdiction of the *British* legislature over her colonies, and for maintaining the authority of the mother-country.—Or if these temporising measures should be found to strengthen and confirm the evil, instead of removing it;—then,

2dly. To attempt to persuade the colonies to send over a certain number of deputies, or representatives, to sit and vote in the *British* Parliament; in order to incorporate *America* and *Great-Britain* into one common empire.—Or if this proposal should be found impracticable, whether on account of the difficulties attending it on this side of the *Atlantic*, or because that the *Americans* themselves would not concur in such a measure;—then,

3dly. To declare open war against them as rebels and revolters; and after having made a perfect conquest of the country, then to govern it by military force and despotic sway.—Or if this scheme should be judged (*as it ought to be*) the most destructive, and the least eligible of any;—then,

4thly. To propose to consent that *America* should become the general seat of empire; and that *Great-Britain* and *Ireland*

should be governed by vice-roys sent over from the court residencies, either at *Philadelphia* or *New-York*, or at some other *American* imperial city.—Or if this plan of accommodation should be ill-digested by home-born *Englishmen*, who, I will venture to affirm, would never submit to such an indignity;—then,

5thly. To propose to separate entirely from the colonies, by declaring them to be a free and independent people, over whom we lay no claim; and then by offering to guarantee this freedom and independence against all foreign invaders whomsoever. ...

And, in fact, what is all this but the natural and even the necessary corollary to be deduced from each of the former reasons and observations? For if we neither can govern the *Americans*, nor be governed by them; if we can neither unite with them, nor ought to subdue them;—what remains, but to part with them on as friendly terms as we can? And if any man should think that he can reason better from the above premises, let him try.

But as the idea of separation, and the giving up the colonies for ever will shock many weak people, who think, that there is neither happiness nor security but in an over-grown unwieldy empire, I will for their sakes enter into a discussion of the *supposed* disadvantages attending such a disjunction; and then shall set forth the manifold advantages.

The first and capital *supposed* Advantage is, *That, if we separate from the colonies, we shall lose their trade.* But why so? And how does this appear? The colonies, we know by experience, will trade with any people, even with their bitterest enemies, during the hottest of a war, and a war undertaken at their own earnest request, and for their own sakes;—the colonies, I say, will trade even with them, provided they shall find it their interest so to do. Why then should any man suppose, that the same self-interest will not induce them to trade with us? ...

The 2d. objection against giving up the colonies is, that such a measure would greatly decrease our shipping and navigation, and consequently diminish the breed of sailors. But this objection has been fully obviated already: For if we shall not lose our trade, at least in any important degree, even with the northern colonies (and most probably we shall encrease it with other countries) then it follows, that neither the quantity of shipping, nor the breed of sailors, can suffer any considerable diminution: So that this supposition is merely a panic, and has no foundation. . . .

The 3d. objection is, That if we were to give up these colonies, the *French* would take immediate possession of them. Now this objection is entirely built on the following very wild, very extravagant, and absurd supposition . . . that the colonists themselves, who cannot brook our government, would like a *French* one much better. . . .

Let us now hasten briefly to point out *the manifold advantages attendant on such a scheme.*

And 1st. A disjunction from the northern colonies would effectually put a stop to our present emigrations. By the laws of the land it is made a capital offense to inveigle artificers and mechanics to leave the kingdom. But this law is unhappily superseded at present as far as the colonies are concerned. . . .

2dly. Another great advantage to be derived from a separation is, that we shall then save between 3 and £400,000 a year, by being discharged from the payment of any civil or military establishment belonging to the colonies:—For which generous benefaction we receive at present no other return than invectives and reproaches.

3dly. The ceasing of the payment of bounties on certain colony productions will be another great saving; perhaps not less than £200,000 a year. . . .

4thly. When we are no longer connected with the colonies by the imaginary tie of an identity of government, then our merchant-exporters and manufacturers will have a better chance of having their debts paid, than they have at present: For as matters now stand, the colonists chuse to carry their ready cash to other nations, while they are contracting debts with their mother-country; with whom they think they can take greater liberties.

5thly. After a separation from the colonies, our influence over them will be much greater than ever it was, since they began to feel their own weight and importance: For at present we are looked upon in no better a light than that of robbers and usurpers; whereas, we shall then be considered as their protectors, mediators, benefactors. The moment a separation takes effect, intestine quarrels will begin: For it is well known, that the seeds of discord and dissention between province and province are now ready to shoot forth; and that they are only kept down by the present combination of all the colonies against us, whom they unhappily fancy to be their *common enemy.* . . .

But after all, there is one thing more, to which I must make some reply.—many, perhaps most of my readers, will be apt to ask,—What is all this about? And what doth this author really mean?—Can he seriously think, that because he hath taken such pains to prove a separation to be a right measure, that therefore we shall separate in good earnest? . . .

I frankly acknowledge, I propose no *present* convenience or advantage to either; nay, I firmly believe, that no minister, as things are now circumstanced, will dare to do so much good to his country; and as to the herd of anti-ministers, they, I am persuaded, would not wish to see it done; because it would deprive them of one of their most plentiful sources for clamor and detraction: And yet I have observed, and have myself had some experience, that measures evidently right will prevail at last. . . . Indeed almost all people are apt to startle at first at bold truths:—But it is observable, that in proportion as they grow familiarized to them, and can see and consider them from different points of view, their fears subside, and they become reconciled by degrees:—Nay, it is not an uncommon thing for them to adopt those salutary measures afterward with as much zeal and ardor as they had rejected them before with anger and indignation. . . .

GEORGE III Royal Proclamation for Suppressing Rebellion and Sedition in North America (August 1775)

On August 23, 1775, four months after the battle of Lexington, the king formally acknowledges that war has broken out within the British Empire.

Whereas many of our subjects in divers parts of our colonies and plantations in North America, misled by dangerous and ill designing men, and forgetting the allegiance which they owe to the power that has protected and sustained them, after various disorderly acts committed in disturbance of the public peace, to the obstruction of lawful commerce and to the oppression of our loyal subjects carrying on the same, have at length proceeded to an open and avowed rebellion by arraying themselves in hostile manner to withstand the execution of the law, and traitorously preparing, ordering, and levying war against us; and whereas there is reason to apprehend that such rebellion hath been much promoted and encouraged by the traitorous correspondence, counsels, and comfort of divers wicked and desperate persons within this realm; to the end therefore that none of our subjects may neglect or violate their duty through ignorance thereof, or through any doubt of the protection which the law will afford to their loyalty and zeal; we have thought fit, by and with the advice of our Privy Council, to issue this our royal proclamation, hereby declaring that not only all our officers, civil and military, are obliged to exert their utmost endeavors to suppress such rebellion and to bring the traitors to

justice; but that all our subjects of this realm and the dominions thereunto belonging are bound by law to be aiding and assisting in the suppression of such rebellion, and to disclose and make known all traitorous conspiracies and attempts against us, our crown, and dignity; and we do accordingly strictly charge and command all our officers, as well civil as military, and all other our obedient and loyal subjects, to use their utmost endeavors to withstand and suppress such rebellion, and to disclose and make known all treasons and traitorous conspiracies which they shall know to be against us, our crown and dignity; and for that purpose, that they transmit to one of our principal secretaries of state, or other proper officer, due and full information of all persons who shall be found carrying on correspondence with, or in any manner or degree aiding or abetting the persons now in open arms and rebellion against our government within any of our colonies and plantations in North America, in order to bring to condign punishment the authors, perpetrators and abettors of such traitorous designs.

Given at our court at St. James the twenty-third day of August, one thousand seven hundred and seventy-five, in the fifteenth year of our reign.

GEORGE III Speech from the Throne (October 1775)

George III sets forth the position of the Lord North ministry (and his own) toward the American rebellion that had broken out during the previous spring.

The present situation of America, and my constant desire to have your advice, concurrence, and assistance on every important

occasion, have determined me to call you thus early together.

Those who have long too successfully la-

SOURCE: From Clarence Saunders Brigham, ed., *British Royal Proclamations Relating to North America, 1603–1783* (Worcester, Mass., 1911), pp. 228–229.

SOURCE: From Cobbett's *Parliamentary History of England*, Vol. XVIII, cols. 695–697.

bored to inflame my people in America by gross misrepresentation and to infuse into their minds a system of opinions repugnant to the true constitution of the colonies, and to their subordinate relation to Great Britain, now openly avow their revolt, hostility, and rebellion. They have raised troops, and are collecting a naval force; they have seized the public revenue, and assumed to themselves legislative, executive, and judicial powers, which they already exercise in the most arbitrary manner over the persons and properties of their fellow subjects; and although many of these unhappy people may still retain their loyalty and may be too wise not to see the fatal consequence of this usurpation, and wish to resist it; yet the torrent of violence has been strong enough to compel their acquiescence till a sufficient force shall appear to support them.

The authors and promoters of this desperate conspiracy have in the conduct of it derived great advantage from the difference of our intentions and theirs. They meant only to amuse by vague expressions of attachment to the parent state and the strongest protestations of loyalty to me, whilst they were preparing for a general revolt. On our part, though it was declared in your last session that a rebellion existed within the province of the Massachusetts Bay, yet even that province we wished rather to reclaim than to subdue. The resolutions of Parliament breathed a spirit of moderation and forbearance; conciliatory propositions accompanied the measures taken to enforce authority, and the coercive acts were adapted to cases of criminal combinations amongst subjects not then in arms. I have acted with the same temper; anxious to prevent, if it had been possible, the effusion of the blood of my subjects and the calamities which are inseparable from a state of war; still hoping that my people in America would have discerned the traitorous views of their leaders and have been convinced that to be a subject of Great Britain, with all its consequences, is to be the freest member of any civil society in the known world.

The rebellious war now levied is become more general and is manifestly carried on for the purpose of establishing an independent empire. I need not dwell upon the fatal effects of the success of such a plan. The object is too important, the spirit of the British nation too high, the resources with which God hath blessed her too numerous, to give up so many colonies which she has planted with great industry, nursed with great tenderness, encouraged with many commercial advantages, and protected and defended at much expense of blood and treasure.

It is now become the part of wisdom, and (in its effects) of clemency to put a speedy end to these disorders by the most decisive exertions. For this purpose I have increased my naval establishment, and greatly augmented my land forces, but in such a manner as may be the least burdensome to my kingdoms.

I have also the satisfaction to inform you that I have received the most friendly offers of foreign assistance; and if I shall make any treaties in consequence thereof, they shall be laid before you. And I have, in testimony of my affection for my people who can have no cause in which I am not equally interested, sent to the garrisons of Gibraltar and Port Mahon a part of my Electoral troops[5] in order that a larger number of the established forces of this kingdom may be applied to the maintenance of its authority; and the national militia, planned and regulated with equal regard to the rights, safety, and protection of my crown and people, may give a farther extent and activity to our military operations.

When the unhappy and deluded multitude against whom this force will be directed shall become sensible of their error, I shall be ready to receive the misled with tenderness and mercy; and in order to prevent the inconveniences which may arise from the great distance of their situation,

---

[5]*Electoral troops:* soldiers loyal to King George in his position as Elector of Hanover

and to remove as soon as possible the calamities which they suffer, I shall give authority to certain persons upon the spot to grant general or particular pardons and indemnities, in such manner and to such persons as they shall think fit, and to receive the submission of any province or colony which shall be disposed to return to its allegiance. It may be also proper to authorize the persons so commissioned to restore such province or colony so returning to its allegiance to the free exercise of its trade and commerce and to the same protection and security as if such province or colony had never revolted.

Gentlemen of the House of Commons:

I have ordered the proper estimates for the ensuing year to be laid before you; and I rely on your affection to me and your resolution to maintain the just rights of this country, for such supplies as the present circumstances of our affairs require. Among the many unavoidable ill consequences of this rebellion none affects me more sensibly than the extraordinary burden which it must create to my faithful subjects.

My Lords and Gentlemen:

I have fully opened to you my views and intentions. The constant employment of my thoughts, and the most earnest wishes of my heart tend wholly to the safety and happiness of all my people, and to the reestablishment of order and tranquillity through the several parts of my dominions, in a close connection and constitutional dependence. You see the tendency of the present disorders and I have stated to you the measures which I mean to pursue for suppressing them. Whatever remains to be done that may farther contribute to this end, I commit to your wisdom. And I am happy to add that as well from the assurances I have received as from the general appearance of affairs in Europe, I see no probability that the measures which you may adopt will be interrupted by disputes with any foreign power.

The Declaration of Independence (1776)

The declaration adopted by the American Continental Congress on July 4, 1776, indicts King George III as a tyrant.

The Unanimous Declaration of the Thirteen United States of America

When in the course of human events, it becomes necessary for one people to dissolve the political bands, which have connected them with another, and to assume among the powers of the earth, the separate and equal station to which the laws of nature and of nature's God entitle them, a decent respect to the opinions of mankind requires that they should declare the causes which impel them to the separation.—We hold these truths to be self-evident, that all men are created equal, that they are endowed by their Creator with certain unalienable rights, that among these are life, liberty and the pursuit of happiness.—That to secure these rights, governments are instituted among men, deriving their just powers from the consent of the governed,—That whenever any form of government becomes destructive of these ends, it is the right of the people to alter or to abolish it, and to institute new government, laying its foundation on such principles and organizing its powers in such form, as to them shall seem most likely to effect their safety and happiness. Prudence, indeed, will dictate that governments long established should not be

SOURCE: Transcribed from the parchment copy.

changed for light and transient causes; and accordingly all experience hath shewn, that mankind are more disposed to suffer, while evils are sufferable, than to right themselves by abolishing the forms to which they are accustomed. But when a long train of abuses and usurpations, pursuing invariably the same object evinces a design to reduce them under absolute despotism, it is their right, it is their duty, to throw off such government, and to provide new guards for their future security.—Such has been the patient sufferance of these colonies; and such is now the necessity which constrains them to alter their former systems of government. The history of the present king of Great Britain is a history of repeated injuries and usurpations, all having in direct object the establishment of an absolute tyranny over these states. To prove this, let facts be submitted to a candid world.—He has refused his assent to laws, the most wholesome and necessary for the public good.—He has forbidden his governors to pass laws of immediate and pressing importance, unless suspended in their operation till his assent should be obtained; and when so suspended, he has utterly neglected to attend to them.—He has refused to pass other laws for the accommodation of large districts of people, unless those people would relinquish the right of representation in the legislature, a right inestimable to them and formidable to tyrants only.—He has called together legislative bodies at places unusual, uncomfortable, and distant from the depository of their public records, for the sole purpose of fatiguing them into compliance with his measures.—He has dissolved representative houses repeatedly, for opposing with manly firmness his invasions on the rights of the people.—He has refused for a long time, after such dissolutions, to cause others to be elected; whereby the legislative powers, incapable of annihilation, have returned to the people at large for their exercise; the state remaining in the meantime exposed to all the dangers of invasion from without, and convulsions within.—He has endeavored to prevent the population of these states; for that purpose obstructing the laws for naturalization of foreigners; refusing to pass others to encourage their migrations hither, and raising the conditions of new appropriations of lands.—He has obstructed the administration of justice, by refusing his assent to laws for establishing judiciary powers.—He has made judges dependent on his will alone, for the tenure of their offices, and the amount and payment of their salaries.—He has erected a multitude of new offices, and sent hither swarms of officers to harrass our people, and eat out their substance.—He has kept among us, in times of peace, standing armies without the consent of our legislatures.—He has affected to render the military independent of and superior to the civil power.—He has combined with others to subject us to a jurisdiction foreign to our constitution, and unacknowledged by our laws; giving his assent to their acts of pretended legislation.—For quartering large bodies of armed troops among us:—For protecting them, by a mock trial, from punishment for any murders which they should commit on the inhabitants of these states:—For cutting off our trade with all parts of the world:—For imposing taxes on us without our consent:—For depriving us in many cases, of the benefits of trial by jury:—For transporting us beyond seas to be tried for pretended offenses:—For abolishing the free system of English laws in a neighboring province, establishing therein an arbitrary government, and enlarging its boundaries so as to render it at once an example and fit instrument for introducing the same absolute rule into these colonies:—For taking away our charters, abolishing our most valuable laws, and altering fundamentally the forms of our governments:—For suspending our own legislatures, and declaring themselves invested with power to legislate for us in all cases whatsoever.—He has abdicated government here, by declaring us out of his protection and waging war against us.—He has plundered our seas, ravaged our coasts, burnt our towns, and destroyed the lives of our people.—He is at this time transporting large armies of foreign mercenaries to complete the works of death, desolation and tyranny, already begun with circumstances of cruelty & perfidy scarcely paralleled in the most barbarous ages, and totally unworthy the head of a civilized nation.—He has constrained our fellow citizens taken captive on the high seas to bear arms against their country, to become the executioners of their friends and brethren, or to fall themselves by their hands.—He has excited domestic insurrections amongst us, and has endeavored to bring on the inhabitants of our frontiers, the merciless Indian savages, whose known rule of warfare, is an undistinguished destruction of all ages, sexes and conditions. In every stage of these oppressions we have petitioned for redress in the most humble terms: Our repeated petitions have been answered only by repeated injury. A prince whose character is thus marked by every act which may define a tyrant, is unfit to be the ruler of a free people. Nor have we been wanting in attentions to our Brittish [sic] brethren. We have warned them from time to time of attempts by their legislature to extend an unwarrantable jurisdiction over us. We have reminded them of the circumstances of our emigration and settlement here. We have appealed to their native justice and magnanimity, and we have conjured them by the ties of our common kindred to disavow these usurpations, which would inevitably interrupt our connections and correspondence. They too have been deaf to the voice of justice and of consanguinity. We must, therefore, acquiesce in the necessity, which denounces our separation, and hold them, as we hold the rest of mankind, enemies in war, in peace friends.—

We, therefore, the representatives of the United States of America, in general congress, assembled, appealing to the Supreme Judge of the world for the rectitude of our intentions do, in the name, and by the authority of the good people of these colonies, solemnly publish and declare, That these united colonies are, and of right ought to be free and independent states; that they are absolved from all allegiance to the British crown, and that all political connection between them and the state of Great Britain, is and ought to be totally dissolved; and that as free and independent states, they have full power to levy war, conclude peace, contract alliances, establish commerce, and to do all other acts and things which independent states may of right do.—And for the support of this declaration, with a firm reliance on the protection of divine Providence, we mutually pledge to each other our lives, our fortunes and our sacred honor.

A Criticism of the Declaration of Independence (1776)

An anonymous Englishman is unimpressed by the Declaration of Independence.

The declaration is without doubt of the most extraordinary nature both with regard to sentiment and language, and considering that the motive of it is to assign some justifiable reasons of their separating themselves from Great Britain, unless it had been fraught with more truth and sense, might well have been spared, as it reflects no honor upon either their erudition or honesty.

We hold, they say, these truths to be self-evident: that all men are created equal. In what are they created equal? Is it in size, strength, understanding, figure, moral or civil accomplishments, or situation of life? Every ploughman knows that they are not created equal in any of these. All men, it is true, are equally created, but what is this to the purpose? It certainly is no reason why the Americans should turn rebels because the people of Great Britain are their fellow-creatures, i.e., are created as well as themselves. It may be a reason why they should not rebel, but most indisputably is

SOURCE: From *Gentleman's Magazine*, September, 1776, pp. 403–404.

none why they should. They therefore have introduced their self-evident truths, either through ignorance or by design, with a self-evident falsehood; since I will defy any American rebel, or any of their patriotic retainers here in England, to point out to me any two men, throughout the whole world, of whom it may with truth be said that they are created equal.

The next of their self-evident truths is that all men are endowed by their Creator with certain unalienable rights (the meaning of which words they appear not at all to understand); among which are life, liberty and the pursuit of happiness. Let us put some of these words together. All men are endowed by their Creator with the unalienable right of life. How far they may be endowed with this unalienable right I do not yet say, but sure I am these gentry assume to themselves an unalienable right of talking nonsense. Was it ever heard since the introduction of blunders into the world that life was a man's right? Life or animation is of the essence of human nature, and is that without which one is not a man, and therefore to call life a right is to betray a total ignorance of the meaning of words. A living man, i.e., a man with life, hath a right to a great many things; but to say that a man with life hath a right to be a man with life is so purely American that I believe the texture of no other brain upon the face of the earth will admit the idea. . . .

The next assigned cause and ground of their rebellion is that every man hath an unalienable right to liberty; and here the words, as it happens, are not nonsense, but then they are not true: slaves there are in America, and where there are slaves there liberty is alienated.

If the Creator hath endowed man with an unalienable right to liberty, no reason in the world will justify the abridgment of that liberty, and a man hath a right to do everything that he thinks proper without control or restraint; and upon the same principle there can be no such things as servants, subjects, or government of any kind whatsoever. In a word, every law that hath been in the world since the formation of Adam, gives the lie to this self-evident truth (as they are pleased to term it), because every law, divine or human, that is or hath been in the world, is an abridgment of man's liberty. . . .

Their next self-evident truth and ground of rebellion is that they have an unalienable right to the pursuit of happiness. The pursuit of happiness an unalienable right! This surely is outdoing everything that went before. Put into English, the pursuit of happiness is a right which the Creator hath endowed me, and which can neither be taken from me nor can I transfer it to another. Did ever any mortal alive hear of taking a pursuit of happiness from a man? . . .

AN ENGLISHMAN

George III A Proclamation for a General Fast (1776)

The Royal Proclamation of October 30, 1776, suggests that, for the king, the American Revolution possesses a spiritual as well as a political and military dimension.

We, taking into our most serious consideration the just and necessary measures of force which we are obliged to use against our rebellious subjects in our colonies and provinces in North America, and putting our trust in Almighty God, that he will vouchsafe a special blessing on our arms, both by sea and land, have resolved, and do, by and with the advice of our Privy Council, hereby command, That a public fast and humiliation be observed throughout the part of our kingdom of Great Britain called England, our dominion of Wales, and town of Berwick upon Tweed, upon the Friday

SOURCE: From *Gentleman's Magazine*, November, 1776, p. 505.

the 13th of December next, that so both we and our people may humble ourselves before Almighty God, in order to obtain pardon of our sins, and may, in the most devout and solemn manner, send up our prayers and supplications to the Divine Majesty, for averting those heavy judgments which our manifold sins and provocations have most justly deserved, and for imploring his intervention and blessing speedily to deliver our loyal subjects within our colonies and provinces in North America from the violence, injustice, and tyranny of those daring rebels, who have assumed to themselves the exercise of arbitrary power; to open the eyes of those who have been deluded by specious falsehoods, into acts of treason and rebellion; to turn the hearts of the authors of these calamities; and finally to restore our people in those distracted provinces and colonies to the happy condition of being free subjects of a free state, under which heretofore they flourished so long and prospered so much.

And we do strictly charge and command, that the said public fast be reverently and devoutly observed by all our loving subjects in England, our dominion of Wales, and town of Berwick upon Tweed, as they tender the favor of Almighty God, & would avoid his wrath and indignation; and upon pain of such punishment as we may justly inflict upon all such as contemn and neglect the performance of so religious a duty. And, for the better and more orderly solemnizing the same, we have given directions to the most reverend the archbishops, and the right reverend the bishops of England, to compose the form of prayer, suitable to this occasion, to be used in churches, chapels, and places of worship, and to take care the same be timely dispersed throughout the respective dioces. Given at our court at St. James, the 30th of October, 1776, in the 17th year of our reign.

GOD SAVE THE KING.

GEORGE III **Letter to Lord North (November 26, 1778)**

The king urges Lord North not to despair.

It has been a certain position with me that firmness is the characteristic of an Englishman, that consequently when a minister will shew a resolution boldly to advance that he will meet with support; consequently Lord North's report that the gentlemen who attended the meeting in Downing Street last night will cordially support during the next session is what I expected; and if on the opening of the session the Speech from the Throne is penned with firmness, and shews no other end is sought but benevolence to all the branches, provided the empire is kept entire, and invite all who will cordially unite in that point and in a resolution to withstand the natural enemies of

the country, and the ministers in their speeches shew that they will never consent to the independence of America, and that the assistance of every man will be accepted on that ground, I am certain the cry will be strong in their favor.

I should have concluded here, had not the letter contained the following expression, that Lord North *is conscious and certain that he neither has the authority nor abilities requisite for the conduct of affairs at this time;* the word *authority* puzzles me, for from the hour of Lord North's so handsomely devoting himself on the retreat of the D. of Grafton,[6] I have never had a political thought which I have not communi-

SOURCE: From W. Bodham Donne, ed., *The Correspondence of King George III with Lord North, 1768 to 1783* (London: John Murray, 1867), Vol. II, pp. 214–216.

[6]*retreat . . . Grafton:* the resignation of the duke of Grafton, Lord North's predecessor as prime minister

cated unto him, have accepted of persons highly disagreable [sic] to me, because he thought they would be of advantage to his conducting public affairs, and have yielded to measures my own opinion did not quite approve. . . .

If Lord North can see with the same degree of enthusiasm I do the beauty, excellence, and perfection of the British Constitution as by law established, and consider that, if any one branch of the empire is alowed [sic] to cast off its dependency, that the others will infalably [sic] follow the ex-

ample, that consequently, though an arduous struggle, that is worth going through any difficulty to preserve to latest posterity what the wisdom of our ancestors have carefully transmitted to us, he will not allow despondency to find a place in his breast, but resolve not merely out of duty to fill his post, but will resolve with vigor to meet every obstacle that may arise, he shall meet with most cordial support from me; but the times require vigor, or the state will be ruined.

JOHN ADAMS Report on Meeting King George III (1785)

John Adams reports to John Jay (secretary of foreign affairs of the American Congress under the Articles of Confederation) on the occasion of his presenting to King George III his credentials as first United States minister to Great Britain.

To Secretary Jay

Bath Hotel, Westminster
2 June, 1785

Dear Sir:

. . . When we arrived in the antechamber . . . of St. James's, the master of the ceremonies met me and attended me, while the secretary of state went to take the commands of the king. While I stood in this place, where it seems all ministers stand upon such occasions, always attended by the master of ceremonies, the room very full of ministers of state, Lords, and bishops, and all sorts of courtiers, as well as the next room, which is the king's bedchamber, you may well suppose I was the focus of all eyes. I was relieved, however, from the embarrassment of it by the Swedish and Dutch ministers, who came to me, and entertained me in a very agreeable conversation during the whole time. Some other gentlemen, whom I had seen before, came to make their compliments too, until the marquis of Carmarthen returned and desired me to go

with him to his Majesty. I went with his Lordship through the levee room into the king's closet. The door was shut, and I was left with his Majesty and the secretary of state alone. I made the three reverences,— one at the door, another about half way, and a third before the presence,—according to the usage established at this and all the northern courts of Europe, and then addressed myself to his Majesty in the following words:

> Sir: The United States of America have appointed me their minister plenipotentiary to your Majesty, and have directed me to deliver to your Majesty this letter which contains the evidence of it. It is in obedience to their express commands, that I have the honor to assure your Majesty of their unanimous disposition and desire to cultivate the most friendly and liberal intercourse between your Majesty's subjects and their citizens, and of their best wishes for your Majesty's health and happiness, and for that of your royal family. The appointment of a minister from the United States to your Majesty's court will form an epoch in the history of England and of America.

SOURCE: From Charles Francis Adams, ed., *The Works of John Adams* (Boston: 1850–1856), 10 vols.: Vol. VIII, pp. 255–259.

I think myself more fortunate than all my fellow-citizens, in having the distinguished honor to be the first to stand in your Majesty's royal presence in a diplomatic character; and I shall esteem myself the happiest of men, if I can be instrumental in recommending my country more and more to your Majesty's royal benevolence, and of restoring an entire esteem, confidence, and affection, or, in better words, the old good nature and the old good humor between people, who, though separated by an ocean, and under different governments, have the same language, a similar religion, and kindred blood.

I beg your Majesty's permission to add, that, although I have some time before been intrusted by my country, it was never in my whole life in a manner so agreeable to myself.

The king listened to every word I said, with dignity, but with an apparent emotion. Whether it was the nature of the interview, or whether it was my visible agitation, for I felt more than I did or could express, that touched him, I cannot say. But he was much affected, and answered me with more tremor than I had spoken with, and said:

Sir: The circumstances of this audience are so extraordinary, the language you have now held is so extremely proper, and the feelings you have discovered so justly adapted to the occasion, that I must say that I not only receive with pleasure the assurance of the friendly dispositions of the United States, but that I am very glad the choice has fallen upon you to be their minister. I wish you, Sir, to believe, and that it may be understood in America, that I have done nothing in the late contest but what I thought myself indispensably bound to do, by the duty which I owed to my people. I will be very frank with you. I was the last to consent to the separation; but the separation having been made, and having become inevitable, I have always said, as I say now, that I would be the first to meet the friendship of the United States as an independent power. The moment I see such sentiments and language as yours prevail, and a disposition to give to this country the preference, that moment I shall say, let the circumstances of language, religion, and blood have their natural and full effect.

I dare not say that these were the King's precise words, and, it is even possible, that I may have in some particular mistaken his meaning: for, although his pronunciation is as distinct as I ever heard, he hesitated some time between his periods, and between the members of the same period. He was indeed much affected, and I confess I was not less so, and, therefore I cannot be certain that I was so cool and attentive, heard so clearly, and understood so perfectly, as to be confident of all his words or sense; and, I think, that all which he said to me should at present be kept secret in America, unless his Majesty or his secretary of state, who alone was present, should judge proper to report it. This I do say, that the foregoing is his Majesty's meaning as I then understood it, and his own words as nearly as I can recollect them.

The King then asked me whether I came last from France, and upon my answering in the affirmative, he put on an air of familiarity, and smiling, or rather laughing, said, "There is an opinion among some people that you are not the most attached of all your countrymen to the manners of France." I was surprised at this, because I thought it an indiscretion and a departure from the dignity. I was a little embarrassed, but determined not to deny the truth on one hand, nor leave him to infer from it any attachment to England on the other. I threw off as much gravity as I could, and assumed an air of gayety and a tone of decision as far as was decent, and said, "That opinion, sir, is not mistaken: I must avow to your Majesty, I have no attachment but to my own country." The king replied, as quick as lightning, "An honest man will never have any other."

The king then said a word or two to the secretary of state, which, being between them, I did not hear, and then turned round and bowed to me, as is customary with all kings and princes when they give the signal to retire. I retreated, stepping backward, as is the etiquette, and, making my last reverence at the door of the chamber, I went my way. The master of the ceremonies joined me the moment of my coming out of the king's closet, and accompanied me through the apartments down to my carriage, several stages of servants, gentlemen-porters and under-porters, roaring out like thunder, as I went along, "Mr. Adams's servants, Mr. Adams's carriage, etc." I have been thus minute, as it may be useful to others hereafter to know.

The conversation with the king Congress will form their own judgment of. I may expect from it a residence less painful than I once expected, as so marked an attention from the king will silence many grumblers; but we can infer nothing from all this concerning the success of my mission. . . .

With great respect, etc.
JOHN ADAMS

Sir Nathaniel Wraxall The Character of King George III (1815)

As a young man, Wraxall (1751–1831) was in the employ of the East India Company. He returned to England in 1772, and from 1780 to 1794 he served as Member of Parliament. His character sketch of George III is one of the few written during the king's lifetime.

In the king's countenance a physiognomist would have distinguished two principal characteristics; firmness, or, as his enemies denominated it, obstinancy, tempered with benignity. The former expression was, however, indisputably more marked and prominent than the latter sentiment. . . . The king seemed to have a tendency to become corpulent, if he had not repressed it by systematic and unremitting temperance. On this subject I shall relate a fact which was communicated to me by a friend, Sir John Macpherson, who received it from the great earl of Mansfield, to whom the king himself mentioned it, forcibly demonstrating that strength of mind, renunciation of all excesses, and dominion over his appetites, which have characterized George III at every period of his life. Conversing with William, duke of Cumberland, his uncle, not long before that prince's death in 1765, his Majesty observed that it was with concern he remarked the duke's augmenting corpulency. "I lament it not less, Sir," replied he, "but it is constitutional, and I am much mistaken if your Majesty will not become as large as myself, before you attain to my age." "It arises from your not using sufficient exercise," answered the king. "I use, nevertheless," said the Duke, "constant and severe exercise of every kind. But there is another effort requisite in order to repress this tendency which is much more difficult to practice, and without which no exercise, however violent, will suffice. I mean great renunciation and temperance. Nothing else can prevent your Majesty from growing to my size." The king made little reply, but the duke's words sunk deep and produced a lasting impression on his mind. From that day he formed the resolution, as he assured Lord Mansfield, of checking his constitutional inclination to corpulency by unremitting restraint upon his appetite, a determination which he carried into complete effect in defiance of every temptation.

Perhaps no sovereign of whom history, ancient or modern, makes mention in any age of the earth, has exceeded him in the practice of this virtue. It is a fact that during many years of his life, after coming up from Kew or from Windsor, often on horseback and sometimes in heavy rain, to the queen's house, he has gone in a sedan-chair to St. James's, dressed himself, held a levée, passed through all the forms of that long and tedious ceremony, for such it was in the way that he performed it, without leaving any individual in the circle unnoticed, and has afterwards assisted at a Privy Council, or given audience to his cabinet ministers and others, till five, and even sometimes till six o'clock. After so much fatigue of body and of mind, the only refreshment or sustenance that he usually took consisted of a

SOURCE: From Sir Nathaniel William Wraxall, *Historical and Posthumous Memoirs*, H. B. Wheatley, ed. (London, 1884), Vol. I, pp. 280–285.

few slices of bread and butter and a dish of tea, which he sometimes swallowed as he walked up and down, previous to getting into his carriage in order to return into the country. His understanding, solid and sedate, qualified him admirably for business, though it was neither of a brilliant, lively, nor imposing description. But his manner did injustice to the endowments of his intellect, and unfortunately, it was in public that these minute personal defects or imperfections became more conspicuous. Dr. Johnson, indeed, thought otherwise on the subject; for after the conversation with which his Majesty was pleased to honor that great literary character in the library of the queen's house in February 1767, he passed the highest encomiums on the elegant manners of the sovereign. Boswell, in Johnson's Life, speaking of this circumstance, adds, "He said to Mr. Barnard, the librarian, 'Sir, they may talk of the king as they will, but he is the finest gentleman I have ever seen.' And he afterwards observed to Mr. Langton, 'Sir, his manners are those of as fine a gentleman as we may suppose Louis XIV or Charles II.'"

Independent of the effect necessarily produced on Johnson's mind by so unexpected and flattering a mark of royal condescension, which may well be imagined to have operated most favorably on the opinions of the moralist, he was perhaps of all men the least capable of estimating personal elegance of deportment. His vast intellectual powers lay in another line of discrimination. Had Johnson been now living, he might indeed witness the finest model of grace, dignity, ease, and affability which the world has ever beheld united in the same person. In *him*[7] are really blended the majesty of Louis XIV with the amenity of Charles II. But George III was altogether destitute of these ornamental and adventitious endowments. The oscillations of his body, the precipitation of his questions, none of which, it was said, would wait for

an answer, and the hurry of his articulation afforded, on the contrary, to little minds, or to malicious observers, who only saw him at a drawing room, (or, as the duchess of Chandos called it, the *drawling* room), occasion for calling in question the soundness of his judgment, or the strength of his faculties. None of his ministers, however, and Mr. Fox, if possible, less than any other, entertained such an opinion. His whole reign forms, indeed, the best answer to the imputation. That he committed many errors, nourished many prejudices, formed many erroneous estimates, and frequently adhered too pertinaciously to his determinations, where he conceived, perhaps falsely, that they were founded in reason, or in justice—all these allegations may be admitted. Nor can the injurious effects to himself and to his people, necessarily flowing in various instances from such defects of character and of administration, be altogether denied. But these infirmities, from which no man is exempt, cannot impugn his right to the affectionate veneration of posterity for the inflexible uprightness of his public conduct; and as little can they deprive him of the suffrages of the wise and good of every age, who will bear testimony to the expansion of his mind and the invariable rectitude of his intentions.

It would indeed be difficult for history to produce an instance of any prince who has united and displayed on the throne during near half a century, so many personal and private virtues. In the flower of youth, unmarried, endowed with a vigorous constitution, and surrounded with temptations to pleasure or indulgence of every kind when he succeeded to the crown, he never yielded to these seductions. Not less affectionately attached to the queen than Charles I was to his consort Henrietta Maria, he remained, nevertheless, altogether exempt from the uxoriousness[8] which characterized his unfortunate predecessor, and which operated so fatally in the course of his reign.

---

[7]*him:* the Prince Regent and later King George IV   [8]*uxoriousness:* the tendency to be dotingly or submissively fond of a wife

6

The Impact of the French Revolution upon England: Threat or Promise?

The 1780s in the British Isles witnessed a recovery from the War of American Independence, a quickening of economic change, and an increased willingness on the part of the British Parliament to discuss, if not necessarily to enact, fundamental changes in the structure of government. Major political issues of the day included such controversial proposals as abolishing the slave trade, ending or easing of legal disadvantages faced by non-Anglican Protestants and by Roman Catholics, creating a single national budget, and reforming the system of parliamentary representation.

In the years after 1789, debates on reform within the British Isles were increasingly influenced by a succession of events in France, which are generally summed up as the French Revolution. The new French National Assembly (and its successors) first limited and then abolished the power of the supposedly absolute French monarchy. The separate castes of nobility and clergy were also abolished. The remnants of medieval serfdom were ended. Old regional divisions were supplanted by a new system of "departments." The right to suffrage was broadened until it approached universal manhood suffrage. The people of Europe were invited to follow the French example. At the same time "counter-revolutionaries" were harried out of the country or, by 1793-1794, executed by the thousands. Since France was the most populous and most powerful of European nations, events there necessarily affected and influenced all of France's neighbors.

Edmund Burke (1729–1797), an Irish-born British politician, had sympathized in the 1760s and 1770s with American claims to justice founded on their "rights as Englishmen." In 1789 and 1790, however, he turned out to be among the first to see events in France as a threat to Britain. The first selection consists of excerpts from his book *Reflections on the Revolution in France* (1790), in which Burke explores the dangers posed by revolutionary France. The most famous reply to Burke was penned within a year by Thomas Paine (1737–1809), an Englishman who in 1774 had emigrated to North America, where he had served as secretary to the Continental Congress and inspired the cause of American independence.

Fashion Before Ease: or, A Good Constitution Sacrificed, for a Fantastick Form

In a 1793 cartoon by William Gillray, Thomas Paine seeks to lace Britannia into a French corset.

During the early months of the French Revolution Paine had lived in France, an experience upon which he drew in writing *The Rights of Man* (1791). The second selection consists of significant excerpts from that work. Paine and Burke were concerned both with the immediate impact of events in France and with perennial questions of political philosophy.

Why does Burke fear and Paine embrace the example of the French Revolution? For Richard Price, the Unitarian minister whom Burke criticizes, England in its Revolution of 1688 had provided a model for the France of 1789 and after. Does Burke agree with this assessment? Does Paine? How do Burke and Paine differ on the questions of how governments originated and why human beings do (and ought) to obey them? How do they differ in their definition of "the rights of man"? How do they differ in their style of writing? What evidence do they provide that the British people would or would not find the French example appealing? Did Burke—often seen as the philosophical founder of modern Anglo-American conservatism—perhaps place too much emphasis on prescription (authority based on precedent)? Did Paine—the philosophical father of nineteenth-century British radicalism—place perhaps too much faith in the power of human reason and in the significance of paper constitutions? How do Burke and Paine compare as prophets of the course that the French Revolution would take?

Events in France inspired numerous other Britons to take pen in hand. Mary Wollstonecraft (1757–1797), a writer, educator, and political radical, not only wrote her own popular reply to Burke, *A Vindication of the Rights of Men* (1791), but also followed it a year later with *A Vindication of the Rights of Woman* (1792). The latter work was dedicated to Charles Maurice de Talleyrand, a French aristocrat (and future foreign minister) who sided with the revolutionaries and who wrote an educational treatise lamenting the fact that most women received an inferior education. He went on: "To see one half of the human race excluded by the other from all participation in government, was a political phenomenon that, according to abstract principles, it was impossible to explain." In what fashion does Mary Wollstonecraft expand on that observation? On what basis does she justify a broader public role for women? What changes in law and custom does she advocate? In the mid-1790s Mary Wollstonecraft became first the mistress and then the wife of William Godwin, perhaps the best-known English political radical of the day. In 1797 she died in childbirth; her daughter Mary was to become the author of *Frankenstein* and the wife of the poet Percy Bysshe Shelley. Wollstonecraft's pioneering feminism bore no immediate fruit, but her views were to be echoed seven decades later in works like John Stuart Mill's *On the Subjection of Women* (1869). (See Chapter 8.)

Hannah More (1745–1833) was, at the time, a far better-known writer than Mary Wollstonecraft. A pioneer of the English Sunday School movement and a founder of the Religious Tract Society (1799), she also wrote plays, a novel, and innumerable essays and reviews. Her purpose, unlike that of Mary Wollstonecraft, was not to expand on the ideas of Thomas Paine and the French revolutionaries but to combat them. In *Village Politics* (1793) she sought to persuade ordinary "mechanics, journeymen, and laborers" that, although French ideals of "liberty, equality, and fraternity" sounded appealing they would have deplorable consequences if applied to Britain. For Hannah More, what are the merits of English society and the demerits of French revolutionary society? What types of liberty, if any, does she favor? On what basis does she justify the type of social inequality to be found in the Britain of her day?

By 1792 the new French revolutionary republic was at war with its immediate neighbors, Austria and Prussia. Early in 1793, after the execution of King Louis XVI, France declared war on Britain as well. In the course of the long era of war that ensued (1793–1802; 1803–1815), the revolutionary French government underwent numerous changes. In 1799 Napoleon Bonaparte took power as First Consul; five years later he crowned himself emperor. Only in 1815, after the Battle of Waterloo and Napoleon's abdication, was the French Bourbon monarchy restored. In the meantime the political reform movement within Britain rapidly ebbed, and British sympathizers with revolutionary France came to be suspected—and sometimes tried—as traitors. Paine, himself, was charged with "seditious libel" by the British crown in 1792, but before he came up for trial, he had left for France, where he was elected deputy to the National Convention that had replaced the National Assembly. In England Paine was found guilty *in absentia;* in France within a year Paine was arrested as a "counterrevolutionary" during the Reign of Terror. He escaped the guillotine, however, and eventually returned to the United States, where he died in relative obscurity.

EDMUND BURKE **Reflections on the Revolution in France (1790)**

The revolution in France had been under way for little more than a year when the veteran parliamentarian and author wrote this lengthy pamphlet in the form of a letter to a Frenchman.

Dear Sir,

. . . Though I do most heartily wish that France may be animated by a spirit of rational liberty, and that I think you bound, in all honest policy, to provide a permanent body, in which that spirit may reside, and an effectual organ, by which it may act, it is my misfortune to entertain great doubts concerning several material points in your late transactions. . . .

The circumstances are what render every civil and political scheme beneficial or noxious to mankind. Abstractedly speaking, government, as well as liberty, is good; yet could I, in common sense, ten years ago, have felicitated France on her enjoyment of a government (for she then had a government) without enquiry what the nature of that government was, or how it was administered? Can I now congratulate the same nation upon its freedom? Is it because liberty in the abstract may be classed amongst

the blessings of mankind, that I am seriously to felicitate a madman, who has escaped from the protecting restraint and wholesome darkness of his cell, on his restoration to the enjoyment of light and liberty? Am I to congratulate an highwayman and murderer, who has broke prison, upon the recovery of his natural rights? . . .

I must be tolerably sure, before I venture publicly to congratulate men upon a blessing, that they have really received one. Flattery corrupts both the receiver and the giver; and adulation is not of more service to the people than to kings. I should therefore suspend my congratulations on the new liberty of France, until I was informed how it had been combined with government; with public force; with the discipline and obedience of armies; with the collection of an effective and well-distributed revenue; with morality and religion; with the solidity of property; with peace and order; with civil and social manners. All these (in

SOURCE: Burke's essay has been reprinted many times. The excerpts cited here may be found on the following pages of the Doubleday Dolphin edition of the same title (Garden City, N.Y., 1961), pp. 17, 19–21, 27, 29–30, 33–34, 38–43, 45–46, 48, 57–65, 71–75, 89–92, 99, 101–105, 110, 137–139, 167, 236–237, 264.

their way) are good things too; and, without them, liberty is not a benefit whilst it lasts, and is not likely to continue long. The effect of liberty to individuals is, that they may do what they please: We ought to see what it will please them to do, before we risque congratulations which may be soon turned into complaints. . . .

It looks to me as if I were in a great crisis, not of the affairs of France alone, but of all Europe, perhaps of more than Europe. All circumstances taken together, the French revolution is the most astonishing that has hitherto happened in the world. . . .

[Dr. Richard Price of the Revolution Society][1] proceeds dogmatically to assert, that by the principles of the Revolution [of 1688] the people of England have acquired three fundamental rights, all which, with him, compose one system, and lie together in one short sentence; namely, that we have acquired a right

1. "To choose our own governors."
2. "To cashier them for misconduct."
3. "To frame a government for ourselves."

. . . Unquestionably there was at the Revolution, in the person of King William, a small and a temporary deviation from the strict order of a regular hereditary succession; but it is against all genuine principles of jurisprudence to draw a principle from a law made in a special case, and regarding an individual person. . . .

The two houses, in the act of King William, did not thank God that they had found a fair opportunity to assert a right to choose their own governors, much less to make an election the *only lawful* title to the crown. Their having been in a condition to avoid the very appearance of it, as much as possible, was by them considered as a providential escape. They threw a politic, well-wrought veil over every circumstance tending to weaken the rights, which in the meliorated order of succession they

meant to perpetuate; or which might furnish a precedent for any future departure from what they had then settled for ever.

A state without the means of some change is without the means of its conservation. Without such means it might even risque the loss of that part of the Constitution which it wished the most religiously to preserve. The two principles of conservation and correction operated strongly at the two critical periods of the Restoration [of 1660] and Revolution [of 1688], when England found itself without a king. At both those periods the nation had lost the bond of union in their antient edifice; they did not, however, dissolve the whole fabric. . . . It was still a line of hereditary descent; still an hereditary descent in the same blood, though an hereditary descent qualified with Protestantism. When the legislature altered the direction, but kept the principle, they showed that they held it inviolable. . . .

The second claim of the Revolution Society is "a right of cashiering their governors for *misconduct*.". . .

No government could stand a moment, if it could be blown down with any thing so loose and indefinite as an opinion of "*misconduct*." They who led at the Revolution, grounded the virtual abdication of King James upon no such light and uncertain principle. They charged him with nothing less than a design, confirmed by a multitude of illegal overt acts, to *subvert the Protestant church and state,* and their *fundamental,* unquestionable laws and liberties: they charged him with having broken the *original contract* between king and people. This was more than *misconduct.* . . .

By the statute of the 1st of King William, sess. 2d, called "*the act for declaring the rights and liberties of the subject, and for settling the succession of the crown,*" they enacted, that the ministers should serve the crown on the terms of that declaration. They secured soon after the *frequent meetings of Parliament,* by which the whole

---

[1]*Richard Price (1723–1791),* a Nonconformist minister and political reformer who sympathized strongly with the aims of the French revolutionaries

government would be under the constant inspection and active controul of the popular representative and of the magnates of the kingdom. . . .

Kings, in one sense, are undoubtedly the servants of the people, because their power has no other rational end than that of the general advantage; but it is not true that they are, in the ordinary sense (by our Constitution, at least) any thing like servants; the essence of whose situation is to obey the commands of some other, and to be removeable at pleasure. But the king of Great Britain obeys no other person; all other persons are individually, and collectively too, under him, and owe to him a legal obedience. . . .

The ceremony of cashiering kings, of which these gentlemen talk so much at their ease, can rarely, if ever, be performed without force. It then becomes a case of war, and not of constitution. . . . The question of dethroning, or, if these gentlemen like the phrase better, "cashiering kings, " will always be, as it has always been, an extraordinary question of state, and wholly out of the law; a question (like all other questions of state) of dispositions, and of means, and of probable consequences, rather than of positive rights. . . .

The third head of right, asserted by [Dr. Price and the Revolution Society], namely, the "right to form a government for ourselves, " has, at least as little countenance from any thing done at the Revolution [of 1688], either in precedent or principle, as the two first of their claims. The Revolution was made to preserve our *antient* indisputable laws and liberties, and that *antient* Constitution of government which is our only security for law and liberty. . . . The very idea of the fabrication of a new government, is enough to fill us with disgust and horror. We wished at the period of the Revolution, and do now wish, to derive all we possess as *an inheritance from our forefathers*. . . .

You will observe, that from Magna Charta [in 1215] to the Declaration of Right [in 1689], it has been the uniform policy of our Constitution to claim and assert our

liberties, as an *entailed inheritance* derived to us from our forefathers, and to be transmitted to our posterity; as an estate specially belonging to the people of this kingdom without any reference whatever to any other more general or prior right. By this means our Constitution preserves an unity in so great a diversity of its parts. We have an inheritable crown; an inheritable peerage; and an House of Commons and a people inheriting privileges, franchises, and liberties from a long line of ancestors.

This policy appears to me to be the result of profound reflection; or rather the happy effect of following nature, which is wisdom without reflection, and above it. A spirit of innovation is generally the result of a selfish temper and confined views. People will not look forward to posterity, who never look backward to their ancestors. Besides, the people of England well know, that the idea of inheritance furnishes a sure principle of conservation, and a sure principle of transmission; without at all excluding a principle of improvement. It leaves acquisition free; but it secures what it acquires. . . .

In what we improve we are never wholly new; in what we retain we are never wholly obsolete. By adhering in this manner and on those principles to our forefathers, we are guided not by the superstition of antiquarians, but by the spirit of philosophic analogy. In this choice of inheritance we have given to our frame of polity the image of a relation in blood; binding up the Constitution of our country with our dearest domestic ties; adopting our fundamental laws into the bosom of our family affections; keeping inseparable, and cherishing with the warmth of all their combined and mutually reflected charities, our state, our hearths, our sepulchres, and our altars.

You [in France] had all these advantages in your antient [Estates of the Realm]; but you chose to act as if you had never been moulded into civil society, and had every thing to begin anew. You began ill, because you began by despising every thing that belonged to you. You set up your trade without a capital. If the last generations of your country appeared without much lustre in your eyes, you might have passed them by, and derived your claims from a more early race of ancestors. . . .

[But] your National Assembly . . . has no fundamental law, no strict convention, no respected usage to restrain it. Instead of finding themselves obliged to conform to a fixed constitution, they have a power to make a constitution which shall conform to their designs. . . . But—*"fools rush in where angels fear to tread."* In such a state of unbounded power, for undefined and undefinable purposes, the evil of a moral and almost physical inaptitude of the man to the function must be the greatest we can conceive to happen in the management of human affairs. . . .

Turbulent, discontented men of quality, in proportion as they are puffed up with personal pride and arrogance, generally despise their own order. One of the first symptoms they discover of a selfish and mischievous ambition, is a profligate disregard of a dignity which they partake with others. To be attached to the subdivision, to love the little platoon we belong to in society, is the first principle (the germ as it were) of public affections. It is the first link in the series by which we proceed toward a love to our country and to mankind. . . .

Every person in your country, in a situation to be actuated by a principle of honor, is disgraced and degraded, and can entertain no sensation of life, except in a mortified and humiliated indignation. But this generation will quickly pass away. The next generation of the nobility will resemble the artificers and clowns, and money-jobbers, usurers, and Jews, who will be always their fellows, sometimes their masters. Believe me, Sir, those who attempt to level, never equalize. In all societies, consisting of various descriptions of citizens, some description must be uppermost. The levellers therefore only change and pervert the natural order of things; they load the edifice of society, by setting up in the air what the solidity of the structure requires to be on the ground. The associations of taylors and carpenters, of which the republic (of Paris,

for instance) is composed, cannot be equal to the situation, into which, by the worst of usurpations, an usurpation on the prerogatives of nature, you attempt to force them.

The chancellor of France at the opening of the states, said, in a tone of oratorial flourish, that all occupations were honorable. If he meant only, that no honest employment was disgraceful, he would not have gone beyond the truth. But in asserting, that any thing is honorable, we imply some distinction in its favor. The occupation of an hair-dresser, or of a working tallow-chandler, cannot be a matter of honor to any person—to say nothing of a number of other more servile employments. Such descriptions of men ought not to suffer oppression from the state; but the state suffers oppression, if such as they either individually or collectively, are permitted to rule. In this you think you are combating prejudice, but you are at war with nature.

You do not imagine, that I wish to confine power, authority, and distinction to blood, and names, and titles. No, Sir. There is no qualification for government, but virtue and wisdom, actual or presumptive. Wherever they are actually found, they have, in whatever state, condition, profession or trade, the passport of heaven to human place and honor. Woe to the country which would madly and impiously reject the service of the talents and virtues, civil, military, or religious, that are given to grace and to serve it; and would condemn to obscurity every thing formed to diffuse lustre and glory around a state. Woe to that country too, that passing into the opposite extreme, considers a low education, a mean contracted view of things, a sordid mercenary occupation, as a preferable title to command. Every thing ought to be open; but not indifferently to every man. No rotation; no appointment by lot; no mode of election operating in the spirit of sortition or rotation, can be generally good in a government conversant in extensive objects. Because they have no tendency, direct or indirect, to select the man with a view to the duty, or to accommodate the one to the other, I do not hesitate to say, that the road to eminence and power, from obscure condition, ought not to be made too easy, nor a thing too much of course. If rare merit be the rarest of all rare things, it ought to pass through some sort of probation. The temple of honor ought to be seated on an eminence. If it be open through virtue, let it be remembered too, that virtue is never tried but by some difficulty, and some struggle.

Nothing is a due and adequate representation of a state, that does not represent its ability, as well as its property. . . . The characteristic essence of property, formed out of the combined principles of its acquisition and conservation, is to be *unequal.* The great masses therefore which excite envy, and tempt rapacity, must be put out of the possibility of danger. . . . The plunder of the few would indeed give but a share inconceivably small in the distribution to the many. But the many are not capable of making this calculation; and those who lead them to rapine, never intend this distribution.

The power of perpetuating our property in our families is one of the most valuable and interesting circumstances belonging to it, and that which tends the most to the perpetuation of society itself. It makes our weakness subservient to our virtue; it grafts benevolence even upon avarice. The possessors of family wealth, and of the distinction which attends hereditary possession (as most concerned in it) are the natural securities for this transmission. . . .

It is said, that twenty-four millions ought to prevail over two hundred thousand. True; if the constitution of a kingdom be a problem of arithmetic. This sort of discourse does well enough with the lamp-post for its second: to men who *may* reason calmly, it is ridiculous. The will of the many, and their interest, must very often differ; and great will be the difference when they make an evil choice. A government of five hundred country attornies and obscure curates is not good for twenty-four millions of men, though it were chosen by eight and forty millions; nor is it the better for being guided by a dozen of persons of quality, who have betrayed their trust in order to obtain

that power. At present, you seem in every thing to have strayed out of the high road of nature. The property of France does not govern it. Of course property is destroyed, and rational liberty has no existence. All you have got for the present is a paper circulation, and stock-jobbing constitution: and as to the future, do you seriously think that the territory of France, upon the republican system of eighty-three independent municipalities (to say nothing of the parts that compose them) can ever be governed as one body, or can ever be set in motion by the impulse of one mind?

Far am I from denying in theory; full as far is my heart from withholding in practice (if I were of power to give or to withhold) the *real* rights of men. . . . They have a right to justice; as between their fellows, whether their fellows are in politic function or in ordinary occupation. They have a right to the fruits of their industry; and to the means of making their industry fruitful. They have a right to the acquisitions of their parents; to the nourishment and improvement of their offspring; to instruction in life, and to consolation in death. Whatever each man can separately do, without trespassing upon others, he has a right to do for himself; and he has a right to a fair portion of all which society, with all its combinations of skill and force can do in his favor. In this partnership all men have equal rights; but not to equal things. He that has but five shillings in the partnership, has as good a right to it, as he that has five hundred pound has to his larger proportion. But he has not a right to an equal dividend in the product of the joint stock; and as to the share of power, authority, and direction which each individual ought to have in the management of the state, that I must deny to be amongst the direct original rights of man in civil society; for I have in my contemplation the civil social man, and no other. It is a thing to be settled by convention.

If civil society be the offspring of convention, that convention must be its law. That convention must limit and modify all the descriptions of constitution which are formed under it. . . . Government is a contrivance of human wisdom to provide for human *wants*. Men have a right that these wants should be provided for by this wisdom. Among these wants is to be reckoned the want, out of civil society, of a sufficient restraint upon their passions. Society requires not only that the passions of individuals should be subjected, but that even in the mass and body as well as in the individuals, the inclinations of men should frequently be thwarted, their will controlled, and their passions brought into subjection. This can only be done *by a power out of themselves;* and not, in the exercise of its function, subject to that will and to those passions which it is its office to bridle and subdue. In this sense the restraints on men, as well as their liberties, are to be reckoned among their rights. . . . What is the use of discussing a man's abstract right to food or to medicine? The question is upon the method of procuring and administering them. In that deliberation I shall always advise to call in the aid of the farmer and the physician, rather than the professor of metaphysics.

The science of constructing a commonwealth, or renovating it, or reforming it, is, like every other experimental science, not to be taught *a priori*. Nor is it a short experience that can instruct us in that practical science; because the real effects of moral causes are not always immediate; but that which in the first instance is prejudicial may be excellent in its remoter operation; and its excellence may arise even from the ill effects it produces in the beginning. . . . The science of government [is] a matter which requires experience, and even more experience than any person can gain in his whole life, however sagacious and observing he may be, it is with infinite caution that any man ought to venture upon pulling down an edifice which has answered in any tolerable degree for ages the common purposes of society, or on building it up again,

without having models and patterns of approved utility before his eyes. . . .

The pretended rights of these theorists are all extremes; and in proportion as they are metaphysically true, they are morally and politically false. The rights of men are in a sort of *middle*, incapable of definition, but not impossible to be discerned. The rights of men in governments are their advantages; and these are often in balances between differences of good; in compromises sometimes between good and evil, and sometimes, between evil and evil. . . .

It is now sixteen or seventeen years since I saw the queen of France,[1] then the dauphiness, at Versailles; and surely never lighted on this orb, which she hardly seemed to touch, a more delightful vision. I saw her just above the horizon, decorating and cheering the elevated sphere she just began to move in,—glittering like the morningstar, full of life, and splendor, and joy. Oh! what a revolution! and what an heart must I have, to contemplate without emotion that elevation and that fall! Little did I dream when she added titles of veneration to those of enthusiastic, distant, respectful love, that she should ever be obliged to carry the sharp antidote against disgrace concealed in that bosom; little did I dream that I should live to see such disasters fallen upon her in a nation of gallant men, in a nation of men of honor and of cavaliers. I thought ten thousand swords must have leaped from their scabbards to avenge even a look that threatened her with insult.—But the age of chivalry is gone.—That of sophisters, economists, and calculators, has succeeded; and the glory of Europe is extinguished for ever. Never, never more, shall we behold that generous loyalty to rank and sex, that proud submission, that dignified obedience, that subordination of the heart, which kept alive, even in servitude itself, the spirit of an exalted freedom. . . .

But now all is to be changed. All the pleasing illusions, which made power

[1]*Queen of France:* Marie Antoinette (1755–1793), the wife of King Louis XVI, was still technically queen in 1790. Two years later both were deposed, and in 1793 both were executed by guillotine after being found guilty of treason to the French republic.

gentle, and obedience liberal, which harmonized the different shades of life, and which, by a bland assimilation, incorporated into politics the sentiments which beautify and soften private society, are to be dissolved by this new conquering empire of light and reason. All the decent drapery of life is to be rudely torn off. . . .

On this scheme of things, a king is but a man; a queen is but a woman; a woman is but an animal; and an animal not of the highest order. All homage paid to the sex in general as such, and without distinct views, is to be regarded as romance and folly. Regicide, and parricide, and sacrilege, are but fictions of superstition, corrupting jurisprudence by destroying its simplicity. The murder of a king or a queen, or a bishop, or a father, are only common homicide; and if the people are by any chance, or in any way gainers by it, a sort of homicide much the most pardonable, and into which we ought not to make too severe a scrutiny.

On the scheme of this barbarous philosophy, which is the offspring of cold hearts and muddy understandings, and which is as void of solid wisdom, as it is destitute of all taste and elegance, laws are to be supported only by their own terrors, and by the concern, which each individual may find in them, from his own private speculations, or can spare to them from his own private interests. . . .

But power, of some kind or other, will survive the shock in which manners and opinions perish; and it will find other and worse means for its support. . . . Kings will be tyrants from policy when subjects are rebels from principle. . . .

Nothing is more certain, than that our manners, our civilization, and all the good things which are connected with manners, and with civilization, have, in this European world of ours, depended for ages upon two principles; and were indeed the result of both combined; I mean the spirit of a gentleman, and the spirit of religion. The nobility and the clergy, the one by profession, the other by patronage, kept learning in existence, even in the midst of arms and confusions, and whilst governments were rather in their causes than formed. Learning paid

back what it received to nobility and to priesthood; and paid it with usury, by enlarging their ideas, and by furnishing their minds. Happy if they had all continued to know their indissoluble union, and their proper place! . . .

We are not the converts of Rousseau; we are not the disciples of Voltaire; Helvetius has made no progress amongst us. Atheists are not our preachers; madmen are not our lawgivers. We know that *we* have made no discoveries; and we think that no discoveries are to be made, in morality; nor many in the great principles of government, nor in the ideas of liberty, which were understood long before we were born, altogether as well as they will be after the grave has heaped its mould upon our presumption, and the silent tomb shall have imposed its law on our pert loquacity. . . .

Your literary men, and your politicians . . . conceive, very systematically, that all things which give perpetuity are mischievous, and therefore they are at inexpiable war with all establishments. They think that government may vary like modes of dress, and with as little ill effect; that there needs no principle of attachment, except a sense of present conveniency, to any constitution of the state. They always speak as if they were of opinion that there is a singular species of compact between them and their magistrates, which binds the magistrate, but which has nothing reciprocal in it, but that the majesty of the people has a right to dissolve it without any reason, but its will.
. . .

Formerly your affairs were your own concern only. We felt for them as men; but we kept aloof from them, because we were not citizens of France. But when we see the model held up to ourselves, we must feel as Englishmen, and feeling, we must provide as Englishmen. Your affairs, in spite of us, are made a part of our interest; so far at least as to keep at a distance your panacea, or your plague. If it be a panacea, we do not want it. We know the consequences of unnecessary physic. If it be a plague; it is such a plague, that the precautions of the most severe quarantine ought to be established against it. . . .

We know, and what is better we feel inwardly, that religion is the basis of civil society, and the source of all good and of all comfort. In England we are so convinced of this, that there is no rust of superstition, with which the accumulated absurdity of the human mind might have crusted it over in the course of ages, that ninety-nine in an hundred of the people of England would not prefer to impiety. . . .

We know, and it is our pride to know, that man is by his constitution a religious animal; that atheism is against, not only our reason but our instincts; and that it cannot prevail long. But if, in the moment of riot, and in a drunken delirium from the hot spirit drawn out of the alembick[3] of hell, which in France is now so furiously boiling, we should uncover our nakedness by throwing off that Christian religion which has hitherto been our boast and comfort, and one great source of civilization amongst us, and among many other nations, we are apprehensive (being well aware that the mind will not endure a void) that some uncouth, pernicious, and degrading superstition, might take the place of it.

Instead of quarrelling with establishments, as some do, who have made a philosophy and a religion of their hostility to such institutions, we cleave closely to them. We are resolved to keep an established church, an established monarchy, an established aristocracy, and an established democracy, each in the degree it exists, and in no greater. . . .

Society is indeed a contract. Subordinate contracts for objects of mere occasional interest may be dissolved at pleasure—but the state ought not to be considered as nothing better than a partnership agreement in a trade of pepper and coffee, callico or tobacco, or some other such low concern, to be taken up for a little temporary interest, and to be dissolved by the fancy of the parties. It is to be looked on with other reverence; because it is not a partnership in things subservient only to the gross animal existence of a temporary and perishable nature. It is a partnership in all science; a partnership in all art; a partnership in every virtue, and in all perfection. As the ends of such a partnership cannot be obtained in many generations, it becomes a partnership not only between those who are living, but between those who are living, those who are dead, and those who are to be born. Each contract of each particular state is but a clause in the great primaeval contract of eternal society, linking the lower with the higher natures, connecting the visible and invisible world, according to a fixed compact sanctioned by the inviolable oath which holds all physical and all moral natures, each in their appointed place. . . .

When all the fraud, impostures, violences, rapines, burnings, murders, confiscations, compulsory paper currencies, and every description of tyranny and cruelty employed to bring about and to uphold this revolution, have their natural effect, that is, to shock the moral sentiments of all virtuous and sober minds, the abettors of this philosophic system immediately strain their throats in a declamation against the old monarchical government of France. . . . Have these gentlemen never heard, in the whole circle of the worlds of theory and practice, of any thing between the despotism of the monarch and the despotism of the multitude? Have they never heard of a monarchy directed by laws, controlled and balanced by the great hereditary wealth and hereditary dignity of a nation; and both again controlled by a judicious check from the reason and feeling of the people at large acting by a suitable and permanent organ? Is it then impossible that a man may be found who, without criminal ill intention, or pitiable absurdity, shall prefer such a mixed and tempered government to either of the extremes. . . .

I do not know under what description to class the present ruling authority in France. It affects to be a pure democracy, though I think it in a direct train of becoming shortly a mischievous and ignoble oligarchy. But for the present I admit it to be a contrivance of the nature and effect of what it pretends to. I reprobate no form of govern-

---

[3]*alembick:* a gourd-shaped vessel used to distill liquor

ment merely upon abstract principles. There may be situations in which the purely democratic form will become necessary. There may be some (very few, and very particularly circumstanced) where it would be clearly desireable. This I do not take to be the case of France, or of any other great country. Until now, we have seen no examples of considerable democracies. The antients [ancients] were better acquainted with them. Not being wholly unread in the authors, who had seen the most of those constitutions, and who best understood them, I cannot help concurring with their opinion, that an absolute democracy, no more than absolute monarchy, is to be reckoned among the legitimate forms of government. They think it rather the corruption and degeneracy, than the sound constitution of a republic. . . . Of this I am certain, that in a democracy, the majority of the citizens is capable of exercising the most cruel oppressions upon the minority whenever strong divisions prevail in that kind of polity, as they often must; and that oppression of the minority will extend to far greater numbers, and will be carried on with much greater fury, than can almost ever be apprehended from the dominion of a single sceptre. . . .

I see the confiscators begin with bishops, and chapters, and monasteries; but I do not see them end there. I see the princes of the blood, who, by the oldest usages of that kingdom, held large landed estates, (hardly with the compliment of a debate) deprived of their possessions, and in lieu of their stable independent property, reduced to the hope of some precarious, charitable pension, at the pleasure of an assembly, which of course will pay little regard to the rights of pensioners at pleasure, when it despises those of legal proprietors. Flushed with the insolence of their first inglorious victories, and pressed by the distresses caused by their lust of unhallowed lucre, disappointed but not discouraged, they have at length ventured completely to subvert all property of all descriptions throughout the extent of a great kingdom. They have compelled all men, in all transactions of commerce, in

the disposal of lands, in civil dealing, and through the whole communion of life, to accept as perfect payment and good and lawful tender, the symbols of their speculations on a projected sale of their plunder. What vestiges of liberty or property have they left? The tenant-right of a cabbage-garden, a year's interest in a hovel, the goodwill of an ale-house or a baker's shop, the very shadow of a constructive property, are more ceremoniously treated in our Parliament than with you the oldest and most valuable landed possessions in the hands of the most respectable personages, or than the whole body of the monies and commercial interest of your country. We entertain an high opinion of the legislative authority; but we have never dreamt that parliaments had any right whatever to violate property, to overrule prescription, or to force a currency of their own fiction in the place of that which is real, and recognized by the law of nations. But you, who began with refusing to submit to the most moderate restraints have ended by establishing an unheard of despotism. . . .

[The] relation of your army to the crown will, if I am not greatly mistaken, become a serious dilemma in your politics. . . . In the weakness of one kind of authority, and in the fluctuation of all, the officers of an army will remain for some time mutinous and full of faction, until some popular general, who understands the art of conciliating the soldiery, and who possesses the true spirit of command, shall draw the eyes of all men upon himself. Armies will obey him on his personal account. There is no other way of securing military obedience in this state of things. But the moment in which that event shall happen, the person who really commands the army is your master; . . . the master of your assembly, the master of your whole republic. . . .

The improvements of the National Assembly are superficial, their errors fundamental. . . . Whatever they are, I wish my countrymen rather to recommend to our neighbors the example of the British Constitution, than to take models from them for the improvement of our own. . . .

Thomas Paine **The Rights of Man (1791)**

Burke's Reflections evoked numerous responses. The most widely read was penned by Thomas Paine, the English advocate of the American Revolution who had become an advocate of the French Revolution. The Rights of Man became the bible of British political radicals in the 1790s and in the early nineteenth century.

TO GEORGE WASHINGTON,
PRESIDENT OF THE UNITED STATES OF AMERICA

Sir,

I present you a small treatise in defense of those principles of freedom which your exemplary virtue hath so eminently contributed to establish. That the Rights of Man may become as universal as your benevolence can wish, and that you may enjoy the happiness of seeing the New World regenerate the Old, is the prayer of

Sir,
Your much obliged, and
Obedient humble servant,
THOMAS PAINE

Preface to the English Edition

From the part Mr. Burke took in the American Revolution, it was natural that I should consider him a friend to mankind; and as our acquaintance commenced on that ground, it would have been more agreeable to me to have had cause to continue in that opinion, than to change it.

At the time Mr. Burke made his violent speech last winter in the English Parliament against the French Revolution and the National Assembly, I was in Paris, and had written to him but a short time before, to inform him how prosperously matters were going on. Soon after this, I saw his advertisement of the pamphlet he intended to publish.

As the attack was to be made in a language but little studied, and less understood, in France, and as everything suffers by translation, I promised some of the friends of the revolution in that country, that whenever Mr. Burke's pamphlet came forth, I would answer it.

This appeared to me the more necessary to be done, when I saw the flagrant misrepresentations which Mr. Burke's pamphlet contains; and that while it is an outrageous abuse on the French Revolution, and the principles of liberty, it is an imposition on the rest of the world.

When the French Revolution broke out, it certainly afforded to Mr. Burke an opportunity of doing some good, had he been disposed to it; instead of which, no sooner did he see the old prejudices wearing away, than he immediately began sowing the seeds of a new inveteracy, as if he were afraid that England and France would cease to be enemies.

That there are men in all countries who get their living by war, and by keeping up the quarrels of nations, is as shocking as it is true; but when those who are concerned in the government of a country, make it their study to sow discord, and cultivate prejudices between nations, it becomes the more unpardonable.

Part First

Among the incivilities by which nations or individuals provoke and irritate each other, Mr. Burke's pamphlet on the French Revolution is an extraordinary instance. Neither the people of France, nor the National Assembly, were troubling themselves about the affairs of England, or the English Parliament; and that Mr. Burke should com-

SOURCE: Paine's essay has been reprinted many times. The excerpts cited here may be found on the following pages of the Doubleday Dolphin edition of the same title (Garden City, N.Y., 1961): pp. 270–271, 275–278, 280–282, 285, 288, 294, 296, 302–305, 307–312, 322–326, 328, 331, 349–351, 353–355, 357, 371, 381–383, 410, 505.

mence an unprovoked attack upon them, both in Parliament and in public, is a conduct that cannot be pardoned on the score of manners, nor justified on that of policy. There is scarcely an epithet of abuse to be found in the English language, with which Mr. Burke has not loaded the French nation and the National Assembly. Every thing which rancor, prejudice, ignorance, or knowledge could suggest, are poured forth in the copious fury of near four hundred pages. . . .

Not sufficiently content with abusing the National Assembly, a great part of his work is taken up with abusing Dr. Price (one of the best-hearted men that lives), and the two societies in England known by the name of the Revolution Society, and the Society for Constitutional Information.

Dr. Price had preached a sermon on the 4th of November, 1789, being the anniversary of what is called in England the Revolution, which took place in 1688. Mr. Burke, speaking of this sermon, says, "The political divine proceeds dogmatically to assert that, by the principles of the Revolution, the people of England have acquired three fundamental rights:

1. To choose our own governors.
2. To cashier them for misconduct.
3. To frame a government for ourselves.

Dr. Price does not say that the right to do these things exists in this or in that person, or in this or in that description of persons, but that it exists in the *whole*; that it is a right resident in the nation. Mr. Burke, on the contrary, denies that such a right exists in the nation, either in whole or in part, or that it exists any where; and, what is still more strange and marvelous, he says, "that the people of England utterly disclaim such a right, and that they will resist the practical assertion of it with their lives and fortunes."

That men should take up arms, and spend their lives and fortunes, *not* to maintain their rights, but to maintain they have *not* rights, is an entirely new species of discovery, and suited to the paradoxical genius of Mr. Burke.

The English Parliament of 1688 did a certain thing, which, for themselves and their constituents, they had a right to do, and which it appeared right should be done: But, in addition to this right, which they possessed by delegation, *they set up another right by assumption*, that of binding and controlling posterity to the end of time. . . .

There never did, there never will, and there never can exist a parliament, or any description of men, or any generation of men, in any country, possessed of the right or the power of binding and controlling posterity to the "end of time, " or of commanding forever how the world shall be governed, or who shall govern it; and therefore, all such clauses, acts or declarations, by which the makers of them attempt to do what they have neither the right nor the power to do, nor the power to execute, are in themselves null and void.

Every age and generation must be as free to act for itself, *in all cases*, as the ages and generation which preceded it. The vanity and presumption of governing beyond the grave, is the most ridiculous and insolent of all tyrannies.

Man has no property in man; neither has any generation a property in the generations which are to follow. . . . Every generation is, and must be, competent to all the purposes which its occasions require. It is the living, and not the dead, that are to be accommodated. . . .

It requires but a very small glance of thought to perceive, that although laws made in one generation often continue in force through succeeding generations, yet they continue to derive their force from the consent of the living. A law not repealed continues in force, not because it *cannot* be repealed, but because it is *not* repealed; and the non-repealing passes for consent. . . .

We now come more particularly to the affairs of France. Mr. Burke's book has the appearance of being written as instruction to the French nation; but if I may permit myself the use of an extravagant metaphor, suited to the extravagance of the case, it is darkness attempting to illuminate light.

It was not against Louis XVI, but against the despotic principles of the government, that the nation revolted. These principles had not their origin in him, but in the original establishment, many centuries back; and they were become too deeply rooted to be removed, and the Augean stable of parasites and plunderers too abominably filthy to be cleansed, by anything short of a complete and universal revolution. . . . There were, if I may so express it, a thousand despotisms to be reformed in France, which had grown up under the hereditary despotism of the monarchy, and became so rooted as to be in a great measure independent of it. . . .

When we see a man dramatically lamenting in a publication intended to be believed, that, "*The age of chivalry is gone! that The glory of Europe is extinguished forever! that The unbought grace of life* (if any one knows what it is), *the cheap defense of nations, the nurse of manly sentiment and heroic enterprise, is gone!*" and all this because the Quixotic age of chivalric nonsense is gone, what opinion can we form of his judgment, or what regard can we pay to his facts?

In the rhapsody of his imagination, he has discovered a world of wind-mills, and his sorrows are, that there are no Quixotes to attack them. . . .

From his violence and his grief, his silence on some points, and his excess on others, it is difficult not to believe that Mr. Burke is sorry, extremely sorry, that arbitrary power, the power of the pope, and the Bastille, are pulled down.

Not one glance of compassion, not one commiserating reflection, that I can find throughout his book, has he bestowed on those who lingered out the most wretched of lives, a life without hope, in the most miserable of prisons.

It is painful to behold a man employing his talents to corrupt himself. Nature has been kinder to Mr. Burke than he is to her.

He is not affected by the reality of distress touching his heart, but by the showy resemblage of it striking his imagination. He pities the plumage, but forgets the dying bird. . . .

More of the citizens fell in this struggle than of their opponents; but four or five persons were seized by the populace, and instantly put to death; the governor of the Bastille, and the mayor of Paris, who was detected in the act of betraying them; and afterwards Foulon, one of the new ministry, and Berthier, his son-in-law, who had accepted the office of intendant of Paris. Their heads were stuck upon spikes, and carried about the city; and it is upon this mode of punishment that Mr. Burke builds a great part of his tragic scenes. . . .

These outrages are not the effect of the principles of the revolution, but of the degraded mind that existed before the revolution, and which the revolution is calculated to reform. Place them then to their proper cause, and take the reproach of them to your own side. . . .

Mr. Burke, with his usual outrage, abuses the *Declaration of the Rights of Man,* published by the National Assembly of France, as the basis on which the constitution of France is built. This he calls "paltry and blurred sheets of paper about the rights of man."

Does Mr. Burke mean to deny that *man* has any rights? If he does, then he must mean that there are no such things as rights any where, and that he has none himself; for who is there in the world but man? But if Mr. Burke means to admit that man has rights, the question then will be, what are those rights, and how came man by them originally?

The error of those who reason by precedents drawn from antiquity, respecting the rights of man, is that they do not go far enough into antiquity. They do not go the whole way. They stop in some of the intermediate stages of an hundred or a thousand years, and produce what was then done as a rule for the present day. This is no authority at all. If we travel still further into antiquity, we ... shall come to the time when man came from the hand of his Maker. What was he then? Man. Man was his high and only title, and a higher cannot be given him. . . .

The Mosaic account of the Creation, whether taken as divine authority or merely historical, is full to this point *the unity or equality of man*. The expressions admit of no controversy. "And God said, let us make man in our own image. In the image of God created he him; male and female created he them." The distinction of sexes is pointed out, but no other distinction is even implied. If this be not divine authority, it is at least historical authority, and shows that the equality of man, so far from being a modern doctrine, is the oldest upon record. . . .

It is not among the least of the evils of the present existing governments in all parts of Europe, that man, considered as man, is thrown back to a vast distance from his Maker, and the artificial chasm filled up by a succession of barriers, or a sort of turnpike gates, through which he has to pass.

I will quote Mr. Burke's catalogue of barriers that he has set up between man and his Maker. Putting himself in the character of a herald, he says—"We fear God—we look with *awe* to kings—with affection to parliaments—with duty to magistrates—with reverence to priests, and with respect to nobility." . . .

The duty of man is not a wilderness of turnpike gates, through which he is to pass by tickets from one to the other. It is plain and simple, and consists but of two points. His duty to God, which every man must feel; and with respect to his neighbor, to do as he would be done by. . . .

Hitherto we have spoken only (and that but in part) of the natural rights of man. We have now to consider the civil rights of man, and to show how the one originates from the other. Man did not enter into society to become *worse* than he was before, nor to have fewer rights than he had before, but to have those rights better secured. His natural rights are the foundation of all his civil rights. . . .

In casting our eyes over the world, it is extremely easy to distinguish the governments which have arisen out of society, or out of the social compact, from those which have not: but to place this in a clearer light than what a single glance may afford, it will be proper to take a review of the several sources from which the governments have arisen, and on which they have been founded.

They may be all comprehended under three heads. First, superstition. Secondly, power. Thirdly, the common interests of society, and the common rights of man.

The first was a government of priestcraft, the second of conquerors, and the third of reason.

When a set of artful men pretended, through the medium of oracles, to hold intercourse with the Deity, as familiarly as they now march up the back-stairs in European courts, the world was completely under the government of superstition. The oracles were consulted, and whatever they were made to say, became the law; and this sort of government lasted as long as this sort of superstition lasted.

After these a race of conquerors arose, whose government, like that of William the Conqueror, was founded in power, and the sword assumed the name of a sceptre. Governments thus established, last as long as the power to support them lasts; but that they might avail themselves of every engine in their favor, they united fraud to force, and set up an idol which they called *Divine Right*. . . .

We have now to review the governments which arise out of society, in contradistinction to those which arose out of superstition and conquest.

It has been thought a considerable advance toward establishing the principles of freedom, to say, that government is a compact between those who govern and those who are governed: but this cannot be true, because it is putting the effect before the cause; for as a man must have existed before governments existed, there necessarily was a time when governments did not exist, and consequently there could originally exist no governments to form such a compact with.

The fact therefore must be, that the *individuals themselves*, each in his own personal and sovereign right, *entered into a compact with each other* to produce a government: and this is the only mode in which governments have a right to arise, and the only principle on which they have a right to exist. . . . The constitution of a country is not the act of its government, but of the people constituting a government. . . .

Can then Mr. Burke produce the English Constitution? If he cannot, we may fairly conclude, that though it has been so much talked about, no such thing as a constitution exists, or ever did exist, and consequently that the people have yet a constitution to form. Mr. Burke will not, I presume, deny the position I have already advanced; namely, that governments arise, either *out* of the people, or *over* the people. The English government is one of those which arose out of a conquest, and not out of society, and consequently it arose over the people; and though it has been much modified from the opportunity of circumstances since the time of William the Conqueror, the country has never yet regenerated itself, and is therefore without a constitution. . . .

The authority of the present [National] Assembly [of France] is different to what the authority of future assemblies will be. The authority of the present one is to form a constitution; the authority of future assemblies will be to legislate according to the principles and forms prescribed in that constitution; and if experience should hereafter show that alterations, amendments, or additions are necessary, the constitution will point out the mode by which such things shall be done, and not leave it to the discretionary power of the future government. . . .

The Constitution of France says, that every man who pays a tax of sixty *sous* per annum (2s. and 6d. English) is an elector. What article will Mr. Burke place against this? Can any thing be more limited, and at the same time more capricious, than what the qualifications are in England? . . .

The French Constitution says, that the number of representatives for any place shall be in a ratio to the number of taxable inhabitants or electors. What article will Mr. Burke place against this? The county of Yorkshire, which contains near a million souls, sends two county members; and so does the county of Rutland, which contains not a hundredth part of that number. . . .

The French Constitution says, there shall be no game laws; that the farmer on whose land wild game shall be found (for it is by the produce of those lands they are fed) shall have a right to what he can take. That there shall be no monopolies of any kind, that all trades shall be free, and every man free to follow any occupation by which he can procure an honest livelihood, and in any place, town, or city, throughout the nation. What will Mr. Burke say to this? . . .

The French Constitution says, *there shall be no titles*; and of consequence, all that class of equivocal generation, which in some countries is called *"aristocracy,"* and in others *"nobility,"* is done away, and the *peer* is exalted into *man*.

Titles are but nicknames, and every nickname is a title. The thing is perfectly harmless in itself, but it marks a sort of foppery in the human character which degrades it. . . .

The French Constitution has reformed the condition of the clergy. It has raised the income of the lower and middle classes, and taken from the higher. None is now less than twelve hundred *livres* (fifty pounds sterling), nor any higher than about two or three thousand pounds. What will Mr. Burke place against this? . . .

The French Constitution has abolished tithes, that source of perpetual discontent between the tithe-holder and the parishioner. . . .

The French Constitution hath abolished or renounced *toleration*, and *intolerance* also, and hath established UNIVERSAL RIGHT OF CONSCIENCE. . . .

Persecution is not an original feature in *any* religion; but it is always the strongly marked feature of all law-religions, or religions established by law. Take away the law-establishment, and every religion reassumes its original benignity. In America, a Catholic priest is a good citizen, a good character, and a good neighbor; an Episcopal minister is of the same description: and this proceeds, independently of the men, from there being no law-establishment in America. . . .

By the French Constitution, the nation is always named before the king. The third article of the Declaration of Rights says, *"The nation is essentially the source* (or fountain) *of all sovereignty."* Mr. Burke argues, that, in England, a king is the fountain— that he is the fountain of all honor. . . . In contemplating the French Constitution, we see in it a rational order of things. . . .

One of the first works of the National Assembly, instead of vindictive proclamations, as has been the case with other governments, published a Declaration of the Rights of Man, as the basis on which the new Constitution was to be built, and which is here subjoined.

Declaration of the Rights of Man and of Citizens

By the National Assembly of France

The representatives of the people of FRANCE, *formed into a* NATIONAL ASSEMBLY, considering that ignorance, neglect, or contempt of human rights, are the sole causes of public misfortunes and corruptions of government, have resolved to set forth in a solemn declaration, these natural, imprescriptible, and unalienable rights; . . .

I. *Men are born, and always continue, free, and equal in respect of their rights. Civil distinctions, therefore, can be founded only on public utility.*

II. *The end of all political associations, is, the preservation of the natural and imprescriptible rights of man; and these rights are liberty, property, security, and resistance of oppression.*

III. *The nation is essentially the source of all sovereignty; nor can any* INDIVIDUAL, *or* ANY BODY OF MEN, *be entitled to any au-*

thority which is not expressly derived from it.

IV. Political liberty consists in the power of doing whatever does not injure another. The exercise of the natural rights of every man has no other limits than those which are necessary to secure to every *other* man the free exercise of the same rights; and these limits are determinable only by the law.

V. The law ought to prohibit only actions hurtful to society. What is not prohibited by the law, should not be hindered; nor should any one be compelled to that which the law does not require.

VI. The law is an expression of the will of the community. All citizens have a right to concur, either personally, or by their representatives, in its formation. It should be the same to all, whether it protects or punishes; and *all being equal in its sight, are equally eligible to all honors, places, and employments, according to their different abilities, without any other distinction than that created by their virtues and talents.* . . . [Eleven additional articles follow.]

. . . We see the solemn and majestic spectacle of a nation opening its commission, under the auspices of its Creator, to establish a government; a scene so new, and so transcendently unequalled by any thing in the European world, that the name of a revolution is diminutive of its character, and it rises into a regeneration of man.

What are the present governments of Europe, but a scene of iniquity and oppression? What is that of England? Do not its own inhabitants say? It is a market where every man has his price, and where corruption is common traffic, at the expense of a deluded people? No wonder, then, that the French Revolution is traduced. . . .

Notwithstanding the nonsense, for it deserves not better name, that Mr. Burke has asserted about hereditary rights, and hereditary succession, and that a nation has not a right to form a government for itself; it happened to fall in his way to give some account of what government is. *"Government,"* say he, *"is a contrivance of human wisdom."*

Admitting that government is a contrivance of human *wisdom*, it must necessarily follow, that hereditary succession, and hereditary rights (as they are called), can make no part of it, because it is impossible to make wisdom hereditary; and on the other hand, *that* cannot be a wise contrivance, which in its operation may commit the government of a nation to the wisdom of an idiot. The ground which Mr. Burke now takes, is fatal to every part of his cause. . . .

When once any object has been seen, it is impossible to put the mind back to the same condition it was in before it saw it. Those who talk of a counter-revolution in France show how little they understand of man. . . .

As the present generation of people in England did not make the government, they are not accountable for its defects; but that sooner or later it must come into their hands to undergo a national reformation, is as certain as that the same thing has happened in France. . . .

Reason and Ignorance, the opposites of each other, influence the great bulk of mankind. If either of these can be rendered sufficiently extensive in a country, the machinery of government goes easily on. Reason obeys itself; and Ignorance submits to whatever is dictated to it.

The two modes of government which prevail in the world, are, *First*, government by election and representation: *Secondly*, government by hereditary succession. The former is generally known by the name of republic; the latter by that of monarchy and aristocracy. . . . Government in a well constituted republic, requires no belief from man beyond what his reason can give.

When men are spoken of as kings and subjects, or when government is mentioned under the distinct or combined heads of monarchy, aristocracy, and democracy, what is it that *reasoning* man is to understand by the terms? If there really existed in the world two or more distinct and separate *elements* of human power, we should then see the several origins to which those terms would descriptively apply; but as there is but one species of man, there can be but one element of human power, and that element is man himself. Monarchy, aristocracy, and democracy, are but creatures of imagination; and a thousand such may be contrived, as well as three. . . .

What were formerly called revolutions, were little more than a change of persons, or an alteration of local circumstances. . . . But what we now see in the world, from the revolutions of America and France, is a renovation of the natural order of things, a system of principles as universal as truth and the existence of man, and combining moral with political happiness and national prosperity. . . .

Government on the old system is an assumption of power, for the aggrandizement of itself; on the new, a delegation of power, for the common benefit of society. The former supports itself by keeping up a system of war; the latter promotes a system of peace, as the true means of enriching a nation. The one encourages national prejudices; the other promotes universal society, as the means of universal commerce. The one measures its prosperity, by the quantity of revenue it extorts; the other proves its excellence, by the small quantity of taxes it requires. . . . The representative system takes society and civilization for its basis; nature, reason, and experience for its guide. . . .

Never did so great an opportunity offer itself to England, and to all Europe, as is produced by the two revolutions of America and France. By the former, freedom has a national champion in the western world; and by the latter, in Europe. When another nation shall join France, despotism and bad government will scarcely dare to appear. To use a trite expression, the iron is becoming hot all over Europe. The insulted German and the enslaved Spaniard, the Russ and the Pole are beginning to think. The present age will hereafter merit to be called the Age of Reason, and the present generation will appear to the future as the Adam of a new world. . . .

MARY WOLLSTONECRAFT   **A Vindication of the Rights of Woman (1792)**

The radical British author, inspired by the French Revolution and Thomas Paine, not only pens her own reply to Edmund Burke but goes beyond Paine. Excerpts from her pamphlet follow.

Contending for the rights of woman, my main argument is built on this simple principle, that if she be not prepared by education to become the companion of man, she will stop the progress of knowledge and virtue; for truth must be common to all, or it will be inefficacious with respect to its influence on general practice. And how can woman be expected to co-operate unless she know why she ought to be virtuous? unless freedom strengthen her reason till she comprehend her duty, and see in what manner it is connected with her real good? If children are to be educated to understand the true principle of patriotism, their mother must be a patriot; and the love of mankind, from which an orderly train of virtues spring[s], can only be produced by considering the moral and civil interest of mankind; but the education and situation of woman, at present, shuts her out from such investigations. . . .

Consider, I address you as a legislator, whether, when men contend for their freedom, and to be allowed to judge for themselves respecting their own happiness, it be not inconsistent and unjust to subjugate women, even though you firmly believe that you are acting in the manner best calculated to promote their happiness? Who made man the exclusive judge, if woman partake with him the gift of reason?

In this style, argue tyrants of every denomination, from the weak king to the weak father of a family; they are all eager to crush reason; yet always assert that they usurp its throne only to be useful. Do you not act a similar part, when you *force* all women, by denying them civil and political rights, to remain immured in their families groping in the dark? For surely, Sir, you will not assert, that a duty can be binding which is not founded on reason? If indeed this be their destination, arguments may be drawn from reason: and thus augustly supported, the more understanding women acquire, the more they will be attached to their duty—comprehending it—for unless they comprehend it, unless their morals be fixed on the same immutable principle as those of man, no authority can make them discharge it in a virtuous manner. They may be convenient slaves, but slavery will have its constant effect, degrading the master and the abject dependent.

But, if women are to be excluded, without having a voice, from a participation of the natural rights of mankind, prove first, to ward off the charge of injustice and inconsistency, that they want reason—else this flaw in your NEW CONSTITUTION, will ever shew that man must, in some shape, act like a tyrant, and tyranny, in whatever part of society it rears its brazen front, will ever undermine morality.

I have repeatedly asserted, and produced what appeared to me irrefragable arguments drawn from matters of fact, to prove my assertion, that women cannot, by force, be confined to domestic concerns; for they will, however ignorant, intermeddle with more weighty affairs, neglecting private duties only to disturb, by cunning tricks, the orderly plans of reason which rise above their comprehension. . . .

Let there be then no coercion *established* in society, and the common law of gravity prevailing, the sexes will fall into their proper places. And, now that more equitable laws are forming your citizens, marriage may become more sacred: your young men may choose wives from motives of af-

SOURCE: Mary Wollstonecraft, *A Vindication of the Rights of Woman* (1792). The book was reprinted many times. The passages cited may be found on the following pages of the original edition: 20–25, 34, 54–55, 60–61, 87–89, 409.

fection, and your maidens allow love to root out vanity.

The father of a family will not then weaken his constitution and debate his sentiments, by visiting the harlot, nor forget, in obeying the call of appetite, the purpose for which it was implanted. And, the mother will not neglect her children to practise the arts of coquetry, when sense and modesty secure her the friendship of her husband.

But, till men become attentive to the duty of a father, it is vain to expect women to spend that time in their nursery which they, "wife in their generation, " choose to spend at their glass[4]; for this exertion of cunning is only an instinct of nature to enable them to obtain indirectly a little of that power of which they are unjustly denied a share: for, if women are not permitted to enjoy legitimate rights, they will render both men and themselves vicious, to obtain illicit privileges.

I wish, Sir, to set some investigations of this kind afloat in France; and should they lead to a confirmation of my principles, when your constitution is revised the Rights of Woman may be respected, if it be fully proved that reason calls for this respect, and loudly demands JUSTICE for one half of the human race. . . .

My own sex, I hope, will excuse me, if I treat them like rational creatures, instead of flattering their *fascinating* graces, and viewing them as if they were in a state of perpetual childhood, unable to stand alone. I earnestly wish to point out in what true dignity and human happiness consists—I wish to persuade women to endeavor to acquire strength, both of mind and body, and to convince them that the soft phrases, susceptibility of heart, delicacy of sentiment, and refinement of taste, are almost synonymous with epithets of weakness, and that those beings who are only the objects of pity and that kind of love, which has been termed its sister, will soon become objects of contempt.

Dismissing then those pretty feminine phrases, which the men condescendingly use to soften our slavish dependence, and despising that weak elegancy of mind, exquisite sensibility, and sweet docility of manners, supposed to be the sexual characteristics of the weaker vessel, I wish to shew that elegance is inferior to virtue, that the first object of laudable ambition is to obtain a character as a human being, regardless of the distinction of sex; and that secondary views should be brought to this simple touchstone. . . .

If then women are not a swarm of ephemeron triflers, why should they be kept in ignorance under the specious name of innocence? Men complain, and with reason, of the follies and caprices of our sex, when they do not keenly satirize our headstrong passions and groveling vices.—Behold, I should answer, the natural effect of ignorance! The mind will ever be unstable that has only prejudices to rest on, and the current will run with destructive fury when there are no barriers to break its force. Women are told from their infancy, and taught by the example of their mothers, that a little knowledge of human weakness, justly termed cunning, softness of temper, *outward* obedience, and a scrupulous attention to a puerile kind of propriety, will obtain for them the protection of man; and should they be beautiful, every thing else is needless, for, at least, twenty years of their lives. . . .

Many are the causes that, in the present corrupt state of society, contribute to enslave women by cramping their understandings and sharpening their senses. One, perhaps, that silently does more mischief than all the rest, is their disregard of order.

To do every thing in an orderly manner, is a most important precept, which women, who, generally speaking, receive only a disorderly kind of education, seldom attend to with that degree of exactness that men, who from their infancy are broken into method, observe. This negligent kind of guess-work, (for what other epithet can be used to point out the random exertions of

---

[4]*to spend at their glass:* to look in their mirror

a sort of instinctive common sense, never brought to the test of reason?) prevents their generalizing matters of fact—so they do to-day, what they did yesterday, merely because they did it yesterday.

This contempt of the understanding in early life has more baneful consequences than is commonly supposed; for the little knowledge which women of strong minds attain, is, from various circumstances, of a more desultory kind than the knowledge of men, and it is acquired more by sheer observations on real life, than from comparing what has been individually observed with the results of experience generalized by speculation. Led by their dependent situation and domestic employments more into society, what they learn is rather by snatches; and as learning is with them, in general, only a secondary thing, they do not pursue any one branch with that persevering ardor necessary to give vigor to the faculties, and clearness to the judgment.

. . .

If, I say, for I would not impress by declamation when Reason offers her sober light, if they are really capable of acting like rational creatures, let them not be treated like slaves; or, like the brutes who are dependent on the reason of man, when they associate with him; but cultivate their minds, give them the salutary, sublime curb of principle, and let them attain conscious dignity by feeling themselves only dependent on God. . . .

I love man as my fellow; but his scepter, real, or usurped, extends not to me, unless the reason of an individual demands my homage; and even then the submission is to reason, and not to man. In fact, the conduct of an accountable being must be regulated by the operations of its own reason; or on what foundation rests the throne of God?

It appears to me necessary to dwell on these obvious truths, because females have been insulated, as it were; and, while they have been stripped of the virtues that should clothe humanity, they have been decked with artificial graces that enable them to exercise a short-lived tyranny. Love, in their bosoms, taking place of every nobler passion, their sole ambition is to be fair, to raise emotion instead of inspiring respect; and this ignoble desire, like the servility in absolute monarchies, destroys all strength of character. Liberty is the mother of virtue, and if women be, by their very constitution, slaves, and not allowed to breathe the sharp invigorating air of freedom, they must ever languish like exotics, and be reckoned beautiful flaws in nature.

. . .

Brutal force has hitherto governed the world, and that the science of politics is in its infancy, is evident from philosophers scrupling to give the knowledge most useful to man that determinate distinction.

I shall not pursue this argument any further than to establish an obvious inference, that as found politics diffuse liberty, mankind, including woman, will become more wise and virtuous. . . .

Let woman share the rights and she will emulate the virtues of man; for she must grow more perfect when emancipated.

HANNAH MORE Village Politics (1793)

The prolific author and Sunday School reformer published this pamphlet anonymously during the year that the French Revolution led to the onset of a lengthy era of war between France and Britain (1793–1802, 1803–1815). By means of an imagined dialogue between two village artisans, blacksmith Jack Anvil and mason Tom Hod, Hannah More popularized Burke's ideas among tens of thousands of lower-class Britons.

SOURCE: *The Complete Works of Hannah More* (New York: Harper's, 1835), Vol. I, pp. 357–366, 369.

JACK. What's the matter Tom? Why dost look so dismal?

TOM. Dismal indeed! Well enough I may.

JACK. What! is the old mare dead? or work scarce?

TOM. No, no, work's plenty enough, if a man had but the heart to go to it.

JACK. What book art reading? Why dost look so like a hang-dog?

TOM (*looking on his book*). Cause enough. Why, I find here that I am very unhappy, and very miserable; which I should never have known, if I had not had the good luck to meet with this book. O, 'tis a precious book!

JACK. A good sign, tho'—that you can't find out you're unhappy, without looking into a book for it! What is the matter?

TOM. Matter? Why, I want liberty.

JACK. Liberty! That's bad, indeed! What! has any one fetched a warrant for thee? Come, man, cheer up, I'll be bound for thee. Thou art an honest fellow in the main, tho' thou dost tipple and prate a little too much at the Rose and Crown.

TOM. No, no, I want a new constitution.

JACK. Indeed! Why, I thought thou hadst been a desperate healthy fellow. Send for the doctor directly.

TOM. I'm not sick; I want liberty and equality, and the rights of man.

JACK. O, now I understand thee. What! thou art a leveller and a republican, I warrant?

TOM. I'm a friend of the people. I want a reform.

JACK. Then the shortest way is to mend thyself.

TOM. But I want a *general* reform.

JACK. Then let every one mend one.

TOM. Pooh! I want freedom and happiness, the same as they have got in France.

JACK. What, Tom, we imitate them! We follow the French! Why, they only began all this mischief at first, in order to be just what *we* are already; and what a blessed land must this be, to be in actual possession of all they ever hoped to gain by all their hurly-burly! Imitate them, indeed! Why, I'd

sooner go to the Negroes to get learning, or to the Turks to get religion, than to the French for freedom and happiness.

TOM. What do you mean by that? ar'n't the French free?

JACK. Free, Tom! ay, free with a witness. They are all so free, that there's nobody safe. They make free to rob whom they will, and kill whom they will. If they don't like a man's looks, they make free to hang him, without judge or jury, and the next lamp-post serves for the gallows; so then, they call themselves free, because you see they have no law left to condemn them, and no king to take them up and hang them for it.

TOM. Ah, but, Jack, didn't their king formerly hang people for nothing, too? and besides, were not they all Papists before the revolution?

JACK. Why, true enough, they had but a poor sort of religion; but bad is better than none, Tom. And so was the government bad enough too; for they could clap an innocent man into prison, and keep him there too, as long as they would, and never say, with your leave, or by your leave, gentlemen of the jury. But what's all that to us?

TOM. To us! Why, don't our governors put many of our poor folks in prison against their will? What are all the jails for? Down with the jails, I say! all men should be free.

JACK. Harkee, Tom, a few rogues in prison keep the rest in order, and then honest men go about their business in safety, afraid of nobody; that's the way to be free. And let me tell thee, Tom, thou and I are tried by our peers as much as a lord is. Why, the *king* can't send me to prison, if I do no harm; and if I do, there's reason good why I should go there. I may go to law with Sir John at the great castle yonder; and he no more dares lift his little finger against me than if I were his equal. A lord is hanged for hanging matter, as thou or I should be; and if it be any comfort to thee, I myself remember a peer of the realm being hanged for killing his man, just the same as the man would have been for killing *him*.[5]

---

[5]*A peer . . . for killing him:* refers to the 1760 case of Lord Ferrers, found guilty by the House of Lords of killing his steward and hanged for the crime

TOM. A lord! Well, that is some comfort, to be sure,—But have you read the "Rights of Man"?

JACK. No, not I; I had rather by half read the "Whole Duty of Man." I have but little time for reading, and such as I should therefore only read a bit of the best. . . . I'll tell thee a story. When Sir John married, my lady, who is a little fantastical, and likes to do every thing like the French, begged him to pull down yonder fine old castle, and build it up in her frippery way. "No, " says Sir John; "what! shall I pull down this noble building, raised by the wisdom of my brave ancestors; which outstood the civil wars, and only underwent a little needful repair at the Revolution; a castle which all my neighbors come to take a pattern by—shall I pull it all down, I say, only because there may be a dark closet, or an awkward passage, or an inconvenient room or two in it? Our ancestors took time for what they did. They understood foundation work; no running up your little slight lath-and-plaster buildings, which are up in a day, and down in a night." My lady mumped and grumbled; but the castle was let stand, and a glorious building it is; tho' there may be a trifling fault or two, and tho' a few decays want stopping; so now and then they mend a little thing, and they'll go on mending, I dare say, as they have leisure, to the end of the chapter, if they are let alone. But no pull-me-down works. What is it you are crying out for, Tom?

TOM. Why, for a perfect government.

JACK. You might as well cry for the moon. There's nothing perfect in this world, take my word for it: tho' Sir John says, we come nearer to it than any country in the world ever did.

TOM. I don't see why we are to work like slaves, while others roll about in their coaches, feed on the fat of the land, and do nothing.

JACK. My little maid brought home a little story-book from the charity-school t'other day, in which was a bit of a fable about the belly and the limbs. The hands said, "I won't work any longer to feed this lazy belly, who sits in state like a lord, and does nothing." Said the feet, "I won't walk and tire myself to carry him about; let him shift for himself;" so said all the members; just as your levellers and republicans do now. And what was the consequence? Why, the belly was pinched, to be sure, and grew thin upon it; but the hands and the feet, and the rest of the members, suffered so much for want of their old nourishment, which the belly had been all the time administering, while they accused him of sitting in idle state, that they all fell sick, pined away, and would have died, if they had not come to their senses just in time to save their lives, as I hope all you will do. . . .

TOM. Well, I know what's what, as well as another; and I'm as fit to govern—

JACK. No, Tom, no. You are indeed as good as another man, seeing you have hands to work, and a soul to be saved. But are all men fit for all kinds of things? Solomon says, "How can he be wise, whose talk is of oxen?" Every one in his way. I am a better judge of a horse-shoe than Sir John; but he has a deal better notion of state affairs than I; and I can no more do without his employ than he can do without my farriery. Besides, few are so poor, but they may get a vote for a Parliament-man; and so, you see the poor have as much share in the government as they well know how to manage.

TOM. But I say all men are equal. Why should one be above another?

JACK. If that's thy talk, Tom, thou dost quarrel with Providence, and not with government. For the woman is below her husband, and the children are below their mother, and the servant is below his master.

TOM. But the subject is not below the king; all kings are "crowned ruffians"; and all governments are wicked. For my part, I'm resolved I'll pay no more taxes to any of them.

JACK. Tom, Tom, if thou didst go oftener to church, thou wouldst know where it is said, "Render unto Caesar the things that are Caesar's"; and also, "Fear God, honor the king." *Your* book tells you that we need obey no government but that of the people; and that we may fashion and alter the government according to our whimseys: but *mine* tells me, "Let every one be subject to the higher powers, for all power is of God; the powers that be, are ordained of God; whosoever, therefore, resisteth the power, resisteth the ordinance of God."

TOM. I say we shall never be happy, till we do as the French have done.

JACK. The French and we contending for liberty, Tom, is just as if thou and I were to pretend to run a race; thou to set out from the starting-post when I am in already; thou to have all the ground to travel, when I have reached the end. Why, we've got it, man! we've no race to run! we're there already! . . .

TOM. I don't see, for all that, why one man is to ride in his coach-and-six, while another mends the highway for him.

JACK. I don't see why the man in the coach is to drive over the man on foot, or hurt a hair of his head, any more than you. And as to our great folks, that you levellers have such a spite against, I don't pretend to say they are a bit better than they should be; but that's no affair of mine; let them look to that; they'll answer for that in another place. To be sure, I wish they'd set us a better example about going to church, and those things; but still *hoarding's* not the sin of the age; they don't lock up their *money*—away it goes, and every body's the better for it. They do spend too much, to be sure, in feastings and fandangoes; and so far from commending them for it, if I was a parson, I'd go to work with 'em, but it should be in another kind of way; but as I am only a poor tradesman, why, 'tis but bringing more grist to my mill. It all comes among the people. Their very extravagance, for which, as I said before, their parsons should be at them, is a fault by which, as poor men, we are benefited; so you cry out just in the wrong place. Their coaches, and their furniture, and their buildings, and their planting, employ a power of tradesmen and laborers. Now, in this village, what should we do without the castle? Tho' my lady is too rantipolish, and flies about all summer to hot water and cold water, and fresh water and salt water, when she ought to stay at home

with Sir John; yet when she does come down, she brings such a deal of gentry, that I have more horses than I can shoe, and my wife more linen than she can wash. Then all our grown children are servants in the family, and rare wages they have got. Our little boys get something every day by weeding their gardens, and the girls learn to sew and knit at Sir John's expense; who sends them all to school of a Sunday, besides.

TOM. Ay, but there's not Sir Johns in every village.

JACK. The more's the pity. But there's other help. 'Twas but last year you broke your leg, and was nine weeks in the Bristol infirmary, where you was taken as much care of as a lord, and your family was maintained all the while by the parish. No poor-rates in France, Tom; and here there's a matter of two million and a half paid for the poor every year, if 'twas but a little better managed.

TOM. Two million and a half!

JACK. Ay, indeed. Not translated into ten-pences, as your French millions are, but twenty good shillings to the pound. But, when this levelling comes about, there will be no infirmaries, no hospitals, no charity-schools, no Sunday-schools, where so many hundred thousand poor souls learn to read the word of God for nothing. For who is to pay for them? *Equality* can't afford it; and those that may be willing won't be able.

TOM. But we shall be one as good as another, for all that.

JACK. Ay, and bad will be the best. But we must work as we do now, and with this difference, that no one will be able to pay us. Tom! I have got the use of my limbs, of my liberty, of the laws, and of my Bible. The two first I take to be my *natural* rights; the two last my *civil* and *religious* rights: these, I take it, are the *true rights of man*, and all the rest is nothing but nonsense, and madness, and wickedness. My cottage is my castle. . . .

TOM. What, then, dost think all the men on our side wicked?

JACK. No—not so, neither. . . . I judge no man, Tom; I hate no man. Even republicans and levellers, I hope, will always enjoy the protection of our laws; though I hope they will never be our law-*makers*. There are many true dissenters, and there are some hollow churchmen; and a good man is a good man, whether his church has got a steeple to it or not. The new–fashioned way of proving one's religion is to *hate* somebody. Now, though some folks pretend that a man's hating a Papist, or a Presbyterian, proves him to be a good *churchman*, it don't prove him to be a good *Christian*, Tom. As much as I hate republican works, I'd scorn to *live* in a country where there was not liberty of conscience, and where every man might not worship God in his own way. Now, that liberty they had not in France; the bible was shut up in an unknown, heathenish tongue [Latin]. While here, thou and I can make as free use of ours as a bishop; can no more be sent to prison unjustly, than the judge who tries us; and

are as much taken care of by the laws as the Parliament-man who makes them. . . .

TOM. And thou art very sure we are not ruined?

JACK. I'll tell thee how we are ruined. We have a king, so loving, that he would not hurt the people if he could: and so kept in, that he could not hurt the people if he would. We have as much liberty as can make us happy, and more trade and riches than allows us to be good. We have the best laws in the world, if they were more strictly enforced; and the best religion in the world, if it was but better followed. While Old England is safe, I'll glory in her, and pray for her; and when she is in danger, I'll fight for her, and die for her.

TOM. And so will I too, Jack, that's what I will. *(Sings)* "O the roast beef of Old England!"

JACK. Thou art an honest fellow, Tom. . . .

7

The Industrial Revolution: Problem or Solution?

During the reigns of King George III and George IV—the years from 1760 to 1830—the life of the British people was affected not only by the American Revolution and the French Revolution but also by a "population explosion" and what traditionally has been called the Industrial Revolution.

The population of England and Wales, which had probably increased by less than 20 percent between 1690 and 1760 (from approximately 5.5 million to approximately 6.5 million), more than doubled during the next seventy years (from that 6.5 million to almost 14 million). Indirectly, this unexpected development inspired in 1798 one of the most influential—and controversial—books of the past three centuries, Thomas Malthus's *Essay on the Principle of Population* (1798, 1807), excerpts from which comprise the first document. Malthus (1766–1834) was an Anglican parson who later spent many years as professor of economics at a college founded to train English East India Company administrators. Although in some respects a disciple of Adam Smith (see Chapter 3) and, like the Enlightenment *philosophes*, eager to seek out fundamental axioms explaining the operations of the natural world, Malthus challenged the disciples of the Enlightenment on the prospect of human improvement, one of their most widely held beliefs. What is, for Malthus, the "fly in the ointment" of human perfectibility? Which solutions to the problem of poverty does Malthus regard as plausible but fallacious? Which solution does he see as theoretically possible though very difficult?

The Industrial Revolution is often discussed independently of either the population explosion or of the era of war with France (1793–1815) with which it coincided, though clearly it did not take place in a demographic or ideological or military vacuum. The Industrial Revolution poses, in any event, one of the oldest and most fundamental of all the problems in historical interpretation that have preoccupied historians of Britain during the past three centuries. As the remaining documents in this chapter illustrate, the questions still debated by historians of our own day were anticipated by direct observers of the process of industrialization.

Historians are generally in agreement as to what happened—that is, the significance of Watt's steam engine as a source of power for cotton

A print by R. Seymour (1830) depicts the prosperity created by factories run by steam engines (note the coin-laden smoke) coexisting with large-scale unemployment, rapacious tax collectors and callous parish relief officers.

mills, ships, railway locomotives, and other machines; the growth of factory towns; the fact that industrialization took place largely under the auspices of private factory owners and investors rather than under the direction of the state. Historians agree also that many examples of human misery may be found in the Britain of the first half of the nineteenth century. At the same time they often disagree as to the reasons for that distress. Were the social ills of the day the result of too much industrialization or of too little? Were phenomena like child labor new, or were they old activities now more concentrated and more visible? Would the process of industrialization have proceeded more smoothly if the state had played an immediate directing role, or would that process have never got under way at all? Even if material standards did not (on average) deteriorate, did the Industrial Revolution widen the gap between the rich and the poor, the powerful and the powerless? Was the Industrial Revolution first and foremost a problem to be ameliorated by parliamentary legislation and to be "solved" by a complete change of social systems or was the Industrial Revolution at bottom a dramatic solution to the "Malthusian dilemma" imposed by population explosion?

John Aikin was a late eighteenth-century physician who took an interest in geography. His book *A Description of . . . Manchester* (1795) is one of the very first to recognize that the unparalleled increase in cotton manufacture was transforming Manchester into Britain's first industrial city. How does Aiken describe the nature of Manchester's expansion? What was its scope?

Though he served for a number of years as a paternalistic factory owner and manager at New Lanark, Scotland, Robert Owen (1771–1859) is better remembered as a pioneer socialist, the inspirer and organizer of model communities, of trade unions, and of cooperative shops and enterprises. Owen's *Observations on the Effects of the Manufacturing System* suggest that by 1815 the "evils" of such a system had in his view come to outweigh the benefits. Why?

The next two selections, "A Petition Against Scribbling Machines" by Yorkshire textile workers (1786) and a "Defense of Machinery" by the wool merchants of Leeds (1791), remind us of some of the chief characteristics of an industrializing society: the machinery and the techniques keep changing; the lives and the work routines of the laboring population require frequent readjustment. Who is right, the cloth makers or the cloth merchants? Either or both?

By the time Dr. James Kay (1804–1877) and Dr. Andrew Ure (1778–1857) wrote about Manchester in the early 1830s, it had become a community of more than 200,000 people, three times larger than the town described by Aikin in 1795. Both Kay and Ure were doctors, and they were describing the same community in the same decade, but their reactions differ dramatically. Kay served as secretary to the Manchester board of health during the cholera epidemic of 1832. Later, he became Assistant Poor Law Commissioner and (as Kay-Shuttleworth) an influential educator. Like Kay, Ure had received his medical education in Scotland, where he also served as professor of chemistry at the University of Glasgow; a pioneer in the scientific education of working men, he was the author of a *Dictionary of Arts, Manufactures, and Mines* (1839). On which aspects of Manchester life do Kay and Ure differ? On which aspects do they agree?

In some respects—as in the large influx of Irish immigrants during the 1820s and 1830s—Manchester was an atypical English city, but young Friedrich Engels (1820–1895) helped make the Manchester experience the basis, indeed the epitome, of the Marxist socialist critique of industrial capitalism. Engels was the son of a successful German textile manufacturer with a branch in Manchester. Already in rebellion against his father, young Engels utilized a six-month visit to Manchester to gather information for a book indicting both industrial society and the British middle class, *The Condition of the Working Class in England in 1844.* The book helped to make Engels the lifelong friend and collaborator of Karl Marx—who became an exile in London after the unsuccessful German Revolution of 1848—and who utilized the work of Engels in his theoretical writings. What is for Engels the most significant consequence of the Industrial Revolution? What are his predictions for the future?

James Wilson (1805–1860) was an English hat manufacturer who in the late 1830s and early 1840s wrote several influential pamphlets advocating a policy of free trade and currency reform. In 1843 he founded and, until a year before his death, he edited *The Economist*, a weekly journal that soon established the reputation it still holds today, that of being the most highly regarded British weekly concerned with financial and commercial trends. In the final document of this chapter, "The First Half of the Nineteenth Century: Progress of the Nation and the Race" (1851), Wilson attempts to stand back from his week-by-week analyses of the British economy in order to take a broader look at the events of the first half of the nineteenth century. How do his assumptions and his approach differ from those of Engels? What type of evidence does he cite to justify a belief in progress?

THOMAS MALTHUS **An Essay on the Principle of Population (1798, 1807)**

A late eighteenth-century clergyman/economist discovers a fundamental flaw in the assumptions on which the thinkers of the Enlightenment have based their confidence in the likelihood of human progress.

The great and unlooked for discoveries that have taken place of late years in natural philosophy . . . have all concurred to lead able men into the opinion, that we were touching upon a period big with the most important changes, changes that would in some measure be decisive of the future fate of mankind.

It has been said, that the great question is now at issue, whether man shall henceforth start forward with accelerated velocity toward illimitable, and hitherto unconceived improvement; or be condemned to a perpetual oscillation between happiness and misery, and after every effort remains still at an immeasurable distance from the wished-for goal. . . .

I have read some of the speculations on the perfectibility of man and of society with great pleasure. I have been warmed and delighted with the enchanting picture which they hold forth. I ardently wish for such happy improvements. But I see great, and, to my understanding, unconquerable difficulties in the way to them. These difficulties it is my present purpose to state; declaring, at the same time, that so far from exulting in them, as a cause of triumphing over the friends of innovation, nothing

would give me greater pleasure than to see them completely removed. . . .

I think I may fairly make two postulata.

First, That food is necessary to the existence of man.

Secondly, That the passion between the sexes is necessary, and will remain nearly in its present state.

These two laws ever since we have had any knowledge of mankind, appear to have been fixed laws of our nature; and, as we have not hitherto seen any alteration in them, we have no right to conclude that they will ever cease to be what they are now, without an immediate act of power in that Being who first arranged the system of the universe; and for the advantage of his creatures, still executes, according to fixed laws, all its various operations. . . .

Assuming, then, my postulata as granted, I say, that the power of population is indefinitely greater than the power in the earth to produce subsistence for man.

Population, when unchecked, increases in a geometrical ratio. Subsistence only increases in an arithmetical ratio. A slight acquaintance with numbers will show the immensity of the first power in comparison of the second.

SOURCE: These excerpts are taken from *An Essay on the Principle of Population*, Chap. I of original (1798) edition; and from Book I, Chaps. I and II; Book III, Chap. V; and Book IV, Chap. III of the fourth edition (London, 1807).

By that law of our nature which makes food necessary to the life of man, the effects of these two unequal powers must be kept equal.

This implies a strong and constantly operating check on population from the difficulty of subsistence. This difficulty must fall some where; and must necessarily be severely felt by a large portion of mankind.

Through the animal and vegetable kingdoms, nature has scattered the seeds of life abroad with the most profuse and liberal hand. She has been comparatively sparing in the room, and the nourishment necessary to rear them. The germs of existence contained in this spot of earth, with ample food, and ample room to expand it, would fill millions of worlds in the course of a few thousand years. Necessity, that imperious, all-pervading law of nature, restrains them within the prescribed bounds. The race of plants, and the race of animals shrink under this great restrictive law. And the race of man cannot, by any efforts of reason, escape from it. Among plants and animals its effects are waste of seed, sickness, and premature death. Among mankind, misery and vice. The former, misery, is an absolutely necessary consequence of it. Vice is a highly probable consequence, and we therefore see it abundantly prevail; but it ought not, perhaps, to be called an absolutely necessary consequence. The ordeal of virtue is to resist all temptation to evil.

This natural inequality of two powers of population, and of production in the earth, and that great law of our nature which must constantly keep their effects equal, form the great difficulty that to me appears insurmountable in the way to perfectibility of society. All other arguments are of slight and subordinate consideration in comparison of this. I see no way by which man can escape from the weight of this law which pervades all animated nature. No fancied equality, no agrarian regulations in their utmost extent, could remove the pressure of it even for a single century. And it appears, therefore, to be decisive against the possible existence of a society, all the members of which should live in ease, happiness, and compara-

tive leisure; and feel no anxiety about providing the means of subsistence for themselves and families.

Consequently, if the premises are just, the argument is conclusive against the perfectibility of the mass of mankind. . . .

The ultimate check to population appears then to be a want of food arising necessarily from the different ratios according to which population and food increase. But this ultimate check is never the immediate check, except in cases of actual famine.

The immediate check may be stated to consist in all those customs, and all those diseases which seem to be generated by a scarcity of the means of subsistence; and all those causes, independent of this scarcity, whether of a moral or physical nature, which tend prematurely to weaken and destroy the human frame.

These checks to population, which are constantly operating with more or less force in every society, and keep down the number to the level of the means of subsistence, may be classed under two general heads—the preventive and the positive checks.

The preventive check, as far as it is voluntary, is peculiar to man, and arises from that distinctive superiority in his reasoning faculties which enables him to calculate distant consequences. . . . But man cannot look around him and see the distress which frequently presses upon those who have large families; he cannot contemplate his present possessions or earnings, which he now nearly consumes himself and calculate the amount of each share, when with very little addition they must be divided, perhaps, among seven or eight, without feeling a doubt whether, if he follow the bent of his inclinations, he may be able to support the offspring which he will probably bring into the world. . . .

If this restraint [does] not produce vice, it is undoubtedly the least evil that can arise from the principle of population. . . .

When this restraint produces vice, the evils which follow are but too conspicuous. A promiscuous intercourse to such a degree as to prevent the birth of children seems to lower, in the most marked manner, the dignity of human nature. It cannot be without its effect on men, and nothing can be more obvious than its tendency to degrade the female character, and to destroy all its most amiable and distinguishing characteristics. Add to which, that among those unfortunate females, with which all great towns abound, more real distress and aggravated misery are, perhaps, to be found than in any other department of human life. . . .

The positive checks to population are extremely various, and include every cause, whether arising from vice or misery, which in any degree contributes to shorten the natural duration of human life. Under this head, therefore, may be enumerated all unwholesome occupations, severe labor and exposure to the seasons, extreme poverty, bad nursing of children, great towns, excesses of all kinds, the whole train of common diseases and epidemics, wars, plague, and famine. . . .

In every country some of these checks are, with more or less force, in constant operation; yet, notwithstanding their general prevalence, there are few states in which there is not a constant effort in the population to increase beyond the means of subsistence. This constant effort as constantly tends to subject the lower classes of society to distress, and to prevent any great permanent melioration of their condition.

These effects, in the present state of society, seem to be produced in the following manner. We will suppose the means of subsistence in any country just equal to the easy support of its inhabitants. The constant effort toward population, which is found to act even in the most vicious societies, increases the number of people before the means of subsistence are increased. The food, therefore, which before supported eleven millions, must now be divided among eleven millions and a half. The poor consequently must live much worse, and many of them be reduced to severe distress. The number of laborers also being above the proportion of work in the market, the price of labor must tend to fall, while the

price of provisions would at the same time tend to rise. The laborer therefore must do more work to earn the same as he did before. During this season of distress, the discouragements to marriage and the difficulty of rearing a family are so great, that the progress of population is retarded. In the meantime, the cheapness of labor, the plenty of laborers, and the necessity of an increased industry among them, encourage cultivators to employ more labor upon their land, to turn up fresh soil, and to manure and improve more completely what is already in tillage, till ultimately the means of subsistence may become in the same proportion to the population as at the period from which we set out. The situation of the laborer being then again tolerably comfortable, the restraints to population are in some degree loosened; and, after a short period, the same retrograde and progressive movements, with respect to happiness, are repeated. . . .

To remedy the frequent distresses of the poor, laws to enforce their relief have been instituted; and in the establishment of a general system of this kind England has particularly distinguished herself. But it is to be feared, that, though it may have alleviated a little the intensity of individual misfortune, it has spread the evil over a much larger surface.

It is a subject often started in conversation, and mentioned always as a matter of great surprise, that, notwithstanding the immense sum which is annually collected for the poor in this country, there is still so much distress among them. Some think that the money must be embezzled for private use; others, that the churchwardens and overseers consume the greatest part of it in feasting. All agree, that somehow or other it must be very ill managed. In short, the fact, that even before the late scarcities three millions were collected annually for the poor, and yet that their distresses were not removed, is the subject of continual astonishment. But a man who looks a little below the surface of things would be much more astonished, if the fact were otherwise than it is observed to be; or even if a collection universally of eighteen shillings in the pound, instead of four, were materially to alter it.

Suppose, that by a subscription of the rich the eighteen pence or two shillings, which men earn now, were made up five shillings: it might be imagined, perhaps, that they would then be able to live comfortably, and have a piece of meat every day for their dinner. But this would be a very false conclusion. The transfer of three additional shillings a day to each laborer would not increase the quantity of meat in the country. There is not at present enough for all to have a moderate share. What would then be the consequence? The competition among the buyers in the market of meat would rapidly raise the price from eight pence or nine pence to two or three shillings in the pound, and the commodity would not be divided among many more than it is at present. . . .

It might be said, perhaps, that the increased number of purchasers in every article would give a spur to productive industry, and that the whole produce of the island would be increased. But the spur that these fancied riches would give to population would more than counter-balance it; and the increased produce would have to be divided among a more than proportionably increased number of people.

A collection from the rich of eighteen shillings in the pound, even if distributed in the most judicious manner, would have an effect similar to that resulting from the supposition which I have just made; and no possible sacrifices of the rich, particularly in money, could for any time prevent the recurrence of distress among the lower members of society, whoever they were. Great changes might indeed be made. The rich might become poor, and some of the poor rich: but while the present proportion between population and food continues, a part of the society must necessarily find it difficult to support a family, and this difficulty will naturally fall on the least fortunate members. . . .

[Yet] it does not seem entirely visionary to suppose that, if the true and permanent cause of poverty were clearly explained and forcibly brought home to each man's bosom, it would have some, and perhaps not an inconsiderable influence on his conduct; at least the experiment has never yet been fairly tried. Almost everything that has been hitherto done for the poor has tended, as if with solicitous care, to throw a veil of obscurity over this subject, and to hide from them the true cause of their poverty. When the wages of labor are hardly sufficient to maintain two children, a man marries and has five or six; he of course finds himself miserably distressed. He accuses the insufficiency of the price of labor to maintain a family. He accuses his parish for their tardy and sparing fulfillment of their obligation to assist him. He accuses the avarice of the rich, who suffer him to want what they can so well spare. He accuses the partial and unjust institutions of society, which have awarded him an inadequate share of the produce of the earth. He accuses perhaps the dispensations of Providence, which have assigned to him a place in society so beset with unavoidable distress and dependence. In searching for objects of accusation, he never adverts to the quarter from which his misfortunes originate. The last person that he would think of accusing is himself, on whom in fact the principal blame lies, except so far as he has been deceived by the higher classes of society. . . .

We are not . . . to relax our efforts in increasing the quantity of provisions, but to combine another effort with it; that of keeping the population, when once it has been overtaken, at such a distance behind as to effect the relative proportion which we desire; and thus unite the two grand *desiderata*, a great actual population and a state of society in which abject poverty and dependence are comparatively but little known; two objects which are far from being incompatible.

If we be really serious in what appears to be object of such general research, the mode of essentially and permanently bettering the condition of the poor, we must explain to them the true nature of their situation, and show them that the withholding of the supplies of labor is the only possible way of really raising its price, and that they themselves, being the possessors of this commodity, have alone the power to do this. . . .

JOHN AIKIN A Description of . . . Manchester (1795)

A contemporary observer is surprised by the manner in which Manchester, a small seventeenth-century village, has become a thriving industrial city by the 1790s.

. . . No exertions of the masters or workmen could have answered the demands of trade without the introduction of *spinning machines.*

These were first used by the country people on a confined scale, twelve spindles being thought a great matter; while the awkward posture required to spin on them was discouraging to grown up people, who saw with surprise children from nine to twelve years of age manage them with dexterity, whereby plenty was brought into families formerly overburthened with children, and the poor weavers were delivered from the bondage in which they had lain from the insolence of spinners. . . .

The improvements kept increasing, till the capital engines for twist were perfected, by which thousands of spindles are put in motion by a water wheel, and managed mostly by children, without confusion and with less waste of cotton than by the former methods. But the carding and slubbing preparatory to twisting required a greater range of invention. The first attempts were in carding engines, which are very curious, and now brought to a great degree of perfection; and an engine has been contrived for converting the carded wool to slubbing, by drawing it to about the thickness of candlewick preparatory to throwing it into twist. . . .

These machines exhibit in their construction an aggregate of clock-maker's work and machinery most wonderful to behold. The cotton to be spun is introduced through three sets of rollers, so governed by the clock-work, that the set which first receives the cotton makes so many more revolutions than the next in order, and these more than the last which feed the spindles, that it is drawn out considerably in passing through the rollers; being lastly received by spindles, which have every one on the bobbin a fly like that of a flax wheel; . . .

Upon these machines twist is made of any fineness proper for warps; but as it is drawn length way of the staple, it was not so proper for weft; wherefore on the introduction of fine callicoes and muslins, mules were invented, having a name expressive of their species, being a mixed machinery between jennies and the machines for twisting, and adapted to spin weft as fine as could be desired. . . .

These mules carry often to a hundred and fifty spindles, and can be set to draw weft to an exact fineness up to 150 hanks in the pound, of which muslin has been made, which for a while had a prompt sale; but the flimsiness of its fabric has brought the finer sorts into discredit, and a stagnation of trade damped the sale of the rest. . . .

The prodigious extension of the several branches of the Manchester manufactures has likewise greatly increased the business of several trades and manufactures connected with or dependent upon them. The

SOURCE: From John Aikin, *A Description of the Country From Thirty to Forty Miles Round Manchester* (London, 1795), pp. 167–184.

making of paper at mills in the vicinity has been brought to great perfection, and now includes all kinds, from the strongest parcelling paper to the finest writing sorts, and that on which banker's bills are printed. To the ironmongers shops, which are greatly increased of late, are generally annexed smithies, where many articles are made, even to nails. A considerable iron foundry is established in Salford, in which are cast most of the articles wanted in Manchester and its neighborhood, consisting chiefly of large cast wheels for the cotton machines; cylinders, boilers, and pipes for steam engines; cast ovens, and grates of all sizes. This work belongs to Batemen and Sharrard, gen[tle]men every way qualified for so great an undertaking. Mr. Sharrard is a very ingenious and able engineer, who has improved upon and brought the steam engine to great perfection. . . .

Some few are also erected in this neighborhood by Messrs. Bolton and Watts of Birmingham, who have far excelled all others in their improvement of the steam engine, for which they have obtained a patent, that has been the source of great and deserved emolument. The boilers are generally of plate iron or copper; but some few for the smaller engines are of cast iron. . . .

The tin-plate workers have found additional employment in furnishing many articles for spinning machines; as have also the braziers in casting wheels for the motion-work of the rollers used in them; and the clock-makers in cutting them. Harness-makers have been much employed in making bands for carding engines, and large wheels for the first operation of drawing out the cardings, whereby the consumption of strong curried leather has been much increased. . . .

To this sketch of the progress of the *trade* of Manchester, it will be proper to subjoin some information respecting the condition and manners of its *tradesmen*, the gradual advances to opulence and luxury, and other circumstances of the domestic history of the place, which are in reality some of the most curious and useful subjects of speculation on human life. The following facts and observations have been communicated by an accurate and well-informed inquirer.

The trade of Manchester may be divided into four periods. The first is that, when the manufacturers worked hard merely for a livelihood, without having accumulated any capital. The second is that, when they had begun to acquire little fortunes, but worked as hard, and lived in as plain a manner as before, increasing their fortunes as well by economy as by moderate gains. The third is that, when luxury began to appear, and trade was pushed by sending out riders for orders to every market town in the kingdom. The fourth is the period in which expense and luxury had made a great progress, and was supported by a trade extended by means of riders and factors through every part of Europe. . . .

When the Manchester trade began to extend, the chapmen used to keep gangs of pack-horses, and accompany them to the principal towns with goods in packs, which they opened and sold to shopkeepers, lodging what was unsold in small stores at the inns. The pack-horses brought back sheep's wool, which was bought on the journey, and sold to the makers of worsted yarn at Manchester, or to the clothiers of Rochdale, Saddleworth, and the West-Riding of Yorkshire. On the improvement of turnpike roads waggons were set up, and the pack-horses discontinued; and the chapmen only rode out for orders, carrying with them patterns in their bags. It was during the forty years from 1730 to 1770 that trade was greatly pushed by the practice of sending these riders all over the kingdom, to those towns which before had been supplied from the wholesale dealers in the capital places before mentioned. . . .

Within the last twenty or thirty years the vast increase of foreign trade has caused many of the Manchester manufacturers to travel abroad, and agents or partners to be fixed for a considerable time on the continent, as well as foreigners to reside at Manchester. And the town has now in every respect assumed the style and manners of one of the commercial capitals of Europe. . . .

Robert Owen **Observations on the Effect of the Manufacturing System (1815)**

A paternalistic cotton mill owner looks upon the coming of industrialization as more of a curse than a blessing—unless the government intervenes.

Those who were engaged in the trade, manufactures, and commerce of this country thirty or forty years ago formed but a very insignificant portion of the knowledge, wealth, influence, or population of the Empire.

Prior to that period, Britain was essentially agricultural. But, from that time to the present, the home and foreign trade have increased in a manner so rapid and extraordinary as to have raised commerce to an importance, which it never previously attained in any country possessing so much political power and influence. . . .

This change has been owing chiefly to the mechanical inventions which introduced the cotton trade into this country, and to the cultivation of the cotton tree in America. The wants which this trade created for the various materials requisite to forward its multiplied operations, caused an extraordinary demand for almost all the manufactures previously established, and, of course, for human labor. The numerous fanciful and useful fabrics manufactured from cotton soon became objects of desire in Europe and America: and the consequent extension of the British foreign trade was such as to astonish and confound the most enlightened statesmen both at home and abroad.

The immediate effects of this manufacturing phenomenon were a rapid increase of the wealth, industry, population, and political influence of the British Empire; and by the aid of which it has been enabled to contend for five-and-twenty years against the most formidable military and *immoral* power [France] that the world perhaps ever contained.

These important results, however, great as they really are, have not been obtained without accompanying evils of such a magnitude as to raise a doubt whether the latter do not preponderate over the former.

Hitherto, legislators have appeared to regard manufactures only in one point of view, as a source of national wealth.

The other mighty consequences which proceed from extended manufactures *when left to their natural progress*, have never yet engaged the attention of any legislature. Yet the political and moral effects to which we allude, well deserve to occupy the best faculties of the greatest and the wisest statesmen.

The general diffusion of manufactures throughout a country generates a new character in its inhabitants; and as this character is formed upon a principle quite unfavorable to individual or general happiness, it will produce the most lamentable and permanent evils, unless its tendency be counteracted by legislative interference and direction. . . .

The acquisition of wealth, and the desire which it naturally creates for a continued increase, have introduced a fondness for essentially injurious luxuries among a numerous class of individuals who formerly never thought of them, and they have also generated a disposition which strongly impels its possessors to sacrifice the best feelings of human nature to this love of accumulation. To succeed in this career, the industry of the lower orders, from whose labor this wealth is now drawn, has been carried by new competitors striving against those of longer standing, to a point of real oppression, reducing them by successive changes, as the spirit of competition increased and the ease of acquiring wealth diminished, to a state more wretched than can be imagined by those who have not attentively observed the changes as they have gradually occurred. In consequence, they

SOURCE: From Robert Owen, *Observations on the Effect of the Manufacturing System* (London, 1815).

are at present in a situation infinitely more degraded and miserable than they were before the introduction of these manufactories, upon the success of which their bare subsistence now depends. . . .

The inhabitants of every country are trained and formed by its great leading existing circumstances, and the character of the lower orders in Britain is now formed chiefly by circumstances arising from trade, manufactures, and commerce; and the governing principle of trade, manufactures, and commerce is immediate pecuniary gain, to which on the great scale every other is made to give way. All are sedulously trained to buy cheap and to sell dear; and to succeed in this art, the parties must be taught to acquire strong powers of deception; and thus a spirit is generated through every class of traders, destructive of that open, honest sincerity, without which man cannot make others happy, nor enjoy happiness himself.

Strictly speaking, however, this defect of character ought not to be attributed to the individuals possessing it, but to the overwhelming effect of the system under which they have been trained.

But the effects of this principle of gain, unrestrained, are still more lamentable on the working classes, those who are employed in the operative parts of the manufactures; for most of these branches are more or less unfavorable to the health and morals of adults. Yet parents do not hesitate to sacrifice the well-being of their children by putting them to occupations by which the constitution of their minds and bodies is rendered greatly inferior to what it might and ought to be under a system of common foresight and humanity. . . .

In the manufacturing districts it is common for parents to send their children of both sexes at seven or eight years of age, in winter as well as summer, at six o'clock in the morning, sometimes of course in the dark, and occasionally amidst frost and snow, to enter the manufactories, which are often heated to a high temperature, and contain an atmosphere far from being the most favorable to human life, and in which all those employed in them very frequently continue until twelve o'clock at noon, when an hour is allowed for dinner, after which they return to remain, in a majority of cases, till eight o'clock at night.

The children now find they must labor incessantly for their bare subsistence: they have not been used to innocent, healthy, and rational amusements; they are not permitted the requisite time, if they had been previously accustomed to enjoy them. They know not what relaxation means, except by the actual cessation from labor. They are surrounded by others similarly circumstanced with themselves; and thus passing on from childhood to youth, they become gradually initiated, the young men in particular, but often the young females also, in the seductive pleasures of the pot-house and inebriation: for which their daily hard labor, want of better habits, and the general vacuity of their minds, tend to prepare them. . . .

Such a system of training cannot be expected to produce any other than a population weak in bodily and mental faculties, and with habits generally destructive of their own comforts, of the well-being of those around them, and strongly calculated to subdue all the social affections. Man so circumstanced sees all around him hurrying forward, at a mail-coach speed, to acquire individual wealth, regardless of him, his comforts, his wants, or even his sufferings, except by way of a *degrading parish charity*, fitted only to steel the heart of man against his fellows, or to form the tyrant and the slave. To-day he labors for one master, to-morrow for a second, then for a third, and a fourth, until all ties between employers and employed are frittered down to the consideration of what immediate gain each can derive from the other.

The employer regards the employed as mere instruments of gain, while these acquire a gross ferocity of character, which, if legislative measures shall not be judiciously devised to prevent its increase, and ameliorate the condition of this class, will sooner or later plunge the country into a formidable and perhaps inextricable state of danger.

Yorkshire Cloth Workers **A Petition Against Scribbling Machines (1786)**

Yorkshire cloth workers protest against the introduction of scribbling machines, which separated and straightened wool fibers before spinning.

To the merchants, clothiers and all such as wish well to the staple manufactory of this nation.

The humble ADDRESS and PETITION of thousands, who labor in the cloth manufactory.

SHEWETH, That the scribbling-machines have thrown thousands of your petitioners out of employ, whereby they are brought into great distress, and are not able to procure a maintenance for their families, and deprived them of the opportunity of bringing up their children to labor: We have therefore to request, that prejudice and self-interest may be laid aside, and that you may pay that attention to the following facts, which the nature of the case requires.

The number of scribbling-machines extending about seventeen miles south-west of LEEDS, exceed all belief, being no less than *one hundred and seventy!* and as each machine will do as much work in twelve hours, as ten men can in that time do by hand, (speaking within bounds) and they working night and day, one machine will do as much work in one day as would otherwise employ twenty men.

As we do not mean to assert any thing but what we can prove to be true, we allow four men to be employed at each machine twelve hours, working night and day, will take eight men in twenty-four hours; so that, upon a moderate computation twelve men are thrown out of employ for every single machine used in scribbling; and as it may be supposed the number of machines in all the other quarters together, nearly equal those in the south-west, full four thousand men are left to shift for a living how they can, and must of course fall to the parish, if not timely relieved. Allowing one boy to be bound apprentice from each family out of work, eight thousand hands are

deprived of the opportunity of getting a livelihood.

We therefore hope, that the feelings of humanity will lead those who have it in their power to prevent the use of those machines, to give every discouragement they can to what has a tendency so prejudicial to their fellow-creatures. . . .

We wish to propose a few queries to those who would plead for the further continuance of these machines:

Men of common sense must know, that so many machines in use, take the work from the hands employed in scribbling,—and who did that business before machines were invented.

How are those men, thus thrown out of employ to provide for their families;—and what are they to put their children apprentice to, that the rising generation may have something to keep them at work, in order that they may not be like vagabonds strolling about in idleness? Some say, Begin and learn some other business.—Suppose we do; who will maintain our families, whilst we undertake the arduous task; and when we have learned it, how do we know we shall be any better for all our pains; for by the time we have served our second apprenticeship, another machine may arise, which may take away that business also; so that our families, being half pined whilst we are learning how to provide them with bread, will be wholly so during the period of our third apprenticeship.

But what are our children to do; are they to be brought up in idleness? Indeed as things are, it is no wonder to hear of so many executions; for our parts, though we may be thought illiterate men, our conceptions are, that bringing children up to industry, and keeping them employed, is the way to keep them from falling into those

SOURCE: The notice was printed in the *Leeds Intelligencer* and *Leeds Mercury* on June 13, 1786.

crimes, which an idle habit naturally leads to.

These things impartially considered will we hope, be strong advocates in our favor; and we conceive that men of sense, religion and humanity, will be satisfied of the reasonableness, as well as necessity of this ad-

dress, and that their own feelings will urge them to espouse the cause of us and our families—

Signed, in behalf of THOUSANDS, by
JOSEPH HEPWORTH   THOMAS LOBLEY
ROBERT WOOD   THOS. BLACKBURN.

LEEDS WOOLLEN MERCHANTS **In Defense of Machinery (1791)**

The cloth merchants of Leeds justify the introduction and the utilization of new machines.

Being informed that various kinds of MACHINERY, for the better and more expeditious DRESSING OF WOOLLEN-CLOTH, have been lately invented, that many such machines are already made and set to work in different parts of this county, and that great numbers more are contracted for, to be used in the dressing of cloth in other parts of Yorkshire, and in the counties of Lancaster, Derby, Chester, Wilts and Gloucester, thought it necessary to meet together on the eighteenth of October, to take into their most serious consideration what steps were needful to be taken, to prevent the merchants and cloth-dressers in other parts, from diminishing the staple trade of this town, by the enjoyment of superior implements in their business.

At the said meeting, attended by almost every merchant in the town, the above facts did clearly appear, and after a discussion of the merits of various inventions, and the improvement in dressing likely to be derived from them, it appeared to them all, absolutely necessary that this town should partake of the benefit of all sorts of improvements that are, or can be made in the dressing of their cloths, to prevent the decline of that business, of which the town of Leeds has for ages had the greatest share, and which from its local advantages, we presume may be maintained and increased,

provided the merchants, and dressers of cloth, in Leeds, do not neglect to use the best means in their power, of performing their work to the utmost perfection.

In order that the matter should be undertaken on a plan to afford every possible information, a committee was then appointed for the purpose of obtaining one of each of the different machines now in use, on the most approved construction, and a subscription was entered into for defraying the expense thereof, and to enable them to obtain an eligible situation for erecting and working them, for the inspection of the trade, previous to their being brought into general use.

At a time when the people, engaged in every other manufacture in the kingdom, are exerting themselves to bring their work to market at reduced prices, which can alone be effected by the aid of machinery, it certainly is not necessary that the cloth merchants of Leeds, who depend chiefly on a foreign demand, where they have for competitors the manufacturers of other nations, whose taxes are few, and whose manual labor is only half the price it bears here, should have occasion to defend a conduct, which has for its aim the advantage of the kingdom in general, and of the cloth trade in particular; yet anxious to prevent misrepresentations, which have usually attended

SOURCE: The proclamation, issued as a broadside in 1791, is reprinted from W. B. Crump, ed., *The Leeds Woollen Industry, 1780–1820* (Leeds: The Council, Thoresby Society, 1931). Reproduced by kind permission of The Thoresby Society, Leeds.

the introduction of the most useful machines, they wish to remind the inhabitants of this town, of the advantages derived to every flourishing manufacture from the application of machinery; they instance that of cotton in particular, which in its internal and foreign demand is nearly alike to our own, and has in a few years by the means of machinery advanced to its present importance, and is still increasing.

If then by the use of machines, the manufacture of cotton, an article which we import, and are supplied with from other countries, and which can every where be procured on equal terms, has met with such amazing success, may not greater advantages be reasonably expected from cultivating to the utmost the manufacture of wool, the produce of our own island, an article in demand in all countries, and almost the universal cloathing [sic] of mankind?

In the manufacture of woollens, the scribbling mill, the spinning frame, and the fly shuttle, have reduced manual labor nearly one-third, and each of them at its first intro-

duction carried an alarm to the work people, yet each has contributed to advance the wages and to increase the trade, so that if an attempt was now made to deprive us of the use of them, there is no doubt, but every person engaged in the business, would exert himself to defend them.

From these premises, we the undersigned merchants, think it a duty we owe to ourselves, to the town of Leeds, and to the nation at large, to declare that we will protect and support the free use of the proposed improvements in cloth-dressing, by every legal means in our power; and if after all, contrary to our expectations, the introduction of machinery should for a time occasion a scarcity of work in the cloth dressing trade, we have unanimously agreed to give a preference to such workmen as are now settled inhabitants of this parish, and who give no opposition to the present scheme.

APPLEBY & SAWYER
BERNARD BISCHOFF & SONS
[and 59 other names]

JAMES KAY **The Moral and Physical Condition of the Working Classes . . . in Manchester (1832)**

Dr. Kay investigates conditions in the cotton-manufacturing capital of the world and is discouraged by his findings.

The township of Manchester chiefly consists of dense masses of houses, inhabited by the population engaged in the great manufactories of the cotton trade. Some of the central divisions are occupied by warehouses and shops, and a few streets by the dwellings of some of the more wealthy inhabitants; but the opulent merchants chiefly reside in the country, and even the superior servants of their establishments inhabit the suburbal [sic] townships. Manchester, properly so called, is chiefly in-

habited by shopkeepers and the laboring classes. Those districts where the poor dwell are of very recent origin. The rapid growth of the cotton manufacture has attracted hither operatives from every part of the kingdom, and Ireland has poured forth the most destitute of her hordes to supply the constantly increasing demand for labor. This immigration has been, in one important respect, a serious evil. The Irish have taught the laboring classes of this country a pernicious lesson. The system of

SOURCE: From James Phillips Kay, *The Moral and Physical Condition of the Working Classes Employed in the Cotton Manufacture in Manchester* (London: Ridgeway, 1832), pp. 6–12, 19, 25–27, 42–43, 49, 55–56, 71–72.

cottier farming,[1] the demoralization and barbarism of the people, and the general use of the potato as the chief article of food, have encouraged the population in Ireland more rapidly than the available means of subsistence have increased. Debased alike by ignorance and pauperism, they have discovered, with the savage, what is the minimum of the means of life, upon which existence may be prolonged. They have taught this fatal secret to the population of this country. . . . Instructed in the fatal secret of subsisting on what is barely necessary to life, the laboring classes have ceased to entertain a laudable pride in furnishing their houses, and in multiplying the decent comforts which minister to happiness. What is superfluous to the mere exigencies of nature, is too often expended at the tavern; and for the provision of old age and infirmity, they too frequently trust either to charity, to the support of their children, or to the protection of the Poor Laws.

When the example is considered in connexion with the unremitting labor of the whole population engaged in the various branches of the cotton manufacture, our wonder will be less excited by their fatal demoralization. Prolonged and exhausting labor, continued from day to day, and from year to year, is not calculated to develop the intellectual or moral faculties of man. The dull routine of a ceaseless drudgery, in which the same mechanical process is incessantly repeated, resembles the torment of Sisyphus—the toil, like the rock, recoils perpetually on the wearied operative. The mind gathers neither stores nor strength from the constant extension and retraction of the same muscles. The intellect slumbers in supine inertness; but the grosser parts of our nature attain a rank development. To condemn man to such severity of toil is, in some measure, to cultivate in him the habits of an animal. He becomes reckless. He disregards the distinguishing appetites and habits of his species. He neglects the comforts and delicacies of life. He lives in squalid wretchedness, on meagre food, and expends his superfluous gains on debauchery.

The population employed in the cotton factories rises at five o'clock in the morning, works in the mills from six till eight o'clock, and returns home for half an hour to forty minutes to breakfast. This meal generally consists of tea or coffee with a little bread. Oatmeal porridge is sometimes, but of late rarely used, and chiefly by the men; but the stimulus of tea is preferred, and especially by the women. The tea is almost always of a bad, and sometimes of a deleterious quality, the infusion is weak, and little or no milk is added. The operatives return to the mills and workshops until twelve o'clock, when an hour is allowed for dinner. Amongst those who obtain the lowest rates of wages this meal generally consists of boiled potatoes. The mess of potatoes is put into one large dish; melted lard and butter are poured upon them, and a few pieces of fried fat bacon are sometimes mingled with them, and but seldom a little meat. Those who obtain better wages, or families whose aggregate income is larger, add a greater proportion of animal food to this meal, at least three times a week; but the quantity consumed by the laboring population is not great. The family sits round the table, and each rapidly appropriates his portion on a plate, or, they all plunge their spoons into the dish, and with an animal eagerness satisfy the cravings of their appetite. At the expiration of the hour, they are all again employed in the workshops or mills, where they continue until seven o'clock or a later hour, when they generally again indulge in the use of tea, often mingled with spirits accompanied by a little bread. Oatmeal or potatoes are however taken by some a second time in the evening.

The comparatively innutritious qualities of these articles of diet are most evident. We are, however, by no means prepared to say that an individual living in a healthy

---

[1]*cottier farming:* a custom whereby a landlord rented small plots for a year to the tenant farmers who placed the highest bids

atmosphere, and engaged in active employment in the open air, would not be able to continue protracted and severe labor, without any suffering, whilst nourished by this food. . . . But the population nourished on this aliment is crowded into one dense mass, in cottages separated by narrow, unpaved, and almost pestilential streets; in an atmosphere loaded with the smoke and exhalations of a large manufacturing city. The operatives are congregated in rooms and workshops during twelve hours in the day, in an enervating, heated atmosphere, which is frequently loaded with dust or filaments of cotton, and impure from constant respiration, or from other causes. They are engaged in an employment which absorbs their attention, and unremittingly employs their physical energies. They are drudges who watch the movements, and assist the operations, of a mighty material force, which toils with an energy ever unconscious of fatigue. The persevering labor of the operative must rival the mathematical precision, the incessant motion, and the exhaustless power of the machine. . . .

The artisan has neither moral dignity nor intellectual nor organic strength to resist the seductions of appetite. His wife and children, too frequently subjected to the same process, are unable to cheer his remaining moments of leisure. Domestic economy is neglected, domestic comforts are unknown. A meal of the coarsest food is prepared with heedless haste, and devoured with equal precipitation. Home has no other relation to him than that of shelter— few pleasures are there—it chiefly presents to him a scene of physical exhaustion, from which he is glad to escape. Himself impotent to all the distinguishing aims of his species, he sinks into sensual sloth, or revels in more degrading licentiousness. His house is ill-furnished, uncleanly, often ill ventilated, perhaps damp; his food, through want of forethought and domestic economy, is meagre and innutritious; he is debilitated and hypochondriacal, and falls the victim of dissipation.

These artisans are frequently subject to . . . disease. . . . We cannot wonder that the wretched victim . . . invited by those haunts of misery and crime, the gin shop and the tavern, as he passes to his daily labor, should endeavor to cheat his sufferings of a few moments, by the false excitement procured by ardent spirits; or that the exhausted artisan, driven by ennui and discomfort from his squalid home, should strive, in the delirious dreams of a continued debauch, to forget the remembrance of his reckless improvidence, of the destitution, hunger, and uninterrupted toil, which threaten to destroy the remaining energies of his enfeebled constitution. . . .

Some idea of the want of cleanliness prevalent in their habitations, may be obtained from the report of the number of houses requiring white-washing; but this column fails to indicate their gross neglect of order, and absolute filth. Much less can we obtain satisfactory statistical results concerning the want of furniture, especially of bedding, and of food, clothing, and fuel. In these respects, the habitations of the Irish are the most destitute. They can scarcely be said to be furnished. They contain one or two chairs, a mean table, the most scanty culinary apparatus, and one or two beds, loathsome with filth. A whole family is sometimes accommodated in a single bed, and sometimes a heap of filthy straw and a covering of old sacking hide them in one undistinguished heap, debased alike by penury, want of economy, and dissolute habits. Frequently, the inspectors found two or more families crowded into one small house, containing only two apartments, in one of which they slept, and another in which they ate; and often more than one family lived in a damp cellar, containing only one room, in whose pestilential atmosphere from twelve to sixteen persons were crowded. To these fertile sources of disease were sometimes added the keeping of pigs and other animals in the house, with other nuisances of the most revolting character. . . .

The houses of the poor . . . are too generally built back to back, having therefore only one outlet, no yard, no privy, and no receptacle for refuse. Consequently the narrow, unpaved streets, in which mud and water stagnate, become the common receptacle of offal and ordure. . . .

These districts are inhabited by a turbulent population, which, rendered reckless by dissipation and want—misled by the secret intrigues, and excited by the inflammatory harangues of demagogues, has frequently committed daring assaults on the liberty of the more peaceful portions of the working classes, and the most frightful devastations on the property of their masters. Machines have been broken, and factories gutted and burned at mid-day, and the riotous crowd has dispersed ere the insufficient body of police arrived at the scene of disturbance. . . . The police form, in fact, so weak a screen against the power of the mob, that popular violence is now, in almost every instance, controlled by the presence of a military force.

The wages obtained by operatives in the various branches of the cotton manufacture are, in general, such, as with the exercise of that economy without which wealth itself is wasted, would be sufficient to provide them with all the decent comforts of life— the average wage of all persons employed (young and old) being from nine to twelve shillings per week. Their means are consumed by vice and improvidence. But the wages of certain classes are exceedingly meagre. The introduction of the power-loom, though ultimately destined to be productive of the greatest general benefits, has, in the present restricted state of commerce, occasioned some temporary embarrassment, by diminishing the demand for certain kinds of labor, and, consequently, their price. The hand-loom weavers, existing in the state of transition, still continue a very extensive class, and though they labor fourteen hours and upwards daily, earn only from five to seven shillings per week. . . .

With unfeigned regret, we are . . . constrained to add, that the standard of morality is exceedingly debased, and that religious observances are neglected amongst the operative population of Manchester. . . .

The children . . . are often neglected by their parents. The early age at which girls are admitted into the factories, prevents their acquiring much knowledge of domestic economy; and even supposing them to have had accidental opportunities of making this acquisition, the extent to which women are employed in the mills, does not, even after marriage, permit the general application of its principles. The infant is the victim of the system; it has not lived long, ere it is abandoned to the care of a hireling or neighbor, whilst its mother pursues her accustomed toil. Sometimes a little girl has care of the child, or even of two or three collected from neighboring houses. Thus abandoned to one whose sympathies are not interested in its welfare, or whose time is too often also occupied in household drudgery, the child is ill-fed, dirty, ill-clothed, exposed to cold and neglect, and, in consequence, more than one-half of the offspring of the poor (as may be proved by the bills of mortality of the town) die before they have completed their fifth year. . . .

The increase of the manufacturing establishments, and the consequent colonization of the district, have been exceedingly more rapid than the growth of its civic institutions. The eager antagonization of commercial enterprise, has absorbed the attention, and concentrated the energies, of every member of the community. In this strife, the remote influence of arrangements has sometimes been neglected, not from the want of humanity, but from the pressure of occupation, and the deficiency of time. . . .

Distrust of the capitalists has long been sown in the minds of the working classes— separation has succeeded to suspicion, and many causes have tended to widen the gulf over which the golden chain of charity seldom extends. We would not have this so. The contest, thus engendered, too often assumes an appalling aspect. Capital is but accumulated labor: their strife is unnatural. Greed does not become the opulent; nor does turbulence the poor. The general combinations of workmen to protect the price of labor are ultimately destined to have a beneficial influence on trade, by the destruction of partial monopolies and petty oppressions, but in these contests the poisonous shafts of personal malice should not be launched. . . .

If the higher classes are unwilling to diffuse intelligence among the lower, those exist who are ever ready to take advantage of their ignorance; if they will not seek their confidence, others will excite their distrust; if they will not endeavor to promote domestic comfort, virtue, and knowledge among them, their misery, vice, and prejudice will prove volcanic elements, by whose explosive violence the structure of society may be destroyed. . . .

ANDREW URE The Philosophy of Manufactures (1835)

Like fellow physician James Kay, Dr. Ure also investigated the city of Manchester; unlike Kay, he was cheered by his findings.

When the wandering savage becomes a citizen, he renounces many of his dangerous pleasures in return for tranquility and protection. He can no longer gratify at will a revengeful spirit upon his foes, nor seize with violence a neighbor's possessions. In like manner, when the handicraftsman exchanges hard work with fluctuating employment and pay, for continuous work of a lighter kind with steady wages, he must necessarily renounce his old prerogative of stopping when he pleases, because he would thereby throw the whole establishment into disorder. Of the amount of injury resulting from the violation of the rules of automatic labor he can hardly ever be the proper judge; just as mankind at large can never fully estimate the evils consequent upon an infraction of God's moral law. Yet the factory operative, little versant in the great operations of political economy, currency, and trade, and actuated too often by an invidious feeling toward the capitalist who animates his otherwise torpid talents, is easily persuaded by artful demagogues, that his sacrifice of time and skill is beyond the proportion of his recompense, or that fewer hours of industry would be an ample equivalent for his wages. This notion seems

to have taken an early and inveterate hold of the factory mind, and to have been riveted from time to time by the leaders of those secret combinations, so readily formed among a peculiar class of men, concentrated in masses within a narrow range of country.

Instead of repining as they have done at the prosperity of their employers, and concerting odious measures to blast it, they should, on every principle of gratitude and self-interest, have rejoiced at the success resulting from their labors, and by regularity and skill have recommended themselves to monied men desirous of engaging in a profitable concern, and of procuring qualified hands to conduct it. Thus good workmen would have advanced their condition to that of overlookers, managers, and partners in new mills, and have increased at the same time the demand for their companions' labor in the market. It is only by an undisturbed progression of this kind that the rate of wages can be permanently raised or upheld. Had it not been for the violent collisions and interruptions resulting from erroneous views among the operatives, the factory system would have developed still more rapidly and beneficially for all con-

SOURCE: From Andrew Ure, *The Philosophy of Manufactures, or, an Exposition of the Scientific, Moral, and Commercial Economy of the Factory System of Great Britain*, 3rd ed. (London: Bohn, 1861), pp. 278–280, 300–301, 309–312, 328–330, 333–336, 349–350, 379–380, 385–388. (The first edition was published in 1835.)

cerned than it has, and would have exhibited still more frequently gratifying examples of skilful workmen becoming opulent proprietors. Every misunderstanding either repels capital altogether, or diverts it from flowing, for a time, in the channels of trade liable to strikes.

No master would wish to have any wayward children to work within the walls of his factory, who do not mind their business without beating, and he therefore usually fines and turns away any spinners who are known to maltreat their assistants. Hence, ill-usage of any kind is a very rare occurrence. I have visited many factories, both in Manchester and in the surrounding districts, during a period of several months, entering the spinning rooms, unexpectedly, and often alone, at different times of day, and I never saw a single instance of corporal chastisement inflicted on a child, nor indeed did I ever see children in ill-humor. They seemed to be always cheerful and alert, taking pleasure in the light play of their muscles—enjoying the mobility natural to their age. The scene of industry, far from exciting sad emotions in my mind, was always exhilarating. It was delightful to observe the nimbleness with which they pieced the broken ends, as the mule-carriage began to recede from the fixed roller-beam, and to see them at leisure, after a few seconds' exercise of their tiny fingers, to amuse themselves in any attitude they chose, till the stretch and winding-on were once more completed. The work of these lively elves seemed to resemble a sport, in which habit gave them a pleasing dexterity. Conscious of their skill, they were delighted to show it off to any stranger. As to exhaustion by the day's work, they evinced no trace of it on emerging from the mill in the evening; for they immediately began to skip about any neighboring play-ground, and to commence their little amusements with the same alacrity as boys issuing from a school. It is moreover my firm conviction, that if children are not ill-used by bad parents or guardians, but receive in food and raiment the full benefit of what they earn,

they would thrive better in our modern factories than if left alone in apartments too often ill-aired, damp and cold.

Of all the modern prejudices that exist with regard to factory labor, there is none more unfounded than that which ascribes to it excessive tedium and irksomeness above other occupations, owing to its being carried on in conjunction with the "unceasing motion of the steam-engine." In an establishment for spinning or weaving cotton, all the hard work is performed by the steam-engine, which leaves for the attendant no hard labor at all, and literally nothing to do in general; but at intervals to perform some delicate operation, such as joining the threads that break, taking the cops off the spindles, etc. And it is so far from being true that the work in a factory is incessant, because the motion of the steam-engine is incessant, that the labor is not incessant on that very account, because it is performed in conjunction with the steam-engine. Of all manufacturing employments, those are by far the most irksome and incessant in which steam-engines are not employed, as in lace-running and stocking-weaving; and the way to prevent an employment from being incessant is to introduce a steam-engine into it. . . .

Occupations which are assisted by steam-engines require for the most part a higher, or at least a steadier, species of labor than those which are not; the exercise of the mind being then partially substituted for that of the muscles, constituting skilled labor, which is always paid more highly than unskilled. On this principle we can readily account for the comparatively high wages which the inmates of a cotton factory, whether children or adults, obtain. Batting cotton by hand for fine spinning seems by far the hardest work in a factory; it is performed wholly by women, without any assistance from the steam-engine, and is somewhat similar in effort to threshing corn; yet it does not bring those who are engaged in it more than 6s. 6d. weekly, while close by it the stretching-frame, which remunerates its tenters or superintendents, women, and even children fourteen years old, with double wages for far lighter labor. In power-loom weaving also, the wages are good, and the muscular effort is trifling, as those who tend it frequently exercise themselves by following the movements of the lay, and leaning on it with their arms. It is reckoned a very healthy occupation, as is shown by the appearance of the females engaged in it, in every well-regulated establishment in England and Scotland. . . .

Under what pretext, or with what face of pretension, operatives, whose labor is assisted by steam or water power, can lay claim to a peculiar privilege of exemption from more than ten hours' daily labor it is hard to conjecture. They compare their toil with that of the small class, comparatively, of artisans, such as carpenters, bricklayers, stone-masons, etc., who, they say, work only from six to six, with two one-hour intervals for meals: a class, however, in this material respect distinguished from most factory operatives, that their work is done entirely by muscular effort, and after serving a long apprenticeship with no little outlay. But what do the factory operatives think of the numerous class of domestic operatives, the stocking or frame-work knitters, the hand-loom weavers, the wool-combers, the lace-manufacturers, and a variety of others, who work, and very hardly too, from twelve to sixteen hours a day, to earn a bare subsistence; and this frequently from a very early age, and in a state of confinement irksome to the mind and injurious to the body? . . .

The factory system, then, instead of being detrimental to the comfort of the laboring population, is its grand Palladium; for the more complicated and extensive the machinery required for any manufacture, the less risk is there of its agents being injured by the competition of foreign manufactures, and the greater inducement and

ability has the mill-owner to keep up the wages of his work-people. The main reason why they are so high is, that they form a small part of the value of the manufactured article, so that if reduced too low by a sordid master, they would render his operatives less careful, and thereby injure the quality of their work more than could be compensated by his saving in wages. . . .

It deserves to be remembered, moreover, that hand-working is more or less discontinuous from the caprice of the operative, and never gives an average weekly or annual product at all comparable to that of a like machine equally driven by power. . . .

In hand-weaving . . . the depreciation of wages has been extraordinary. Annexed are the prices paid at different periods in Manchester for weaving a sixty reed 6/4 cambric, as taken in the month of March each year; the weaver paying threepence out of each shilling, for winding his warp, for brushes, paste, etc.

In 1795	39s. 6d.
1800	25s.
1810	15s.
1820	8s.
1830	5s.

The [admittedly] painful statements made to the factory commissioners will show in how abject a condition are our so-called independent handicraft laborers, compared with that of those much-lamented laborers who tend the power-driven machines of the factories. The former class needs all the sympathy which Mr. Sadler's faction[2] so perniciously expended upon the latter. . . .

Mr. T. Ashton's cotton-works are agreeably grouped together on a gentle declivity, which is traversed by a little tributary stream of the Mersey. This supplies the condensing power to his steam-engines,

---

[2]*Michael Sadler (1780–1835):* a banker, Tory M. P. for Leeds, and chairman of the parliamentary investigating committee whose findings led to the Factory Act of 1833.

while their expansive force is furnished from rich coal-measures immediately under the factory lands. This is the motive-element which pervades and animates the region all around. The houses occupied by his work-people lie in streets, all built of stone, and are commodious; consisting each of at least four apartments [i.e., rooms] in two stories, with a small back-yard and a mews lane. The rent for a good lodging, containing an improved kitchen-grate, with boiler and oven, is only £8 per annum, and good fuel may be had for 9s. a ton. I looked into several of the houses, and found them more richly furnished than any common work-people's dwellings which I had ever seen before. In one I saw a couple of sofas, with good chairs, an eight-day clock in a handsome mahogany case, several pictures in oil on the walls, freshly painted for the family, . . . In another house I observed a neat wheel barometer, with its attached thermometer, suspended against the snow-white wall. In a third there was a piano, with a little girl learning to play upon it.

My notice was particularly attracted to a handsome house and shop, in one of the streets where Mr. Ashton's operatives dwell. On asking who occupied it, I learned it was a spinner, who having saved from his earnings £200, had embarked this capital in a retail business, now managed by his wife, a tidy-looking person, while the husband continued to pursue his profitable avocations in the mill.

The most recent, and perhaps most convincing, evidence regarding the healthiness of factory children is that given in the official report of Mr. Harrison, the inspecting surgeon appointed for the mills of Preston and its vicinity. There are 1,656 under 18 years of age, of whom 952 are employed in spinning-rooms, 468 in carding rooms, 128 at power-looms, and 108 in winding, skewering cops, etc. "I have made very particular inquiries respecting the health of every child whom I have examined, and I find that the average annual sickness of each child is not more than four days; at least, that not more than four days on an average

are lost by each child in a year, in consequence of sickness. This includes disorders of every kind, for the most part induced by causes wholly unconnected with factory labor. I have been not a little surprised to find so little sickness which can fairly be attributed to mill work. I have met with very few children who have suffered from injuries occasioned by machinery; and the protection, especially in new factories, is so complete, that accidents will, I doubt not, speedily become rare. I have not met with a single instance out of the 1,656 children whom I have examined, of deformity, that is referable to factory labor. It must be admitted, that factory children do not present the same blooming robust appearance as is witnessed among children who labor in the open air, but I question if they are not more exempt from acute diseases, and do not, on the average, suffer less sickness than those who are regarded as having more healthy employments. The average age at which the children of this district enter the factories is ten years and two months; and the average age of all the young persons together is fourteen years."

I examined samples of bacon as sold in several respectable shops in Manchester, and found it to be much more rank than the average of the London shops. In this piquant state, it suits vitiated palates accustomed to the fiery impression of tobacco and gin. These three stimulants are too much used by that order of work-people in Manchester who receive the highest wages, and they are quite sufficient to account for many chronic maladies of the stomach, liver, or spleen, without tracing them to mere factory labor or confinement. Were a judicious plan of cookery and diet, combining abundance of vegetable matter with light animal food, introduced among them, as it is among the families of the work-people at Belper, Hyde, New Lanark, Catrine, etc., joined to abstinence from tobacco and alcohol, I am confident that the health of the Manchester spinners would surpass that of any class of operatives in the kingdom. . . .

FRIEDRICH ENGELS   The Condition of the Working Class in England in 1844

The youthful visitor from Germany encounters a new society, a new class structure, and grounds for political revolution in the England of the 1840s.

This in brief has been the development of British industry over the last sixty years, a development which has no parallel in the annals of mankind. Eighty, even sixty years ago England was no different from any other country, with its little townships, only a few simple domestic manufactures and a relatively large but widely-scattered agricultural population. Today England is a unique country with a capital city of 2 ½ million inhabitants, with huge factory towns; with industries which supply the needs of the whole world, making practically everything by means of the most complicated machines. England has an industrious, intelligent and dense population, two-thirds of which is engaged in industry. The population is composed of quite different classes than it used to be and these social groups make up a quite different sort of nation, with new customs and new needs. The Industrial Revolution has been as important for England as the political revolution for France and the philosophical revolution for Germany. The gulf between the England of 1760 and that of 1844 is at least as great as that between France under the *ancien régime* and the France of the July Revolution. The most important result of this Industrial Revolution has been the creation of the English proletariat. . . .

But this process of social change was not confined to industry in the narrow sense of the term. It occurred also in craft work and even in commerce. Former masters and apprentices were replaced by large capitalists

and workers. There was now no possibility that the workers would ever improve their position and rise out of their social group. Craftsmanship was now replaced by factory production. There was a strict division of labor. The result was that the small master could not compete with the big factories and so sank to the position of a mere worker. The disappearance of handicraft work and of the middle-class groups dependent upon it deprived the workers of the possibility of rising into this class of society. Hitherto there had always been a possibility that the craftsman might establish himself as an independent master and might eventually employ apprentices himself. The disappearance of the old independent small masters and the large amount of capital required to start a factory made it impossible for the worker to rise out of his social class. The proletariat now became a definite class in the population whereas formerly it had only been a transitional stage toward entering into the middle classes. Today he who is born a worker must remain a worker for the rest of his life. This is why it is only now possible for an organized working-class movement to spring up.

This is how the great masses of workers who now cover the whole of the United Kingdom have been brought together. The social problems of these workers are daily claiming more and more of the attention of the whole of the civilized world.

Since the Reform Act of 1832[3] the most important social issue in England has been

SOURCE: From Friedrich Engels, *The Condition of the Working Class in England in 1844* (New York, 1887). (First published in 1844.)

[3]*Reform Act of 1832:* the measure that increased the size of the electorate by at least 50 percent and gave industrial cities like Manchester direct representation in Parliament for the first time

the condition of the working classes, who form the vast majority of the English people. The problems are these: What is to become of these propertyless millions who own nothing and consume today what they earned yesterday? What fate is in store for the workers who by their inventions and labor have laid the foundations of England's greatness? What is to be the future of those who are now daily becoming more and more aware of their power and are pressing more and more strongly for their share of the social advantages of the new era? All the parliamentary debates of any consequence are in fact concerned with these questions.

It is in vain that the English middle classes have hitherto tried to ignore the issue. It is useless for them to ignore these problems and to pretend that the interests of the middle classes are really identical with those of the nation as a whole. . . . It is high time the English middle classes learned that they must be prepared to make concessions before it is too late, not only to the worker who begs, but to the worker who threatens to secure his demands by force. But the English middle classes prefer to ignore the distress of the workers, and this is particularly true of the industrialists, who grow rich on the misery of the mass of wage earners. . . . The middle classes are living in frivolous unconcern, although the very ground beneath their feet is undermined and may give way at any moment. The imminence of this collapse may be foretold with the certainty of the laws of mathematics and mechanics. It is astonishing that there is not a single adequate account of the condition of the working classes, although for heaven knows how many years the middle classes have been enquiring into this problem and tinkering with it. No wonder that all the workers from Glasgow to London are deeply incensed against the wealthy, who systematically exploit the wage-earners and then cal-

lously leave them to their fate. The wrath of the workers must very soon—one can very nearly fix the date—lead to a revolution compared with which the French Revolution and the year 1794[4] will seem like child's play. . . .

Capital is the all-important weapon in the class war. Power lies in the hands of those who own, directly or indirectly, foodstuffs and the means of production. The poor, having no capital, inevitably bear the consequences of defeat in the struggle. Nobody troubles about the poor as they struggle helplessly in the whirlpool of modern industrial life. The working man may be lucky enough to find employment, if by his labor he can enrich some member of the middle classes. But his wages are so low that they hardly keep body and soul together. If he cannot find work, he can steal, unless he is afraid of the police; or he can go hungry and then the police will see to it that he will die of hunger in such a way as not to disturb the equanimity of the middle classes. . . .

The only difference between the old-fashioned slavery and the new is that while the former was openly acknowledged the latter is disguised. The worker *appears* to be free, because he is not bought and sold outright. He is sold piecemeal by the day, the week, or the year. Moreover he is not sold by one owner to another, but he is forced to sell himself in this fashion. He is not the slave of a single individual, but of the whole capitalist class. As far as the worker is concerned, however, there can be no doubt as to his service status. It is true that the apparent liberty which the worker enjoys does give him some *real* freedom. Even this genuine freedom has the disadvantage that no one is responsible for providing him with food and shelter. His real masters, the middle-class capitalists, can discard him at any moment and leave him to starve, if they have no further use for his services and no further interest in his survival. . . .

---

[4]*1794:* the year of the Reign of Terror that followed the French Revolution

JAMES WILSON   **The First Half of the Nineteenth Century:**
Progress of the Nation and the Race (1851)

At mid-century, the editor of The Economist *looks back upon fifty years of progress for the people of Britain.*

Too many of us are disposed to place our golden age in the past. . . . Nearly everybody agrees by common consent to undervalue and abuse the present. We confess that we cannot share their disappointment, nor echo their complaints. We look upon the past with respect and affection as a series of stepping-stones to that high and advanced position which we actually hold, and from the future we hope for the realization of those dreams, almost of perfectibility, which a comparison of the past with the present entitles us to indulge in. But we see no reason to be discontented either with our rate of progress or with the actual stage which we have reached. . . .

Perhaps the best way of realizing . . . the actual progress of the last half-century would be to fancy ourselves suddenly transferred to the year 1800, with all our habits, expectations, requirements, and standard of living formed upon the luxuries and appliances collected round us in 1850. In the first year of the century we should find ourselves eating bread at 1s. 10½d. the quartern [four-pound] loaf, and those who could not afford this price driven to short commons, to entire abstinence, or to some miserable substitute. We should find ourselves grumbling at heavy taxes laid on nearly all the necessaries and luxuries of life—even upon salt; blaspheming at the high price of coffee, tea, and sugar, which confined these articles, in any adequate abundance, to the rich and easy classes of society; paying fourfold for our linen shirts, threefold for our flannel petticoats, and above fivefold for our cotton handkerchiefs and stockings; receiving our newspapers seldom . . . and some days after date; receiving our Edinburgh letters in London a week after they were written, and paying thirteen pence-halfpenny for them when delivered, exchanging the instantaneous telegraph for the slow and costly express by chaise and pair; travelling with soreness and fatigue by the "old heavy" [coach] at the rate of seven miles an hour, instead of by the Great Western [railway] at fifty; and relapsing from the blaze of light which gas now pours along our streets, into a perilous and uncomfortable darkness made visible by a few wretched oil lamps scattered at distant intervals.

But these would by no means comprise the sum total, nor the worst part, of the descent into barbarism. We should find our criminal law in a state worthy of Draco; executions taking place by the dozen; the stealing of five shillings punishable and punished as severely as rape or murder; slavery and the slave trade flourishing in their palmiest atrocity. We should find the liberty of the subject at the lowest ebb; freedom of discussion and writing always in fear and frequently in jeopardy; religious rights trampled under foot; Catholics, slaves and not citizens; Dissenters still disabled and despised. Parliament was unreformed; public jobbing[5] flagrant and shameless; gentlemen drank a bottle where they now drink a glass, and measured their capacity by their cups; and the temperance medal was a thing undreamed of. Finally, the *people* in those days were little thought of, where they are now the main topic of discourse and statesmanship; steamboats were unknown, and a voyage to America occupied eight weeks instead of ten days;

SOURCE: From "The First Half of the Nineteenth Century: Progress of the Nation and the Race," *The Economist* (January 18, 1851), pp. 57–59; (January 25, 1851), pp. 81–83; (February 1, 1851), pp. 109–111.

[5]*jobbing:* using a public office for private gain

and while in 1850, a population of nearly 30, 000, 000 paid £50, 000, 000 of taxes, in 1801 a population of 15, 000, 000 paid no less than £63, 000, 000.

We have ample means of showing by indisputable facts that wealth has been *diffused* as well as increased during the period under review; that so far from "the rich having become richer and the poor poorer," as is so often and so inconsiderately asserted, the middle classes have advanced faster than the great, and the command over the comforts and luxuries of life, even among peasants and artisans, is far greater now than at any former period. . . .

In the first place let us look at the savings banks, which are entirely the growth of this century, the first having been established about 1806, and which are confined to the savings of the peasant and artisan class, of domestic servants, and of the humbler portion of the middle class. . . . The deposits in savings banks must . . . be considered as so much capital accumulated since 1800 by the humbler classes of the community. These amounted in 1846 to no less a sum than £31, 743, 250. But this is not all; the amount deposited in proportion to the population shows a steady increase [from 13s. 6d. per head in England, Wales and Ireland in 1831 to 20s. 11d. per head in 1848].

Let us now collect together a few facts showing the increase in the consumption of those articles of necessity, or luxury, which are used indiscriminately *among all classes.*

We have no means of comparing the amount of butchers' meat consumed now with that consumed at the beginning of the century, but the price we know has fallen from 5s.8d. to 3s.4d. a stone, and M'Culloch considers the quantity *per head* eaten in London to have doubled since 1750. . . . During the latter part of the 18th century rye and barley bread were very extensively used in many parts of England, the former being . . . the habitual food of one-seventh of the population; it is now unknown, except in Durham, while the use of wheaten bread is almost universal among the poorer classes.

In the use of coffee, tea, and sugar also, a marked advance has taken place. . . .

The truth is, that the relief to the population generally, and to the working classes especially, which has been given by the remission of taxation, has been something quite unprecedented. . . . If we except the excise on soap, it may be said that no tax now remains on a single one of the strict necessaries of life. If a poor man is content to live, as wise and great men have often thought it well to live, in health and comfort, but with strict frugality . . . he may escape taxation almost entirely. The whole tendency of our fiscal changes for the last twenty years has been to release the working classes from all financial burdens. . . . To this enumeration of our increased command over the comforts and essentials of life must be added one more item, not the least important in its influence. In 1800 the poor man paid from 6d. to a shilling for each letter he received; it now costs him only one penny.

In no one point is the half-century we have just closed more distinguished from its predecessors than in the share of PUBLIC ATTENTION AND SYMPATHY WHICH THE CONDITION OF THE POORER CLASSES HAS OBTAINED. Formerly the lower orders were regarded, even by the kindly disposed, simply as hewers of wood and drawers of water. . . . The idea of studying them, of raising them, of investigating into the operation of the causes which affected them for good or evil, had scarcely taken rise. There was kindness, there was charity, there was sympathy toward the poor as *individuals,* but not any interest in their condition as a class. We are far from considering the multiplication of charitable institutions as a . . . source of unalloyed good to the indigent and industrious of the community, but it at least shows the increase of sympathy towards them on the part of the rich. . . . In the metropolis alone the charitable institutions reach 491 in number, and have an annual income of £1, 765, 000. Of these 109 were established in the last, and no less than 294 in the present century.

But a far stronger proof of the general

interest now taken in the working classes, is to be found in the various commissions that have of late years been issued to inquire into the state of the people in various occupations. Wherever there was a rumor of an abuse, a tyranny, or an injustice, a representation was made in Parliament, and an investigation immediately took place. We have had a factory commission, a children's employment commission, a commission to inquire into the condition of those employed in mines and manufactures, and a commission to inquire into the employment of women and children in agriculture. We have had inspectors of mines and inspectors of factories appointed. . . .

On the novel and extraordinary attention which is now being paid to SANITARY MATTERS we can look with . . . unmingled satisfaction. . . . Our progress since 1800 has been far from contemptible. The population is less crowded than it was, and roomier dwellings are constantly in process of erection. The average number of individuals in a house which was 5.67 in 1801 had fallen to 5.44 in 1841; and the census which is to be taken this year, will, we have no doubt, show a still further diminution. . . . Many removable causes of premature death yet remain, but the four or five years which the last half-century has added to the average duration of life are a hopeful earnest of what may yet be done to prolong it, now that the subject has awakened public interest, and that administrative exertions are conducted under the guidance of scientific skill.

We hope we [have] succeeded in satisfying those who [have] followed our facts and figures that the national advance in wealth and all the material appliances of civilization . . . has not been turned solely to the benefit of the more favored children of fortune, but that all classes of the community, the humbler as well as the richer, have participated in the blessings of the change. Indeed, it scarcely could be otherwise. The cheapness of the necessaries and of the commoner, and therefore more indispensable comforts of daily life, *must* redound more especially to the advantage of those whose income is most exclusively devoted to the purchase of those needful articles. A reduction in the price of bread, meat, coffee, sugar, and calico, affects the comforts of the poor man far more immediately and extensively than that of the rich or the easy classes. . . . The only way in which our conclusion could be shown to be erroneous, would be by proving that the wages of labor had fallen to an equal or a greater ratio; but this, it is well known, is far from having been generally the case. . . . While unquestionably wages have fallen considerably in a few departments of industry, this fall has been confined to those departments in which a change in the machinery employed has taken place, and in which the artisans have obstinately refused to accommodate themselves to the new state of things, and have continued to overstock an impoverished and doomed employment, as in the case of plain hand-loom weaving; or to those where senseless *strikes* have introduced supernumerary hands or new mechanism into the trade, as in the cases of coarse cotton spinners and of the London tailors; or to those where the easiness and collateral conveniences of the occupation have attracted to it excessive numbers, as in the case of needlework. In these branches wages have undoubtedly fallen, and the hours of work have become in some instances longer; but the general tendency in most departments of industry has been the reverse;—a desire for shorter hours has been of late rapidly spreading. The hours of labor in factories have been reduced for adults from 74 to 60 a week, and for children from 72 to 40; shops are beginning to be closed much earlier, and great, and in some cases already successful, efforts are making to secure a weekly half-holiday for the generality of tradespeople. All these, where not pursued by illegitimate means, are steps in the right direction. The progress of scientific discovery has been magnificent, and its application to the arts of life more remarkable still. . . . The first steamship constructed in the British Empire carried passengers upon the Clyde in 1811: in 1816 we had 15 steamboats with a burden of 2,612 tons; in 1848, we had 1,253, registered at 168,078 tons. Many of these are ocean steamers, and ply between England and America at an average speed of ten miles an hour. Between Holyhead and Dublin we have attained a speed of 15 miles an hour.

But this advance is nothing compared to that which has taken place in LOCOMOTION BY LAND within the last twenty years. It is here that our progress has been most stupendous—surpassing all previous steps since the creation of the human race. In 1829 the first railway for the transport of passengers was opened between Liverpool and Manchester;—it opened at the modest speed of 20 miles an hour. At the period at which we write, the whole of England is traversed by almost countless railways in every direction. . . . In the days of Adam the average speed of travel, if Adam ever did such things, was four miles an hour . . . in the year 1828, or *4,000 years afterward, it was still only ten miles*, and sensible and scientific men were ready to affirm and eager to prove that this rate could never be materially exceeded;—in 1850, it is habitually forty miles an hour, and *seventy* for those who like it. We have reached in a single bound from the speed of a horse's canter, to the utmost speed comparable with the known strength and coherence of brass and iron.

Now, who have specially benefited by this vast invention? The rich, whose horses and carriages carried them in comfort over the known world?—the middle classes to whom stage coaches and mails were an accessible mode of conveyance?—or the poor, whom the cost of locomotion condemned often to an almost vegetable existence? Clearly the latter. The railroad is the Magna Charter [*sic*] of their motive freedom. How few among the last generation ever stirred beyond their own village? How few among the present will die without visiting London?. . . . The number who left Manchester by cheap trips in one week of holiday time last year exceeded 202,000; against 150,000 in 1849, and 116,000 in 1848.

But even the rapid augmentation of our locomotive speed shrinks into nothing when compared to that which has taken place in the last five years in the transmission of intelligence. If Abraham had wished to communicate to Lot some important tidings by express, he must have sent a man on horseback with the news, and even then he could not have transmitted it much faster than 10 miles an hour. . . . In the year 1800, the case was exactly the same; the most important expresses could seldom average more than 10 miles an hour. The same was the case in 1830 and 1840, except where the old signal telegraphs enabled governments to transmit their orders in fine weather, by the raising and lowering of certain clumsy arms attached to a high tower. But now in 1850, for a sum varying from 5s. to 12s. 6d., any private individual may send a message or summon a friend [by telegraph], the distance of many hundred miles in a space of time reckoned by seconds rather than by minutes. . . .

Economists as we are, we should be little satisfied with even these signs of astounding progress . . . were there not ample reason to believe that a corresponding improvement has taken place in EDUCATION, SOCIAL MORALS, AND PUBLIC PRINCIPLE. . . .

When we remember that it is only within our own recollection that the propriety or wisdom of educating the lower orders at all was seriously and very generally questioned; that before 1800 the only provision for popular instruction was to be found in grammar and other endowed schools (the funds for the support of a large proportion of which had been scandalously jobbed away or misapplied), together with a few dame schools in towns, and a few squires' and ladies' schools in the rural districts; and that now not only is the paramount necessity of general education universally insisted upon, but every sect vies with every other in the number and excellence of its schools; that even pauper schools are systematically good; that even ragged schools for the most desolate and depraved of our town population have been established with great success in many localities . . . that Lancasterian schools, national schools, model schools, and normal schools, are all the product of this century; that a committee on education now forms a recognized department of the government; and finally, that Parliament, which in 1833 could with difficulty be persuaded to vote £20,000 for educational purposes in aid of private munificence, now votes liberally and ungrudgingly £150,000 a year:—when we remember all those things, we shall scarcely be disposed to deem our national progress under this head unsatisfactory or slow.

The general tone of morals in the middle and higher classes has unquestionably become much higher and purer in the last generation. Language which was common in our fathers' days would not be tolerated now. A higher sense, both of duty and of decency, has taken possession of all ranks. . . . *Debt*, which used to be considered as an indispensable characteristic of a man of fashion, is now almost everywhere scouted as disreputable; and reckless extravagance is no longer regarded as an indication of cleverness and spirit. . . . *Labor* has ceased to be looked down upon—exertion is no longer regarded as derogatory, nor a life of languid indolence as the supreme felicity. The bees are more considered than the butterflies of society; wealth is valued less as an exemption from toil, than as a call to effort, and

an instrument of influence and power; the duties of property are, far less than formerly, forgotten in its rights; if the poor do not yet work less, the rich certainly work more. . . .

The third point to which we wish to draw attention, is the marked improvement which has taken place in one generation in habits of *temperance*, especially among the upper circles. Within the memory of men still in middle life, excess in wine was the rule, not the exception; few left the dinner-table without having taken more than was good for them; many got drunk every day. . . . *Now*, intemperance is as disreputable as any other kind of low debauchery, and, except in Ireland and at the universities, a drunken gentleman is one of the rarest sights in society. . . .

On no account has this country greater ground for self-congratulation than on the vast improvement which is observable in the CHARACTER and tone of feeling among PUBLIC MEN. . . . Statesmen have now learned to feel not merely that they are playing a noble game . . . but that they are called upon to guide a glorious vessel through fluctuating shoals, and sunken rocks, and storms of terrific violence . . . the greatest nation that ever stood in the vanguard of civilization and of freedom. . . .

8

The Status of Women in Victorian England: Zenith or Nadir?

What was the status of women in Victorian society? Were women repressed dependents deprived of the opportunity to enter upon any career but that of housewife? Alternatively, were they placed on a pedestal as the inspirers, the educators, and the moral guides of fallible men? As the documents cited in this chapter will suggest, the answer depends in part upon whether our concern is with the state of the law or with social custom. It depends also, to a very large degree, upon which class in society we are assessing.

Victorian ideas and ideals as to the proper role of women are usually identified with the middle class. How does Sarah Stickney Ellis (1812–1872) define "middle class" in *The Women of England?* How does she describe the proper role of women? What is her reply to those who consider the sphere she allots to women as humiliating or degrading? The wife of a Christian missionary, Mrs. Ellis was a prolific writer. *The Women of England* sold so widely during the years after its publication in 1838 that she went on to produce three companion volumes *The Daughters of England, The Wives of England,* and *The Mothers of England.*

The middle-class women whose role Mrs. Ellis extolled are not even mentioned in the list of principal occupation groups in Britain derived from the census of 1851. As that document demonstrates, at least three women in ten (above the age of ten) did work full time outside the home for pay and were thus part of the labor market. The selection that follows throws light on the lives and activities of the single largest class of women workers, the live-in domestic servants. Isabella Beeton (1836–1865) lived a short life, but her *Book of Household Management* was to be reissued on numerous occasions after its first appearance in 1861. It came to serve as a veritable household bible to several generations of Victorians. What light does it shed upon the Victorian "servant problem"? To which now forgotten household tasks does it call our attention?

Some three-quarters of the early Victorian population was neither upper class nor middle class, in the sense that Mrs. Ellis defined the latter phrase. Mrs. B., the anonymous wife of a Manchester cotton spinner (who was interviewed in 1833 by a factory commission investigator), tells us about *Life at Home.* In what type of house does she live? What is her

Natural Religion

BISHOP (*reproving delinquent page*). "Wretched boy! *Who* is it that sees and hears all we do, and before whom *even I* am but as a crushed worm?"
PAGE. "The Missus, my Lord!"

(*Punch, August 14, 1880*)

family's diet like? What role does her eldest daughter play in helping to support the family? Has Mrs. B. ever worked outside the house?

As Mrs. B.'s account reminds us, early Victorian Britain was acquainted not only with women domestics but also with women factory workers, and during the 1830s and 1840s the British Parliament subjected cotton mills to investigation, to a system of regular inspection, and to a statutory limitation of working hours for women and for young people of both sexes. One of the leading advocates in the House of Commons was Lord Ashley (Anthony Ashley Cooper), the future seventh earl of Shaftesbury (1801–1885). In the speech of 1844, "Women Factory Workers" (1844), he advocated a maximum working day of ten hours for women.

Although he failed to attain his goal that year, Parliament did enact such a measure three years later. On what basis does Ashley justify legislative interference in the "freedom of contract" of women to work for hours longer than ten? On what underlying premises do Ashley's attitudes toward women factory workers rest?

A significant number of early and mid-Victorian women were engaged in occupations unrelated to either domestic service or industrialization. The costermongers, described by Henry Mayhew (1812–1887) in his pioneering venture into sociological journalism, *London Labour and the London Poor* (1851), are a case in point. How do they earn their living? How do the lives led by the coster girls compare with the ideals of Mrs. Ellis or, for that matter, Mrs. Beeton?

In works such as *The Principles of Political Economy* (1848), *Considerations on Representative Government* (1861), *Utilitarianism* (1863), and, most importantly, *On Liberty* (1859), John Stuart Mill (1806–1873) established himself as the foremost philosophical prophet of Victorian liberalism. In many respects his most remarkable work was *The Subjection of Women*, a feminist manifesto written in consultation with Harriet Taylor, Mill's associate and (from 1851 until her much lamented death in 1858) his wife. Though first drafted during the late 1850s, the work was not published until 1869, by which time Mill, as Member of Parliament, had attempted to include women voters in what became the Reform Bill of 1867. In what historical and philosophical context does Mill place the subject? What were the legal restrictions imposed upon British women at the time that Mill wrote? What is Mill's goal?

During the remaining years of the nineteenth century, most legal restrictions on women with regard to property and child custody were ended, and women won the vote in local elections, but the parliamentary franchise was to be deferred until 1918. Although Mill's essay had implications for all women, the legal changes it advocated had a more immediate relevance for the lives of women in the upper ranks of society than for costermongers or factory girls. This statement holds true to an even greater degree for the writings of Eliza Lynn Linton and Hyppolite Taine—not that their approaches are identical to either Mill's or each other's. Mrs. Linton (1822–1898) was a novelist and the first English female journalist under regular contract to a newspaper. "The Girl of the Period" created a minor sensation when it appeared in 1868. How do her concerns about the state of women in the higher ranks of society differ from those of Mill? What is her feminine ideal? Hyppolite Taine (1828–1893) was a historian of English literature, of modern France, and of art. From 1864 to 1884 he served as professor of esthetics and art history at the École des Beaux-Arts. His context for appraising the women of mid-Victorian England, as outlined in the chapter's final document, "English Womanhood" (1871), is neither all of human history nor "the good old days." Rather, Taine is concerned with how English women differ from women in the same social ranks in his native France. What are those differences? What other aspects of upper-class Victorian society do Taine's comments highlight?

SARAH STICKNEY ELLIS   **The Women of England: Their Social Duties and Domestic Habits (1838)**

Mrs. Ellis, a widely-read, early-Victorian authority, assigns an exalted role to the women of England.

Every country has its peculiar characteristics, not only of climate and scenery, of public institutions, government, and laws; but every country has also its *moral characteristics*, upon which is founded its true title to a station, either high or low, in the scale of nations. . . .

One of the noblest features in her national character . . . is the domestic character of England—the home comforts, and fireside virtues for which she is so justly celebrated. These I hope to be able to speak of without presumption, as intimately associated with, and dependent upon, the moral feelings and habits of the women of this favored country. . . .

In order to speak with precision of the characteristics of any class of people, it is necessary to confine our attention as much as possible to that portion of the class where such characteristics are most prominent. . . . It is not . . . from the aristocracy of the land that the characteristics of English women should be taken. . . . Neither is it entirely amongst the indigent and most laborious of the community, that we can with propriety look for those strong features of nationality, which stamp the moral character of different nations. . . .

In looking around, then, upon our "nation of shop-keepers," we readily perceive that by dividing society into three classes, as regards what is commonly called rank, the middle class must include so vast a portion of the intelligence and moral power of the country at large, that it may not improperly be designated the pillar of our nation's strength, its base being the important class of the laborious poor, and its rich and highly ornamental capital, the ancient nobility of the land. In no other country is society thus beautifully proportioned, and England should beware of any deviation from the order and symmetry of her national column. . . .

Perhaps it may be necessary to be more specific in describing the class of women to which this work relates. It is, then, strictly speaking, to those who belong to that great mass of the population of England which is connected with trade and manufactures;—or, in order to make the application more direct, to that portion of it who are restricted to the services of from one to four domestics,—who, on the one hand, enjoy the advantages of a liberal education, and, on the other, have no pretension to family rank. . . .

It is from the class of females above described, that we naturally look for the highest tone of moral feeling, because they are at the same time removed from the pressing necessities of absolute poverty, and admitted to the intellectual privileges of the great: and thus, while they enjoy every facility in the way of acquiring knowledge, it is their still higher privilege not to be exempt from the domestic duties which call forth the best energies of the female character.
. . .

It is perhaps the nearest approach we can make toward any thing like a definition of what is most striking in the characteristics of the women of England, to say, that the nature of their domestic circumstances is such as to invest their characters with the threefold recommendation of *promptitude in action, energy of thought, and benevolence of feeling*. With all the responsibilities of family comfort and social enjoyment resting upon them, and unaided by those troops of menials who throng the halls of

SOURCE: From Mrs. Ellis, *The Women of England: Their Social Duties and Domestic Habits* (New York: D. Appleton & Co., 1839), pp. 13–14, 16–17, 20–26, 30–31, 33–34, 38–39, 41–42, 44, 46–47, 50–51.

the affluent and the great, they are kept alive to the necessity of making their own personal exertions conducive to the great end of promoting the happiness of those around them. . . .

"What shall I do to gratify myself—to be admired—or to vary the tenor of my existence?" are not the questions which a woman of right feelings asks on first awaking to the avocations of the day. Much more congenial to the highest attributes of woman's character, are inquiries such as these: "How shall I endeavor through this day to turn the time, the health, and the means permitted me to enjoy, to the best account? Is any one sick, I must visit their chamber without delay, and try to give their apartment an air of comfort, by arranging such things as the wearied nurse may not have thought of. Is any one about to set off on a journey, I must see that the early meal is spread, to prepare it with my own hands, in order that the servant, who was working late last night, may profit by unbroken rest. Did I fail in what was kind or considerate to any of the family yesterday; I will meet her this morning with a cordial welcome, and show, in the most delicate way I can, that I am anxious to atone for the past. Was any one exhausted by the last day's exertion, I will be an hour before them this morning, and let them see that their labor is so much in advance. Or, if nothing extraordinary occurs to claim my attention, I will meet the family with a consciousness that, being the least engaged of any member of it, I am consequently the most at liberty to devote myself to the general good of the whole, by cultivating cheerful conversation, adapting myself to the prevailing tone of feeling, and leading those who are least happy, to think and speak of what will make them more so."

. . . Good household management, conducted on this plan, is indeed a science well worthy of attention. It comprises so much, as to invest it with an air of difficulty on the first view; but no woman can reasonably complain of incapability, because nature has endowed the sex with perceptions so lively and acute, that where benevolence

is the impulse, and principle the foundation upon which they act, experience will soon teach them by what means they may best accomplish the end they have in view. . . .

The domestic woman, moving in a comparatively limited circle, is not necessarily confined to a limited number of ideas, but can often expatiate upon subjects of mere local interest with a vigor of intellect, a freshness of feeling, and a liveliness of fancy, which create in the mind of the uninitiated stranger, a perfect longing to be admitted into the home associations from whence are derived such a world of amusement, and so unfailing a relief from the severer duties of life. . . .

Above all other characteristics of the women of England, the strong moral feeling pervading even their most trifling and familiar actions, ought to be mentioned as most conducive to the maintenance of that high place which they so justly claim in the society of their native land. . . . The women of England are not surpassed by those of any other country for their clear perception of the right and the wrong of common and familiar things, for their reference to principle in the ordinary affairs of life, and for their united maintenance of that social order, sound integrity, and domestic peace, which constitute the foundation of all that is most valuable in the society of our native land.

Much as I have said of the influence of the domestic habits of my country-women, it is, after all, to the prevalence of religious instruction, and the operation of religious principle upon the heart, that the consistent maintainance of their high tone of moral character is to be attributed. . . . Women are said to be more easily brought under this influence than men; and we consequently see, in places of public worship, and on all occasions in which a religious object is the motive for exertion, a greater proportion of women than of men. . . .

If . . . all was confusion and neglect at home—filial appeals unanswered—domestic comforts uncalculated—husbands, sons, and brothers referred to servants for all the little offices of social kindness, in order that the ladies of the family might hurry away at the appointed time to some committee-room, scientific lecture, or public assembly: however laudable the object for which they met, there would be sufficient cause why their cheeks should be mantled with the blush of burning shame ... which those whose charity has not begun at home, ought never to appropriate to themselves.

It is a widely mistaken notion to suppose that the sphere of usefulness recommended here, is a humiliating and degraded one.... With [some women] it is a favorite plea, brought forward in extenuation of their own uselessness, that they have no influence—that they are not leading women—that society takes no note of them. . . .

It is an important consideration, that from such women as these, myriads of immortal beings derive that early bias of character, which under Providence decides their fate, not only in this world, but in the world to come. And yet they flutter on, and say they have no influence—they do not aspire to be leading women—they are in society but as grains of sand on the sea-shore. Would they but pause one moment to ask how will this plea avail them, when as daughters without gratitude, friends without good faith, wives without consideration, and mothers without piety, they stand before the bar of judgment, to render an account of the talents committed to their trust! . . .

Amongst this unpretending class are found striking and noble instances of women, who apparently feeble and insignificant, when called into action by pressing and peculiar circumstances, can accomplish great and glorious purposes, supported and carried forward by that most valuable of all faculties—*moral power.* And just in proportion as women cultivate this faculty (under the blessing of heaven) ... is their influence over their fellow-creatures, and consequently their power of doing good.

It is not to be presumed that women *possess* more moral power than men; but happily for them, such are their early impressions, associations, and general position in the world, that their moral feelings are less liable to be impaired by the pecuniary ob-

jects which too often constitute the chief end of man, and which, even under the limitations of better principle, necessarily engage a large portion of his thoughts. . . .

How often has man returned to his home with a mind confused by the many voices, which in the mart, the exchange, or the public assembly, have addressed themselves to his inborn selfishness or his worldly pride; and while his integrity was shaken, and his resolution gave way beneath the pressure of apparent necessity, or the insidious pretences of expediency, he has stood corrected before the clear eye of woman, as it looked directly to the naked truth, and detected the lurking evil of the specious act he was about to commit. Nay, so potent may have become this secret influence, that he may have borne it about with him like a kind of second conscience, for mental reference, and spiritual counsel, in moments of trial: and when the snares of the world were around him, and temptations from within and without have bribed over the witness in his own bosom, he has thought of the humble monitress who sat alone, guarding the fireside comforts of his distant home; and the remembrance of her character, clothed in moral beauty, has scattered the clouds before his mental vision, and sent him back to that beloved home, a wiser and a better man. . . .

There is another point of consideration by which this necessity for a higher degree of female influence is greatly increased, and it is one which comprises much that is interesting to those who aspire to be the supporters of their country's worth. The British throne being now graced by a female sovereign, the auspicious promise of whose early years seems to form a new era in the annals of our nation, and to inspire with brighter hopes and firmer confidence the patriot bosoms of her expectant people; it is surely not a time for the female part of the community to fall away from the high standard of moral excellence, to which they have been accustomed to look, in the formation of their domestic habits. Rather let them show forth the benefits arising from their more enlightened systems of education, by proving to their youthful sovereign, that whatever plan she may think it right to sanction for the moral advancement of her subjects, and the promotion of their true interests as an intelligent and happy people, will be welcomed by every female heart throughout her realm, and faithfully supported in every British home by the female influence prevailing there. . . .

Principal Occupation Groups (1851)

The census of 1851 identified the following as the principal ways in which mid-Victorian men and women earned their living.

	Male	Female
Total population	10,224,000	10,736,000
Population of ten years old and upward	7,616,000	8,155,000
Agriculture: farmer, grazier, laborer, servant	1,563,000	227,000
Domestic service (excluding farm service)	134,000	905,000
Cotton worker, every kind, with printer, dyer	255,000	272,000
Building craftsman: carpenter, bricklayer, mason, plasterer, plumber, etc.	442,000	1,000
Laborer (unspecified)	367,000	9,000
Milliner, dress-maker, seamstress (seamster)	494	340,000
Wool worker, every kind, with carpet-weaver	171,000	113,000
Shoe-maker	243,000	31,000
Coal-miner	216,000	3,000
Tailor	135,000	18,000
Washerwoman		145,000
Seaman (merchant), pilot	144,000	
Silk worker	53,000	80,000
Blacksmith	112,000	592
Linen, flax worker	47,000	56,000
Carter, carman, coachman, postboy, cabman, busman, etc.	83,000	1,000
Iron worker, founder, moulder (excluding iron-mining, nails, hardware, cutlery, files, tools, machines)	79,000	590
Railway driver, etc., porter, etc., laborer, platelayer	65,000	54
Hosiery worker	35,000	30,000
Lace worker	10,000	54,000
Machine, boiler maker	63,000	647
Baker	56,000	7,000
Copper, tin, lead-miner	53,000	7,000
Charwoman		55,000
Commercial clerk	44,000	19
Fisherman	37,000	1,000
Miller	37,000	562
Earthenware worker	25,000	11,000
Sawyer	35,000	23
Shipwright, boat-builder, block and mast maker	32,000	28
Straw-plait worker	4,000	28,000
Wheelwright	30,000	106
Glover	4,500	25,000
Nailer	19,000	10,000
Iron-miner	27,000	910
Tanner, currier, fellmonger	25,000	276
Printer	22,000	222

SOURCE: Adapted from J. H. Clapham, *An Economic History of Modern Britain* (Cambridge, England: Cambridge University Press, 1932), 3 vols.: Vol. II, p. 24. By permission of the publisher.

Isabella Beeton **Domestic Servants (1861)**

Women who worked for pay in Victorian Britain were most likely to be employed as domestic servants. In her bible for homemakers, The Book of Household Management, *Mrs. Beeton outlines the duties of both servants and their mistresses.*

The custom of "society" is to abuse its servants: a *façon de parler* such as leads their lords and masters to talk of the weather, and, when ruefully inclined, of the crops, leads matronly ladies, and ladies just entering on their probation in that honored and honorable state, to talk of servants, and, as we are told, wax eloquent over the greatest plague in life while taking a quiet cup of tea. . . . It is a conviction of "society" that the race of good servants has died out, at least in England, although they do order these things better in France; that there is neither honesty, conscientiousness, nor the careful and industrious habits which distinguished the servants of our grandmothers and great-grandmothers; that domestics no longer know their place; that the introduction of cheap silks and cottons, and, still more recently, those ambiguous "materials" and tweeds, have removed the landmarks between the mistress and her maid, between the master and his man.

CHOICE OF SERVANTS.—When the distinction really depends on things so insignificant as dress, when the lady of fashion chooses her footman without any other consideration than his height, shape, and *tournure* of calf, it is not surprising that she should find a domestic who has no attachment for the family, who considers the figure he cuts behind her carriage, and the late hours he is compelled to keep, a full compensation for the wages he exacts, for the food he wastes, and for the perquisites he can lay his hands on. Nor should the fast young man, who chooses his groom for his knowingness in the ways of the turf and in the tricks of low horse-dealers, be surprised if he is sometimes the victim of these learned ways. But these are the exceptional cases, which prove the existence of a better state of things. The great masses of society

among us are not thus deserted: there are few families of respectability, from the shopkeeper in the next street to the nobleman whose mansion dignifies the next square, which do not contain among their dependents attached and useful servants; and where these are absent altogether, there are good reasons for it.

MASTERS AND MISTRESSES.—It has been said that good masters and mistresses make good servants, and this to a great extent is true. There are certainly some men and women in the wide field of servitude whom it would be impossible to train into good servants, but the conduct of both master and mistress is seldom without its effect upon these dependents. They are not mere machines, and no one has a right to consider them in that light. The sensible master and the kind mistress know, that if servants depend on them for their means of living, in their turn they are dependent on their servants for very many of the comforts of life; and that, using a proper amount of care in choosing servants, treating them like reasonable beings, and making slight excuses for the shortcomings of human nature, they will, save in some exceptional cases, be tolerably well served, and, in most instances, surround themselves with attached domestics. . . .

WOMEN SERVANTS are specially likely to be influenced by their mistress's treatment of them, and yet we venture to assert that good mistresses are rarer than good masters, so many of the former lacking consideration for their servants.

In many cases they do not give them the help which it is their duty to afford. A timely hint or even a few words of quiet reproof may be lacking when needed, and still more so the kind words and the deserved praise for work well and carefully done. It

SOURCE: From Isabella Beeton, *The Book of Household Management* (London, 1888), pp. 1453–1481. (First published in 1861.)

is a fact that we must take some *trouble* with our servants. The wheels of domestic machinery will not run well without constant care. There is no necessity for a mistress to be continually fussing round and superintending her servants' work, but she must first make sure that they do it thoroughly and well. Also she must take time and pains to show her domestics *how* she likes the work done. . . .

THE NUMBER OF MEN-SERVANTS IN A FAMILY varies according to the wealth and position of the master, from the owner of the ducal mansion, with a retinue of attendants, at the head of which is the chamberlain and house-steward, to the occupier of the humbler house, where a single footman, or even the odd man-of-all-work, is the only male retainer. The majority of gentlemen's establishments probably comprise a servant out of livery, or butler, a footman and coachman, or coachman and groom, where the horses exceed two or three.

To a certain extent the number of men-servants kept is regulated by the number of women servants, this statement, of course, not applying to such out-door servants as coachman, groom, or gardener.

Occasionally a parlor-maid is kept instead of a second footman, or a kitchen or scullery-maid does the work in the way of boot-cleaning, etc., that would fall to a third footman or page. A man cook is now more rarely to be found in private service than formerly, women having found it expedient to bring their knowledge of the culinary art more to the level of the *chef;* while in many cases those who have a talent for cooking have risen superior to him both in the way they flavor and serve the various dishes that call for skill and taste. . . .

THE FIRST DUTY OF THE HOUSEMAID in winter is to open the shutters of all the lower rooms in the house, and take up the hearth-rugs in those rooms which she is going to "do" before breakfast. In some families, where there are only a cook and housemaid kept, and where the drawing-rooms are large, the cook has the care of the dining-room, and the housemaid that of the breakfast-room, library and drawing-rooms. After the shutters are all opened, she sweeps the breakfast-room, sweeping the dust toward the fireplace, of course previously removing the fender. She should then lay a cloth (generally made of coarse wrappering) over the carpet in front of the stove, and on this should place her housemaid's box, containing black-lead brushes, leathers, emery-paper, cloth, black-lead, and all utensils necessary for cleaning a grate, with the cinder-pail on the other side. She now sweeps up the ashes, and deposits them in her cinder-pail, which is a japanned tin pail, with a wire sifter inside, and a closely-fitting top. In this pail the cinders are sifted, and reserved for use in the kitchen or under the copper, the ashes only being thrown away. The cinders disposed of, she proceeds to black-lead the grate, producing the black lead, the soft brush for laying it on, her blacking and polishing brushes, from the box which contains her tools. The housemaid's box should be kept well stocked. Having blackened, brushed and polished every part, and made all clean and bright, she now proceeds to lay the fire. Sometimes it is very difficult to get a proper polish to black grates, particularly if they have been neglected and allowed to rust at all. But later on we give recipes for treating them that will be found useful.

Bright grates require unceasing attention to keep them in perfect order. A day should never pass without the housemaid rubbing with a dry leather the polished parts of a grate, as also the fender and fire-irons. A careful and attentive housemaid should have no occasion ever to use emery-paper for any part but the bars, which, of course, become blacked by the fire. (Some mistresses, to save labor, have a double set of bars, one set bright for the summer, and another black set to use when fires are in requisition.)

The several fires lighted, the housemaid proceeds with her dusting, and polishing the several pieces of furniture in the breakfast-parlor, leaving no corner unvisited. Before sweeping the carpet, it is a good practice to sprinkle it all over with tea-leaves, which not only lay all dust, but give a slightly fragrant smell to the room. It is now in order for the reception of the family, and where there is neither footman or parlor-maid, she now proceeds to the dressing-room, and lights her mistress's fire, if she is in the habit of having one to dress by. Her mistress is called, hot water placed in the dressing-room for her use, her clothes—as far as they are under the housemaid's charge—put before the fire, hanging a fire-guard on the bars where there is one, while she proceeds to prepare the breakfast. . . .

BEDROOM WORK.—Breakfast served, the housemaid proceeds to the bed-chambers, throws up the sashes, if not already done, pulls up the blinds, throwing back the curtains at the same time, and opens the beds, by removing the clothes, placing them over a horse, or failing that, over the backs of chairs. She now proceeds to empty the slops. In doing this, everything is emptied into the slop-pail, leaving a little scalding-hot water for a minute in vessels that require it; adding a drop of turpentine to the water, when that is not sufficient to cleanse them. The basin is emptied, well rinsed with clean water, and carefully wiped; the ewers emptied and washed; finally, the water-jugs themselves emptied out and rinsed, and wiped dry. As soon as this is done, she should remove and empty the pails, taking care that they also are well washed, scalded and wiped as soon as they are empty. Next follows bed-making, at which one of the other servants usually assists; but, before beginning, velvet chairs, or other things injured by dust, should be removed to another room. In bed-making, the fancy of its occupant should be consulted: some like beds sloping from the top toward the feet, swelling slightly in the middle; others, perfectly flat; a good housemaid will accommodate each bed to the taste of the sleeper, taking

care to shake, beat and turn it well in the process. Some persons prefer sleeping on the mattress; in which case a feather bed is usually beneath, resting on a second mattress, and a straw palliasse at the bottom. In this case, the mattresses should change places daily; the feather bed placed on the mattress shaken, beaten, taken up and opened several times, so as thoroughly to separate the feathers; if too large to be thus handled, the maid should shake and beat one end first, and then the other, smoothing it afterward equally all over into the required shape, and place the mattress gently over it. Any feathers which escape in this process a tidy servant will put back through the seam of the tick; she will also be careful to sew up any stitch that gives way the moment it is discovered. The bed-clothes are laid on, beginning with an under blanket and sheet, which are tucked under the mattress at the bottom. The bolster is then beaten and shaken, and put on, the top of the sheet rolled round it, and the sheet tucked in all round. The pillows and other bed-clothes follow, and the counterpane over all, which should fall in graceful folds, and at equal distance from the ground all round. The curtains are drawn to the head and folded neatly across the bed, and the whole finished in a smooth and graceful manner. Where spring mattresses are used, care should be taken that the over one is turned every day. The housemaid should now take up in a dustpan any pieces that may be on the carpet; she should dust the room, shut the door, and proceed to another room. When all the bedrooms are finished, she should dust the stairs and polish the hand-rail of the banisters, and see that all ledges, window-sills, etc., are quite free from dust.

THE WIFE OF A COTTON SPINNER   Life at Home (1833)

An investigator for the factory commission interviews Mrs. B., the wife of a Manchester cotton spinner, about her family's life. In the first portion of the report, he summarizes his observations and her responses. In the second, he prints both his questions and her answers.

SOURCE: *Reports from Factory Commissioners. Parliamentary Papers*, Vol. 20 (1833), pp. 39–41.

Her husband is a fine spinner, at Mr.——, where he has been from 1816, has five children. Her eldest daughter, now going on fourteen, has been her father's piecer for three years. At her present age, her labor is worth 4s. 6d. a week, and has been worth as much for these last four months; before, it was worth less. At present her husband's earnings and her daughter's together amount to about 25s. a week—at least she sees no more than 25s. a week[1]; and before his daughter could piece for him, and when he had to pay for a piecer in her stead, he only brought home 19s. or 20s. a week.

Rent of house, 3s. 6d. a week.

Breakfast is generally porridge, bread and milk, lined with flour or oatmeal. On Sunday, a sup of tea and bread and butter.—*Dinner*, on week days, potatoes and bacon, and bread, which is generally white. On a Sunday, a little flesh meat; no butter, egg, or pudding.—*Tea-time*, every day, tea, and bread and butter; nothing extra on Sunday at tea.—*Supper*, oatmeal porridge and milk; sometimes potatoes and milk. Sunday, sometimes a little bread and cheese for supper: never have this on week days. Now and then buys eggs when they are as low as a halfpenny apiece, and fries them to bacon.

They never taste any other vegetables than potatoes; never use any beer or spirits; now and then may take a gill of beer when ill, which costs a penny. Perhaps she and her husband may have two gills a week. Her husband never drinks any beer or spirits that she knows of beyond this. The house consists of four rooms, two on each floor; the furniture consists of two beds in the same room, one for themselves, the other for the children; have four chairs, one table in the house, boxes to put clothes in, no chest of drawers, two pans and a tea kettle

Consumption by the week, of different articles, by her husband, herself, and five children.

	£	s.	d.
Butter, 1½ lb, at 10d.	0	1	3
Tea, 1½ oz.	0	0	4½
Bread she makes herself: buys 24 lb. of flour—flour, barm, salt, and baking, cost	0	4	6
Half a peck of oatmeal	0	0	6½
Bacon, 1½ lb.	0	0	9
Potatoes, two score a week, at 8d. a score[2]	0	1	4
Milk, a quart a day, at 3d. a quart	0	1	9
Flesh meat on Sunday, about a pound	0	0	7
Sugar, 1½ lb. a week, at 6d.	0	0	9
Pepper, mustard, salt, and extras, say	0	0	3
Soap and candles	0	1	0
Coals	0	1	6
Rent	0	3	6
	£0	18	1
Alleged total of weekly income	£1	5	0
Deduct foregoing expenses	0	18	1
Leaves for clothing, sickness of seven persons, } schooling, etc. a surplus of	£0	6	11

[1]The investigator notes that the standard wage for a spinner like the husband of Mrs. B. must be at least 28s. a week. (A pound [£.] was worth 20 shillings [s.], and each shilling was worth 12 pence [d.].) [2]*a score:* twenty pounds

for boiling, a gridiron and frying-pan, half-a-dozen large and small plates, four pair of knives and forks, several pewter spoons. They subscribe 1*d*. a week for each child to a funeral society[3] for the children. Two of the children go to school at 3*d*. a week each: they are taught reading for this, but not writing. Have a few books, such as a Bible, hymn-book, and several small books that the children have got as prizes at the Sunday School. Four children go to Stott's Sunday School.

QUESTION. Does your daughter, who pieces for her father, seem much fatigued when she comes home at night?

ANSWER. No, she does not seem much fatigued. She is coming of an age that perhaps she may be. She has a good appetite. Hears her complain of headache sometimes; does not hear her complain of not sleeping.

Q. Do you think that people in your own way of life, spinners and such like, and their families, are better off than yourselves, or worse off, or just about the same?

A. Well, some's better, some's worse, some's the same. It is according to their work—whether they work upon fine or coarse work.

Q. I want to know whether the most are like off to yourselves. Now, at Mr.——mill, are most of the parents of children as well off, or better off, than yourself?

A. Well, they are most of them at his mill as well off as we ourselves, because it is one of the best mills in the town. There is not many better than his.

In answer to questions concerning herself, she said she should be forty years old on Whitsun Monday: that at fourteen years old she began frame-tenting, and worked at it for two years every day, from six in the morning till eight in the evening—sometimes from half-past five in the morning. She then went to stretching, at which she worked till twenty-five years old: at that she worked fourteen hours a day regularly every day. At twenty-five years old she married, and has staid at home ever since. Her father was a bleacher, her mother a spinner. Has eight brothers and sisters; but can't give no idea whether her brothers and sisters are bigger or less than her parents, because her mother took them all away to America when she was a child.

Q. Should you say you were as healthy a woman now, as if you had not been a frame tenter or a stretcher?

A. Well, I don't know but what I am. I have not my health very well at present. I do not know that work injured it.

Q. How many different mills were you in when you were young?

A. In four mills. Has heard different language at some from others; some very bad, some very well. A child may pick up much bad in mills. Better to put a child in a mill than let it run in the streets; it won't get as much harm in a mill.

Q. Do girls run a chance of being bad by living in mills; in short, to be unchaste?

A. I can't say. I never see'd nothing of bad wherever I worked. It is according to their own endeavors a good deal.

LORD ASHLEY **Women Factory Workers (1844)**

The future earl of Shaftesbury, a leading social reformer, is sorely troubled by the type of life led by women factory workers.

Sir, look at the physical effect of this system on the women. See its influence on the delicate constitutions and tender forms of the female sex. Let it be recollected that the

SOURCE: From *Hansard's Parliamentary Debates*, 3rd Series, Vol. 73 (1844), cols. 1089, 1092–1096, 1100–1101.

[3]The society provided an insurance policy that would pay for the cost of funeral and burial.

age at which the "prolonged labor," as it is called, commences, is at the age of thirteen. That age, according to the testimony of medical men, is the tenderest period of female life. Observe the appalling progress of female labor; and remember that the necessity for particular protection to females against overwork is attested by the most eminent surgeons and physicians. . . .

There are [says Mr. Saunders] among them, females who have been employed for some weeks, with an interval only of a few days, from six o'clock in the morning until twelve o'clock at night, less than two hours for meals, thus giving them for five nights in the week, six hours out of its twenty-four to go to and from their homes, and to obtain rest in bed. . . . A vast majority [says Mr. Saunders, in January, 1844] of the persons employed at night, and for long hours during the day, are females; their labor is cheaper, and they are more easily induced to undergo severe bodily fatigue than men.

Where, Sir, under this condition, are the possibilities of domestic life? How can its obligations be fulfilled? Regard the woman as wife or mother, how can she accomplish any portion of her calling? And if she cannot do that which Providence has assigned her, what must be the effect on the whole surface of society? . . .

Look again to the effects on domestic economy; out of thirteen married females taken at one mill, only one knew how to make her husband a shirt, and only four knew how to mend one. I have the evidence of several females, who declare their own ignorance of every domestic accomplishment—the unmarried declare, "not a single qualification of any sort for household servants." The married; "untidy, slovenly, dirty; cannot work, sew, take care of children, or the house; cannot manage expenses; perpetual waste and extravagance."

. . . So much, Sir, for their physical, and, if I may so speak, their financial condition; the picture of their moral state will not be more consolatory. And, first, their exces-

sive intemperance: Mr. Roberton, a distinguished surgeon at Manchester, says, in a published essay:—

I regard it as a misfortune for an operative to be obliged to labor for so long hours at an exhausting occupation, and often in an impure atmosphere. I consider this circumstance as one of the chief causes of the astounding inebriety of our population. . . .

Mr. Braidley, when boroughreeve[4] of Manchester, stated, "that in one gin shop, during eight successive Saturday evenings, from seven till ten o'clock, he observed, on an average rate, 412 persons enter by the hour, of which the females were 60 per cent." Many females state, that the labor induces "an intolerable thirst; they can drink, but not eat." . . .

But listen to another fact, and one deserving of serious attention; that the females not only perform the labor, but occupy the places of men; they are forming various clubs and associations, and gradually acquiring all those privileges which are held to be the proper portion of the male sex. These female clubs are thus described:— "Fifty or sixty females, married and single, form themselves into clubs, ostensibly for protection; but, in fact, they meet together, to drink, sing, and smoke; they use, it is stated, the lowest, most brutal, and most disgusting language imaginable." Here is a dialogue which occurred in one of these clubs, from an ear witness:—"A man came into one of these club-rooms, with a child in his arms; 'Come lass,' said he, addressing one of the women, 'come home, for I cannot keep this bairn quiet, and the other I have left crying at home.' 'I won't go home, idle devil,' she replied, 'I have thee to keep, and the bairns too, and if I can't get a pint of ale quietly, it is tiresome. This is the only second pint that Bess and me have had between us; thou may sup if thou likes, and sit thee down, but I won't go home yet.'" Whence is it that this singular and unnatural change is taking place? Because that on

---

[4]*boroughreeve:* the chief municipal officer

women are imposed the duty and burthen of supporting their husbands and families, a perversion as it were of nature, which has the inevitable effect of introducing into families disorder, insubordination, and conflict. What is the ground on which the woman says she will pay no attention to her domestic duties, nor give the obedience which is owing to her husband? Because on her devolves the labor which ought to fall to his share, and she throws out the taunt, "If I have the labor, I will also have the amusement."

... The toil of the females has hitherto been considered the characteristic of savage life; but we, in the height of our refinement, impose on the wives and daughters of England a burthen from which, at least during pregnancy, they would be exempted even in slave-holding states, and among the Indians of America. But every consideration sinks to nothing compared with that which springs from the contemplation of the moral mischiefs this system engenders and sustains. You are poisoning the very sources of order and happiness and virtue; you are tearing up root and branch, all the relations of families to each other; you are annulling, as it were, the institution of domestic life, decreed by Providence himself, the wisest and kindest of earthly ordinances, the mainstay of social peace and virtue, and therein of national security. . . .

It matters not whether it be prince or peasant, all that is best, all that is lasting in the character of a man, he has learnt at his mother's knees. Search the records, examine the opening years of those who have been distinguished for ability and virtue, and you will ascribe, with but few exceptions, the early culture of their minds, and above all, the first discipline of the heart, to the intelligence and affection of the mother, or at least of some pious woman, who with the self-denial and tenderness of her sex, has entered as a substitute, on the sacred office. No, Sir, these sources of mischief must be dried up; every public consideration demands such an issue; the health of the females; the care of their families; their conjugal and parental duties; the comfort of their homes; the decency of their lives; the rights of their husbands; the peace of society; and the laws of God. . . .

HENRY MAYHEW **The Costermongers (1851)**

Britain's pioneer journalist-sociologist reports on the lives of London's 30,000 coster-mongers—or streetsellers of fruit and vegetables.

Only one-tenth—at the outside one-tenth—of the couples living together and carrying on the costermongering trade, are married. In Clerkenwell parish, however, where the number of married couples is about a fifth of the whole, this difference is easily accounted for, as in Advent and Easter the incumbent of that parish marries poor couples without a fee. Of the rights of "legitimate" or "illegitimate" children the costermongers understand nothing, and account it a mere waste of money and time to go through the ceremony of wedlock when a pair can live together, and be quite as well regarded by their fellows, without it. The married women associate with the unmarried mothers of families without the slightest scruple. There is no honor attached to the marriage state, and no shame to concubinage. Neither are the unmarried women less faithful to their "partners" than the married; but I understand that, of the two classes, the unmarried betray the most jealousy.

As regards the fidelity of these women I was assured that, "in anything like good

SOURCE: From Henry Mayhew, *London Labour and the London Poor* (London: Charles Griffin and Co., 1861), 4 vols.: Vol. I, pp. 22–23, 45–48. (First published in 1851.)

times," they were rigidly faithful to their husbands or paramours; but that, in the worst pinch of poverty, a departure from this fidelity—if it provided a few meals or a fire—was not considered at all heinous. An old costermonger, who had been mixed up with other callings, and whose prejudices were certainly not in favor of his present trade, said to me, "What I call the working girls, are as industrious and as faithful a set as can well be. I'm satisfied that they're more faithful to their mates than other poor working women. I never knew one of these working girls do wrong that way. They're strong, hearty, healthy girls, and keep clean rooms. Why, there's numbers of men leave their stockmoney with their women, just taking out two or three shillings to gamble with and get drunk upon. They sometimes take a little drop themselves, the women do, and get beaten by their husbands for it, and hardest beaten if the man's drunk himself. They're sometimes beaten for other things too, or for nothing at all. But they seem to like the men better for their beating them. I never could make that out." Notwithstanding this fidelity, it appears that the "larking and joking" of the young, and sometimes of the middle-aged people, among themselves is anything but delicate. The unmarried separate as seldom as the married. The fidelity characterizing the women does not belong to the men.

The dancing-rooms are the places where matches are made up. There the boys go to look out for "mates" and sometimes a match is struck up the first night of meeting, and the couple live together forthwith. The girls at these dances are all the daughters of costermongers, or of persons pursuing some other course of street life. Unions take place when the lad is but 14. Two or three out of 100 have their female helpmates at that early age; but the female is generally a couple of years older than her partner. Nearly all the costermongers form such alliances as I have described, when both parties are under twenty. One reason why these alliances are contracted at early ages is, that when a boy has assisted his father, or any one engaging him, in the busi-

ness of a costermonger, he knows that he can borrow money, and hire a shallow or a barrow—or he may have saved 5s—"and then if the father vexes him or snubs him," said one of my informants, "he'll tell his father to go to h—l, and he and his gal will start on their own account."

Most of the costermongers have numerous families, but not those who contract alliances very young. The women continue working down to the day of their confinement.

"Chance children," as they are called, or children unrecognized by any father, are rare among the young women of the costermongers. . . .

The story of one coster girl's life may be taken as a type of the many. When quite young she is placed out to nurse with some neighbor, the mother—if a fond one—visiting the child at certain periods of the day, for the purpose of feeding it, or sometimes, knowing the round she has to make, having the infant brought to her at certain places, to be "suckled." As soon as it is old enough to go alone, the court is its playground, the gutter its school-room, and under the care of an elder sister the little one passes the day, among children whose mothers like her own are too busy out in the streets helping to get the food, to be able to mind the family at home. When the girl is strong enough, she in her turn is made to assist the mother by keeping guard over the younger children, or, if there be none, she is lent out to carry about a baby, and so made to add to the family income by gaining her sixpence weekly. Her time is from the earliest years fully occupied; indeed, her parents cannot afford to keep her without doing and getting *something*. Very few of the children receive the least education. "The parents," I am told, "never give their minds to learning, for they say, 'What's the use of it? *That* won't yarn a gal a living.'" Everything is sacrificed—as, indeed, under the circumstances it must be—in the struggle to live— aye! and to live *merely*. Mind, heart, soul, are all absorbed in the belly. The rudest form of animal life, physiologists tell us, is simply a locomotive stomach. Verily, it would appear as if our social state had a tendency to make the highest animal sink to the lowest.

At about seven years of age the girls first go into the streets to sell. A shallow-basket is given to them, with about two shillings for stock-money, and they hawk, according to the time of year, either oranges, apples, or violets; some begin their street education with the sale of water-cresses. The money earned by this means is strictly given to the parents. Sometimes—though rarely—a girl who has been unfortunate during the day will not dare return home at night, and then she will sleep under some dry arch or about some market, until the morrow's gains shall ensure her a safe reception and shelter in her father's room.

The life of the coster-girls is as severe as that of the boys. Between four and five in the morning they have to leave home for the markets, and sell in the streets until about nine. Those that have more kindly parents, return then to breakfast, but many are obliged to earn the morning's meal for themselves. After breakfast, they generally remain in the streets until about ten o'clock at night; many having nothing during all that time but one meal of bread and butter and coffee, to enable them to support the fatigue of walking from street to street with the heavy basket on their heads. In the course of a day, some girls eat as much as a pound of bread, and very seldom get any meat, unless it be on a Sunday.

Mayhew interviews a particular coster girl, "a fine-grown young woman of eighteen."

"There's six on us in family, and father and mother makes eight. Father used to do odd jobs with the gas-pipes in the streets, and when work was slack we had very hard times of it. Mother always liked being with us at home, and used to manage to keep us employed out of mischief—she'd give us an old gown to make into pinafores for the children and such like! She's been very good

to us, has mother, and so's father. She always liked to hear us read to her whilst she was washing or such like! and then we big ones had to learn the little ones. But when father's work got slack, if she had no employment charing,[5] she'd say, 'Now I'll go and buy a bushel of apples,' and then she'd turn out and get a penny that way. I suppose by sitting at the stall from nine in the morning till the shops shut up—say ten o'clock at night, I can earn about 1*s.*6*d.* a day. It's all according to the apples—whether they're good or not—what we makes. If I'm unlucky, mother will say, 'Well, I'll go out to-morrow and see what *I* can do'; and if I've done well, she'll say 'Come, you're a good hand at it; you've done famous.' Yet, mother's very fair that way. Ah! there's many a gal I knows whose back has to suffer if she don't sell her stock well; but, thank God! I never get more than a blowing up. My parents is very fair to me.

"I dare say there ain't ten out of a hundred gals what's living with men, what's been married Church of England fashion. I know plenty myself, but I don't, indeed, think it right. It seems to me that the gals is fools to be 'ticed away, but, in coorse, they needn't go without they likes. This is why I don't think it's right. Perhaps a man will have a few words with his gal, and he'll say, 'Oh! I ain't obligated to keep her!' and he'll turn her out: and then where's that poor gal to go? Now, there's a gal I knows as came to me no later than this here week, and she had a dreadful swole face and a awful black eye; and I says, 'Who's done that?' and she says, says she, 'Why, Jack'—just in that way; and then she says, says she, 'I'm going to take a warrant out to-morrow.' Well, he gets the warrant that same night, but she never appears again him, for fear of getting more beating. That don't seem to me to be like married people ought to be. Besides, if parties is married, they ought to bend to each other; and they won't, for sartain, if they're only living together. A man as is married is obligated to keep his wife if they quarrels or not; and he says to himself, says

---

[5]*charing:* cleaning house

he, 'Well, I may as well live happy, like.' But if he can turn a poor gal off, as soon as he tires of her, he begins to have noises with her, and then gets quit of her altogether. Again, the men takes the money of the gals, and in coorse ought to treat 'em well—which they don't. This is another reason: when the gal is in the family way, the lads mostly sends them to the workhouse to lay in, and only goes sometimes to take them a bit of tea and shuggar; but, in course, married men wouldn't behave in such likes to their poor wives. After a quarrel, too, a lad goes and takes up with another young gal, and that isn't pleasant for the first one. The first step to ruin is them places of 'penny gaffs,'[6] for they hears things there as oughtn't to be said to young gals. Besides, the lads is very insinivating, and after leaving them places will give a gal a drop of beer, and make her half tipsy, and then they makes their arrangements. I've often heerd the boys boasting of having ruined gals, for all the world as if they was the first noblemen in the land.

"It would be a good thing if these sort of goings on could be stopped. It's half the parents' fault; for if a gal can't get a living, they turns her out into the streets, and then what's to become of her? I'm sure the gals, if they was married, would be happier, because they couldn't be beat worse. And if they was married, they'd get a nice home about 'em; whereas, if they's only living together, they takes a furnished room. I'm sure, too, that it's a bad plan; for I've heerd the gals themselves say, 'Ah! I wish I'd never seed Jack' (or Tom, or whatever it is); 'I'm sure I'd never be half so bad but for him.'"

JOHN STUART MILL **The Subjection of Women (1869)**

The author of On Liberty *issues a manifesto calling for the complete legal equality of the sexes.*

The object of this essay is to explain as clearly as I am able, the grounds of an opinion which I have held from the very earliest period when I had formed any opinions at all on social or political matters, and which, instead of being weakened or modified, has been constantly growing stronger by the progress of reflection and the experience of life: That the principle which regulates the existing social relations between the two sexes—the legal subordination of one sex to the other—is wrong in itself, and now one of the chief hindrances to human improvement; and that it ought to be replaced by a principle of perfect equality, admitting no power or privilege on the one side, nor disability on the other. . . .

In the first place, the opinion in favor of the present system, which entirely subordinates the weaker sex to the stronger, rests upon theory only; for there never has been trial made of any other: so that experience, in the sense in which it is vulgarly opposed to theory, cannot be pretended to have pronounced any verdict. And in the second place, the adoption of this system of inequality never was the result of deliberation, or forethought, or any social ideas, or any notion whatever of what conduced to the benefit of humanity or the good order of society. It arose simply from the fact that from the very earliest twilight of human society, every woman (owing to the value attached to her by men, combined with her inferiority in muscular strength) was found in a state of bondage to some man. Laws and systems of polity always begin by recognizing the relations they find already

SOURCE: From John Stuart Mill, *The Subjection of Women*, 2nd ed. (London: Longmans, Green, 1869), pp. 1, 8–10, 20–21, 24–31, 33–35, 38–39, 48–49, 51, 53–60, 62–63, 66–71, 78–79, 83.

[6]*'penny gaffs'*: low-class theatres or music halls

existing between individuals. They convert what was a mere physical fact into a legal right, give it the sanction of society, and principally aim at the substitution of public and organized means of asserting and protecting these rights, instead of the irregular and lawless conflict of physical strength. . . . No presumption in its favor, therefore, can be drawn from the fact of its existence. The only such presumption which it could be supposed to have, must be grounded on its having lasted till now, when so many other things which came down from the same odious source have been done away with. . . .

Some will object, that a comparison cannot fairly be made between the government of the male sex and the forms of unjust power which I have adduced in illustration of it [e.g., absolute monarchy; the enslavement of blacks by whites], since these are arbitrary, and the effect of mere usurpation, while it on the contrary is natural. But was there ever any domination which did not appear natural to those who possessed it? . . .

It will be said, the rule of men over women differs from all these others in not being a rule of force: it is accepted voluntarily; women make no complaint, and are consenting parties to it. In the first place, a great number of women do not accept it. Ever since there have been women able to make their sentiments known by their writings (the only mode of publicity which society permits to them), an increasing number of them have recorded protests against their present social condition: and recently many thousands of them, headed by the most eminent women known to the public, have petitioned Parliament for their admission to the parliamentary suffrage. The claim of women to be educated as solidly, and in the same branches of knowledge, as men, is urged with growing intensity, and with a great prospect of success; while the demand for their admission into professions and occupations hitherto closed against them, becomes every year more urgent. . . .

There is never any want of women who complain of ill usage by their husbands. There would be infinitely more, if complaint were not the greatest of all provocatives to a repetition and increase of the ill usage. . . .

All causes, social and natural, combine to make it unlikely that women should be collectively rebellious to the power of men. They are so far in a position different from all other subject classes, that their masters require something more from them than actual service. Men do not want solely the obedience of women, they want their sentiments. All men, except the most brutish, desire to have, in the woman most nearly connected with them, not a forced slave but a willing one, not a slave merely, but a favorite. They have therefore put everything in practice to enslave their minds. . . . All women are brought up from the very earliest years in the belief that their ideal of character is the very opposite to that of men; not self-will, and government by self-control, but submission, and yielding to the control of others. All the moralities tell them that it is the duty of women, and all the current sentimentalities that it is their nature, to live for others; to make complete abnegation of themselves, and to have no life but in their affections. . . . When we put together three things—first, the natural attraction between opposite sexes; secondly, the wife's entire dependence on the husband, every privilege or pleasure she has being either his gift, or depending entirely on his will; and lastly, that the principal object of human pursuit, consideration, and all objects of social ambition, can in general be sought or obtained by her only through him, it would be a miracle if the object of being attractive to men had not become the polar star of feminine education and formation of character. . . .

The preceding considerations are amply sufficient to show that custom, however universal it may be, affords in this case no presumption, and ought not to create any prejudice, in favor of the arrangements which place women in social and political subjection to men. But I may go farther, and maintain that the course of history, and the tendencies of progressive human society, afford not only no presumption in favor of this system of inequality of rights, but a strong one against it. . . .

For, what is the peculiar character of the modern world—the difference which chiefly distinguishes modern institutions, modern social ideas, modern life itself, from those of times long past? It is, that human beings are no longer born to their place in life, and chained down by an inexorable bond to the place they are born to, but are free to employ their faculties, and such favorable chances as offer, to achieve the lot which may appear to them most desirable. Human society of old was constituted on a very different principle. All were born to a fixed social position, and were mostly kept in it by law. . . . In modern Europe, and most in those parts of it which have participated most largely in all other modern improvements, diametrically opposite doctrines now prevail. Law and government do not undertake to prescribe by whom any social or industrial operation shall or shall not be conducted, or what modes of conducting them shall be lawful. These things are left to the unfettered choice of individuals. . . .

But if the principle is true, we ought to act as if we believed it, and not to ordain that to be born a girl instead of a boy, any more than to be born black instead of white, or a commoner instead of a nobleman, shall decide the person's position through all life—shall interdict people from all the more elevated social positions, and from all, except a few, respectable occupations. . . .

At present, in the more improved countries, the disabilities of women are the only case, save one, in which laws and institutions take persons at their birth, and ordain that they shall never in all their lives be allowed to compete for certain things. The one exception is that of royalty. . . . All other dignities and social advantages are open to the whole male sex: many indeed are only attainable by wealth, but wealth may be striven for by any one, and is actually obtained by many men of the very

humblest origin. The difficulties, to the majority, are indeed insuperable without the aid of fortunate accidents; but no male human being is under any legal ban: neither law nor opinion superadd artificial obstacles to the natural ones. . . .

Neither does it avail anything to say that the *nature* of the two sexes adapt them to their present functions and position, and renders these appropriate to them. Standing on the ground of common sense and the constitution of the human mind, I deny that any one knows, or can know, the nature of the two sexes, as long as they have only been seen in their present relation to one another. . . . What is now called the nature of women is an eminently artificial thing—the result of forced repression in some directions, unnatural stimulation in others. . . .

One thing we may be certain of—that what is contrary to women's nature to do, they never will be made to do by simply giving their nature free play. The anxiety of mankind to interfere in behalf of nature, for fear lest nature should not succeed in effecting its purpose, is an altogether unnecessary solicitude. What women by nature cannot do, it is quite superfluous to forbid them from doing. What they can do, but not so well as the men who are their competitors, competition suffices to exclude them from; since nobody asks for protective duties and bounties in favor of women; it is only asked that the present bounties and protective duties in favor of men should be recalled. If women have a greater natural inclination for some things than for others, there is no need of laws or social inculcation to make the majority of them do the former in preference to the latter. Whatever women's services are most wanted for, the free play of competition will hold out the strongest inducements to them to undertake. . . .

Those who attempt to force women into marriage by closing all other doors against them . . . are afraid, not lest women should be unwilling to marry, for I do not think that any one in reality has that apprehension; but lest they should insist that marriage should be on equal conditions; lest all women of spirit and capacity should prefer doing almost anything else, not in their own eyes degrading, rather than marry, when marrying is giving themselves a master, and a master too of all their earthly possessions. . . .

Originally women were taken by force, or regularly sold by their father to the husband. Until a late period in European history, the father had the power to dispose of his daughter in marriage at his own will and pleasure, without any regard to hers. . . . After marriage, the man had anciently (but this was anterior to Christianity) the power of life and death over his wife. She could invoke no law against him; he was her sole tribunal and law. . . . By the old laws of England, the husband was called the *lord* of the wife; he was literally regarded as her sovereign, inasmuch that the murder of a man by his wife was called treason. . . . Because the various enormities have fallen into disuse . . . men suppose that all is now as it should be in regard to the marriage contract; and we are continually told that civilization and Christianity have restored to the woman her just rights. Meanwhile the wife is the actual bond-servant of her husband: no less so, as far as legal obligation goes, than slaves commonly so called. She vows a life-long obedience to him at the altar, and is held to it all through her life by law. . . . She can do no act whatever but by his permission, at least tacit. She can acquire no property but for him; the instant it becomes hers, even if by inheritance, it becomes *ipso facto* his. In this respect the wife's position under the common law of England is worse than that of slaves in the laws of many countries. . . .

By means of settlements, the rich usually contrive to withdraw the whole or part of the inherited property of the wife from the absolute control of the husband. . . . In the immense majority of cases there is no settlement: and the absorption of all rights, all property, as well as all freedom of action, is complete. The two are called "one person

in law," for the purpose of inferring that whatever is hers is his, but the parallel inference is never drawn that whatever is his is hers; the maxim is not applied against the man, except to make him responsible to third parties for her acts, as a master is for the acts of his slaves or of his cattle. I am far from pretending that wives are in general no better treated than slaves; but no slave is a slave to the same lengths, and in so full a sense of the word, as a wife is. . . .

Though she may know that he hates her, . . . he can claim from her and enforce the lowest degradation of a human being, that of being made the instrument of an animal function contrary to her inclinations. While she is held in this worst description of slavery as to her own person, what is her position in regard to the children in whom she and her master have a joint interest? They are by law *his* children. He alone has any legal rights over them. . . .

It is only legal separation by a decree of a court of justice, which entitles her to live apart, without being forced back into the custody of an exasperated jailer—or which empowers her to apply any earnings to her own use, without fear that a man whom perhaps she has not seen for twenty years will pounce upon her some day and carry all off. This legal separation, until lately,[7] the courts of justice would only give at an expense which made it inaccessible to any one out of the higher ranks. Even now it is only given in cases of desertion, or of the extreme of cruelty; and yet complaints are made every day that it is granted too easily. . . . But no amount of ill usage, without adultery superadded, will in England free a wife from her tormentor.

I have no desire to exaggerate, nor does the case stand in any need of exaggeration. I have described the wife's legal position, not her actual treatment. The laws of most countries are far worse than the people who execute them, and many of them are only able to remain laws by being seldom or never carried into effect. If married life were all that it might be expected to be,

---

[7]*until lately:* the Divorce Act of 1857

looking to the laws alone, society would be a hell upon earth. Happily there are both feelings and interests which in many men exclude, and in most, greatly temper, the impulses and propensities which lead to tyranny: and of those feelings, the tie which connects a man and his wife affords, in a normal state of things, incomparably the strongest example. The only tie which at all approaches to it, that between him and his children, tends, in all save exceptional cases, to strengthen, instead of conflicting with, the first. Because this is true; because men in general do not inflict, nor women suffer, all the misery which could be inflicted and suffered if the full power of tyranny with which the man is legally invested were acted on; the defenders of the existing form of the institution think that all its iniquity is justified, and that any complaint is merely quarrelling with the evil which is the price paid for every great good. . . .

Whether the institution to be defended is slavery, political absolutism, or the absolutism of the head of a family, we are always expected to judge of it from its best instances; and we are presented with pictures of loving exercise of authority on one side, loving submission to it on the other—superior wisdom ordering all things for the greatest good of the dependents, and surrounded by their smiles and benedictions. All this would be very much to the purpose if any one pretended that there are no such things as good men. Who doubts that there may be great goodness, and great happiness, and great affection, under the absolute government of a good man? Meanwhile, laws and institutions require to be adapted, not to good men, but to bad. Marriage is not an institution designed for a select few. Men are not required, as a preliminary to the marriage ceremony, to prove by testimonials that they are fit to be trusted with the exercise of absolute power. The tie of affection and obligation to a wife and children is very strong with those whose general social feelings are strong, and with many who are little sensible to any other social ties; but there are all degrees of sensi-

bility and insensibility to it, as there are all grades of goodness and wickedness in men, down to those whom no ties will bind, and on whom society has no action but through its *ultima ratio*, the penalties of the law. . . .

If the family in its best forms is, as it is often said to be, a school of sympathy, tenderness, and loving forgetfulness of self, it is still oftener, as respects its chief, a school of wilfulness, overbearingness, unbounded self-indulgence, and a double-dyed and idealized selfishness, of which sacrifice itself is only a particular form: the care for the wife and children being only care for them as parts of the man's own interests and belongings, and their individual happiness being immolated in every shape to his smallest preferences. What better is to be looked for under the existing form of the institution? . . . I know that there is another side to the question. I grant that the wife, if she cannot effectually resist, can at least retaliate; she, too, can make the man's life extremely uncomfortable, and by that power is able to carry many points which she ought, and many which she ought not, to prevail in. But this instrument of self-protection—which may be called the power of the scold, or the shrewish sanction—has the fatal defect, that it avails most against the least tyrannical superiors, and in favor of the least deserving dependents. . . . The amiable cannot use such an instrument, the highminded disdain it. And on the other hand, the husbands against whom it is used most effectively are the gentler and more inoffensive; those who cannot be induced, even by provocation, to resort to any very harsh exercise of authority. The wife's power of being disagreeable generally only establishes a counter-tyranny, and makes victims in their turn chiefly of those husbands who are least inclined to be tyrants.

What is it, then, which really tempers the corrupting effects of the power, and makes it compatible with such amount of good as we actually see? . . . The real mitigating causes are, the personal affection which is the growth of time, in so far as the man's nature is susceptible of it, and the woman's character sufficiently congenial with his to excite it; their common interests as regards the children, and their general community of interest as concerns third persons . . . ; the real importance of the wife to his daily comforts and enjoyments, and the value he consequently attaches to her on his personal account, which, in a man capable of feeling for others, lays the foundation of caring for her on her own. . . . Through these various means, the wife frequently exercises even too much power over the man; she is able to affect his conduct in things in which she may not be qualified to influence it for good—in which her influence may be not only unenlightened, but employed on the morally wrong side; and in which he would act better if left to his own prompting. But neither in the affairs of families nor in those of states is power a compensation for the loss of freedom. . . .

But how, it will be asked, can any society exist without government? In a family, as in a state, some one person must be the ultimate ruler. . . .

It is not true that in all voluntary association between two people, one of them must be absolute master: still less that the law must determine which of them it shall be. The most frequent case of voluntary association, next to marriage, is partnership in business: and it is not found or thought necessary to enact that in every partnership, one partner shall have entire control over the concern, and the others shall be bound to obey his orders. . . .

There are, no doubt, women, as there are men, whom equality of consideration will not satisfy; with whom there is no peace while any will or wish is regarded but their own. Such persons are a proper subject for the law of divorce. They are only fit to live alone, and no human beings ought to be compelled to associate their lives with them. . . .

The equality of married persons before the law, is not only the sole mode in which that particular relation can be made consistent with justice to both sides, and conducive to the happiness of both, but it is the only means of rendering the daily life of mankind, in any high sense, a school of moral cultivation. . . .

I readily admit (and it is the very foundation of my hopes) that numbers of married people even under the present law, (in the higher classes of England probably a great majority), live in the spirit of a just law of equality. Laws never would be improved, if there were not numerous persons whose moral sentiments are better than the existing laws. Such persons ought to support the principles here advocated; of which the only object is to make all other married couples similar to what these are now. . . .

E. LYNN LINTON   The Girl of the Period (1868)

In an article that startled the readers of the prestigious Saturday Review *and added a new phrase to the vocabulary of Victorian society, Mrs. Lynn Linton condemns "The Girl of the Period."*

Time was when the phrase, "a fair young English girl," meant the ideal of womanhood; to us, at least, of home birth and breeding. It meant a creature generous, capable, modest; something franker than a Frenchwoman, more to be trusted than an Italian, as brave as an American but more refined, as domestic as a German and more graceful. It meant a girl who could be trusted alone if need be, because of the innate purity and dignity of her nature, but who was neither bold in bearing nor masculine in mind; a girl who, when she married, would be her husband's friend and compan-

SOURCE: Reprinted in E. Lynn Linton, *The Girl of the Period and Other Social Essays* (London: Richard Bentley & Son, 1883), 2 vols.: Vol. I, pp. 1–9.

ion, but never his rival; one who would consider his interests as identical with her own, and not hold him as just so much fair game for spoil; who would make his house his true home and place of rest, not a mere passage-place for vanity and ostentation to pass through; a tender mother, an industrious housekeeper, a judicious mistress.

We prided ourselves as a nation on our women. We thought we had the pick of creation in this fair young English girl of ours, and envied no other men their own.... This was in the old time, and when English girls were content to be what God and nature had made them. Of late years we have changed the pattern, and have given to the world a race of women as utterly unlike the old insular ideal as if we had created another nation altogether. The Girl of the Period, and the fair young English girl of the past, have nothing in common save ancestry and their mother-tongue; and even of this last the modern version makes almost a new language, through the copious additions it has received from the current slang of the day.

The Girl of the Period is a creature who dyes her hair and paints her face, as the first articles of her personal religion—a creature whose sole idea of life is fun; whose sole aim is unbounded luxury; and whose dress is the chief object of such thought and intellect as she possesses. Her main endeavor is to outvie her neighbors in the extravagance of fashion. No matter if, in the time of crinolines, she sacrifices decency; in the time of trains, cleanliness; in the time of tied-back skirts, modesty; no matter either, if she makes herself a nuisance and an inconvenience to every one she meets;—the Girl of the Period has done away with such moral muffishness as consideration for others, or regard for counsel and rebuke. It was all very well in old-fashioned times, when fathers and mothers had some authority and were treated with respect, to be tutored and made to obey, but she is far too fast and flourishing to be stopped in mid-career by these slow old morals; and as she lives to please herself, she does not care if she displeases every one else.... She cannot be

made to see that modesty of appearance and virtue in deed ought to be inseparable; and that no good girl can afford to appear bad, under pain of receiving the contempt awarded to the bad.

This imitation of the *demi-monde* in dress leads to something in manner and feeling, not quite so pronounced perhaps, but far too like to be honorable to herself or satisfactory to her friends. It leads to slang, bold talk and general fastness; to the love of pleasure and indifference to duty; to the desire of money before either love or happiness; to uselessness at home, dissatisfaction with the monotony of ordinary life, horror of all useful work; in a word, to the worst forms of luxury and selfishness—to the most fatal effects arising from want of high principle and absence of tender feeling....

It is this envy of the pleasures, and indifference to the sins, of these women of the *demi-monde* which is doing such infinite mischief to the modern girl. They brush too closely by each other, if not in actual deeds, yet in aims and feelings; for the luxury which is bought by vice with the one is that thing of all in life most passionately desired by the other, though she is not yet prepared to pay quite the same price....

Love indeed is the last thing she thinks of, and the least of the dangers besetting her. Love in a cottage—that seductive dream which used to vex the heart and disturb the calculations of the prudent mother—is now a myth of past ages. The legal barter of herself for so much money, representing so much dash, so much luxury and pleasure—that is her idea of marriage; the only idea worth entertaining. For all seriousness of thought respecting the duties or the consequences of marriage, she has not a trace. If children come, they find but a stepmother's cold welcome from her; and if her husband thinks that he has married anything that is to belong to him—a *tacens et placens uxor* pledged to make him happy—the sooner he wakes from his hallucination and understands that he has simply married some one who will condescend to spend his money on herself, and who will shelter her indiscretions behind the shield of his name, the less severe will be his disappointment. She has married his house, his carriage, his balance at the banker's, his title; and he himself is just the inevitable condition clogging the wheel of her fortune; at best an adjunct, to be tolerated with more or less patience as may chance. For it is only the old-fashioned sort, not Girls of the Period *pur sang*, who marry for love, or put the husband before the banker. But the Girl of the Period does not marry easily. Men are afraid of her; and with reason. They may amuse themselves with her for an evening, but they do not readily take her for life. . . .

At whatever cost of shocked self-love or pained modesty it may be, it cannot be too plainly told to the modern English girl that the net result of her present manner of life is to assimilate her as nearly as possible to a class of women whom we must not call by their proper—or improper—name. And we are willing to believe that she has still some modesty of soul left hidden under all this effrontery of fashion, and that, if she could be made to see herself as she appears to the eyes of men, she would mend her ways before too late. . . .

When women become again what they were once, they will gather round them the love and homage and chivalrous devotion which were then an Englishwoman's natural inheritance. . . .

HYPPOLITE TAINE **English Womanhood (1871)**

The French literary critic and historian, after touring the England of the 1860s, appraises—among other subjects—the distinctive qualities of English women.

How simple and affable they are! On two out of three occasions when one converses with a woman here, one feels at ease, touched, almost happy. Their greeting is kindly and friendly, with a smile of such gentle and quiet goodness! No ulterior motives; their intention, expression, everything is open, natural, cordial. One feels much more at ease than with a Frenchwoman; one has not the vague fear of being judged or made fun of. One does not feel oneself in the presence of a sharp wit, a keen and cutting mind apt to cut you in four pieces at any moment; nor of a vivid, exacting, tiring imagination that demands of you anecdotes, amusement, flattery, all kinds of morsels, and that abandons you if you have no tid-bits to offer her. Conversation here is neither a duel nor a competition. . . .

I can vouch from personal experience the great degree of freedom that they enjoy. I see many of them riding in the morning in Hyde Park with no companion other than a groom. Only two days after arriving at a country estate, I was asked to escort one of the young daughters of the family to a place a mile distant. S——, who has spent a year here in England, finds this free and candid sociability charming. A gentleman to whom he was introduced said: "Come home with me and make the acquaintance of my daughters." They are comrades as men might be but more amiable and polite. One can go riding with them, accompany them to "archery meetings," chat familiarly with them on all, or nearly all, subjects; one can joke with them without ulterior motives. It would be impossible even for a conceited ass to treat them otherwise than as sisters. . . . In this we are deficient. An Englishman who has visited our country is astonished and shocked at the insolent way in which men stare at women in Paris and fail to make way for them on the sidewalk. It is necessary to have lived abroad to real-

SOURCE: From H. Taine, *Notes on England*, translated and with an introductory chapter by W. F. Rae (London: Strahan and Co., 1872), pp. 84, 87–101. Parts of Rae's translation have been revised by the editor in order to bring them closer to contemporary American usage.

ize how much our manners and ways of talking are in this respect displeasing and even offensive. . . .

Dined at F——'s house. The ladies told me about the education received here by girls. In well-to-do or wealthy families they all learn French, German, Italian, as a rule from childhood, from foreign nursemaids and governesses. Generally they begin with French; nearly all of them speak it fluently, and some without any accent. . . . They read Dante, Manzoni, Schiller, and Goethe, our own classics, Chateaubriand, and a few moderns. Many learn a little Latin, which will be useful for teaching their own children or their younger brothers. Many learn natural history, botany, mineralogy, geology; they have a taste for all things natural. In the country, at the seaside, in their frequent journeys, they have a chance to see minerals, herbs, and shells, and to collect them. This fits well with the English habit of storing up facts; as a result they are better instructed than are our own girls. Another motive is that many girls do not marry and must prepare for employment. . . . [Maiden aunts] help to bring up the children, take charge of part of the household, like fruit-bottling or the linen cupboard, make albums of pressed plants, paint in water-colors, read, write, and become learned. A number of them write moral novels, sometimes very good ones. Miss Yonge, Miss Kavanaugh, Miss Bronte, the author of *John Halifax*,[8] Miss Thackeray, and others are well known. Many of these "authoresses" are highly talented—Mrs. Gaskell, Miss Evans [George Eliot], Elizabeth Browning; the last two possess genius. Think also of the translations; numerous German and French works have been translated—and well translated—by women. Others write for magazines, compose short popular treatises, join associations, teach classes of poor children. Their continual concern is to find a use for their abilities or to acquire a talent to serve as a remedy for boredom. . . .

In none of the London or country houses that I have visited have I ever noticed a fashion journal. One of my English friends who has lived in France informs me that here no well brought up woman reads such rubbish. Indeed there is a journal of the very opposite character, *The English Women's Review*. The issue that I am leafing through contains documents and letters on emigration to Australia, articles on state education in France, and other equally serious matters—no novels, no gossip about the theater, no fashion notes, etc. Everything is serious and solid. . . .

Here are the titles of some of the articles written by women in the *Transactions of the National Association for the Promotion of Social Science:* "Education in the Workhouses" by Louisa Twining; "District Schools for the Poor in England" by Barbara Collett; "Application of the Principles of Education in Schools for the Lower Classes" by Mary Carpenter; "The Present State of the Colony of Mettray" by Florence Hill; "Hospital Statistics" by Florence Nightingale; "The Condition of Working Women in England and France" by Bessie Parkes; "Slavery in America and Its Influence Upon Great Britain" by Sarah Redmond; "Improvement of Nurses in Agricultural Districts" by Mrs. Wiggins; "Report of the Society for Furnishing Employment to Women" by Jane Crowe. Most of these authoresses are not married. Several of them are secretaries of active associations of which the review I have just cited is the central organ. One of these associations supplies women with work; another visits workhouses; another visits the sick. All these articles are instructive and useful. The custom of holding classes, of visiting the poor, of conversing with men, of discussion, study, and personal observation of facts have borne fruit. These women know how to observe and to reason; they get to the bottom of things, and they understand the true principle of all progress. . . . In

---

[8]*Miss Bronte . . . Halifax:* refers to *John Halifax, Gentleman* (1856), a novel written by Dinah Maria Mulock Craik, not one of the Bronte sisters

France we believe too readily that if a woman ceases to be a doll she ceases to be a woman. . . .

An English girl wants to marry only for love. She creates a romance for herself, and this dream forms part of her pride, her chastity. Thus some of them, and those of the highest character, would think that they were falling below the proper standard if they married without feeling an enthusiasm proper to absolute preference. To marry is to give oneself wholly and for ever. . . . In this private romance, the English girl remains English, that is to say positive and practical. She does not dream of outpourings, of sentimental walks hand-in-hand in the moonlight, but of her share in an undertaking. She wants to be her husband's helper and partner in his long journeys and his difficult enterprises however tiring or dangerous. Such, for example, were Mrs. Livingstone and Lady Samuel Baker: the first crossed Africa, the second went to the source of the Nile and narrowly escaped death. I have met an English bishop of the Sunda Isles, a country of wild beasts and cannibals; his poor wife bears on her face the marks of that terrible climate. A girl of the neighborhood (where I am staying), rich and of good family, is at present engaged in making preparations; they include crating her piano, etc. The gentleman she is about to marry will take her to Australia, and she will return only once in five or six years to see her aged parents. . . .

As a rule dowries are very small. I have been told of several families in which the eldest son has from one hundred thousand to two hundred thousand pounds sterling; the daughters receive from three to five thousand pounds. Consequently, in order to marry, they must inspire a man with passion. As a result of an unrequited love, many do not marry, and then they live with their eldest brother.

Every Englishman has a touch of romance in his heart with regard to marriage. He pictures a home with the wife of his choice, domestic talk, children. That is his own little universe, closed to the world. So long as he does not possess it he feels dissat-

isfied in contrast to a Frenchman, for whom marriage is the end of something, a makeshift. Often he is obliged to wait, especially if he is a younger son who does not earn enough to maintain a wife. He goes to India or Australia, works as hard as he can, comes home, and marries; here the passions are deep and tenacious. When an Englishman is in love, so one of my hosts assured me, there is nothing he is incapable of doing. . . .

I have already observed that young people of both sexes mingle in perfect freedom without surveillance; they are thus able to study and get to know each other as much as they please. For four or five months or longer, during several successive seasons in the country, they ride and chat with one another. When the young man has made up his mind, it is the young woman to whom he declares himself first; only then does he ask her parents for their consent. This is the reverse of the custom in France, where the man would consider it indelicate to utter one word, however vague, to the girl before speaking to her parents. . . .

The wife's dowry is nearly always placed in the hands of trustees, who take responsibility for its management and pay only the income to the couple. As a rule this income constitutes the wife's pocket money; with it she must clothe herself and her children. Her fortune thus becomes a kind of endowment, safe from any accident that may befall her husband or his business. This precaution is taken, because, according to the law, all the wife's property belongs to her husband. Without such an arrangement, she would begin married life absolutely penniless; she can own nothing in her own right and she is, in the eyes of the law, a minor. This was one of the considerations that drove Mr. J. Stuart Mill to protest so vigorously against the subjection of women. They are indeed kept in subjection here before the law, in religion, in manners and customs, far more vigorously than among us. A woman's husband is her lord, and very often he takes that title seriously. Because the wife contributes little money into the establishment and because her little nest-egg is kept separate, the husband thinks he has the right to tell her nothing about his business. . . .

She is merely a housekeeper, and her business is to look after her household and her children. As a rule she feels content with that role; conscience and training have made her gentle and submissive. Nevertheless, as one of my friends assures me, this inequality has serious disadvantages: the husband is often a despot, and, should he die, his widow, having been kept all her life in ignorance and dependence, is not capable, as in France, of understanding his business, governing the children, and becoming the head of the family.

Marriage is regarded with profound respect, and public opinion concerning it is rigid. If one reads the kinds of books or periodicals in which anonymous writers generally allow themselves the greatest measure of license—for example, novels and comic papers—one finds that adultery is never excused; even in private conversations between two men it is always treated as a crime. . . . In the great body of the nation, among well-brought-up people, wives are almost always faithful. . . . Public opinion has become strict, and the queen has labored to that end with all her might, first by her example, second by her influence. She excludes ladies of doubtful reputation from her court. The extreme urgency and pressure of business of the Crimean War were needed for her to tolerate, under the same roof with her at Windsor, a statesman with a reputation as a profligate.[9] Another safeguard is the fear of publicity and of the newspapers. In this regard our free and rakish manners offend them grievously. C—— related to me that in a Paris club he heard one man of the world say to another: "Is it true, then, that your wife has got herself a lover?" This remark he considers monstrous, and he is right. . . .

According to my friends, the good conduct of English ladies may be explained by the following causes:

1. They are more used to taking care of themselves, having been free since childhood.
2. They are less open to illusions and romantic dreams, being used to the company of young men and having some knowledge of the world.
3. They are accustomed to thinking things over, and having received a more serious education, they possess a fund of good sense. They have studied several languages, gained a smattering of sciences, traveled at least in England and often abroad, and heard their father discuss politics and serious subjects with his friends. Besides, Protestantism develops habits of reflection and reasoning. Finally, novels are always moral, and charitable societies have brought them into contact with the poor and have enabled them to acquire some knowledge of real life.
4. They live for eight or nine months of the year in the country; there they are sheltered from temptation.
5. They have many children to occupy their time. A full nursery with its staff of nursery-maids and governesses requires continual supervision.
6. They undertake all manner of additional work: Sunday School classes; needle-work classes for the poor in the country; visits to the poor; botany, mineralogy, collections of plants and butterflies; reading.

---

[9]*statesman . . . profligate:* Lord Palmerston

9

Religion in Victorian England: How Significant?

Most historians tend to agree that religion played a significant role in the lives of Victorian Englishmen and women, but what form did its influence take? Did it involve all social classes or just the upper and middle classes? Was its influence felt primarily in individual lives or in the corporate role of the Church of England and other religious bodies? How was faith related to social reform and to developments in science? Was religion primarily a source of unity or of division?

The purpose of this chapter is to help answer all those questions. The first document provides excerpts from the report of the commissioners who conducted the unique Religious Census of 1851. The report (prepared in large part by Horace Mann, a London barrister) is a combination of fact and reflection. Some of the questions it seeks to answer are statistical: Is there enough pew space to accommodate all worshipers? What are the religious preferences of church-goers in the England and Wales of 1851? A consideration of the religious census raises other questions as well: What assumptions about church attendance guide the author of the report? How does he account for the number of absentees? In his judgment, what role does social class play? What recommendations does he make?

There was considerable dispute in early Victorian England about the religious life of the working classes. What conclusions does Edward Baines (1774–1848) reach about the situation in Yorkshire and Lancashire in the second document, *The . . . Religious State of the Manufacturing Districts* (1843)? Baines, publisher of the influential *Leeds Mercury*, was a champion of the Whig (Liberal) Party in Yorkshire. How does his assessment compare with that made by Henry Mayhew (1812–1887), the journalist/social investigator, about a rather different segment of the working classes, London's streetsellers? "The Religion of the Costermongers" (1851) is, like the selection in Chapter 8, drawn from Mayhew's *London Labour and the London Poor*.

For many Victorian Englishmen, religion was far less a matter of statistics or of detached analysis than a matter of all-encompassing personal significance. That conclusion is illustrated by a chapter from *The Anxious Inquirer After Salvation* (1838) by John Angell James (1785–1859). An apprentice linen-draper, James in due course became one of the most

Charles Darwin Caricatured as the Very Recent Product of Biological Evolution (*The Hornet,* **March 22, 1871**)

respected ministers in Birmingham, where he preached at a large Independent (or Congregationalist) chapel. The work was frequently republished and helped gain James a high reputation and honorary Doctor of Divinity degrees from institutions as distant as America's Princeton University. Why is Christian faith so important, so urgent, to James? What seem to be his underlying assumptions about the place of human beings in the world?

For John Henry Newman (1801–1890), a young Church of England clergyman at Oxford, it was the Church that was in danger in the 1830s. *Tracts for the Times,* No. 1 (1833), was the first in a series of pamphlets by which Newman and his associates in the Oxford Movement sought to alert their fellow clergy and countrymen during the 1830s. What dangers do they see as threatening their Church? On which aspects of their Church's history and tradition do they lay the greatest stress?

Newman and some of his Oxford associates eventually became converts to Roman Catholicism, but not before the Church of England had experienced both a sense of revival and an accentuated sense of division among its various wings: High (or Tractarian), Low (or Evangelical), and Broad (or undogmatic).

Religion in Victorian Britain had important political as well as personal implications. Thus Victorian Nonconformists challenged the assumption of Anglican clergy that the Church of England should dominate elementary education in the country. Religion also influenced the course of parliamentary legislation. Lord Ashley (after 1851 the seventh earl of Shaftesbury) became the era's prime example of the evangelical (Church of England) layman whose life was devoted to the cause of bettering the lives of the poor. "Religion and Social Reform" consists of part of a speech he gave in the House of Commons and of a series of diary entries concerned with Ashley's drive in the parliamentary session of 1842 to enact a law to ban women and children from underground work in the mines. Although Ashley was a member of Sir Robert Peel's Conservative Party, he was not in 1842 a member of Peel's ministry; rather he was a private member with a cause. For the purposes of this chapter, the various names that Ashley mentions in passing are of little importance. Of far greater importance are the revelations the speech and the diary entries provide about the problems faced by a private M. P. seeking to push a bill through Parliament and about the way in which Ashley's mind worked. What problems did a private member face? What appear to have been Ashley's political motivations?

Another link between religion and social reform may be found in the temperance movement that galvanized the energies of so many Victorians. A remarkable example of this link was Father (Theobald) Mathew (1790–1856), an Irish Roman Catholic priest who during the late 1830s launched an unprecedented one-man crusade on behalf of total abstinence from alcohol. At the highpoint of his influence in the early 1840s, almost half the population of Ireland, Protestant and Catholic alike, was enrolled in his movement, and government revenue from excise taxes on liquor fell by more than one-third. Father Mathew's influence was considerable also in England and in the United States. The description of the temperance apostle in the next document is by Jane Welsh Carlyle (1801–1866), the gifted wife of the Scottish-born historian and social critic, Thomas Carlyle (1795–1881). What impression does she convey of the character of Father Mathew and of the nature of his appeal?

During the nineteenth century, as in earlier centuries, the world view conveyed by science collided from time to time with the world view of Christianity expounded by churchmen of the day. A famous example of such a conflict is to be found in the rather different reactions to Charles Darwin's *On the Origin of Species* expressed in the selections following—"Darwin's Faults" (1860) by the Anglican bishop of Oxford, Samuel Wilberforce (1805–1873), a son of the antislavery crusader, and "Darwin's Virtues" (1860) by Thomas Henry Huxley (1825–1895), scientist and educator. On what grounds do Wilberforce and Huxley judge Darwin's theory? How do they differ on the implications of the theory for religion?

A number of upper-class Victorians brought up in a religious tradition experienced a loss of faith in the course of their life, and Matthew Arnold (1822–1888)—poet, critic, and son of the "public school" reformer Dr. Thomas Arnold—is a case in point. What are the implications of Arnold's poem, "Dover Beach" (1867), for his own loss of faith? How does his attitude seem to differ from that of Huxley, who turned from revealed religion to "agnosticism" (a word he coined)?

The Religious Census of 1851

The census commissioners report on, and then reflect on the only attempt ever made to count all of the religious worshipers in England and Wales on the same Sunday.

If, by a happy miracle, on Sunday, March the 30th 1851, an universal feeling of devotion had impressed our population, and impelled toward the public sanctuaries all whom no impediment, of physical inability or needful occupation, hindered; if the morning or the evening invitation of the service-bell had called, no less from the crowded courts of populous towns and the cottages of scattered villages than from the city mansions and the rural halls, a perfect complement of worshippers; for what proportion of the 17,927,609 inhabitants of England would accommodation in religious buildings have been necessary?

The reply to this inquiry will determine mainly the extent by which our actual supply of spiritual ministration is inadequate to the demand. . . .

From many valid causes, there will always be a considerable number of persons absent from public worship. First, a large deduction from the total population must be made on account of *infants and young children:* of whom there were in England and Wales, in 1851, as many as 4,440,466 under ten years of age—2,348,107 of this number being under five. Of course, opinions vary as to the earliest age at which a child, in order to acquire a habit of devo-

tion, should be taken to a place of worship: some begin occasional attendance before they reach five years of age, while others are retained at home much later. Many parents too, no doubt, conceive that the attendance of their children at a Sunday-school is a sufficient tax upon their tender strength. Perhaps it will not, therefore, be unreasonable to assume that, either on account of immaturity or Sunday-school engagements, about 3,000,000 children will be always justifiably away from public worship.

There will also always be in any large community a certain number kept at home by *sickness.* . . . We shall probably not err in taking nearly seven per cent. of the 15,000,000 . . . and putting down 1,000,000 persons as the number usually and lawfully away from public worship on the ground of *sickness or debility.*

Another large deduction must be made for those who are necessarily left in charge of houses and in attendance upon the two preceding classes. There were, in 1851, in England and Wales, 3,278,039 inhabited houses. If some of these in country parishes were left untenanted, locked up, while the inmates were at service, others doubtless were in charge of more than one domestic; so that we may safely take the whole

SOURCE: From *Parliamentary Papers, 1852–1853*, as supplemented by Horace Mann, "On the Statistical Position of Religious Bodies in England and Wales," *Journal of the Statistical Society of London* (June 1855), Vol. 18, pp. 151–152.

3,278,039 houses as representing so many individuals legitimately absent from religious edifices on account of *household duties.* . . .

A fourth considerable class, of which a certain number will be always absent from religious worship, is the class employed in connexion with the various *public conveyances;* as railways, steamboats, omnibuses, coaches, barges on canals, etc. . . .

The summary result of this inquiry with respect to accommodation is, that there are in England and Wales 10,398,013 persons able to be present at one time in buildings for religious worship. . . . Of the total existing number of 10,212,563 sittings, the Church of England contributes 5,317,915, and the other churches, together, 4,894,648. . . .

An inquirer . . . anxious to discover more precisely the extent to which religious sentiments pervade the nation, would desire to know not merely the amount of accommodation *offered* to the people, but also what proportion of the means at their command is actually *used.* A knowledge, therefore, of the number of ATTENDANTS on the various services of public worship is essential. . . .

Comparing the number of actual attendants with the number of persons *able* to attend, we find that out of 10,398,013 (58 per cent. of the total population) who would be at liberty to worship at one period of the day, there were actually worshipping but 4,647,482 in the morning, 3,184,135 in the afternoon, and 3,064,449 in the evening. So that, taking any one service of the day, there were actually attending public worship less than half the number who, as far as physical impediments prevented, *might* have been attending. In the *morning* there were absent, without physical hindrance, 5,750,531; in the afternoon, 7,213,878; in the evening, 7,333,564. There exist no *data* for determining how many persons attended twice, and how many three times on

Religious body	Number of Attendants
Church of England	3,773,474
Methodists (all sections)	1,566,097
Independents (or Congregationalists)	793,142
Baptists	587,978
Presbyterians	60,131
Unitarians	37,156
Mormons	18,800
Quakers	18,172
Miscellaneous Protestants	89,019
Roman Catholics	305,393
Jews	4,150
All others	7,520
TOTAL	7,261,032

This table shews the computed number of persons who attended *at one service or another,* on the census Sunday, and therefore, represents the entire number of worshippers on that day. The position of the Church of England, as compared with those not belonging to her communion, is thus seen, according to this view, to be 3,773,474 worshippers against 3,487,558.

But it is clear that these 7,261,032 persons, who attended service *on one particular Sunday,* cannot be taken to represent the total number of persons who are in the habit of worshipping, *more or less frequently,* with some particular communion. A considerable number, doubtless, attend on one Sunday who may not attend the next; *some* perhaps worship only on alternate Sundays; others still more occasionally. And yet these occasional attendants must unquestionably be reckoned, in any calculation of the total number of persons who, by frequenting public services, give evidence of their connection with particular religious bodies. But, it is just at this point that we are destitute of information, and I fear, without the means of forming any very probable conjecture. This is unfortunate, because a knowledge of the number of these casual or irregular attendants is very essential to a fair comparison between the different communions; since some are much more constant than others in their attendance at religious worship. Thus, there can be little doubt that, whatever may be the cause, the great body of Protestant dissenters are more assiduous in this matter than are churchmen. That is, our of a given number (say 1,000,000) of dissenters, the proportion found attending service on any particular Sunday will be greater than the proportion of churchmen out of a similar number; so that 1,000,000 attendants at church would represent a greater number of professed churchmen, than 1,000,000 attendants at chapel would represent of professed dissenters. In this respect, the Roman Catholics are probably in much the same position as the Church of England; while the Jews and some other sects are altogether exceptional. . . .

the Sunday; nor, consequently, for deciding how many altogether attended on *some* service of the day; but if we suppose that half of those attending service in the afternoon had not been present in the morning, and that a third of those attending service in the evening had not been present at either of the previous services, we should obtain a total of 7,261,032 separate persons who attended service either once or oftener upon the Census-Sunday. But as the number who would be able to attend at *some* time of the day is more than 58 per cent. (which is the estimated number able to be present *at one and the same time*)—probably reaching 70 per cent.—it is with this latter number (12,549,326) that this 7,261,032 must be compared, and the result of such comparison would lead to the conclusion that, upon the Census-Sunday, 5,288,294 persons, able to attend religious worship once at least, neglected altogether so to do.

It is clear that, unless they should all select the *same service*, there is ample room for all the 70 percent., who, according to the estimate, are able to attend at least *once* upon the Sunday. So that it is tolerably certain that the 5,288,294 who every Sunday, neglect religious ordinances, do so of their own free choice, and are not compelled to be absent on account of a deficiency of sittings. . . .

The most important fact which this investigation as to attendance brings before us is, unquestionably, the alarming number of the non-attendants. Even in the least unfavourable aspect of the figures just presented, and assuming (as no doubt is right) that the 5,288,294 absent every Sunday are not always the same individuals, it must be apparent that a sadly formidable portion of the English people are habitual neglecters of the public ordinances of religion. Nor is it difficult to indicate to what particular class of the community this portion in the main belongs. The middle classes have augmented rather than diminished that devotional sentiment and strictness of attention to religious services by which, for several centuries, they have so eminently been distinguished. With the upper classes, too, the subject of religion has obtained of late a

marked degree of notice, and a regular church-attendance is now ranked amongst the recognized properties of life. It is to satisfy the wants of these two classes that the number of religious structures has of late years so increased. But while the *laboring* myriads of our country have been multiplying with our multiplied material prosperity, it cannot, it is feared, be stated that a corresponding increase has occurred in the attendance of this class in our religious edifices. More especially in cities and large towns it is observable how absolutely insignificant a portion of the congregations is composed of artizans. They fill, perhaps, in youth, our national, British, and Sunday schools, and there receive the elements of a religious education; but, no sooner do they mingle in the active world of labor than, subjected to the constant action of opposing influences, they soon become as utter strangers to religious ordinances as the people of a heathen country. . . . They are *unconscious seculars*—engrossed by the demands, the trials, or the pleasures of the passing hour, and ignorant or careless of a future. These are never or but seldom seen in our religious congregations; and the melancholy fact is thus impressed upon our notice that the classes which are most in need of the restraints and consolations of religion are the classes which are most without them. . . .

As was to be expected, in an age so prone to self-inquiry and reform, this attitude of our increasing population toward religion and religious institutions has occasioned much solicitude and many questions; and the Christian church has not been backward to investigate the causes of her ill success with these the more especial objects of her mission. It is only purposed here to point out some of the more prominent results of this investigation. . . .

1. One chief cause of the dislike which the laboring population entertain for religious services is thought to be the maintenance of those distinctions by which they are separated as a class from the class above them. Working men, it is contended, cannot enter our religious structures without having pressed upon their notice some me-

mento of inferiority. The existence of pews and the position of the free seats are, it is said, alone sufficient to deter them from our churches; and religion has thus come to be regarded as a purely middle-class propriety or luxury. . . . It is urged that the influence of that broad line of demarcation which on week days separates the workman from his master cannot be effaced on Sundays by the mere removal of a physical barrier. The laboring myriads, it is argued, forming to themselves a world apart, have no desire to mingle, even though ostensibly on equal terms, with persons of a higher grade. . . .

2. A second cause of the alienation of the poor from religious institutions is supposed to be an insufficient sympathy exhibited by professed Christians for the alleviation of their social burdens—poverty, disease and ignorance.

3. A third cause of the ill-success of Christianity among the laboring classes is supposed to be a misconception on their part of the motives by which Christian ministers are actuated in their efforts to extend the influence of the gospel. From the fact that clergymen and other ministers receive in exchange for their services pecuniary support, a hasty inference is often drawn, that it is wholly by considerations of a secular and selfish kind that their activity and zeal are prompted. Or, even if no sordid motives are imputed, an impression is not seldom felt that the exhortations and the pleadings of the ministry are matters merely of professional routine—the requisite fulfilment of official duty. It is obvious that these misapprehensions would be dissipated by a more familiar knowledge. . . .

4. Another and a potent reason why so many are forgetful of religious obligations is attributable to their *poverty;* or rather, probably, to certain conditions of life which seem to be inseparable from less than moderate incomes. The scenes and associates from which the poor, however well disposed, can never, apparently, escape; the vice and filth which riot in their crowded dwellings, and from which they cannot fly to any less degraded homes. . . . Better dwellings, therefore, for the laboring classes are suggested as a most essential aid and introduction to the labors of the Christian agent. . . .

Probably, however, the grand requirement of the case is, after all, a multiplication of the various *agents* by whose zeal religious truth is disseminated. Not chiefly an additional provision of *edifices*. The supply of these perhaps, will not much longer, if the present wonderful exertions of the Church of England (aided in but little less degree by other churches) be sustained, prove very insufficient for the wants of the community. But what is eminently needed is, an agency to bring into the buildings thus provided those who are indifferent or hostile to religious services.

It is not, perhaps, sufficiently remembered that the process by which men in general are to be brought to practical acceptance of Christianity is necessarily aggressive. There is no attractiveness, at first, to them in the proceedings which take place within a church or chapel: all is either unintelligible or disagreeable. . . . Something more, then, it is argued, must be done. The people who refuse to hear the gospel in the church must have it brought to them in their own haunts. If ministers, by standing every Sunday in the desk or pulpit, fail to attract the multitudes around, they must by some means make their invitations heard beyond the church or chapel walls. The myriads of our laboring population, really as ignorant of Christianity as were the heathen Saxons at Augustine's landing, are as much in need of missionary enterprise to bring them into practical acquaintance with its doctrines. . . . In illustration, the conspicuous achievements of the patriarchs of Methodism are referred to; and a further proof is found in the success of Mormon emissaries. It is argued that the vast effect produced upon the populace by Wesley and Whitfield, in the course of their unceasing labors, shows that the masses are by no means inaccessible to earnest importunity; while the very progress of the Mormon faith reveals the presence in its votaries of certain dim, unsatisfied religious aspirations. . . .

EDWARD BAINES   The . . . Religious State of the Manufacturing Districts (1843)

One of the leading newspaper proprietors and editors of the North of England surveys· the state of religion in industrial Lancashire and Yorkshire and denies that the interests of the working classes have been neglected.

[The returns made to our committee] establish the following important CONCLUSIONS, namely:

1st. That in these manufacturing districts there is *church and chapel room for 45 per cent. of the entire population;* and, deducting the Catholics, who fill their chapels several times in the day, the church and chapel room for Protestants cannot fall greatly short of 50 *per cent.*

2d. That that provision for the religious instruction of the community has been made, and is still supported, almost wholly by the *voluntary zeal and liberality of the inhabitants,*—no less than 682,795 sittings in churches and chapels having been provided within the present century, of which only 70,611 are in parliamentary churches.

3d. That the provision for religious instruction is *far more abundant, in proportion to the population, now than it was at the beginning of the century.* The church and chapel accommodation has been increased 219 per cent., whilst the population has only increased 127 per cent.

4th. That *Sunday Schools* have been provided, and are supported and taught, by the voluntary zeal of the inhabitants, in which *one in every* $5\frac{2}{5}$ *of the population* are enrolled on the books,—which must include an immense proportion of all the children of the working classes.

5th. That $55\frac{2}{5}$ *per cent.* of the children in Sunday Schools are *able* to read, and are *actually reading, the Holy Scriptures.*

6. That *sixty-six thousand teachers* are gratuitously engaged in the benevolent and pious duty of Sunday School instruction.

7th. That *one in every ten of the population* are taught in *day schools,* of whom only a small proportion in dame and factory schools.

8th. That the proportions of the established Church and other religious bodies, so far as the sittings in churches and chapels would indicate, are as follow, viz.:—established Church, 377,104 sittings,—other religious denominations, 617,479: but probably the proportion actually attending the churches would be less than this, in comparison with the other sects.

9th. That the proportions of Sunday scholars taught are as follow, viz.;—in the schools of the established Church, 123,451,—in the schools of all other denominations, 285,080. . . .

I might dwell upon the many institutions and associations for the diffusion of knowledge, and for the dispensing of every kind of good, which have arisen within the present or the last generation, and which flourish most in the manufacturing towns and villages;—such as mechanics' institutes, literary societies, circulating libraries, youths' guardian societies, friendly societies, temperance societies, medical charities, clothing societies, benevolent and district visiting societies, etc.,—forty-nine fiftieths of which are of quite recent origin. The moral, intellectual, and physical good done by these associations is beyond calculation; and their existence is one of the most decisive proofs possible of the growth and commanding influence of true Christian principle in the communities where they have been formed.

SOURCE: From Edward Baines, *The Social, Educational, and Religious State of the Manufacturing Districts* (London, 1843), pp. 27–28, 62.

HENRY MAYHEW The Religion of the Costermongers (1851)

An inquiring investigative reporter assesses the state of religion among London's 30,000 streetsellers of fruits and vegetables.

An intelligent and trustworthy man, until very recently actively engaged in coster-mongering, computed that not 3 in 100 costermongers had ever been in the interior of a church, or any place of worship, or knew what was meant by Christianity. The same person gave me the following account, which was confirmed by others:

"The costers have no religion at all, and very little notion, or none at all, of what religion or a future state is. Of all things they hate tracts. They hate them because the people leaving them never give them anything, and as they can't read the tract—not one in forty—they're vexed to be bothered with it. And really what is the use of giving people reading before you've taught them to read? Now, they respect the city missionaries, because they read to them—and the costers will listen to reading when they don't understand it—and because they visit the sick, and sometimes give oranges and such like to them and the children. I've known a city Missionary buy a shilling's worth of

oranges of a coster, and give them away to the sick and the children—most of them belonging to the costermongers—down the court, and that made him respected there. I think the city missionaries have done good. But I'm satisfied that if the costers had to profess themselves of some religion to-morrow, they would all become Roman Catholics, every one of them. This is the reason:—London costers live very often in the same courts and streets as the poor Irish, and if the Irish are sick, be sure there comes to them the priest, the sisters of charity—they *are* good women—and some other ladies. Many a man that's not a Catholic, has rotted and died without any good person near him. Why, I lived a good while in Lambeth, and there wasn't one coster in 100, I'm satisfied, knew so much as the rector's name,—though Mr. Dalton's a very good man. But the reason I was telling you of, sir, is that the costers reckon *that* religion's the best that gives the most in charity, and they think the Catholics do this."

JOHN ANGELL JAMES The Anxious Inquirer After Salvation (1838)

The Reverend John Angell James, a popular independent (Congregationalist) minister from Birmingham, in one of the religious best sellers of the early Victorian era, asks and answers a timeless question.

Deep Solicitude about Salvation Reasonable and Necessary

Reader, you have lately been awakened by the mercy of God, to ask, with some degree of anxiety, that momentous question, *"What shall I do to be saved?"* No wonder

you should be anxious; the wonder is, that you were not concerned about this matter before, that you are not more deeply solicitous now, and that all who possess the word of God do not sympathize with you in this anxiety. Every thing justifies solicitude and condemns indifference. Unconcern about

SOURCE: From Henry Mayhew, *London Labour and the London Poor* (London: Charles Griffin and Co., 1861), 4 vols.: Vol. I, p. 23.

SOURCE: From Rev. John Angell James, *The Anxious Inquirer After Salvation* (New York: American Tract Society, n.d.), pp. 13–20. (First published in England in 1838.)

the soul, indifference to salvation, is a most irrational as well as a most guilty state of mind. The wildest enthusiasm on the subject of religion is less surprising and unreasonable than absolute carelessness, as will appear from the following considerations:

1. *You are an immortal creature, a being born for eternity, a creature that will never go out of existence.* Millions of ages, as numerous as the sands upon the shore, and the drops of the ocean, and the leaves of all the forests on the globe, will not shorten the duration of your being; eternity, vast eternity, incomprehensible eternity, is before you. Every day brings you nearer to everlasting torments or felicity. You may die any moment, and you are as near to heaven or hell as you are to death. No wonder you are asking, "What shall I do to be saved?"

2. But the reasonableness of this anxiety appears, *if you add to this consideration that you are a sinner.* You have broken God's law; you have rebelled against his authority; you have acted as an enemy to him, and made him *your* enemy. If you had committed only one single act of transgression, your situation would be alarming. *One* sin would have subjected you to the sentence of his law, and exposed you to his displeasure; but you have committed sins more in number and greater in magnitude than you know or can conceive of. Your whole life has been one continued course of sin; you have, as relates to God, done nothing but sin. Your transgressions have sent up to heaven a cry for vengeance. You are actually under the curse of the Almighty.

3. *Consider what the loss of the soul includes.* The loss of the soul is the loss of every thing dear to man as an immortal creature: it is the loss of heaven, with all its honors, felicities, and glories; it is the loss of God's favor, which is the life of all rational creatures; it is the loss of every thing that can contribute to our happiness; and it is the loss of hope, the last refuge of the wretched. The loss of the soul includes in it all that is contained in that dreadful word, *hell:* it is the eternal endurance of the wrath of God; it is the lighting down of the

curse of the Almighty upon the human spirit; or rather, it is the falling of the human spirit into that curse, as into a lake that burneth with fire and brimstone. How true as well as solemn are the words of Christ, "What shall it profit a man, if he gain the whole world, and lose his own soul; or what shall a man give in exchange for his soul?" All the tears that ever have been or ever will be shed on the face of the earth; all the groans that ever have been or ever will be uttered; all the anguish that ever has been or ever will be endured by all the inhabitants of the world, through all the ages of time, do not make up an equal amount of misery to that which is included in the loss of one human soul. Justly, therefore, do *you* say, who are exposed to this misery, *"What shall I do to be saved?"*

4. This solicitude is reasonable, *if we consider that the eternal loss of the soul is not a rare, but a very common occurrence.* It is so tremendous a catastrophe, that if it happened only once in a year, or once in a century, so as to render it barely possible that it should happen to you, it would be unpardonable carelessness not to feel some solicitude about the matter: how much more then, when, alas, it is every day occurring? So far from its being a rare thing for men to go to hell, it is a much rarer thing for them to go to heaven. Our Lord tells us that the road to destruction is thronged, while the way to life is travelled by few. Hell opens its mouth wide, and swallows up multitudes in perdition. How alarming is the idea, and how probable the fact, that *you* may be among this number. Some that read these pages will very likely spend their eternity with lost souls: it is therefore your wisdom, as well as your duty, to cherish the anxiety which says, *"What shall I do to be saved?"*

5. *Salvation is possible:* if it were not, it would be useless to be anxious about it. It would be cruel, and only tormenting you before your time, to encourage an anxiety which could never be relieved by the possession of the object which excites it. Who, if such a thing were possible, would say any

thing to "lost souls in prison," by way of encouraging in them a solicitude to be saved? But *your* case is not hopeless: you may be saved; you are invited to be saved. Christ has died for your salvation, and God waits to save you; all the opportunities and advantages and helps and encouragements to salvation are around you; the blessing is within your reach; it is brought near to you; and it will be your own fault if you do not possess it. Your solicitude is not therefore directed to an unattainable object.

6. *Salvation has been obtained by multitudes, and why may it not be obtained by you?* Millions in heaven are already saved; myriads more are on the road to salvation. God is still as willing, and Christ is still as able to save you as he was them; why then should not *you* be saved?

7. *And then, what a blessing is salvation*—a blessing that includes all the riches of grace, and all the greater riches of glory; deliverance from sin, death, and hell; the possession of pardon, peace, holiness, and heaven; a blessing, in short, immense, infinite, everlasting—which occupied the mind of Deity from eternity, was procured by the Son of God upon the cross, and which will fill eternity with its happiness. O, how little, how insignificant, how contemptible is the highest object of human ambition, to say nothing of the *lower* matters of men's desires, compared with SALVATION. Riches, rank, fame, honors, are but as the small dust of the balance when compared with the salvation that is in Christ Jesus, with eternal glory. Who that pretends to the least regard to his own happiness would not say, "What shall I do to be saved?"

8. *The circumstances in which you are placed for obtaining this blessing, are partly favorable and partly unfavorable.* The love of God is infinite; the merit of Christ is infinite; the power of the Holy Spirit is infinite; Jehovah is willing and waiting to save you; Christ invites; all things are ready, and the grace of God offered for your conversion. On the other hand you have a corrupt heart, and are placed in a world where every thing seems

to combine to draw off your attention from salvation, and to cause you to neglect it. Satan is busy to blind your mind, the world to fill your imagination and heart with other objects, so that even the "righteous are *scarcely* saved." You cannot quit the world and go into monasteries and convents, but must seek the salvation of your soul amidst the engrossing cares of this busy and troublesome world, where anxiety about the body is so liable to put away anxiety about the soul, and things seen and temporal are likely to withdraw the attention from things that are unseen and eternal. O, how difficult is it to pay just enough regard to present things, and yet not too much. How difficult to attend properly to the affairs both of earth and heaven; to be busy for two worlds at once. These circumstances may well excite your solicitude.

Anxiety, then, deep anxiety about salvation, is the most reasonable thing in the world; and we feel almost ready to ask, Can that man have a soul, or know that he has one, who is careless about its eternal happiness? Is he a man or a brute? Is he in the exercise of his reason, or is he a maniac? Ever walking on the edge of the precipice that hangs over the bottomless pit, and not anxious about salvation! O fatal, awful, destructive indifference! Cherish then *your* solicitude. You *must* be anxious, you *ought* to be so, you *cannot be saved without it,* for no man ever was, or ever will be. The salvation of a lost soul is such a stupendous deliverance, such an infinitely momentous concern, that it is impossible, in the very nature of things, it should be bestowed on any one who is not in earnest to obtain it. This is the very end of your existence, the purpose for which God created you. Apart from this, you are an enigma in creation, a mystery in nature. Why has God given you faculties which seem to point to eternity, and desires which go forward to it, if he has not destined you for it? ETERNAL SALVATION IS THE GREAT END OF LIFE: GET WHAT YOU WILL, IF YOU LOSE THIS YOU HAVE LOST THE PURPOSE OF EXISTENCE. . . .

JOHN HENRY NEWMAN　Tracts for the Times, No. 1 (1833)

One of the leading clergymen in the university community launches the Oxford (or Tractarian) Movement, a call to revive and to restore the independent role and status of the Church of England.

To My Brethren in the Sacred Ministry, the Presbyters and Deacons of the Church of Christ in England, Ordained Thereunto by the Holy Ghost and the Imposition of Hands.

Fellow-Laborers,

I am but one of yourselves—a Presbyter; and therefore I conceal my name, lest I should take too much on myself by speaking in my own person. Yet speak I must; for the times are very evil, yet no one speaks against them.

Is not this so? Do not we "look one upon another," yet perform nothing? Do we not all confess the peril into which the Church is come, yet sit still each in his own retirement, as if mountains and seas cut off brother from brother? Therefore suffer me, while I try to draw you forth from those pleasant retreats, which it has been our blessedness hitherto to enjoy, to contemplate the condition and prospects of our Holy Mother in a practical way; so that one and all may unlearn that idle habit, which has grown upon us, of owning the state of things to be bad, yet doing nothing to remedy it.

Consider a moment. Is it fair, is it dutiful, to suffer our bishops to stand the brunt of the battle without doing our part to support them? Upon them comes "the care of all the churches." This cannot be helped; indeed it is their glory. Not one of us would wish in the least to deprive them of the duties, the toils, the responsibilities of their high office. And, black event as it would be for the country, yet (as far as they are concerned) we could not wish them a more blessed termination of their course than the spoiling of their goods and martyrdom.

To them then we willingly and affectionately relinquish their high privileges and honors; we encroach not upon the rights of the SUCCESSORS OF THE APOSTLES; we touch not their sword and crozier. Yet surely we may be their shield-bearers in the battle without offense; and by our voice and deeds be to them what Luke and Timothy were to St. Paul.

Now then let me come at once to the subject which leads me to address you. Should the government and the country so far forget their God as to cast off the Church, to deprive it of its temporal honors and substance, *on what* will you rest the claim of respect and attention which you make upon your flocks? Hitherto you have been upheld by your birth, your education, your wealth, your connexions; should these secular advantages cease, on what must Christ's ministers depend? Is not this a serious practical question? We know how miserable is the state of religious bodies not supported by the state. Look at the dissenters on all sides of you, and you will see at once that their ministers, depending simply upon the people, become the *creatures* of the people. Are you content that this should be your case? Alas! can a greater evil befall Christians, than for their teachers to be guided by them, instead of guiding? How can we "hold fast the form of sound words," and "keep that which is committed to our trust," if our influence is to depend simply on our popularity? Is it not our very office to *oppose* the world? Can we then allow ourselves to *court* it? to preach smooth things and prophesy deceits? to make the way of life easy to the rich and indolent, and to bribe the humbler classes by excitements and strong intoxicating doctrine? Surely it must not be so;—and the question

SOURCE: These tracts were first published anonymously by "Members of the University of Oxford" in 1833.

recurs, *on what* are we to rest our authority when the state deserts us?

Christ has not left His Church without claim of its own upon the attention of men. Surely not. Hard Master He cannot be, to bid us oppose the world, yet give us no credentials for so doing. There are some who rest their divine mission on their own unsupported assertion; others, who rest it upon their popularity; others, on their success; and others, who rest it upon their temporal distinctions. This last case has, perhaps, been too much our own; I fear we have neglected the real ground on which our authority is built—OUR APOSTOLICAL DESCENT.

We have been born, not of blood, nor of the will of the flesh, nor of the will of man, but of God. The Lord Jesus Christ gave His Spirit to His Apostles; they in turn laid their hands on those who should succeed them; and these again on others; and so the sacred gift has been handed down to our present bishops, who have appointed us as their assistants, and in some sense representatives.

Now every one of us believes this. I know that some will at first deny they do; still they do believe it. Only, it is not sufficiently, practically impressed on their minds. They *do* believe it; for it is the doctrine of the ordination service, which they have recognised as truth in the most solemn season of their lives. In order, then, not to prove, but to remind and impress, I entreat your attention to the words used when you were made ministers of Christ's Church.

The office of deacon was thus committed to you: "Take thou authority to execute the office of a deacon in the Church of God committed unto thee: In the name, etc."

And the priesthood thus:

"Receive the Holy Ghost, for the office and work of a priest, in the Church of God, now committed unto thee by the imposition of our hands. Whose sins thou dost forgive, they are forgiven; and whose sins thou dost retain, they are retained. And be thou a faithful dispenser of the Word of God, and of His Holy Sacraments: In the name, etc."

These, I say, were words spoken to us, and received by us, when we were brought nearer to God than at any other time of our lives. I know the grace of ordination is contained in the laying on of hands, not in any form of words;—yet in our own case (as has ever been usual in the Church) words of blessing have accompanied the act. Thus we have confessed before God our belief that the bishop who ordained us gave us the Holy Ghost, gave us the power to bind and to loose, to administer the sacraments, and to preach. Now *how* is he able to give these great gifts? *Whence* is his right? Are these words idle (which would be taking God's name in vain), or do they express merely a wish (which surely is very far below their meaning), or do they not rather indicate that the speaker is conveying a gift? Surely they can mean nothing short of this. But whence, I ask, his right to do so? Has he any right, except as having received the power from those who consecrated him to be a bishop? He could not give what he had never received. It is plain then that he but *transmits*; and that the Christian ministry is a *succession*. And if we trace back the power of ordination from hand to hand, of course we shall come to the apostles at last. We know we do, as a plain historical fact; and therefore all we, who have been ordained clergy, in the very form of our ordination acknowledged the doctrine of the APOSTOLICAL SUCCESSION. . . .

Therefore, my dear brethren, act up to your professions. Let it not be said that you have neglected a gift; for if you have the spirit of the apostles on you, surely this *is* a great gift. "Stir up the gift of God which is in you." Make much of it. Show your value of it. Keep it before your minds as an honorable badge, far higher than that secular respectability, or cultivation, or polish, or learning, or rank, which gives you a hearing with the many. Tell *them* of your gift. The times will soon drive you to do this, if you mean to be still anything. But wait not for the times. Do not be compelled, by the world's forsaking you, to recur as if unwillingly to the high source of your authority. Speak out now, before you are forced, both as glorying in your privilege and to insure your rightful honor from your people. A notion has gone abroad that they can take away your power. They think they have given and can take it away. They think it lies in the Church property, and they know that they have politically the power to confiscate that property. They have been deluded into a notion that present palpable usefulness, produceable results, acceptableness to your flocks, that these and such like are the tests of your divine commission. Enlighten them in this matter. Exalt our holy fathers the bishops, as the representatives of the apostles, and the angels of the churches; and magnify your office, as being ordained by them to take part in their ministry.

But, if you will not adopt my view of the subject, which I offer to you, not doubtingly, yet (I hope) respectfully, at all events, CHOOSE YOUR SIDE. To remain neuter much longer will be itself to take a part. *Choose your side;* since side you shortly must, with one or other party, even though you do nothing. Fear to be of those whose line is decided for them by chance circumstances, and who may perchance find themselves with the enemies of Christ, while they think but to remove themselves from worldly politics. Such abstinence is impossible in troublous times. HE THAT IS NOT WITH ME IS AGAINST ME, AND HE THAT GATHERETH NOT WITH ME SCATTERETH ABROAD.

LORD ASHLEY   **Religion and Social Reform (1842)**

One of England's most prominent evangelical laymen appeals to the House of Commons to ban the labor of women and children in the coal mines.

Sir, we can estimate our loss or acquisition of territory by geographical measurement; and so we can calculate in finance by increase or deficiency of revenue; but it is not so easy to arrive at the moral statistics of a country. Many persons love to estimate the condition of a kingdom by its criminal tables; but surely these figures exhibit very scantily the moral state of a people. A people may be in a frightful condition as citizens, and yet but few appear before the magistrate or infringe the laws. . . . Criminal statistics are only a symptom, and not the extent of the internal disorder. . . . I do fear the progress of a cancer, a perilous, and, if we much longer delay, an incurable cancer, which has seized upon the body, social, moral, and political; and then in some day, when there shall be required on the part of our people an unusual energy, an unprecedented effort of virtue and patriotism, the

strength of the empire will be found prostrate, for the fatal disorder will have reached its vitals.

There are, I well know, many other things to be done; but this, I must maintain, is an indispensable preliminary; for it is a mockery to talk of education to people who are engaged, as it were, in unceasing toil from their cradle to their grave. I have endeavored for many years to attain this end by limiting the hours of labor, and so bringing the children and young persons within the reach of a moral and religious education. I have hitherto been disappointed, and I deeply regret it, because we are daily throwing away a noble material!—for, depend upon it, the British people are the noblest and the most easily governed of any on the face of the earth. Their fortitude and obedience under the severest privations sufficiently prove it. . . .

SOURCES: From *Hansard's Parliamentary Debates*, 3rd Series, Vol. LXIII, cols. 1349–1352. The excerpts from his diary are taken from Edwin Hodder, *The Life and Work of the 7th Earl of Shaftesbury, K. G.* (London: Cassell & Co., 1887), 3 vols.: Vol. I, pp. 421–422, 426–432.

Is it not enough to announce these things to an assembly of Christian men and British gentlemen? For twenty millions of money you purchased the liberation of the negro; and it was a blessed deed. You may, this night, by a cheap and harmless vote, invigorate the hearts of thousands of your countrypeople, enable them to walk erect in newness of life, to enter on the enjoyment of their inherited freedom, and avail themselves (if they will accept them) of the opportunities of virtue, of morality, and religion. These, Sir, are the ends that I venture to propose. The House will, I am sure, forgive me for having detained them so long; and still more will they forgive me for venturing to conclude, by imploring them, in the words of Holy Writ, "To break off our sins by righteousness, and our iniquities by showing mercy to the poor, if it may be a lengthening of our tranquility."

In successive diary entries, Ashley records his feelings as his bill makes its tortuous way through Parliament.

June 9th [1842] —Oh that I had the tongue of an angel to express what I ought to feel! God grant that I may never forget it, for I cannot record it. On the 7th, brought forward my motion—the success has been *wonderful*, yes really wonderful—for two hours the House listened so attentively that you might have heard a pin drop, broken only by loud and repeated marks of approbation—at the close a dozen members at least followed in succession to give me praise, and express their sense of the holy cause. . . .

As I stood at the table, and just before I opened my mouth, the words of God came forcibly to my mind, "Only be strong and of a good courage"—praised be His Holy Name, I was as easy from that moment as though I had been sitting in an armchair. Many men, I hear, shed tears—Beckett Denison confessed to me that he did, and that he left the House lest he should be seen. Sir G. Grey told William Cowper that he "would rather have made that speech than any he ever heard." Even Joseph Hume was touched. Members took me aside, and spoke in a *very serious* tone of thanks and admiration. I must and will sing an everlasting "non nobis."—Grant, oh blessed God, that I may not be exalted above measure, but that I may ever creep close by the ground, knowing, and joyfully confessing, that I am Thy servant, that without Thee I am nothing worth, and that from Thee alone cometh all counsel, wisdom, and understanding for the sake of our most dear and only Savior, God manifest in the flesh, our Lord Jesus Christ! It has given me hopes for the empire, hopes for its permanence, hopes for its service in the purposes of the Messiah. God prosper the issue! . . .

June 23rd. —Last night pushed the bill through committee; a feeble and discreditable opposition! "Sinners" were with me, "saints" against me—strange the contradiction in human nature! . . . Had I trusted in man, I should have been lamentably forlorn: not a member of the government, except Manners Sutton, who was necessarily present. Graham, it is true, apologized, as summoned to the queen; but where were the rest? It is very curious (but so I have invariably found it) that those who promised support, failed, and those who made no promises, were present. I must except a few. Bell and his northern gentry behaved admirably. Some who came down to support me spoke against me!

June 24th. —A notice given last night, by Mr. Ainsworth, to refer the bill to a select committee, to see whether it would not abate the wages of the working classes! This involves delay—long and serious delay. I suffer much from anxiety. George Anson gave me a kind message from Prince Albert, expressive of his sympathy and the queen's, adding that he had read every syllable of it [the speech] to the queen. . . .

June 25. —Late last night, or rather at two o'clock in the morning, forced my bill through the report, despite the resistance of Mr. Ainsworth. Thank God! but the day is not yet won. There may be difficulty on the third reading.

June 28. —Deputation from South Staffordshire; very positive, very unreasonable. But they have secured Hatherton's co-operation in the Lords; and I, meanwhile, have not found any one to take charge of the bill.... The whole struggle is reserved for the upper House. God be with us!

June 29. —A day of expectation and hope. Disappointed at the last. The House was counted out, and my bill again delayed. The mercy of God is ever qualifying evil. I have lost the day, but I have gained the duke of Buccleuch. He will undertake the charge [sponsorship] of the bill; for him I will extend the time of operation to 1st of March.

July 2. —Resisted again last night. Two divisions on the adjournment of the debate late at night. Peel and Graham voted with me on the first, but went away on the second. *Neither of them said a word in my favor.* ...

July 8. —Much, very much trouble to find a peer who would take charge of the bill. It is "the admiration of everybody, but the choice of none." So often refused, that I felt quite humbled. ...

At last, this very evening, a debate still raging in the House of Lords, I obtained Lord Devon, who spoke, with shame, of the indifference of the peers to such a measure.

Never did one body present such a contrast to another as the House of Lords to the House of Commons—the question seemed to have no friends.... But God will overrule, and turn all things to His glory at last. There is, I doubt not, and will be, more success than I now see, for disappointment and apprehension lie heavy on me. I sent the bill to the Lords with deep and fervent prayer, consecrating, and committing it to God, as Hannah consigned her son Samuel, to His blessed service. May He, in His mercy, have "respect unto me and my offering!"

July 13th. —Last night fixed for debate in the House of Lords, postponed to Thursday. Lord Londonderry attacked me, Clanricarde defended me. Misery makes one acquainted with strange bedfellows! He did it kindly and well. Government at last declared, by the voice of Lord Wharncliffe, that it would *"be quite passive, it would give no support to the Bill."* ...

Now then I am impotent—nothing remains (humanly speaking) but public opinion—were it not for this I should not be able to carry *one* article of the bill; but something, please God, I shall attain through that His instrument; yet a very small portion of what I desired. It is impossible to keep terms with this ministry, their promises are worth nothing.

July 26th. —Bill passed through committee last night. In this work, which should have occupied one hour, they spent nearly six, and left it far worse than they found it; never have I seen such a display of selfishness, frigidity to every human sentiment, such ready and happy self-delusion. Three bishops only present. Chichester (Gilbert), Norwich (Stanley), Gloucester (Monk), who came late, but he intended well. The bishop of London and the archbishop of Canterbury went away! It is my lot, should I, by God's grace, live so long, to be hereafter among them [in the House of Lords]; but may He avert the day on which my means of utility in public life would be for ever concluded! ...

Aug. 1. —Redesdale moved the third reading. I was much buoyed up with the notion (which papers, bills, peers, and clerks confirmed) that the amendments (!) admitting the women into pits "only not to work," had been omitted; full of excitement and thankfulness; then I suddenly discovered that the words were added on a slip of paper. God forgive me for my bitter disappointment; God strengthen my faith and patience! I am in a fix, shall I accept the words, or endeavor to strike them out? If they remain, the bill is neutralized; if they be objected to, the bill is lost. [On August 7, 1842, the bill passed.]

August 8th. —Took the sacrament on Sunday in joyful and humble thankfulness to Almighty God for the undeserved measure of success with which He has blessed my effort for the glory of His name, and the welfare of His creatures. Let a new order of the century be born! *Novus saeculorum nascitur ordo!*[1] Whatever had been done, is but the millionth part of what there is to do; and *even then,* should such an end be accomplished, which man never yet saw, we should still be "unprofitable servants." The more I labor, the more I see of labor to be performed, and vain at the last will be the labor of us all. Our prayer must be for the Second Advent, our toil "that we be found watching."

JANE WELSH CARLYLE **Father Mathew (1843)**

The wife of one of Britain's leading social critics, Thomas Carlyle, reports to him on her encounter with the remarkable Irish temperance advocate, Father Mathew.

. . . And now let me tell you something which you will perhaps think questionable, a piece of hero-worship that I have been after. My youthful enthusiasm, as John Sterling calls it, is not extinct then, as I had supposed; but must certainly be immortal! Only think of its blazing up for Father Mathew! You know I have always had the greatest reverence for that priest; and when I heard he was in London, attainable to me, I felt that I must see him, shake him by the hand, and tell him I loved him considerably! I was expressing my wish to see him, to Robertson, the night he brought the ballad collector; and he told me it could be gratified quite easily. Mrs. Hall had offered him a note of introduction to Father Mathew, and she would be pleased to include my name in it. "Fix my time, then." "He was administering the pledge all day long in the Commercial Road." I fixed next evening.

Robertson, accordingly, called for me at five, and we rumbled off in omnibus, all the way to Mile End, that hitherto for me unimaginable goal! Then there was still a good way to walk; the place, the "new lodging," was a large piece of waste ground, boarded off from the Commercial Road, for a Catholic cemetery. I found "my youthful enthusiasm" rising higher and higher as I got on the ground, and saw the thousands of people all hushed into awful silence, with not a single exception that I saw—the only religious meeting I ever saw in cockneyland which had not plenty of scoffers hanging on its outskirts. The crowd was all in front of a narrow scaffolding, from which an American captain was then haranguing it; and Father Mathew stood beside him, so good and simple-looking! Of course, we could not push our way to the front of the scaffold, where steps led up to it; so we went to one end, where there were no steps or other visible means of access, and handed up our letter of introduction to a policeman; he took it and returned presently, saying that Father Mathew was coming. And he came; and reached down his hand to me, and I grasped it; but the boards were higher than my head, and it seemed our communication must stop there. But I have told you that I was in a moment of enthusiasm; I felt the need of getting closer to that good man. I saw a bit of rope hanging, in the form of a festoon, from the end of the boards; I put my foot on it; held still by Father Mathew's hand; seized the end of the boards with the other; and, in some, to myself (up to this moment), incomprehensible way, flung

SOURCE: Excerpt from a letter of August 9, 1843, reprinted in James Anthony Froude, ed., *Letters and Memorials of Jane Welsh Carlyle* (New York: Scribners, 1903), 2 vols.: Vol. I, pp. 164–167.

---

[1]*Novus . . . ordo?:* "Is a new secular order born?"

myself horizontally on to the scaffolding at Father Mathew's feet! He uttered a scream, for he thought (I suppose) I must fall back; but not at all; I jumped to my feet, shook hands with him and said—what? "God only knows." He made me sit down on the only chair a moment; then took me by the hand as if I had been a little girl, and led me to the front of the scaffold, to see him administer the pledge. From a hundred to two hundred took it; and all the tragedies and theatrical representations I ever saw, melted into one, could not have given me such emotion as that scene did. There were faces both of men and women that will haunt me while I live; faces exhibiting such concentrated wretchedness, making, you would have said, its last deadly struggle with the powers of darkness. There was one man, in particular, with a baby in his arms; and a young girl that seemed of the "unfortunate" sort, that gave me an insight into the lot of humanity that I still wanted. And in the face of Father Mathew, when one looked from them to him, the mercy of heaven seemed to be laid bare. Of course I cried; but I longed to lay my head down on the good man's shoulder and take a hearty cry there before the whole multitude! He said to me one such nice thing. "I dare not be absent for an hour," he said: "I think always if some dreadful drunkard were to come, and me away, he might never muster determination perhaps to come again in all his life; and there would be a man lost!"

I was turning sick, and needed to get out of the thing, but, in the act of leaving him—never to see him again through all time, most probably—feeling him to be the very best man of modern times (you excepted), I had another movement of youthful enthusiasm which you will hold up your hands and eyes at. Did I take the pledge then? No; but I would, though, if I had not feared it would be put in the newspapers! No, not that; but I drew him aside, having considered if I had any ring on, any handkerchief, anything that I could leave with him in remembrance of me, and having bethought me of a pretty memorandum-book in my reticule, I drew him aside and put it in his hand, and bade him keep it for my sake; and asked him to give me one of his medals to keep for his! And all this in tears and in the utmost agitation! Had you any idea that your wife was still such a fool! I am sure I had not. The father got through the thing admirably. He seemed to understand what it all meant quite well, inarticulate though I was. He would not give me a common medal, but took a little silver one from the neck of a young man who had just taken the pledge for example's sake, telling him he would get him another presently, and then laid the medal into my hand with a solemn blessing. I could not speak for excitement all the way home. When I went to bed I could not sleep; the pale faces I had seen haunted me, and Father's Mathew's smile; and even next morning, I could not anyhow subside into my normal state, until I had sat down and written Father Mathew a long letter—accompanying it with your "Past and Present"! Now, dear, if you are ready to beat me for a distracted Gomeril[2] I cannot help it. All that it was put into my heart to do, *Ich konnte nicht anders.*[3]

SAMUEL WILBERFORCE Darwin's Faults (1860)

Bishop Samuel Wilberforce's anonymous book review points out grave defects in Charles Darwin's On the Origin of Species.

SOURCE: From *The Quarterly Review*, Vol. 108 (1860), pp. 225–226, 230–231, 233, 247–248, 250, 256–260.

[2]*Gomeril:* a Scottish expression meaning "good-natured fool"

[3]*Ich . . . anders:* "I could do no other" (Luther's statement to the Diet of Worms)

Any contribution to our natural history literature from the pen of Mr. C. Darwin is certain to command attention. His scientific attainments, his insight and carefulness as an observer, blended with no scanty measure of imaginative sagacity, and his clear and lively style, make all his writings unusually attractive. His present volume on the "Origin of Species" is the result of many years of observation, thought, and speculation; and is manifestly regarded by him as the "opus" upon which his future fame is to rest. . . .

The essay is full of Mr. Darwin's characteristic excellences. It is a most readable book; full of facts in natural history, old and new, of his collecting and of his observing; and all of these are told in his own perspicuous language, and all thrown into picturesque combinations, and all sparkle with the colors of fancy and the lights of imagination. It assumes, too, the grave proportions of a sustained argument upon a matter of the deepest interest, not to naturalists only, or even to men of science exclusively, but to every one who is interested in the history of man and of the relations of nature around him to the history and plan of creation.

With Mr. Darwin's "argument" we may say in the outset that we shall have much and grave fault to find. . . .

The conclusion, then, to which Mr. Darwin would bring us is, that all the various forms of vegetable and animal life with which the globe is now peopled, or of which we find the remains preserved in a fossil state in the great earth-museum around us, which the science of geology unlocks for our instruction, . . . "have descended from some one primordial form into which life was first breathed by the Creator." This is the theory which really pervades the whole volume. Man, beast, creeping thing, and plant of the earth, are all the lineal and direct descendants of some one individual *ens*, whose various progeny have been simply modified by the action of natural and ascertainable conditions into the multiform aspect of life which we see around us. This is undoubtedly at first sight a some-

what startling conclusion to arrive at. To find that mosses, grasses, turnips, oaks, worms, and flies, mites and elephants, infusoria and whales, tadpoles of to-day and venerable saurians, truffles and men, are all equally the lineal descendants of the same aboriginal common ancestor. . . . —This, to say the least of it, is no common discovery—no very expected conclusion. . . .

Now, the main propositions by which Mr. Darwin's conclusion is attained are these:—

1. That observed and admitted variations spring up in the course of descents from a common progenitor.
2. That many of these variations tend to an improvement upon the parent stock.
3. That, by a continued selection of these improved specimens as the progenitors of future stock, its improvement may be unlimitedly increased.
4. And, lastly, that there is in nature a power continually and universally working out this selection, and so fixing and augmenting these improvements. . . .

That such a struggle for life then actually exists, and that it tends continually to lead the strong to exterminate the weak, we readily admit; and in this law we see a merciful provision against the deterioration, in a world apt to deteriorate, of the works of the Creator's hands. Thus it is that the bloody strifes of the males of all wild animals tend to maintain the vigor and full development of their race; because, through this machinery of appetite and passion, the most vigorous individuals become the progenitors of the next generation of the tribe. And this law, which thus maintains through the struggle of individuals the high type of the family, tends continually, through a similar struggle of species, to lead the stronger species to supplant the weaker. . . .

We come then to these conclusions. All the facts presented to us in the natural world tend to show that none of the variations produced in the fixed forms of animal life, when seen in its most plastic condition under domestication, give any promise of a true transmutation of species; first, from the difficulty of accumulating and fixing variations within the same species; secondly, from the fact that these variations, though most serviceable for man, have no tendency to improve the individual beyond the standard of his own specific type, and so to afford matter, even if they were infinitely produced, for the supposed power of natural selection on which to work; whilst all variations from the mixture of species are barred by the inexorable law of hybrid sterility. Further, the embalmed records of 3,000 years show that there has been no beginning of transmutation in the species of our most familiar domesticated animals; and beyond this, that in the countless tribes of animal life around us, down to its lowest and most variable species, no one has ever discovered a single instance of such transmutation being now in prospect; no new organ has ever been known to be developed—no new natural instinct to be formed—whilst, finally, in the vast museum of departed animal life which the strata of the earth imbed for our examination, whilst they contain far too complete a representation of the past to be set aside as a mere imperfect record, yet afford no one instance of any such change as having ever been in progress, or give us anywhere the missing links of the assumed chain, or the remains which would enable now existing variations, by gradual approximations, to shade off into unity.

On what then is the new theory based? We say it with unfeigned regret, in dealing with such a man as Mr. Darwin, on the merest hypothesis, supported by the most unbounded assumptions. . . .

In the name of all true philosophy we protest against such a mode of dealing with nature, as utterly dishonorable to all natural science, as reducing it from its present lofty level of being one of the noblest trainers of man's intellect and instructors of his mind, to being a mere idle play of the fancy, without the basis of fact or the discipline of observation. In the "Arabian Nights" we are not offended as at an impossibility when Amina sprinkles her husband with water and transforms him into a dog, but we cannot open the august doors of the venerable temple of scientific truth to the genii and magicians of romance. We plead guilty to Mr. Darwin's imputation that "the chief cause of our natural unwillingness to admit that the species has given birth to other and distinct species is that we are always slow in admitting any great change of which we do not see the intermediate steps." . . .

Our readers will not have failed to notice that we have objected to the views with which we have been dealing solely on scientific grounds. We have done so from our fixed conviction that it is thus that the truth or falsehood of such arguments should be tried. We have no sympathy with those who object to any facts or alleged facts in nature, or to any inference logically deduced from them, because they believe them to contradict what it appears to them is taught by revelation. We think that all such objections savor of a timidity which is really inconsistent with a firm and well-instructed faith. . . .

He who is as sure as he is of his own existence that the God of truth is at once the God of nature and the God of revelation, cannot believe it to be possible that His voice in either, rightly understood, can differ, or deceive His creatures. To oppose facts in the natural world because they seem to oppose revelation, or to humor them so as to compel them to speak its voice, is, he knows, but another form of the ever-ready feebleminded dishonesty of lying for God, and trying by fraud or falsehood to do the work of the God of truth. It is with another and a nobler spirit that the true believer walks amongst the works of nature. The words graven on the everlasting rocks are the words of God, and they are graven by His hand. No more can they contradict His Word written in His book, than could the words of the old covenant graven by His hand on the stony tables contradict the writings of His hand in the volume of the new dispensation. There may be to man difficulty in reconciling all the utterances of the two voices. But what of that? . . .

Few things have more deeply injured the cause of religion than the busy fussy energy with which men, narrow and feeble alike in faith and in science, have bustled forth to reconcile all new discoveries in physics with the word of inspiration. For it continually happens that some larger collection of facts, or some wider view of the phenomena of nature, alter the whole philosophic scheme; whilst revelation has been committed to declare an absolute agreement with what turns out after all to have been a misconception or an error. We cannot, therefore, consent to test the truth of natural science by the word of revelation. But this does not make it the less important to point out on scientific grounds scientific errors, when those errors tend to limit God's glory in creation, or to gainsay the revealed relations of that creation to Himself. To both these classes of error, though, we doubt not, quite unintentionally on his part, we think that Mr. Darwin's speculations directly tend.

Mr. Darwin writes as a Christian, and we doubt not that he is one. We do not for a moment believe him to be one of those who retain in some corner of their hearts a secret unbelief which they dare not vent; and we therefore pray him to consider well the grounds on which we brand his speculations with the charge of such a tendency. First, then, he not obscurely declares that he applies his scheme of the action of the principle of natural selection to MAN himself, as well as to the animals around him. Now, we must say at once, and openly, that such a notion is absolutely incompatible not only with single expressions in the word of God on that subject of natural science with which it is not immediately concerned, but, which in our judgment is of far more importance, with the whole representation of that moral and spiritual condition of man which is its proper subject-matter. Man's derived supremacy over the earth; man's power of articulate speech; man's gift of reason; man's free-will and responsi-

bility; man's fall and man's redemption; the incarnation of the Eternal Son; the indwelling of the Eternal Spirit,—all are equally and utterly irreconcilable with the degrading notion of the brute origin of him who was created in the image of God, and redeemed by the Eternal Son assuming to himself his nature. Equally inconsistent, too, not with any passing expressions, but with the whole scheme of God's dealings with man as recorded in His word, is Mr. Darwin's daring notion of man's further development into some unknown extent of powers, and shape, and size, through natural selection acting through that long vista of ages which he casts mistily over the earth upon the most favored individuals of his species. . . .

Nor can we doubt, secondly, that this view, which thus contradicts the revealed relation of creation to its Creator, is equally inconsistent with the fulness of His glory. It is, in truth, an ingenious theory for diffusing throughout creation the working and so the personality of the Creator. And thus, however unconsciously to him who holds them, such views really tend inevitably to banish from the mind most of the peculiar attributes of the Almighty.

How, asks Mr. Darwin, can we possibly account for the manifest plan, order, and arrangement which pervade creation, except we allow to it this self-developing power through modified descent? . . .

How can we account for all this? By the simplest and yet the most comprehensive answer. By declaring the stupendous fact that all creation is the transcript in matter of ideas eternally existing in the mind of the Most High—that order in the utmost perfectness of its relation pervades His works, because it exists as in its center and highest fountain-head in Him the Lord of all. Here is the true account of the fact which has so utterly misled shallow observers, that man himself, the prince and head of this creation, passes in the earlier stages of his being through phases of existence closely analogous, so far as his earthly tabernacle is concerned, to those in which the lower animals ever remain. At that point of being the development of the proto-zoa is arrested. Through it the embryo of their chief passes to the perfection of his earthly frame. But the types of those lower forms of being must be found in the animals which never advance beyond them—not in man for whom they are but the foundation for an after-development; whilst he too, creation's crown and perfection, thus bears witness in his own frame to the law of order which pervades the universe. . . .

That reverence for the work of God's hands with which a true belief in the All-wise Worker fills the believer's heart is at the root of all great physical discovery; it is the basis of philosophy. He who would see the venerable features of nature must not seek with the rudeness of a licensed royst-erer violently to unmask her countenance; but must wait as a learner for her willing unveiling. . . . This temper must beset those who do in effect banish God from nature. And so Mr. Darwin not only finds in it these bungling contrivances which his own greater skill could amend, but he stands aghast before its mightier phenomena. The presence of death and famine seems to him inconceivable on the ordinary idea of creation: and he looks almost aghast at them

until reconciled to their presence by his own theory that "a ratio of increase so high as to lead to a struggle for life, and as a consequence to natural selection entailing divergence of character and the extinction of less improved forms, is decidedly followed by the most exalted object which we are capable of conceiving, namely, the production of the higher animals." But we can give him a simpler solution still for the presence of these strange forms of imperfection and suffering amongst the works of God.

We can tell him of the strong shudder which ran through all this world when its head and ruler fell. When he asks concerning the infinite variety of these multiplied works which are set in such an orderly unity, and run up into man as their reasonable head, we can tell him of the exuberance of God's goodness and remind him of the deep philosophy which lies in those simple words—"All thy works praise Thee, O God, and thy saints give thanks unto Thee." For it is one office of redeemed man to collect the inarticulate praises of the material creation, and pay them with conscious homage into the treasury of the supreme Lord. . . .

THOMAS HENRY HUXLEY Darwin's Virtues (1860)

The youthful biologist and educator who is to become Darwin's foremost champion declares that Darwin's work "inaugurates a new epoch in natural history."

Mr. Darwin's long-standing and well-earned scientific eminence probably renders him indifferent to that social notoriety which passes by the name of success; but if the calm spirit of the philosopher have not yet wholly superseded the ambition and the vanity of the carnal man within him, he must be well satisfied with the results of his venture in publishing the "Origin of Species." . . . Everybody has read Mr. Dar-

win's book, or, at least, has given an opinion upon its merits or demerits; pietists, whether lay or ecclesiastic, decry it with the mild railing which sounds so charitable; bigots denounce it with ignorant invective; old ladies of both sexes consider it a decidedly dangerous book, and even savants, who have no better mud to throw, quote antiquated writers to show that its author is no better than an ape himself;

SOURCE: From a review published in the April 1860 issue of the *Westminster Review*, reprinted in Thomas Henry Huxley, *Lay Sermons, Addresses, and Reviews* (New York: D. Appleton & Co., 1871), pp. 255, 276–283, 292–298.

while every philosophical thinker hails it as a veritable Whitworth gun in the armory of liberalism; and all competent naturalists and physiologists, whatever their opinions as to the ultimate fate of the doctrines put forth, acknowledge that the work in which they are embodied is a solid contribution to knowledge and inaugurates a new epoch in natural history. . . .

. . . Whatever may be his theoretical views, no naturalist will probably be disposed to demur to the following summary of that exposition:—

Living beings, whether animals or plants, are divisible into multitudes of distinctly definable kinds, which are morphological species. They are also divisible into groups of individuals, which breed freely together, tending to reproduce their like, and are physiological species. Normally resembling their parents, the offspring of members of these species are still liable to vary, and the variation may be perpetuated by selection, as a race, which race, in many cases, presents all the characteristics of a morphological species. But it is not as yet proved that a race ever exhibits, when crossed with another race of the same species, those phenomena of hybridization which are exhibited by many species when crossed with other species. On the other hand, not only is it not proved that all species give rise to hybrids infertile *inter se*, but there is much reason to believe that, in crossing, species exhibit every gradation from perfect sterility to perfect fertility.

Such are the most essential characteristics of species. Even were man not one of them—a member of the same system and subject to the same laws—the question of their origin, their causal connexion, that is, with the other phenomena of the universe, must have attracted his attention, as soon as his intelligence had raised itself above the level of his daily wants.

Indeed history relates that such was the case, and has embalmed for us the speculations upon the origin of living beings, which were among the earliest products of the dawning intellectual activity of man. . . . The myths of paganism are as dead as Osiris or Zeus, and the man who should revive them, in opposition to the knowledge of our time, would be justly laughed to scorn; but the coeval imaginations current among the rude inhabitants of Palestine, recorded by writers whose very name and age are admitted by every scholar to be unknown, have unfortunately not shared their fate, but, even at this day, are regarded by nine-tenths of the civilized world as the authoritative standard of fact and the criterion of the justice of scientific conclusions, in all that relates to the origin of things, and, among them, of species. In this nineteenth century, as at the dawn of modern physical science, the cosmogony of the semi-barbarous Hebrew is the incubus of the philosopher and the opprobrium of the orthodox. Who shall number the patient and earnest seekers after truth, from the days of Galileo until now, whose lives have been embittered and their good name blasted by the mistaken zeal of bibliolaters? Who shall count the host of weaker men whose sense of truth has been destroyed in the effort to harmonize impossibilities—whose life has been wasted in the attempt to force the generous new wine of science into the old bottles of Judaism, compelled by the outcry of the same strong party?

It is true that if philosophers have suffered, their cause has been amply avenged. Extinguished theologians lie about the cradle of every science as the strangled snakes beside that of Hercules; and history records that whenever science and orthodoxy have been fairly opposed, the latter has been forced to retire from the lists, bleeding and crushed, if not annihilated; scotched, if not slain. But orthodoxy is the Bourbon of the world of thought. It learns not, neither can it forget; and though, at present, bewildered and afraid to move, it is as willing as ever to insist that the first chapter of Genesis contains the beginning and the end of sound science; and to visit, with such petty thunderbolts as its half-paralyzed hands can hurl, those who refuse to degrade nature to the level of primitive Judaism.

Philosophers, on the other hand, have no such aggressive tendencies. With eyes fixed on the noble goal to which "per aspera et ardua"[4] they tend, they may, now and then, be stirred to momentary wrath by the unnecessary obstacles with which the ignorant, or the malicious, encumber, if they cannot bar, the difficult path; but why should their souls be deeply vexed? The majesty of fact is on their side, and the elemental forces of nature are working for them. Not a star comes to the meridian at its calculated time but testifies to the justice of their methods—their beliefs are "one with the falling rain and with the growing corn." By doubt they are established, and open inquiry is their bosom friend. Such men have no fear of traditions however venerable, and no respect for them when they become mischievous and obstructive; but they have better than mere antiquarian business in hand, and if dogmas, which ought to be fossil but are not, are not forced upon their notice, they are too happy to treat them as nonexistent.

The hypotheses respecting the origin of species which profess to stand upon a scientific basis, and, as such, alone demand serious attention, are of two kinds. The one, the "special creation" hypothesis, presumes every species to have originated from one or more stocks, these not being the result of the modification of any other form of living matter—or arising by natural agencies—but being produced, as such, by a supernatural creative act.

The other, the so-called "transmutation" hypothesis, considers that all existing species are the result of the modification of preexisting species, and those of their predecessors, by agencies similar to those which at the present day produce varieties and races, and therefore in an altogether natural way; and it is a probable, though not a necessary consequence of this hypothesis, that all living beings have arisen from a single stock. With respect to the origin of this primitive stock, or stocks, the doctrine of the origin of species is obviously not necessarily concerned. The transmutation hypothesis, for example, is perfectly consistent either with the conception of a special creation of the primitive germ, or with the supposition of its having arisen, as a modification of inorganic matter, by natural causes.

The doctrine of special creation owes its existence very largely to the supposed necessity of making science accord with the Hebrew cosmogony; but it is curious to observe that, as the doctrine is at present maintained by men of science, it is as hopelessly inconsistent with the Hebrew view as any other hypothesis. . . .

Deserving no aid from the powerful arm of bibliolatry, then, does the received form of the hypothesis of special creation derive any support from science or sound logic? Assuredly not much. The arguments brought forward in its favor all take one form: If species were not supernaturally created, we cannot understand the facts x, or y, or z; we cannot understand the structure of animals or plants, unless we suppose they were contrived for special ends; we cannot understand the structure of the eye, except by supposing it to have been made to see with; we cannot understand instincts, unless we suppose animals to have been miraculously endowed with them.

As a question of dialectics, it must be admitted that this sort of reasoning is not very formidable to those who are not to be frightened by consequences. It is an *argumentum ad ignorantiam*—take this explanation or be ignorant. But suppose we prefer to admit our ignorance rather than adopt a hypothesis at variance with all the teachings of nature? Or, suppose for a moment we admit the explanation, and then seriously ask ourselves how much the wiser are we; what does the explanation explain? . . .

But the hypothesis of special creation is not only a mere specious mask for our ignorance; its existence in biology marks the youth and imperfection of the science. For what is the history of every science but the history of the elimination of the notion of creative, or other interferences, with the natural order of the phenomena which are

---

[4]*"per aspera et ardua"*: through difficulty and adversity

the subject-matter of that science? When astronomy was young "the morning stars sang together for joy," and the planets were guided in their courses by celestial hands. Now, the harmony of the stars has resolved itself into gravitation according to the inverse squares of the distances, and the orbits of the planets are deducible from the laws of the forces which allow a schoolboy's stone to break a window. . . .

Harmonious order governing eternally continuous progress—the web and woof of matter and force interweaving by slow degrees, without a broken thread, that veil which lies between us and the infinite—that universe which alone we know or can know; such is the picture which science draws of the world, and in proportion as any part of that picture is in unison with the rest, so may we feel sure that it is rightly painted. Shall biology alone remain out of harmony with her sister sciences? . . .

The Darwinian hypothesis has the merit of being eminently simple and comprehensible in principle, and its essential positions may be stated in a very few words: all species have been produced by the development of varieties from common stocks by the conversion of these first into permanent races and then into new species, by the process of *natural selection*, which process is essentially identical with that artificial selection by which man has originated the races of domestic animals—the *struggle for existence* taking the place of man, and exerting, in the case of natural selection, that selective action which he performs in artificial selection.

The evidence brought forward by Mr. Darwin in support of his hypothesis is of three kinds. First, he endeavors to prove that species may be originated by selection; secondly, he attempts to show that natural causes are competent to exert selection; and thirdly, he tries to prove that the most remarkable and apparently anomalous phenomena exhibited by the distribution, development, and mutual relations of species, can be shown to be deducible from the general doctrine of their origin, which he propounds, combined with the known facts of

geological change; and that, even if all these phenomena are not at present explicable by it, none are necessarily inconsistent with it. . . .

There is no fault to be found with Mr. Darwin's method, . . . but it is another question whether he has fulfilled all the conditions imposed by that method. Is it satisfactorily proved, in fact, that species may be originated by selection? that there is such a thing as natural selection? that none of the phenomena exhibited by species are inconsistent with the origin of species in this way? If these questions can be answered in the affirmative, Mr. Darwin's view steps out of the ranks of hypotheses into those of proved theories; but, so long as the evidence at present adduced falls short of enforcing that affirmation, so long, to our minds, must the new doctrine be content to remain among the former—an extremely valuable, and in the highest degree probable, doctrine, indeed the only extant hypothesis which is worth anything in a scientific point of view; but still a hypothesis, and not yet the theory of species.

After much consideration, and with assuredly no bias against Mr. Darwin's views, it is our clear conviction that, as the evidence stands, it is not absolutely proven . . . but we do not hesitate to assert that it is as superior to any preceding or contemporary hypothesis, in the extent of observational and experimental basis on which it rests, in its rigorously scientific method, and in its power of explaining biological phenomena, as was the hypothesis of Copernicus to the speculations of Ptolemy. But the planetary orbits turned out not to be quite circular after all, and grand as was the service Copernicus rendered science, Kepler and Newton had to come after him. What if the orbit of Darwinism should be a little too circular? . . . Viewed as a whole, we do not believe that [in thirty years] any work has appeared calculated to exert so large an influence, not only on the future of biology, but in extending the domination of science over regions of thought into which she has, as yet, hardly penetrated.

MATTHEW ARNOLD **Dover Beach (1867)**

The poet and social and literary critic Matthew Arnold ponders the implications of "the loss of faith."

Dover Beach

The sea is calm to-night.
The tide is full, the moon lies fair
Upon the straits;—on the French coast the
    light
Gleams and is gone; the cliffs of England
    stand,
Glimmering and vast, out in the tranquil
    bay.
Come to the window, sweet is the night-
    air
Only, from the long line of spray
Where the sea meets the moon-blanch'd
    land,
Listen! you hear the grating roar
Of pebbles which the waves draw back,
    and fling,
At their return, up the high strand,
Begin, and cease, and then again begin,
With tremulous cadence slow, and bring
The eternal note of sadness in.

Sophocles long ago
Heard it on the Aegean, and it brought
Into his mind the turbid ebb and flow
Of human misery; we
Find also in the sound a thought,
Hearing it by this distant northern sea.

The Sea of Faith
Was once, too, at the full, and round
    earth's shore
Lay like the folds of a bright girdle furl'd.
But now I only hear
Its melancholy, long, withdrawing roar,
Retreating, to the breath
Of the night-wind, down the vast edges
    drear
And naked shingles of the world.

Ah, love, let us be true
To one another! for the world, which
    seems
To lie before us like a land of dreams,
So various, so beautiful, so new,
Hath really neither joy, nor love, nor light,
Nor certitude, nor peace, nor help for
    pain;
And we are here as on a darkling plain
Swept with confused alarms of struggle
    and flight,
Where ignorant armies clash by night.

SOURCE: This poem was first published in 1867 and has been reprinted in most collections of Arnold's poems as well as in numerous anthologies.

10

The Coming of Political
Democracy: Threat or Promise?

For many mid-Victorian Englishmen, the political arrangement worked out in the aftermath of the Reform Act of 1832 had proved a happy one: it included an admired queen (who had "the right to be consulted, the right to encourage and the right to warn") to head the state; a respected House of Lords to serve as a bulwark against too rapid change; and a powerful House of Commons to enact legislation and also to uphold (and sometimes to dismiss) the prime minister and his cabinet, who ran the national government. Members of the cabinet linked the executive and legislative parts of the government: they were ministers of the Crown who, at the same time, served as Members of Parliament. The House of Commons in turn was chosen by country gentlemen and by an urban electorate made up largely of "ten-pound householders"—owners of substantial houses who served in the professions or as merchants, shopkeepers, and well-to-do artisans, a group that was gradually expanding as the country grew more prosperous but that involved no more than one adult male in five. The "political nation" was clearly upper class and upper-middle class, yet the political atmosphere was "liberal" in spirit; a host of earlier restrictions upon freedom of religion, freedom of the press, and freedom of enterprise had been stricken from the statute book.

During the 1830s and 1840s this political arrangement had been challenged vigorously by the Chartists, but during the 1850s the spirit of militant reform ebbed. Thus when John Stuart Mill (1806–1873) published *Considerations on Representative Government* in 1861, his readers included many who feared that a nation noted for constitutional government and for a high degree of civil liberty might be injured rather than aided by a democratic expansion of the franchise. By profession an administrator in the East India Company's London office until 1858, Mill was well known as a child prodigy raised by the founders of utilitarianism, Jeremy Bentham and John's father, James Mill. By 1861 John Stuart Mill had already produced fundamental works on logic and economics as well as *On Liberty*, but his book *The Subjection of Women* (cited in Chapter 8) had not yet been published. On what grounds does Mill justify the coming of political democracy? What advantages for Britain does he see in such a change? Are there any groups that, in Mill's judgment, might justifiably be excluded from the expanded franchise? What methods does

The Workingman, from the Royal Westminster Exhibition

Number 450 presents the workingman as depicted by John Bright; number 1002 shows the workingman as portrayed by Robert Lowe. (Punch, May 20, 1865)

Mill propose to deal with the pitfalls of democracy, such as the possibility that the twin ideals of an expanded electorate and of individual liberty might come into conflict?

Although John Stuart Mill was to serve as Member of Parliament for only three years (1865–1868), Robert Lowe (1811–1892) was a member of the House of Commons for almost three decades and John Bright (1811–1889), for more than four. Like Mill, both Lowe and Bright were members of the Liberal Party, and on subjects such as civil service reform, education, and the extension of religious liberty they were in close accord. In

1866 and 1867, however, when the expansion of the franchise became the most important issue in parliamentary politics, Bright and Lowe headed opposite sides. Bright approached the question of political reform more as stump orator than as political philosopher, and his speech in Birmingham in 1865, "The Case for Democracy," helped inspire the Liberal Reform Bill of 1866 and, indirectly, the Conservative Reform Bill of 1867. A cotton manufacturer by trade, a Quaker by religion, Bright had entered politics as a champion of the Anti-Corn Law League and, at the time he spoke, he had never held ministerial office. How does he utilize the experience of Canada, Australia, and the United States in his stock of arguments? How does he deal with the fears of his opponents? Does he threaten revolution or does his militant surface conceal a moderate core?

Unlike Bright, Lowe had actually lived in Australia and had served for a time in the legislature of New South Wales. But as "The Case Against Democracy" (1867) illustrates, his approach to politics differed sharply from that of both Mill and Bright. How does Lowe himself define that difference? What does Lowe see as the practical (as opposed to theoretical) arguments in favor of retaining the political status quo? How important a role in promoting human happiness does he assign to government?

In the parliamentary debates of 1866 and 1867, a majority of M.P.s ultimately followed Bright and Mill rather than Lowe. Although Mill failed in his attempt to extend the franchise to some women as well as to male members of the urban working class, his advocacy did much to launch the women's suffrage movement as a serious force in Victorian Britain. And Gladstone, who became Liberal prime minister in 1868, was so impressed by Bright's eloquence and by Lowe's brilliance that he induced both men to become members of his cabinet.

By the time Sir Henry Maine (1822–1888) wrote *Popular Government* in 1885, not merely the Reform Bill of 1867 but also the Reform Bill of 1884 had been passed. The vast majority of males had been enfranchised (though rigid registration rules kept a considerable number from electoral participation), and the House of Commons had ceased to argue the virtues or the deficiencies of political democracy. Maine never became a Member of Parliament, but he won a high reputation as a jurist at Cambridge, Oxford, and London's Inns of Court, as an administrator in India, and as a legal historian. His book, *Popular Government,* was repeatedly republished during the late Victorian years and constitutes a reminder that not all Victorians were persuaded that their nation had taken the right course. Why is Maine doubtful that democratic governments will prove either stable or enduring? Which rival historical forces does he see as injuring the prospects of democracy? What built-in defects does he attribute to democracy? How does his utilization of the American experience compare with that of Bright? In the aftermath of a century, which of the four—Mill, Bright, Lowe, and Maine—has proved to be the truest prophet?

JOHN STUART MILL **Considerations on Representative Government (1861)**

Mid-Victorian Britain's most notable philosophical champion of political liberalism argues in favor of democracy—with safeguards.

To inquire into the best form of government in the abstract (as it is called) is not a chimerical, but a highly practical employment of scientific intellect; and to introduce into any country the best institutions which, in the existing state of that country, are capable of, in any tolerable degree, fulfilling the conditions, is one of the most rational objects to which practical effort can address itself. . . .

There is no difficulty in showing that the ideally best form of government is that in which the sovereignty, or supreme controlling power in the last resort, is vested in the entire aggregate of the community; every citizen not only having a voice in the exercise of that ultimate sovereignty, but being, at least occasionally, called on to take an actual part in the government, by the personal discharge of some public function, local or general. . . . It is both more favorable to present good government, and promotes a better and higher form of national character, than any other polity whatsoever.

Its superiority in reference to present well-being rests upon two principles, of as universal truth and applicability as any general propositions which can be laid down respecting human affairs. The first is, that the rights and interests of every or any person are only secure from being disregarded, when the person interested is himself able, and habitually disposed, to stand up for them. The second is, that the general prosperity attains a greater height, and is more widely diffused, in proportion to the amount and variety of the personal energies enlisted in promoting it.

Putting these two propositions into a shape more special to their present application; human beings are only secure from evil at the hands of others, in proportion as

they have the power of being, and are, self-*protecting*; and they only achieve a high degree of success in their struggle with nature, in proportion as they are self-*dependent*, relying on what they themselves can do, either separately or in concert, rather than on what others do for them. . . . We need not suppose that when power resides in an exclusive class, that class will knowingly and deliberately sacrifice the other classes to themselves: it suffices that, in the absence of its natural defenders, the interest of the excluded is always in danger of being overlooked; and, when looked at, is seen with very different eyes from those of the persons whom it directly concerns. In this country, for example, what are called the working classes may be considered as excluded from all direct participation in the government. I do not believe that the classes who do participate in it, have in general any intention of sacrificing the working classes to themselves. They once had that intention; witness the persevering attempts so long made to keep down wages by law. But in the present day, their ordinary disposition is the very opposite: they willingly make considerable sacrifices, especially of their pecuniary interest, for the benefit of the working classes, and err rather by too lavish and indiscriminating beneficence; nor do I believe that any rulers in history have been actuated by a more sincere desire to do their duty toward the poorer portion of their countrymen. Yet does Parliament, or almost any of the members composing it, ever for an instant look at any question with the eyes of a working man? When a subject arises in which the laborers as such have an interest, is it regarded from any point of view but that of the employers of labor? I do not say that the

SOURCE: From John Stuart Mill, *Considerations on Representative Government*, 2nd ed. (London, 1861), pp. 11, 53–59, 63–65, 69, 105–106, 127–129, 163, 165–167, 169–172, 175–176.

working men's view of these questions is in general nearer to truth than the other: but it is sometimes quite as near; and in any case it ought to be respectfully listened to, instead of being, as it is, not merely turned away from, but ignored. . . .

All free communities have both been more exempt from social injustice and crime, and have attained more brilliant prosperity, than any others, or than they themselves after they lost their freedom. Contrast the free states of the world, while their freedom lasted, with the contemporary subjects of monarchical or oligarchical despotism: the Greek cities with the Persian satrapies; the Italian republics, and the free towns of Flanders and Germany, with the feudal monarchies of Europe; Switzerland, Holland, and England, with Austria or ante-revolutionary France. Their superior prosperity was too obvious ever to have been gainsayed: while their superiority in good government and social relations, is proved by the prosperity, and is manifest besides in every page of history. . . .

Thus stands the case as regards present well-being; the good management of the affairs of the existing generation. If we now pass to the influence of the form of government upon character, we shall find the superiority of popular government over every other to be, if possible, still more decided and indisputable. . . .

The striving, go-ahead character of England and the United States is only a fit subject of disapproving criticism, on account of the very secondary objects on which it commonly expends its strength. In itself it is the foundation of the best hopes for the general improvement of mankind. . . .

Now there can be no kind of doubt that the passive type of character is favored by the government of one or a few, and the active self-helping type by that of the many. Irresponsible rulers need the quiescence of the ruled, more than they need any activity but that which they can compel. Submissiveness to the prescriptions of men as necessities of nature, is the lesson inculcated by all governments upon those who are wholly without participation in them. . . .

Between subjection to the will of others, and the virtues of self-help and self-government, there is a natural incompatibility. This is more or less complete, according as the bondage is strained or relaxed. . . .

From these accumulated considerations it is evident, that the only government which can fully satisfy all the exigencies of the social state, is one in which the whole people participate; that any participation, even in the smallest public function, is useful; that the participation should everywhere be as great as the general degree of improvement of the community will allow; and that nothing less can be ultimately desirable, than the admission of all to a share in the sovereign power of the state. But since all cannot, in a community exceeding a single small town, participate personally in any but some very minor portions of the public business, it follows that the ideal type of a perfect government must be representative. . . .

Instead of the function of governing, for which it is radically unfit, the proper office of a representative assembly is to watch and control the government: to throw the light of publicity on its acts: to compel a full exposition and justification of all of them which any one considers questionable; to censure them if found condemnable, and, if the men who compose the government abuse their trust, or fulfil it in a manner which conflicts with the deliberate sense of the nation, to expel them from office, and either expressly or virtually appoint their successors. This is surely ample power, and security enough for the liberty of the nation. In addition to this, the Parliament has an office, not inferior even to this in importance; to be at once the nation's Committee of Grievances, and its Congress of Opinions: an arena in which not only the general opinion of the nation, but that of every section of it, and as far as possible of every eminent individual whom it contains, can produce itself in full light and challenge discussion; where every person in the country may count upon finding somebody who speaks his mind, as well or better than he could speak it himself. . . . Where every party or opinion in the country can muster its strength, and be cured of any illusion concerning the number or power of its adherents; where the opinion which prevails in the nation makes itself manifest as prevailing, and marshals its hosts in the presence of the government, which is thus enabled and compelled to give way to it on the mere manifestation, without the actual employment, of its strength; where statesmen can assure themselves, far more certainly than by any other signs, what elements of opinion and power are growing, and what declining, and are enabled to shape their measures with some regard not solely to present exigencies, but to tendencies in progress.

One of the greatest dangers . . . of democracy, as of all other forms of government, lies in the sinister interest of the holders of power: it is the danger of class legislation; of government intended for (whether really effecting it or not) the immediate benefit of the dominant class, to the lasting detriment of the whole. And one of the most important questions demanding consideration, in determining the best constitution of a representative government, is how to provide efficacious securities against this evil.

If we consider as a class, politically speaking, any number of persons who have the same sinister interest,—that is, whose direct and apparent interest points toward the same description of bad measures; the desirable object would be that no class, and no combination of classes likely to combine, should be able to exercise a preponderant influence in the government. A modern community, not divided within itself by strong antipathies of race, language, or nationality, may be considered as in the main divisible into two sections, which, in spite of partial variations, correspond on the whole with two divergent directions of apparent interest. Let us call them (in brief general terms) laborers on the one hand, employers of labor on the other: including however along with employers of labor, not only retired capitalists, and the possessors of inherited wealth, but all that highly paid description of laborers (such as the profes-

sions) whose education and way of life assimilate them with the rich, and whose prospect and ambition it is to raise themselves into that class. With the laborers, on the other hand, may be ranked those smaller employers of labor, who by interests, habits, and educational impressions, are assimilated in wishes, tastes, and objects to the laboring classes; comprehending a large proportion of petty tradesmen. In a state of society thus composed, if the representative system could be made ideally perfect, and if it were possible to maintain it in that state, its organization must be such, that these two classes, manual laborers and their affinities on one side, employers of labor and their affinities on the other, should be, in the arrangement of the representative system, equally balanced, each influencing about an equal number of votes in Parliament. . . .

Democracy is not the ideally best form of government unless this weak side of it can be strengthened; unless it can be so organized that no class, not even the most numerous, shall be able to reduce all but itself to political insignificance, and direct the course of legislation and administration by its exclusive class interest. The problem is, to find the means of preventing this abuse, without sacrificing the characteristic advantages of popular government. . . .

Whoever, in an otherwise popular government, has no vote, and no prospect of obtaining it, will either be a permanent malcontent, or will feel as one whom the general affairs of society do not concern; for whom they are to be managed by others; who "has no business with the laws except to obey them," nor with the public interests and concerns except as a looker-on. . . .

Independently of all these considerations, it is a personal injustice to withhold from any one, unless for the prevention of greater evils, the ordinary privilege of having his voice reckoned in the disposal of affairs in which he has the same interest as other people. If he is compelled to pay, if he may be compelled to fight, if he is required implicitly to obey, he should be legally entitled to be told what for; to have his consent asked, and his opinion counted at its worth, though not at more than its worth. . . .

There are, however, certain exclusions, required by positive reasons, which do not conflict with this principle, and which, though an evil in themselves, are only to be got rid of by the cessation of the state of things which requires them. I regard it as wholly inadmissible that any person should participate in the suffrage, without being able to read, write, and, I will add, perform the common operations of arithmetic. Justice demands, even when the suffrage does not depend on it, that the means of attaining these elementary acquirements should be within the reach of every person, either gratuitously, or at an expense not exceeding what the poorest, who earn their own living, can afford. . . .

It is also important, that the assembly which votes the taxes, either general or local, should be elected exclusively by those who pay something toward the taxes imposed. Those who pay no taxes, disposing by their votes of other people's money, have every motive to be lavish, and none to economize. . . . But to reconcile this, as a condition annexed to the representation, with universality, it is essential, as it is on many other accounts desirable, that taxation, in a visible shape, should descend to the poorest class. . . .

I regard it as required by first principles, that the receipt of parish relief should be a peremptory disqualification for the franchise. He who cannot by his labor suffice for his own support, has no claim to the privilege of helping himself to the money of others. By becoming dependent on the remaining members of the community for actual subsistence, he abdicates his claim to equal rights with them in other respects. . . .

To be an uncertificated bankrupt, or to have taken the benefit of the Insolvent Act, should disqualify for the franchise until the person has paid his debts, or at least proved that he is not now, and has not for some long period been, dependent on eleemosy-

nary support.[1] Non-payment of taxes, when so long persisted in that it cannot have arisen from inadvertence, should disqualify while it lasts. . . .

In the long run, therefore (supposing no restrictions to exist but those of which we have now treated), we might expect that all, except that (it is to be hoped) progressively diminishing class, the recipients of parish relief, would be in possession of votes, so that the suffrage would be, with that slight abatement, universal. . . .

Yet in this state of things, the great majority of voters, in most countries, and emphatically in this, would be manual laborers; and the twofold danger that of too low a standard of political intelligence, and that of class legislation, would exist, in a very perilous degree. . . .

The only thing which can justify reckoning one person's opinion as equivalent to more than one, is individual mental superiority; and what is wanted is some approximate means of ascertaining that. If there existed such a thing as a really national education, or a trustworthy system of general examination, education might be tested directly. In the absence of these, the nature of a person's occupation is some test. An employer of labor is on the average more intelligent than a laborer; for he must labor with his head, and not solely with his hands. A foreman is generally more intelligent than an ordinary laborer, and a laborer in the skilled trades than in the unskilled. A banker, merchant, or manufacturer, is likely to be more intelligent than a tradesman, because he has larger and more complicated interests to manage. In all these cases it is not the having merely undertaken the superior function, but the successful performance of it, that tests the qualifications. . . . Two or more votes might be allowed to every person who exercises any of these superior functions. The liberal professions, when really and not nominally practiced, imply, of course, a still higher degree of instruction; and wherever a sufficient examination, or any serious condi-

---

[1]*eleemosynary support:* charity

tions of education, are required before entering on a profession, its members could be admitted at once to a plurality of votes. The same rule might be applied to graduates of universities; and even to those who bring satisfactory certificates of having passed through the course of study required by any school at which the higher branches of knowledge are taught, under proper securities that the teaching is real, and not a mere pretense. . . .

In the preceding argument for universal, but graduated suffrage, I have taken no account of difference of sex. I consider it to be as entirely irrelevant to political rights, as difference in height, or in the color of the hair. All human beings have the same interest in good government; the welfare of all is alike affected by it, and they have equal need of a voice in it to secure their share of its benefits. If there be any difference, women require it more than men, since, being physically weaker, they are more dependent on law and society for protection. Mankind have long since abandoned the only premises which will support the conclusion that women ought not to have votes. No one now holds that women should be in personal servitude; that they should have no thought, wish, or occupation, but to be the domestic drudges of husbands, fathers, or brothers. It is allowed to unmarried, and wants but little of being conceded to married women, to hold property, and have pecuniary and business interests, in the same manner as men. It is considered suitable and proper that women should think, and write, and be teachers. As soon as these things are admitted, the political disqualification has no principle to rest on. The whole mode of thought of the modern world is, with increasing emphasis, pronouncing against the claim of society to decide for individuals what they are and are not fit for, and what they shall and shall not be allowed to attempt. If the principles of modern politics and political economy are good for anything, it is for proving that these points can only be rightly judged of by the individuals themselves. . . .

JOHN BRIGHT **The Case for Democracy (1865)**

The foremost parliamentary champion of suffrage expansion during the 1860s pleads for his cause at Birmingham on January 18, 1865.

Well, then, there is this question that will not sleep—the question of the admission of the people of this country to the rights which are guaranteed to them, and promised to them by everything that we comprehend as the Constitution of this United Kingdom. . . .

That bill or question is not dead; it takes shape again, and you perceive that the Tories, and those Whigs who are like Tories— all Whigs are not like Tories, therefore I make the distinction—the Tories, and those Whigs who are like Tories, have an uncomfortable feeling which approaches almost to a shiver. What is this apparition which alarms them? . . . I will tell you what it is.

They are afraid of the five or six millions of Englishmen, grown up men who are allowed to marry, to keep house, to rear children, who are expected to earn their living, who pay taxes, who must obey the law, who must be citizens in all honorable conduct— they are afraid of the five or six millions who by the present system of representation are shut out, and insultingly shut out, from the commonest rights of citizenship.

We are proud of our country; and there are many things in it which, as far as men may rightly be proud, we may be proud of. We may be proud of this, that England is the ancient country of parliaments. . . . You know the boast we have of what takes place

SOURCE: From James E. Thorold Rogers, ed., *The Speeches of John Bright, M.P.* (London, 1868), Vol. II, pp. 110–114, 118–129.

when negro-slaves land in England; you know what one of our best poets has said, that if their lungs but breathe our air, that moment they are free; they touch our country, and their shackles fall. But how is it with an Englishman? An Englishman, if he goes to the Cape [of Good Hope], can vote; if he goes farther, to Australia, to the nascent empires of the New World, he can vote; if he goes to the Canadian Confederation, he can vote; and if he goes to those grandest colonies of England not now dependent upon the English crown, there, in twenty free, and, in the whole, in thirty-five different states, he can give his free and independent vote. It is only in his own country, on his own soil, where he was born, the very soil which he has enriched with his labor and with the sweat of his brow, that he is denied the right which in every other community of Englishmen in the world would be freely accorded to him. . . .

It may happen, as it happened thirty years ago, that the eyes of the five millions all through the United Kingdom may be fixed with an intense glare upon the doors of Parliament; it was so in the years 1831–32. There are men in this room who felt then, and know now, that it required but an accident—but one spark to the train, and this country would have been in the throes of revolution. . . . If the five millions should once unitedly fix their eyes with an intense look upon the door of that House where my hon. Friend[2] and I expect so soon to enter, I would ask who shall say them nay? Not the mace upon the table of the House; not the four hundred easy gentlemen of the House of Lords who lounge in and out of that decorated chamber; not the dozen gentlemen who call themselves statesmen, and who meet in Downing-street. . . . I say there is no power in this country, as opinion now stands, and as combination is now possible, there is no power in this country that can say "Nay" for one single week to the five millions, if they are intent upon making their way within the doors of Parliament. . . .

I have always thought that it was one of the great objects of statesmen in our time not to separate the people into sections and classes, but rather to unite them all in one firm and compact body of citizenship, equally treated by the law, and equally loyal to the law and to the government of the country. . . .

I want to know whence this fear of the people is. Will somebody undertake to tell us why is this fear of the people? It does not exist elsewhere. It does not exist in the various countries of Europe, where representative systems are being daily established. It does not exist anywhere amongst Englishmen, except in these two islands. I have spoken to you already of Australia. The franchise in Australia, doubtless, is lower than it is in this country: but Australian governments legislate in accordance with the opinions of the Australian people. . . . You know that . . . all the British North American provinces are about to make a confederation—a state of considerable magnitude. . . . Therefore our Parliament is this session about to pass a bill affecting the British North American provinces which these gentlemen tell us will be wholly destructive if applied to this country. . . .

I want to ask you, the men of Birmingham, who have recently been reading the papers a good deal, especially with regard to what is taking place in the United States—and I shall, like my honorable Friend, avoid any allusion to that terrible revolution which is taking place there—if you have observed that in the state of New York alone 700,000 men voted at the last presidential election, and that throughout the whole of free states not less than 4,000,000 votes were given, and that they were all given with the most perfect order and tranquillity throughout the whole of the states?

But perhaps our friends who oppose us will say, "We do not fear about elections and order. What we fear is this—the legislative results of this wide extension of the franchise." I am ready to test it in any country by the results of legislation. I say,

---

[2]*Friend:* William Scholefield, Bright's fellow Liberal M.P. for Birmingham

whether you go to South Africa, or to Australia, or to the British North American provinces, or the the states of the American Union, you will find—excluding always those states where slavery injures the state of society—you will find that life and property are as secure, you will find that education is much more extended amongst the people, that there is quite as wide a provision for their religious interests, that the laws are as merciful and just, that taxes are imposed and levied with as great equality, and that the millions of your countrymen who are now established in those countries are at least as well off in all the circumstances of life as are the people of this country whom they have left behind them. I confess that I never yet heard of a man who returned to this country from any of those countries under the impression that he would be more secure here than he would be there.

I have sought a good deal into this question, and it seems to me as if they [the opponents of reform] had a notion that in this country we have some institutions which have come down to us from the Middle Ages—from what some people call the Dark Ages—and that these institutions may not permanently harmonize with the intelligence and the necessities of the nineteenth century in which we live. The "institutions" are truly safe enough if the government be in the hands of the institution; and if the peerage and the established Church are to rule in England, then I presume that the peerage and the established Church, in their present condition, will be permanently safe; and if the great patronage of our vast expenditure is to be dispensed perpetually amongst the ruling class, the ruling class as a matter of course will take extreme care of the patronage. There is something very sacred in that patronage. There are many families in this country with long lines of ancestry, who, if patronage were curtailed, would feel very much as some of us feel in Lancashire when the American war has stopped our supplies of cotton. They look upon patronage as a holy

thing, not to be touched by profane hands. . . .

But, Sir, I protest against this theory. I protest against the theory that the people of this country have an unreasonable and violent desire to shake or overturn institutions which they may not theoretically approve of. . . . I am perfectly content to live under the institutions which the intelligence, and the virtue, and the experience of my countrymen fairly represented in Parliament shall determine upon. . . .

The House of Commons is in reality the only guarantee we have for freedom. If you looked at any other country, and saw nothing but a monarch, he might be a good king and might do his best, but you would see that there is no guarantee for freedom—you know not who will be his successor. If you saw a country with no crown, but with a handful of nobles, administering the government of the country, you would say there is no guarantee there for freedom, because a number of individuals acting together have not the responsibility, or the feeling of responsibility, that one man has, and they do things which one man would not dare to do. . . . It is only the existence of that House which makes the institution they are so fond of safe and permanent at all—and they are afraid that the five millions somehow or other will get into it. Now, I beg to tell them that the five millions will get into it, though they may not get into it all at once; and perhaps few men desire that they should, for I am opposed myself to great and violent changes, which create needless shocks, and which are accepted, if they are accepted, with great alarm.

But I will undertake to say that some portion, a considerable and effective portion, of those five millions will before many years are passed be freely allowed to vote for members of the House of Commons. It is not the democracy which these gentlemen are always afraid of that is the peril of this country. It was not democracy in 1832 that was the peril. It was the desperate antagonism of the class that then had power to the just claims and rights of the people. . . . Conservatism, be it Tory or be it Whig, is the true national peril which we have to face. They may dam the stream, they may keep back the waters, but the volume is ever increasing, and it descends with accelerated force, and the time will come when, in all probability, and to a certainty, if wisdom does not take the place of folly, the waters will burst their banks, and these men, who fancy they are stemming this imaginary apparition of democracy, will be swept away by the resolute will of a united and determined people. . . .

England has long been famous for the enjoyment of personal freedom by her people. They are free to think, the are free to speak, they are free to write; and England has been famed of late years, and is famed now the world over, for the freedom of her industry and the greatness and the freedom of her commerce. I want to know then why it is that her people should not be free to vote. Who is there that will meet me on this platform, or will stand upon any platform, and will dare to say, in the hearing of an open meeting of his countrymen, that these millions for whom I am now pleading are too degraded, too vicious, and too destructive to be entrusted with the elective franchise? I at least will never thus slander my countrymen. I claim for them the right of admission, through their representatives, into the most ancient and the most venerable Parliament which at this hour exists among men; and when they are thus admitted, and not till then, it may be truly said that England, the august mother of free nations, herself is free.

ROBERT LOWE **The Case Against Democracy (1867)**

Although Lowe, like Mill and Bright, looked upon himself as Liberal, he became the foremost parliamentary opponent of suffrage expansion in 1866 and 1867. Here he sets forth the dangers of democracy.

No assertion is more frequently met with in the speeches of the supporters of a democratic reform than this,—that the arguments are all on one side, that the question is an easy one, depending merely on arithmetic, and such as any man possessed of ordinary common sense may decide on the first inspection. To me the question appears very difficult to treat in a popular, and, at the same time, in a fair and intelligible way, because it involves not merely the balancing of adverse arguments, but a decision as to what kind of argument should have weight on such a subject. A consideration of the speeches delivered on both sides will show that the arguments in favor of democracy are mostly metaphysical, resting on considerations prior to, and therefore independent of, experience, appealing to abstract maxims and terms, and treating this peculiarly practical subject as if it were a problem of pure geometry. The arguments against a democratic change, on the other hand, are all drawn, or profess to be drawn, from considerations purely practical. The one side deals in such terms as right, equality, justice; the other, with the working of institutions, with their faults, with their remedies, with the probable influence which such changes will exert. Are both these methods right, and if not both, which of the two? There are, as a great thinker has taught, three ways of treating political subjects:—the theological, the metaphysical, and the inductive, or experimental. The doctrine of the divine right of kings is an instance of the first kind of treatment of a political subject; the argument so much relied on at reform meetings in favor of extended suffrage, and the writings of James

SOURCE: From Robert Lowe, *Speeches and Letters on Reform* (London, 1867), pp. 3–16.

and John Mill, are examples of the second; and discussions of the House of Commons on almost every other subject except reform, and the arguments against reform, of the third. It is considered, I believe, by most thinkers that the second of these methods is superior to the first, and the third superior to the first and second—so superior as entirely to supersede them, and to afford the only safe guide in political and in many other branches of speculation. I certainly entertain this opinion. When I find a book or a speech appealing to abstract *a priori* principles I put it aside in despair, being well aware that I can learn nothing useful from it. Such works only present to us the limited and qualified propositions which experience has established, without their limitations and qualifications, and elevate them into principles by a rash generalization which strips them of whatever truth they originally possessed. Thus the words *right* and *equality* have a perfectly clear and defined meaning when applied to the administration of justice under a settled law, but are really without meaning, except as vague and inappropriate metaphors, when applied to the distribution of political power. The proper answer to a statement, for instance, that all men free from crime or pauperism have a right to the franchise, is—that this is a question of experience, not of *a priori* assumption, and that the assertion, whether true or false, is inadmissible in political discussion. But how is this truth to be made evident to a large multitude when we find men from whom better things might have been expected, speaking of those who deny the existence of rights as if they sought to deprive men of something they really possess, instead of to explode a vague and meaningless assumption? The position may be further illustrated by observing, that if the propositions of this nature which we hear were true, they would not lead, as they do, to false conclusions, such as—that men, women, and children, should have the franchise; that this right applies to every race in the world; that this right being prior to and independent of experience cannot be limited by experience,

and that it is therefore the duty of a state to do what may be foreseen to lead to immediate ruin in order to satisfy these abstract principles which it has imposed on itself as its guides. The first step, therefore, in the discussion of democratic changes is to clear the mind of these delusive notions, and to employ the teaching of experience, not to qualify or limit, but absolutely to supersede them.

What, then, is the professed object of reform? It is to improve the structure of the House of Commons. The natural order of investigation is—What are the faults which require correction, and then how will the proposed measures cure those faults? Passion or party spirit may drive men to plunge into the details of a Reform Bill without clearly putting to themselves and answering these questions, but no really conscientious investigator can pass them by unconsidered.

... It is not for the evils that exist, but for the evils which it is in its power to prevent, that Parliament should be held responsible. Everybody admits this when he judges another in private life, but when we are dealing with public bodies, we cast candor aside, and censure them for things over which they have no control, or which they have done very wisely to let alone. The theory of uneducated or half-educated persons in general is, that government is almost omnipotent, and that when an evil is not remedied the fault lies in the indolence, the selfishness, or the shortsightedness of Parliament. It is much pleasanter to an audience of non-electors to be told that the franchise would enable them to remedy the evils of their condition than to be told the real truth, that the evils they endure are remediable by themselves, in their individual rather than in their collective capacity—by their own thrift and self-denial, not by pressing on government to do that for them which they are able, if they will, to do without it. It were ludicrous, if it were not so sad, to hear speeches which urge workingmen to seek for the franchise, that they may compel Parliament to compel them to educate their children, or to practise an involuntary abstinence from intoxicating liquors. When one man is willing to sell his vote and another to buy it, what machinery does Parliament possess to prevent a secret bargain for its purchase? The ballot nowhere secures secrecy, and the elections of America show that in large constituencies bribery is used as well as in small, especially when parties are evenly divided. Till Parliament can give health, strength, providence, and self-control, how can it deal with the evil of pauperism? If the poor were willing to pay a rent sufficient to provide them with decent and healthy dwellings, capital would flow into the business just as it does into the business of building public-houses and gin-shops. With what justice can Parliament be called upon to tax the community at large for that which it is in the power of all who receive fair wages to provide for themselves? These may suffice as specimens of the complaints of neglect of the interests of the poor which are brought against Parliament. Parliament does not command boundless resources. A course of the kind indicated would be felt very sensibly in heavier taxation, and a violation of sound principles would avenge itself on the very classes for whose supposed interest they were violated.

The attempts to enlarge the sphere of government action, which the impatience of benevolent persons urges upon us, can only be made at a heavy sacrifice of individual liberty. It is said Parliament should remedy the unequal distribution of land. This can only be done by curtailing individual liberty of disposition. That it should give compensation for improvements to tenants, this can only be done by invading the freedom of contract. Is it not at least conceivable that a legislature which declines to enter on this retrograde course may be in the right, and actuated by better motives than prejudice in favor of one class or antipathy to another?

For my own part, I disclaim such motives. The end of good government appears to me to be the good of all, and, if that be not attainable, the good of the majority; but I must pause when I am told that the majority, told by the head, should have the supreme power because they will be sure to do that which is for their own interest. If this be so, the solution of all questions is easy indeed. Let us burn our books, and send round the ballot-box on every question as it arises? No position can be more unsound. If the queen's council, as the men of Kent complained, be no good craftsmen, neither are good craftsmen necessarily wise councillors. I cannot blow a glass bottle because it would be my interest to do so, nor discern political truth merely because I shall suffer if I am wrong. *Cuique in suâ arte credendum.*[3] The popular view of the obstacles which prevent the accomplishment of our wishes for the happiness of our fellow-creatures is, that there is a want of good-will in those who have the power to make laws, while the view which is forced on every thoughtful man who has practical experience of human affairs, is, that the real obstacle is most frequently the difficulty of knowing how the end is to be gained. The more complicated and artificial society becomes, and the better we know the principles which underlie all sound legislation, the more difficult do we find it to do things which to our ancestors, three hundred years ago, presented no difficulty at all. Protection, for instance, is the political economy of the poor, simply because they are not able to follow the chain of reasoning which demonstrates that they themselves are sure to be the victims of the waste of capital which protection implies. I dare say that a democratic House of Commons would deal with many of these questions, especially those relating to protection, to the distribution of wealth, and the giving direct assistance to the poor from the public purse; but that does not prove that they would, by doing so, benefit the poor, or that the interest of the poor would be promoted by placing in their hands a more extended power of injuring themselves. From these considerations, it follows that, of those things

---

[3]*Cuique in suâ arte credendum:* Each profession possesses its own specialized knowledge.

which Parliament is blamed for not doing, many are impossible, others inexpedient, while some, such as the regulation of sanitary matters, have actually been attained without our censors being aware of it; that what is wanted is not more power to urge on change, but more intelligence to decide on what that change ought to be, and therefore that the standard of intelligence, in constituencies or members, should on no account be lowered, nor the impulse to inconsiderate action increased.

. . . I would point out that the working classes, under the modest claim to share in electoral power, are really asking for the whole of it. Their claim is to pass from the position of non-electors to the position of sovereign arbiters in the last resort of the destinies of the nation. They who set up such a claim must show that they are masters of themselves before they can hope to be masters of others. One of the first qualifications for power should be the willingness to hear both sides—those who say what is unpleasing, as well as those who say what is smooth. They must not seek to limit the field of discussion by their own susceptibilities. They must expect to be critically surveyed and canvassed before they can persuade the present depositories of power to abdicate in their favor. If it is competent to me to argue that with a little self-denial the franchise is already within the reach of many of them; that they will swamp the less numerous classes; that the expenses of elections will be increased, and the character of the House of Commons impaired; it is also competent for me to urge that since corruption and the other electoral vices prevail most in the lower ranks of the present constituencies, it is unwise and unsafe to go lower in search of electoral virtue. It is no answer to such an argument to abuse its author. Either the statement is false, in which case it can be refuted, and will only recoil upon him who made it, or it is true, in which case it is worthy of the most serious consideration, not only by the upper classes, but by the very class which is instructed to resent it, because that class more than any other will suffer if Parliament should, through any ill-considered change, becomes less fit for the discharge of its duties.

Sir Henry Maine **Popular Government (1885)**

One of late Victorian Britain's leading jurists and legal historians assesses the prospects of democracy in Britain and the world.

The democratic principle has gone forth conquering and to conquer, and its gainsayers are few and feeble. Some Catholics, from whose minds the diplomacy of the present pope has not banished the Syllabus[4] of the last, a fairly large body of French and Spanish legitimists,[5] and a few aged courtiers in the small circles surrounding exiled German and Italian princes, may still believe that the cloud of democratic ascendency will pass away. Their hopes may be as vain as their regrets; but nevertheless those who recollect the surprises which the future had in store for men equally confident in the perpetuity of the present, will ask themselves whether it is really true that the expectation of virtual permanence for governments of the modern type rests upon solid grounds of historical experience as regards the past, and of rational probabil-

SOURCE: From Sir Henry Sumner Maine, *Popular Government* (London, 1885), pp. 5–8, 13–16, 42, 44–45, 49–56.

[4]*Syllabus:* the Syllabus of Errors (1864), which denounced the doctrine that "the Roman Pontiff can, and ought to, reconcile himself to, and agree with, progress, liberalism, and modern civilization"   [5]*legitimists:* supporters of a restoration of the Bourbon monarchy

ity as regards the time to come. I endeavor in these pages to examine the question in a spirit different from that which animates most of those who view the advent of democracy either with enthusiasm or with despair.

Out of the many names commonly applied to the political system prevailing or tending to prevail in all the civilized portions of the world, I have chosen "popular government" as the name which, on the whole, is least open to objection. But what we are witnessing in west European politics is not so much the establishment of a definite system, as the continuance, at varying rates, of a process. . . .

The states of Europe are now regulated by political institutions answering to the various stages of the transition from the old view, that "rulers are presumably wise and good, the rightful rulers and guides of the whole population," to the newer view, that "the ruler is the agent and servant, and the subject the wise and good master, who is obliged to delegate his power to the so-called ruler because, being a multitude, he cannot use it himself." Russia and Turkey are the only European states which completely reject the theory that governments hold their powers by delegation from the community, the word "community" being somewhat vaguely understood, but tending more and more to mean at least the whole of the males of full age living within certain territorial limits. . . .

The principle of modern popular government was . . . affirmed less than two centuries ago, and the practical application of that principle outside these islands and their dependencies is not quite a century old. What has been the political history of the commonwealths in which this principle has been carried out in various degrees? The inquiry is obviously one of much importance and interest; . . . I undertake it solely with the view of ascertaining, within reasonable limits of space, how far actual experience countenances the common assumption of our day, that popular government is likely to be of indefinitely long duration. I will first take France, which began

with the imitation of the English, and has ended with the adoption of the American model. Since the introduction of political freedom into France, the existing government, nominally clothed with all the powers of the state, has been three times overturned by the mob of Paris, in 1792, in 1830, and in 1848. It has been three times overthrown by the army. . . . The French government has also been three times destroyed by foreign invasion, in 1814, 1815, and 1870; the invasion having been in each case provoked by French aggression, sympathized in by the bulk of the French people. In all, putting aside the anomalous period from 1870 to 1885, France, since she began her political experiments, has had forty-four years of liberty and thirty-seven years of stern dictatorship. But it has to be remembered, and it is one of the curiosities of this period of history, that the elder Bourbons, who in practice gave very wide room to political freedom, did not expressly admit the modern theory of popular government; while the Bonapartes, who proclaimed the theory without qualification, maintained in practice a rigid despotism.

There are some places in South America where the people date events, not from the great earthquakes, but from the years in which, by a rare intermission, there is no earthquake at all. On the same principle we may note that during the nine years following 1845, and the nine years following 1857, there was comparative, though not complete, freedom from military insurrection in Spain. As to the residue of her political history, my calculation is that between the first establishment of popular government in 1812 and the accession of the present king, there have been forty military risings of a serious nature, in most of which the mob took part. Nine of them were perfectly successful, either overthrowing the Constitution for the time being, or reversing the principles on which it was administered. . . .

The real beginning of popular or parliamentary government in Germany and the Austrian dominions, other than Hungary, cannot be placed earlier than 1848. . . .

Taking Europe as a whole, the most durably successful experiments in popular government have been made either in small states, too weak for foreign war, such as Holland and Belgium, or in countries, like the Scandinavian states, where there was an old tradition of political freedom.

If we look outside Europe and beyond the circle of British dependencies, the phenomena are much the same. The civil war of 1861–1865, in the United States, was as much a war of revolution as the war of 1775–1782.... It would be absurd, however, to deny the relative stability of the government of the United States, which is a political fact of the first importance; but the inferences which might be drawn from it are much weakened, if not destroyed, by the remarkable spectacle furnished by the numerous republics set up from the Mexican border-line to the Straits of Magellan. It would take many of these pages even to summarize the whole political history of the Spanish-American communities. There have been entire periods of years during which some of them have been disputed between the multitude and the military, and again when tyrants, as brutal as Caligula or Commodus, reigned over them like a Roman emperor in the name of the Roman people. It may be enough to say of one of them, Bolivia, ... that out of fourteen presidents of the Bolivian republic thirteen have died assassinated or in exile....

I have now given shortly the actual history of popular government since it was introduced, in its modern shape, into the civilized world. I state the facts, as matter neither for congratulation nor for lamentation, but simply as materials for opinion. It is manifest that so far as they go, they do little to support the assumption that popular government has an indefinitely long future before it. Experience rather tends to show that it is characterized by great fragility, and that, since its appearance, all forms of government have become more insecure than they were before.... The convinced partisans of democracy care little for instances which show democratic governments to be unstable. These are merely isolated triumphs of the principle of evil. But the conclusion of the sober student of history will not be of this kind. He will rather note it as a fact, to be considered in the most serious spirit, that since the century during which the Roman emperors were at the mercy of the Praetorian soldiery, there has been no such insecurity of government as the world has seen since rulers became delegates of the community.

Is it possible to assign any reasons for this singular modern loss of political equilibrium? I think that it is possible to a certain extent. It may be observed that two separate national sentiments have been acting on western Europe since the beginning of the present century. To call them by names given to them by those who dislike them, one is imperialism and the other is radicalism.... But for the first of these coveted objects, imperial rank, great armies and fleets are indispensable, and it becomes ever more a necessity that the men under arms should be nearly coextensive with the whole of the males in the flower of life. It has yet to be seen how far great armies are consistent with popular government resting on a wide suffrage. No two organizations can be more opposed to one another than an army scientifically disciplined and equipped, and a nation democratically governed. The great military virtue is obedience; the great military sin is slackness in obeying. It is forbidden to decline to carry out orders, even with the clearest conviction of their inexpediency. But the chief democratic right is the right to censure superiors; public opinion, which means censure as well as praise, is the motive force of democratic societies. The maxims of the two systems flatly contradict one another, and the man who would loyally obey both finds his moral constitution cut into two halves. It has been found by recent experience that the more popular the civil institutions, the harder it is to keep the army from meddling with politics....

Popular governments have been repeatedly overturned by the army and the mob in combination; but on the whole the violent destruction of these governments in their more extreme forms has been effected by the army, while in their more moderate shapes they have had the mob for their principal assailant. . . . At present, whenever in Europe there is a disturbance like those created by the old mobs, it is in the interest of the parties which style themselves irreconcileable, and which refuse to submit their opinions to the arbitration of any governments, however wide be the popular suffrage on which they are based. . . . Still more recently, however, the mob has obtained new arms. . . . The bomb of nitroglycerine and the parcel of dynamite are as characteristic of the new enemies of government as their irreconcileable opinions.

There can be no more formidable symptom of our time, and none more menacing to popular government, than the growth of irreconcileable bodies within the mass of the population. Church and state are alike convulsed by them; but, in civil life, irreconcileables are associations of men who hold political opinions as men once held religious opinions. . . . They are doubtless a product of democratic sentiment; they have borrowed from it its promise of a new and good time at hand, but they insist on the immediate redemption of the pledge, and they utterly refuse to wait until a popular majority gives effect to their opinions. . . .

Of all modern irreconcileables, the nationalists appear to be the most impracticable and of all governments, popular governments seem least likely to cope with them successfully. Nobody can say exactly what nationalism is, and indeed the dangerousness of the theory arises from its vagueness. It seems full of the seeds of future civil convulsion. As it is sometimes put, it appears to assume that men of one particular race suffer injustice if they are placed under the same political institutions with men of another race. But race is quite as ambiguous a term as nationality. . . . The Irish are an extremely mixed race, and it is only by a perversion of language that the Italians can be called a race at all. The fact is that any portion of a political society, which has had a somewhat different history from the rest of the parts, can take advantage of the theory and claim independence, and can thus threaten the entire society with dismemberment. Where royal authority survives in any vigor, it can to a certain extent deal with these demands. Almost all the civilized states, derived their national unity from common subjection, past or present, to royal power; the Americans of the United States, for example, are a nation because they once obeyed a king. Hence too it is that such a miscellany of races as those which make up the Austro-Hungarian monarchy can be held together, at all events temporarily, by the authority of the emperor-king. But democracies are quite paralyzed by the plea of nationality. . . .

The difficulties of popular government, which arise from the modern military spirit and from the modern growth of irreconcileable parties, could not perhaps have been determined without actual experience. But there are other difficulties which might have been divined, because they proceed from the inherent nature of democracy. . . .

Political liberty, said Hobbes, is political power. When a man burns to be free, he is not longing for the "desolate freedom of the wild ass"; what he wants is a share of political government. But, in wide democracies, political power is minced into morsels and each man's portion of it is almost infinitesimally small. . . .

There is no doubt that, in popular governments resting on a wide suffrage, either without an army or having little reason to fear it, the leader, whether or not he be cunning, or eloquent, or well provided with commonplaces, will be the Wire-puller. The process of cutting up political power into petty fragments has in him its most remarkable product. The morsels of power are so small that men, if left to themselves, would not care to employ them. In England, they would be largely sold, if the law permitted it; in the United States, they are extensively sold in spite of the law. . . . The Wire-puller is not intelligible unless we take into account one of the strongest forces acting on human nature—party feeling. Party feeling is probably far more a survival of the primitive combativeness of mankind than a consequence of conscious intellectual differences between man and man. It is essentially the same sentiment which in certain states of society leads to civil, intertribal, or international war; and it is as universal as humanity. It is better studied in its more irrational manifestations than in those to which we are accustomed. . . .

Once a year, large numbers of English ladies and gentlemen, who have no serious reason for preferring one university to the other, wear dark or light blue colors to signify good wishes for the success of Oxford or Cambridge in a cricket-match or boat-race. Party differences, properly so called, are supposed to indicate intellectual, or moral, or historical preferences; but these go a very little way down into the population, and by the bulk of partisans they are hardly understood and soon forgotten. . . . Some men are Tories or Whigs by conviction; but thousands upon thousands of electors vote simply for yellow, blue, or purple, caught at most by the appeals of some popular orator.

It is through this great natural tendency to take sides that the Wire-puller works. Without it he would be powerless. His business is to fan its flame; to keep it constantly acting upon the man who has once declared himself a partisan; to make escape from it difficult and distasteful. His art is that of the Nonconformist preacher, who gave importance to a body of commonplace religionists by persuading them to wear a uniform and take a military title.[6] . . . Lastly, the wire-pulling system, when fully developed, will infallibly lead to the constant enlargement of the area of suffrage. What is called universal suffrage has greatly declined in the estimation not only of philosophers who follow Bentham, but of the *a priori* theorists who assumed that it was the inseparable accompaniment of a republic, but who found that in practice it was the natural basis of a tyranny. But extensions of the suffrage, though no longer believed to be good in themselves, have now a perma-

nent place in the armory of parties, and are sure to be a favorite weapon of the Wire-puller. The Athenian statesmen who, worsted in a quarrel of aristocratic cliques, "took the people into partnership," have a close parallel in the modern politicians who introduce household suffrage into towns to "dish" one side, and into countries to "dish" the other.

Let us now suppose the competition of parties, stimulated to the utmost by the modern contrivances of the Wire-puller, to have produced an electoral system in which every adult male has a vote, and perhaps every adult female. . . . One of the strangest of vulgar ideas is that a very wide suffrage could or would promote progress, new ideas, new discoveries and inventions, new arts of life. Such a suffrage is commonly associated with radicalism; and no doubt amid its most certain effects would be the extensive destruction of existing institutions; but the chances are that, in the long-run, it would produce a mischievous form of conservatism. . . . A moment's reflection will satisfy any competently instructed person that this is not too broad a proposition. Let him turn over in his mind the great epochs of scientific invention and social change during the last two centuries, and consider what would have occurred if universal suffrage had been established at any one of them. Universal suffrage, which today excludes free trade from the United States, would certainly have prohibited the spinning-jenny and the power-loom. It would certainly have forbidden the threshing-machine. It would have prevented the adoption of the Gregorian calendar; and it would have restored the Stuarts. It would have proscribed the Roman Catholics with the mob which burned Lord Mansfield's house and library in 1780, and it would have proscribed the dissenters with the mob which burned Dr. Priestley's house and library in 1791.

There are possibly many persons who, without denying these conclusions in the past, tacitly assume that no such mistakes

---

[6]*military title*: refers to the Salvation Army

will be committed in the future, because the community is already too enlightened for them, and will become more enlightened through popular education. But without questioning the advantages of popular education under certain aspects, its manifest tendency is to diffuse popular commonplaces, to fasten them on the mind at the time when it is most easily impressed, and thus to stereotype average opinion. . . . The progress of mankind has hitherto been effected by the rise and fall of aristocracies, by the formation of one aristocracy within another, or by the succession of one aristocracy to another. . . .

What is to be the nature of the legislation by which the lot of the artisan and of the agricultural laborer is to be not merely altered for the better, but exchanged for whatever station and fortune they may think it possible to confer on themselves by their own supreme authority? . . .

It is perfectly possible, I think . . . to revive even in our day the fiscal tyranny which once left even European populations in doubt whether it was worth while preserving life by thrift and toil. You have only to tempt a portion of the population into temporary idleness by promising them a share in a fictitious hoard lying (as [John Stuart] Mill puts it) in an imaginary strongbox which is supposed to contain all human wealth. You have only to take the heart out of those who would willingly labor and save, by taxing them *ad misericordiam* for the most laudable philanthropic objects. For it makes not the smallest difference to the motives of the thrifty and industrious part of mankind whether their fiscal oppressor be an Eastern despot, or a feudal baron, or a democratic legislature, and whether they are taxed for the benefit of a corporation called Society, or for the advantage of an individual styled King or Lord. Here then is the great question about democratic legislation, when carried to more than a moderate length. How will it affect human motives? What motives will it substitute for those now acting on men? The

motives, which at present impel mankind to the labor and pain which produce the resuscitation of wealth in ever-increasing quantities, are such as infallibly to entail inequality in the distribution of wealth. They are the springs of action called into activity by the strenuous and never-ending struggle for existence, the beneficent private war which makes one man strive to climb on the shoulders of another and remain there through the law of the survival of the fittest.

These truths are best exemplified in the part of the world to which the superficial thinker would perhaps look for the triumph of the opposite principle. The United States have justly been called the home of the disinherited of the earth. . . . The government of the United States . . . now rests on universal suffrage, but then it is only a political government. It is a government under which coercive restraint, except in politics, is reduced to a minimum. There has hardly ever before been a community in which the weak have been pushed so pitilessly to the wall, in which those who have succeeded have so uniformly been the strong, and in which in so short a time there has arisen so great an inequality of private fortune and domestic luxury. And at the same time, there has never been a country in which, on the whole, the persons distanced in the race have suffered so little from their ill-success. . . . It all reposes on the sacredness of contract and the stability of private property, the first the implement, and the last the reward, of success in the universal competition. These, however, are all principles and institutions which the British friends of the "artisan" and "agricultural laborer" seem not a little inclined to treat as their ancestors did agricultural and industrial machinery. The Americans are still of opinion that more is to be got for human happiness by private energy than by public legislation. The Irish, however, even in the United States, are of another opinion, and the Irish opinion is manifestly rising into favor here.[7] But on the question, whether

---

[7]*Irish opinion . . . here:* refers to the Irish Land Acts of 1870 and 1881, by which the traditional property rights of Irish landlords were significantly curtailed

future democratic legislation will follow the new opinion, the prospects of popular government to a great extent depend. . . .

I have thus shown that popular governments of the modern type have not hitherto proved stable as compared with other forms of political rule, and that they include certain sources of weakness which do not promise security for them in the near or remote future. . . . It is not too much to say, that the only evidence worth mentioning for the duration of popular government is to be found in the success of the British Constitution during two centuries under special conditions, and in the success of the American Constitution during one century under conditions still more peculiar and more unlikely to recur. Yet, so far as our own Constitution is concerned, that nice balance of attractions, which caused it to move evenly on its stately path, is perhaps destined to be disturbed. One of the forces governing it may gain dangerously at the expense of the other; and the British political system, with the national greatness and material prosperity attendant on it, may yet be launched into space and find its last affinities in silence and cold.

11

The Proper Solution for Ireland: Conciliation or Separation?

During the nineteenth century the "Irish Question" was an almost continual preoccupation of British governments. It presented itself in a variety of ways. In the 1820s the question had been: Should Roman Catholics be admitted to serve as members of Parliament at Westminster, which had included Irish as well as Scottish and English representatives since the Act of Union of 1800? Once "Catholic Emancipation" (1829) had answered that question in the affirmative, other questions came to fore, questions of local government, of how to deal with the disastrous famine caused by the potato blight during the later 1840s, question of religion, of land law, and—time and again—the question of whether Ireland had been or ever could be completely amalgamated within a single United Kingdom.

But what were the Irish? A "nation"? a "race"? a group with a distinct language or historical tradition or religion? The first two documents provide some late Victorian answers. Isaac Butt (1813–1879), a distinguished Dublin lawyer and the son of a rector in the Church of Ireland (the Irish branch of the Anglican Church), became in the early 1870s the leader of the Home Rule Party, a group of Irish Members of Parliament who designated themselves as neither Liberals nor Conservatives but as independently pledged to achieve once again a separate Parliament for Ireland. Butt's initial proposal, "Irish Affairs for an Irish Parliament" (1874), was opposed by both major parties. On what basis does Butt justify the partial separation of Ireland's government from that of the rest of the British Isles?

Douglas Hyde (1860–1949) was born a generation and a half later than Butt, and he too was the son of a Church of Ireland clergyman, the descendant of sixteenth-century English settlers. How does he define "Irishness" in his speech of 1892, "On the Necessity for De-Anglicizing Ireland"? Is Irishness an actuality or more a potentiality? According to Hyde, have all historical migrants to Ireland become Irish or only some? Unlike the other persons represented in this chapter Douglas Hyde was primarily a poet rather than a politician. Shortly after giving this speech Hyde became the founder of the Gaelic League, an organization dedicated to the revival of Gaelic, the Irish language. Within a decade the Gaelic League had established more than 500 branches; although not overtly

The "Divided Skirt"

GRAND OLD MAN-MILLINER (*persuasively*). "Fits beautifully, Madam! A little alteration here and there—"

MRS. BRITANNIA. "It's very uncomfortable,—and I'm sure it isn't becoming. I shall never get along with it as it is!!"

Cartoon inspired by Gladstone's Home Rule Bill of 1886 (Punch, April 24, 1886).

political, the league necessarily gave implicit support to movements seeking political separation. Hyde himself was to live long enough to become the first president of an independent Irish Republic (1937–1945).

The Home Rule movement that Butt had helped organize became both more militant and more powerful as a consequence of the agricultural depression that hit Ireland in the later 1870s and the early 1880s. By 1886, the Home Rule Party led by Butt's successor Charles Stewart Parnell (1846–1891) numbered eighty-six members and held the balance of power in the British House of Commons. It was at this time and in this context that William Ewart Gladstone (1809–1898) became both a convert to Home Rule and for the third time Liberal prime minister. The speech in which Gladstone introduced the 1886 bill to provide Ireland with its own parliament, "The Case for Home Rule," sets forth Gladstone's justification. Gladstone's conversion was to cause one-third of the Liberal Members of Parliament to break away from his leadership. One of the most influential of the disenchanted Liberals was the marquess of Hartington (1833–1908), who had served Gladstone as chief secretary for Ireland, as secretary of state for India, an as secretary of state for war, and who headed the Liberal Party in the House of Commons during Gladstone's temporary retirement in the later 1870s. Despite his title, Hartington spent most of his political career in the House of Commons; not until 1891 was he to succeed his father as the eighth duke of Devonshire and enter the House of Lords. His speech, "The Case Against Home Rule" (1886), summarizes Hartington's objections to Gladstone's proposal. To what extent do Gladstone's and Hartington's analyses of the state of Ireland in the 1880s concur or differ? How do they differ on the relevance or lack of relevance of arguments drawn from Irish history and from the example of Britain's overseas colonies? Do they expect Home Rule to conciliate the Irish or to encourage them to seek complete independence? How does Hartington deal with a fact that Gladstone cites, that five out of six of Ireland's elected representatives were pledged to support Home Rule?

Hartington's prediction that a majority of the representatives of the United Kingdom (as opposed to Ireland alone) would oppose Home Rule proved correct in June 1886, when the House of Commons defeated Gladstone's measure by a vote of 343–313. A new general election and six years of Conservative rule followed. Although Gladstone's second Home Rule Bill (1893), similar to the first except that it allowed for some continuing Irish representation in the imperial Parliament, was approved by the House of Commons, it was defeated by the House of Lords. Only after the Parliament Act of 1911 had curbed the powers of the House of Lords did a Liberal government headed by H. H. Asquith introduce a third Home Rule Bill. Opposition to that bill was centered in the northeastern corner of Ireland, part of the ancient province of Ulster, where Roman Catholics were in the minority and where the Home Rule Party had never found favor. The movement was led by a Protestant lawyer, Edward Carson (1854–1935), who had made a distinguished reputation for himself first in Dublin, the city of his birth, and then in London, where he had served as a member of the Conservative government from 1900 to 1905. "The Case for Ulster" (1912) gives us the flavor of Carson's style. How does Carson justify an action that would seem to constitute rebellion against a legally elected government? Does his purpose appear to be to stop Home Rule for all of Ireland or simply to exempt Ulster from such a plan? John Redmond (1856–1918) was Parnell's successor as leader of the Home Rule Party in the House of Commons during the early twentieth century. Like the vast majority of his followers, he was a Roman Catholic. "The Case Against Ulster" (1913) provides Redmond's answer to Carson and his campaign. How does Redmond meet Carson's implicit claim that the Ulster Protestant minority within Ireland is as deserving of special treatment as is the entire Irish minority within the United Kingdom? What is Redmond's attitude toward the prospect of partition?

The immediate consequence of the outbreak of World War I in August 1914 was to delay an Irish settlement; the war also inspired the Irish "Easter Rebellion" of 1916. When, after six years of intermittent guerrilla warfare, a settlement was reached in 1922, it disappointed the followers of both Carson and Redmond. To Carson's dismay, most of Ireland was granted not merely Home Rule but almost complete independence as the Irish Free State. To the disappointment of Redmond's followers and also of the I.R.A. (the Irish Republican Army), Ireland was to be partitioned. The northern six counties of Ireland would receive a Home Rule Parliament of their own; at the same time they would remain part of the United Kingdom. In the light of the evidence presented in these six documents, what other solution was either likely or possible?

Isaac Butt Irish Affairs for an Irish Parliament (1874)

The leader of the new Irish Home Rule Party speaks to the House of Commons on June 30, 1874, in support of his resolution "that it is expedient and just to restore to the Irish nation the right and power of managing all exclusively Irish affairs in an Irish Parliament. . . ."

I propose no change in the imperial Parliament. . . . The only change would be to take from this assembly some of the duties which it now discharges in reference to Irish business, and to relegate them to another. . . .

The English Parliament . . . would meet to discuss purely English affairs, and when there was any question affecting the empire at large, Irish members might be summoned to attend. I see no difficulty in the matter. The English Parliament could manage English affairs as before the Union; but now the English Parliament undertakes a duty it is unable to perform—namely to manage the internal affairs of Ireland to the satisfaction of the Irish people. I do not seek to interfere with the right of taxing Ireland

for imperial purposes, providing always that Ireland has a voice in imperial matters. I am asking only for a constitutional government, and the benefit of those free institutions which make England great. If I succeed in showing that Ireland has not a constitutional government, then I think I can rely on the justice and generosity of the English Parliament and of the Commons at large to give it to her. What is constitutional government? It consists of adequate representation in Parliament—a control of the administration of affairs by a representative assembly of the people, so as to bring the government of the country into harmony with the feeling, the wants, and the wishes of the people. Does the representation by 103 Irish members in the English

SOURCE: From *Hansard's Parliamentary Debates*, 3rd Series, Vol. CCXX, cols. 700–717.

House of Commons amount to that? Can it be said that this House discharges the great function of constitutional government to Ireland? If it does not, then it follows that Ireland is deprived of that constitutional government which is its inherent right. I know it may be said that this involves the question whether Ireland and England are not so blended into one nation, that the same House may discharge the duties of a representative assembly for both. This, again, is a matter of fact. The House may wish that we were all West Britons, but wishes will not alter facts. . . . An Irishman travelling through England, while admiring the people and their manufacturing prosperity, and wishing they may long enjoy it, will think with bitter regret that his own country is not likewise prosperous. The two countries are not blended together, because in every department in Ireland the distinction was marked. We have a separate government, a separate lord lieutenant, separate courts of law; and exceptional laws are passed for Ireland which would never be tolerated for England. How, then, can one representative assembly act for both? . . . Is there a department of the Irish administration which does not consider it its highest policy to thwart the wishes of the Irish people? ("Oh!") That I say deliberately. Apart from the office of lord chancellor there are five great and important administrative offices in Ireland:—that of the chief secretary, the chief of the Irish constabulary—that Irish army of occupation which is not placed in that country for police—the first commissioner of police in Dublin, the chief of the local government board, and the chief of . . . the board of works. How many of these are Irishmen? Not a single one. And these are offices the owners of which are brought into daily contact with the life of the people. They are all filled at this moment by Englishmen and Scotchmen.

The whole record of the legislation for Ireland since the Union is made up of successive Arms Acts, suspensions of the Habeas Corpus Act, to Party Procession Prevention Acts, and Coercion Acts, each one more severe than its predecessor. And this record is the more gloomy because it is a record of the doings of well-intentioned parliaments. Notwithstanding all that has been done, the curfew bell of the Norman conquerors is rung in many parts of the country, and in others blood money is exacted after the example of the Saxons. . . . I am therefore justified in saying that up to now the government of the country has failed, and in asking that Irish people may have an opportunity of managing their own affairs. I am told that Parliament having passed the Land Act and the Church Act, the Irish people are ungrateful in coming forward and demanding Home Rule also. It is even said that such a course is an act of ingratitude towards the individual minister [Gladstone] who was mainly instrumental in passing these acts. All I can say is that such assertions show the faultiness of the system under which they can be possible. Who ever speaks of the English people being grateful for the passing of a good act? . . . Wrong has driven a large proportion of the Irish people into the madness of insurrection or sympathy with insurrection. It was, indeed, the consciousness of this fact which made me set myself earnestly to work to devise a means of stopping this miserable series of abortive insurrections and revolts by which Ireland has been torn and some of the best and bravest of her sons driven into exile. I believe I have devised a plan which will satisfy the just demands of the people without producing a disintegration of the empire. . . . I believe the Irish people are essentially Conservative. It is only misgovernment that has driven us into revolt. Give us fair play, and there is no people on earth who will be more attached to true Conservative principles than the Irish nation. . . . Give us a full participation in your freedom, and make us sharers in those free institutions which have made England so great and glorious. Give us our share which we have not now in that greatest and best of all free institutions—a free parliament.

Douglas Hyde **On the Necessity for De-Anglicizing Ireland (1892)**

A young Irish poet is less concerned with the setting up of a separate Irish Parliament. than with the restoration and creation of a separate Irish culture.

If we take a bird's-eye view of our island to-day, and compare it with what it used to be, we must be struck by the extraordinary fact that the nation which was once, as every one admits, one of the most classically learned and cultured nations in Europe, is now one of the least so; how one of the most reading and literary peoples has become one of the *least* studious and most *un*literary, and how the present art products of one of the quickest, most sensitive, and most artistic races on earth are now only distinguished for their hideousness.

I shall endeavor to show that this failure of the Irish people in the recent times has been largely brought about by the race diverging during this century from the right path, and ceasing to be Irish without becoming English. I shall attempt to show that with the bulk of the people this change took place quite recently, much more recently than most people imagine, and is, in fact, still going on. I should also like to call attention to the illogical position of men who drop their own language to speak English, of men who translate their euphonious Irish names into English monosyllables, of men who read English books, and know nothing about Gaelic literature, nevertheless protesting as a matter of sentiment that they hate the country which at every hand's turn they rush to imitate.

I wish to show you that in anglicizing ourselves wholesale we have thrown away with a light heart the best claim which we have upon the world's recognition of us as a separate nationality. What did Mazzini say? What is Goldwin Smith never tired of declaiming? What do the *Spectator* and *Saturday Review* harp on? That we ought to be content as an integral part of the United Kingdom because we have lost the notes of nationality, our language and customs.

It has always been very curious to me how Irish sentiment sticks in this half-way house—how it continues to apparently hate the English, and at the same time continues to imitate them; how it continues to clamor for recognition as a distinct nationality, and at the same time throws away with both hands what would make it so. If Irishmen only went a little further they would become good Englishmen in sentiment also. But—illogical as it appears—there seems not the slightest sign or probability of their taking that step. It is the curious certainty that come what may Irishmen will continue to resist English rule, even though it should be for their good, which prevents many of our nation from becoming unionists upon the spot. It is a fact, and we must face it as a fact, that although they adopt English habits and copy England in every way, the great bulk of Irishmen and Irishwomen over the whole world are know to be filled with a dull, ever-abiding animosity against her, and—right or wrong—to grieve when she prospers, and joy when she is hurt. Such movements as Young Irelandism, Fenianism, Land Leagueism, and parliamentary obstruction seems always to gain their sympathy and support. It is just because there appears no earthly chance of their becoming good members of the empire that I urge that they should not remain in the anomalous position they are in, but since they absolutely refuse to become the one thing, that they become the other; cultivate what they have rejected, and build up an Irish nation on Irish lines.

But you ask, why should we wish to make Ireland more Celtic than it is—why should we de-anglicize it all? I answer because the Irish race is at present in a most anomalous position, imitating England and

SOURCE: From *The Revival of Irish Literature and Other Addresses* (London, 1894), pp. 118–129.

yet apparently hating it. How can it produce anything good in literature, art or institutions as long as it is actuated by motives so contradictory? Besides, I believe it is our Gaelic past which, though the Irish race does not recognize it just at present, is really at the bottom of the Irish heart, and prevents us becoming citizens of the empire, as, I think, can be easily proved. . . .

Let us suppose for a moment—which is idea that was Irish, and left us, at last, after ries of Cromwells in England for the space of one hundred years, able administrators of the empire, careful rulers of Ireland, developing to the utmost our national resources, whilst they unremittingly stamped out every spark of national feeling, making Ireland a land of wealth and factories, whilst they extinguished every thought and every idea that was Irish, and left us, at last after a hundred years of good government, fat, wealthy, and populous, but with all our characteristics gone, with every external that at present differentiates us from the English lost or dropped; all our Irish names of places and people turned into English names; the Irish language completely extinct; the O's and Macs dropped; our Irish intonation changed, as far as possible by English schoolmasters into something English; our history no longer remembered or taught; the names of our rebels and martyrs blotted out; our battlefields and traditions forgotten; the fact that we are not of Saxon origin dropped out of sight and memory, and let me now put the question—How many Irishmen are there who would purchase material prosperity at such a price? It is exactly such a question as this and the answer to it that shows the difference between the English and Irish race. Nine Englishmen out of ten would jump to make the exchange, and I as firmly believe that nine Irishmen out of ten would indignantly refuse it.

And yet this awful idea of complete anglicization, which I have put here before you in all its crudity is, and has been, making silent inroads upon us for nearly a century. . . .

What lies at the back of the sentiments of nationality with which the Irish millions seem so strongly leavened, what can prompt them to applause such sentiment as:

They say the British empire owes much
   to Irish hands,
That Irish valor fixed her flag o'er many
   conquered lands;
And ask if Erin takes no pride in these
   her gallant sons,
Her Wolseleys and her Lawrences, her
   Wolfes and Wellingtons.
Ah! these were of the empire—we yield
   them to her fame,
And ne'er in Erin's orisons are heard their
   alien name;
But those for whom her heart beats high
   and benedictions swell,
They died upon the scaffold and they
   pined within the cell.

Of course it is a very composite feeling which prompts them; but I believe that what is largely behind it is the half unconscious feeling that the race which at one time held possession of more than half Europe, which established itself in Greece, and burned infant Rome, is now—almost extirpated and absorbed elsewhere—making its last stand for independence in this island of Ireland; and do what they may the race of to-day cannot wholly divest itself from the mantle of its own past. Through early Irish literature, for instance, we can best form some conception of what that race really was, which, after overthrowing and trampling on the primitive peoples of half Europe, was itself forced in turn to yield its speech, manners, and independence to the victorious eagles of Rome. We alone of the nations of western Europe escaped the claws of those birds of prey; we alone developed ourselves naturally upon our own lines outside of and free from all Roman influence; we alone were thus able to produce an early art and literature, *our* antiquities can best throw light upon the pre-Romanized inhabitants of half Europe, and—we are our father's sons. . . .

What we must endeavor to never forget is this, that the Ireland of to-day is the descendant of the Ireland of the seventh century, then the school of Europe and the torch of learning. It is true that Northmen made some minor settlements in it in the ninth and tenth centuries, it is true that the Normans made extensive settlements during the succeeding centuries, but none of these broke the continuity of the social life of the island. Dane and Norman drawn to the kindly Irish breast issued forth in a generation or two fully Irishized, and more Hibernian than the Hibernians themselves, and even after the Cromwellian plantation the children of numbers of the English soldiers who settled in the south and midlands, were after forty years' residence, and after marrying Irish wives, turned into good Irishmen, and unable to speak a word of English, while several Gaelic poets of the last century have, like Father English, the most unmistakably English names. In two points only was the continuity of the Irishism of Ireland damaged. First, in the northeast of Ulster, where the Gaelic race was expelled and the land planted with aliens, whom our dear mother Erin, assimilative as she is, has hitherto found it difficult to absorb, and in the ownership of the land, eight-ninths of which belongs to people many of whom

have always lived, or live, abroad, and not half of whom Ireland can be said to have assimilated.

During all this time the continuation of Erin's national life centered, according to our way of looking at it, not so much in the Cromwellian or Williamite landholders who sat in College Green, and governed the country, as in the mass of the people. . . . But, alas, *quantum mutatus ab illo!*[1] What the battleaxe of the Dane, the sword of the Norman, the wile of the Saxon were unable to perform, we have accomplished ourselves. We have at last broken the continuity of Irish life, and just at the moment when the Celtic race is presumably about to largely recover possession of its own country, it finds itself deprived and stripped of its Celtic characteristics, cut off from the past, . . . language, traditions, music, genius and ideas. Just when we should be starting to build up anew the Irish race and the Gaelic nation—as within our own recollection Greece has been built up anew—we find ourselves despoiled of the bricks of nationality. The old bricks that lasted eighteen hundred years are destroyed; we must now set to, to bake new ones, if we can, on other ground and of other clay.

WILLIAM EWART GLADSTONE   **The Case for Home Rule (1886)**

The veteran Liberal prime minister shakes the political world with his speech of April 8, 1886, in which he asks the British House of Commons to grant Home Rule to Ireland.

. . . Our intention is, Sir, to propose to the House of Commons that which, as we think, if happily accepted, will liberate Parliament from the restraints under which of late years it has ineffectually struggled to perform the business of the country; will restore legislation to its natural, ancient, unimpeded course; and will, above all, obtain an answer—a clear, we hope, and definite answer—to the question whether it is or is not

possible to establish good and harmonious relations between Great Britain and Ireland on the footing of those free institutions to which Englishmen, Scotchmen, and Irishmen are alike unalterably attached. . . .

And, Sir, the first point to which I would call your attention is this, that whereas exceptional legislation—legislation which introduces exceptional provisions into the law—ought itself to be in its own nature es-

SOURCE: From *Hansard's Parliamentary Debates*, 3rd Series, Vol. CCCIV, cols. 1038-1085.

[1]*quantum mutatus ab illo!*: how great a change since then

sentially and absolutely exceptional, it has become for us not exceptional, but habitual. We are like a man who, knowing that medicine may be the means of his restoration to health, endeavors to live upon medicine. Nations, no more than individuals, can find a subsistence in what was meant to be a cure. But has it been a cure? Have we attained the object which we desire, and honestly desired, to attain? No, Sir, agrarian crime[2] has become, sometimes upon a larger and sometimes upon a smaller scale, as habitual in Ireland as the legislation which has been intended to repress it, and that agrarian crime, although at the present time it is almost at the low watermark, yet has a fatal capacity of expansion under stimulating circumstances, and rises from time to time, as it rose in 1885, to dimensions, and to an exasperation which becomes threatening to general social order, and to the peace of private and domestic life. . . .

But the agrarian crime in Ireland is not so much a cause as it is a symptom. It is a symptom of a yet deeper mischief of which it is only the external manifestation. That manifestation is mainly threefold. In the first place, with certain exceptions for the case of winter juries, it is impossible to depend in Ireland upon the finding of a jury in a case of agrarian crime according to the facts as they are viewed by the government, by the judges, and by the public, I think, at large. . . . It is also, Sir, undoubtedly a mischief that . . . cases of eviction, good, bad, and indifferent as to their justification, stand pretty much in one and the same discredit with the rural population of Ireland, and become, as we know, the occasion of transactions that we all deeply lament. Finally, Sir, it is not to be denied that there is great interference in Ireland with individual liberty in the shape of intimidation. . . .

The consequence of that is to weaken generally the respect for law, and the respect for contract, and that among a people who, I believe, are as capable of attaining to

the very highest moral and social standard as any people on the face of the earth. . . .

Nothing has been more painful to me than to observe that, in this matter, we are not improving, but, on the contrary, we are losing ground. . . . In the fifty-three years since we advanced far in the career of Liberal principles and actions—in those fifty-three years, from 1833 to 1885—there were but two years which were entirely free from the action of this special legislation for Ireland. . . . In point of fact, law is discredited in Ireland, and discredited in Ireland upon this ground especially—that it comes to the people of that country with a foreign aspect, and in a foreign garb. These Coercion Bills of ours, of course—for it has become a matter of course—I am speaking of the facts and not of the merits—these Coercion Bills are stiffly resisted by the members who represent Ireland in parliament. The English mind, by cases of this kind and by the tone of the press toward them, is estranged from the Irish people and the Irish mind is estranged from the people of England and Scotland. . . .

I will not assume, I will not beg, the question, whether the people of England and Scotland will ever administer that sort of effectual coercion which I have placed in contrast with our timid and hesitating repressive measures; but this I will say, that the people of England and Scotland will never resort to that alternative until they have tried every other. Have they tried every other? . . . There is one—not unknown to human experience—on the contrary, widely known to various countries in the world, where this dark and difficult problem has been solved by the comparatively natural and simple, though not always easy, expedient of stripping law of its foreign garb, and investing it with a domestic character. I am not saying that this will succeed; I by no means beg the question at this moment; but this I will say, that Ireland, as far as I know, and speaking of the great majority of the people of Ireland, be-

---

[2]*Agrarian crime:* tenant farmers evicted for failing to pay rents often engaged in the burning of hayricks and the maiming of cattle.

lieves it will succeed, and that experience elsewhere supports that conclusion. The case of Ireland, though she is represented here not less fully than England or Scotland, is not same as that of England or Scotland. . . .

The mainspring of law in England is felt by the people to be English; the mainspring of law in Scotland is felt by the people to be Scotch; but the mainspring of law in Ireland is not felt by the people to be Irish. . . . It is a problem not unknown in the history of the world; it is really this—there can be no secret about it as far as we are concerned—how to reconcile imperial unity with diversity of legislation. Mr. Grattan[3] not only held these purposes to be reconcilable, but he did not scruple to go to the length of saying this—

> I demand the continued severance of the Parliaments with a view to the continued and everlasting unity of the empire.

. . . We ourselves may be said to have solved it, for I do not think that anyone will question the fact that, out of the six last centuries, for five centuries at least Ireland has had a Parliament separate from ours. That is a fact undeniable. Did that separation of Parliament destroy the unity of the British Empire? Did it destroy it in the 18th century? . . . It was, in a preeminent sense, the century of empire, and it was in a sense, but too conspicuous, the century of wars. Those wars were carried on, that empire was maintained and enormously enlarged, that trade was established, that navy was brought to supremacy when England and Ireland had separate Parliaments.

I define the essence of the Union to be this—that before the Act of Union there were two independent, separate, coordinate parliaments; after the Act of Union there was but one. A supreme statutory authority of the imperial Parliament

over Great Britain, Scotland, and Ireland as one United Kingdom was established by the Act of Union. That supreme statutory authority it is not asked, so far as I am aware, and certainly it is not intended, in the slightest degree to impair. . . .

There are those who say—"Let us abolish the Castle;"[4] and I think that gentlemen of very high authority, who are strongly opposed to giving Ireland a domestic legislature, have said nevertheless that they think there ought to be a general reconstruction of the administrative government in Ireland. . . . Without providing a domestic legislature for Ireland, without having an Irish Parliament, I want to know how you will bring about this wonderful, superhuman, and, I believe, in this condition, impossible result, that your administrative system shall be Irish, and not English? . . .

Well, Sir, what we seek is the settlement of that question, and we think that we find that settlement in the establishment, by the authority of Parliament, of a legislative body sitting in Dublin, for the conduct of both legislation and administration under the conditions which may be prescribed by the act defining Irish, as distinct from imperial, affairs. There is the head and front of our offending. . . .

I will deviate from my path for a moment to say a word upon the state of opinion in that wealthy, intelligent, and energetic portion of the Irish community which, as I have said, predominates in a certain portion of Ulster. . . . I cannot conceal the conviction that the voice of Ireland, as a whole, is at this moment clearly and constitutionally spoken. I cannot say it is otherwise when five-sixths of its lawfully chosen representatives are of one mind in this matter. There is a counter voice; and I wish to know what is the claim of those by whom that counter voice is spoken, and how much is the scope and allowance we can give them. Certainly, Sir, I cannot allow it to be said that a Protes-

---

[3]*Henry Grattan (1746–1820):* the most influential member of the Irish Parliament in Dublin that became largely autonomous in 1782 and that maintained a separate existence until the Act of Union of 1800   [4]*The Castle:* Dublin Castle, seat of the British viceroy in Ireland and the symbol of the executive branch of the government

tant minority in Ulster, or elsewhere, is to rule the question at large for Ireland. . . .

The capital article of that legislative body will be that it should have the control of the executive government of Ireland as well as of legislative business. . . .

I will now tell the House—and I would beg particular attention to this—what are the functions that we propose to withdraw from the cognizance of this legislative body. The three grand and principal functions are, first, everything that relates to the crown. . . . The next would be all that belongs to defense—the army, the navy, the entire organization of armed force. . . . And the third would be the entire subject of foreign and colonial relations. . . . We propose to provide that the legislative body should not be competent to pass a law for the establishment or the endowment of any particular religion. Those I may call exceptions of principle. . . .

There is only one subject more on which I feel it still necessary to detain the House. It is commonly said in England and Scotland—and in the main it is, I think, truly said—that we have for a great number of years been struggling to pass good laws for Ireland. We have sacrificed our time; we have neglected our own business; we have advanced our money—which I do not think at all a great favor conferred on her—and all this in the endeavor to give Ireland good laws. . . . Sir, I do not deny the general good intentions of Parliament on a variety of great and conspicuous occasions, and its desire to pass good laws for Ireland. But let me say that, in order to work out the purposes of government, there is something more in this world occasionally required than even the passing of good laws. It is sometimes requisite not only that good laws should be passed, but also that they should be passed by the proper persons. . . .

The principle that I am laying down I am not laying down exceptionally for Ireland. It is the very principle upon which, within my recollection, to the immense advantage of the country, we have not only altered, but revolutionized our method of governing the colonies. I had the honor to hold office

in the colonial department—perhaps I ought to be ashamed to confess it—51 years ago. At that time the colonies were governed from Downing Street. . . . England tried to pass good laws for the colonies at that period; but the colonies said—"We do not want your good laws; we want our own." We admitted the reasonableness of the principle, and it is now coming home to us from across the seas. We have to consider whether it is applicable to the case of Ireland. Do not let us disguise this from ourselves. We stand face to face with what is termed Irish nationality. . . .

These, Sir, are great facts. I hold that there is such a thing as local patriotism, which, in itself, is not bad, but good. The Welshman is full of local patriotism—the Scotchman is full of local patriotism. . . . I believe it is stronger in Ireland even than in Scotland. Englishmen are eminently English; Scotchmen are profoundly Scotch; and, if I read Irish history aright, misfortune and calamity have wedded her sons to her soil. The Irishman is more profoundly Irish; but it does not follow that, because his local patriotism is keen, he is incapable of imperial patriotism. There are two modes of presenting the subject. The one is to present what we now recommend as good, and the other to recommend it as a choice of evils. Well, Sir, I have argued the matter as if it were a choice of evils; . . . But, in my own heart, I cherish the hope that this is not merely the choice of the lesser evil, but may prove to be rather a good in itself. . . .

Looking forward, I ask the House to assist us in the work which we have undertaken and to believe that no trivial motive can have driven us to it—to assist us in this work which, we believe, will restore Parliament to its dignity and legislation to its free and unimpeded course. I ask you to stay the waste of public treasure which is involved in the present system of government and legislation in Ireland, and which is not a waste only, but which demoralizes while it exhausts. . . . I ask that in our own case we should practice with firm and fearless hand, what we have so often preached. . .

namely, that the concession of local self-government is not the way to sap or impair, but the way to strengthen and consolidate unity . . . and it is thus, by the decree of the Almighty, that we may be enabled to secure at once the social peace, the fame, the power, and the permanence of empire.

THE MARQUESS OF HARTINGTON **The Case Against Home Rule (1886)**

A major figure in the Liberal Party since the 1860s, Hartington takes issue with Gladstone's plan for Ireland in a speech delivered to the House of Commons on April 9, 1886.

. . . Well, Sir, it is not possible for any member of this House to say that, if it had been known at the time of the last general election that the first work and task of the present Parliament was going to be the entire resettlement of the relations between Great Britain and Ireland—the creation of a statutory power, with the sole legislative power in Irish affairs, and with complete control over the Irish administration and executive—it would not be possible for any of us to maintain that the result, in numberless elections in this country, might not have been very different from what it was. . . . I must protest at the outset against the competence—the normal competence, for I do not deny the constitutional competence—of this Parliament, in the presence of no adequate emergency, to initiate legislation such as that which is involved in the proposal unfolded to us last night by my right hon. Friend. . . .

It may be that this measure will really be accepted by the Irish Party only as an instalment; and it may be especially under these circumstances, that the people of this country will not be willing that changes so vast and so wide-reaching should be made. But, whatever may be the fate of this measure, its mere introduction by a responsible government, by a minister wielding, and justly wielding, the influence and authority of my right hon. Friend, will have done much that can never be recalled. This measure will be henceforth the minimum of the Irish national demand; it will be the starting-point

and the vantage-ground of whatever proposals they may hereafter think it necessary to bring forward. . . . From this point of view it seems to me that if, as I think is extremely likely, this measure does not command the support—the intelligent and informed support—of the majority of the people of this country, its introduction without, as I think, adequate preparation or consideration will have vastly added in the future to the already great difficulties of the government of Ireland.

And now let me say a word or two upon the historical argument, by which a concession of this kind is sometimes justified. My right hon. Friend referred last night to the history of Grattan's Parliament. . . . Grattan's Parliament was a Protestant Parliament, a Parliament in which the influence of the landlords was entirely paramount; and it is just as probable that a Parliament so composed might have delayed, rather than have forwarded, those reforms in Irish administration, which we all now acknowledge to have been delayed too long. We may grant that the Parliament of the United Kingdom delayed too long Catholic Emancipation; we may grant that it too long maintained Protestant ascendancy in Ireland; we may grant that the land legislation of the imperial Parliament was too long conceived in the interests of the landlord class and in disregard of those of the occupiers and cultivators; but it is beyond the possibility of proof that an Irish Parliament, composed as Grattan's Parliament

SOURCE: From *Hansard's Parliamentary Debates*, 3rd Series, Vol. CCCIV, cols. 1245-1263.

was, would have initiated and carried out the reforms that were needed before the imperial Parliament did so. It is just as likely that the authority of the imperial Parliament might have had to be invoked for the protection of the oppressed majority of the Irish people as that the Grattan Parliament would have carried out those reforms one day sooner than they did take place. It is equally impossible to prove that any government or parliament could have averted any of the evils that have befallen Ireland since that time. We are a great deal too apt to attribute omnipotence to parliaments and to governments. In the presence of physical and economical causes and changes I believe it is much nearer the truth to say that parliaments and governments, whatever they may be, are almost powerless. . . .

I maintain that the restoration of an Irish Parliament, or of anything approaching to an Irish Parliament, will not be the restoration of that which existed before the Union, but will be the creation of a state of things as absolutely and entirely different from that as it is possible to conceive. . . . The Parliament which would be restored now would not be a Protestant, but would be a Roman Catholic Parliament. The established Church has been swept away; and instead of a Roman Catholic priesthood, which at the time of the Union was without political influence at all, we have a Roman Catholic clergy wielding a large political influence. The owners of land in Ireland have been deprived of almost all control over their estates; and with the loss of that control they have lost the political influence which they formerly enjoyed. Now, Sir, it is not a question whether all these changes have been wise and just changes. I believe, in the main, that the changes have been wise and have been just; but they are changes which have been made by the paramount and superior authority of the imperial Parliament. They are not changes which have been made by the efforts or exertions of the people of Ireland themselves. They are changes which have been imposed by the superior and overwhelming authority of the people of the United Kingdom of Great Britain and Ireland. It may have been, and I believe it was, substantially just that those changes should be made in the interests of the great majority of the people of Ireland; but, at the same time, it is not less just that the minority which has been deprived by our action, and not by the action of the people of Ireland, of almost all the rights and privileges and power which they possessed at the time of the Union, should not be handed over without due and adequate protection at the hands of that power by whose influence those vast and far-reaching changes have been effected, and by whose influence the whole balance of the political situation in Ireland has been changed since the time of the Union. . . .

Now, Sir, my right hon. Friend, having resolved to make some concession to the demands of the Irish Parliament, as expressed by their representatives, had no lack of choice between plans and policies which he might adopt. It was open to him to adopt a plan in the direction of what has, up to now, been generally understood as the extension of local government in Ireland. It was open to him to adopt something in the nature of the plan which has been referred to to-night by my right hon. Friend the member for Birmingham (Mr. Chamberlain) as a plan of national councils. . . . When the time comes, let Ireland share in whatever is granted to England, Scotland, or to Wales; but when it comes it will be, in my opinion, the outgrowth of institutions which have not yet been created. The superstructure will be raised on foundations which have not yet been laid; and it would be, in my opinion, unwise and impolite in reference to either England or to any of the Three Kingdoms to attempt to begin at the top instead of allowing the natural result of a growth of reform in local government which the Three Kingdoms equally desire, and which is naturally developed. But, Sir, I conceived that in the progress of the examination which my right hon. Friend has undertaken he has discovered that the demand which the Irish people make is not a demand for the reform or the extension of local self-government—as that term is here understood—at all. What that demand really is, is a demand for practical separation from this country, for natural independence, for the power to make their own laws and to shape their own institutions, without any reference whatever to the opinion that may be held here in respect to the wisdom, the justice, the equity of those laws, or to the fitness or the wisdom of those institutions. . . .

My right hon. Friend referred yesterday to the case of [the] colonies. He attached great importance to the 60 miles of sea which divide Great Britain from Ireland. He did not refer to the 3,000 miles which separate England from her nearest self-governing colony, or the still greater number of thousands of miles which separate her from the most distant of those colonies. The distance which separates our colonies from us makes any analogy which may be drawn between their case and that of Ireland utterly fallacious. Beyond this, it is perfectly well known that the connection which exists between our self-governing colonies and the United Kingdom is purely a voluntary connection. We have granted to these colonies practical independence. If they are willing still to be bound to, and to form part of, the British Empire; if they are willing to have their foreign policy regulated by the imperial government; if they are willing to submit to the nominal superiority of British law and British authority over their internal affairs, it is by virtue of a voluntary compact by which they accept our direction of their foreign relations that they gain the imperial protection of our fleets and armies. But everyone knows that the real interference or authority exercised by the imperial government in the domestic affairs of the colonies is practically nothing. . . .

My right hon. Friend would never dream of saying that it was the first duty of every representative of the people to maintain under all or any circumstances the unity of this country with Canada or with the colony of Victoria[5]; and, therefore, it must be considered, when he himself agreed that we cannot permit absolute separation between England and Ireland, that he must have had some other unity in his mind than the unity which binds these colonial dependencies to this country, and which it is our first duty to maintain. . . .

I have said that I do not want to go into any details in this matter; but there is, I admit, one consideration which is not one of detail which seems to be absolutely fatal to the existence of this legislature. If this is a plan which is good for Ireland, I conceive that it ought to be good and must be good for England, Scotland, and Wales. If Scotland or Wales demand that this plan should be extended to them, I do not see how that demand can possibly be refused. Supposing they make the demand, what would be the resulting state of things? We should have in Ireland, Scotland, and Wales domestic legislatures, having full control over their own affairs. So far, very well. We should have in England a domestic legislature also, with full control over English affairs; but we should, in addition to this, find this House, from which every Irish, Scotch, and Welsh member was excluded, having full control, not only over the domestic legislation of England, but over the imperial legislation of the whole of the empire. All the foreign policy of this empire, all the colonial policy, all the Indian policy of this empire would in future be controlled by representatives of English constituencies alone. . . . It would be unfair, financially, to the Irish, Scotch, and Welsh people that they should contribute to the expense of an imperial policy—in the case of Ireland it would be a fixed contribution—when they would have no voice whatever in controlling it. . . .

Well, Sir, what will remain of the unity

---

[5]*Victoria:* one of the self-governing states that in 1900 became part of the federated Dominion of Australia

of the empire when this bill shall have passed? We shall be under one sovereign; but the question is, shall we be under one sovereign power? The sovereign power, as I have already ventured to remind the House, is the power of the imperial Parliament. Will the power of the imperial Parliament remain sovereign in Ireland? . . . It may be said that the military forces of the crown will remain under the entire control of the imperial government and the imperial Parliament. But if that is all we are to rely upon, it appears to me to be nothing less than to call in civil war as the sanction— the ordinary sanction—of the proceedings of the government. It is impossible to administer the affairs of the country by means of an army. . . .

I maintain that, as far as I can understand, there is no legal or constitutional means by which the imperial Parliament will be able henceforth to exert authority in Ireland contrary to the will of the Irish Parliament. Well, it may be said that it is to be hoped occasions of difference may not arise. I do not cherish this hope. We have had the experience of the last few years. . . . The people of Great Britain—England and Scotland—have relatives, and connections, and friends in Ireland, and great interests in Ireland, and the people of Great Britain will not be indifferent to what passes in Ireland; and if—I will not say injustice or oppression occur—but if they think that oppression or injustice is taking place, the minority in Ireland will appeal to the people of England and Scotland, and will not appeal in vain. The occasions of collision will be too likely, in fact will be certain, to occur; and I firmly believe that this measure, which is brought forward by my right hon. Friend in the interests of peace, will be of all measures the measure which is most likely to furnish occasions of even more serious differences than have ever arisen in Ireland in the past. . . .

I cannot help thinking that my right hon. Friend, for the purpose of his argument, has somewhat overstated the difficulties and the inefficiency and the impossibility of

continuing to govern Ireland by the mingled system of remedial and repressive legislation. . . . Sir, I think it is necessary that we should clear our ideas a little on this subject of coercion. We have accepted far too readily the term "coercion" which has been applied to it by its opponents, and which has been generally interpreted as a sort of synonym for tyranny. What, Sir, is the reason? Why is it that powers in excess of those of the ordinary law have had very generally to be conferred upon the executive government in Ireland? It is because the ordinary law has not received that ready and willing assent from the people of Ireland that it receives in the remaining parts of the kingdom. But the law in support of which these extraordinary powers have been evoked is the same law, the same system of law, administered on the same principle which prevails over the whole of the United Kingdom. If that law is an unjust law, it is in our power, without the creation of a domestic legislature in Ireland, to alter it. If it is a just law it is our duty to maintain it. . . .

There are other causes to be found for the failure of our system of government in Ireland, and among them has been the fact that Irish questions and the government of Ireland have too long and too habitually been made the battle-ground of political parties. . . . I believe, at all events, that now, if ever—now that the people of this country have been brought face to face with the alternative of the disruption of the empire on the one hand, or all the evils and calamities which I admit will follow on the rejection of this unfortunate scheme, I believe that now, at all events, the people of this country will require that their representatives shall, in relation to Irish affairs, agree to sink all minor differences, and to unite as one man for the maintenance of this great empire, to hand it down to our successors compact and complete, as we have inherited it from our forefathers, and at the same time to maintain throughout its length and breadth the undisputed supremacy of the law.

Sir Edward Carson **The Case for Ulster (1912)**

The leader of the opposition to the third Home Rule Bill speaks in Belfast on the day before the following "Solemn League and Covenant" was to be signed by 471,000 persons.

"Being convinced in our consciences that Home Rule would be disastrous to the material well-being of Ulster as well as of the whole of Ireland, subversive of our civil and religious freedom, destructive of our citizenship, and perilous to the unity of the empire, we, whose names are underwritten, men of Ulster, loyal subjects of His Gracious Majesty King George V, humbly relying on the God whom our fathers in days of stress and trial confidently trusted, do hereby pledge ourselves in solemn covenant throughout this our time of threatened calamity to stand by one another in defending for ourselves and our children our cherished position of equal citizenship in the United Kingdom, and in using all means which may be found necessary to defeat the present conspiracy to set up a Home Rule Parliament in Ireland. And in the event of such a Parliament being forced upon us we further solemnly and mutually pledge ourselves to refuse to recognize its authority. In sure confidence that God will defend the right we hereto subscribe our names. And further, we individually declare that we have not already signed this covenant. God save the King."

This night is the eve of Ulster Day, which, I hope and expect, will be a solemn landmark in the history, not merely of Ireland, but in the history of the United Kingdom. . . . The truth of the matter is that we have been challenged by the government. We were challenged by the government when they told us we had no way out of the Irish difficulty but to bend the knee to John Redmond. *(Hisses)* I said in the Albert Hall, and without having the time to consult with the people of Ulster, "I willingly accept the challenge." I said then, "We will take deliberately a step forward, not in defiance, but in defence." *(Loud cheers)* And the covenant which we shall most willingly sign to-morrow will be a great step forward, in no spirit of aggression, in no spirit of ascendancy, but with a full knowledge that if necessary you and I—you trusting me and I trusting you—will follow out everything that covenant means to the very end, whatever the consequences. *(Loud cheers)*

Let the government remember—and I say it in all seriousness—that in the future, after we have signed the covenant, they will have on their own responsibility not only to ask us to accept Home Rule but to break one of the most sacred and solemn pledges that had ever been entered into by any men. We shall take no unnecessary steps, but we shall shrink from no necessary steps. *(Cheers)* . . . Never under any circumstances will we accept a Home Rule Parliament in Ireland. *(Cheers).* . . .

When they tell us the Union has failed, I say, "Look at Belfast." When they tell me that Irish industries cannot flourish under the Union, I say "Look at Belfast." When they say that these flourish only in Belfast under a number of bigots, I say, "Do communities flourish under bigotry or free institutions?" Let me give you a few startling figures about Belfast. At the time of the Union the down-trodden city *(laughter)* numbered something like 20,000 inhabitants. Now it has nearly 400,000 inhabitants. . . . The valuation of Belfast has more than doubled even since the last Home Rule Bill. *(Cheers)* In 1892 . . . the customs and inland revenue returns at Belfast amounted to £3,250,000; last year the figure was £4,915,000—not a bad contribution to the imperial exchequer. *(Cheers)* . . . Is it any wonder that Mr. Redmond says he will not take Home Rule if they keep Ulster out of

SOURCE: From *The Times* (London), September 28, 1912, p. 10. Parts of the speech have been changed from the third person to the first person.

it? *(Laughter and cheers)* Our policy is not merely a negative policy. It does not merely mean that we want to trample under foot this wretched project of a log-rolling party of tricksters. No! It means far more—it means the continuation of the policy of development which can alone be carried on under an imperial Parliament. It means the completion of land purchase and the removal of many difficulties that will enable Ireland to take her share in all measures for uplifting our people.

Home Rule from a nationalist point of view is only the beginning and not the end of a great controversy. You remember the suppressed paragraph in the resolution of the Ancient Order of Hibernians at their convention in America in which they stated that nothing else than absolute independence could ever be considered by the Irish race at home and abroad as a final settlement for the Irish question. . . . The government has thrown down the challenge. It is the challenge of the Constitution wreckers to the upholders of the Constitution; it is the challenge of the champions of ascendancy to the champions of equality; of the preachers of separation to the congregation of unity; of retrogression to progress; of men who want to put back the hands of the clock instead of forward. This is the struggle upon which we enter without any qualms and, may I say, without any fears. *(Cheers)* A great man in the American War of Independence said, and I give it to you as a motto this night, "Blandishments will not fascinate us, nor will threats intimidate us, for under God we are determined that wheresoever, whosoever, and howsoever we shall be called upon to make our exit, we shall die as free men." *(Cheers)* My last word to you before you sign the covenant is "Be ready." *(Loud cheers)*

JOHN REDMOND **The Case Against Ulster (1913)**

In a speech given in Limerick on October 12, 1913, the leader of the Irish Home Rule Party in the British Parliament reasserts his opposition to the exclusion of Ulster from the prospective Irish Parliament in Dublin.

Let me ask what is the meaning of this unparalleled demonstration, the like of which has not been witnessed in Limerick or in Munster in this generation? The first object of this gathering is to give the lie to those men who have been declaring that Ireland has grown apathetic in the struggle for Home Rule. *(Cries of "No.")* If there were, which, thank God, there is not, any serious danger to the immediate triumph of our cause, the men who talk in this way would soon find out their mistake. *(Cheers)* The second object of this gathering I take to be to strengthen the hands of those who have thrown upon them the weight of responsibility of conducting the Irish national movement in its last but triumphant phase. *(Cheers)* . . .

Fellow-countrymen, the struggle for Home Rule, the old, old struggle in which your great-grandfathers, aye, and further back still, took a part, is now practically ended. That Ireland shall have Home Rule in the immediate future is now recognized as inevitable, not only in Ireland, but all through Great Britain and through the British Empire. *(Cheers)* The argumentative opposition to Home Rule is absolutely dead, and all the violent language, all the extravagant action, all the bombastic threats, are but indications that the battle is over. They are tactics of despair. They are not really methods of warfare at all. They are simply the maneuvers of defeated men seeking to cover their retreat. Our opponents, even the most extreme of them, no longer hope to win, and their one object in life at this moment is to find some means of saving their

SOURCE: From *The Times* (London), October 13, 1913, pp. 9–10.

faces. *(Cheers)* I am a man who is always willing to build a golden bridge for a retreating enemy, and I say here to-day I am quite willing to assist in saving the faces of Sir Edward Carson and his friends. They must realize to-day, if they did not realize before, from the speeches that have recently been made in England, that their policy, well described by Mr. Churchill as "the bullies' veto," is not going to be submitted to by the government or the people. *(Cheers)* The British people have made up their minds to give Home Rule to Ireland, and they will not submit to the insolent threats and intimidation of Sir Edward Carson and his friends. *(Cheers)* . . .

Early next year the Home Rule Bill will be passed the third time in the House of Commons. Whether it be rejected by the House of Lords or not, it will become the law of the land next year. It will become operative in the normal course, and, after the normal and necessary and short interval, an Irish Parliament will be elected and sitting in College Green. *(Cheers)* . . .

I see that the Tory Party seems to think that, if they were returned to power at the next general election, they could repeal Home Rule. *(Laughter)* What I have to say is that, if they think they can, with ease or impunity, violate another treaty, they know very little of the Ireland they would have to deal with to-day. I make them a present of that prospect. *(Laughter and cheers)* Now it looks as if the Ulster rebels were seeking for terms. Personally, I always thought they would be, and I always regarded the warlike preparations of the provisional government simply as a means of raising the price. . . .

I have repeatedly stated that there are practically no limits, short of the betrayal of Home Rule, to which, personally, I would not be unwilling to go to bring about an absolutely united Ireland. *(Cheers)* If our opponents in Ulster desire still further provisions in the Home Rule Bill to safeguard them against the possibility of oppression, persecution, or injustice; if they have any claim to urge even for a further representation in the Irish Parliament; if they have any

claim to urge for a greater control of local administration, and they say it is administration and not legislation they fear—if they have any claims of that sort to put forward I can conceive no reasonable demand that would not be considered fairly and sympathetically by my colleagues and myself. *(Cheers)*

But Mr. Churchill, in his speech in Scotland, alluded to a possible exclusion of a part of Ireland on condition that both parties in England agree to pass the bill and make it a real settlement. I have to say here, today, that that suggestion is a totally impracticable and unworkable one. Let me point out that it has no friends in Ireland. No section of national opinion has ever suggested or tolerated the idea. No responsible leader of the Unionist Party in Ireland has ever put forward that idea as a means of settlement of the Irish question, and when it was proposed in the House of Commons the men who proposed it declared, in so many words, that they put it forward simply as a means of wrecking and killing the Home Rule Bill. . . .

It is my duty, I think, to declare that that suggestion is impracticable and unworkable, and to repeat the statement that I have many times made in Parliament and out of it that Irish nationalists can never be assenting parties to the mutilation of the Irish nation. *(Cheers)*

Ireland is a unit from north to south and from east to west. It is true that, within the bosom of a nation, there is room for many local diversities of treatment, of government, and of administration, but a unit Ireland is and Ireland must remain, and we can never assent to any proposal which would create a sharp, eternal dividing line between Irish Catholics and Irish Protestants. *(Cheers)* . . .

Our ideal is the exact reverse. We want all Irishmen to join together in defense of their common Motherland, and we take our stand on the immortal and historic words of Parnell, who declared in the House of Commons, in 1886, that Ireland could not spare a single son, and that, no matter how good an Irish Protestant might be, he was not too good to take his share with his Catholic brothers in making an Irish Parliament the instrument of religious and civil liberty of Ireland. *(Cheers)* . . .

We know, in our ideal of the Irish nation, no district, no country, no province. We know no race, no creed, no class. Ireland, and all Ireland, for the Irish, Ireland emancipated, Ireland united, Ireland indivisible, these are our unchanged and unchangeable ideals. *(Cheers)* And, let me say it with reverence and seriousness to you, we ought reverently to thank God that we have lived to see the day when those ideals are accepted by the democracy of Great Britain. . . .

12

Britain's Victorian Empire: Asset or Burden?

Overseas empire has played an important role in British thinking and action ever since permanent settlements were first projected in the age of Queen Elizabeth I, yet both the scope and the significance of that empire have varied greatly through the years. By the middle of the nineteenth century, the empire was made up of enormous stretches of land and relatively few people in both Canada and Australia, as well as vast claims in India (accumulated under the English East India Company) and smaller settlements in South America and Africa and on islands in the Atlantic, Indian, and Pacific oceans. Attitudes toward that empire varied as greatly as did its nature. In the 1840s and 1850s, for example, many Britons wondered how colonies could be justified at all in a world that seemed to be moving from an age of mercantilism into an age of free trade.

That is the question to which William Rathbone Greg (1809–1881) addressed himself in an article he contributed to the prestigious *Edinburgh Review* in 1851, "Shall We Retain Our Colonies?" Greg was an industrialist and later a civil servant who at the same time contributed numerous essays to the major journals of the day. Why does the argument for decolonization impress Greg as "lucid, plausible, and attractive"? On what grounds does he ultimately reject that argument? In assessing Greg's article as well as the subsequent documents in this chapter, we should pay attention to matters that the authors take for granted (such as racial or ethnic superiority) as well as those they seek to prove or disprove (such as whether colonies are profitable or costly to the mother country). We should also take note of the varied ways in which they cite the example of the United States and the implications of the American War of Independence in order to buttress an argument.

Although "Little Englanders" did not dominate mid-Victorian British ministries and although the empire continued to grow in population and size, except for the Indian Mutiny of 1857–1858, imperial questions played a secondary role in British thought and politics during the 1840s, 1850s, and 1860s. During the 1870s, empire-building did become a party issue, however, and the so-called "scramble for Africa" of the 1880s and the Boer War of 1899–1902 tended for a time to make questions of empire of overriding interest to Britons of all classes. Benjamin Disraeli

The White Elephant

PRESENT PROPRIETOR. "See here, Governor! He's a likely-looking animal,—but I can't manage him. If you won't take him, I must let him go!!" (*Punch*, 1892)

In the midst of the "Scramble for Africa" John Bull ponders whether he should take over direct responsibility for Uganda from the financially hard-pressed British East Africa Company or permit the territory to fall into German hands. In 1894 the British government agreed to take Uganda over as a protectorate.

(1804–1881), the leader of the Conservative Party in the House of Commons from 1849 until 1876 and the leader of the Conservative Party generally from 1868 until his death, is often credited with deliberately tying his party's fortunes to the cause of the empire. What role does he assign to empire in his Crystal Palace Speech of 1872, a speech in which he outlined his party's platform for the next election? In 1874, his party won that election and Disraeli became prime minister for the next six years. His administration became known for its "forward" foreign policy and for an attitude favorable to imperial expansion in Africa and Asia.

Disraeli's rival from the 1850s on, and the leader of the opposing Liberal Party from 1868 on, was William Ewart Gladstone (1809–1898). In "England's Mission," an article he published in the journal *The Nine-*

teenth Century in 1878, Gladstone outlined forcefully the ways in which he disagreed with Disraeli's policies. What does he discern as the underlying basis of his opponent's actions? On the basis of this article, would it be fair to classify Gladstone as a "Little Englander"? On balance, does Gladstone see the empire more as a burden or as an asset?

Although attitudes of the sort expressed in "England's Mission" helped Gladstone and the Liberal Party to return to power in 1880, Gladstone found it difficult to resist altogether the imperialistic tide that seemed to be sweeping the whole European world. Joseph Chamberlain (1836–1914), a Birmingham businessman who for a time headed the radical wing of Gladstone's Liberal Party, did not resist at all. He broke with Gladstone on the subject of Irish Home Rule in 1886, and in 1895 he joined Lord Salisbury's predominantly Conservative cabinet as colonial secretary, a post he rapidly made the second most important in the ministry. In a speech he gave in 1897, Chamberlain outlined his own definition of "The True Conception of Empire." How does he define the three stages of Britain's involvement with the empire? How does he differentiate Britain's relationship with colonies dominated by people of British descent (as was the case in much of Canada and most of Australia) from those like India and parts of Africa in which "native peoples" predominated?

The theme of empire was central not merely to late Victorian politics and social thought but also to imaginative literature and even to some of the poems composed by the poet laureate Alfred, Lord Tennyson (1809–1892). Two examples of this genre are included—"Hands All Round" (1885) and "Opening of the Indian and Colonial Exhibition by the Queen" (1886). How does the poet tie together what may impress us as the separate themes of nation, empire, and freedom? Rudyard Kipling (1865–1936), who was born in India and who spent much of his early life there, is often described as a poet who celebrated the British Empire. Yet there is a deep strain of pessimism in his message, as "The White Man's Burden" (1898) suggests. Kipling had an American wife and lived for a time in Vermont, and the poem was specifically addressed to the citizens of the United States, which was about to annex the Philippine Islands. What are the purposes of colonization, according to the poem? Are those purposes ever likely to be accomplished?

The most difficult problem that the Salisbury government of the late 1890s encountered was how the British colonies of Cape Colony and Natal might continue to coexist peacefully with the Boer Republics of the Transvaal (headed by President Paul Kruger) and the Orange Free State. The discovery of gold and diamonds had made the Transvaal's Johannesburg one of the world's great boomtowns in the 1890s, and the unwillingness of the Transvaal's President Kruger to give the immigrant miners (many of them British) full rights of citizenship ultimately led to war between Britain and the Boer Republics. As the next two documents illustrate, the war did not merely lead to bloody fighting in South Africa; it also provoked heated differences of opinion within Britain. In "The Boer War Defended" (1900), Colonial Secretary Joseph Chamberlain justifies the British decision both to go to war and (at a time when British victory seemed near) to annex the Boer Republics. In "The Boer War Criticized" (1900), David Lloyd George (1863–1945), a future prime minister and war leader but then a youthful Liberal backbencher from Wales, takes sharp exception to Chamberlain's arguments. How do Chamberlain and Lloyd George differ on both the justification for Britain's entry into the war and on the consequences of the war for Britain's position in the world?

Many aspects of empire-building have been debated by historians— as indeed they were by contemporaries—and the contribution of no author has proved either more influential or more controversial than that of the Liberal journalist and economist, J. A. Hobson (1858–1940). Excerpts from his book, *Imperialism: A Study* (1902), constitute the last document. In Hobson's judgment, has the British nation benefited from imperialism? If not, on what basis does Hobson account for late nineteenth-century empire-building? What does Hobson look upon as an appropriate substitute for "economic imperialism"?

WILLIAM RATHBONE GREG **Shall We Retain Our Colonies? (1851)**

A mid-Victorian government official and writer ponders the pros and cons of Britain giving up her colonies at a time when a policy of free trade seemed to make those colonies no more than expensive burdens.

The line of argument we have to meet is lucid, plausible, and attractive. It may be stated thus. In former times, and under the old mercantile system, we valued our colonies as outlets for our manufactures, and as sources of supply for needful products which we could not obtain, or could not obtain so cheaply or so well, elsewhere. We valued them as the principal and the surest channels for that commerce which we felt to be the life-blood of the nation. They were secure, increasing, and favored markets for those articles of British produce which other nations excluded as far as they could by severe and prohibitory tariffs; and they produced for us exclusively those valuable raw materials and articles of luxury which we wished to debar other nations from procuring. In conformity with these ideas, we bound them to the mother country in the bands of a strict and mutually favoring system of customs duties: we compelled them to trade with us exclusively; to take from us exclusively all the articles with which we could supply them; and to send to us exclusively all the produce of their soil. In return, we admitted their produce to our markets at lower rates than that of other countries, or excluded the produce of other countries altogether. This was a consistent, intelligible, and mutually fair system. Under it our colonies were *customers who could not escape us,* and *vendors who could sell to us alone.*

But a new system has risen up, not only differing from the old one, but based upon radically opposite notions of commercial policy. We have discovered that under this system our colonies have cost us, in addition to the annual estimate for their civil government and their defense, a sum amounting to many millions a year in the extra price which we have paid for their produce beyond that at which other coun-

SOURCE: From "Shall We Retain Our Colonies?", *Edinburgh Review* (April, 1851), pp. 479–485, 488–494, 496–498.

tries could have supplied it to us. In obedience to our new and wiser commercial policy, we have abolished all discriminating and protective duties; we have announced to our colonies that we shall no longer favor their productions and, as a necessary and just corollary, that we shall no longer compel them to favor ours—that we shall supply ourselves with our sugar, coffee, cotton and indigo wherever we can buy them cheapest and that they are at liberty to follow the same principle in the purchase of their calicoes, silks and woolens. They are therefore to us now, in a commercial point of view, friendly trading communities and nothing more. The very object for which we founded, governed, defended and cherished them, has been abandoned: why, then, should we any longer incur the cost of their maintenance?

Being, then, on the footing of independent states as far as their tariffs are concerned, they yield us nothing and benefit us in nothing as colonies that they would not yield us and serve us were they altogether independent. Nay, they are even less serviceable to us; for the experience of the United States has shown us how immeasurably faster colonies advance in population, in enterprise, in agriculture and in commerce—in everything which makes them valuable as customers—when separated from the mother country than when still attached to it by the bonds of allegiance and the clumsy fetters of remote and injudicious control. . . .

In the next place, our colonies used to be regarded as inexhaustible storehouses of waste and fertile land and as outlets for our dense and often-suffering population; and it is in this view, perhaps, that most persons are still disposed especially to value them. But what is the fact? Have we not the plainest indications that even in this respect they would be more valuable if they were independent and that even now the United States, because independent, are preferred by our emigrants? According to Sir William Molesworth's statement in 1848, of 1,673,600 persons who had emigrated during the preceding twenty years,

825,564 went direct to the United States, and how many more went indirectly through Canada we can only guess. . . .

Again—we used to make some of our colonies serviceable as prisons for our convicts—distant and safe receptacles for the disposal of our metropolitan villany and filth—places for "burying our dead out of our sight." *Now* we can use them as such no longer. Our colonies have one and all remonstrated; have refused to receive the sweepings of our jails any longer; have threatened to rebel if we persist in sending them; and we have ourselves, on more than one occasion, admitted the system to be an indefensible one and have announced our determination to abandon it.

We have been taught to believe that our colonial empire, "on which the sun never sets," is about the most important element in our national greatness and that these vast dominions in every part of the world add incalculably, though in some mysterious way, to our imperial dignity and strength. . . . [Now we are told] that this "prestige of empire" is a hollow show . . . ; that outlying dependencies which require to be garrisoned in time of peace and protected in time of war draft off from this country the forces which are needed for our defense at home; dissipate our army and navy . . . ; and waste the funds which should be devoted to the protection of the mother country.

It is idle, [we learn,] to pretend that a system which gives us such a vast additional territory to defend without giving us any additional means of defending it can be other than a source of dangerous weakness; that if we had no dependencies, we should be impregnable and invulnerable at home; and that half our navy and a fourth of our army would suffice for the protection of our hearths and homes. If, indeed, the colonies paid tribute into our treasury, if they furnished contingents to our military force and supplied a fixed quota of ships and stores toward the augmentation of our navy,—the case might be different. But they do nothing of all this; overtaxed and overburdened, England pays for a great part of their civil government, and nearly the whole of their naval and military requirements; the impoverished and struggling peasant of Dorsetshire—the suffering artisan of Lancashire—the wretched needlewomen of London—all have to pay their contribution to the defense and the civil rule of the comfortable Australian farmer, the wealthy Canadian settler, and the luxurious Jamaica negro. If Sir W. Molesworth's statistics may be taken as approaching to accuracy, our colonial empire costs us at least £4,000,000 a year—a sum nearly equal to the income-tax—to the malt-tax—to the sugar tax;—any one of which might be repealed, to the infinite relief of our people, in case our colonies were abandoned.

Lastly, we govern them ill. . . . They are perpetual sources of difficulty and dispute; they are always quarreling with us, and complaining of us, and not unfrequently breaking out into open rebellion; they yearn for independence, and would gladly purchase immunity from our vexatious interference and ignorant control by encountering all the risks and difficulties to which a severance of the imperial connexion might expose them.—Since, then, the colonies are commercially as free as America or Spain; since they are no longer favored or enforced customers for our productions; since they would be at least as available to our emigrants if independent as if still subject to our rule; since they refuse to help us by relieving us of our convict population; since they are sources of weakness and not of strength to us in times of peril or of war; since they pay no part of the expenses of the mother country, and only a small portion of their own; since we mismanage their affairs and impede their progress; and since they themselves wish to be set free from a fettering and galling yoke;—what argument, which will bear the test of close investigation, can be adduced to warrant our retaining them in tutelage?

Such is . . . the reasoning we have to meet. Such are the conclusions, deduced to all appearance from the premises by the legitimate process of logic, against which we are to show cause. The position is undoubt-

edly a strong one: nevertheless, we hold that there are sufficient grounds for maintaining inviolate the connexion actually existing between the colonies and the mother country.

And, first, let us look a little more closely into the question of their actual cost. Sir W. Molesworth's estimate in his speech of July, 1848, is as follows: . . . £2,500,000 per annum. . . .

Let us separate the sum, which Sir W. Molesworth lumps under one head, into its proper divisions. The total cost in 1843–4, charged upon the military purse of Great Britain was (throwing out £48,941 of "general charges" which we cannot well appropriate) £2,509,026, thus:—

Military and maritime stations	£ 952,934
Penal settlements	189,005
Plantations and colonies proper	1,367,087
	£2,509,026

The military expenditure for our colonies, then, instead of being as Sir W. Molesworth stated, above two millions and a half, was little more than *one million and a quarter.* . . .

The just proportion of our naval expenditure, which should be charged to colonial account, it is impossible to estimate with any precision; because, though we know the number of vessels attendant on our purely military and maritime stations, it is impossible to say what proportion of the force employed on foreign service is required for the protection of our commerce, and what for the defense and supervision of our colonies. With our ships spread over the whole world, even to the remotest corners, with our merchants settled in all parts, constantly claiming the interference and protection of government, and prompt and vehement in their complaints whenever their representations do not meet with instant attention, a numerous and widely-scattered naval force would still be required, even if our colonies were independent, or abandoned to other alliances. . . .

Since, then, there is no foundation for the idea that we need to abandon our colonies from sheer inability to retain them, we may proceed to point out a few of the reasons which may be urged for preserving the connexion inviolate, and which we think will be deemed conclusive by the nation at large, if not by all political parties in it.

In the first place, not a single one of our colonies is inhabited by a homogeneous population. In none, is the British race the sole one; in scarcely any, is it the most numerous. Some of the dependencies have been taken from savage tribes; others have been conquered from other European nations. In Trinidad we have *seven* distinct races; in the Cape Colony at least *five*; in Canada *four*; in Mauritius *four*; in Ceylon at least *three*; in Australia and New Zealand *two*. . . .

Now, with what show of decency or justice could England abandon to their own guidance and protection countries peopled by such various, heterogeneous, and often hostile races,—even if any very considerable number of their inhabitants were unwise enough to wish it? What inevitable injustice such a step must entail upon one or other section of the colonists, what certain peril to the interests of them all, and of humanity at large! Let us follow out this inquiry in the case of two or three of them. We will assume that Canada would go on without any serious disturbances, now that the various populations which inhabit it have been so much more amalgamated than before by being pressed together into one legislature. We will suppose that the Australian colonies would be able to stand on their own feet, and to maintain their own interests, and would manifest that marvelous faculty for self-government and social organization which has always been the proud distinction of the Anglo-Saxon race. . . .

But what would be the result in Jamaica, in Mauritius, at the Cape [of Good Hope], and in Ceylon, where the blacks outnumber the whites in overwhelming proportion, and where the whites themselves belong to disunited and hostile nations? In Jamaica, and our other West Indian possessions, one of three results would follow,—either the whites would remain as now, the dominant class, and would use their legislative power for the promotion of their own interests, and for the compression of the subject race;—would induce large immigration, would prohibit squatting, would compel work; would tax the necessaries of life rather than their own property or their own commerce,—perhaps might even strive to restore a modified slavery: or, the blacks, easily excited, but not easily restrained when once aroused by their demagogues and missionaries, would seize upon the supreme power, either by sudden insurrection, or by gradual and constitutional, but not open force; and in this event few who know the negroes well, who have watched them during the prevalence of cholera in Jamaica, or who have the example of Haiti before their eyes, will doubt that another Haiti would ere long, though not perhaps at once, be the issue of the experiment: or, lastly, the whites, fearing the second alternative, and finding themselves too feeble to enforce the first, would throw themselves into the arms of the United States, who would, as we are well aware, receive them with a warm welcome and a covetous embrace, and would speedily reconvert 800,000 free men into slaves. This we think far the most probable alternative of the three. But is there one of the three which any philanthropist, any Briton, any friend to progress and civilization, could contemplate without grief and dismay? . . .

We have simply *no right* to abandon the blacks to the possible oppression of the whites, nor the whites to the dubious mercies of the blacks. We cannot do so without a dereliction of duty, amounting to a crime. Toward both races we have incurred the solemn obligations of protection and control; both have acted or suffered under a tacit covenant, which it would be flagrant dishonesty to violate; toward both we have assumed a position which we may not without dishonor abdicate, on the miserable plea that it would be convenient and economical to do so. . . .

Colonies with mixed and aboriginal populations such as these, then, we simply *could not* abandon; colonies, with a population exclusively or overpoweringly British, come under a different category. But even with these, we think it is not difficult to see that the interests of civilization will be far more effectually served by their retention than by their abandonment,—by still maintaining them as integral portions by the British Empire,—than by casting them adrift to run the chances of a hazardous voyage unassisted and alone. They would "go ahead" far faster, we are told, if independent, than if still subject to the hampering rule of the mother country; and the example of the United States is triumphantly appealed to in confirmation of the assertion. We reply, that we can well believe that they would go ahead far faster if free than if fettered, but not than they will now, when colonial legislatures have been created and endowed with the powers of managing all strictly colonial concerns. There is scarcely an advantage, conferrable by freedom, possessed by the United States since their separation from Britain, that will not now be enjoyed in an equal degree by our North American and our Australian dependencies. . . .

If, indeed, it were true, as is often ignorantly alleged, that the colonies hated Great Britain, and were anxious to cast off their allegiance to her, much might be urged against the policy of retaining unwilling and therefore troublesome and dangerous dependencies. But, we believe the statement to be the reverse of true. They may hate the colonial office: they do not hate England. They are often indignant, and sometimes we think they have been so with justice, at the vexatious interference, the injudicious control, the irritating vacillations, the sad mistakes of the authorities at home; they often bluster and sometimes rebel; they nurture in their bosom, as does every community, a noisy knot of turbulent and disaffected men; they talk largely at time of their desire of independence, and occasionally even forget themselves so far as to hint at "annexation." But this is the mere effervescence of political excitement.
. . .

If, in an evil hour, the counsels of the counterfeit economists were to prevail, and England were to resign her children to the vanity and feebleness of independence, we feel certain that the very first peril they encountered from without, the very first time they were menaced either with insult or with conquest by a foreign power, they would instinctively and undoubtingly appeal to England for assistance and protection; and England would respond to their confidence with the most prompt and generous aid. . . . We should have to bear the expense of defending them from attack, without having any control over their conduct in incurring it.

Finally: there is one other consequence which would ensue from the abandonment of our colonial empire which demands to be most deliberately weighed. . . . If we emancipate our colonies, and cast them on their own unaided resources both for self-government and self-defense, they will of course immediately look about them for the means of securing these primary objects. However economically they may manage— however small the salary they may assign their governors—however homely and republican the style of life they may require their officials to adopt—they can neither govern themselves, nor defend themselves, without a considerable revenue. An appeal to the example of the United States has no validity as a reply. The United States are surrounded by no ambitious neighbors; they are liable to no attack from without; they have no wars or quarrels to fear but such as they pertinaciously insist upon bringing upon themselves. They are an aggressive, not a defensive people. . . .

The first effect, then, of our proclaiming the independence of our colonies must inevitably be, the enactment by them of *a high tariff on all imported commodities;* and as the commodities required by new countries are, by the nature of the case, articles of manufactured rather than of agricultural produce, and as England is the chief manufacturing country in the world, it would be chiefly on our productions that this high tariff would press, however unintentional such a result might be, and however, in diplomatic language, it might be "regretted and deplored."

The rate of the duties imposed by such a tariff it is in vain to guess; this must depend primarily on the necessities of the state imposing it. If, however, the example of the United States is of any service in helping us to a conjecture, it may be observed that her tariff imposes duties of from 30 to 50 per cent on all our chief productions, and that a powerful section of her people are clamorous for an augmentation of these rates. We have no reason to suppose that a lower scale would meet the requirements of Canada, Australia, or the Cape. . . .

No, if Mr. Cobden,[1] after having spent the last ten years of his energetic and useful life in abolishing protective tariffs at home, should wish to spend the next ten years in establishing them in every other corner of the world, and in laying the foundation of a reactionary policy which shall close the markets we ourselves have planted in the wilderness, one after another, to the produce of our spindles and our looms,—we cannot hinder him;—but we should wish him to do it with his eyes open.

We hope we have succeeded in making it clear that our colonies are far too valuable portions of our empire to be lightly laid down or put away; and that if they should not continue to be so, the fault will lie in some sad mismanagement of our own. Many of them, in simple justice to the native population, or to those British subjects who have settled there on the faith of the imperial connexion, we *could not* possibly

abandon. Others the interests of civilization and humanity compel us to retain. All of them ought to be, and will be if we govern them aright, sources of strength and pride to us. The very interests of that free and enlightened commercial policy for which we have fought so long and sacrificed so much, forbid us to entertain the thought of severing the time-hallowed connexion between Great Britain and the communities which have gone forth from her bosom. Nor is there any call or motive for such a step: the cost of our colonies, though less by one half than it has been represented, we could easily sustain were it twice as great: the affection of the colonists it is easy to preserve, or to recover where, through misjudgment or misunderstanding, it has been shaken or impaired. By ruling them with forbearance, steadiness, and justice; by leading them forward in the path of freedom with an encouraging but cautious hand; by bestowing on them the fullest powers of self-government wherever the infusion of British blood is large enough to warrant such a course. . . . To cast our colonial empire to the winds, with the sole aim of saving two millions a year,—is a line of policy which, we sincerely think, is worthy only of a narrow and a niggard school; which will be counselled only by men who are merchants rather than statesmen, and whose mercantile wisdom even is confined, short-sighted, and unenlightened; one, which, we feel assured, can never be adopted by England till the national spirit which has made her what she is, shall have begun to wane and fade away.

BENJAMIN DISRAELI **The Maintenance of Empire (1872)**

In his Crystal Palace Speech of 1872, Disraeli, the leader of the Conservative Party (then in opposition), constructs a party platform made up of three planks: (1) monarchy and the nation's other established institutions; (2) empire; and (3) social reform. In the following excerpts, Disraeli describes the second plank.

SOURCE: From T. E. Kebbel, ed., *Selected Speeches of the Earl of Beaconsfield* (London, 1882), 2 vols.: Vol. II, pp. 529–534.

[1]*Richard Cobden (1804–1865):* the parliamentary leader of the Anti–Corn Law League and a prime champion of a policy of decolonization

Gentlemen, there is another and second great object of the Tory party. If the first is to maintain the institutions of the country, the second is, in my opinion, to uphold the empire of England. If you look to the history of this country since the advent of Liberalism—forty years ago—you will find that there has been no effort so continuous, so subtle, supported by so much energy, and carried on with so much ability and acumen, as the attempts of Liberalism to effect the disintegration of the empire of England.

And, gentlemen, of all its efforts, this is the one which has been the nearest to success. Statesmen of the highest character, writers of the most distinguished ability, the most organized and efficient means, have been employed in this endeavor. It has been proved to all of us that we have lost money by our colonies. It has been shown with precise, with mathematical demonstration, that there never was a jewel in the crown of England that was so truly costly as the possession of India. How often has it been suggested that we should at once emancipate ourselves from this incubus. Well, that result was nearly accomplished. When those subtle views were adopted by the country under the plausible plea of granting self-government to the colonies, I confess that I myself thought that the tie was broken. Not that I for one object to self-government. I cannot conceive how our distant colonies can have their affairs administered except by self-government. But self-government, in my opinion, when it was conceded, ought to have been conceded as part of a great policy of imperial consolidation. It ought to have been accompanied by an imperial tariff, by securities for the people of England for the enjoyment of the unappropriated lands which belonged to the sovereign as their trustee, and by a military code which should have precisely defined the means and the responsibilities by which the colonies should be defended, and by which, if necessary, this country should call for aid from the colonies themselves. It ought, further, to have been accompanied by the institution of some representative council in the metropolis, which would have brought the colonies into constant and continuous relations with the home government. All this, however, was omitted because those who advised that policy—and I believe their convictions were sincere—looked upon the colonies of England, looked even upon our connection with India, as a burden upon this country, viewing everything in a financial aspect, and totally passing by those moral and political considerations which make nations great, and by the influence of which alone men are distinguished from animals.

Well, what has been the result of this attempt during the reign of Liberalism for the disintegration of the empire? It has entirely failed. But how has it failed? Through the sympathy of the colonies with the mother country. They have decided that the empire shall not be destroyed, and in my opinion no minister in this country will do his duty who neglects any opportunity of reconstructing as much as possible our colonial empire, and of responding to those distant sympathies which may become the source of incalculable strength and happiness to this land. Therefore, gentlemen, with respect to the second great object of the Tory party also—the maintenance of the empire—public opinion appears to be in favor of our principles—that public opinion which, I am bound to say, thirty years ago, was not favorable to our principles, and which, during a long interval of controversy, in the interval had been doubtful. . . .

When you return to your homes, when you return to your counties and to your cities, you must tell to all those whom you can influence that the time is at hand, that, at least, it cannot be far distant, when England will have to decide between national and cosmopolitan principles. The issue is not a mean one. It is whether you will be content to be a comfortable England, modelled and moulded upon continental principles and meeting in due course an inevitable fate, or whether you will be a great country,—an imperial country—a country where your sons, when they rise, rise to paramount positions, and obtain not merely the esteem of their countrymen, but command the respect of the world. . . .

WILLIAM EWART GLADSTONE **England's Mission (1878)**

Gladstone agrees that England has a mission in the world, but his definition differs from Disraeli's. At the time this article was written, Disraeli (now earl of Beaconsfield) and his foreign secretary, Lord Salisbury, had just returned in triumph from the Congress of Berlin. Gladstone was in theory no more than a member of the Liberal opposition, having retired from the Liberal Party leadership in 1875. In 1880 he would reassume both the party leadership and the role of prime minister.

"Gentlemen, we bring you peace; and peace with honor." Such are the reputed words, with which Lord Beaconsfield and Lord Salisbury, the two British plenipotentiaries at Berlin, rewarded the admiring crowds who, on their return to London in July, formed part of the well-organized machinery of an obsequious reception, unexampled, I suppose, in the history of our civilians; and meant, perhaps, to recall the pomp of the triumphs which Rome awarded to her most successful generals. . . .

Whether honor is the right name for it must depend upon what is held to constitute honor. The honor to which the recent British policy is entitled is this: that, from the beginning of the Congress to the end, the representatives of England, instead of taking the side of freedom, emancipation, and national progress, took, in every single point where a practical issue was raised, the side of servitude, of reaction, and of barbarism. With a zeal worthy of a better cause, they labored to reduce the limits within which the populations of European Turkey are to be masters of their own destinies; to keep as much as they could of direct Turkish rule; and to enfeeble as much as they could the limitations upon that rule. . . .

The honor, which the government have earned for us at Berlin, is that of having used the name and influence, and even, by their preparations, the military power of England, to set up the principles of Metternich, and to put down the principles of Canning. We, who have helped Belgium, Spain, and Portugal to be free, we who led the way in the establishment of free Greece, and gave no mean support to the liberation and union of Italy, have at Berlin

wrought actively to limit everywhere the area of self-government, and to save from the wreck as much as possible of a domination which has contributed more than any other that ever existed to the misery, the debasement, and the extermination of mankind. . . . The honor which is claimed is, then, a spurious birth, which tarnishes the fame of the England that has been and is, and only can be coveted in an England that has unlearned her best traditions, and that is willing to be known to the world not as the friend of freedom, but as its consistent foe. . . .

And what is this Cyprus, which has shown in so singular a manner its possession of the tempter's power, for which we are to pay so heavily in the good name and fame which are "better than rubies"? . . . Cyprus is above and before all things a symbol and a counter: negative and valueless for any purpose of ours in itself, but a sign of the vastness of our empire, and an effectual sign that, in the opinion of our government, that empire is not yet vast enough.

Viewed in this sense, as the earnest of a policy, the acquisition of Cyprus, instead of silly and unmeaning, becomes eloquent enough, even if mischievous. The most devoted adherent of the ministry must inwardly feel a wish, that it had been acquired with cleaner hands: but, on the other hand, their most resolute opponent must admit that this assumption of new dominion is thoroughly in keeping with their behavior throughout. . . . Since their accession to office we have taken to ourselves, by way of proving to the world our equity and moderation, (1) the Fiji Islands; (2) the Transvaal Republic, in the teeth, as it is now alleged,

SOURCE: From "England's Mission," *The Nineteenth Century* (September 1878), pp. 560–563, 566–570, 572–573, 581, 584.

of the wishes of more than four-fifths of the enfranchised population; (3) the island of Cyprus; (4) if recent information be correct, the island of Socotra, lying a little beyond the Straits of Babelmandeb; (5) we have begun to protrude our military garrisons beyond our Indian frontier: in order to warn Russia how justly indignant we shall be, if she should take, at Merv or elsewhere, any corresponding step. I do not speak in condemnation of each one of these proceedings. It may be true that annexations are sometimes necessary, but it ought to be understood that they are, as a rule, new burdens added to the old, and that in augmenting space they diminish power. I look at them, as a whole, in connection with the doctrine of the first minister that the people do not dislike to see the empire increased, and of his faithful echo and mirror, the foreign secretary, who proclaims that commerce only flourishes with or through territorial dominion. When authority thus appeals to cupidity, when the lips of the state-priest, that should speak wisdom, are given to its opposite, the wonder is not that many are misled by those who pollute the fountain-heads of knowledge, but that many are still found to confute, if they cannot stay, their rulers, and to check the present deviation from those ways of sober, measured, and considerate energy, by which it is that England has grown great. Some seem actually to believe they are increasing strength, when they multiply the points they are to occupy and defend, without adding a single man to the force they can arm, or a pound to the fund by which that force is to be sustained. But it is well to cherish no illusions, and to look the matter in the face. Territorial aggrandizement, backed by military display, is the *cheval de bataille*[2] of the administration. Empire is greatness; leagues of land are empire; your safety is measured by the fear you strike into other nations; trade follows the flag: he that doubts is an enemy to his country. This creed of aggrandizement, made real to the public imagination by the acquisition

of a Mediterranean and virtually European island, has operated a relative success: it has covered the miscarriages of the government, and it enables them to say that they have not been condemned to capital punishment by the country.

It is very disagreeable for an Englishman to hint to Englishmen that the self-love and pride, which all condemn in individuals, have often lured nations to their ruin or their loss; that they are apt to entail a great deal of meanness, as well as a great deal of violence; that they begin with a forfeiture of respect abroad, and end even in the loss of self-respect; that their effect is to destroy all sobriety in the estimation of human affairs, and to generate a temperament of excitability which errs alternately on the side of arrogance, and of womanish and unworthy fears. For the performance of this disagreeable duty, we are entitled to look in the first place to the queen's government; which ought in foreign affairs invariably to play, and which in other times usually has played, the part of moderator. . . .

The doctrines of national self-restraint, of the equal obligations of states to public law, and of their equal rights to fair construction as to words and deeds, have been left to unofficial persons. The government, not uniformly nor consistently, but in the main and on the whole, have opened up and relied on an illegitimate source of power, which never wholly fails: they have appealed, under the prostituted name of patriotism, to exaggerated fears, to imaginary interests, and to the acquisitiveness of a race which has surpassed every other known to history in the faculty of appropriating to itself vast spaces of the earth, and establishing its supremacy over men of every race and language. Now I hold that to stimulate these tendencies, to overlook the proportion between our resources and our obligations, and above all to claim anything more than equality of rights in the moral and political intercourse of the world, is not the way to make England great, but to make it both morally and materially little.

---

[2]*cheval de bataille:* war-horse

The sentiment of empire may be called innate in every Briton. If there are exceptions, they are like those of men born blind or lame among us. It is part of our patrimony: born with our birth, dying only with our death; incorporating itself in the first elements of our knowledge, and interwoven with all our habits of mental action upon public affairs. It is a portion of our national stock, which has never been deficient, but which has more than once run to rank excess, and brought us to mischief accordingly, mischief that for a time we have weakly thought was ruin. In its normal action, it made for us the American colonies, the grandest monument ever erected by a people of modern times, and second only to the Greek colonization in the whole history of the world. In its domineering excess, always under the name of British interests and British honor, it lost them by obstinacy and pride. Lord Chatham who forbade us to tax, Mr. Burke who forbade us to legislate for them, would have saved them. But they had to argue for a limitation of English power; and to meet the reproach of the political wiseacres, who first blustered on our greatness, and then, when they reaped as they had sown, whined over our calamities. Undoubtedly the peace of 1782–3, with its adjuncts in exasperated feeling, was a terrible dismemberment. But England was England still: and one of the damning signs of the politics of the school is their total blindness to the fact, that the central strength of England lies in England. Their eye travels with satisfaction over the wide space upon the map covered by the huge ice-bound deserts of North America or the unpenetrated wastes of Australasia, but rests with mortification on the narrow bounds of latitude and longitude marked by nature for the United Kingdom. They are the materialists of politics: Their faith is in acres and in leagues, in sounding titles and long lists of territories. They forget that the entire fabric of the British Empire was reared and consolidated by the energies of a people, which was (though it is not now) insignificant in numbers, when compared with the leading states of the Continent; and that if

by some vast convulsion our transmarine possessions could be all submerged, the very same energies of that very same people would either discover other inhabited or inhabitable spaces of the globe on which to repeat its work, or would without them in other modes assert its undiminished greatness. Of all the opinions disparaging to England, there is not one which can lower her like that which teaches that the source of strength for this almost measureless body lies in its extremities, and not in the heart which has so long propelled the blood through all its regions, and in the brain which has bound and binds them into one.

. . .

The dominant passion of France was military glory. Twice, in this century, it has towered beyond what is allowed to man; and twice has paid the tremendous forfeit of opening to the foe the proudest capital in the world. The dominant passion of England is extended empire. It has heretofore been kept in check by the integrity and sagacity of her statesmen, who have not shrunk from teaching her the lessons of self-denial and self-restraint. But a new race has arisen; and the most essential or the noblest among all the duties of government, the exercise of moral control over ambition and cupidity, have been left to the intermittent and feeble handling of those who do not govern. . . .

The prospective multiplication of possessions oversea [sic] is, to say the least, far from desirable. It is difficult to regard without anxiety the formidable extension, which has been given to our boundaries at the Cape. During the last forty years, those possessions have cost us probably from twenty to thirty millions sterling in wars and military establishments; and an annexation like that of the Transvaal will entail the heaviest responsibility on the government, should it be found that our sovereignty has been imposed by force on an unwilling population. We do not want Bosnian submissions. Especially is it inexpedient to acquire possessions which, like Cyprus, never can become truly British, because they have acquired indelibly an ethnical character of their own. In them we remain as masters and as foreigners, and the connection at its best has not the ennobling features which, in cases like America and Australasia, give a high moral purpose to the subsisting relation, and compensate for the serious responsibilities which in given contingencies it may entail. . . .

The truth is that, turn where we will, we are met on every side with proofs that the cares and calls of the British Empire are already beyond the strength of those who govern and have governed it. A protracted experience of public affairs, not unattended with a high estimate of the general diligence, devotion, and ability of the Parliamentary as well as the civil servants of the Crown, has long convinced me that of the more difficult descriptions of the public business, apart from simple routine, it is only a small part that is transacted with the requisite knowledge, care, and thoroughness. We have undertaken, in the matter of government, far more than ever in the history of the world has been previously attempted by the children of men. . . .

England, which has grown so great, may easily become little; through the effeminate selfishness of luxurious living; through neglecting realities at home to amuse herself everywhere else in stalking phantoms; through putting again on her resources a strain like that of the great French war, which brought her people to misery, and her throne to peril; through that denial of equal rights to others, which taught us so severe a lesson at the epoch of the Armed Neutrality. But she will never lose by the modesty in thought and language, which most of all beseems the greatest of mankind; never by forwardness to allow, and to assert, the equal rights of all states and nations; never by refusing to be made the tool of foreign cunning, for ends alien to her principles and feelings; never by keeping her engagements in due relation to her means, or by husbanding those means for the day of need, and for the noble duty of defending, as occasion offers, the cause of public right, and of rational freedom, over the broad expanse of Christendom.

JOSEPH CHAMBERLAIN **The True Conception of Empire (1897)**

The colonial secretary in Lord Salisbury's Unionist government (1895–1902) sets forth "The True Conception of Empire" in a speech delivered at the annual Royal Colonial Institute dinner on March 31, 1897.

It seems to me that there are three distinct stages in our imperial history. We began to be, and we ultimately became a great imperial power in the eighteenth century, but, during the greater part of that time, the colonies were regarded, not only by us, but by every European power that possessed them, as possessions valuable in proportion to the pecuniary advantage which they brought to the mother country, which, under that order of ideas, was not truly a mother at all,

but appeared rather in the light of a grasping and absentee landlord desiring to take from his tenants the utmost rents he could exact. The colonies were valued and maintained because it was thought that they would be a source of profit—of direct profit—to the mother country.

That was the first stage, and when we were rudely awakened by the War of Independence in America from this dream that the colonies could be held for our profit

SOURCE: From Charles W. Boyd, ed., *Mr. Chamberlain's Speeches* (Boston: Houghton Mifflin & Co., 1914), 2 vols.: Vol. II, pp. 1–6.

alone, the second chapter was entered upon, and public opinion seems then to have drifted to the opposite extreme; and, because the colonies were no longer a source of revenue, it seems to have been believed and argued by many people that their separation from us was only a matter of time, and that that separation should be desired and encouraged lest haply they might prove an encumbrance and a source of weakness.

It was while those views were still entertained, while the little Englanders were in their full career, that this institute was founded to protest against doctrines so injurious to our interests and so derogatory to our honor; and I rejoice that what was then, as it were, "a voice crying in the wilderness" is now the expressed and determined will of the overwhelming majority of the British people. Partly by the efforts of this institute and similar organizations, partly by the writings of such men as Froude and Seeley, but mainly by the instinctive good sense and patriotism of the people at large, we have now reached the third stage in our history, and the true conception of our empire.

What is that conception? As regards the self-governing colonies we no longer talk of them as dependencies. The sense of possession has given place to the sentiment of kinship. We think and speak of them as part of ourselves, as part of the British Empire, united to us, although they may be dispersed throughout the world, by ties of kindred, of religion, of history, and of language, and joined to us by the seas that formerly seemed to divide us.

But the British Empire is not confined to the self-governing colonies and the United Kingdom. It includes a much greater area, a much more numerous population in tropical climes, where no considerable European settlement is possible, and where the native population must always vastly outnumber the white inhabitants; and in these cases also the same change has come over the imperial idea. Here also the sense of possession has given place to a different sentiment—the sense of obligation. We feel now that our rule over these territories can only be justified if we can show that it adds to the happiness and prosperity of the people, and I maintain that our rule does, and has, brought security and peace and comparative prosperity to countries that never knew these blessings before.

In carrying out this work of civilization we are fulfilling what I believe to be our national mission, and we are finding scope for the exercise of those faculties and qualities which have made of us a great governing race. I do not say that our success has been perfect in every case, I do not say that all our methods have been beyond reproach; but I do say that in almost every instance in which the rule of the queen has been established and the great *Pax Britannica* has been enforced, there has come with it greater security to life and property, and a material improvement in the condition of the bulk of the population. No doubt, in the first instance, when these conquests have been made, there has been bloodshed, there has been loss of life among the native populations, loss of still more precious lives among those who have been sent out to bring these countries into some kind of disciplined order, but it must be remembered that that is the condition of the mission we have to fulfil. There are, of course, among us—there always are among us, I think—a very small minority of men who are ready to be the advocates of the most detestable tyrants, provided their skin is black—men who sympathize with the sorrows of Prempeh and Lobengula,[3] and who denounce as

---

[3]*Prempeh:* an Ashanti ruler (in the area of present-day Nigeria) deposed by a British military force in 1896; *Lobengula:* ruled the most powerful native kingdom of South-Central Africa (in present-day Zimbabwe) before it was overthrown by Cecil Rhodes's British South Africa Company in 1893–1894

murderers those of their countrymen who have gone forth at the command of the queen, and who have redeemed districts as large as Europe from the barbarism and the superstition in which they had been steeped for centuries. I remember a picture by Mr. Selous of a philanthropist—an imaginary philanthropist, I will hope—sitting cozily by his fireside and denouncing the methods by which British civilization was promoted. This philanthropist complained of the use of Maxim guns and other instruments of warfare, and asked why we could not proceed by more conciliatory methods, and why the impis[4] of Lobengula could not be brought before a magistrate, and fined five shillings and bound over to keep the peace.

No doubt there is a humorous exaggeration in this picture, but there is gross exaggeration in the frame of mind against which it was directed. You cannot have omelettes without breaking eggs; you cannot destroy the practices of barbarism, of slavery, of superstition, which for centuries have desolated the interior of Africa, without the use of force; but if you will fairly contrast the gain to humanity with the price which we are bound to pay for it, I think you may well rejoice in the result of such expeditions as those which have been recently conducted with such signal success in Nyassaland, Ashanti, Benin, and Nupé—expeditions which may have, and indeed have, cost valuable lives, but as to which we may rest assured that for one life lost a hundred will be gained, and the cause of civilization and the prosperity of the people will in the long run be eminently advanced. But no doubt such a state of things, such a mission as I have described, involves heavy responsibility. In the wide dominions of the queen the doors of the temple of Janus are never closed, and it is a gigantic task that we have undertaken when we have determined to wield the sceptre of empire. Great is the task, great is the responsibility, but great is the honor; and I am convinced that the conscience and the spirit of the country will rise to the height of its obligations, and that we shall have the strength to fulfil the mission which our history and our national character have imposed upon us.

In regard to the self-governing colonies our task is much lighter. We have undertaken, it is true, to protect them with all the strength at our command against foreign aggression, although I hope that the need for our intervention may never arise. But there remains what then will be our chief duty—that is, to give effect to that sentiment of kinship to which I have referred and which I believe is deep in the heart of every Briton. We want to promote a closer and a firmer union between all members of the great British race, and in this respect we have in recent years made great progress—so great that I think sometimes some of our friends are apt to be a little hasty, and to expect even a miracle to be accomplished. I would like to ask them to remember that time and patience are essential elements in the development of all great ideas. Let us, gentlemen, keep our ideal always before us. For my own part, I believe in the practical possibility of a federation of the British race, but I know that it will come, if it does come, not by pressure, not by anything in the nature of dictation from this country, but it will come as the realization of a universal desire, as the expression of the dearest wish of our colonial fellow-subjects themselves.

That such a result would be desirable, would be in the interest of all of our colonies as well as of ourselves, I do not believe any sensible man will doubt. It seems to me that the tendency of the time is to throw all power into the hands of the greater empires, and the minor kingdoms—those which are non-progressive—seem to be destined to fall into a secondary and subordinate place. But, if Greater Britain remains united, no empire in the world can ever surpass it in area, in population, in wealth, or in the diversity of its resources. . . .

---

[4]*impis:* warriors

ALFRED LORD TENNYSON **Hands All Round (1885), Opening of the Indian and Colonial Exhibition by the Queen (1886)**

The poet laureate celebrates the theme of empire in the 1880s.

Hands All Round

First pledge our Queen this solemn night,
  Then drink to England, every guest;
That man's the true Cosmopolite
  Who loves his native country best.
May freedom's oak for ever live
  With stronger life from day to day;
That man's the best Conservative
  Who lops the moulder'd branch away.
    Hands all round!
  God the traitor's hope confound!
To this great cause of Freedom drink, my
  friends,
  And the great name of England, round
  and round.

To all the loyal hearts who long
  To keep our English Empire whole!
To all our noble sons, the strong
  New England of the Southern Pole!
To England under Indian skies,
  To those dark millions of her realm!
To Canada whom we love and prize,

Whatever statesmen hold the helm.
    Hands all round!
  God the traitor's hope confound!
To this great name of England drink, my
  friends,
  And all her glorious empire, round and
  round.

To all our statesmen so they be
  True leaders of the land's desire!
To both our Houses, may they see
  Beyond the borough and the shire!
We sail'd wherever ship could sail,
  We founded many a mighty state;
Pray God our greatness may not fail
  Through craven fears of being great.
    Hands all round!
  God the traitor's hope confound!
To this great cause of Freedom drink, my
  friends,
  And the great name of England, round
  and round.

Opening of the Indian and Colonial Exhibition by the Queen

I

Welcome, welcome with one voice!
In your welfare we rejoice,
Sons and brothers that have sent,
From isle and cape and continent,
Produce of your field and flood,
Mount and mine, and primal wood;
Works of subtle brain and hand,
And splendours of the morning land,
Gifts from every British zone;
  Britons, hold your own!

II

May we find, as ages run,
The mother featured in the son;
And may yours for ever be
That old strength and constancy
Which has made your fathers great
In our ancient island State,
And wherever her flag fly,
Glorying between sea and sky,
Makes the might of Britain known;
  Britons, hold your own!

SOURCE: From Alfred, Lord Tennyson, *Tiresias and Other Poems* (London, 1885), pp. 195–197.

III

Britain fought her sons of yore—
Britain fail'd; and never more,
Careless of our growing kin,
Shall we sin our fathers' sin,
Men that in a narrower day—
Unprophetic rulers they—
Drove from out the mother's nest
That young eagle of the West
To forage for herself alone;
  Britons, hold your own!

IV

Sharers of our glorious past,
Brothers, must we part at last?
Shall we not thro' good and ill
Cleave to one another still?
Britain's myriad voices call,
"Sons, be welded each and all,
Into one imperial whole,
One with Britain, heart and soul!
One life, one flag, one fleet, one throne!"
  Britons, hold your own!

RUDYARD KIPLING The White Man's Burden (1898)

The author of The Jungle Book *and of stories and poems about the British army in India urges his fellow Britons and his American cousins to fulfill their imperial obligations.*

Take up the White Man's burden—
Send forth the best ye breed—
Go bind your sons to exile
To serve your captives' need;
To wait in heavy harness,
On fluttered folk and wild—
Your new-caught, sullen peoples,
Half-devil and half-child.

Take up the White Man's burden—
In patience to abide,
To veil the threat of terror
And check the show of pride;
By open speech and simple,
An hundred times made plain
To seek another's profit,
And work another's gain.

Take up the White Man's burden—
The savage wars of peace—
Fill full the mouth of Famine
And bid the sickness cease;
And when your goal is nearest
The end for others sought,
Watch sloth and heathen Folly
Bring all your hopes to nought.

Take up the White Man's burden—
No tawdry rule of kings,
But toil of serf and sweeper—
The tale of common things.
The ports ye shall not enter,
The roads ye shall not tread,
Go make them with your living,
And mark them with your dead.

Take up the White Man's burden—
And reap his old reward:
The blame of those ye better,
The hate of those ye guard—
The cry of hosts ye humour
(Ah, slowly!) toward the light:—
"Why brought he us from bondage,
Our loved Egyptian night?"

Take up the White Man's burden—
Ye dare not stoop to less—
Nor call too loud on Freedom
To cloke your weariness;
By all ye cry or whisper,
By all ye leave or do,
The silent, sullen peoples
Shall weight your Gods and you.

SOURCE: From Alfred, Lord Tennyson, *Locksley Hall Sixty Years After, Etc.* (London, 1886), pp. 43–45. From "The White Man's Burden" from *Rudyard Kipling's Verse*, Definitive Edition (New York: Doubleday & Company, Inc., 1924), pp. 371–372. Reprinted by permission of the Executors of the Estate of Mrs. George Bambridge and Doubleday & Company, Inc.

Take up the White Man's burden—
Have done with childish days—
The lightly proffered laurel,
The easy, ungrudged praise.

Comes now, to search your manhood
Through all the thankless years,
Cold, edged with dear-bought wisdom,
The judgment of your peers!

JOSEPH CHAMBERLAIN The Boer War Defended (1900)

The colonial secretary defends the conduct of the British government in South Africa, where war broke out the year before and where British troops are in the process of conquering the Boer Republics (the Transvaal and the Orange Free State).

We are engaged in the greatest war of our generation. The cost of life and treasure has been tremendous. The whole question, then, of the policy of the war, of the continuance of the war, and of the results of the war—all that is the greatest question which this House has had to consider. And upon that there can be no neutral ground. [A member of the Opposition has] laid a great deal of stress on, and spoke with much feeling of, the misery which has been caused by this war—the loss of life and money, and so forth. But surely the hon. and learned Gentleman must know as well as everyone else that all that is absolutely irrelevant. It is an appeal to sentiment which has nothing to do with the issue we are trying. Of course it may be an argument against all war. . . . It is irrelevant language. You must not judge the war by the loss of life and limb incurred, but by other considerations altogether. The greatest war of our times— a war in which thousands lost their lives where in this war only units have done so— the great Civil War of America, even Mr. [John] Bright defended as a just and righteous war. Yet the loss and suffering caused by it was infinite in comparison with that of the present war. . . .

We were fully aware that if we did enter into this war it would be a great calamity, and, therefore, we had every reason to avoid it. Our contention . . . is that we could not avoid the war, that the war was inevitable as well as just, and that we have to take these consequences, terrible as they are, as a result of a war which we believe to be just. . . .

The policy of Her Majesty's government is not a vindictive policy. Revenge does not enter into our minds, nor, as I believe, does it enter into the minds of any reasonable people in this country. What we want is prevention. We do not want rebellion to be made so easy and so profitable that if any difficulty at any future time recurs, the same men may again go out in arms against us. What do we propose in the case of the men who have behaved as I have described [i.e., the disloyal Boers of the British Cape Colony]? We do not propose to submit them to the death penalty or to imprison them; we do not propose to even fine them, but we propose to disarm them politically for five years. This is the whole punishment. It was said we should disarm them as far as possible. Is it not illogical to say you are to take away the rifles which these people have used for certain purposes injurious to the British Empire, and that you are going to give them votes in order to do the same thing by other means?

The hon. and learned Gentleman opposite, although I do not think he defined his position very clearly, as I understand is against the annexation of the two republics. If so, will he bear this in mind, that in the first place he is opposing himself to the unanimous opinion of all the great self-governing colonies who have assisted us in this matter. That is one point on which through all their governments they had officially

SOURCE: From *Hansard's Parliamentary Debates*, 4th Series (July 25, 1900), Vol. 86, cols. 1187–1189, 1194–1199.

communicated their opinion before we came to a decision. He is going against the opinion of every loyal Englishman and Dutchman in the Cape Colony. He is going against the opinion, I believe, of nine out of ten of his own countrymen. It is true the hon. Baronet says the country has gone mad. Well, we know that frame of mind; there are a good number of people who hold that opinion, that all the rest of the world is mad, but then they are generally shut up. But, although the hon. Gentlemen are perfectly at liberty to hold their opinion, and to press it upon the House, I do ask the committee to consider what would be the result of adopting it. What would be the position then of these loyal colonists, whose desires you would have rejected? Might you not then be accused of having "flouted" them? You would be doing that, and at the same time you would be doing worse than that, you would be discouraging all your loyal subjects in South Africa. . . . I do not conceal from myself the terrible divisions among families, among peoples, among races, among religions, which exist at the present time in South Africa. But it seems to me that those who know most of the country are of opinion that hitherto those divisions have been based upon a misunderstanding on the part of the Boers of the English character and the English power, and that now that that misunderstanding has been removed by the war the probability is that after a short time they will settle down to a condition of things in which certainly they will not have anything to complain of. We have publicly declared it to be our desire and intention to give to them at the earliest possible moment self-government similar to that enjoyed by our own colonies. When hon. Members in this debate have spoken of disfranchisement and other punishments, and have said that, while the object of the war was to enfranchise the Uitlanders, the result of the war would be to disfranchise the Boers, they ignore the fact, which they know perfectly well, that while for a period, which I hope may be brief, it is absolutely necessary that the country should be governed with large military forces present in it, yet we regard that as only a temporary situation, and one which we hope will be altered at the earliest possible moment. . . .

We remember what happened when the Transvaal was annexed on the last occasion; we remember how difficulties were created by military administration; we believe that there are difficulties essential to military administration, and that without in any way implying blame to the military authorities. But the military authorities are not trained for the purposes of civil administration, and certainly, in our opinion, at the very earliest moment civil administration must be set up, and a civil administration as opposed to a military administration is what we call crown colony government. But the fact that we establish such a government with a view to make the condition of the country as easy as possible, to make as few breaks as possible with the past, is not to be taken as an indication that the government will last for long, or indeed as any indication whatever on the subject. The question of the length of such an administration must depend on many circumstances which we now cannot anticipate, but especially, of course, on the way in which the Boers take to the new government which we shall set up. I am advised by those who, as I say, are most intimate with the country that it is the most improbable thing in the world that anything like continuous guerrilla warfare will be maintained, that it is not in the habits of the Boers at the present moment. . . .

In sitting down I can only say that, although I recognize the enormous difficulties of the task which has been imposed upon us, I am hopeful, I am sanguine, that we shall bring it to a successful conclusion if we have the clear, the undoubted support of the nation behind us. If we could have had the warm authoritative support of the Opposition in this House, that is what I would have been best pleased to have had; if we could have shown that there was absolutely no party in this country on the question, I firmly believe, as I am standing here, that the war would have been brought to a conclusion before now. I believe, and I have some evidence to justify it, that the hope of reaction has prolonged the war, just as in the earlier stages of the war the Boers were encouraged to greater efforts by the hope of intervention. There may be no ground for accusing anybody, but there is ground for wishing, in the interest of this country, that, at all events, we shall have substantially a unanimous House behind us, and substantially a unanimous people behind us, in the difficulties we have still to face.

DAVID LLOYD GEORGE **The Boer War Criticized (1900)**

Within a decade and a half, Lloyd George was to lead his country in a far greater war, but in 1900 the youthful Liberal M.P. from Wales was a mere Opposition backbencher. He takes pointed issue with Chamberlain on both the origins and the consequences of the war.

I think it is one of the most extraordinary speeches I have ever heard in this House. For my part, I rather admired it for what I would call its audacity. The right hon. Gentleman held up his hands in holy horror, and exclaimed that he could not imagine how anybody could regard his conduct with regard to South Africa with suspicion.... The history of the last four or five years in South Africa is simply one record of facts, each and every one of them affording good, solid, substantial ground for suspecting the attitude of the right hon. Gentleman in everything that he does in South Africa. . . .

Anybody who listened to his speech knows perfectly well that that speech had nothing whatever to do with South Africa. It was not a speech directed to South Africa, or having any connection with South Africa, and it was not intended to deal with the South African business. It was a speech intended purely for the hustings. It was an electioneering performance.... He is determined that this war should have one result—that is, a Chamberlain ministry in the next Parliament. That is electioneering; it is not statesmanship; and it is not the way to settle the peace of South Africa. The worst of the whole business is that these are the considerations that have directed his entire policy, instead of considerations of statesmanship and conciliation which

might have settled the whole thing without war. . . .

When you come to the effect of your policy in South Africa upon the empire at large, it is found to be most disastrous. We have been obliged to drop all those great proposals for domestic reform of which the right hon. Gentleman claimed to be the apostle. And when you come to consider how it has paralyzed the power and arms of Great Britain abroad the policy might very well be described in the phrase of the right hon. Gentleman himself as calamitous. One thing has struck me. Hon. and right hon. Gentlemen opposite are wont to congratulate themselves upon the fact that the European powers have not offered to intervene. But has it never occurred to them to consider what is the reason why those European powers which are hostile to us, who hate us, and are willing to strike a blow at the very existence of this empire, have not intervened and have not talked of intervening? . . . The reason is that the powers that hate and dislike us do not want to stop the terrible exhaustion of our power going on in South Africa. There is nothing that suits them better. . . .

The right hon. Gentleman . . . said that to talk of suffering was irrelevant. That is an extraordinary declaration to make. He said, "What is the loss of 8,000 men killed on the one side and 3,000 or 4,000 on the

SOURCE: From *Hansard's Parlimentary Debates*, 4th Series (July 25, 1900), Vol. 86, cols. 1200–1202, 1204–1212.

other; what is the maiming of 40,000 for life?—and that is only the beginning of it. All that is perfectly irrelevant!" Surely in a question of this kind the suffering undergone is more or less relevant. Does not the price you are to pay come in when you are considering whether you should go to war?

. . . It was because the right hon. Gentleman did not foresee what would happen, because he was misled by his own prejudices and prepossessions and by the men "who know the country" that he went into this terrible war in South Africa. I would ask the committee what is it we have gained by this war? . . . We entered into the war in order to establish equal rights between the white races in the Transvaal. That was the avowed, open, and declared object. How do we stand now, even according to the declaration of the colonial secretary? Equal rights! Not at all. The first thing is that you have got to conquer the territory, and that will take at least a year. And then there is to be a military occupation. Afterwards you will set up a Crown colony, which is to last according to the behavior of the Boers. But, taking the right hon. Gentleman's own previous declaration, this feud may last for generations. Does he believe that if he annexes these two republics he will restore peace and amity in ten or fifteen years, so that you can trust them with self-government? . . . He deprives everybody of votes, and governs that state by means of nominees of the crown. We started the war in order to obtain the franchise for everybody, and we end it with a franchise for nobody. It is true that you establish a kind of equality between the white races there, but it is not equal rights, but equal wrongs. . . .

If we had not gone into this wretched war, we would have had the franchise and equal rights in seven or ten years at the outside; and what would have been spared to humanity? Eight thousand and more of our own soldiers dead! And the worst of a war like this is, that it is not the guilty persons who are punished, but the innocent. I know not who is responsible for this war. President Kruger? It may be; but he is not the man to be punished. It may be the right

hon. Gentleman himself—as I believe—but he is not the man to be punished for it. What had these 8,000 British troops who had been killed done? What had the 450,000 men, women, and children who have been turned out of their homes and are roaming over the veldt in the Transvaal done? . . . If we had only waited with patience all would have come out well in five or ten years, and the suffering, the detestation, and the stain of the name of Great Britain would have been spared. (HON. MEMBERS: "Oh!") Yes, all that would have been saved. . . .

I ask hon. Members, will they venture to say that this war has re-established British prestige in South Africa or elsewhere? A force of 250,000 of the picked and trained men, not only of this country, but of the colonies, is required to crush 35,000 peasants. (HON. MEMBERS: "Oh!")

. . . British prestige has suffered, and no one will deny that this great war has done nothing more than to multiply grief and poverty. As for our military reverses, it is not for me to dwell upon them; but, at any rate, there is in them no restoring of prestige. I remember perfectly well the great cry at the last general election was "Support home industries," and the government, and above all, the minister who got his party into power on the prohibition of foreign brushes, is now engaged in the task of restoring British prestige with guns made in Germany, soldiers fed on French vegetables and South American meat, Hungarian horses provided with American saddles, and foreign fodder carried by Spanish mules. That is how we are restoring British prestige and the credit of the country. The fact is that this war was based on a gross miscalculation—upon a series of miscalculations.

The miscalculation was a miscalculation of statesmanship—a miscalculation as to the character, disposition, ideals, and tenacity of the men with whom we had to deal. And that miscalculation must rest entirely on the shoulders of the right hon. Gentleman himself. He has led us into two blunders. The first was the war. But worse than the war is the change that has been effected in the purpose for which we are prosecuting the war. We went into the war for equal rights; we are prosecuting it for annexation. . . .

It is exactly as if you had entered into a man's house to protect the children, and started to steal his plate. You entered into these two republics for philanthropic purposes, and remained to commit burglary. In changing the purpose of the war you have made a bad change. That is the impression you are creating abroad. Our critics say you are not going to war for equal rights and to establish fair play, but to get hold of the goldfields; and you have justified that criticism of our enemies by that change. But, worst of all, a change has been effected in the character of the war. Up to a certain point it was conducted with considerable chivalry, and, so far as war can be so conducted, with apparent good temper on both sides. A war of annexation, however, against a proud people must be a war of extermination, and that is unfortunately what it seems we are now committing ourselves to—burning homesteads and turning women and children out of their homes. . . .

JOHN A. HOBSON Imperialism: A Study (1902)

An economist and journalist by trade and a "left-wing" Liberal by political conviction, Hobson was motivated by the events in South Africa not only to condemn the Boer War but also to reexamine in a critical spirit what he considered to be the underlying basis of late-Victorian imperial expansion.

Seeing that the imperialism of the last six decades is clearly condemned as a business policy, in that at enormous expense it has procured a small, bad, unsafe increase of markets, and has jeopardized the entire wealth of the nation in rousing the strong resentment of other nations, we may ask, "How is the British nation induced to embark upon such unsound business?" The only possible answer is that the business interests of the nation as a whole are subordinated to those of certain sectional interests that usurp control of the national resources and use them for their private gain.

Although the new imperialism has been bad business for the nation, it has been good business for certain classes and certain trades within the nation. The vast expenditure on armaments, the costly wars, the grave risks and embarrassments of foreign policy, the checks upon political and social reforms within Great Britain, though fraught with great injury to the nation, have served well the present business interests of certain industries and professions. . . .

What is the direct economic outcome of imperialism? A great expenditure of public money upon ships, guns, military and naval equipment and stores, growing and productive of enormous profits when a war, or an alarm of war, occurs; new public loans and important fluctuations in the home and foreign bourses;[5] more posts for soldiers and sailors and in the diplomatic and consular services; improvement of foreign investments by the substitution of the British flag for a foreign flag; acquisition of markets for certain classes of exports and some protection and assistance for British trades in these manufactures; employment for engineers, missionaries, speculative miners, ranchers and other emigrants.

Certain definite business and professional interests feeding upon imperialistic

SOURCE: From J. A. Hobson, *Imperialism: A Study* (London: George Allen & Unwin, Ltd., 1938), pp. 46–61, 71, 80–83, 85, 88. (First published in 1902.) By permission of The University of Michigan Press.

[5]*bourses:* stock exchanges

expenditure, or upon the results of that expenditure, are thus set up in opposition to the common good and, instinctively feeling their way to one another, are found united in strong sympathy to support every new imperialist exploit.... Some ... , especially the shipbuilding, boilermaking and gun and ammunition making trades, are conducted by large firms with immense capital whose heads are well aware of the uses of political influence for trade purposes.

These men are imperialists by conviction; a pushful policy is good for them.

With them stand the great manufacturers for export trade who gain a living by supplying the real or artificial wants of the new countries we annex or open up. Manchester, Sheffield, Birmingham, to name three representative cases, are full of firms which compete in pushing textiles and hardware, engines, tools, machinery, spirits, guns, upon new markets. The public debts which ripen in our colonies, and in foreign countries that come under our protectorate or influence, are largely loaned in the shape of rails, engines, guns and other materials of civilization made and sent out by British firms. The making of railways, canals and other public works, establishment of factories, the development of mines, the improvement of agriculture in new countries, stimulate a definite interest in important manufacturing industries which feeds a very firm imperialist faith in their owners.

The proportion which such trade bears to the total industry of Great Britain is not great, but some of it is extremely influential and able to make a definite impression upon politics through chambers of commerce, parliamentary representatives and semi-political, semi-commercial bodies like the imperial South African Association or the China Society.

The shipping trade has a very definite interest which makes for imperialism. This is well illustrated by the policy of state subsidies now claimed by shipping firms as a retainer and in order to encourage British shipping for purposes of imperial safety and defense.

The services are, of course, imperialist by conviction and by professional interest and every increase of the army, navy and air force enhances the political power they exert.... To the military services we may add the Indian civil service and the numerous official and semi-official posts in our colonies and protectorates. Every expansion of the empire is also regarded by these same classes as affording new openings for their sons as ranchers, planters, engineers or missionaries.... From this standpoint our colonies still remain what James Mill cynically described them as being, "a vast system of outdoor relief for the upper classes."

In all the professions, military and civil, the army, diplomacy, the church, the bar, teaching and engineering, Greater Britain serves for an overflow, relieving the congestion of the home market and offering chances to more reckless or adventurous members, while it furnishes a convenient limbo for damaged characters and careers. ...

By far the most important economic factor in imperialism is the influence relating to investments.... In dealing with ... foreign investments we are facing the most important factor in the economics of imperialism. Whatever figures we take, two facts are evident. First, that the income derived as interest upon foreign investments enormously exceeded that derived as profits upon ordinary export and import trade. Secondly, that while our foreign and colonial trade, and presumably the income from it, were growing but slowly, the share of our import values representing income from foreign investments was growing very rapidly....

... The modern foreign policy of Great Britain has been primarily a struggle for profitable markets of investment. To a larger extent every year Great Britain has been becoming a nation living upon tribute from abroad, and the classes who enjoy this tribute have had an ever-increasing incentive to employ the public policy, the public purse and the public force to extend the field of their private investments and to safeguard and improve their existing investments. This is, perhaps, the most important fact in modern politics and the obscurity in which it is wrapped has constituted the gravest danger to our state.

What was true of Great Britain was true likewise of France, Germany, the United States and of all countries in which modern capitalism has placed large surplus savings in the hands of a plutocracy or of a thrifty middle class. . . .

[It is a] popular delusion that the use of national force to secure new markets by annexing fresh tracts of territory is a sound and a necessary policy for an advanced industrial country like Great Britain. It has indeed been proved that recent annexations of tropical countries, procured at great expense, have furnished poor and precarious markets, that our aggregate trade with our colonial possessions is virtually stationary, and that our most profitable and progressive trade is with rival industrial nations, whose territories we have no desire to annex, whose markets we cannot force, and whose active antagonism we are provoking by our expansive policy.

Overproduction in the sense of an excessive manufacturing plant, and surplus capital which could not find sound investments within the country, forced Great Britain, Germany, Holland, France to place larger and larger portions of their economic resources outside the area of their present political domain, and then stimulate a policy of political expansion so as to take in the new areas. . . .

The process, we may be told, is inevitable, and so it seems upon a superficial inspection. Everywhere appear excessive powers of production, excessive capital in search of investment. It is admitted by all business men that the growth of the powers of production in their country exceeds the growth in consumption, that more goods can be produced than can be sold at a profit, and that more capital exists than can find remunerative investment.

It is this economic condition of affairs that forms the taproot of imperialism. If the consuming public in this country raised its standard of consumption to keep pace with every rise of productive powers, there could be no excess of goods or capital clamorous to use imperialism in order to find markets. . . .

But it may be asked, "Why should there be any tendency to over-savings? Why should the owners of consuming power withhold a larger quantity for savings than can be serviceably employed?" Another way of putting the same question is this, "Why should not the pressure of present wants keep pace with every possibility of satisfying them?" The answer to these pertinent questions carries us to the broadest issue of the distribution of wealth. If a tendency to distribute income or consuming power according to needs were operative, it is evident that consumption would rise with every rise of producing power, for human needs are illimitable, and there could be no excess of saving. But it is quite otherwise in a state of economic society where distribution has no fixed relation to needs, but is determined by other conditions which assign to some people a consuming power vastly in excess of needs or possible uses, while others are destitute of consuming power enough to satisfy even the full demands of physical efficiency. . . .

The fallacy of the supposed inevitability of imperial expansion as a necessary outlet for progressive industry is now manifest. It is not industrial progress that demands the opening up of new markets and areas of investment, but maldistribution of consuming power which prevents the absorption of commodities and capital within the country. . . .

The struggle for markets, the greater eagerness of producers to sell than of consumers to buy, is the crowning proof of a false economy of distribution. Imperialism is the fruit of this false economy; "social reform" is its remedy. The primary purpose of "social reform," using the term in its economic signification, is to raise the wholesome standard of private and public consumption for a nation, so as to enable the nation to live up to its highest standard of production. . . .

13

Which Road Toward
the Welfare State: Socialist,
Conservative, or Liberal?

One of the central developments in British history during the first half of the twentieth century was the creation of the welfare state. A welfare state may be defined as a society that accords an important role to private and corporate enterprise while using the powers and revenues of the national government to assure minimum standards of well-being for the young, the old, the sick, the out-of-work, and those poor for yet other reasons. At the same time the state sets standards of safety, minimum wages, and maximum hours at the workplace and comparable standards of safety and reliability for foods and drugs, housing, and transportation. In Britain such developments would eventually reach fruition with Sir William Beveridge's reports during World War II and with the legislative measures of the 1945–1951 Labour Government (see Chapter 15).

But which group in British society was primarily responsible for altering mid-Victorian attitudes as to the proper limits of national government authority? Who did most—during the final years of the nineteenth century and the early years of the twentieth—to lay the philosophical and legislative foundations of the welfare state? Was it the late-Victorian and early-twentieth-century socialists, many of whom sought a revolutionary transformation of society, looking upon welfare state measures as half-way steps at best? Was it early twentieth-century Conservatives who, building on aristocratic notions of *noblesse oblige* and Disraeli's concept of "Tory Democracy," hoped to use the income from restored protective tariffs on imports to build a network of social services? Or was it the Edwardian Liberals who controlled British ministries between 1905 and 1915? Was it those Liberals who sought to build on their party's nineteenth-century tradition of expanding political, religious, and economic liberties by adding examples of "constructive" government in the form of a range of government social services and minimum standards? A survey of the readings in this chapter may suggest that no one group was responsible and that Britain's emerging welfare state was a curious hybrid, a development founded on no single social theory but on an amalgam of such theories as well as on *ad hoc* experimentation and political compromise.

The Philanthropic Highwayman

MR. LLOYD GEORGE. "I'll make 'em pity the aged poor!" (*Sambourne*, 1909)

The selections in this chapter can do little but sample the profusion of manifestos, reports, and appraisals by means of which a variety of Britons between the 1890s and the 1910s sought to cope with the subject of how to assure a minimum of social security for all without destroying either individual liberty and initiative or the productive enterprises within the nation that were, decade by decade, increasing its total wealth.

Robert Blatchford (1851–1943) was the most widely read of an array of late-Victorian socialist pioneers. In 1891 he founded the weekly *Clarion*. The first selection is an excerpt from a collection of articles drawn from that journal in 1893 under the title *Merrie England*; it sold more than a million copies within two years. What is Blatchford's professed purpose? Why did his readers presumably find his ideas appealing? Do some of his statements raise questions as well as provide answers? A somewhat different version of the socialist case was presented in 1896 by George Bernard Shaw (1856–1950), at that time just beginning a brilliant career as social critic and acerbic playwright. What claims for socialism does he make in his *Report on Fabian Policy?* How does he distinguish the members of the Fabian Society from other professed socialists (including Marxists)? What is the prime purpose of the Fabian Society? What are the limits of Fabian socialism as outlined by Shaw?

The dominant political party in Britain as the twentieth century began was not a socialist party (or even a Labour party) but the Unionist Party, an alliance of Conservatives and Liberal Unionists pledged to oppose Home Rule for Ireland. In 1903 one of the leaders of that party, Joseph Chamberlain (1836–1914), rocked the Unionist ministry then headed by Arthur J. Balfour by seeking to have his party and his country readopt the protective tariffs that Britain had abandoned half a century before. Which other types of social-reform legislation for the working classes does Chamberlain tie to the cause of tariff reform? How does the experience of other countries affect his argument? How does he respond to the criticism that tariff reform will raise the cost of living?

In the short run Chamberlain failed to convert fully either his party or his country, and the general election of 1906 brought electoral victory to the Liberal Party led by Sir Henry Campbell-Bannerman and (from 1908 on) Herbert Henry Asquith. Two of its most imaginative members were Winston Spencer Churchill (1874–1965) and David Lloyd George (1863–1945). Churchill, a convert from the Conservative Party of his father, had recently joined the Liberal ministry as under-secretary for the colonies when he made the speech at Glasgow on *Liberalism and Socialism* (1906). Afterward he was to serve as president of the board of trade, home secretary, and First Lord of the Admiralty in that same Liberal government. Does Churchill seem aware of the threat to the Liberal party posed by a separate Labour Party? What dangers does he foresee for working people if labourites were to replace liberals? What types of policies would he like the Liberal government to sponsor? In his judgment, should government be primarily "individualistic" or "collectivistic"? David Lloyd George, who became Liberal Chancellor of the Exchequer in 1908 and author of the controversial "People's Budget" in 1909, grew up at the shoemaker shop owned by his Welsh uncle rather than in the shadow of Blenheim Palace. Nevertheless, he expresses a philosophy very similar to that of Churchill in *The New Liberalism*, a speech he gave in Wales in 1908. Which parts of his speech appeal to nineteenth-century Liberal values? Which appeal to "the New Liberalism"?

It was under Liberal Party auspices that, between 1906 and 1914, many of the foundations of the welfare state were laid in the form of initiatives like old-age pensions, a graduated income tax, national health insurance for full-time workers, and a system of unemployment insurance. World War I (1914–1918) was to expand yet further the role of Britain's government in the economy and in the mandating of social services. The war would also gravely weaken the influence of the Liberal party and enhance the power of a Labour party committed to advancing socialist ideals.

ROBERT BLATCHFORD   **Merrie England (1893)**

The editor of a radical journal, The Clarion, *publicizes, praises, and promotes the doctrine of socialism in late Victorian England.* Merrie England, *a collection of articles from the journal, sold a million copies in just two years.*

John Smith, do you know what socialism is? You have heard it denounced many a time, and it is said that you do not believe in it; but do you know what it is?

Good or bad, wise or foolish, it is all I have to offer as a remedy of the many evils of which I have been complaining.

Good or bad, wise or foolish, socialism is the only remedy in sight. None of its opponents, none of your friends, the Members of Parliament, old trade union leaders, Tory and Liberal editors, parsons, priests, lawyers, and men of substance have any remedy to offer at all.

Some of them are sorry, or profess to be sorry, that there is much misery in the land; some of them offer a little mild charity, some a little feeble legislation, but there is no great radical cure to be heard of except socialism.

What is socialism? I am going to tell you, and I ask you to listen patiently, and to judge fairly. You have heard socialism reviled by speakers and writers. You know that the pope has denounced it, and that the bishop of Manchester has denounced it. You know that men like Herbert Spencer, Charles Bradlaugh, and John Morley have written and spoken against it, and doubtless you have got an idea that it is as unworthy, as unwise, and as unworkable as such men say it is. Now I will describe it for you and you shall draw your own conclusions.

But before I tell you what socialism is, I must tell you what socialism is not. For half our time as champions of socialism is wasted in denials of false descriptions of socialism; and to a large extent the anger, the ridicule, and the argument of the opponents of socialism are hurled against a socialism which has no existence except in their own heated minds.

Socialism does not consist in violently seizing upon the property of the rich and sharing it out amongst the poor.

Socialists do not propose by a single act of Parliament or by a sudden revolution, to put all men on an equality, and compel them to remain so. Socialism is not a wild dream of a happy land where the apples will drop off the trees into our open mouths, the fish come out of the rivers and fry themselves for dinner, and the looms turn out ready-made suits of velvet with gold buttons without the trouble of coaling the engine. Neither is it a dream of a nation of stained-glass angels, who never say damn, who always love their neighbors better than themselves, and who never need to work unless they wish to.

No. Socialism is none of these things. It is a scientific scheme of national government, entirely wise, just and practical. And now let us see.

For convenience sake, socialism is usually divided into two kinds. These are called—

1. Practical socialism.
2. Ideal socialism.

Really they are only part of one whole; practical socialism being a kind of preliminary step toward ideal socialism, so that we might with more reason call them elementary and advanced socialism.

I am an ideal socialist, and desire to have the whole socialist program carried out.

Practical socialism is so simple that a child may understand it. It is a kind of national scheme of co-operation, managed by the state. Its program consists, essentially, of one demand, that the land and other instruments of production shall be the com-

SOURCE: From Robert Blatchford, *Merrie England* (London, 1893), pp. 43–45.

mon property of the people, and shall be used and governed by the people for the people.

Make the land and all the instruments of production state property; put all farms, mines, mills, ships, railways, and shops under state control, as you have already put the postal and telegraphic services under state control, and practical socialism is accomplished.

The postal and telegraphic service is the standing proof of the capacity of the state to manage the public business with economy and success.

That which has been done with the post-offices may be done with mines, trams, railways, and factories.

The difference between socialism and the state of things now in existence will now be plain to you.

At present the land—that is, England—does not belong to the people—to the English—but to a few rich men. The mines, mills, ships, shops, canals, railways, houses, docks, harbors and machinery do not belong to the people, but to a few rich men.

Therefore, the land, the factories, the railways, ships, and machinery are not used for the general good of the people, but are used to make wealth for the few rich men who own them.

Socialists say that this arrangement is unjust and unwise, that it entails waste as well as misery, and that it would be better for all, even for the rich, that the land and other instruments of production should become the property of the state, just as the post-office and the telegraphs have become the property of the state.

Socialists demand that the state shall manage the railways and the mines and the mills just as it now manages the post-offices and the telegraphs.

Socialists declare that if it is wicked and foolish and impossible for the state to manage the factories, mines and railways, then it is wicked and foolish and impossible for the state to manage the telegraphs.

Socialists declare that as the state carries the people's letters and telegrams more cheaply and more efficiently than they were carried by private enterprise, so it could grow corn and weave cloth and work the railway systems more cheaply and more efficiently than they are now worked by private enterprise.

Socialists declare that as our government now makes food and clothing and arms and accoutrements for the army and navy and police, so it could make them for the people.

Socialists declare that as many [municipal] corporations make gas, provide and manage the water-supply, look after the paving and lighting and cleansing of the streets, and often do a good deal of building and farming, so there is no reason why they should not get coal and spin yarn, and make boots, and bread, and beer for the people.

Socialists point out that if all the industries of the nation were put under state control, all the profit which now goes into the hands of a few idle men, would go into the coffers of the state—which means that the people would enjoy the benefits of all the wealth they create.

This, then, is the basis of socialism, that England should be owned by the English, and managed for the benefit of the English, instead of being owned by a few rich idlers, and mismanaged by them for the benefit of themselves.

But socialism means more than the mere transference of the wealth of the nation to the nation.

Socialism would not endure competition. Where it found two factories engaged in under-cutting each other at the price of long hours and low wages to the workers, it would step in and fuse the two concerns into one, save an immense sum in cost of working, and finally produce more goods and better goods at a lower figure than were produced before.

But practical socialism would do more than that. It would educate the people. It would provide cheap and pure food. It would extend and elevate the means of study and amusement. It would foster literature and science and art. It would encourage and reward genius and industry. It would abolish sweating and jerry work. It would demolish the slums and erect good and handsome dwellings. It would compel all men to do some kind of useful work. It would recreate and nourish the craftsman's pride in his craft. It would protect women and children. It would raise the standard of health and morality; and it would take the sting out of pauperism by paying pensions to honest workers no longer able to work.

Why nationalize the land and instruments of production? To save waste; to save panics; to avert trade depressions, famines, strikes, and congestion of industrial cen-

ters; and to prevent greedy and unscrupulous sharpers from enriching themselves at the cost of the national health and prosperity. In short, to replace anarchy and war by law and order. To keep the wolves out of the fold, to tend and fertilize the field of labor instead of allowing the wheat to be strangled by the tares, and to regulate wisely the distribution of the seed-corn of industry so that it might no longer be scattered broadcast—some falling on rocks and some being eaten up by the birds of the air.

GEORGE BERNARD SHAW **Report on Fabian Policy (1896)**

Music critic, fledgling playwright, and a founding father of the Fabian Society, Shaw outlines the policies of this most literate of late-Victorian socialist organizations.

1. The Mission of the Fabians

The object of the Fabian Society is to persuade the English people to make their political constitution thoroughly democratic and so to socialize their industries as to make the livelihood of the people entirely independent of private capitalism.

The Fabian Society endeavors to pursue its socialist and democratic objects with complete singleness of aim. For example:

It has no distinctive opinions on the marriage question, religion, art, abstract economics, historic evolution, currency, or any other subject than its own special business of practical democracy and socialism.

It brings all the pressure and persuasion in its power to bear on existing forces, caring nothing by what name any party calls itself, or what principles, socialist or other, it professes, but having regard solely to the tendency of its actions, supporting those which make for socialism and democracy, and opposing those which are reactionary.

It does not propose that the practical steps toward social-democracy should be carried out by itself, or by any other specially organized society or party.

It does not ask the English people to join the Fabian Society.

II. Fabian Electoral Tactics

The Fabian Society does not claim to be the people of England, or even the Socialist Party, and therefore does not seek direct political representation by putting forward Fabian candidates at elections. But it loses no opportunity of influencing elections and inducing constituencies to select socialists as their candidates. . . .

III. Fabian Toleration

The Fabian Society, far from holding aloof from other bodies, urges its members to lose no opportunity of joining them and permeating them with Fabian ideas as far as possible. Almost all organizations and movements contain elements making for socialism, no matter how remote the sympathies and intentions of their founders may be from those of the socialists. On the other hand, unintentionally reactionary proposals are constantly being brought forward in socialist bodies. Fabians are there-

SOURCE: From Tract No. 70, *Report on Fabian Policy* (London, 1896).

fore encouraged to join all other organizations, socialist or nonsocialist, in which Fabian work can be done.

IV. Fabian Constitutionalism

The Fabian Society is perfectly constitutional in its attitude; and its methods are those usual in political life in England.

The Fabian Society accepts the conditions imposed on it by human nature and by the national character and political circumstances of the English people. It sympathizes with the ordinary citizen's desire for gradual, peaceful changes, as against revolutionary, conflict with the army and police, and martyrdom. . . .

V. Fabian Democracy

Democracy, as understood by the Fabian Society, means simply the control of the administration by freely elected representatives of the people. The Fabian Society energetically repudiates all conceptions of democracy as a system by which the technical work of government administration and the appointment of public officials, shall be carried on by referendum or any other form of direct popular decision. Such arrangements may be practical in a village community, but not in the complicated industrial civilizations which are ripening for social democracy. When the House of Commons is freed from the veto of the House of Lords and thrown open to candidates from all classes by an effective system of payment of representatives and a more rational method of election, the British parliamentary system will be, in the opinion of the Fabian Society, a first-rate practical instrument of democratic government.

Democracy, as understood by the Fabian Society, makes no political distinction between men and women.

VI. Fabian Compromise

The Fabian Society, having learnt from experience that socialists cannot have their own way in everything any more than other people, recognizes that in a democratic community compromise is a necessary condition of political progress.

VII. Fabian Socialism

Socialism, as understood by the Fabian Society, means the organization and conduct of the necessary industries of the country and the appropriation of all forms of economic rent of land and capital by the nation as a whole, through the most suitable public authorities, parochial, municipal, provincial, or central.

The socialism advocated by the Fabian Society is state socialism exclusively. . . . Since England now possesses an elaborate democratic state machinery, graduated from the parish council or vestry up to the central Parliament, and elected under a franchise which enables the working class vote to overwhelm all others, . . . the difficulty in England is not to secure more political power for the people, but to persuade them to make any sensible use of the power they already have.

VIII. Fabian Individualism

The Fabian Society does not suggest that the state should monopolize industry as against private enterprise or individual initiative further than may be necessary to make the livelihood of the people and their access to the sources of production completely independent of both. The freedom of individuals to test the social value of new inventions; to initiate improved methods of production; to anticipate and lead public enterprise in catering for new social wants; to practise all arts, crafts, and professions independently; in short, to complete the social organization by adding the resources of private activity and judgment to those of public routine, is, subject to the above conditions, as highly valued by the Fabian Society as freedom of speech, freedom of the press or any other article in the charter of popular liberties.

IX. Fabian Freedom of Thought

The Fabian Society strenuously maintains its freedom of thought and speech with regard to the errors of socialist authors, economists, leaders and parties, no less than to those of its opponents. For instance, it insists on the necessity of maintaining as critical an attitude toward Marx and Lassalle, some of whose views must by this time be discarded as erroneous or obsolete, as these eminent socialists themselves maintained toward their predecessors, St. Simon and Robert Owen.

X. Fabian Journalism

The Fabian Society, in its relations with the press, makes no such distinction as that indicated by the phrase "the Capitalist Press." In England all political papers without exception are conducted with private capital under the control of the owners of the capital. Some of them profess socialist opinions, other conservative opinions, others liberal and radical opinions, and so forth. The socialists papers are in no way more independent of social pressure than the others; and the superiority of a socialist paper from the socialist point of view is of exactly the same nature as the superiority of a conservative paper from the conservative point of view. The Fabian Society, in securing journalistic expression for its ideas, has no preference, except for the largest circulation.

XI. Fabians and the Middle Class

In view of the fact that the socialist movement has been hitherto inspired, instructed, and led by members of the middle class or "bourgeoisie," the Fabian Society though not at all surprised to find these middle class leaders attacking with much bitterness the narrow social ideals current in their own class, protests against the absurdity of socialists denouncing the very class from which socialism has sprung as specially hostile to it. The Fabian Society

has no romantic illusions as to the freedom of the proletariat from these same narrow ideals. Like every other socialist society, it can only educate the people in socialism by making them conversant with the conclusions of the most enlightened members of all classes. The Fabian Society, therefore, cannot reasonably use the words "bourgeoisie" or "middle class" as terms of reproach, more especially as it would thereby condemn a large proportion of its own members.

XII. Fabian Natural Philosophy

The Fabian Society endeavors to rouse social compunction by making the public conscious of the evil condition of society under the present system. This it does by the collection and publication of authentic and impartial statistical tracts, compiled, not from the works of socialists, but from official sources. . . . The Fabian Society . . . concludes that in the natural philosophy of socialism, light is a more important factor than heat.

XIII. Fabian Repudiations

The Fabian Society discards such phrases as "the abolition of the wage system," which can only mislead the public as to the aims of socialism. Socialism does not involve the abolition of wages, but the establishment of standard allowances for the maintenance of all workers by the community in its own service, as an alternative to wages fixed by the competition of destitute men and women for private employment, as well as to commercial profits, commissions, and all other speculative and competitive forms of remuneration. In short, the Fabian Society, far from desiring to abolish wages, wishes to secure them for everybody.

The Fabian Society resolutely opposes all pretentions to hamper the socialization of industry with equal wages, equal hours of labor, equal official status, or equal authority for everyone. Such conditions are not only impracticable, but incompatible with the equality of subordination to the common interest which is fundamental in modern socialism.

The Fabian Society steadfastly discountenances all schemes for securing to any person, or any group of persons "the entire product of their labor." It recognizes that wealth is social in its origin and must be social in its distribution, since the evolution of industry has made it impossible to distinguish the particular contribution that each person makes to the common product, or to ascertain its value.

The Fabian Society desires to offer all projectors and founders of utopian communities in South America, Africa, and other remote localities, its apologies for its impatience of such adventures. To such projectors, and all patrons of schemes for starting similar settlements and workshops at home, the society announces emphatically that it does not believe in the establishment of socialism by private enterprise.

XIV. Finally

The Fabian Society does not put socialism forward as a panacea for the ills of human society, but only for those produced by defective organization of industry and by a radically bad distribution of wealth.

JOSEPH CHAMBERLAIN **Tariff Reform and Unemployment (1904)**

In 1903 Joseph Chamberlain launched the last great political crusade of his career. He sought to persuade both his party and his country that, after an interval of half a century, Britain's government should once again guard the nation's and the empire's economy by instituting a policy of protective tariffs. In a speech given in December 1904 to an audience of poor London workers, Chamberlain seeks to persuade them that they would be the greatest beneficiaries of such tariff reform.

I am very grateful to those who have organized this meeting, and to you who have attended it, for giving me an opportunity of addressing representatives of the working classes in the East of London. This is a district in which the condition of the majority of the people is certainly very hard, in which the margin of subsistence is very small. . . . [I] come amongst you because I believe in my heart and conscience that the greatest evil from which you suffer is the antiquated policy of our fiscal system. . . .

I venture to assert that the most retrograde Tory in the most retrograde of times never committed himself to such an insane policy of stagnation as has now been accepted by the party which calls itself Radical, which professes to be the party of progress, in regard to a dogma which it treats as sacred and inspired, but which history and experience have already discredited.

But if the probabilities are in my favor, so are the facts. What has happened in that interval of sixty years? One by one every civilized nation, every civilized state, including the great democratic nation which dominates on the other side of the Atlantic, including every colony under the British flag—one by one they have rejected this extreme doctrine of free trade or of free imports. One by one they have found it wanting; and we alone remain still adhering to this old superstition. . . .

It is not a question of whether we are richer now than we were fifty years ago or a thousand years ago. It is a question which of us in the race for existence, that has been going on ever since the world began, is pro-

SOURCE: Excerpts from "Tariff Reform and Unemployment" in Charles W. Boyd, ed., *Mr. Chamberlain's Speeches* (Boston, 1914), Vol. II, pp. 257–270.

gressing more rapidly, and which of us is going further.

The doctrine of Mr. Cobden[1] was a consistent doctrine. His view was that there should be no interference by the state in our domestic concerns. He believed that individuals should be left to themselves to make the best of their abilities and circumstances, and that there should be no attempt to equalize the conditions of life and happiness. To him, accordingly, protection of labor was quite as bad as protection of trade. To him a trade union was worse than a landlord. To him all factory legislation was as bad as the institution of tariffs. That is a consistent doctrine. I am not arguing now whether it was right or wrong, but it was upon the basis of that doctrine that we had imposed upon us our present fiscal system by a Parliament which, in those days, was not in the slightest degree representative of the majority of the country, and above all of the working classes.

Now, it cannot be denied that all parties have given up these harsh theories. We now no longer think that we ought to leave human beings like ourselves, born into the world for no fault of their own, to struggle against the overpowering pressure of circumstances. We do not believe in the theory of every one for himself and the devil take the hindmost. Accordingly, we have for years been engaged in considering—I think I may say without conceit no one more seriously than myself—these questions of social reform. Now, note something. During the last thirty or fifty years there has been a great deal of what is called social legislation. By whom has it been promoted? By the Conservative Party, and latterly by the Unionist Party. You owe all your factory legislation to Lord Shaftesbury as its originator. You owe to the Unionist Party free education, and that provision for allotments and small holdings which has,

at all events, secured for the laborers in the country something like 100,000 holdings which they had not before. You owe to us compensation for workmen in the case of accidents during the course of their business. Now, why is that? I do not pretend that the Liberal or Radical Party, either now or formerly, are or have been less anxious to do good—less philanthropic, or less considerate for the poor than we are; but they have been prevented from taking this course by the theories by which they have been governed. All this legislation is inconsistent with what they call free trade. You must no more interfere to raise the standard of living, to raise the wages of working men, than you must interfere to raise the price of goods or the profits of manufacturers. . . .

Let me give you an illustration. I was myself concerned largely in the act which gave compensation for accidents.[2] I got very little help from the other side while that measure was passing. On the contrary, if they did not openly oppose it, they did everything they could to embarrass me in the work of carrying it out and to delay its operation. . . . Since then it has been extended with universal consent, and I shall not be satisfied until it is extended to every class of labor throughout the country. But it cannot stand alone. By that act what is it we do? We put upon the employer everywhere an additional obligation. We add thereby to his cost of production. We put him at a disadvantage with his foreign competitor, who has no such legislation. Now, if we do not make a balance somehow or another, one of two things will happen. Either the working classes of this country will have to accept lower wages in proportion to the extra cost which has been put upon the manufacturer, or else they will lose their employment. Trade will go to those foreign countries which are not troubled by any of these hu-

---

[1]*Richard Cobden (1804–1865):* the cofounder of the Anti–Corn Law League of the 1830s and 1840s, here presented by Chamberlain (somewhat misleadingly) as the symbol of mid-Victorian laissez-faire capitalism   [2]*the act . . . accidents:* Chamberlain's Workmen's Compensation Act (1897), which made business proprietors financially responsible for the costs of accidents that befell employees at the workplace

manitarian considerations. This attempt of ours to protect the weak, to raise the general standard of living, to regulate the conditions of trade in the interest of the working men—it is very good; but—take this to heart—remember that it is inconsistent with free trade. You cannot have free trade in goods in the sense in which our opponents use the word, and at the same time have protection of labor.

What is the experience of the world? Take the United States of America: take our own colonies. . . . You will not find, I believe, a single man of influence or importance, whether among the manufacturing classes or amongst the working men of America and the colonies, who will not tell you that the principle of a tariff is part of a system for the elevation of the working classes, and that if they adopted our policy of free imports it would absolutely be impossible for them to maintain the high level of general prosperity to which they have attained.

Take the case of Germany. . . . Whether at the present moment the German workman is better off than our workman or not is an open question. But what is not an open question, what is certain, is that the progress of the German workman, since a tariff was adopted in that country under the strong influence of Prince Bismarck, has been much greater, quicker, and more evident than the progress of the working man in this country. . . .

You are suffering from the unrestricted imports of cheaper goods. You are suffering also from the unrestricted immigration of the people who make these goods. . . .

The evils of this immigration have increased during recent years. And behind those people who have already reached these shores, remember there are millions of the same kind who, under easily conceivable circumstances, might follow in their track, and might invade this country in a way and to an extent of which few people have at present any conception. The same causes that brought ten thousand and twenty thousand, and tens of thousands, may bring hundreds of thousands, or even millions. . . .

Now a word as to the [immigrants] themselves. I, for one, am not going to press hardly upon these poor people.[3] They have been driven from their homes by the pressure of want, by the grossest and the most brutal persecution, and I think they are subjects for pity and for practical sympathy. The problem is how are they to be saved from the fate which is befalling them, how is their salvation to be accomplished without the ruin of our own people at home?

They come here—I do not blame them, I am speaking of the results—they come here and change the whole character of a district. The speech, the nationality, of whole streets has been altered; and British workmen have been driven by the fierce competition of famished men from trades which they previously followed. I ask you, is it good for the people themselves that they should be tempted to come here? Is it good for men to be herded together like beasts in a pen, to starve upon a few pence a day, doled out to them by employers who seem to be deficient in the bowels of compassion? I say it is bad for you, that it is bad for them; and so far as I am concerned I have always been, and I am now, in favor of giving to the Executive Government the strongest power of control over this alien immigration.[4]

But the party of free imports is against any reform. How could they be otherwise? If they were openly to admit that the policy which I recommend ought to be adopted, they would be giving up their whole theory. Where would Mr. Cobden be? Where would the doctrine of free imports be? Where would the doctrine of cheap goods be? They are perfectly consistent. If sweated goods are to be allowed in this country without restriction, why not the people who make

---

[3]*these poor people:* Mostly Jews fleeing the Russian Empire   [4]*Control . . . immigration:* In 1905 the Unionist (Conservative) government passed an Aliens Act that placed limited restrictions on the tradition of political asylum in Britain.

them? Where is the difference? There is no difference either in the principle or in the results. It all comes to the same thing—less labor for the British working man. This alien problem is only part of a greater problem—the problem of the employment of our people. . . .

This matter is very much in your own hands. You are the judges. You are Caesar to whom I appeal. If your verdict goes against me, I have nothing but to submit; and if you think, all of you, that you are as well off as you ought to be, if you think that your condition cannot be improved, if you believe that all is well with you, and that all these tales we hear of people being on the verge of hunger, of people unemployed seeking for work, of people who are starving in the midst of plenty—if you believe that all these are idle fancies of mistaken philanthropists, then, gentlemen, it is I who wish you to vote against me. If you are happy, I am quite content that you should leave well alone. But if, on the contrary, you find that somehow or another this apparent prosperity shown by the figures is not represented in the actual condition of the people, then try with me to see if you can find out the reason. Now, what is the reason? I think that a great change is going on in the condition of trade in this country. . . . Whereas at one time England was the greatest manufacturing country, now its people are more and more employed in finance, in distribution, in domestic service, and in other occupations of the same kind. That state of things is consistent with ever-increasing wealth. It may mean more money, but it means less men. It may mean more wealth, but it means less welfare; and I think it is worth while to consider—whatever its immediate effects may be—whether that state of things will not be the destruction ultimately of all that is best in England, all that has made us what we are, all that has given us our prestige and power in the world. . . .

I have tried in what I have said to you to force you to see that this is not, as our opponents say, a rich man's question. I have never been able to see how a rich man—a man already rich—would be materially benefited by my policy. Of course, if the whole country profited, I suppose he would profit in a like manner. But as he would probably have to pay more for his luxuries, I think it is possible he would lose more than he would gain. But to the working man it is life and death. . . .

But, I am told, "You will increase the cost of living." Well, suppose I did; which is the better for a working man—to have a loaf a farthing[5] dearer and plenty of money in his pocket, or to have a loaf for twopence or threepence and no money to buy it? Therefore I am not afraid of that argument. I would be willing for the sake of argument, although I believe it to be utterly untrue, to argue the question on the assumption that there was going to be a trifling rise in the cost of living, because I should say, "You are sensible men, you will do what everybody else would do in similar circumstances—you will draw a balance, you will not mind paying more if you get more in proportion." In my view the cost of living is not the most important thing for the working man to consider. What he has to consider as most important to him is the price which he gets for his labor.

But, gentlemen, do not be deceived; it so happens that all that I want for the purposes of this crusade does not involve a farthing's increased cost of living to any working man. All that it requires is a scientific, a reasonable transposition of taxation. A government has to take out of the pockets even of the poorest of working men a certain amount of money. I am not going to increase that amount, but it is possible that I may take it out of one pocket rather than out of the other. He has to bear the burden in any case; I may put it on his right shoulder instead of on his left. That is the whole of the change which I propose in the taxation of this country. . . .

---

[5]*farthing:* a fourth of a penny

WINSTON S. CHURCHILL **Liberalism and Socialism (1906)**

Churchill, a junior member of the Liberal government that had taken office the year before, discusses the meaning of both "liberalism" and "socialism" and goes on to outline the tasks that lie ahead for Britain's Liberal party.

The fortunes and the interests of liberalism and labor are inseparably interwoven; they rise by the same forces, and in spite of similar obstacles, they face the same enemies, they are affected by the same dangers, and the history of the last thirty years shows quite clearly that their power of influencing public affairs and of commanding national attention fluctuate together. Together they are elevated, together they are depressed, and any Tory reaction which swept the Liberal Party out of power would assuredly work at least proportionate havoc in the ranks of labor. That may not be a very palatable truth, but it is a truth none the less.

Labor! It is a great word. It moves the world, it comprises the millions, it combines many men in many lands in the sympathy of a common burden. Who has the right to speak for labor? A good many people arrogate to themselves the right to speak for labor. How many political flibbertigibbets are there not running up and down the land calling themselves the people of Great Britain, and the social democracy, and the masses of the nation! But I am inclined to think, so far as any body of organized opinion can claim the right to speak for this immense portion of the human race, it is the trade unions that more than any other organization must be considered the responsible and deputed representatives of labor. They are the most highly organized part of labor! they are the most responsible part; they are from day to day in contact with reality. They are not mere visionaries or dreamers weaving airy utopias out of tobacco smoke....

The fortunes of the trade unions are interwoven with the industries they serve. The more highly organized trade unions are, the more clearly they recognize their responsibilities; the larger their membership, the greater their knowledge, the wider their outlook. Of course, trade unions will make mistakes, like everybody else, will do foolish things, and wrong things, and want more than they are likely to get, just like everybody else. But the fact remains that for thirty years trade unions have had a charter from Parliament which up to within a few years ago protected their funds, and gave them effective power to conduct a strike; and no one can say that these thirty years were bad years of British industry, that during these thirty years it was impossible to develop great business and carry on large manufacturing operations, because, as everybody knows perfectly well, those were good and expanding years of British trade and national enrichment.

A few years ago a series of judicial decisions utterly changed the whole character of the law regarding trade unions.[6] It became difficult and obscure. The most skilful lawyers were unable to define it.... We have determined to give back that charter to the trade unions. The bill is even now passing through the House of Commons.

We are often told that there can be no progress for democracy until the Liberal Party has been destroyed. Let us examine that. Labor in this country exercises a great influence upon the government. That is not so everywhere. It is not so, for instance, in Germany, and yet in Germany there is no Liberal party worth speaking of. Labor there

SOURCE: From a speech at Glasgow, October 11, 1906, reprinted in Robert Rhodes James, ed., *The Complete Speeches of Winston Churchill* (New York: Chelsea House Publishers, 1974), pp. 673–677.

[6]*judicial decisions:* refers primarily to the Taff Vale Railway decision of 1901

is very highly organized, and the Liberal party there has been destroyed. In Germany there exists exactly the condition of affairs, in a party sense, that Mr. Keir Hardie and his friends are so anxious to introduce here. A great social democratic party on the one hand, are bluntly and squarely face to face with a capitalist and military confederation on the other. That is the issue, as it presents itself in Germany, that is the issue, as I devoutly hope it may never present itself here. And what is the result? In spite of the great numbers of the Socialist Party in Germany, in spite of the high ability of its leaders, it has hardly any influence whatever upon the course of public affairs. It has to submit to food taxes and to conscription; and I observe that Herr Bebel, the distinguished leader of that party, at Mannheim the other day was forced to admit, and admitted with great candor, that there was no other country in Europe so effectively organized as Germany to put down anything in the nature of a violent socialist movement. That is rather a disquieting result to working men of having destroyed the Liberal party.

But we are told to wait a bit; the Socialist party in Germany is only three millions. How many will there be in ten years' time? That is a fair argument. I should like to say this. A great many men can jump four feet, but very few can jump six feet. After a certain distance the difficulty increases progressively. . . .

In France, before the Revolution, property was divided among a very few people. A few thousand nobles and priests and merchants had all the wealth in the country; twenty-five million peasants had nothing. But in modern states, such as we see around us in the world to-day, property is very widely divided. I do not say it is evenly divided. I do not say it is fairly divided, but it is very widely divided. Especially is that true in Great Britain. Nowhere else in the world, except, perhaps, in France and the United States, are there such vast numbers of persons who are holders of interest-bearing, profit-bearing, rent-earning property, and the whole tendency of civilization and

of free institutions is to an ever-increasing volume of production and an increasingly wide diffusion of profit. And therein lies the essential stability of modern states. There are millions of persons who would certainly lose by anything like a general overturn, and they are everywhere the strongest and best organized millions. And I have no hesitation in saying that any violent movement would infallibly encounter an overwhelming resistance, and that any movement which was inspired by mere class prejudice, or by a desire to gain a selfish advantage, would encounter from the selfish power of the "haves" an effective resistance which would bring it to sterility and to destruction.

And here is the conclusion to which I lead you. Something more is needed if we are to get forward. There lies the function of the Liberal party. Liberalism supplies at once the higher impulse and the practicable path; it appeals to persons by sentiments of generosity and humanity; it proceeds by courses of moderation. By gradual steps, by steady effort from day to day, from year to year, Liberalism enlists hundreds of thousands upon the side of progress and popular democratic reform whom militant socialism would drive into violent Tory reaction. That is why the Tory party hate us. . . . The cause of the Liberal party is the cause of the left-out millions; and because we believe that there is in all the world no other instrument of equal potency and efficacy available at the present time for the purposes of social amelioration, we are bound in duty and in honor to guard it from all attacks, whether they arise from violence or from reaction.

There is no necessity to-night to plunge into a discussion of the philosophical divergencies between socialism and liberalism. It is not possible to draw a hard-and-fast line between individualism and collectivism. You cannot draw it either in theory or in practice. That is where the socialist makes a mistake. Let us not imitate that mistake. No man can be a collectivist alone or an individualist alone. He must be both an individualist and a collectivist. The nature of man is a dual nature. The character of the organization of human society is dual. Man is at once a unique being and a gregarious animal. For some purposes he must be collectivist, for others he is, and he will for all time remain, an individualist. Collectively we have an army and a navy and a civil service; collectively we have a post office, and a police, and a government; collectively we light our streets and supply ourselves with water; collectively we indulge increasingly in all the necessities of communication. But we do not make love collectively, and the ladies do not marry us collectively, and we do not eat collectively, and we do not die collectively, and it is not collectively that we face the sorrows and the hopes, the winnings and the losings of this world of accident and storm.

No view of society can possibly be complete which does not comprise within its scope both collective organization and individual incentive. The whole tendency of civilization is, however, towards the multiplication of the collective functions of society. The evergrowing complications of civilization create for us new services which have to be undertaken by the state, and create for us an expansion of the existing services. There is a growing feeling, which I entirely share, against allowing those services which are in the nature of monopolies to pass into private hands. There is a pretty steady determination, which I am convinced will become effective in the present Parliament, to intercept all future unearned increment which may arise from the increase in the speculative value of the land. There will be an ever-widening area of municipal enterprise. I go further; I should like to see the state embark on various novel and adventurous experiments. I am delighted to see that Mr. Burns is now interesting himself in afforestation. I am of opinion that the state should increasingly assume the position of the reserve employer of labor. I am very sorry we have not got the railways of this country in our hands. We may do something better with the canals, and we are all agreed, every one in this hall who belongs to the Progressive

Party, that the state must increasingly and earnestly concern itself with the care of the sick and the aged, and, above all, of the children.

I look forward to the universal establishment of minimum standards of life and labor, and their progressive elevation as the increasing energies of production may permit. I do not think that Liberalism in any circumstances can cut itself off from this fertile field of social effort, and I would recommend you not to be scared in discussing any of these proposals, just because some old woman comes along and tells you they are socialistic. If you take my advice, you will judge each case on its merits. Where you find that state enterprise is likely to be ineffective, then utilize private enterprises, and do not grudge them their profits.

The existing organization of society is driven by one mainspring—competitive selection. It may be a very imperfect organization of society, but it is all we have got between us and barbarism. It is all we have been able to create through unnumbered centuries of effort and sacrifice. It is the whole treasure which past generations have been able to secure, and which they have been able to bequeath: and great and numerous as are the evils of the existing condition of society in this country, the advantages and achievements of the social system are greater still. Moreover, that system is one which offers an almost indefinite capacity for improvement. We may progressively eliminate the evils; we may progressively augment the goods which it contains. I do not want to see impaired the vigor of competition, but we can do much to mitigate the consequences of failure. We want to draw a line below which we will not allow persons to live and labor, yet above which they may compete with all the strength of their manhood. We want to have free competition upward: we decline to allow free competition to run downward. We do not want to pull down the structures of science and civilization; but to spread a net over the abyss; and I am sure that if the vision of a fair utopia which cheers the hearts and lights the imagination of the toiling multitudes, should ever break into reality, it will be by developments through, and modifications in, and by improvements out of, the existing competitive organization of society; and I believe that Liberalism mobilized, and active as it is to-day, will be a principal and indispensable factor in that noble evolution.

DAVID LLOYD GEORGE   The New Liberalism (1908)

One of the leading members of the pre–World War I Liberal government was David Lloyd George, who became Chancellor of the Exchequer in 1908. In the following speech, delivered on October 1 of that year at Swansea, Wales, he outlines the tasks of "the New Liberalism."

What is the work still waiting the Liberal Party in this country? It is to establish complete religious equality in our institutions. There is no religious equality so long as men of capacity and character are debarred from competing for teacherships in 14,000 state schools because they cannot conscientiously conform to the doctrines of some dominant sect. There is no religious equality as long as one sect whose dogmas, in Wales at any rate, are repudiated by the vast majority of the people, is able to pose as the official exponent of the faith of the Welsh people, and to enjoy all the privileges, emoluments, and endowments attached to that position. I place the establishment of complete religious equality in the forefront, because it lies in the domain of conscience . . . and nothing can save a people afflicted by such institutions from the spirit of bondage but an incessant protest against them. . . .

The same observations apply to the question of civil equality. We have not yet attained it in this country—far from it. You will not have established it in this land until the child of the poorest parent shall have the same opportunity for receiving the best education as the child of the richest. . . . It will never be established so long as you have five hundred men nominated by the lottery of birth to exercise the right of thwarting the wishes of the majority of forty millions of their countrymen in the determination of the best way of governing the country. I hope no prospect of a temporary material advantage will blind the people of this country to the permanent good for them of vindicating in the laws and institutions of the land these great principles, which lie at the root of freedom and good government for the people.

On the other hand, I think there is a danger that Liberals may imagine that their task begins and ends there. If they do so, then they will not accomplish even that task.

British Liberalism is not going to repeat the fate of continental liberalism. The fate of continental liberalism should warn them of that danger. It has been swept on one side before it had well begun its work, because it refused to adapt itself to new conditions. The liberalism of the continent concerned itself exclusively with mending and perfecting the machinery which was to grind corn for the people. It forgot that the people had to live whilst the process was going on, and people saw their lives pass away without anything being accomplished. British Liberalism has been better advised. It has not abandoned the traditional ambition of the Liberal Party to establish freedom and equality; but side by side with this effort it promotes measures for ameliorating the conditions of life for the multitude.

The old Liberals in this country used the natural discontent of the people with the poverty and precariousness of the means of subsistence as a motive power to win for them a better, more influential, and more honorable status in the citizenship of their native land. The new Liberalism, while pur-

SOURCE: From David Lloyd George, *Better Times* (London, 1910), pp. 49–54.

suing this great political ideal with unflinching energy, devotes a part of its endeavor also to the removing of the immediate causes of discontent. It is true that men cannot live by bread alone. It is equally true that a man cannot live without bread. . . . It is a recognition of that elemental fact that has promoted legislation like the Old-Age Pensions Act. It is but the beginning of things. . . . Poverty is the result of a man's own misconduct or misfortune. In so far as he brings it on himself, the state cannot accomplish much. It can do something to protect him. In so far as poverty is due to circumstances over which the man has no control, then the state should step in to the very utmost limit of its resources, and save the man from the physical and mental torture involved in extreme penury. . . . The aged we have dealt with during the present session. We are still confronted with the more gigantic task of dealing with the rest—the sick, the infirm, the unemployed, the widows, and the orphans. No country can lay any real claim to civiliza-tion that allows them to starve. Starvation is a punishment that society has ceased to inflict for centuries on its worst criminals, and at its most barbarous stage humanity never starved the children of the criminal. . . . Is it just, is it fair, is it humane, to let them suffer privation? I do not think the better-off classes, whose comfort is assured, realize the sufferings of the unemployed workmen. What is poverty? Have you felt it yourselves? If not, you ought to thank God for having been spared its sufferings and temptations. Have you ever seen others enduring it? Then pray God to forgive you if you have not done your best to alleviate it. By poverty I mean real poverty, not the cutting down of your establishment, not the limitation of your luxuries. I mean the poverty of the man who does not know how long he can keep a roof over his head, and where he will turn to find a meal for the pinched and hungry little children who look to him for sustenance and protection. That is what unemployment means.

14

British Involvement
in World War I: Honor or Error?

By general consensus, the year 1914 remains a watershed in the history not merely of Britain but of much of the world. It was in August of that year that a century of peace—or at least a century free from all-out conflict among alliances of major powers—gave way to four years of unprecedented bloodshed and destruction. Britain was the last of five major powers—Germany, Austria-Hungary, Russia and France were the others—to be drawn into war in late July and early August. The cabinet that formally led Britain into that conflict was a Liberal one headed by Prime Minister Herbert Henry Asquith (1852–1928). The speech that did most to persuade the House of Commons that it would be altogether proper for Britain to become involved in the war on the anti-German side was given by Sir Edward Grey, "Statement to the House of Commons, August 3, 1914." Grey (1862–1933) had served as secretary of state for foreign affairs since 1905. Although half of the members of Asquith's cabinet, including David Lloyd George, briefly played with the notion of opposing British involvement, ultimately only two resigned from the cabinet on the issue, John Burns and John Morley (1838–1923). Morley, a veteran journalist and biographer, had served in Gladstone's later cabinets and had been secretary of state for India in the Asquith cabinet. Morley's account of the events that led to his decision to leave the cabinet, his "Memorandum on Resignation" (1914), was not to be published until several years after his death. Three days after Grey's speech and Morley's resignation—and after Germany had invaded Belgium and Britain had declared war—Asquith himself publicly upheld his government's actions in a statement to the House of Commons, "Justification for War."

On what grounds does Grey condemn a policy of neutrality for Britain? On what grounds does Morley justify such a policy? How do Grey and Morley differ on the subject of the obligations that Britain owes to France? What are the underlying premises of Grey's argument? Is he primarily guided by considerations of national interest or of national honor? Was concern for the neutrality of Belgium of central importance to most British policymakers or was it a secondary issue that did, however, play a vital role in persuading the undecided?

Differences of opinion with regard to Britain's involvement in World War I did not end with Britain's declaration of war on August 4, 1914.

At The Post of Honour

LIBERTY (*to* BELGIUM). "Take comfort. Your courage is vindicated; your wrongs shall be avenged."

(*Punch*, September 2, 1914)

Some Britons, like poet Siegfried Sassoon (1886–1967), welcomed the war when it began and gladly volunteered for service in the British Army. As the years of trench warfare dragged on in France on the Western Front, however, Sassoon became deeply disenchanted. How do his later poems differ from "France"? Which aspects of trench warfare do his poems emphasize? Do the poems suggest that a gulf had opened between the mental world of soldiers and that of civilian war leaders? Sassoon served in France for more than two years and won a Military Cross for bravery before he was wounded in action and sent home. A diagnosis of "shell shock" caused him to be confined for a time in Craiglockhart War Hospital near Edinburgh; there he composed the final poem in this selection. Sassoon returned to the battlefront in 1918; he was wounded a second time, but he survived the war by four decades. Although he is remembered primarily as a "war poet," he afterward preferred to look back nostalgically on pre-1914 English countryhouse life in books like *Memoirs of a Fox-Hunting Man* (1928).

Other Britons opposed the war from the start. They worked for a negotiated peace, and they resisted military service as conscientious objectors. One of the most prominent objectors to the war was the mathematician and philosopher Bertrand Russell (1872–1970). He appraises the problems that the war resisters faced in *Reflections on Pacifism in Wartime* (1935). Although Russell wrote the essay almost two decades later, in the midst of an era of "appeasement," he evokes the conflicting attitudes of those who opposed the national war effort in his own masterly prose style.

While the war was going on, many of Britain's writers considered it their prime duty to justify Britain's role both to their own countrymen and to the citizens of allied or potentially allied countries. Such a work is *England's Effort: Letters to an American Friend* (1916) by the Victorian novelist, Mary Augusta Ward, who wrote under the name of Mrs. Humphry Ward (1851–1920). At the time she wrote, the United States was still neutral.

How widespread does the internal British resistance to war appear to have been? On what assumptions was such resistance based? How do Russell and Ward differ in their attitudes toward Germany? What does Russell see as the most unfortunate intellectual consequence of war? What aspects of war does Ward consider essentially positive and even constructive?

SIR EDWARD GREY **Statement to the House of Commons (August 3, 1914)**

During the week before Britain's foreign secretary spoke, the international order had crumbled. Austria had declared war on Serbia, and Germany and Russia had declared war on each other. Germany had also threatened war on Russia's ally France, unless the latter pledged strict neutrality. Grey's purpose is to set Britain's commitments in a historical context and to put forward his government's course.

Last week I stated that we were working for peace not only for this country, but to preserve the peace of Europe. To-day events move so rapidly that it is exceedingly difficult to state with technical accuracy the actual state of affairs, but it is clear that the peace of Europe cannot be preserved. Russia and Germany, at any rate, have declared war upon each other.

Before I proceed to state the position of His Majesty's [George V's] government, I would like to clear the ground so that, with regard to the present crisis, the House may know exactly under what obligations the government is, or the House can be said to be, in coming to a decision on the matter. First of all let me say, very shortly, that we have consistently worked with a single mind, with all the earnestness in our power, to preserve peace. The House may be satisfied on that point. We have always done it. During these last years, as far as His Maj-

SOURCE: From *Hansard's Parliamentary Debates*, 5th Series, Vol. LXV, cols. 1809–1827.

esty's government are concerned, we would have no difficulty in proving that we have done so. Throughout the Balkan crisis,[1] by general admission, we worked for peace. The co-operation of the Great Powers of Europe was successful in working for peace in the Balkan crisis. It is true that some of the powers had great difficulty in adjusting their points of view. It took much time and labor and discussion before they could settle their differences, but peace was secured, because peace was their main object, and they were willing to give time and trouble rather than accentuate differences rapidly.

In the present crisis, it has not been possible to secure the peace of Europe; because there has been little time, and there has been a disposition—at any rate in some quarters on which I will not dwell—to force things rapidly to an issue, at any rate, to the great risk of peace, and, as we now know, the result of that is that the policy of peace, as far as the Great Powers generally are concerned, is in danger. I do not want to dwell on that, and to comment on it, and to say where the blame seems to us to lie, which powers were most in favor of peace, which were most disposed to risk or endanger peace, because I would like the House to approach this crisis in which we are now, from the point of view of British interests, British honor, and British obligations, free from all passion, as to why peace has not been preserved. . . .

I come first, now, to the question of British obligations. I have assured the House—and the prime minister has assured the House more than once—that if any crisis such as this arose, we should come before the House of Commons and be able to say to the House that it was free to decide what the British attitude should be, that we would have no secret engagement which we should spring upon the House, and tell the House that, because we had entered into that engagement, there was an obliga-

tion of honor upon the country. I will deal with that point to clear the ground first.

There has been in Europe two diplomatic groups, the Triple Alliance and what came to be called the "Triple *Entente*," for some years past. The Triple *Entente* was not an alliance—it was a diplomatic group. . . .

In this present crisis, up till yesterday, we have also given no promise of anything more than diplomatic support—up till yesterday no promise of more than diplomatic support. Now I must make this question of obligation clear to the House. I must go back to the first Moroccan crisis of 1906. That was the time of the Algeciras Conference, and it came at a time of very great difficulty to his Majesty's government when an election was in progress, and ministers were scattered over the country, and I—spending three days a week in my constituency and three days at the foreign office—was asked the question whether if that crisis developed into war between France and Germany we would give armed support. I said then that I could promise nothing to any foreign power unless it was subsequently to receive the whole-hearted support of public opinion here if the occasion arose. I said, in my opinion, if war was forced upon France then on the question of Morocco—a question which had just been the subject of agreement between this country and France, an agreement exceedingly popular on both sides—that if out of that agreement war was forced on France at that time, in my view public opinion in this country would have rallied to the material support of France.

I gave no promise, but I expressed that opinion during the crisis, as far as I remember, almost in the same words, to the French ambassador and the German ambassador at the time. I made no promise, and I used no threats; but I expressed that opinion. That position was accepted by the French government, but they said to me at

---

[1]*Balkan crisis:* the Balkan Wars of 1912–1913, when Grey took the initiative in organizing peace talks in London

the time—and I think very reasonably—"If you think it possible that the public opinion of Great Britain might, should a sudden crisis arise, justify you in giving to France the armed support which you cannot promise in advance, you will not be able to give that support, even if you wish to give it, when the time comes, unless some conversations have already taken place between naval and military experts." There was force in that. I agreed to it, and authorized those conversations to take place, but on the distinct understanding that nothing which passed between military or naval experts should bind either government, or restrict in any way their freedom to make a decision as to whether or not they would give that support when the time arose. . . .

The Agadir crisis came—another Morocco crisis—and throughout that I took precisely the same line that had been taken in 1906. But subsequently, in 1912, after discussion and consideration in the cabinet it was decided that we ought to have a definite understanding in writing, which was to be only in the form of an unofficial letter, that these conversations which took place were not binding upon the freedom of either government; and on 22 November, 1912, I wrote to the French ambassador the letter which I will now read to the House, and I received from him a letter in similar terms in reply. The letter which I have to read now is the record that, whatever took place between military and naval experts, they were not binding engagements upon the government:

My dear Ambassador—from time to time in recent years the French and British naval and military experts have consulted together. It has always been understood that such consultation does not restrict the freedom of either government to decide at any future time whether or not to assist the other by armed force. We have agreed that consultation between experts is not and ought not to be regarded as an engagement that commits either government to action in a contingency that has not yet arisen and may never arise. The disposition, for instance, of the French and British fleets respectively at the present moment is not based upon an engagement to co-operate in war.

You have, however, pointed out that, if either government had grave reason to expect an unprovoked attack by a third power, it might become essential to know whether it could in that event depend upon the armed assistance of the other.

I agree that, if either government had grave reason to expect an unprovoked attack by a third power, or something that threatened the general peace, it should immediately discuss with the other whether both governments should act together to prevent aggression and to preserve peace, and, if so, what measures they would be prepared to take in common. . . .

That is the starting-point for the government with regard to the present crisis. . . . We do not construe anything which has previously taken place in our diplomatic relations with other powers in this matter as restricting the freedom of government to decide what attitude they should take now, or restrict the freedom of the House of Commons to decide what their attitude should be.

Well, Sir, I will go further, and I will say this: The situation in the present crisis is not precisely the same as it was in the Morocco question. In the Morocco question it was primarily a dispute which concerned France—a dispute which concerned France and France primarily—a dispute, as it seemed to us, affecting France, out of an agreement subsisting between us and France, and published to the whole world, in which we engaged to give France diplomatic support. No doubt we were pledged to give nothing but diplomatic support; we were, at any rate, pledged by a definite public agreement to stand with France diplomatically in that question.

The present crisis has originated differently. It has not originated with regard to Morocco. It has not originated as regards anything with which we had a special agreement with France; it has not originated with anything which primarily concerned France. It has originated in a dispute between Austria and Serbia. I can say this with the most absolute confidence—no government and no country has less desire to be involved in war over a dispute with Austria and Serbia than the government and the country of France. They are involved in it because of their obligation of honor under a definite alliance with Russia. Well, it is only fair to say to the House that the obligation of honor cannot apply in the same way to us. We are not parties to the Franco-Russian Alliance. We do not even know the terms of that alliance. So far I have, I think, faithfully and completely cleared the ground with regard to the question of obligation.

I now come to what we think the situation requires of us. For many years we have had a long-standing friendship with France. (*An hon. Member:* "*And with Germany!*") I remember well the feeling in the House—and my own feeling—for I spoke on the subject, I think, when the late government made their agreement with France—the warm and cordial feeling resulting from the fact that these two nations, who had had perpetual differences in the past, had cleared these differences away. I remember saying, I think, that it seemed to me that some benign influence had been at work to produce the cordial atmosphere that had made that possible. But how far that friendship entails obligation—it has been a friendship between the nations and ratified by the nations—how far that entails an obligation let every man look into his own heart, and his own feelings, and construe the extent of the obligation for himself. I construe it myself as I feel it, but I do not wish to urge upon anyone else more than their feelings dictate as to what they should feel about the obligation. The House, individually and collectively, may judge for itself. I speak my personal view, and I have given the House my own feeling in the matter.

The French fleet is now in the Mediterranean, and the northern and western coasts of France are absolutely undefended. The French fleet being concentrated in the Mediterranean the situation is very different from what it used to be, because the friendship which has grown up between the two countries has given them a sense of security that there was nothing to be feared from us. The French coasts are absolutely undefended. The French fleet is in the Mediterranean, and has for some years been concentrated there because of the feeling of confidence and friendship which has existed between the two countries. My own feeling is that if a foreign fleet engaged in a war which France had not sought, and in which she had not been the aggressor, came down the English Channel and bombarded and battered the undefended coasts of France, we could not stand aside and see this going on practically within sight of our eyes with our arms folded, looking on dispassionately, doing nothing! . . .

But I also want to look at the matter without sentiment, and from the point of view of British interests, and it is on that that I am going to base and justify what I am presently going to say to the House. If we say nothing at this moment, what is France to do with her fleet in the Mediterranean? If she leaves it there, with no statement from us as to what we will do, she leaves her northern and western coasts absolutely undefended, at the mercy of a German fleet coming down the Channel, to do as it pleases in a war which is a war of life and death between them. If we say nothing, it may be that the French fleet is withdrawn from the Mediterranean. We are in the presence of a European conflagration; can anybody set limits to the consequences that may arise out of it? Let us assume that to-day we stand aside in an attitude of neutrality, saying, "No, we cannot undertake and engage to help either party in this conflict." Let us suppose the French fleet is withdrawn from the Mediterranean; and let us assume that the consequences—which are already tremendous in what has happened in Europe even to countries which are at peace—in fact, equally whether countries are at peace or at war—let us assume that out of that come consequences unforeseen, which make it necessary at a sudden moment that, in defense of vital British interests, we should go to war: and let us assume—which is quite possible—that Italy, who is now neutral—(*Hon. Members: "Hear, Hear!"*)—because, as I understand, she considers that this war is an aggressive war, the Triple Alliance being a defensive alliance her obligation did not arise—let us assume that consequences which are not yet foreseen—and which perfectly legitimately consulting her own interests—make Italy depart from her attitude of neutrality at a time when we are forced in defense of vital British interests ourselves to fight, what then will be the position in the Mediterranean? It might be that at some critical moment those consequences would be forced upon us because our trade routes in the Mediterranean might be vital to this country. . . .

We have great and vital interests in the independence—and integrity is the least part—of Belgium. If Belgium is compelled to submit to allow her neutrality to be violated, of course the situation is clear. Even if by agreement she admitted the violation of her neutrality, it is clear she could only do so under duress. The smaller states in that region of Europe ask but one thing. Their one desire is that they should be left alone and independent. The one thing they fear is, I think, not so much that their integrity but that their independence should be interfered with. If in this war which is before Europe the neutrality of one of those countries is violated, if the troops of one of the combatants violate its neutrality and no action be taken to resist it, at the end of the war, whatever the integrity may be, the independence will be gone.

I have one further quotation from Mr. Gladstone as to what he thought about the independence of Belgium. . . . Mr. Gladstone said:

"We have an interest in the independence of Belgium which is wider than that which we may have in the literal operation of the guarantee. It is found in the answer to the question whether under the circumstances of the case, this country endowed as it is with influence and power, would quietly stand by and witness the perpetration of the direst crime that ever stained the pages of history, and thus become participators in the sin."

No, Sir, if it be the case that there has been anything in the nature of an ultimatum to Belgium, asking her to compromise or violate her neutrality, whatever may have been offered to her in return, her independence is gone if that holds. If her independence goes, the independence of Holland will follow. I ask the House from the point of view of British interests, to consider what may be at stake. If France is beaten in a struggle of life and death, beaten to her knees, loses her position as a great power, becomes subordinate to the will and power of one greater than herself—consequences which I do not anticipate, because I am sure that France has the power to defend herself with all the energy and ability and patriotism which she has shown so often—still, if that were to happen, and if Belgium fell under the same dominating influence, and then Holland, and then Denmark, then would not Mr. Gladstone's words come true, that just opposite to us there would be a common interest against the unmeasured aggrandizement of any power?

It may be said, I suppose, that we might stand aside, husband our strength, and that whatever happened in the course of this war at the end of it intervene with effect to put things right, and to adjust them to our own point of view. If, in a crisis like this, we run away from those obligations of honor and interest as regards the Belgian Treaty, I doubt whether, whatever material force we might have at the end, it would be of very much value in face of the respect that we should have lost. And, do not believe, whether a great power stands outside this war or not, it is going to be in a position at the end of it to exert its superior strength. For us, with a powerful fleet, which we believe able to protect our commerce, to protect our shores, and to protect our interests, if we are engaged in war, we shall suffer but little more than we shall suffer even if we stand aside.

We are going to suffer, I am afraid, terribly in this war whether we are in it or whether we stand aside. Foreign trade is going to stop, not because the trade routes are closed, but because there is no trade at the other end. Continental nations engaged in war—all their populations, all their energies, all their wealth, engaged in a desperate struggle—they cannot carry on the trade with us that they are carrying on in time of peace, whether we are parties to the war or whether we are not. I do not believe for a moment, that at the end of this war, even if we stood aside and remained aside, we should be in a position, a material position to use our force decisively to undo what had happened in the course of the war, to prevent the whole of the west of Europe opposite to us—if that has been the result of the war—falling under the domination of a single power, and I am quite sure that our moral position would be such as to have lost us all respect. I can only say that I have put the question of Belgium somewhat hypothetically, because I am not yet sure of all the facts, but, if the facts turn out to be as they have reached us at present, it is quite clear that there is an obligation on this country to do its utmost to prevent the consequences to which those facts will lead if they are undisputed.

I have read to the House the only engagements that we have yet taken definitely with regard to the use of force. I think it is due to the House to say that we have taken no engagement yet with regard to sending an expeditionary armed force out of the country. Mobilization of the fleet has taken place; mobilization of the army is taking place; but we have as yet taken no engagement, because I do feel that in the case of a European conflagration such as this, unprecedented, with our enormous responsibilities in India and other parts of the empire, or in countries of British occupation, with all the unknown factors, we must take very carefully into consideration the use which we make of sending an expeditionary force out of the country until we know how we stand. . . .

The most awful responsibility is resting upon the government in deciding what to advise the House of Commons to do. . . . We [have] worked for peace up to the last moment, and beyond the last moment. How hard, how persistently, and how earnestly we strove for peace last week, the House will see from the papers that will be before it.

But that is over, as far as the peace of Europe is concerned. We are now face to face with a situation and all the consequences which it may yet have to unfold. We believe we shall have the support of the House at large in proceeding to whatever the consequences may be and whatever measures may be forced upon us by the development of facts or action taken by others. I believe the country, so quickly has the situation been forced upon it, has not had time to realize the issue. It perhaps is still thinking of the quarrel between Austria and Serbia, and not the complications of this matter which have grown out of the quarrel between Austria and Serbia. Russia and Germany we know are at war. We do not yet know officially that Austria, the ally whom Germany is to support, is yet at war with Russia. We know that a good deal has been happening on the French frontier. We do not know that the German ambassador has left Paris.

The situation has developed so rapidly that technically, as regards the condition of the war, it is most difficult to describe what has actually happened. I wanted to bring out the underlying issues which would affect our own conduct, and our own policy, and to put them clearly. I have put the vital facts before the House, and if, as seems not improbable, we are forced, and rapidly forced, to take our stand upon those issues, then I believe, when the country realizes what is at stake, what the real issues are, the magnitude of the impending dangers in the west of Europe, which I have endeavored to describe to the House, we shall be supported throughout, not only by the House of Commons, but by the determination, the resolution, the courage, and the endurance of the whole country.

JOHN MORLEY **Memorandum on Resignation (1914)**

The leaders of the Conservative Opposition and all but two of the members of the Liberal government agreed upon the rightness of Britain's declaration of war on Germany—after German troops had invaded neutral Belgium. One of the two cabinet skeptics was the veteran Liberal statesman, biographer, and essayist Lord Morley. The events that led to his resignation from the cabinet were recorded by Morley in 1914 but published only after the war was over and Morley was dead.

I

On or about July 24–27. Grey took a very important line in the Cabinet. He informed us of the contents of Buchanan's[2] telegram of July 24 from Petersburg: describing Sazonoff's[3] hopes that England would not fail to proclaim her solidarity with France and Russia; his warnings to us that the general European question was involved and England could not afford to efface herself from the problems now at issue; that she would sooner or later be dragged into war if it did break out; and, as Buchanan thought, even if England declined to join, France and Russia were determined to make a strong stand, *i.e.* in plain language, to fight Austria and Germany.

Then Grey in his own quiet way, which is none the less impressive for being so simple, and so free from the *cassant* and over-emphatic tone that is Asquith's vice on such occasions, made a memorable pronouncement. The time had come, he said, when the cabinet was bound to make up its mind plainly whether we were to take an active part with the two other powers of the Entente, or to stand aside in the general European question, and preserve an absolute neutrality.

We could no longer defer decision. Things were moving very rapidly. We could no longer wait on accident, and postpone. If the cabinet was for neutrality, he did not think that he was the man to carry out such a policy. Here he ended in accents of unaffected calm and candor. The cabinet seemed to heave a sort of sigh, and a moment or two of breathless silence fell upon us. I followed him, expressing my intense satisfaction that he had brought the inexorable position, to which circumstances had now brought us, plainly and definitely before us. It was fairer to France and everybody else, ourselves included. Though he had at least once, talking to an ambassador, drawn a distinction between diplomatic and military intervention, it was henceforth assumed that intervention meant active resort to arms. We rambled, as even the best cabinets are apt to do, from the cogent riddle that the European sphinx or sphinxes had posed, into incidental points and secondary aspects. I could not, on the instant, gather with any certainty in which direction opinion was inclining. No wonder. Everybody had suddenly awakened to the startling fact that nothing less than the continued existence of the ministry was this time—the first time—in sharp peril from differences within, and not from the House of Commons.

Later, we were pressed by the prime minister and Grey to examine the neutrality of Belgium and our obligations under the Treaty of 1839. But it was thrown back day after day as less urgent than France. . . . A cabinet usually thinks of one thing at once, and the question of Belgium was up to this date, and in truth up to the morning of

SOURCE: From John Viscount Morley, *Memorandum on Resignation: August 1914* (London: Macmillan, London and Basingstoke, 1928), pp. 1–8, 10–14, 16–27, 30–31.

[2]*George Buchanan:* the British ambassador to Russia   [3]*Sergei Sazonoff:* the Russian foreign minister

August 3rd, when Grey had to set out his whole case in the House of Commons, secondary to the pre-eminent controversy of the Anglo-French Entente. One of these days Grey rather suddenly let fall his view, in the pregnant words that German policy was that of a great "European aggressor, as bad as Napoleon." "I have no German partialities," I observed, "but you do not give us evidence." Perhaps he might have cited the series of naval laws.[4]

Meanwhile Harcourt had been busy in organizing opinion among his cabinet colleagues in favor of neutrality. This was meant for a counter-move [to] that [which] was being openly worked with his best demonic energy by Winston,[5] with strenuous simplicity by Grey, and *sourdement*[6] by the Lord Chancellor—the prime minister seeing and waiting. There was no intrigue about it either way. All was above-board. Harcourt got me to his room in the House of Commons one night as I was passing along the corridor and I found Beauchamp, M'Kinnon Wood, Hobhouse, Pease, very zealous against extension of entente to alliance. They calculated to a tune of eight or nine men in the cabinet likely to agree with us. I think I attended one other meeting of this peace group in the same place, and under the same auspices. Harcourt this week two or three times threw me little slips at the cabinet table, "That I must resign is more and more evident." One of these days I tapped Winston on the shoulder, as he took his seat next me. "Winston, we have beaten you after all." He smiled cheerfully. Well he might. *O pectora caeca!*[7]

Lloyd George, not by design, furthered the good cause by a very remarkable piece of intelligence communicated to the cabinet, acquired I think at the suggestion of the prime minister. He informed us that he had been consulting the governor and deputy governor of the Bank of England, other men of light and leading in the City, also cotton men, and steel and coal men, etc., in the North of England, in Glasgow, etc., and they were all *aghast* at the bare idea of our plunging into the European conflict; how it would break down the whole system of credit with London as its center, how it would cut up commerce and manufacture—they told him—how it would hit labor and wages and prices, and, when the winter came, would inevitably produce violence and tumult. When I pressed this all-important prospect in a later debate, the Chancellor of the Exchequer said rather tartly that he had never said he believed it all. "In the present temper of labor," said I, "this tremendous dislocation of industrial life must be fraught with public danger. The atmosphere of war cannot be friendly to order, in a democratic system that is verging on the humour of '48."[8] But then the wisest saws, as I have many a time found before now, count for little in the hour of practical emergency. This first-class and vital element in settling our policy received little of the attention that it well deserved; it vanished in the diplomatic hurry.

Then they were rather surprised at the stress I laid upon the Russian side of things. "Have you ever thought," I put to them, "what will happen if Russia wins? If Germany is beaten and Austria is beaten, it is not England and France who will emerge preeminent in Europe. It will be Russia. Will that be good for western civilization? I at least don't think so. If she says she will go to Constantinople, or boldly annex both northern and neutral zone in Persia, or insist on railways up to the Indian and Afghan frontier, who will prevent her? Germany is unpopular in England, but Russia is more

---

[4]*Naval laws:* The German naval-building program, begun in 1897, which had led to intense rivalry with Britain, especially during the years 1908–1912   [5]*Winston:* Winston Churchill, the First Lord of the Admiralty   [6]*sourdement:* secretly   [7]*O pectora caeca:* Oh, blind heart!
[8]*'48:* 1848, a year of revolution in continental Europe, and of a major Chartist demonstration in England

unpopular still. And people will rub their eyes when they realise that cossacks are their victorious fellow-champions for freedom, justice, equality of man (especially Jew man), and respect for treaties (in Persia for instance)." They listened rather intently, and Lloyd George told me after that he had never thought of all this.

I think it was to-day [July 26] I put a really strong point. Grey has more than once congratulated Europe on the existence of two great confederacies, Triple Alliance and Triple Entente, as healthily preserving the balance of power. Balance! What a beautiful euphemism for the picture of two giant groups armed to the teeth, each in mortal terror of the other, both of them passing year after year in an incurable fever of jealousy and suspicion!

The cabinet for the first time became seriously uneasy about the danger of these foreign affairs to our own cohesion. For the very first time something of the old cleavage between the Liberal League[9] and the faithful Campbell Bannerman, Harcourt and myself began to be very sensibly felt. Hitherto not a whisper of the old schism of the Boer war. As I walked away with Burns after the cabinet of the 29th, he pressed my arm and said with vehement emphasis, *"Now mind, we look to you to stand firm."* He repeated it on Friday. I was not keen in response, as to my taking any lead. We were all first alarmed on the Saturday evening. Burns himself took the lead, to good purpose, and intimated in his most downright tones that the warning to Germany not to try it on against French coasts or ships in the Channel, was more than he could stand, not only because it was practically a declaration of war on sea leading inevitably to a war on land, but mainly because it was the symbol of an alliance with France with whom no such understanding had hitherto existed. . . .

II

Sunday, August 2.—Cabinet. Main question resumed was the language to be held by Grey to Cambon in the afternoon. Neutrality of Belgium, though Asquith pressed for attention to that topic, was secondary to the question of our neutrality in the struggle between Germany and France; and to our liability to France under the Entente. The situation now was this: Grey admitted that we were not bound by the same obligation of honor to France as bound France to Russia. He professed to stand by what he had told Cambon in his letter of 1912, that we were left perfectly free to decide whether we would assist France by armed force. We were not committed, he always said, to action in a contingency that had not yet arisen and might never arise. No immediate aggressive action was entailed upon us, unless there was action against France in the Channel or the North Sea. So much then for the point of honor arising on the French Entente.

On August 3rd Grey received news that Germany would be prepared, if we would pledge ourselves to neutrality, to agree that its fleet would not attack the north coast of France. Grey replied that this was far too narrow an engagement for us. Why? And if it was too narrow, why not at least take it as a basis for widening and enlargement? Pure precipitancy! At any rate there had as yet been no word said in the Cabinet about an expeditionary force. But I had been too virtuous an attendant at the C.I.D.[10] for several years, not to know that this was a settled aim in the minds of many, if not most, of its members.

Harcourt assured me before discussion began, that he believed he could count on ten or eleven men against Grey's view that we had both moral obligations of honor and substantial obligations of policy in taking

---

[9]*Liberal League:* a group of Liberals, including Asquith and Grey, who had loyally supported the British war effort against the Boers of South Africa (1899–1902) [10]*C.I.D.:* Committee of Imperial Defense

sides with France. After a very fair discussion Grey was authorized to give an assurance to Cambon that "if the German fleet comes into the Channel or through the North Sea to undertake hostile operations against French coasts or shipping, the British fleet will give all the protection in its power. This assurance of course subject to the policy of His Majesty's government receiving the support of Parliament, and must not be taken as binding His Majesty's government to take any action until the above contingency of action by the German fleet takes place." There were two lines of argument for this warning to Germany. (1) We owed it to France, in view of the Entente, and also of her value to us in the Mediterranean. (2) We could not acquiesce in Franco-German naval conflict in the narrow seas, on our doorstep so to say. This authorization, however, was not unanimous.

The Belgian question took its place in today's discussion, but even now only a secondary place. Grey very properly asked leave to warn the German ambassador that, unless Germany was prepared to give us a reply in the sense of the reply we had from France, it would be hard to restrain English feeling on any violation of Belgian neutrality by either combatant. This leave of course we gave him. There was a general, but vague, assent to our liabilities under the Treaty of 1839, but there was no assent to the employment of a land force, and, I think, no mention of it.

The German line on Belgian neutrality might be met in two ways. One, we might at once make it a *casus belli*;[11] the other we might protest with direct energy, as the British government protested on the Russian repudiation in 1870 of the Black Sea articles of the Treaty of Paris, and push on by diplomatizing. What was the difficulty of the second course? Why, our supposed entanglement with France, and nothing else. The precipitate and peremptory blaze about Belgium was due less to indignation

at the violation of a treaty, than to natural perception of the plea that it would furnish for intervention on behalf of France, for expeditionary force, and all the rest of it. Belgium was to take the place, that had been taken before as pleas for war, by Morocco and Agadir. . . .

The dissolution of the ministry was that afternoon in full view. Would even the break-up of the ministry be less of an evil both for Liberal principles, and the prospects and power of the Liberal Party, than their wholesale identification with a cabinet committed to intervention in arms by sea and land in central Europe and all the meshes of the continental system? It is easy to get a question into a false position. Never easier than now. The significance of the French Entente had been rather disingenuously played with, before both the cabinet and Parliament. An entente was evidently something even more dangerous for us than an alliance. An alliance has definite covenants. An entente is vague, rests on point of honor, to be construed by accident and convenience. The prime minister and Grey had both of them assured the House of Commons that we had no engagements unknown to the country. Yet here we were confronted by engagements that were vast indeed, because indefinite and undefinable. . . . In reply to anxious protests from Harcourt and myself, [Asquith and Grey had] minimized the significance of the systematic conferences constantly going on between the military and naval officers of the two countries. Then the famous letter to Cambon of November 1912, which we had extorted from Grey—what a singularly thin and deceptive document it was turning out!

No political rumination of mine, again, could ever leave out the effect of a war upon Home Rule. What more certain to impair the chances of a good settlement of Home Rule [for Ireland] than the bottomless agitations of a great war? I travelled in my mind over all the well-trodden ground of the di-

---

[11]*casus belli*: occasion for war

plomacies of the last fortnight. I recalled a conversation, recorded in some blue print, between Grey and Lichnowsky,[12] in which there was almost a glow and fervor not common in such affairs, over the blessed improvement in the relations of England and Germany during the last three or four years. Why was not this great new fact, instead of the Entente, made the center, the pivot, the starting-point of new negotiations? Grey's fine character had achieved an influence in Europe that was the noblest asset for the fame of England and the glory of peace. In a few hours it would be gone. I could not but be penetrated by the precipitancy of it all. What grounds for expecting that the ruinous waste and havoc of war would be repaid by peace on better terms than were already within reach of reason and persistent patience. When we counted our gains, what would they amount to, when reckoned against the ferocious hatred that would burn with inextinguishable fire, for a whole generation at least, between two great communities better fitted to understand one another than any other pair in Europe? This moral devastation is a worse incident of war even than human carnage, and all the other curses with which war lashes its victims and its dupes. With a fleet of overwhelming power, a disinterestedness beyond suspicion, a foreign minister of proved ability, truthfulness and self-control, when the smoke of battle-fields had cleared from the European sky, England might have exerted an influence not to be acquired by a hundred of her little expeditionary forces. Grey, after too long delay, had wisely and manfully posed the issue of the hour for his colleagues, when he declared that we must now decide between intervention and neutrality, and that for neutrality he was not the man. Nor am I the man, said I to myself, to sit in the council of war into which Campbell Bannerman's cabinet is to be transformed. It is after all not to be endured that not even two

men in it should be found to "testify" for convictions. Nor were these convictions merely abstract or general. They were supported by my full and accurate knowledge of the facts of the particular situation. I could not be sure that the fervid tone of the colleagues whom I had just left, sincere though it was, would last. I saw no standard-bearer. The power of Asquith and Grey, and the natural "cohesion of office," would prove too hard for an isolated group to resist. The motives of Lloyd George were a riddle. He knew that his "stock" had sunk dangerously low; peace might be the popular card against the adventurous energy of Winston; war would make mince-meat of the land question. And the break-up of government and party might well make any man pause quite apart from demagogic calculations. In plain truth the Liberal Party was already shattered and could not win the approaching election, mainly owing to Lloyd George himself. He was on the eve of the mistake of his life. Let him and others do what they would, and with a balance of motives in their minds as legitimate as my own. For me at any rate—*the future being what it must inevitably be*—no choice was open.

So I wrestled all the afternoon, and in this vein I made my way through the crowds in Whitehall to Downing Street. My decision was due to no one particular conversation, telegram, despatch; to none of the private correspondence from abroad, which Grey used to confide to me as representing the Foreign Office in the House of Lords. It was the result of a whole train of circumstance and reflection. . . .

III

Monday, August 3. After breakfast, composed my letter to Asquith, copied it fair at the Privy Council office, and sent it in to him.

---

[12]*Lichnowsky:* the German ambassador to England

J. M. TO ASQUITH.

August 3, 1914.

My dear Asquith,

I have, as you wished, taken a night to think over my retirement. I have given earnest pains to reach a sensible conclusion.

The thing is clear. Nothing can be so fatal in present circumstances as a cabinet with divided counsels. Grey has pointed out the essential difference between two views of neutrality in the present case. Well, I deplore to think that I incline one way, and three or four of my leading colleagues incline the other way. This being so, I could contribute nothing useful to your deliberations, and my presence could only hamper the concentrated energy, the zealous and convinced accord, that are indispensable. . . .

You will believe that I write this with heartfelt pain.

Ever yours,
M.

Privy Council at the palace and talked with the king. Nothing particular passed, though he seemed to scent what was afoot. Then to cabinet. Saw Lloyd George, and told him that I had sent in my resignation. He seemed astonished. *"But if you go, it will put us who don't go, in a great hole."* I made the obvious reply to this truly singular remark. He asked if I had considered the news of Germany bullying Belgium, etc. "Yes," said I, "and it is bad enough, but, in my view, war is not the only reply, and it does not alter my aversion to the French entente policy and its extended application." He told me that it changed Runciman's[13] line and his own. My impression is that he must have begun the day with one of his customary morning talks with the splendid *condottiere*[14] at the Admiralty, had revised his calculations, as he had a perfect right to

do; had made up his mind to swing round, as he had done about the *Panther*[15] in 1911 to the politics of adventure; and found in the German ultimatum to Belgium a sufficiently plausible excuse. . . .

After luncheon, I went to the club to rest an hour; then to House of Lords where everybody was talking of Grey's "convincing" exposition of his policy. Nothing passed in the House of Lords, and I soon found myself with the trees and fresh grass and open skies of my home.

After Prime Minister Asquith pleaded with Morley to reconsider his resignation, the latter wrote a second letter.

August 4, 1914.

My dear Asquith,

Your letter shakes me terribly. It goes to my very core. In spite of temporary moments of difference, my feelings for you have been cordial, deep, close, from your earliest days, and the idea of severing our affectionate association has been the most poignant element in the stress of the last four days.

But I cannot conceal from myself that we—I and the leading men of the cabinet—do not mean the same thing in the foreign policy of the moment. To swear ourselves to France, is to bind ourselves to Russia, and to whatever demands may be made by Russia on France. With this cardinal difference, how could I either decently or usefully sit in a cabinet day after day discussing military and diplomatic details in a policy which I think a mistake. Again I say divided counsels are fatal.

I am more distressed in making this reply to your generous and moving appeal, than I have ever been in writing any letter of all my life.

Ever yours,
M.

---

[13]*Runciman's:* Walter Runciman was president of the board of agriculture.   [14]*condottiere:* war hawks   [15]*Panther:* War between France and Germany threatened after the German warship *Panther* landed troops at a Moroccan port. In a public speech Lloyd George indicated that the British government would give diplomatic support to France.

Herbert Henry Asquith **Justification for War (1914)**

A British ultimatum to Germany demanding the withdrawal of German troops from Belgium expired on August 4, 1914, at midnight. There was no German response. The result was a British declaration of war on Germany and the following statement from the prime minister.

I am entitled to say, and I do so on behalf of this country—I speak not for a party, I speak for the country as a whole—that we made every effort any government could possibly make for peace. But this war has been forced upon us. What is it we are fighting for? Everyone knows, and no one knows better than the government, the terrible, incalculable suffering, economic, social, personal and political, which war, and especially a war between the Great Powers of the world, must entail. There is no man amongst us sitting upon this bench in these trying days—more trying perhaps than any body of statesmen for a hundred years have had to pass through—there is not a man amongst us who has not, during the whole of that time, had clearly before his vision the almost unequalled suffering which war, even in a just cause, must bring about, not only to the peoples who are for the moment living in this country and in the other countries of the world, but to posterity and to the whole prospects of European civilization. Every step we took with that vision before our eyes, and with a sense of responsibility which it is impossible to describe. Unhappily, if in spite of all our efforts to keep the peace, and with what fully and overpowering consciousness of the result, if the issue be decided in favor of war, we have, nevertheless, thought it the duty as well as the interest of this country to go to war, the House may be well assured it was because we believe, and I am certain the country will believe, that we are unsheathing our sword in a just cause.

If I am asked what we are fighting for, I reply in two sentences. In the first place to fulfill a solemn international obligation, an obligation which, if it had been entered into between private persons in the ordinary concerns of life, would have been regarded as an obligation not only of law but of honor, which no self-respecting man could have repudiated. I say, secondly we are fighting to vindicate the principle which, in these days when force, material force, sometimes seems to be the dominant influence and factor in the development of mankind, we are fighting to vindicate the principle that small nationalities are not to be crushed, in defiance of international good faith, by the arbitrary will of a strong and overmastering power.

Siegfried Sassoon **War Poems (1915–1917)**

Like many youthful upper-middle-class country gentlemen, Sassoon volunteered for military service in the British Army, and he served on the Western Front—in the trenches amid the barbed wire and the machine guns—for the greater part of three years. His

SOURCE: From *Hansard's Parliamentary Debates*, 5th Series, Vol. LXV, cols. 2978–2979.

poems illustrate his growing disenchantment with war itself as experienced on the battlefield, however high-minded the professed goals of his nation's leaders.

France

She triumphs, in the vivid green
Where sun and quivering foliage meet;
And in each soldier's heart serene;
When death stood near them they have
seen
The radiant forests where her feet
Move on a breeze of silver sheen.

And they are fortunate, who fight
For gleaming landscapes swept and
shafted
And crowned by cloud pavilions white;
Hearing such harmonies as might
Only from Heaven be downward wafted—
Voices of victory and delight.

A Working Party

Three hours ago he blundered up the
trench,
Sliding and poising, groping with his
boots;
Sometimes he tripped and lurched against
the walls
With hands that pawed the sodden bags of
chalk.
He couldn't see the man who walked in
front;
Only he heard the drum and rattle of feet
Stepping along barred trench boards, often
splashing
Wretchedly where the sludge was ankle-
deep.

Voices would grunt "Keep to your right—
make way!"
When squeezing past some men from the
front-line:
White faces peered, puffing a point of red;
Candles and braziers glinted through the
chinks
And curtain-flaps of dug-outs; then the
gloom
Swallowed his sense of sight; he stooped
and swore
Because a sagging wire had caught his
neck.

A flare went up; the shining whiteness
spread
And flickered upward, showing nimble
rats
And mounds of glimmering sand-bags,
bleached with rain;
Then the slow silver moment died in
dark.
The wind came posting by with chilly
gusts
And buffeting at corners, piping thin.
And dreary through the crannies; rifle-
shots
Would split and crack and sing along the
night,
And shells came calmly through the
drizzling air
To burst with hollow bang below the hill.

Three hours ago he stumbled up the
trench;
Now he will never walk that road again:
He must be carried back, a jolting lump
Beyond all need of tenderness and care.

He was a young man with a meagre wife
And two small children in a Midland
town;
He showed their photographs to all his
mates,
And they considered him a decent chap
Who did his work and hadn't much to say,
And always laughed at other people's
jokes
Because he hadn't any of his own.

That night when he was busy at his job
Of piling bags along the parapet,
He thought how slow time went,
stamping his feet
And blowing on his fingers, pinched with
cold.
He thought of getting back by half-past
twelve,
And tot of rum to send him warm to
sleep
In draughty dug-out frowsty with the
fumes
Of coke, and full of snoring weary men.

He pushed another bag along the top,
Craning his body outward; then a flare
Gave one white glimpse of No Man's
  Land and wire;
And as he dropped his head the instant
  split
His startled life with lead, and all went
  out.

"They"

The Bishop tells us: "When the boys
  come back
"They will not be the same, for they'll
  have fought
"In a just cause: they lead the last attack
"On Anti-Christ; their comrades' blood
  has bought
"New right to breed an honourable race,
"They have challenged Death and dared
  him face to face."

"We're none of us the same!" the boys
  reply.
"For George lost both his legs; and Bill's
  stone blind;
"Poor Jim's shot through the lungs and
  like to die;
"And Bert's gone syphilitic: you'll not
  find
"A chap who's served that hasn't found
  some change."
And the Bishop said: "The ways of God
  are strange!"

The One-Legged Man

Propped on a stick he reviewed the
  August weald;
Squat orchard trees and oasts with painted
  cowls;
A homely, tangled hedge, a corn-stalked
  field,
And sound of barking dogs and farmyard
  fowls.

And he'd come home again to find it
  more
Desirable than ever it was before.
How right it seemed that he should reach
  the span

Of comfortable years allowed to man!
Splendid to eat and sleep and choose a
  wife,
Safe with his wound, a citizen of life.
He hobbled blithely through the garden
  gate,
And thought: "Thank God they had to
  amputate!"

Counter-Attack

We'd gained our first objective hours
  before
While dawn broke like a face with
  blinking eyes,
Pallid, unshaved and thirsty, blind with
  smoke.
Things seemed all right at first. We held
  their line,
With bombers posted, Lewis guns well
  placed,
And clink of shovels deepening the
  shallow trench.
The place was rotten with dead; green
  clumsy legs
High-booted, sprawled and grovelled
  along the saps
And trunks, face downward, in the
  sucking mud,
Wallowed like trodden sand-bags loosely
  filled;
And naked sodden buttocks, mats of
  hair,
Bulged, clotted heads slept in the
  plastering slime.
And then the rain began—the jolly old
  rain!

A yawning soldier knelt against the bank,
Staring across the morning blear with fog;
He wondered when the Allemands would
  get busy;
And then, of course, they started with
  five-nines
Traversing, sure as fate, and never a dud.
Mute in the clamour of shells he watched
  them burst
Spouting dark earth and wire with gusts
  from hell,
While posturing giants dissolved in drifts
  of smoke.

He crouched and flinched, dizzy with
  galloping fear,
Sick for escape—loathing the strangled
  horror
And butchered, frantic gestures of the
  dead.

An officer came blundering down the
  trench:
"Stand-to and man the fire-step!" On he
  went . . .
Gasping and bawling, "Fire-step . . .
  counter-attack!"
Then the haze lifted. Bombing on the
  right
Down the old sap: machine-guns on the
  left;
And stumbling figures looming out in
  front.
"O Christ, they're coming at us!"
Bullets spat,
And he remembered his rifle . . . rapid fire
  . . .
And started blazing wildly . . . then a bang
Crumpled and spun him sideways,
  knocked him out
To grunt and wriggle: none heeded him;
  he choked
And fought the flapping veils of
  smothering gloom,

Lost in a blurred confusion of yells and
  groans . . .
Down, and down, and down, he sank and
  drowned,
Bleeding to death. The counter-attack had
  failed.

Survivors

No doubt they'll soon get well; the shock
  and strain
Have caused their stammering,
  disconnected talk.
Of course they're "longing to go out
  again"—
These boys with old, scared faces,
  learning to walk.
They'll soon forget their haunted nights;
  their cowed
Subjection to the ghosts of friends who
  died—
Their dreams that drip with murder; and
  they'll be proud
Of glorious war that shatter'd all their
  pride . . .
Men who went out to battle, grim and
  glad;
Children, with eyes that hate you, broken
  and mad.

Craiglockart. October 1917.

BERTRAND RUSSELL **Reflections on Pacifism in Wartime (1914–1918)**

*Just as the declaration of war on Germany in August 1914 won the support of most but
not all British leaders, so did the prosecution of the war that followed win the support of
most Britons but rouse the objections of a small but distinguished group of conscientious
objectors. Of these, the philosopher Bertrand Russell was one of the most eminent.*

The most difficult period in which to keep
one's head was the very beginning, before
the battle of the Marne. The rapid advance
of the Germans was terrifying; the newspapers, and still more private conversations,
were full of apparently well-authenticated
atrocity stories; the stream of Belgian refu-
gees seemed to strengthen the case for de-

fending Belgium. One by one, the people
with whom one had been in the habit of
agreeing politically went over to the side of
the war, and as yet the exceptional people,
who stood out, had not found each other.
But the greatest difficulty was the purely
psychological one of resisting mass suggestion, of which the force becomes terrific

SOURCE: From Bertrand Russell, "Some Psychological Difficulties of Pacifism in Wartime," in
Julian Bell, ed., *We Did Not Fight: 1914–18; Experiences of War Resisters* (London: Cobden-
Sanderson, 1935), pp. 329–335.

when the whole nation is in a state of violent collective excitement. As much effort was required to avoid sharing this excitement as would have been needed to stand out against the extreme of hunger or sexual passion, and there was the same feeling of going against instinct.

It must be remembered that we had not then the experience which we gradually acquired during the war. We did not know the wiles of herd-instinct, from which, in quiet times, we had been fairly free. We did not realize that it is stimulated by the cognate emotions of fear and rage and blood-lust, and we were not on the look-out for the whole system of irrational beliefs which war-fever, like every other strong passion, brings in its train. In the case of passions which our neighbors do not share, their arguments may make us see reason; but in war-time our neighbors encourage irrationality, and shrink in horror from the slightest attempt to throw doubt upon prevailing myths.

The great stimulant to herd-instinct is fear; in patriots, the instinct was stimulated by fear of the Germans, but in pacifists fear of the patriots produced a similar result. I can remember sitting in a bus and thinking: "These people would tear me to pieces if they knew what I think about the war." The feeling was uncomfortable, and led one to prefer the company of pacifists. Gradually a pacifist herd was formed. When we were all together we felt warm and cozy, and forgot what an insignificant minority we were. We thought of other minorities that had become majorities. We did not know that one of us was to become prime minister,[16] but if we had known we should have supposed that it would be a good thing when he did.

The pacifist herd was a curious one, composed of very diverse elements. There were those who, on religious grounds, considered all warfare wicked; there were many in the I.L.P.[17] who came to the same conclusion without invoking the authority of the Bible; there were men who subsequently became Communists, who were cynical about capitalist wars but were quite willing to join in a proletarian revolution; and there were men in the Union of Democratic Control,[18] who, without having definite opinions about wars in general, thought that our pre-war diplomacy had been at fault, and that the belief in the sole guilt of Germany was a dangerous falsehood. These different elements did not easily work together. The cynicism of communists-to-be was painful to Quakers, and Quaker gentleness toward the war-mongers was exasperating to those who attributed everything evil to the wickedness of capitalists. The socialism of the I.L.P. repelled many Liberal pacifists, and those who condemned all war were impatient with those who confined their arguments to the particular war then in progress. And so the pacifist herd split into minor herds. In some men, the habit of standing out against the herd became so ingrained that they could not co-operate with anybody about anything.

The atmosphere was very inimical to intelligence. At first, I tried not to "lose, though full of pain, this intellectual being." I observed—or thought I observed—that, in the early months, most people were happier than in peace-time, because they enjoyed the excitement. This observation produced indignation among my pacifist friends, who believed that virtuous democracies had been tricked into war by wicked governments. Arguments as to the origins of the war were thought unimportant by those who were opposed to all war, and were brushed aside as irrelevant by the great bulk of the population, to whom victory was the

---

[16]*one of us . . . minister:* Ramsay MacDonald, prime minister 1924, 1929–35   [17]*I.L.P.:* the Independent Labour Party, a relatively small socialist group affiliated with, but not identical to, the parliamentary Labour Party   [18]*Union of Democratic Control:* an organization founded during the war to work for a negotiated peace; it anticipated Woodrow Wilson in its advocacy of a postwar League of Nations

only thing that mattered. For the sake of unanimity among pacifists, it became necessary for the different sections to suppress all but the broadest issues. We all had to avoid all subtlety, and practice a kind of artificial stupidity.

And gradually the hysteria of the outer world invaded the pacifist herd. I remember hearing a woman at a meeting state, with passion, that if her son were wounded in the war she would not lift a finger to nurse him. The logic was clear, since nursing was war-work; but her position was not calculated to recommend pacifism to waverers. Some pacifists, out of opposition to the patriots, made out such a good case for the German government that they embarrassed German pacifists, who were trying to persuade *their* public that the faults were not all on *our* side. At intervals, the German government made peace offers which were, as the Allies said, illusory, but which all pacifists (myself included) took more seriously than they deserved. Having, with great difficulty, disbelieved what was false in war propaganda, it was impossible to believe what happened to be true.

I remember one evening when I came away from a pacifist meeting with Ramsay MacDonald. He was depressed, and as we walked up Kingsway he said he was afraid of acquiring what he called the "minority mind." Some may think that he has since been only too successful in avoiding this danger, but it cannot be denied that it is a danger. It does not do to think that majorities must be wrong and minorities must be right.

In times of excitement, simple views find a hearing more readily than those that are sufficiently complex to have a chance of being true. Nine people out of ten, in England during the war, never got beyond the view that the Germans were wicked and the Allies were virtuous. (Crude moral categories, such as "virtuous" and "wicked," revived in people who, at most times, would have been ashamed to think in such terms.) The easiest theory to maintain in opposition to the usual one was the Quaker view, that all men are good at heart, and that the way to bring out the good in them is to love them. Christ had taught that we ought to love our enemies, and few people cared to say straight out that He was mistaken. Those who genuinely held the Quaker view were respected, and the government disliked having to send them to prison.

The class-war opinion, that capitalist wars are wicked but proletarian wars are laudable, could be preached with success to working-class audiences; it had the advantage of giving an outlet for hatred, of which many persecuted pacifists felt the need. Frequently, in meetings nominally opposed to all war, the threat of violent revolution was applauded to the echo. This view was, of course, the one of all others most hated by the authorities, but it was psychologically capable of being held by a majority.

The view which I took, and still take, was that, while some wars have been justified (for instance the American Civil War), the Great War was not justified, because it was about nothing impersonal and raised no important issue. This view required too much argument to be effective in such a violent time; it could be put forward in books, but not at meetings. It was also impossible to get a hearing for the view that a war cannot be justified by its causes, but only, if at all, by its effects. A "righteous" war was supposed to be one which had the correct diplomatic preliminaries, not one in which victory would bring some benefit to mankind. One of the most surprising things about the war, to me, was its power of producing intellectual degradation in previously intelligent people, and the way in which intellectual degradation always clothed itself in the language of a lofty but primitive morality.

To stand out against a war, when it comes, a man must have within himself some passion so strong and so indestructible that mass hysteria cannot touch it. The Christian war resister loves his enemies; the Communist war resister hates his government. Neither of these causes of resistance was available for me; what kept me from war fever was a desire for intellectual sobriety, for viewing matters involving passionate emotion as if they were elements in a formula of symbolic logic. I found it useful to think of nation *x*, nation *y*, and nation *z*, instead of England, France and Germany. But the effort was considerable, and hardly left me the mental energy to apply the same process when *x* was the British government and *y* was the imprisoned pacifists. I still think, however, that intellectual sobriety is very desirable in war time, and I should wish all who, in anticipation, expect to stand out against the next war, to practice the habit of translating concretes into abstracts, so as to see whether their reasonings still seem convincing when the emotion has been taken out of them. In theory, we all know that this is essential to scientific thinking, but the war showed that it is more difficult than many people suppose.

MARY AUGUSTA WARD **England's Effort (1916)**

While a minority of war resisters pondered on what grounds and in what manner to oppose their nation's war effort, Mrs. Humphry Ward was representative of the majority of her fellow citizens in defending Britain's war record and in seeking to spur that effort on.

You say that England at the present moment is misunderstood, and even hardly judged in America, and that even those great newspapers of yours that are most friendly to the Allies are often melancholy reading for those with English sympathies. Our mistakes—real and supposed—loom so large. We are thought to be not taking the war seriously—even now. Drunkenness, strikes, difficulties in recruiting the new armies, the losses of the Dardanelles expedition, the failure to save Serbia and Montenegro, tales of luxurious expenditure in the private life of rich and poor, and of waste or incompetence in military administration— these are made much of, even by our friends, who grieve, while our enemies mock.... "Tell me," you say in effect, "what in your belief is the real spirit of your people—of your men in the field and at sea, of your workmen and employers at home, your women, your factory workers, your soldiers' wives, your women of the richer and educated classes, your landowners and politicians. Are you yet fully awake—yet fully in earnest, in this crisis of England's fate?" ...

Yes!—I must answer your questions—to the best of my power. [Britain's effort]

seems to me—it must seem to any one who has seriously attempted to gauge it—amazing, colossal. "What country has ever raised over sixty per cent of its total recruitable strength, for service beyond the seas in a few months?" asks one of our younger historians; and that a country not invaded, protected by the sea, and by a supreme fleet; a country, moreover, without any form of compulsory military service, in which soldiering and the soldier have been rather unpopular than popular, a country in love with peace, and with no intention or expectation of going to war with any one?

For there we come to the root of everything—the *unpreparedness of England*— and what it meant. It meant simply that as a nation we never wished for war with Germany, and, as a nation, we never expected it. . . . Fruitless efforts were made by successive English governments to limit armaments, to promote arbitration, and extend the scope of the Hague Tribunal. In vain. Germany would have none of them. Year by year, in a world of peace her battle-navy grew. "For what can it be intended but to attack England?" said the alarmists. But how few of us believed them! Our tariff reformers protested against the encroach-

SOURCE: From *England's Effort: Letters to an American Friend*, second edition, by Mary A. Ward. Copyright 1916 by Charles Scribner's Sons, pp. 4–6, 10–13, 16–18, 30–33, 35–37, 40–42, 148–149, 173, 180–181.

ments of German trade; but, outside a handful of persons who seemed to most of us fanatics, the emphasis lay always on care for our own people, and not on hostility to Germany. Those who warned us passionately that Germany meant to provoke a struggle, that the struggle must come, were very little heeded. . . .

"There was *no* hatred of Germany in this country"—I quote a cabinet minister. "Even in those parts of the country which had most reason to feel the trade rivalry of Germany, there was no thought of war, no wish for war!" It came upon England like one of those sudden spates through mountain clefts in spring, that fall with havoc on the plains beneath. After such days of wrestling for European peace as have left their indelible mark upon every member of the English cabinet which declared war on August 4th, 1914, we fought because we must, because, in Luther's words, we "could [do] no other." . . .

At the word "Belgium" on August 4th, practically the whole English nation fell into line. We felt no doubts—we knew what we had to do. But the problem was how to do it. Outside the navy and the expeditionary force, both of them ready to the last gun and button, we had neither men nor equipment equal to the fighting of a continental war, and we knew it. The fact is more than our justification—it is our glory. If we had meant war, as Germany still hoarsely but more faintly says, week after week, to a world that listens no longer, could any nation of sane men have behaved as we did in the years before the war?— 233,000 men on active service—and 263,000 territorials, against Germany's millions!—with arsenals and equipment to match. . . .

Then as to munitions: in many ways, as you will perhaps say, and as I agree, a tragic story. If we had possessed last spring the ammunition—both for ourselves and our allies we now possess, the war would have gone differently. Drunkenness, trade-union difficulties, a small—very small—revolutionary element among our work people— all these have made trouble. But the real

cause of our shortage lay in the fact that no one, outside Germany, realized till far into the war, what the ammunition needs—the absolutely unprecedented needs—of this struggle were going to be. It was the second Battle of Ypres at the end of April last year which burnt them into the English mind. We paid for the grim knowledge in thousands of our noblest lives. But since then?

In a later letter I propose to draw some picture in detail of the really marvellous movement which since last July, under the impulse given by Mr. Lloyd George, has covered England with new munition factories and added enormously to the producing power of the old and famous firms, has drawn in an army of women—now reckoned at something over a quarter of a million—and is at this moment not only providing amply for our own armies, but is helping those of the Allies against those final days of settlement with Germany which we believe to be now steadily approaching. American industry and enterprise have helped us substantially in this field of munitions. We are gratefully conscious of it. But England is now fast overtaking her own needs. . . .

And at the foundation of it all—the human and personal effort!—the lives given for England, the blood so generously shed for her, the homes that have sacrificed their all, our "golden lads" from all quarters and classes, whose young bodies lie mingled with an alien dust that "is for ever England," since they sleep there and hallow it; our mothers who mourn the death or the wreck of the splendid sons they reared; our widowed wives and fatherless children. And this, in a quarrel which only very slowly our people have come to feel as in very deed their own. At first we thought most often and most vividly of Belgium, of the broken treaty, and of France, so wantonly attacked, whose people no Englishman or woman could ever have looked in the face again, had we forsaken her. Then came the hammer blows that forged our will—Louvain, Aerschot, Rheims, the airraids on our defenseless towns, the senseless murder of our women and children, the

Bryce report, the *Lusitania*, the execution of Edith Cavell—the whole stupefying revelation of the German hatred and greed toward this country, and of the qualities latent in the German character. Now we *know*—that it is they, or we—since they willed it so. And this old, illogical, unready country is only just arriving at its full strength, only just fully conscious of the sternness of its own resolve. . . .

A new ministry was created—the ministry of munitions, and Mr. Lloyd George was placed at its head. The work that Mr. Lloyd George and his ministry—now employing vast new buildings, and a staff running into thousands—have done since June, 1915, is nothing less than colossal. Much no doubt had been done earlier for which the new ministry has perhaps unjustly got the credit, and not all has been smooth sailing since. One hears, of course, criticism and complaints. What vast and effective stir, for a great end, was ever made in the world without them?

Mr. Lloyd George has incurred a certain amount of unpopularity among the working classes, who formerly adored him. In my belief he has incurred it for the country's sake, and those sections of the working class who have smarted under his criticisms most bitterly will forgive him when the time comes. In his passionate determination to *get the thing done*, he has sometimes let his theme—of the national need, and the insignificance of all things else in comparison with it—carry him into a vehemence which the workmen have resented, and which foreign or neutral countries have misunderstood.

He found in his path, which was also the nation's path, three great foes—drunkenness, the old envenomed quarrel between employer and employed, and that deep-rooted industrial conservatism of England, which shows itself on the one hand in the trade-union customs and restrictions of the working class, built up, as they hold, through long years, for the protection of their own standards of life, and, on the other, in the slowness of many of the smaller English employers (I am aston-ished, however, at the notable exceptions everywhere!) to realize new needs and processes, and to adapt themselves to them. Could any one have made such an omelet without breaking a great many eggs? . . . What the workmen of England did in the first year of the war in her docks and shipyards, history will tell some day. . . .

I, too, have seen that utter fatigue stamped on a certain percentage of faces through the Midlands, or the districts of the Tyne and the Clyde—fatigue which is yet indomitable, which never gives way. How fresh, beside that look, are the faces of the women, for whom workshop life is new! In its presence one forgets all hostile criticism, all talk of strikes and drink, of trade-union difficulties, and the endless worries of the employers.

The English workman is not tractable material—far from it—and he is not imaginative; except in the persons of some of his chosen leaders, he has never seen a ruined French or Flemish village, and he was slow to realize the bitterness of that silence of the guns on the front, when ammunition runs short, and lives must pay. But he has sent his hundreds of thousands to the fighting line; there are a million and a half of him now working at munitions, and it is he, in a comradeship with the brain workers, the scientific intelligence of the nation, closer than any he has yet known, and lately, with the new and astonishing help of women—it is he, after all, who is "delivering the goods," . . .

There will be a new wind blowing through England when this war is done. Not only will the scientific intelligence, the general education, and the industrial plant of the nation have gained enormously from this huge impetus of war; but men and women, employers and employed, shaken perforce out of their old grooves, will look at each other surely with new eyes, in a world which has not been steeped for nothing in effort and sacrifice, in common griefs and a common passion of will. . . .

I am soon listening to the report of the works superintendent. . . . "As to the women!"—he throws up his hands—

"they're saving the country. They don't mind what they do. Hours? They work ten and a half or, with overtime, twelve hours a day, seven days a week. At least, that's what they'd like to do. The government are insisting on one Sunday—or two Sundays—a month off. I don't say they're not right. But the women resent it. *'We're* not tired!' they say. And you look at them!—they're not tired."

"If I go down to the shed and say: 'Girls!—there's a bit of work the government are pushing for—they say they must have—can you get it done?' Why, they'll stay and get it done, and then pour out of the works, laughing and singing. I can tell you of a surgical-dressing factory near here, where for nearly a year the women never had a holiday. They simply wouldn't take one. 'And what'll our men at the front do, if we go holiday-making?'

"Last night" (the night of the Zeppelin raid) "the warning came to put out lights. We daren't send them home. They sat in the dark among the machines, singing, 'Keep the home fires burning,' 'Tipperary,' and the like. I tell you, it made one a bit choky to hear them. They were thinking of their sweethearts and husbands I'll be bound!—not of themselves." . . .

As it is, by the sheer body of work the women have brought in, by the deftness, energy, and enthusiasm they throw into the simpler but quite indispensable processes, thereby setting the unskilled man free for the army, and the skilled man for work which women cannot do, Great Britain has become possessed of new and vast resources of which she scarcely dreamed a year ago. . . .

Meanwhile, as Mr. Asquith will explain next Tuesday, the expenditure on the war, not only on our own needs but on those of our Allies is colossal—terrifying. The most astonishing budget of English history, demanding a fourth of his income from every well-to-do citizen, has been brought in since I began to write these letters, and quietly accepted. Five hundred millions sterling ($2,500,000,000) have been already lent to our Allies. We are spending at the yearly rate of 600,000,000 sterling ($3,000,000,000) on the army; 200,000,000 on the navy as compared with 40,000,000 in 1913; while the munitions department is costing about two-thirds as much (400,000,000 sterling) as the rest of the army, and is employing close upon 2,000,000 workers, one-tenth of them women. The export trade of the country, in spite of submarines and lack of tonnage, is at the moment greater than it was in the corresponding months of 1913. . . .

The nation is behind the war, and behind the government—solidly determined to win this war, and build a new world after it. . . .

Sympathy with France—France, the invaded, the heroic—is easy for America—for us all. She is the great tragic figure of the war—the whole world does her homage. We are not invaded—and so less tragic, less appealing. But we are fighting the fight which is the fight of all freemen everywhere—against the wantonness of military power, against the spirit that tears up treaties and makes peaceful agreement between nations impossible—against a cruelty and barbarism in war which brings our civilization to shame. We have a right to your sympathy—you who are the heirs of Washington and Lincoln, the trustees of liberty in the New World as we, with France, are in the Old. You are concerned—you must be concerned—in the triumph of the ideals of ordered freedom and humane justice over the ideals of unbridled force and ruthless cruelty, as they have been revealed in this war, to the horror of mankind. The nation that can never, to all time, wash from its hands the guilt of the Belgium crime, the blood of the *Lusitania* victims, of the massacres of Louvain and Dinant, of Aerschot and Termonde, may some day deserve our pity. Today it has to be met and conquered by a will stronger than its own, in the interests of civilization itself. . . .

15

What Answer to the Great Depression: Communism, Fascism, or the British "Middle Way"?

For the continent of Europe, World War I (1914–1918) constituted a cataclysm of destruction in the course of which old empires were demolished, old political institutions dramatically transformed, and ancient boundary lines redrawn. Britain emerged from the war technically victorious, but with a generation of young men either dead (ca. 750,000) or wounded (ca. 1,700,000) and a gigantic national debt. An immediate post-war boom gave way to economic depression in 1921; a partial recovery during the later 1920s gave way to an even more severe depression between 1929 and 1932 and a gradual if partial recovery thereafter. Both World War I and the Great Depression helped evoke the mood of self-questioning illustrated by several of the selections in this chapter.

One of the consequences of the war was the decline of the Liberal Party and the transformation of Labour from a small third party into one of the nation's two most powerful political organizations. *Labour and the New Social Order* (1918), a document largely drafted by the veteran Fabian Socialist Sydney Webb (1859–1947), sets forth the party's long-range goals. What lessons does *Labour and the New Social Order* draw from World War I? What does Webb mean by the "Democratic Control of Industry"? How does the party expect to reduce the national debt? What future does it foresee for private industry?

The Labour Party under Ramsay MacDonald was able to form a government both in 1924 and again from 1929 to 1931, but on neither occasion did the party control an overall majority of seats in the House of Commons. The party that did control such a majority from 1924 to 1929 and again from 1931 on—as part of a coalition National Government—was the Conservative Party, headed by Stanley Baldwin. Shortly after the Conservative government took office in 1924, Neville Chamberlain (1869–1940), the new minister of health, sent his prime minister a memorandum, *Program of Legislation*, in which he outlined the social reform measures that he hoped to sponsor in Parliament on behalf of the government. What types of government involvement in the economy and in

March 23, 1933

PLEASANT EVENINGS ROUND THE FIRESIDE.

society does Chamberlain take for granted? How does his program differ in approach and in tone from Webb's in *Labour and the New Social Order?*

Most of Chamberlain's program had been enacted by 1929, but neither the Labour government of 1929–1931 nor the National Government that followed could at first halt the worldwide depression of the early 1930s. By late 1932 almost one Briton in four was out of work. It was in this context that John Strachey published *The Case for Communism* (1932) and Sir Oswald Mosley *The Case for Fascism* (1932). Both Strachey and Mosley came from well-established, upper-middle-class English families. John Strachey (1901–1963), an aspiring journalist and Labour Member of Parliament (1929–1931), had become convinced by 1932 that Britain's economy and political system required a revolutionary transformation. Although he never became an official member of Britain's Communist Party, his became "the most powerful intellectual voice in the Communist movement . . . throughout most of the thirties."[1] At the same time Oswald Mosley (1896–1980), erstwhile Conservative, Labour, and independent Member for Parliament (1918–1924, 1926–1931), became the founder and leader of the British Union of Fascists. What glaring faults do Strachey and Mosley find in the British economy and political system of their day? How are their proposals for dramatic change both alike and different? How is Strachey's program related to Stalin's Russia and Mosley's to Mussolini's Italy?

---

[1]"John Strachey," *Dictionary of National Biography, 1961–1970,* p. 988.

As matters worked out, neither Strachey's nor Mosley's political hopes were realized. Although Stalin's Soviet Union secretly subsidized the British Communist Party and Mussolini's Italy secretly subsidized the British Union of Fascists, neither movement ever won more than a relative handful of votes in Britain. (The Communist party did succeed, however, in winning the support of certain British intellectuals and in recruiting spies for the Soviet Union.) Strachey broke with the Communist party during the early years of World War II and became minister of food in the post–World War II Labour government. In the meantime Mosley and his Black Shirts came to be increasingly influenced by Hitler's National Socialism and antisemitism, and during World War II Mosley was placed under arrest for three years by the British government.

A considerable degree of economic recovery had taken place by the time Sir Ernest Barker (1874–1960) surveyed the reign of King George V in an article, "The Movement of National Life, 1910–1935," for *The Fortnightly Review.* The occasion was the king's Silver Jubilee. Barker was a distinguished historian of political thought who served at the time as professor of political science at Cambridge University. On which changes in technology and attitudes does he place the greatest emphasis? What changes had taken place among the classes, the sexes, and the cultures that made up Britain? Although he does not use the phrase "welfare state," which welfare state assumptions and institutions does Barker seem to take for granted? How does his article help explain why the Britain of 1935 remained a society notably different from Mussolini's Italy, Hitler's Germany, and Stalin's Soviet Union?

The relative political consensus about welfare state legislation that could be discerned during the 1930s was given an additional boost by Britain's fight for national survival during World War II (1939–1945). Late in 1942 a government committee headed by the veteran Liberal social reformer Sir William Beveridge (1879–1963) published its *Report on Social Insurance,* a blueprint for the postwar era that captured the imagination of a generation. How does Beveridge's proposal differ from the earlier pattern of social legislation in Britain? What personal and family needs does the plan seek to address? What type of work pattern and family structure does Beveridge take for granted? Much of the Beveridge Report of 1942 was to be enacted into law between 1946 and 1948 by the post-1945 Labour government.

THE LABOUR PARTY **Labour and the New Social Order (1918)**

The expansion of trade unionism spurred by World War I and the extension of the franchise brought about by the Reform Act of 1918 made a separate Labour Party an influential political force for the first time. Its program, outlined below, was drafted initially by Sydney Webb of the Fabian Society.

SOURCE: From the Labour Party, *Labour and the New Social Order* (London, 1918), pp. 3–22. By permission of the Labour Party.

It behooves the Labour party, in formulating its own program for reconstruction after the war, and in criticizing the various preparations and plans that are being made by the present government, to look at the problem as a whole. We have to make clear what it is that we wish to construct. It is important to emphasize the fact that, whatever may be the case with regard to other political parties, our detailed practical proposals proceed from definitely held principles.

The End of a Civilization

We need to beware of patchwork. The view of the Labour party is that what has to be reconstructed after the war is not this or that government department, or this or that piece of social machinery; but, so far as Britain is concerned, society itself. The individual worker, or for that matter the individual statesman, immersed in daily routine—like the individual soldier in a battle—easily fails to understand the magnitude and far-reaching importance of what is taking place around him. How does it fit together as a whole? How does it look from a distance? Count Okuma, one of the oldest, most experienced and ablest of the statesmen of Japan, watching the present conflict from the other side of the globe, declares it to be nothing less than the death of European civilization. . . .

What this war is consuming is not merely the security, the homes, the livelihood and the lives of millions of innocent families, and an enormous proportion of all the accumulated wealth of the world, but also the very basis of the peculiar social order in which it has arisen. The individualist system of capitalist production, based on the private ownership and competitive administration of land and capital, which has in the past couple of centuries become the dominant form, with its reckless "profiteering" and wage-slavery; with its glorification of the unhampered struggle for the means of life and its hypocritical pretence of the "survival of the fittest"; with the monstrous inequality of circumstances

which it produces and the degradation and brutalization, both moral and spiritual, resulting therefrom, may, we hope, indeed have received a death-blow. With it must go the political system and ideas in which it naturally found expression. We of the Labour party, whether in opposition or in due time called upon to form an administration, will certainly lend no hand to its revival. On the contrary, we shall do our utmost to see that it is buried with the millions whom it has done to death. . . .

The Pillars of the House

We need not here recapitulate, one by one, the different items in the Labour party's program, which successive party conferences have adopted. These proposals, some of them in various publications worked out in practical detail, are often carelessly derided as impracticable, even by the politicians who steal them piecemeal from us! . . . The war, which has scared the old political parties right out of their dogmas, has taught every statesman and every government official, to his enduring surprise, how very much more can be done along the lines that we have laid down than he had ever before thought possible. What we now promulgate as our policy, whether for opposition or for office, is not merely this or that specific reform, but a deliberately thought out, systematic, and comprehensive plan for that immediate social rebuilding which any ministry, whether or not it desires to grapple with the problem, will be driven to undertake. The Four Pillars of the house that we propose to erect, resting upon the common foundation of the democratic control of society in all its activities, may be termed, respectively:

(a) The Universal Enforcement of the National Minimum;

(b) The Democratic Control of Industry;

(c) The Revolution in National Finance; and

(d) The Surplus Wealth for the Common Good.

The Universal Enforcement of a National Minimum

The first principle of the Labour party—in significant contrast with those of the capitalist system, whether expressed by the Liberal or by the Conservative party—is the securing to every member of the community, in good times and bad alike (and not only to the strong and able, the well-born or the fortunate), of all the requisites of healthy life and worthy citizenship. . . .

The Legislative Regulation of Employment

Thus it is that the Labour party to-day stands for the universal application of the policy of the national minimum, to which (as embodied in the successive elaborations of the factory, mines, railways, shops, merchant shipping, trade boards, and truck acts, the public health, housing, and education acts, and the minimum wage acts) the spokesmen of Labour have already gained the support of the enlightened statesmen and economists of the world. All these laws purporting to prevent any degradation of the standard of life need considerable improvement and extension. . . .

Securing Employment for All

The Labour party insists [that] . . . it is one of the foremost obligations of the government to find, for every willing worker, whether by hand or by brain, productive work at standard rates.

It is accordingly the duty of the government to adopt a policy of deliberately and systematically preventing the occurrence of unemployment, instead of (as heretofore) letting unemployment occur, and then seeking, vainly and expensively, to relieve the unemployed. . . .

Social Insurance Against Unemployment

In so far as the government fails to prevent unemployment—whenever it finds it impossible to discover for any willing worker, man or woman, a suitable situation at the standard rate—the Labour party holds that

the government must, in the interest of the community as a whole, provide him or her with adequate maintenance, either with such arrangements for honorable employment or with such useful training as may be found practicable, according to age, health and previous occupation. . . .

The Democratic Control of Industry

. . . Unlike the Conservative and Liberal Parties, the Labour party insists on democracy in industry as well as in government. It demands the progressive elimination from the control of industry of the private capitalist, individual or joint-stock; and the setting free of all who work, whether by hand or by brain, for the service of the community, and of the community only. And the Labour party refuses absolutely to believe that the British people will permanently tolerate any reconstruction or perpetuation of the disorganization, waste and inefficiency involved in the abandonment of British industry to a jostling crowd of separate private employers, with their minds bent, not on the service of the community, but—by the very law of their being—only on the utmost possible profiteering. . . .

Immediate Nationalization

The Labour party stands not merely for the principle of the common ownership of the nation's land, to be applied as suitable opportunities occur, but also, specifically, for the immediate nationalization of railways, mines and the production of electrical power. . . .

In quite another sphere the Labour party sees the key to temperance reform in taking the entire manufacture and retailing of alcoholic drink out of the hands of those who find profit in promoting the utmost possible consumption. . . .

Local Government

The Labour party is alive to the evils of centralization and the drawbacks of bureaucracy. To counteract these disadvantages it intends that the fullest possible scope shall be given, in all branches of social reconstruction, to the democratically elected local governing bodies. . . . The Labour party holds, moreover, that the municipalities and county councils should not confine themselves to the necessarily costly services of education, sanitation, and police, and the functions to be taken over from the boards of guardians, nor yet rest content with acquiring control of the local water, gas, electricity, and tramways, but that they should greatly extend their enterprises in housing and town planning, parks, and public libraries, the provision of music and the organization of popular recreation, and also that they should be empowered to undertake, not only the retailing of coal, but also other services of common utility, particularly the local supply of milk, where this is not already fully and satisfactorily organized by a co-operative society. . . .

By far the most important function of the local authorities is the administration of education. The first step to social reconstruction must be a genuine nationalization of education, which shall get rid of all class distinction and privileges, and bring effectively within the reach, not only of every boy and girl, but also of every adult citizen, all the training, physical, mental and moral, literary, technical, and artistic of which he is capable. . . .

A Revolution in National Finance

In taxation, also, the interests of the professional and housekeeping classes are at one with those of the manual workers. Too long has our national finance been regulated, contrary to the teaching of political economy, according to the wishes of the possessing classes and the profits of the financiers. The colossal expenditure involved in the present war (of which, against the protest of the Labour party, only a quarter has been raised by taxation, whilst three-quarters have been borrowed at onerous rates of interest, to be a burden on the nation's future) brings things to a crisis. . . . How are we to discharge a public debt that

may well reach the almost incredible figure of 7,000 million pounds sterling, and at the same time raise an annual revenue which, for local as well as central government, must probably reach 1,000 millions a year? It is over this problem of taxation that the various political parties will be found to be most sharply divided.

The Labour party stands for such a system of taxation as will yield all the necessary revenue to the government without encroaching on the prescribed national minimum standard of life of any family whatsoever; without hampering production or discouraging any useful personal effort, and with the nearest possible approximation to equality of sacrifice. We definitely repudiate all proposals for a protective tariff, in whatever specious guise they may be cloaked, as a device for burdening the consumer with unnecessarily enhanced prices, to the profit of the capitalist employer or landed proprietor, who avowedly expects his profit or rent to be increased thereby. . . .

For the raising of the greater part of the revenue now required the Labour party looks to the direct taxation of the incomes above the necessary cost of family maintenance; and for the requisite effort to pay off the national debt, to the direct taxation of private fortunes both during life and at death. The income tax and super-tax ought at once to be thoroughly reformed in assessment and collection, in abatements and allowances and in graduation and differentiation, so as to levy the required total sum in such a way as to make the real sacrifice of all the taxpayers as nearly as possible equal. This would involve assessment by families instead of by individual persons, so that the burden is alleviated in proportion to the number of persons to be maintained. It would involve the raising of the present unduly low minimum income assessable to the tax, and the lightening of the present unfair burden on the great mass of professional and small trading classes by a new scale of graduation, rising from a penny in the pound on the smallest assessable income up to sixteen or even nineteen shillings in the pound on the highest income of the millionaires. . . .

At the same time, for the service and redemption of the national debt, the death duties ought to be regraduated, much more strictly collected, and greatly increased. In this matter we need, in fact, completely to reverse our point of view, and to rearrange the whole taxation of inheritance from the standpoint of asking what is the maximum amount that any rich man should be permitted at death to divert, by his will, from the national exchequer, which should normally be the heir to all private riches in excess of a quite moderate amount by way of family provision. But all this will not suffice, . . . and the Labour party stands for what is called the "Conscription of Wealth" —that is to say, for a special capital levy to pay off, if not the whole, a very substantial part of the entire national debt. . . .

The Street of To-morrow

The house which the Labour party intends to build, the Four Pillars of which have now been described, does not stand alone in the world. Where will it be in the Street of To-morrow? If we repudiate, on the one hand, the imperialism that seeks to dominate other races, or to impose our own will on other parts of the British Empire, so we disclaim equally any conception of a selfish and insular "non-interventionism," unregarding of our special obligations to our fellow-citizens overseas; of the corporate duties of one nation to another; of the moral claims upon us of the non-adult races, and of our own indebtedness to the world of which we are part. We look for an ever-increasing intercourse, a constantly developing exchange of commodities, a steadily growing mutual understanding, and a continually expanding friendly co-operation among all the peoples of the world. With regard to that great Commonwealth of all races, all colors, all religions and all degrees of civilization, that we call the British Empire, the Labour party stands for its maintenance and its progressive development on the lines of local autonomy and "Home Rule All Round"; the fullest respect for the rights of each people, whatever its color, to all the democratic self-government of which it is capable, and to the proceeds of its own toil upon the resources of its own territorial home; and the closest possible co-operation among all the various members of what has become essentially not an empire in the old sense, but a Britannic Alliance. . . .

NEVILLE CHAMBERLAIN **Program of Legislation (1924)**

In 1924 a Labour government headed by Prime Minister Ramsay MacDonald briefly came to power, but after the general election of November 1924, it was replaced by a Conservative government headed by Stanley Baldwin. In the following memorandum, Baldwin's new minister of health, Neville Chamberlain, outlines his own legislative program for the next several years. Twenty-one of the twenty-five measures that Chamberlain projects were enacted into law between 1925 and 1929.

1. With a prospect of a continuous administration for a few years ahead, it is possible to make plans in advance, and I have therefore been engaged in preparing a provisional program of legislation dealing with various subjects in which the ministry of health are directly or indirectly concerned.

2. Apart from bills which will be required to replace various expiring enactments and some minor departmental bills, the program represents a connected series of reforms spread over a period of 3 to 4 years, and if this program is to be carried out it will be necessary to make an early

SOURCE: Reprinted from *The Life of Neville Chamberlain* by Keith Feiling, © 1970 (Archon Books, Hamden, Connecticut), pp. 459–462.

start with some parts of it on which the work is more advanced, in order to clear the way for the remainder.

3. I append a schedule showing the proposed bills and their approximate date of introduction.

4. All political parties have repeatedly subscribed to the doctrine of Poor Law reform, and the late government under parliamentary pressure appointed a cabinet committee which instructed the ministry of health to prepare a detailed scheme.

Without recalling the well-known arguments in favor of Poor Law reform, I may note the following points:

(a) The overlapping of the guardians' functions with the health function of the local authorities constitutes an ever-present difficulty in current administration, and until this overlapping is removed there can be no real advance in the direction of a properly organized Health Service. For example, as matters stand, there may be numbers of empty beds in the Poor Law infirmaries and long waiting lists at the voluntary hospitals, and proper use cannot be made of the total hospital accommodation in an area until there is in existence one health authority charged with the responsibility for the health of the area, so far as that responsibility is a public one.

(b) The developments in national health insurance which may be expected to follow from the findings of the Royal Commission now sitting cannot be attained without the creation of a single health authority in each local area. The national health insurance scheme should obviously be linked up with the general public health organization, and the readiest way to do this is to make the insurance committee which now administers medical benefit under the insurance scheme a committee of the local health authority.

(c) The gradual diminution in the number of persons requiring assistance from the guardians, which has been going on since the report of the Royal Commission, was materially accelerated by the recent Unemployment Insurance Act,

and a further step in this direction will be taken if a scheme for widows' pensions and old-age pensions commencing at 65 is adopted.

(d) Unless Poor Law reform is undertaken in 1926 it will be necessary to ask Parliament to renew the Local Authorities (Emergency Provisions) Acts which provide for centralizing the cost of outrelief in London. This would revive in an acute form the problem of London government, which in my view can only be resolved by a prior settlement of the Poor Law question.

5. At the present time valuation and rating are attached chiefly to the Poor Law areas and the Poor Law authorities, and accordingly any schemes of Poor Law reform which proceeds on the lines of transferring the functions of the Poor Law guardians to other bodies would necessarily involve a reconstruction of the machinery of valuation and rating. . . .

7. I accordingly suggest that the Cabinet (a) should give provisional approval to the appended program of legislation, and (b) should appoint a Committee to settle certain points of policy in connection with the Rating and Valuation Bill, and to make recommendations as to the main principles underlying the draft scheme of Poor Law Reform prepared by the Ministry of Health.

N. C.

Ministry of Health
19th November 1924

Provisional Program of Legislation

1925–1926

1. *Agricultural Rates.*—Bill to continue the Agricultural Rates Act, 1923.
2. *Valuation (Metropolis).*—Bill to amend the Repairs Schedule to the Act of 1869 before the next quinquennial valuation in 1925.
3. *Rent Restriction.*—Bill to continue for a further period the Rent Restriction Acts.
4. *Milk.*—Bill to replace the Milk and

Dairies (Amendment) Act, 1922, which postponed the operation of the Milk and Dairies (Consolidation) Act, 1915, until 1st September 1925.

5. *Therapeutic Substances.*—Bill to regulate the manufacture and sale of certain therapeutic substances.

6. *Rating and Valuation.*—Bill to reform the present system of rating and valuation in England and Wales.

7. *Rating of Machinery.*—Bill to amend the laws as to the rating of machinery.

8. *Tithe.*—Bill to deal with the redemption and rating of tithe rent-charge.

9. *Smoke.*—Bill to provide for smoke abatement.

10. *Housing (Consolidation).*

11. *Town Planning (Consolidation).*

1926

12. *Poor Law.*—Bill to reform the Poor Law.

13. *Widows' and Old-Age Pensions.*—Bill to establish contributory schemes of pensions for widows and old-age pensions at 65.

14. *Local Government.*—Bill to give effect to recommendation of Lord Onslow's commission in regard to creation and extension of county boroughs and other local government matters.

15. *Registration Service.*—Bill to reorganize terms and conditions of service of registrars of births, deaths, and marriages.

16. *Public Health (Amendment).*—Bill to amend the Public Health Acts.

17. *Maternity Homes.*—Bill to provide for the better regulation of maternity homes.

18. *Proprietary Medicines.*—Bill to regulate the sale of proprietary medicines.

19. *Food and Drugs.*—Bill to regulate the use of preservatives in food.

20. *National Health Insurance.*—Temporary bill to provide for doctors' remuneration on expiry of present arrangements.

21. *Public Health (Consolidation).*

1927

22. *National Health Insurance.*—Bill to give effect to recommendations of the Royal Commission on Insurance.

23. *Mental Treatment.*—Bill to give effect to recommendations of the Royal Commission on Lunacy.

24. *Local Taxation.*—Bill to reform local taxation, including revision of the present system of exchequer grants.

25. *Housing.*—Bill to deal with slums, including town planning in built-up areas, and (possibly) housing in rural districts.

JOHN STRACHEY **The Case for Communism (1932)**

Writing during the depths of the interwar economic depression, a youthful British journalist and Labour Member of Parliament (1929–1931) seeks to convince his fellow Britons that capitalism—however modified by social reform legislation—has failed and that communism provides the only solution to the difficulties that threaten their country.

Communism is a principle of social organization antithetical to capitalism. It solves the problem of organizing production by entirely different methods. It does not attempt to secure the concentration of the means of production by vesting their own-

SOURCE: John Strachey, *The Coming Struggle for Power* (New York: The Modern Library, 1935), pp. 343–360. First published in London in 1932. Reprinted by permission of the estate of John Strachey.

ership in the hands of a class, nor does it leave the adjustment of the life of the community to the motives of the market. Indeed, communist methods of organizing production cannot be even attempted until the class ownership of the means of production has been ended, and until the economic adjustments of society have been freed from the influence of the motives of the market. . . . Such a society would, of course, be moneyless as well as classless. . . .

[Karl] Marx . . . distinguishes clearly a primary, transitional stage of communism, which must follow the revolution. . . . It must, therefore, be clearly understood that when we use the word communism we use it to denote not ultimate, fully developed, communism, but the primary transitional stage of communism which must follow the overthrow of capitalism. . . .

A communist society (in its primary transitional stages) is one in which the mechanism of the market has been superseded by a planned direction of production; in which this change has been effected by taking the instruments of production from their present owners and vesting them in the hands of the working class. In consequence of this act, the working class gradually becomes identical with the community. . . .

What in practice happens in a communist society is simple. Society, through the institutions (councils, committees, call them what you will) which it sets up for the purpose, frames a body of rules for the duration, conditions, and remuneration, of the work which different categories of its members must perform. And these rules the members of society impose upon themselves. They see the necessity of going each day to factory, mine or field, and utilizing the means of production to satisfy their needs. Naturally, this does not mean that individuals here and there will see any such necessity: that particular individuals will not seek to enjoy the social fruits, without undergoing the social labor necessary to their production. And it will certainly be necessary to enforce compulsorily upon such individuals the rules of work which

society has laid down. And all the other members of society will be strongly in favor of such an enforcement. For no one likes to have the maintenance of his neighbor imposed upon him by that neighbor's idleness. . . .

No community, however, can pass overnight even to the primary transitional stage of communism. In the early stages of a working-class dictatorship, it may even be true to say that the obligation to labor is a compulsion imposed by the conscious and reflecting members of society both on themselves and on those members who, if left to themselves, would not realize the desirability of more labor than would just maintain themselves on the most primitive standards. . . . Moreover, with each advance in the level of technique, the character of necessary labor will change; it will become less irksome and arduous, more interesting and less exhausting. The barrier between mental and physical labor will be broken down. . . .

In order to hasten this process, communism requires, and requires urgently, the very maximum possible application and extension of scientific knowledge. The ruling class, which must rapidly become coterminous with society as a whole, will have a direct and personal interest in minimizing the amount of human toil necessary to a given standard of life. Since under communism there is no longer an antagonism of opposite status—freeman and serf, property owner and proletarian—man will be at last in a position to turn his entire energies to the subjugation of his oldest antagonist, nature. Indeed, just as communism only becomes possible when previous social systems have raised the level of man's comprehensive command over nature to a certain point, so the maintenance of communism is closely associated with a continued development of scientific knowledge and skill. . . . Rapid scientific development will everywhere follow, as it followed in Russia, the establishment of working-class power. . . .

This brings us to a wider consideration. Since there are, by definition, no classes in a communist society, there can be no class friction: there can be no necessity for those immense expenditures of social effort which are to-day necessary in order forcibly to adjust the relationship of inherently antagonistic classes. . . . Remove class conflict in the only way in which it can be removed, namely, by the abolition of classes, and nine-tenths of the present activities of the state become redundant. What are left are not really state activities at all; they are rather economic functions of regulation and distribution which are not part of the original work of the capitalist state at all. . . .

We now come to the most striking of all the contrasts between communism and the present, imperialist, phase of capitalism. Communism is, in its very essence, internationalist. Just as communism provides the only possible solution of the problem of the class conflict by abolishing classes, it also provides the only solution of the problem of the international conflict, by abolishing national sovereignties. It is non-national, both in its economic basis and the system of ideas which it builds upon that basis. A communist economy cannot possibly admit of national boundaries. A single planned economy must extend throughout the area which has become communist. Thus there cannot ever be . . . two communist nations in the world at the same time. . . . For example, when the German working class obtains power, the world will not see a communist Germany and a communist Russia. There will still be one Union of Socialist Soviet Republics, but now it will extend westward to the Rhine. . . . [Similarly] the welfare of the workers of a Soviet Britain will in no way depend upon their power relative to some other constituent part of the worldwide Union of Soviet Republics. Hence, it will be possible for such communities, and for such communities alone, "to cooperate happily together."

Thus we arrive at the crucial contrast between communism and present-day capitalist imperialism. Communism does provide a basis upon which the world can be progressively unified. . . . For just as the capi-

talist class is driven, in order to maintain itself in power, to seek to divide the workers into mutually odious national groups, so the conscious elements in the working class, in order to achieve working-class power, must necessarily urge the basic identity of interest, the basic solidarity, of all workers; must urge the unreality in the modern world of national divisions, and the reality of class divisions. . . . Communism is inherently capable of world unity; capitalist imperialism is inherently incapable of world unity.

But it would be absurd to consider the nature of communism without alluding to the Soviet Union. The first thing, however, which we must observe is that never has a single Soviet leader claimed that the Union is to-day a communist community. The Soviet Union cannot be considered to be as yet a community in even the primary stage of communism, which we have defined. Many capitalists remnants are still present. It is hoped, however, that by the end of the Second Five-Year Plan, in 1937, that is, it will be possible to speak of a communist society in Russia. Both Lenin and Stalin, for example, have been scrupulous to point out that it would be childishly and ridiculously un-Marxian to suppose that the Russian republics could leap in a year or so from the conditions of 1917 into communism. . . . But they showed themselves to be men of incomparable resolution and marvelous historical insight when they determined that the smoking ruins which were bequeathed to them by the Russian imperialists did offer the possibility of a firmly established working-class dictatorship; and that such a dictatorship alone could rebuild Russia. With what dazzling audacity did Lenin conceive his project: with what colossal tenacity has Stalin clung to its execution. The little group of Marxists who helped the Russian worker to build that indispensable instrument for the execution of their class will, the Russian Communist Party, are now passing one by one into history. And it is certain that history will record no parallel to the task which they attempted, and which their survivors and successors are now carrying forward, stage by stage, toward its completion. . . . Hence, the history of the Soviet Union affords an example of the power and achievements of a working-class dictatorship in transforming, in the face of the most adverse circumstances, the basis of the life of a community, rather than an example of communism in existence. But the Soviet Union does of course give us by far the best indications—indeed the only concrete indications which we have—of what communism will be like when it does come into existence. . . .

The coming of communism can alone can render our problems soluble. A working-class dictatorship can alone open the way to communism. A working-class dictatorship can only be successful if the workers as a whole achieve a clear understanding of the historic destiny of their class. And this understanding, in turn, cannot be developed unless the working class succeeds in organizing its most conscious and clear-sighted members into that indispensable instrument of the workers' will, a Communist Party. The assumption of power by the workers can occur by means of revolution alone; by means, that is, of an event which takes place over a limited number of years, and of which there may be a critical moment, such as the conquest of the existing state apparatus in a capital city, which can be "dated" to a given week of a given month of a given year. The coming of communism itself, however, after the achievement of working-class power, must be a gradual process. And it is only gradually, with the emergence of communism, with the creation—and that, we may be sure, only by Herculean labors and painful sacrifices—of the essential economic basis for a classless society, that the problems which to-day threaten civilization with eclipse will actually be solved. . . . Even to-day in the Soviet Union, during the very brunt of the initial struggles of a working-class dictatorship, before a classless society has fully emerged, there is perceptible an exhilaration of living which finds no parallel in the world. To travel from the capitalist world into Soviet territory is to pass from death to birth. . . .

Sir Oswald Mosley   The Case for Fascism (1932)

Writing, like Strachey, during the depths of the Great Depression, a young British Member of Parliament (1918–1924, 1926–1931) seeks to convince his fellow Britons that only the British Union of Fascists can save the country from its economic problems and from Parliament's political impotence.

Introduction

The Breakdown

In Great Britain during the past ten years there have never been less than a million unemployed, and at present unemployment approaches the three million figure. In 1929—a year which is now regarded as the peak of industrial prosperity—British trade was slack, large industrial areas were almost derelict, and only the stock markets enjoyed a semblance of boom conditions.

We have tragic proof that economic life has outgrown our political institutions. Britain has failed to recover from the war period; and this result, however complicated by special causes, is largely due to a system of government designed by, and for, the nineteenth century.

Setting aside any complaint of the conduct or capacity of individual governments,

SOURCE: Sir Oswald Mosley, *The Greater Britain* (London: British Union of Fascists, 1932), pp. 11–25.

I believe that, under the existing system, government cannot be efficiently conducted.

The object of this book is to prove, by analysis of the present situation and by constructive policy, that the necessity for a fundamental change exists. Our political system dates substantially from 1832. The intervening century has seen the invention and development of telegraph, telephone and wireless. At the beginning of the period, railways were a novelty, and a journey of a dozen miles was a serious undertaking. . . . The huge expansion of commerce has made us depend more and more on one another; the building-up of popular newspapers has organized and formulated popular opinion.

From the standpoint of a century ago, all these changes are revolutionary. The sphere of government has widened and the complications of government have increased. It is hardly surprising that the political system of 1832 is wholly out of date to-day. . . . *Our problem is to reconcile the revolutionary changes of science with our system of government, and to harmonize individual initiative with the wider interests of the nation.*

Fascism—the Modern Movement

Hence the need for a New Movement, not only in politics, but in the whole of our national life. The movement is Fascist, (i) because it is based on a high conception of citizenship—ideals as lofty as those which inspired the reformers of a hundred years ago; (ii) because it recognizes the necessity for an authoritative state, above party and sectional interests. Some may be prejudiced by the use of the word "Fascist," because that word has so far been completely misunderstood in this country. It would be easy for us to avoid that prejudice by using another word, but it would not be honest to do so. We seek to organize the Modern Movement in this country by British methods in a form which is suitable to and characteristic of Great Britain. We are essentially a national movement, and if our

policy could be summarized in two words, they would be "Britain First." Nevertheless, the Modern Movement is by no means confined to Great Britain; it comes to all the great countries in turn as their hour of crisis approaches, and in each country it naturally assumes a form and a character suited to that nation. As a world-wide movement, it has come to be known as "Fascism," and it is therefore right to use that name. . . .

Misrepresentation

All new movements are misunderstood. Our British Union of Fascists will without a doubt be misrepresented by politicians of the older schools. The movement did not begin with the wiseacres and the theorists. It was born from a surging discontent with a regime where nothing can be achieved. . . . We are also faced by the fact that a few people have misused the name "Fascism" in this country, and from ignorance or in perversion have represented it as the "White Guard of reaction."

This is indeed a strange perversion of a creed of dynamic change and progress. In all countries, fascism has been led by men who came from the "Left," and the rank and file has combined the conservative and patriotic elements of the nation with ex-socialists, ex-communists and revolutionaries who have forsaken their various *illusions* of progress for the new and orderly *reality* of progress. In our new organization we now combine within our ranks all those elements in this country who have long studied and understood the great constructive mission of fascism; but we have no place for those who have sought to make fascism the lackey of reaction, and have thereby misrepresented its policy and dissipated its strength. In fact fascism is the greatest constructive and revolutionary creed in the world. It seeks to achieve its aim legally and constitutionally, by methods of law and order; *but in objective it is revolutionary or it is nothing.* It challenges the existing order and advances the constructive alternative of the corporate state. To many of us this creed represents the thing which we have sought throughout our political lives. *It combines the dynamic urge to change and progress with the authority, the discipline and the order without which nothing great can be achieved. . . .*

CHAPTER 1

Creed and System

Stability and Progress

In the ranks of conservatism there are many who are attracted there by the party's tradition of loyalty, order and stability—but who are, none the less, repelled by its lethargy and stagnation. In the ranks of Labour there are many who follow the party's humane ideals, and are attracted by its vital urge to remedy social and economic evils—but who are, none the less, repelled by its endless and inconclusive debates, its cowardice, its lack of leadership and decision.

These elements comprise the best of both parties: and to both fascism appeals. The two essential of government are stability and progress; and the tragedy of politics is that the two, essentially coincident, are organized as contradictions. Stability implies order and authority, without which nothing can be done. It is regarded as belonging to the "Right." Progress implies the urge to reform without which society cannot survive. It is regarded as belonging to the "Left." Stability is confused with reaction and a stand-pat resistance to change: progress with ill-considered changes, or with the futile and paralytic discussions so characteristic of a timorous democracy. As a result, neither of these essentials is achieved. This is a dynamic age. . . .

We are faced to-day with the results of government by indecision, compromise and blether. Both political parties, and the remnants of Liberalism as well, stand bound by the great vested interests of "Right" and "Left" which created them. In Opposition, there is the same profusion of promise; in office, the same apathy and inertia. In postwar England, their creeds have become platitudes; they consistently fail to grapple with the problems of the time. Their rule has led, with tragic inevitability, to the present chaos. Therefore our Fascist Movement seeks on the one hand Stability, which envisages order and authority as the basis of all solid achievement; we seek, on the other hand, Progress, which can be achieved only by the executive instrument that order, authority and decision alone can give.

Parliament

Fascism, as we understand it, is not a creed of personal dictatorship in the continental manner. The dictatorship of Mussolini in Italy is merely dictatorship of the revolutionary machine, consequent on the changes having been effected by a violent revolution owing to the collapse and surrender of government. Neither is fascism a creed of government tyranny. But it is definitely a creed of effective government. Parliament is, or should be, the mouthpiece of the will of the people; but, as things stand at present, its time is mainly taken up with matters of which the nation neither knows nor cares. . . . The discussion, too, is usually futile; most of the bills before Parliament demand technical knowledge; but they are discussed, voted on, and their fate decided, by men and women chosen for their assiduity in opening local charity bazaars, or for their lung power at street corners. . . .

In a practical system of government our political philosophy comes to these conclusions. Whatever movement or party be entrusted with government must be given absolute power to act. Let the people preserve, through an elected Parliament, the power to dismiss and to change the government of the day. While such power is retained, the charge of dictatorship has no reality. On the other hand, the power of obstruction, the interminable debate of small points which to-day frustrate the nation's will to action, must be abolished. The present parliamentary system is not the expression, but the negation, of the people's will. *Gov-*

ernment must have power to legislate by order, subject to the power of Parliament to dismiss it by vote of censure. We must eliminate the solemn humbug of six hundred men and women indulging in detailed debate of every technical measure handled by a non-technical assembly in a vastly technical age. Thus only shall we clear the way to the real fulfillment of the nation's desire, which is to get things done in modern conditions.

Liberty

When we propose an effective system of government we are, of course, charged with the negation of liberty by those who have erected liberty into the negation of action. Liberty, by the definition of the old parliamentarians, becomes the last entrenchment of obstruction.

We hear so much glib talk of liberty, and so little understanding of its meaning. Surely nobody can imagine that the British, as a race, are free. The essence of liberty is freedom to enjoy some of the fruits of life, a reasonable standard of life, a decent house, good wages, reasonable hours of leisure after hours of work short enough not to leave a man exhausted, unmolested private happiness with wife, children and friends and, finally, the hope of material success to set the seal on private ambition: these are the realities of liberty to the ordinary man. How many possess this liberty to-day? How can the mass possess such freedom in a period of economic chaos? Many unemployed, the remainder living in the shadow of unemployment, low wages, long hours of exhausting labor, bad houses, shrinking social amenities, the uncertainty of industrial collapse and universal confusion: these are the lot of the average man to-day. What humbug, then, to talk of liberty! *The beginning of liberty is the end of economic chaos.* Yet how can economic chaos be overcome without the power to act?

...In complicated affairs of this kind, *somebody must be trusted, or nothing will ever be done.* The government, once in power, must have power to legislate by or-

der; and Parliament must have power to dismiss the government by vote of censure. This is the kernel of our parliamentary proposals. To some it may seem to imply the suppression of liberty, but *we prefer to believe that it will mean the suppression of chaos.*

Organization of the Modern Movement

The same principles which are essential to government apply, with even greater force, to a political movement of modern and fascist structure. Here we are dealing, not with the mass, but with men who believe in the cause, and are devoting their energy to its aims.

We have seen the political parties of the old democracy collapse into futility through the sterility of committee government and the cowardice and irresponsibility of their leadership. Voluntary discipline is the essence of the Modern Movement. Its leadership may be an individual, or preferably, in the case of the British character, a team with clearly allocated functions and responsibility. In either case, the only effective instrument of revolutionary change is absolute authority. We are organized, therefore, as a disciplined army, not as a bewildered mob with every member bellowing orders. Fascist leadership must lead, and its discipline must be respected. . . .

The immediate task is the firm establishment of the Modern Movement in the life of the British nation. Ultimately, nations are saved from chaos, not by Parliaments, however elected; not by civil servants, however instructed; but by the steady will of an organized movement to victory. . . .

For such purpose is needed the grip of an organized and disciplined movement, grasping and permeating every aspect of national life. In every town and village, in every institution of daily life, the will of the organized and determined minority must be struggling for sustained effort. In moments of difficulty, dissolution and despair it must be the hard core round which the weak and the dismayed may rally. The Modern Movement, in struggle and in victory, must be ineradicably interwoven with the life of the nation. No ordinary party of the past, resting on organizations of old women, teafights and committees, can survive in such a struggle. Our hope is centered in vital and

determined youth, dedicated to the resurrection of a nation's greatness and shrinking from no effort and from no sacrifice to secure that mighty end. We need the sublime enthusiasm of a nation, and the devoted energies of its servants. . . .

SIR ERNEST BARKER   **The Movement of National Life, 1910–1935 (1935)**

On the occasion of the Silver Jubilee of the reign of King George V in 1935, Sir Ernest Barker, a historian of political thought at Oxford University, looks back on twenty-five years of turmoil—and progress.

A center of calm in a blowing wind of change—a signal of comfort and assurance on a ship driving rapidly forward—that is how we think of the king, when we listen to his voice diffused through all the airs of the world, as we did last Christmas. He has seen great changes unrolled before his eyes in the last quarter of a century, as he has stood on the bridge and watched the voyage of his people into a new age and a new temper of life. What stock can we take of the course we have traversed during his reign and under his flag?

I

A gust of mechanical changes has produced a revolution in our material way of life. There has been a great age of applied physics. Perhaps it will be succeeded by a great age of applied biology, which will breed a new race of men, new stocks of animals, new crops of plants and all the kindly fruits of the earth. But we are still in the age of applied physics and all its marvels. The pace of life has been quickened by the motor-car, the aeroplane, the telephone, wireless. We lived at a different tempo. We can move more quickly by land, sea and air; we can communicate thoughts and visual images far more rapidly, by new methods of diffusing sound and sight.

A world in which transport, and all other

means of communication, have been quickened from *andante* to *presto*, is also a world which is far more interconnected. Not only do things move faster and farther than they used to do, men are also brought more together than they used to be, and they share more together in hearing and seeing the same thing. The same film is shown in London and Florence. The same music is heard on the wireless in Cambridge and Stockholm. Our minds are driven to a new rapidity and a new catholicity. More psychological elasticity is demanded of us. We have to stretch our faculties to a quicker exercise and a wider reach. It is a question whether we can keep pace with the pace of our own inventions. But they will not stop. And we, too, cannot stop.

Perhaps some of the social and political movements of our time on the continent of Europe are connected with the physical revolution through which we are going. They tend towards an idolization of the group—the race, the nation, the class. They use the new physical means of mass-propaganda—the staged demonstration of masses of men brought together by new and quicker means of transport: the film, the wireless—to produce the temper and feeling of the group. But perhaps we may also say that the new means use them, or at any rate help to produce them. Physics affects politics: physical inventions which make men move

SOURCE: From "The Movement of National Life, 1910–1935," *The Fortnightly Review*, Vol. CXLIII (1935), pp. 513–526. By permission of *Contemporary Review*.

quicker, and in closer connection, tend to produce political movements of a rapid *élan* and a gregarious or collectivist temper. It is not clear, however, that such consequences have yet ensued, or are likely to ensue, in Great Britain. We are not easily stampeded, and we still have a certain phlegm. But the new physical changes have changed us; and they have changed us in a number of ways.

There has been a movement into new industries. From the building of ships, for example, we have turned to the making of gramophones and wireless sets. The change is simple in itself: it is more complicated, and more serious, when we look at its consequences. One consequence is that the responsible work of a craftsman, whose mistake might cost his employer hundreds of pounds, has become repetitive work which follows an undeviating rule. Another consequence, not less serious than the change in technique and the nature of workmanship, is geographical. Changing its character, industry has also changed its residence. Its chosen home is the Midlands and the South. A process of "industrial transference" is automatically at work; and statesmanship has even addressed itself to the problem of directing and guiding this transference by schemes of internal migration. Along with this change in the character and the residence of industry there has also gone a change of commerce. Publicity and salesmanship have become major commercial arts. The uses of advertisement, never unknown, have been explored and extended. We have perhaps become more suggestible; we have certainly been exposed to a greater pressure and blare of suggestion. The development is not peculiar to us. But it is at work among us—in our politics as well as in our economics; in our newspapers as well as on our hoardings. It is helping to make us a different people from what we were a quarter of a century ago.

There has been a movement of tastes as well as a movement of industry and commerce. Here the shock of the war has collaborated with the physical revolution and its gust of mechanical change to alter our ways of living. We have become more ex-

perimental in our clothes, our food and our habits. Old and set ways were cracked by the war and the years of experimentation which followed the end of the war. But there have also been many changes in mechanism of our enjoyments, which have had nothing to do with the war. The cinema has become a common possession of all classes. It is a leveller within; it is also a link with the world without. The same is true of broadcasting; the same—at any rate in the matter of levelling, and of giving a new access for all into fresh fields of experience and appreciation—is also true of the growth of motor-transport. Joy has been spread in a wider commonalty; a new understanding of one another, and a new feeling for the aspect and the beauty of our country, have been gained.

In particular, we are perhaps less urban in spirit than we used to be. We have discovered that there is an English countryside which is worthy of being kept in its native beauty as our common heritage. . . . All this helps to make our nation better balanced than it was some twenty-five years ago. We may see this better balance even in the love of sport, which is one of our national obsessions. There is more sport and more games than there ever were; but it is less of a tyranny. Sport has fallen into a better proportion in our lives. There is so much else of which we can think, and so many other things for which we have now to find time.

In many ways we have progressed in the art of life since 1910. Not only have we found new tastes; we have also tried to give a new security, by schemes of insurance and pensions and other means, to those who walk on the verge between livelihood and starvation. But there is still a black shadow which attends on all our progress in the art of life; and it is greater now than it was in 1910. This is the shadow of unemployment. A revolution of technique has altered the conditions of production: the political revolutions and perturbations which followed the war have altered the markets for products. We are paying the price of both alterations—or rather the unemployed are paying it for us, and we are paying them back, in benefit and assistance, some of the price which they are vicariously paying in their own persons.

That is one shadow on the last twenty-five years. It is also a shadow, or is it a cloud with a silver lining, that our country has begun to live more to itself than it did when the king ascended the throne? There is less emigration than there was. In 1913 about 320,000 persons emigrated to the British dominions; in 1933 the emigrants were fewer than 90,000. The causes are external as well as internal; they depend on the dominions as well as upon ourselves. But it is the internal causes which illustrate the movement of our national life; and among them we may count partly a greater framework of security, which makes men and women less anxious to leave its shelter, and partly a large provision of amenities and amusements, which acts as a homekeeping magnet. Not only is there less emigration of persons; there is also less export and import of goods to connect us with the world outside. The old England of free trade, which depended on the markets of the world, began to be modified after the war, when the policy of safeguarding industries was introduced in 1921; it has been modified still more drastically during the last few years. We can never be a self-sufficing country, with a purely national economy; but we have moved some stages in that direction during the last fifteen years.

We have not, however, developed any exclusive type of nationalism. Toleration (sometimes based on a healthy spirit of sympathy and compromise, but sometimes resting on mere acquiescence and apathy) has long been one of our qualities; but we have learned to practice the quality in new forms and new directions. Old religious differences have lost their edge. The various branches of Scottish Presbyterianism were united in 1929; the different bodies of the Wesleyan confession became a single Methodist Church in 1932. The people of the Irish Free State, long divided from us in feeling, and dividing us acutely among ourselves by the profound cleavage of Unionists and Home Rulers, has acquired dominion status with general consent; and if there are still disagreements between its government and the government of Great Britain, they do not involve the old cleavage of parties in Great Britain, nor are they conducted with the old rancor between the Irish and the British side. Scotland has bred a new nationalism in the last few years; but no Englishman would ever say "Nay" to its demands if they were pressed with a general ardor and conviction.

Our nationalism in Great Britain, such as it is, is a federal nationalism; it has no unitarian zeal; it will tolerate, and even respect, the claims of its different branches and the feelings of its different nationalities. The same spirit of toleration is abroad in the Commonwealth. . . . Most of us welcome the progressive devolution upon India of the responsibility for carrying the vast orb of her fate. Signor Mussolini has said that "people that rise, or re-arise, are imperialistic; peoples that die are renouncers." If it be a sign of death to renounce power, and to be content with the voluntary bonds of free association, the British people is a dying people. But the renunciation of power may well be the most signal proof of strength and vitality.

Toleration is not only a virtue when it is practiced between different confessions and different peoples; it is also a virtue between different classes, between different sexes, and between youth and age. Is there more tolerance and more understanding between social classes than there was in 1910, or is there a truceless war which has only been accentuated? I remember, when I was a proctor at Oxford just before 1910, seeking in vain to secure a hearing for Mr. Keir Hardie[2]—not because I believed in his views, but because I believed in free speech. I do not think that there would be any difficulty in securing a hearing for a Labour leader today, either in Oxford or anywhere else. The cry of the class war is still ingeminated in England to-day . . . ; and it is all too true that there is still too great a gulf of classes among us—and not least in the field of edu-

---

[2]*Keir Hardie:* a mine-union leader and Labour Member of Parliament, 1892–1895, 1900–1915

cation. But those who lived through the so-called "General Strike" will not readily believe in a truceless war; and I, for one, should note a growth of social equality, and of mutual respect of class for class, in the years since 1910—though I should also note the long road that has still to be travelled before we attain any satisfactory level of equality.

Sex is far more equal to sex than class to class. The enfranchisement of women, in 1918, was not only a political act; it was also a social and moral landmark. Meredith[3] would rejoice in the women of to-day, the peers and the companions of men. There are few things in the king's reign that are more notable than the ending of the subjection of women.

Youth, too, has come more into its own. Perhaps the cause is partly the sinking of the birth rate, which makes the young fewer and therefore more precious; perhaps it is partly the memory of the young gallantry which sacrificed itself twenty years ago (let us hope, "Not in vain"; let us pray, "Never again") in the turmoil of battle and death. To-day the nation gives far more pains to the right training and education of youth. To-day the old are beginning to learn and to practice the doctrine of a fixed age of retirement. Age-limits are coming down; youth feels its freedom and acclaims its responsibility; it is even ready to write autobiographies in the early twenties. There is some effervescence and some bubbles of an imaginary revolt of youth; there is some decay of manners (a precious thing, and a near neighbor of morals), and some wild experimentation in art and literature. But the man of sixty and upward who reads the young poets of to-day, and then remembers what he was reading in the nineties of the last century, will note a new gravity and power and responsibility. . . .

II

The movement of national life is preeminently a movement of social thought, social temper, social habits and social adjustment. But there is another sphere, which also invites and demands attention. This is the sphere of organized institutions, in all its ranges—political and economic; ecclesiastical and educational; internal, imperial; and international.

In 1910 we spoke of the United Kingdom. In 1935 we speak of Great Britain and Northern Ireland. The change in our speech reflects a great change in our political structure. In 1910 there was a single Parliament at Westminster. In 1935 there is also a dominion Parliament in Dublin, and a separate Parliament in Belfast for the North of Ireland, which, however, still continues to send members to the Westminster Parliament.

The second great change has been the increase of the electorate, under the Representation of the People Act of 1918 and the subsequent Act of 1928. Under these acts men and women count alike. . . . The number of the electorate, which in 1910 was 7,700,000 for the whole of the United Kingdom, is now over 30,000,000 for Great Britain and Northern Ireland; it has been more than quadrupled. . . .

The third great change, in addition to the changes in Parliament and the electorate, has been a change in the party system. The Liberal Party, which had been triumphant in the election of 1906, and was still the largest single party in the two elections of 1910, has dwindled and dwindled since 1918 until it has sunk to a tenth, or less, of the House of Commons. The Labour Party, which in 1910 numbered only some 40 members, has grown till its normal strength may be said to vary between one-third and one-half of the House. The strength of the Conservative Party has remained tolerably constant; but the changes in the two other parties have profoundly affected the general working of the whole party system. There has been a tendency, since 1918, towards coalition ministries and formal or informal working agreements between different parties. What the even-

---

[3]*Meredith:* The Victorian novelist and poet George Meredith (1828–1909) affirmed the intellectual equality of men and women.

tual issue will be; whether the Liberal party, after nearly 300 years of history, will disappear; whether we shall have a system of two parties, each widened in scope and altered in character by the absorption of the right and the left wings of the old Liberal party—these are questions we have still to solve.

There are other changes in the world of politics since 1910. . . . Economics has advanced into the foreground: "economics," as it was being said in Germany in 1920, "is destiny." For some fifteen years now there has been the temporary problem (so long protracted that it may almost be called permanent) of the crisis of unemployment; but over and above that there is the enduring problem, which is destined long to engage our thought, of the proper economic basis of our general society—capitalist, socialist, syndicalist, or some form of mixture and compromise. . . .

Meanwhile the immediate and urgent problem of maintaining a stable and decent standard of life for the people, in a period of bewilderingly swift transition, has controlled our actual policies. It has controlled the policy and legislation of the state; it has controlled the policy and the efforts of the trade unions. The state, in the last 25 years, has moved toward the fixing of standard wages in unorganized industries; it has developed schemes of insurance against invalidity and unemployment; it has introduced new methods of pensions and new provision for housing; it has, in a word, guaranteed, by a variety of social services, new rights to security of life and health and livelihood. Public expenditure upon these purposes has been multiplied, and again multiplied; taxation has risen to meet the expenditure; and there has been achieved, in the course of social legislation and in the process of financing such legislation, no inconsiderable redistribution of wealth. The convinced socialist feels that all these measures are, at the most, palliatives offered by a desperate capitalism; but it may at least be said, in answer, that for our day, and in

our circumstances, they are indispensable, and they serve the cause of general human welfare. . . .

In the general movement of national life the growth of national education has been an important factor. The great Education Act of 1902 has gradually matured its consequences. It has issued in powerful and progressive local education authorities; it has issued in a large extension of secondary education, which has opened new opportunities of development to tens of thousands of boys and girls; it has issued, ultimately, in a new entry of students into the universities, which have grown apace both in numbers and in resources, and have come to play a far larger part in the life of the nation.

III

. . . It is a stirring age through which we have travelled; it is a stirring age that lies ahead. The aim of any organized society of men is justice—social justice within, which is fair to all classes and persons; international justice without, which is fair to all states and nations. Can we say of our country, in these last twenty-five years, that it has helped to advance the cause of social and international justice? That is our ultimate criterion. If we apply it, we may fairly say that there has been progress. There is more social justice than there was—more recognition of the just claims of different classes, different sexes, different ages. . . .

But the establishment of justice is a neverending movement, which will last as long as the life of humanity. . . . We have not only to think out the demands of justice by a process of social thought; we have also to realize those demands for ourselves, as far as we can, by a process of voluntary social co-operation. The state is the great organ of justice; but voluntary societies and voluntary effort can also help to build Jerusalem. That is an old English method; but the Prince of Wales,[4] in recent years, has drawn our attention again to its value. Voluntary social effort and social service—in helping

---

[4]*Prince of Wales:* the future King Edward VIII (1936) and then duke of Windsor (1936–1972)

the unemployed to help themselves; in promoting community associations, for the betterment of social life, on the great new housing estates which our municipalities have recently built; in every field in which we can freely serve social purposes—these are the needs, and their increasing fulfillment is the promise of our times.

Our country is being rebuilt. The rebuilding was already at work in 1910: it has gone further, much further, in 1935; it has still to go on, and to go still further. The scope of state action has widened, and is likely to widen still more. But if we are true to our old tradition and our present temper, we shall all seek to join in thinking freely together about the plan of the rebuilding, and we shall all work together, in the free company of voluntary society, to aid in its realization. The state is not all.

SIR WILLIAM BEVERIDGE **The Report on Social Insurance (1942)**

Basing itself on Britain's experience during the interwar era and inspired by a spirit of wartime unity, a committee headed by a veteran Liberal social reformer sets forth Britain's post–World War II social goals. Most of Beveridge's recommendations were enacted into law by the post-1945 Labour government in the form of the National Insurance Act of 1946 and the National Health Act of 1948.

2. The schemes of social insurance and allied services which the Interdepartmental Committee have been called on to survey have grown piece-meal. Apart from the Poor Law, which dates from the time of Elizabeth, the schemes surveyed are the product of the last 45 years beginning with the Workmen's Compensation Act, 1897. That act, applying in the first instance to a limited number of occupations, was made general in 1906. Compulsory health insurance began in 1912. Unemployment insurance began for a few industries in 1912 and was made general in 1920. The first Pensions Act, giving non-contributory pensions subject to a means test at the age of 70, was passed in 1908. In 1925 came the act which started contributory pensions for old age, for widows and for orphans. Unemployment insurance, after a troubled history, was put on a fresh basis by the Unemployment Act of 1934, which set up at the same time a new national service of unemployment assistance. . . .

3. In all this change and development, each problem has been dealt with separately, with little or no reference to allied problems. The first task of the committee has been to attempt for the first time a comprehensive survey of the whole field of social insurance and allied services, to show just what provision is now made and how it is made for many different forms of need. . . .

Three Guiding Principles of Recommendations

7. The first principle is that any proposals for the future, while they should use to the full the experience gathered in the past, should not be restricted by consideration of sectional interests established in the obtaining of that experience. Now, when the war is abolishing landmarks of every kind, is the opportunity for using experience in a clear field. A revolutionary moment in the world's history is a time for revolutions, not for patching.

8. The second principle is that organization of social insurance should be treated as one part only of a comprehensive policy of social progress. Social insurance fully developed may provide income security; it is an attack upon Want. But Want is one only of five giants on the road of reconstruction

SOURCE: *Parliamentary Papers,* "Social Insurance and Allied Services," 1942–1943, VI, Cmd. 6404, pp. 5–17, 153–170.

and in some ways the easiest to attack. The others are Disease, Ignorance, Squalor and Idleness.

9. The third principle is that social security must be achieved by co-operation between the state and the individual. The state should offer security for service and contribution. The state in organizing security should not stifle incentive, opportunity, responsibility; in establishing a national minimum, it should leave room and encouragement for voluntary action by each individual to provide more than that minimum for himself and his family. . . .

Summary of the Plan for Social Security

17. The main feature of the plan for Social Security is a scheme of social insurance against interruption and destruction of earning power and for special expenditure arising at birth, marriage or death. . . .

20. Under the scheme of social insurance, which forms the main feature of this plan, every citizen of working age will contribute in his appropriate class according to the security that he needs, or as a married woman will have contributions made by the husband. Each will be covered for all his needs by a single weekly contribution on one insurance document. All the principal cash payments—for unemployment, disability and retirement will continue so long as the need lasts, without means test, and will be paid from a social insurance fund built up by contributions from the insured persons, from their employers, if any, and from the state. This is in accord with two views as to the lines on which the problem of income maintenance should be approached.

21. The first view is that benefit in return for contributions, rather than free allowances from the state, is what the people of Britain desire. . . .

26. After trial of a different principle, it has been found to accord best with the sentiments of the British people that in insurance organized by the community by use of compulsory powers each individual should

stand in on the same terms; none should claim to pay less because he is healthier or has more regular employment. In accord with that view, the proposals of the report mark another step forward to the development of state insurance as a new type of human institution, differing both from the former methods of preventing or alleviating distress and from voluntary insurance. The term "social insurance" to describe this institution implies both that it is compulsory and that men stand together with their fellows. . . .

31. What is proposed today for unified social security springs out of what has been accomplished in building of security piece by piece. It retains the contributory principle of sharing the cost of security between three parties—the insured person himself, his employer, if he has an employer, and the state. It retains and extends the principle that compulsory insurance should provide a flat rate for benefit, irrespective of earnings, in return for a flat contribution from all. It retains as the best method of contribution the system of insurance documents and insurance stamps. It builds upon the experience gained in the administration of unemployment insurance and later of unemployment assistance, of a national administration which is not centralized at Whitehall but is carried out through responsible regional and local officers, acting at all points in close co-operation with representatives of the communities which they serve. . . .

311. *Eight Primary Causes of Need:* The primary needs for social security are of eight kinds, reckoning the composite needs of a married woman as one and including also the needs of childhood (Assumption A) and the need for universal comprehensive medical treatment and rehabilitation (Assumption B). These needs are set out below; to each there is attached in the security scheme a distinct insurance benefit or benefits. Assistance may enter to deal with any kind of need, where insurance benefit for any reason is inadequate or absent.

Unemployment: that is to say, inability to obtain employment by a person dependent on it and physically fit for it, met by unemployment benefit with removal and lodging grants.

Disability: that is to say, inability of a person of working age, through illness or accident, to pursue a gainful occupation, met by disability benefit and industrial pension.

Loss of Livelihood by person not dependent on paid employment, met by training benefit.

Retirement from occupation, paid or unpaid, through age, met by retirement pension.

Marriage needs of a woman, met by Housewives' Policy including provision for:—

(1) Marriage, met by marriage grant.
(2) Maternity, met by maternity grant in all cases, and, in the case of a married woman in gainful occupation, also by maternity benefit for a period before and after confinement.
(3) Interruption or cessation of husband's earnings by his unemployment, disability or retirement, met by share of benefit or pension with husband.
(4) Widowhood, met by provision varying according to circumstances including temporary widow's benefit for readjustment, guardian benefit while caring for children and training benefit if and when there are no children in need of care.
(5) Separation, i.e., end of husband's maintenance by legal separation, or established desertion, met by adaptation of widowhood provisions, including separation benefit, guardian benefit and training benefit.

(6) Incapacity for household duties, met by provision of paid help in illness as part of treatment.

Funeral Expenses of self or any person for whom responsible, met by funeral grant.

Childhood, provided for by children's allowances if in full-time education, till sixteen.

Physical Disease or *Incapacity,* met by medical treatment, domiciliary and institutional, for self and dependents in comprehensive health service and by post-medical rehabilitation. . . .

455. There are some to whom pursuit of security appears to be a wrong aim. They think of security as something inconsistent with initiative, adventure, personal responsibility. That is not a just view of social security as planned in this report. The plan is not one for giving to everybody something for nothing and without trouble, or something that will free the recipients for ever thereafter from personal responsibilities. The plan is one to secure income for subsistence on condition of service and contribution and in order to make and keep men fit for service. It cannot be got without thought and effort. It can be carried through only by a concentrated determination of the British democracy to free itself once for all of the scandal of physical want for which there is no economic or moral justification. When that effort has been made, the plan leaves room and encouragement to all individuals to win for themselves something above the national minimum, to find and to satisfy and to produce the means of satisfying new and higher needs than bare physical needs. . . .

16

Chamberlain, Churchill, and Hitler: Did "Appeasement" Delay or Invite World War II?

In the aftermath of World War I, historians debated which country had ultimately been most at fault and whether it would ultimately have been wiser for Britain to stay out of the conflict. In the aftermath of World War II, however, they tended to debate little as to which power was instrumental in instigating the war; the case for German aggression appeared too blatant. Instead, controversy raged over the merits and limitations of the British and French policy of appeasement, associated in the case of Britain primarily with the career of Prime Minister Neville Chamberlain (1869–1940), chancellor of the exchequer from 1931 to 1937 and prime minister from 1937 until May 1940. Was his policy of bending over backward to remedy grievances and to seek peaceful solutions not merely understandable but ethically justifiable? Alternatively, did it betray a complete misunderstanding of German aims and of the personality of Germany's leader, Adolf Hitler (1889–1945)? Did conciliation, indeed, ultimately invite the very conflict it was meant to prevent? How deep an impression that historical debate has made is illustrated by the fact that almost all the conflicts that have beset the world since 1945 have been praised or criticized by persons using analogies drawn from the events of the late 1930s. "Munich" and "appeasement" remain terms alive with meaning even in the 1990s. The documents reprinted in this chapter are necessarily only a sample, a sample that, granted, virtually ignores the independent roles played by France, Czechoslovakia, Italy, and Soviet Russia in the events leading to the Munich Agreement of 1938.

Hitler's long-range program as spelled out in the so-called "Hossbach Memorandum" of November 10, 1937, and the plan for the invasion of Czechoslovakia he set forth on April 22, 1938, present us with the private or "Top Secret" Hitler just as his speech at the Berlin Sports Palace on September 26, 1938, presents us with the public Hitler, the Hitler whose voice became familiar to radio listeners and newsreel-viewers throughout the world in the 1930s. In the same fashion, Chamberlain's letter of March 20, 1938, to his sister Ida and his diary entries of September 3 and 11, 1938, give us glimpses of the private prime minister. That he differed

Increasing Pressure

FRANCE (to BRITAIN). "Why should we take a stand about someone pushing someone else when it's all so far away . . ." (David Low, February 18, 1938, a few weeks before the German annexation of Austria)

only in degree of candor from the public prime minister is suggested by the other selections in this chapter. These include excerpts from the speech he gave to Parliament on March 24, 1938 (after the German annexation of Austria), the speech of July 26, 1938 (in which he announced the sending of a British mediator to Czechoslovakia), and the publicly broadcast speech of September 27, 1938 (a time when his peace mission had apparently failed). The last-minute Munich Conference of September 30, 1938—a summit meeting of the leaders of Britain, France, Germany, and Italy—*did* save the European peace for the moment, even if it did not save a militarily defensible Czechoslovakia. In his speech to Parliament of October 3, 1938, Chamberlain defends his policy, the policy that had led to the Munich Agreement itself and to a separate Anglo-German Declaration—both also reprinted in this chapter.

What were the differences between the private and the public Hitler? How did Neville Chamberlain define "appeasement"? Was it for him a passive or an active policy? What were the prime minister's private and public appraisals both of Hitler and of Czechoslovakia and its place in Europe? What formal obligations toward Czechoslovakia did Britain have in the summer of 1938? Since Chamberlain was apparently willing to let the Sudetenland portion of Czechoslovakia be ceded to Hitler's Germany, on what points and assumptions did Hitler and Chamberlain differ? Did Chamberlain appear to fall to any degree under Hitler's spell?

The British policy that led to Munich received its sharpest criticism from Winston Churchill (1874–1965), a man who had first entered Parliament in 1901 and who had held cabinet office most of the time between 1908 and 1929, but who, during the 1930s, served as an independent Conservative backbencher. A long section of his speech to Parliament of October 6, 1938, "In Criticism of the Munich Agreement," is reprinted.

How does Churchill differ with Chamberlain on the implication of the Munich Agreement? Which of the two proved to possess the keener appreciation of the workings of international power politics and, for that matter, which proved the more accurate prophet?

Within a year of the signing of the Munich Agreement, Hitler had swallowed up the rest of Czechoslovakia, had signed a treaty of cooperation with his erstwhile enemy Soviet Russia, and had successfully invaded Poland. As a result, on September 3, 1939, Britain and France declared war on Germany. But Germany kept the initiative; in April 1940 Hitler's armies conquered Denmark and Norway and in May and June 1940—to the astonishment of the world—Holland, Belgium, and France. On the same day, May 10, 1940, that the invasion of the West began, Neville Chamberlain's government gave way to an all-party Coalition Government headed by Winston Churchill. Churchill's speech to Parliament on June 18, 1940—"Britain Stands Alone"—is an example of both his attitudes and rhetoric in the summer of 1940. At that time continental Europe lay at Hitler's feet, with Soviet Russia his silent partner, Japan his ally, and the United States yet neutral. The only major power that still resisted Nazi Germany was Churchill's Britain. What are the distinctive characteristics of Churchill's approach? Which qualities in his personality made him so appropriate a war leader? How does his role in the summer of 1940 relate to his role in October 1938?

ADOLF HITLER Hossbach Memorandum (November 1937)

Late in 1937, Adolf Hitler, chancellor of Germany since early 1933, outlined his long-range plans to his senior military leaders. This document (known as the "Hossbach Memorandum" after the adjutant who took the conference minutes) was not known to anyone outside Germany until after the end of World War II in 1945.

Berlin, November 10, 1937.

MINUTES OF THE CONFERENCE IN THE REICH CHANCELLERY, BERLIN, NOVEMBER 5, 1937, FROM 4:15 TO 8:30 P.M.

PRESENT: The Führer and Chancellor; Field Marshal von Blomberg, War Minister; Colonel General Baron von Fritsch, Commander in Chief, Army; Admiral Dr. h. c. Raeder, Commander in Chief, Navy; Colonel General Goering, Commander in Chief, *Luftwaffe*; Baron von Neurath, Foreign Minister; Colonel Hossbach.

SOURCE: From *Documents on German Foreign Policy 1918–1945*, Series D, Vol. I (Washington, D.C., 1949), No. 19.

The Führer began by stating that the subject of the present conference was of such importance that its discussion would, in other countries, certainly be a matter for a full cabinet meeting, but he—the Führer—had rejected the idea of making it a subject of discussion before the wider circle of the Reich cabinet just because of the importance of the matter. His exposition to follow was the fruit of thorough deliberation and the experiences of his 4½ years of power. He wished to explain to the gentlemen present his basic ideas concerning the opportunities for the development of our position in the field of foreign affairs and its requirements, and he asked, in the interests of a long-term German policy, that his exposition be regarded, in the event of his death, as his last will and testament.

The Führer then continued:

The aim of German policy was to make secure and to preserve the racial community [*Volksmasse*] and to enlarge it. It was therefore a question of space.

The German racial community comprised over 85 million people and, because of their number and the narrow limits of habitable space in Europe, constituted a tightly packed racial core such as was not to be met in any other country and such as implied the right to a greater living space than in the case of other peoples. If, territorially speaking, there existed no political result corresponding to this German racial core, that was a consequence of centuries of historical development, and in the continuance of these political conditions lay the greatest danger to the preservation of the German race at its present peak. To arrest the decline of Germanism [*Deutschtum*] in Austria and Czechoslovakia was as little possible as to maintain the present level in Germany itself. Instead of increase, sterility was setting in, and in its train disorders of a social character must arise in course of time, since political and ideological ideas remain effective only so long as they furnish the basis for the realization of the essential vital demands of a people. Germany's future was therefore wholly conditional upon the solving of the need for space, and such a solution could be sought, of course, only for a foreseeable period of about one to three generations. . . .

Germany's problem could only be solved by means of force and this was never without attendant risk. The campaigns of Frederick the Great for Silesia and Bismarck's wars against Austria and France had involved unheard-of risk, and the swiftness of the Prussian action in 1870 had kept Austria from entering the war. If one accepts as the basis of the following exposition the resort to force with its attendant risks, then there remain still to be answered the questions "when" and "how." In this matter there were three cases [*Fälle*] to be dealt with:

Case I: Period 1943–1945

After this date only a change for the worse, from our point of view, could be expected.

The equipment of the army, navy, and *Luftwaffe* [air force], as well as the formation of the officer corps, was nearly completed. Equipment and armament were modern; in further delay there lay the danger of their obsolescence. In particular, the secrecy of "special weapons" could not be preserved forever. The recruiting of reserves was limited to current age groups; further drafts from older untrained age groups were no longer available.

Our relative strength would decrease in relation to the rearmament which would by then have been carried out by the rest of the world. If we did not act by 1943–45, any year could, in consequence of a lack of reserves, produce the food crisis, to cope with which the necessary foreign exchange was not available, and this must be regarded as a "waningpoint of the regime." Besides, the world was expecting our attack and was increasing its counter-measures from year to year. It was while the rest of the world was still preparing its defenses [*sich abriegele*] that we were obliged to take the offensive.

Nobody knew today what the situation would be in the years 1943–45. One thing only was certain, that we could not wait longer.

On the one hand there was the great *Wehrmacht* [Armed Force], and the necessity of maintaining it at its present level, the aging of the movement and of its leaders; and on the other, the prospect of a lowering of the standard of living and of a limitation of the birth rate, which left no choice but to act. If the Führer was still living, it was his unalterable resolve to solve Germany's problem of space at the latest by 1943–45. The necessity for action before 1943–45 would arise in cases 2 and 3.

Case 2

If internal strife in France should develop into such a domestic crisis as to absorb the French army completely and render it incapable of use for war against Germany, then the time for action against the Czechs had come.

Case 3

If France is so embroiled by a war with another state that she cannot "proceed" against Germany.

For the improvement of our politico-military position our first objective, in the event of our being embroiled in war, must be to overthrow Czechoslovakia and Austria simultaneously in order to remove the threat to our flank in any possible operation against the West. In a conflict with France it was hardly to be regarded as likely that the Czechs would declare war on us on the very same day as France. The desire to join in the war would, however, increase among the Czechs in proportion to any weakening on our part and then her participation could clearly take the form of an attack toward Silesia, toward the north or toward the west.

If the Czechs were overthrown and a common German-Hungarian frontier achieved, a neutral attitude on the part of Poland could be the more certainly counted on in the event of a Franco-German conflict. Our agreements with Poland only retained their force as long as Germany's strength remained unshaken. In the event of German setbacks a Polish action against East Prussia, and possibly against Pomerania and Silesia as well, had to be reckoned with.

On the assumption of a development of the situation leading to action on our part as planned, in the years 1943–45, the attitude of France, Britain, Italy, Poland, and Russia could probably be estimated as follows:

Actually, the Führer believed that almost certainly Britain, and probably France as well, had already tacitly written off the Czechs and were reconciled to the fact that this question would be cleared up in due course by Germany. Difficulties connected with the empire, and the prospect of being once more entangled in a protracted European war, were decisive considerations for Britain against participation in a war against Germany. Britain's attitude would certainly not be without influence on that of France. An attack by France without British support, and with the prospect of the offensive being brought to a standstill on our western fortifications, was hardly probable. Nor was a French march through Belgium and Holland without British support to be expected; this also was a course not to be contemplated by us in the event of a conflict with France, because it would certainly entail the hostility of Britain. It would of course be necessary to maintain a strong defense [*eine Abriegelung*] on our western frontier during the prosecution of our attack on the Czechs and Austria. And in this connection it had to be remembered that the defense measures of the Czechs were growing in strength from year to year, and that the actual worth of the Austrian army also was increasing in the course of time. Even though the populations concerned, especially of Czechoslovakia, were not sparse, the annexation of Czechoslovakia and Austria would mean an acquisition of foodstuffs for 5 to 6 million people, on the assumption that the compulsory emigration of 2 million people from Czechoslovakia and 1 million people from Austria was practicable. The incorporation of these two states with Germany meant, from the politico-military point of view, a substantial advantage because it would mean shorter and better frontiers, the freeing of forces for other purposes, and the possibility of creating new units up to a level of about 12 divisions, that is, 1 new division per million inhabitants.

Italy was not expected to object to the elimination of the Czechs, but it was impossible at the moment to estimate what her attitude on the Austrian question would be; that depended essentially upon whether the Duce [Mussolini] were still alive.

The degree of surprise and the swiftness of our action were decisive factors for Poland's attitude. Poland—with Russia at her rear—will have little inclination to engage in war against a victorious Germany.

Military intervention by Russia must be countered by the swiftness of our operations; however, whether such an intervention was a practical contingency at all was, in view of Japan's attitude, more than doubtful.

Should case 2 arise—the crippling of France by civil war—the situation thus created by the elimination of the most dangerous opponent must be seized upon *whenever it occurs* for the blow against the Czechs.

The Führer saw case 3 coming definitely nearer; it might emerge from the present tensions in the Mediterranean, and he was resolved to take advantage of it whenever it happened, even as early as 1938. . . .

If Germany made use of this war to settle the Czech and Austrian questions, it was to be assumed that Britain—herself at war with Italy—would decide not to act against Germany. Without British support, a warlike action by France against Germany was not to be expected.

The time for our attack on the Czechs and Austria must be made dependent on the course of the Anglo-French-Italian war and would not necessarily coincide with the commencement of military operations by these three states. Nor had the Führer in mind military agreements with Italy, but wanted, while retaining his own independence of action, to exploit this favorable situation, which would not occur again, to begin and carry through the campaign against the Czechs. This descent upon the Czechs would have to be carried out with "lightning speed." . . .

HOSSBACH

Certified Correct:
Colonel (General Staff)

NEVILLE CHAMBERLAIN **Letter to His Sister (March 1938)**

A few days after Germany's annexation of Austria (March 11–12, 1938), Britain's prime minister confides his anxieties to his sister Ida.

March 20, 1938.

With Franco winning in Spain by the aid of German guns and Italian planes, with a French government in which one cannot have the slightest confidence and which I suspect to be in closish touch with our [Labour Party] Opposition, with the Russians stealthily and cunningly pulling all the

strings behind the scenes to get us involved in war with Germany (our Secret Service doesn't spend all its time looking out of the window), and finally with a Germany flushed with triumph, and all too conscious of her power, the prospect looked black indeed. In face of such problems, to be badgered and pressed to come out and give a clear, decided, bold, and unmistakable lead,

SOURCE: Reprinted from *The Life of Neville Chamberlain* by Keith Feiling, © 1970 (Archon Books, Hamden, Connecticut), pp. 347–348. From *Hansard's Parliamentary Debates*, 5th Series, Vol. 333, cols. 1403–1407.

show "ordinary courage," and all the rest of the twaddle, is calculated to vex the man who has to take the responsibility for the consequences. As a matter of fact, the plan of the "Grand Alliance," as Winston [Churchill] calls it, had occurred to me long before he mentioned it. . . . I talked about it to Halifax,[1] and we submitted it to the chiefs of the staff and the F.O.[2] experts. It is a very attractive idea; indeed, there is almost everything to be said for it until you come to examine its practicability. From that moment its attraction vanishes. You have only to look at the map to see that nothing that France or we could do could possibly save Czechoslovakia from being overrun by the Germans, if they wanted to do it. The Austrian frontier is practically open; the great Skoda munition works are within easy bombing distance of the German aerodromes, the railways all pass through German territory, Russia is 100 miles away. Therefore we could not help Czechoslovakia—she would simply be a pretext for going to war with Germany. That we could not think of unless we had a reasonable prospect of being able to beat her to her knees in a reasonable time, and of that I see no sign. I have therefore abandoned any idea of giving guarantees to Czechoslovakia, or the French in connection with her obligations to that country.

NEVILLE CHAMBERLAIN **Statement to the House of Commons (March 1938)**

On March 24, 1938, Prime Minister Chamberlain publicly outlines the formal obligations of the British government to Czechoslovakia, the nation that appeared most likely to be threatened next by Germany.

. . . I now turn to the situation with which we are more particularly concerned this afternoon. His Majesty's government have expressed the view that recent events in Austria have created a new situation, and we think it right to state the conclusions to which consideration of these events has led us. We have already placed on record our judgment upon the action taken by the German government [the invasion of Austria]. I have nothing to add to that. But the consequences still remain. There has been a profound disturbance of international confidence. In these circumstances the problem before Europe, to which in the opinion of His Majesty's government it is their most urgent duty to direct their attention, is how best to restore this shaken confidence, how to maintain the rule of law in international affairs, how to seek peaceful solutions to questions that continue to cause anxiety. Of these the one which is necessarily most present to many minds is that which concerns the relations between the government of Czechoslovakia and the German minority in that country; and it is probable that a solution of this question, if it could be achieved, would go far to re-establish a sense of stability over an area much wider than that immediately concerned.

Accordingly, the government have given special attention to this matter, and in particular they have fully considered the question whether the United Kingdom, in addition to those obligations by which she is already bound by the Covenant of the League and the Treaty of Locarno, should, as a further contribution toward preserving peace in Europe, now undertake new and specific commitments in Europe, and in particular such a commitment in relation to Czechoslovakia. I think it is right that I should here remind the House what are our existing commitments, which might lead to the use of our arms for purposes other than our own defense and the defense of territories of other parts of the British Commonwealth of Nations. They are, first of all, the defense of France and Belgium against unprovoked aggression in accordance with

---

[1]*Halifax:* the foreign secretary   [2]*F.O.:* the Foreign Office

our existing obligations under the Treaty of Locarno, as reaffirmed in the arrangement which was drawn up in London on 19th March 1936. We have also obligations by treaty to Portugal, Iraq, and Egypt. Those are our definite obligations to particular countries.

There remains another case in which we may have to use our arms, a case which is of a more general character, but which may have no less significance. It is the case arising under the Covenant of the League of Nations which was accurately defined by the former foreign secretary[3] when he said:

> In addition, our armaments may be used in bringing help to a victim of aggression in any case where in our judgment it would be proper under the provision of the Covenant to do so.

The case might, for example, include Czechoslovakia. The ex–foreign secretary went on to say:

> I use the word "may" deliberately, since in such an instance there is no automatic obligation to take military action. It is moreover right that this should be so, for nations cannot be expected to incur automatic military obligations save for areas where their vital interests are concerned.

His Majesty's government stand by these declarations. They have acknowledged that in present circumstances the ability of the League to fulfil all the functions originally contemplated for it is reduced; but this is not to be interpreted as meaning that His Majesty's government would in no circumstances intervene as a member of the League for the restoration of peace or the maintenance of international order if circumstances were such as to make it appropriate for them to do so. And I cannot but feel that the course and development of any dispute, should such unhappily arise, would be greatly influenced by the knowledge that such action as it may be in the power of Great Britain to take will be determined by His Majesty's government of the day in accordance with the principles laid down in the Covenant.

The question now arises, whether we should go further. Should we forthwith give an assurance to France that, in the event of her being called upon by reason of German aggression on Czechoslovakia to implement her obligations under the Franco-Czechoslovak Treaty, we would immediately employ our full military force on her behalf? Or, alternatively, should we at once declare our readiness to take military action in resistance to any forcible interference with the independence and integrity of Czechoslovakia, and invite any other nations, which might so desire, to associate themselves with us in such a declaration?

From a consideration of these two alternatives it clearly emerges that under either of them the decision as to whether or not this country should find itself involved in war would be automatically removed from the discretion of His Majesty's government, and the suggested guarantee would apply irrespective of the circumstances by which it was brought into operation, and over which His Majesty's government might not have been able to exercise any control. This position is not one that His Majesty's government could see their way to accept, in relation to an area where their vital interests are not concerned in the same degree as they are in the case of France and Belgium; it is certainly not the position that results from the Covenant. For these reasons His Majesty's government feel themselves unable to give the prior guarantee suggested.

But while plainly stating this decision I would add this. Where peace and war are concerned, legal obligations are not alone involved, and, if war broke out, it would be unlikely to be confined to those who have assumed such obligations. It would be quite impossible to say where it would end and what governments might become involved. The inexorable pressure of facts might well prove more powerful than formal pronouncements, and in that event it would be well within the bounds of probability that

---

[3]*former foreign secretary:* Anthony Eden

other countries, besides those which were parties to the original dispute, would almost immediately become involved. This is especially true in the case of two countries like Great Britain and France, with long associations of friendship, with interests closely interwoven, devoted to the same ideals of democratic liberty, and determined to uphold them. . . .

So far as Czechoslovakia is concerned, it seems to His Majesty's government that now is the time when all the resources of diplomacy should be enlisted in the cause of peace. They have been glad to take note of and in no way underrate the definite assurances given by the German government as to their attitude. On the other side they have observed with satisfaction that the government of Czechoslovakia are address-

ing themselves to the practical steps that can be taken within the framework of the Czechoslovak constitution to meet the reasonable wishes of the German minority. For their part, His Majesty's government will at all times be ready to render any help in their power, by whatever means might seem most appropriate, toward the solution of questions likely to cause difficulty between the German and Czechoslovak Governments. In the meantime, there is no need to assume the use of force, or, indeed, to talk about it. Such talk is to be strongly deprecated. Not only can it do no good; it is bound to do harm. It must interfere with the progress of diplomacy, and it must increase feelings of insecurity and uncertainty. . . .

ADOLF HITLER **Plans for "Operation Green" (April 1938)**

On April 22, 1938, Hitler and Field Marshal Wilhelm Keitel agreed on a plan for "Operation Green," a German attack on Czechoslovakia. The memorandum of that conversation is labeled "Top Secret, Military."

A. Political

1. Idea of strategic attack out of the blue without cause or possibility of justification is rejected. Reason: hostile world opinion which might lead to serious situation. Such measures only justified for elimination of last enemy on the continent.

2. Action after a period of diplomatic discussions which gradually lead to a crisis and to war.

3. Lightning action based on an incident (for example the murder of the German minister in the course of an anti-German demonstration).

B. Military Conclusions

1. Preparations to be made for political contingencies 2 and 3. Contingency 2 is undesirable because "Green" security measures will have been taken.

2. The loss of time through transport by rail of the bulk of the divisions—which is unavoidable and must be reduced to a minimum—must not be allowed to divert from lightning attack at the time of action.

3. "Partial thrusts" toward breaching the defense line at numerous points and in operationally advantageous directions are to be undertaken at once.

These thrusts are to be prepared down to the smallest detail (knowledge of the routes, the objectives, composition of the columns according to tasks allotted them).

Simultaneous attack by land and air forces.

The *Luftwaffe* is to support the individual columns (for instance, dive bombers, sealing off fortification works at the points of penetration; hindering the movement of reserves; destruction of signal communications and thus isolating the garrisons).

SOURCE: From *Documents on German Foreign Policy*, 1918–1945, Series D, Vol. II (Washington, D.C., 1949), No. 133.

4. The first 4 days of military action are, politically speaking, decisive. In the absence of outstanding military successes, a European crisis is certain to arise. *Faits accomplis* must convince foreign powers of the hopelessness of military intervention; call in allies to the scene (sharing the booty!); demoralize "Green."

Hence, bridging the period between first penetration of enemy's lines and throwing into action the advancing troops by the determined ruthless advance of a motorized army (for instance through Pi past Pr).[4]

5. If possible, separation of the transport movement "Red" ["*Rot*"][5] from "Green." A simultaneous deployment of "Red" might cause "Red" to adopt undesirable measures. On the other hand operation "Red" must at all times be ready to come into action.

C. Propaganda

1. Leaflets for the conduct of the Germans in "Green" territory [*Grünland*].

2. Leaflets with threats to intimidate the "Greens."

SCHM[UNDT]

Written by hand of officer

NEVILLE CHAMBERLAIN **Mediation in Czechoslovakia (July 1938)**

As the German minority in Czechoslovakia (the Sudeten Germans) put increasing pressure upon the Czech government to grant semiautonomous powers in those parts of the country in which they constituted a majority, Prime Minister Chamberlain announced to the House of Commons (on July 26, 1938) a new plan to prevent the Czech crisis from leading to German intervention and possible war.

While we have felt that an agreement voluntarily come to, if it could be reached between the Sudeten Germans and the Czech government, would be the best solution, nevertheless, as time has gone on it has begun to appear doubtful whether, without some assistance from outside, such a voluntary agreement could take place. In those circumstances, His Majesty's government have been considering whether there were some other way in which they could lend their help to bring the negotiators together, and, in response to a request from the government of Czechoslovakia, we have agreed to propose a person with the necessary experience and qualities to investigate this subject on the spot and endeavor, if need be, to suggest means for bringing the negotiations to success. Such an investigator and mediator would, of course, be independent of His Majesty's government—in fact, he would be independent of all governments. He would act only in his personal capacity, and it would be necessary, of course, that he should have all the facilities and all the information placed at his disposal in order to enable him to carry through his task.

I cannot assert that a proposal of that kind will necessarily bring about a solution of this problem, but I think it may have two valuable results. First of all, I think it would go far to inform public opinion generally as to the real facts of the case, and, secondly, I hope that it may mean that issues which hitherto have appeared intractable may prove, under the influence of such a mediator, to be less obstinate than we have thought. But it is quite obvious that the task of any one who undertakes this duty is going to be a very exacting, very responsi-

---

SOURCE: From *Hansard's Parliamentary Debates*, 5th Series, Vol. 338, cols. 2957–2960.

[4]*through Pi past Pr:* presumably "through Pilsen past Prague"   [5]*"Red":* Just as all references to "Green" refer to Czechoslovakia and the Czechs, so references to "Red" refer to France and the French.

ble, and very delicate one, and His Majesty's government feel that they are fortunate in having secured from Lord Runciman a promise to undertake it, provided he is assured of the confidence of the Sudeten Germans—I hope he will be—as well as the assistance of the Czechoslovakian government. Lord Runciman was a Member of this House so long that he is well known to many hon. Members. I think they will agree with me that he has outstanding personal qualifications for the task he has undertaken. He has a long experience of public affairs and of men of all sorts and conditions. He is characterized by fearlessness, freedom from prejudice, integrity, and impartiality, and I am quite certain that every one here will wish him all success. . . .

He is an investigator and mediator—that is what I called him. He will try to acquaint himself with all the facts and the views of the two sides, and he will no doubt see them separately, and perhaps later on he will be able to make some proposals to them which will help them. He is in the position, so well known to the hon. Member, of a man who goes down to assist in settling a strike. He has to see two sides who have come to a point when they cannot go any further. He is there as an independent, impartial person. . . .

We have impressed upon the government of Czechoslovakia, and also upon the German government, our own sense of the desirability of restraint. We have noted with satisfaction the efforts which the Czech government have made, and we have also been very happy to receive assurances, only recently renewed, from the German government of their own desire for a peaceful solution. . . .

If only we could find some peaceful solution of this Czechoslovakian question, I should myself feel that the way was open again for a further effort for a general appeasement—an appeasement which cannot be obtained until we can be satisfied that no major cause of difference or dispute remains unsettled. We have already demonstrated the possibility of a complete agreement between a democratic and a totalitarian state, and I do not myself see why that experience should not be repeated. When Herr Hitler made his offer of a naval treaty[6] under which the German fleet was to be restricted to an agreed level bearing a fixed ratio to the size of the British fleet, he made a notable gesture of a most practical kind in the direction of peace, the value of which it seems to me has not ever been fully appreciated as tending toward this general appeasement. There the treaty stands as a demonstration that it is possible for Germany and ourselves to agree upon matters which are vital to both of us. Since agreement has already been reached on that point, I do not think that we ought to find it impossible to continue our efforts at understanding, which, if they were successful, would do so much to bring back confidence. . . .

NEVILLE CHAMBERLAIN **Diary Entries (September 1938)**

The prime minister confides his fears to his private diary.

September 3, 1938.

Is it not positively horrible to think that the fate of hundreds of millions depends on one man, and he is half mad? I keep racking my brains to try and devise some means of averting a catastrophe, if it should seem to be upon us. I thought of one so unconven-

SOURCE: Reprinted from *The Life of Neville Chamberlain* by Keith Feiling, © 1970 (Archon Books, Hamden, Connecticut), pp. 357, 360–361.

[6]*naval treaty:* the Anglo-German Naval Agreement of 1935, according to which Germany was allowed to build up a navy 35 percent as large as that of Britain

tional and daring that it rather took Halifax's breath away. But since Henderson thought it might save the situation at the 11th hour, I haven't abandoned it, though I hope all the time that it won't be necessary to try it.

September 11, 1938.

I fully realize that, if eventually things go wrong and the aggression takes place, there will be many, including Winston, who will say that the British government must bear the responsibility, and that if only they had had the courage to tell Hitler now that, if he used force, we should at once declare war, that would have stopped him. By that time it will be impossible to prove the con-

trary, but I am satisfied that we should be wrong to allow the most vital decision that any country could take, the decision as to peace or war, to pass out of our hands into those of the ruler of another country, and a lunatic at that. I have been fortified in this view by reading a very interesting book on the foreign policy of Canning.[7] . . . Over and over again Canning lays it down that you should never menace unless you are in a position to carry out your threats, and although, if we have to fight I should hope we should be able to give a good account of ourselves, we are certainly not in a position in which our military advisers would feel happy in undertaking to begin hostilities if we were not forced to do so.

ADOLF HITLER   My Last Territorial Demand (September 1938)

Chamberlain put his "unconventional and daring" plan into action, and on September 15 he flew to Germany for a two-man summit conference with Hitler at Berchtesgaden. This was followed by a second meeting on September 22–24 at Godesberg. Although Chamberlain in effect promised Hitler the cession of the Sudetenland to Germany—provided the operation could be carried out over a period of time and by international negotiation—Hitler wanted even faster action. On September 26, at an open-air rally in Berlin, he makes the following statements.

And now before us stands the last problem that must be solved and will be solved. It is the last territorial claim which I have to make in Europe, but it is the claim from which I will not recede and which, God willing, I will make good.

The history of the problem is as follows: in 1918 under the watchword "The Right of the Peoples to Self-Determination" central Europe was torn in pieces and was newly formed by certain crazy so-called "statesmen." Without regard for the origin of the peoples, without regard for either their wish as nations or for economic necessities central Europe at that time was broken up into

atoms and new so-called states were arbitrarily formed. To this procedure Czechoslovakia owes its existence. This Czech state began with a single lie and the father of this lie was named Benes.[8] This Mr. Benes at that time appeared in Versailles and he first of all gave the assurance that there was a Czechoslovak nation. He was forced to invent this lie in order to give to the slender number of his own fellow-countrymen a somewhat greater range and thus a fuller justification. And the Anglo-Saxon statesmen, who were, as always, not very adequately versed in respect of questions of geography or nationality, did not at

SOURCE: From Norman H. Baynes, ed., *The Speeches of Adolf Hitler* (Oxford: Oxford University Press for the Royal Institute of International Affairs, 1942). By permission of Oxford University Press.

[7]*book . . . Canning: The Foreign Policy of Canning* by Harold Temperley   [8]*Edvard Benes (1884–1948):* Czech statesman and, at the time of the speech, president of Czechoslovakia

that time find it necessary to test these assertions of Mr. Benes. Had they done so, they could have established the fact that there is no such thing as a Czechoslovak nation but only Czechs and Slovaks and that the Slovaks did not wish to have anything to do with the Czechs but ... (*the rest of the sentence was drowned in a tumultuous outburst of applause*).

So in the end through Mr. Benes these Czechs annexed Slovakia. Since this state did not seem fitted to live, out of hand three and a half million Germans were taken in violation of their right to self-determination and their wish for self-determination. Since even that did not suffice, over a million Magyars had to be added, then some Carpathian Russians, and at last several hundred thousand Poles.

That is this state which then later proceeded to call itself Czechoslovakia—in violation of the right of the peoples to self-determination, in violation of the clear wish and will of the nations to which this violence had been done. When I speak to you here it goes without saying that I should sympathize with the fate of all these oppressed peoples, with the fate of Poles, Hungarians, and Ukrainians. I am naturally spokesman only for the fate of my Germans.

At the time that Mr. Benes lied this state into being, he gave a solemn pledge to divide it on the model of the Swiss system into cantons; for amongst the democratic statesmen there were some who still had some twinges of conscience. We all know how Mr. Benes has redeemed his pledge to introduce this cantonal system. He began his reign of terror. Even at that time the Germans already attempted to protest against this arbitrary violence. They were shot down. After that a war of extermination began. In these years of the "peaceful" development of Czechoslovakia nearly 600,000 Germans had to leave Czechoslovakia. This happened for a very simple reason: otherwise they would have had to starve!

The whole development from the year 1918 up to 1938 showed one thing clearly:

Mr. Benes was determined slowly to exterminate the German element. And this to a certain extent he has achieved. He has hurled countless people into the profoundest misery. He has managed to make millions of people fearful and anxious. Through the continuous employment of his methods of terrorism he has succeeded in reducing to silence these millions. . . .

Germany had not called a man to the colors: it never thought for a moment to solve this problem by military intervention. Still I always hoped that the Czechs at the last minute would realize that this tyranny could not be maintained any longer. But Mr. Benes adopted the standpoint that, protected by France and by England, one could do anything with Germany with impunity—nothing could happen to him. And above all: when all other strings failed, behind him stood Soviet Russia.

And so the answer of this man was now more than before: Shoot down, arrest, imprison—the fate of all those who in any way failed to please him. Thus it was that there came my demand in Nuremberg. This demand was quite clear: for the first time I there expressed the claim that now at last—almost twenty years since the statements of President Wilson—for these three and a half millions the right of self-determination must come into force. And once again Mr. Benes gave his answer: more deaths, more imprisonments, more arrests. The Germans began perforce to flee.

And then came England. I have told Mr. Chamberlain quite distinctly what we regard now as the sole possibility of a solution. It is the most natural solution that there can be. I know that *all* nationalities no longer wish to remain with Dr. Benes, but I am in the first place spokesman of the Germans, and for these Germans I have now spoken and asserted that I am no longer willing to look on calm and inactive and see how this madman in Prague thinks that he can undisturbed ill-treat three and a half million human beings. And I have left him in no doubt that now at last German patience has really come to an end. . . .

Faced by the declaration of England and of France that they would no longer support Czechoslovakia if at last the fate of these peoples was not changed and the areas liberated, Mr. Benes found a way of escape. He conceded that these districts must be surrendered. That was what he stated, but what did he do? He did not surrender the area but the Germans he now drives out! And that is now the point at which the game comes to an end. Mr. Benes had hardly spoken when he began his military subjugation afresh—only with still greater violence. We see the appalling figures: on one day 10,000 fugitives, on the next 20,000, a day later, already 37,000, again two days later 41,000, then 62,000, then 78,000; now 90,000, 107,000, 137,000 and today 214,000. Whole stretches of country were depopulated, villages are burned down, attempts are made to smoke out the Germans with hand-grenades and gas. Mr. Benes, however, sits in Prague and is convinced: "Nothing can happen to me: in the end England and France stand behind me." . . .

I have now placed a memorandum containing a last and final German proposal in the hands of the British government.

I have demanded that now after twenty years Mr. Benes should at last be compelled to come to terms with the truth. On 1 October he will have to hand over to us this area. . . .

I have only a few statements still to make: I am grateful to Mr. Chamberlain for all his efforts. I have assured him that the German people desires nothing else than peace, but I have also told him that I cannot go back behind the limits set to our patience. I have further assured him, and I re-peat it here, that when this problem is solved there is for Germany no further territorial problem in Europe. And I have further assured him that at the moment when Czechoslovakia solves her problems, that means when the Czechs have come to terms with their other minorities, and that peaceably and not through oppression, then I have no further interest in the Czech state. And that is guaranteed to him! We want no Czechs!

But in the same way I desire to state before the German people that with regard to the problem of the Sudeten Germans my patience is now at an end! I have made Mr. Benes an offer which is nothing but the carrying into effect of what he himself has promised. The decision now lies in his hands: Peace or War! He will either accept this offer and now at last give to the Germans their freedom or we will go and fetch this freedom for ourselves. The world must take note that in four and a half years of war and through the long years of my political life there is one thing which no one could ever cast in my teeth: I have never been a coward!

Now I go before my people as its first soldier and behind me—that the world should know—there marches a people and a different people from that of 1918!

If at that time a wandering scholar was able to inject into our people the poison of democratic catchwords—the people of today is no longer the people that it was then. Such catchwords are for us like wasp-stings: they cannot hurt us: we are now immune.

In this hour the whole German people will unite with me! It will feel my will to be its will. . . .

NEVILLE CHAMBERLAIN Radio Speech to the British People (September 1938)

On the following night, September 27, 1938, Prime Minister Chamberlain speaks, by radio, to his people.

SOURCE: From Neville Chamberlain, *The Struggle for Peace* (London: Hutchinson Publishing Group, Ltd., 1939), pp. 274–276. Reprinted by permission of the publisher.

Tomorrow Parliament is going to meet, and I shall be making a full statement of the events which have led up to the present anxious and critical situation. An earlier statement would not have been possible when I was flying backward and forward across Europe, and the position was changing from hour to hour. But today there is a lull for a brief time, and I want to say a few words to you, men and women of Britain and the empire, and perhaps to others as well.

First of all I must say something to those who have written to my wife or myself in these last weeks to tell us of their gratitude for my efforts and to assure us of their prayers for my success. Most of these letters have come from women—mothers or sisters of our own countrymen. But there are countless others besides—from France, from Belgium, from Italy, even from Germany, and it has been heart-breaking to read of the growing anxiety they reveal and their intense relief when they thought, too soon, that the danger of war was past.

If I felt my responsibility heavy before, to read such letters has made it seem almost overwhelming. How horrible, fantastic, incredible it is that we should be digging trenches and trying on gas-masks here because of a quarrel in a far-away country between people of whom we know nothing. It seems still more impossible that a quarrel which has already been settled in principle should be the subject of war.

I can well understand the reasons why the Czech government have felt unable to accept the terms which have been put before them in the German memorandum. Yet I believe after my talks with Herr Hitler that, if only time were allowed, it ought to be possible for the arrangements for transferring the territory that the Czech government has agreed to give to Germany to be settled by agreement under conditions which would assure fair treatment to the population concerned.

You know already that I have done all that one man can do to compose this quarrel. After my visits to Germany I have realized vividly how Herr Hitler feels that he must champion other Germans, and his indignation that grievances have not been met before this. He told me privately, and last night he repeated publicly, that after this Sudeten German question is settled, that is the end of Germany's territorial claims in Europe.

After my first visit to Berchtesgaden I did get the assent of the Czech government to proposals which gave the substance of what Herr Hitler wanted, and I was taken completely by surprise when I got back to Germany and found that he insisted that the territory should be handed over to him immediately, and immediately occupied by German troops without previous arrangements for safeguarding the people within the territory who were not Germans, or did not want to join the German Reich.

I must say that I find this attitude unreasonable. If it arises out of any doubts that Herr Hitler feels about the intentions of the Czech government to carry out their promises and hand over the territory, I have offered on the part of the British government to guarantee their words, and I am sure the value of our promise will not be underrated anywhere. I shall not give up the hope of a peaceful solution, or abandon my efforts for peace, as long as any chance for peace remains. I would not hesitate to pay even a third visit to Germany if I thought it would do any good. But at this moment I see nothing further that I can usefully do in the way of mediation.

Meanwhile there are certain things we can and shall do at home. Volunteers are still wanted for air-raid precautions, for fire brigade and police services, and for the territorial units. I know that all of you, men and women alike, are ready to play your part in the defense of the country, and I ask you all to offer your services, if you have not already done so, to the local authorities, who will tell you if you are wanted and in what capacity.

Do not be alarmed if you hear of men being called up to man the anti-aircraft defenses or ships. These are only precautionary measures such as a government must take in times like this. But they do not necessarily mean that we have determined on war or that war is imminent.

However much we may sympathize with a small nation confronted by a big and powerful neighbor, we cannot in all circumstances undertake to involve the whole British Empire in war simply on her account. If we have to fight it must be on larger issues than that. I am myself a man of peace to the depths of my soul. Armed conflict between nations is a nightmare to me; but if I were convinced that any nation had made up its mind to dominate the world by fear of its force, I should feel that it must be resisted. Under such a domina-

tion life for people who believe in liberty would not be worth living; but war is a fearful thing, and we must be very clear, before we embark on it, that it is really the great issues that are at stake, and that the call to risk everything in their defense, when all the consequences are weighed, is irresistible.

For the present I ask you to await as calmly as you can the events of the next few days. As long as war has not begun, there is always hope that it may be prevented, and you know that I am going to work for peace to the last moment. Good night.

The Munich Agreement and the Anglo-German Declaration (September 1938)

Just as Britain seemed about to drift into war, reprieve came in the form of an agreement by Hitler—in part at the behest of his ally, Italy's Benito Mussolini—to hold a four-power conference at Munich. There, on September 29, 1938, the representatives of Germany, Italy, France, and Britain signed the Munich Agreement. On the following day, Hitler and Chamberlain signed a separate Anglo-German Declaration of their own, and Chamberlain flew home to England bearing "peace in our time."

Germany, the United Kingdom, France, and Italy, taking into consideration the agreement, which has been already reached in principle for the cession to Germany of the Sudeten German territory, have agreed on the following terms and conditions governing the said cession and the measures consequent thereon, and by this agreement they each hold themselves responsible for the steps necessary to secure its fulfillment.

1. The evacuation will begin on October 1st.

2. The United Kingdom, France, and Italy agree that the evacuation of the terri-

tory shall be completed by October 10th, without any existing installations having been destroyed, and that the Czechoslovak government will be held responsible for carrying out the evacuation without damage to the said installations.

3. The conditions governing the evacuation will be laid down in detail by an international commission composed of representatives of Germany, the United Kingdom, France, Italy, and Czechoslovakia.

4. The occupation by stages of the predominantly German territory by German

SOURCE: The documents dated September 29 are taken from British White Paper, Great Britain, Cmd. 5848: *Further Documents Respecting Czechoslovakia . . .* ; the last document is taken from E. L. Woodward and Rohan Butler, eds., *Documents on British Foreign Policy 1919–1939,* Third Series, Vol. II, No. 1228, Appendix.

troops will begin on October 1st. The four territories marked on the attached map will be occupied by German troops in the following order: the territory marked number I on the 1st and 2d of October, the territory marked number II on the 2d and 3d of October, the territory marked number III on the 3d, 4th, and 5th of October, the territory marked number IV on the 6th and 7th of October. The remaining territory of preponderantly German character will be ascertained by the aforesaid international commission forthwith and be occupied by German troops by the 10th of October.

5. The international commission referred to in paragraph 3 will determine the territories in which a plebiscite is to be held. These territories will be occupied by international bodies until the plebiscite has been completed. The same commission will fix the conditions in which the plebiscite is to be held, taking as a basis the conditions of the Saar plebiscite. The commission will also fix a date, not later than the end of November, on which the plebiscite will be held.

6. The final determination of the frontiers will be carried out by the international commission. This commission will also be entitled to recommend to the four powers, Germany, the United Kingdom, France, and Italy, in certain exceptional cases, minor modifications in the strictly ethnographical determination of the zones which are to be transferred without plebiscite.

7. There will be a right of option into and out of the transferred territories, the option to be exercised within 6 months from the date of this agreement. A German-Czechoslovak commission shall determine the details of the option, consider ways of facilitating the transfer of population and settle questions of principle arising out of the said transfer.

8. The Czechoslovak government will, within a period of 4 weeks form the date of this agreement, release from their military and police forces any Sudeten Germans who may wish to be released, and the Czechoslovak government will within the same period release Sudeten German prisoners who are serving terms of imprisonment for political offenses.

ADOLF HITLER
ED. DALADIER
MUSSOLINI
NEVILLE CHAMBERLAIN
Munich, September 29, 1938.

His Majesty's government in the United Kingdom and the French government have entered into the above agreement on the basis that they stand by the offer, contained in paragraph 6 of the Anglo-French proposals of September 19th, relating to an international guarantee of the new boundaries of the Czechoslovak state against unprovoked aggression.

When the question of the Polish and Hungarian minorities in Czechoslovakia has been settled, Germany and Italy for their part will give a guarantee to Czechoslovakia.

ADOLF HITLER
NEVILLE CHAMBERLAIN
MUSSOLINI
ED. DALADIER
Munich, September 29, 1938.

We, the German Führer and chancellor and the British prime minister, have had a further meeting today and are agreed in recognizing that the question of Anglo-German relations is of the first importance for the two countries and for Europe.

We regard the agreement signed last night and the Anglo-German Naval Agreement as symbolic of the desire of our two peoples never to go to war with one another again.

We are resolved that the method of consultation shall be the method adopted to deal with any other questions that may concern our two countries, and we are determined to continue our efforts to remove possible sources of difference and thus to contribute to assure the peace of Europe.

(Signed) A. HITLER
(Signed) NEVILLE CHAMBERLAIN
September 30, 1938.

Neville Chamberlain **In Defense of the Munich Agreement (October 1938)**

On October 3, 1938, the prime minister justifies his actions at the Munich Conference to the House of Commons.

When the House met last Wednesday, we were all under the shadow of a great and imminent menace. War, in a form more stark and terrible than ever before, seemed to be staring us in the face. Before I sat down, a message had come which gave us new hope that peace might yet be saved, and today, only a few days after, we all meet in joy and thankfulness that the prayers of millions have been answered, and a cloud of anxiety has been lifted from our hearts. . . .

Ever since I assumed my present office my main purpose has been to work for the pacification of Europe, for the removal of those suspicions and those animosities which have so long poisoned the air. The path which leads to appeasement is long and bristles with obstacles. The question of Czechoslovakia is the latest and perhaps the most dangerous. Now that we have got past it, I feel that it may be possible to make further progress along the road to sanity.

My right hon. Friend[9] has alluded in somewhat bitter terms to my conversation last Friday morning with Herr Hitler. I do not know why that conversation should give rise to suspicion, still less to criticism. I entered into no pact. I made no new commitments. There is no secret understanding. Our conversation was hostile to no other nation. The object of that conversation, for which I asked, was to try to extend a little further the personal contact which I had established with Herr Hitler and which I believe to be essential in modern diplomacy. We had a friendly and entirely noncommittal conversation, carried on, on my part, largely with a view to seeing whether there could be points in common between the head of a democratic government and

the ruler of a totalitarian state. We see the result in the declaration which has been published, in which my right hon. Friend finds so much ground for suspicion. What does it say?

There are three paragraphs. The first says that we agree "in recognizing that the question of Anglo-German relations is of the first importance for the two countries and for Europe." Does anyone deny that? The second is an expression of opinion only. It says that: "We regard the agreement signed last night and the Anglo-German Naval Agreement as symbolic of the desire of the two peoples never to go to war with one another again." Once more I ask, does anyone doubt that that is the desire of the two peoples? What is the last paragraph? "We are resolved that the method of consultation shall be the method adopted to deal with any other questions that may concern our two countries, and we are determined to continue our efforts to remove possible sources of difference and thus to contribute to assure the peace of Europe." Who will stand up and condemn that sentence?

I believe there are many who will feel with me that such a declaration, signed by the German chancellor and myself, is something more than a pious expression of opinion. In our relations with other countries everything depends upon there being sincerity and good will on both sides. I believe that there is sincerity and good will on both sides in this declaration. That is why to me its significance goes far beyond its actual words. If there is one lesson which we should learn from the events of these last weeks it is this, that lasting peace is not to be obtained by sitting still and waiting for

SOURCE: From *Hansard's Parliamentary Debates*, 5th Series, Vol. 339, cols. 41, 48–50.

[9]*My right hon. Friend:* Alfred Duff Cooper, First Lord of the Admiralty, and the only member of Chamberlain's cabinet to resign in protest against the Munich Agreement

it to come. It requires active, positive efforts to achieve it. No doubt I shall have plenty of critics who will say that I am guilty of facile optimism, and that I should disbelieve every word that is uttered by rulers of other great states in Europe. I am too much of a realist to believe that we are going to achieve our paradise in a day. We have only laid the foundations of peace. The superstructure is not even begun.

For a long period now we have been engaged in this country in a great program of rearmament, which is daily increasing in pace and in volume. Let no one think that because we have signed this agreement between these four powers at Munich we can afford to relax our efforts in regard to that program at this moment. Disarmament on the part of this country can never be unilateral again. We have tried that once, and we very nearly brought ourselves to disaster. If disarmament is to come it must come by steps, and it must come by the agreement and the active cooperation of other coun-tries. Until we know that we have obtained that cooperation and until we have agreed upon the actual steps to be taken, we here must remain on guard. . . .

While we must renew our determination to fill up the deficiencies that yet remain in our armaments and in our defensive precautions, so that we may be ready to defend ourselves and make our diplomacy effective—(*interruption*)—Yes, I am a realist—nevertheless, I say with an equal sense of reality that I do see fresh opportunities of approaching this subject of disarmament opening up before us, and I believe that they are at least as hopeful today as they have been at any previous time. It is to such tasks (the winning back of confidence, the gradual removal of hostility between nations until they feel that they can safely discard their weapons, one by one) that I would wish to devote what energy and time may be left to me before I hand over my office to younger men.

WINSTON S. CHURCHILL In Criticism of the Munich Agreement (October 1938)

The single most eloquent critic of both the policy of appeasement in general and the Munich Agreement in particular was the independent Conservative backbencher Winston Churchill. This is his reply to Chamberlain.

MR. CHURCHILL. If I do not begin this afternoon by paying the usual, and indeed almost invariable, tributes to the prime minister for his handling of this crisis, it is certainly not from lack of any personal regard. We have always, over a great many years, had very pleasant relations, and I have deeply understood from personal experiences of my own in a similar crisis the stress and strain he has had to bear; but I am sure it is much better to say exactly what we think about public affairs, and this is certainly not the time when it is worth anyone's while to court political popularity. . . .

I will, therefore, begin by saying the most unpopular and most unwelcome thing. I will begin by saying what everybody would like to ignore or forget but which must nevertheless be stated, namely, that we have sustained a total and unmitigated defeat, and that France has suffered even more than we have.

VISCOUNTESS ASTOR.[10] Nonsense!

MR. CHURCHILL. When the noble Lady cries "Nonsense," she could not have heard

SOURCE: From *Hansard's Parliamentary Debates*, 5th Series, Vol. 339, cols. 359–371, 373.

[10]The Virginia-born Lady Astor was elected to the House of Commons in 1922 as a Conservative, the first woman to take a seat in that body.

the Chancellor of the Exchequer admit in his illuminating and comprehensive speech just now that Herr Hitler had gained in this particular leap forward in substance all he set out to gain. The utmost my right hon. Friend, the prime minister, has been able to secure by all his immense exertions, by all the great efforts and mobilization which took place in this country, and by all the anguish and strain through which we have passed in this country, the utmost he has been able to gain [*Hon. Members: "Is Peace"*]. I thought I might be allowed to make that point in its due place, and I propose to deal with it. The utmost he has been able to gain for Czechoslovakia and in the matters which were in dispute has been that the German dictator, instead of snatching his victuals from the table has been content to have them served to him course by course.

The Chancellor of the Exchequer said it was the first time Herr Hitler has been made to retract (I think that was the word) in any degree. We really must not waste time, after all this long debate, upon the difference between the positions reached at Berchtesgaden, at Godesberg and at Munich. They can be very simply epitomized, if the House will permit me to vary the metaphor. One pound was demanded at the pistol's point. When it was given, two pounds were demanded at the pistol's point. Finally, the dictator consented to take one pound, seventeen shillings and six pence, and the rest in promises of good will for the future.

Now I come to the point, which was mentioned to me just now from some quarters of the House, about the saving of peace. No one has been a more resolute and uncompromising struggler for peace than the prime minister. Everyone knows that. Never has there been such intense and undaunted determination to maintain and to secure peace. That is quite true. Nevertheless, I am not quite clear why there was so much danger of Great Britain or France being involved in a war with Germany at this juncture if, in fact, they were ready all along to sacrifice Czechoslovakia. . . .

There never can be any absolute certainty that there will be a fight if one side is determined that it will give way completely. . . .

I have always held the view that the maintenance of peace depends upon the accumulation of deterrents against the aggressor, coupled with a sincere effort to redress grievances. Herr Hitler's victory, like so many of the famous struggles that have governed the fate of the world, was won upon the narrowest of margins. After the seizure of Austria in March, we faced this problem in our debates. I ventured to appeal to the government to go a little further than the prime minister went, and to give a pledge that in conjunction with France and other powers they will guarantee the security of Czechoslovakia, while the Sudeten Deutsch question was being examined either by a League of Nations commission, or some other impartial body, and I still believe that if that course had been followed events would not have fallen into this disastrous state. . . .

France and Great Britain together, especially if they had maintained a close contact with Russia, which certainly was not done, would have been able in those days in the summer, when they had the prestige, to influence many of the smaller states of Europe. . . . Such a combination, prepared at the time when the German dictator was not deeply and irrevocably committed to his new adventure, would, I believe, have given strength to all those forces in Germany which resisted this departure, this new design. . . .

All is over. Silent, mournful, abandoned, broken, Czechoslovakia recedes into the darkness. She has suffered in every respect by her association with the Western democracies and with the League of Nations, of which she has always been an obedient servant. . . . We in this country, as in other liberal and democratic countries, have a perfect right to exalt the principle of self-determination, but it comes ill out of the mouths of those in totalitarian states who deny even the smallest element of toleration to every section and creed within their bounds. But, however you put it, this particular block of land, this mass of human beings to be handed over, has never expressed the desire to go into the Nazi rule. I do not believe that even now—if their opinion could be asked, they would exercise such an option. . . .

I venture to think that in the future the Czechoslovak state cannot be maintained as an independent entity. You will find that in a period of time which may be measured by years, but may be measured only by months, Czechoslovakia will be engulfed in the Nazi regime. . . . It is the most grievous consequence which we have yet experienced of what we have done and of what we have left undone in the last five years: five years of futile good intention, five years of eager search for the line of least resistance, five years of uninterrupted retreat of British power, five years of neglect of cur air defenses. . . .

When I think of the fair hopes of a long peace which still lay before Europe at the beginning of 1933 when Herr Hitler first obtained power, and of all the opportunities of arresting the growth of the Nazi power which have been thrown away, when I think of the immense combinations and resources which have been neglected or squandered, I cannot believe that a parallel exists in the whole course of history. So far as this country is concerned the responsibility must rest with those who have the undisputed control of our political affairs. They neither prevented Germany from rearming, nor did they rearm ourselves in time. They quarrelled with Italy without saving Ethiopia. They exploited and discredited the vast institution of the League of Nations and they neglected to make alliances and combinations which might have repaired previous errors, and thus they left us in the hour of trial without adequate national defense or effective international security. . . .

We are in the presence of a disaster of the first magnitude which has befallen Great Britain and France. Do not let us blind ourselves to that. It must now be accepted that all countries of Central and Eastern Europe will make the best terms they can with the triumphant Nazi power. The system of alliances in central Europe upon which France has relied for her safety has been swept away, and I can see no means by which it can be reconstituted. The road down the Danube Valley to the Black Sea, the resources of corn and oil, the road which leads as far as Turkey, has been opened. In fact, if not in form, it seems to me that all those countries of middle Europe, all those Danubian countries, will, one after another, be drawn into this vast system of power politics (not only power military politics but power economic politics) radiating from Berlin, and I believe this can be achieved quite smoothly and swiftly and will not necessarily entail the firing of a single shot. . . . We are talking about countries which are a long way off and of which, as the prime minister might say, we know nothing. (*Interruption*) The noble Lady says that that very harmless allusion is . . .

VISCOUNTESS ASTOR. Rude.

MR. CHURCHILL. She must very recently have been receiving her finishing course in manners. What will be the position, I want to know, of France and England this year and the year afterward? What will be the position of that Western Front of which we are in full authority the guarantors? . . . Relieved from all anxiety in the East, and having secured resources which will greatly diminish, if not entirely remove, the deterrent of a naval blockade, the rulers of Nazi Germany will have a free choice open to them in what direction they will turn their eyes. If the Nazi dictator should choose to look westward, as he may, bitterly will France and England regret the loss of that fine army of ancient Bohemia which was estimated last week to require not fewer than thirty German divisions for its destruction. . . . Many people, no doubt, honestly believe that they are only giving away the interests of Czechoslovakia, whereas I fear we shall find that we have deeply compromised, and perhaps fatally endangered, the safety and even the independence of Great Britain and France. . . . You have to consider the character of the

Nazi movement and the rule which it implies. The prime minister desires to see cordial relations between this country and Germany. There is no difficulty at all in having cordial relations with the German people. Our hearts go out to them. But they have no power. You must have diplomatic and correct relations, but there can never be friendship between the British democracy and the Nazi power, that power which spurns Christian ethics, which cheers its onward course by a barbarous paganism, which vaunts the spirit of aggression and conquest, which derives strength and perverted pleasure from persecution, and uses, as we have seen, with pitiless brutality, the threat of murderous force. That power cannot ever be the trusted friend of the British democracy.

What I find unendurable is the sense of our country falling into the power, into the orbit and influence of Nazi Germany, and of our existence becoming dependent upon their good will or pleasure. . . . In a very few years, perhaps in a very few months, we shall be confronted with demands with which we shall no doubt be invited to com-ply. Those demands may affect the surrender of territory or the surrender of liberty. I foresee and foretell that the policy of submission will carry with it restrictions upon the freedom of speech and debate in Parliament, on public platforms, and discussions in the press, for it will be said (indeed, I hear it said sometimes now) that we cannot allow the Nazi system of dictatorship to be criticized by ordinary, common English politicians. . . .

We have passed an awful milestone in our history, when the whole equilibrium of Europe has been deranged, and that the terrible words have for the time being been pronounced against the Western democracies:

"Thou art weighed in the balance and found wanting."

And do not suppose that this is the end. This is only the beginning of the reckoning. This is only the first sip, the foretaste of a bitter cup which will be proffered to us year by year unless by a supreme recovery of moral health and martial vigor, we arise again and take our stand for freedom as in the olden times.

WINSTON S. CHURCHILL **Britain Stands Alone (June 1940)**

In March 1939, Hitler's troops marched into Prague and completed the conquest of Czechoslovakia. During the following month, Britain gave guarantees to Poland and Romania, and in September 1939—after the Stalin-Hitler Pact and the German invasion of Poland—Britain and France declared war on Germany. They were unable to prevent the German (and Russian) conquest of Poland or the German acquisition of Denmark and Norway in April 1940. In the aftermath of the latter disaster, Chamberlain gave way to Winston Churchill as prime minister. When Churchill addressed the House of Commons on June 18, 1940, Holland and Belgium had also fallen under German control and Hitler was completing the conquest of France. Britain "stood alone."

The military events which have happened during the past fortnight have not come to me with any sense of surprise. Indeed, I indicated a fortnight ago as clearly as I could to the House that the worst possibilities were open, and I made it perfectly clear then that whatever happened in France would make no difference to the resolve of Britain and the British Empire to fight on, "if necessary for years, if necessary alone." During the last few days we have successfully brought off the great majority of the troops we had on the lines of communication in France—a very large number, scores of thousands—and seven-eighths of the troops we have sent to France since the beginning of the war, that is to say, about 350,000 out of 400,000 men, are safely back in this country. Others are still fighting with the French, and fighting with considerable success in their local encounters with the enemy. We have also brought back a great mass of stores, rifles and munitions of all kinds which had been accumulated in France during the last nine months.

We have, therefore, in this island to-day a very large and powerful military force. This force includes all our best trained and finest troops and includes scores of thousands of those who have already measured their quality against the Germans and found themselves at no disadvantage. We have under arms at the present time in this island over a million and a quarter men. Behind these we have the local defense volunteers, numbering half a million, only a portion of whom, however, are yet armed with rifles or other firearms. We have incorporated into our defense forces every man for whom we have a weapon. We expect a very large addition to our weapons in the near future, and in preparation for this we intend to call up, drill and train further large numbers at once. Those who are not called up or employed upon the vast business of munitions production in all its branches—and it runs through every kind of grade—serve their country best by remaining at their ordinary work until they are required.

We also have dominions armies here. The Canadians had actually landed in France but have now been safely withdrawn, much disappointed, but in perfect order, with all their artillery and equipment. These very high-class forces from the dominions will now take part in the defense of the Mother Country. . . .

. . . It seems to me that as far as seaborne invasion on a great scale is concerned, we are far more capable of meeting it to-day than we were at many periods in the last war and during the early months of this war, before our other troops were trained,

and while the B.E.F.[11] was already abroad and still abroad. The navy have never pretended to be able to prevent raids by bodies of 5,000 or 10,000 men flung suddenly across and thrown ashore at several points on the coast some dark night or foggy morning. The efficacy of sea-power, especially under modern conditions, depends upon the invading force being of large size. It has to be of large size, in view of our military strength, to be of any use. If it is of large size, then the navy have something they can find and meet and as it were, bite on. Now we must remember that even five divisions, however lightly equipped, would require 200 to 250 ships, and with modern air reconnaissance and photography, it would not be easy to collect such an armada, marshal it and conduct it across the sea without any powerful naval forces to escort it, and with the very great possibility that it would be intercepted long before it reached the coast, and the men all drowned in the sea or, at the worst, blown to pieces with their equipment while they were trying to land. We also have a great system of minefields, recently strongly reinforced, . . .

This brings me, naturally, to the great question of invasion from the air and of the impending struggle between the British and German air forces. It seems quite clear that no invasion on a scale beyond the capacity of our land forces to crush speedily is likely to take place from the air until our air force has been definitely overpowered. In the meantime, there may be raids by parachute troops and attempted descents of airborne soldiers. We should be able to give those gentry a warm reception both in the air and if they reach the ground in any condition to continue the dispute. But the great question is, can we break Hitler's air weapon? Now, of course, it is a very great pity that we have not got an air force at least equal to that of the most powerful enemy within striking distance of these shores. But we have a very powerful air force which has proved itself far superior in quality, both in men and in

---

[11]*B.E.F.:* British Expeditionary Force

many types of machine, to what we have met so far in the numerous fierce air battles which have been fought. In France, where we were at a considerable disadvantage and lost many machines on the ground, we were accustomed to inflict losses of as much as two to two and a half to one. In the fighting over Dunkirk, which was a sort of no man's land, we undoubtedly beat the German air force, and this gave us the mastery locally in the air, and we inflicted losses of three or four to one. . . .

There remains the danger of bombing attacks, which will certainly be made very soon upon us by the bomber forces of the enemy. It is true that the German bomber force is superior in numbers to ours, but we have a very large bomber force also which we shall use to strike at military targets in Germany without intermission. I do not at all underrate the severity of the ordeal which lies before us, but I believe our countrymen will show themselves capable of standing up to it, like the brave men of Barcelona, and will be able to stand up to it, and carry on in spite of it, at least as well as any other people in the world. Much will depend upon this, and every man and every woman will have the chance to show the finest qualities of their race and render the highest service to their cause. For all of us at this time, whatever our sphere, our station, our occupation, our duties, it will be a help to remember the famous lines:

He nothing common did, or mean,
Upon that memorable scene.[12]

I have thought it right upon this occasion to give the House and the country some indication of the solid, practical grounds upon which we base our inflexible resolve to continue the war, and I can assure them that our professional advisers of the three services unitedly advise that we should do so, and that there are good and reasonable hopes of final victory. We have also fully in-formed and consulted all the self-governing dominions, and I have received from their prime ministers, Mr. Mackenzie King, Mr. Menzies, Mr. Fraser and General Smuts,[13] messages couched in the most moving terms in which they endorse our decision and declare themselves ready to share our fortunes and to persevere to the end. . . .

. . . During the first four years of the last war the Allies experienced, as my right hon. Friend opposite the Member for Carnarvon Boroughs (Mr. Lloyd George) will remember, nothing but disaster and disappointment, and yet at the end their morale was higher than that of the Germans, who had moved from one aggressive triumph to another. During that war we repeatedly asked ourselves the question, "How are we going to win?" and no one was able ever to answer it with much precision, until at the end, quite suddenly, quite unexpectedly, our terrible foe collapsed before us, and we were so glutted with victory that in our folly we cast it away. . . .

What General Weygand called the "Battle of France" is over. I expect that the battle of Britain is about to begin. Upon this battle depends the survival of Christian civilization. Upon it depends our own British life and the long continuity of our institutions and our empire. The whole fury and might of the enemy must very soon be turned on us. Hitler knows that he will have to break us in this island or lose the war. If we can stand up to him all Europe may be free, and the life of the world may move forward into broad, sunlit uplands; but if we fail then the whole world, including the United States, and all that we have known and cared for, will sink into the abyss of a new dark age made more sinister, and perhaps more prolonged, by the lights of a perverted science. Let us therefore brace ourselves to our duty and so bear ourselves that if the British Commonwealth and Empire lasts for a thousand years men will still say, "This was their finest hour."

---

[12]*He . . . scene:* From a poem by Andrew Marvell (1620–1678); the reference is to King Charles I on the day of his execution.   [13]*King . . . Smuts:* the prime ministers of Canada, Australia, New Zealand, and the Union of South Africa, respectively

17

From Worldwide Empire to European Community: Necessity or Choice?

In the aftermath of World War II, the British people were initially preoccupied with the complexities of postwar reconstruction while a Labour government sought at the same time to build "a Socialist Britain" (or at the very least a welfare state) at home and to combat Soviet expansion on the continent of Europe and elsewhere in the world.

One of the immediate questions faced by the post-1945 Labour government was how best to cope with its imperial responsibilities. Although the decline of overseas empire in the twentieth century is as complex a phenomenon as was the growth of that empire in the nineteenth, the events themselves may fruitfully be interpreted as the combined consequence of colonial nationalism, of the impact of two world wars, and of the erosion within Britain of a once widely felt sense of imperial mission. The single most important event in this process was the granting of independence to India in 1947, an event that foreshadowed the award of independence to other erstwhile British colonies in Southeast Asia, in Africa, and in the Caribbean during the late 1950s and the 1960s. The first document consists of the prosaic statement in which Prime Minister Clement Attlee (1883–1967), the leader of the postwar Labour government (1945–1951), informs the House of Commons that British forces and administrators would leave India within little more than a year, no matter what. In the second document, the then leader of the Conservative Opposition, Winston Churchill (1874–1965), protests that conditions in India are in no sense propitious for an immediate British departure. To what degree do Attlee and Churchill agree on what had been the movement of events in India during the previous half century? About the obstacles then existing to the establishment of a single Indian government to take over the reins of a new nation? Why does Churchill view the departure from India as a "shameful flight"?

The Indian subcontinent *did* become independent in 1947, even though independence involved partition—the creation of the separate nations of India and Pakistan—and prompted Hindu-Moslem riots that took the lives of hundreds of thousands of people. During the prime ministership (1957–1963) of one of Churchill's Conservative successors, Harold

"HE SAYS HE WANTS TO JOIN — ON HIS OWN TERMS ..."

Macmillan (1894–1986), Ghana, Nigeria and several other new African nations were to follow suit. In 1960 Macmillan cautioned the leaders of the Union of South Africa that "the wind of change" was sweeping across the African continent. What kind of racial policy does Macmillan advocate for the British Commonwealth of Nations? What is the tone of his statement?

In his speech, Macmillan described the Union of South Africa's policies of white supremacy and *apartheid* (the legal separation of the races) as policies that Britain could not support "without being false to our own deep convictions about the political destinies of free men . . . ," and a year later the South African government declared itself a republic and quit the Commonwealth of Nations. In 1965 the white-dominated government of neighboring Rhodesia issued its own unilateral declaration of independence against Britain. This is one of several topics that Bernard Levin discusses in *Run It Down the Flagpole,* a description of Britain's decline as a world power during the 1960s. Levin (1928–   ) had emerged during that decade as a drama critic and widely read newspaper columnist. What types of evidence does he cite for Britain's decline? How does the manner in which he assesses that decline differ from Macmillan's a decade earlier? Why does he conclude that Britons have once again been guilty of "appeasement"?

Harold Macmillan, the same Conservative prime minister who had encouraged independence for Britain's one-time colonies in Africa, decided in 1961 that it made sense for Britain to join what was coming to be a new and increasingly powerful force economically in Western Europe, the European Economic Community (EEC) or Common Market, an association made up of France, West Germany, Italy, and the three Benelux countries, Belgium, the Netherlands, and Luxembourg. Although Britain was still connected to a multiracial Commonwealth—an entity that held regular prime ministerial meetings and cooperated on matters ranging from athletics to higher education—it seemed increasingly clear that the Commonwealth would not and could not constitute a unified political, economic, or military force in the world.

Although Britain's initial application for EEC admission led to lengthy negotiations, its entry was vetoed in 1963 by President Charles DeGaulle of France, who was suspicious of a continuing "special relationship" between Britain and the United States. In 1967 a Labour government headed by Prime Minister Harold Wilson made a second attempt at admission only to face a second veto by DeGaulle. When the Conservatives returned to power in 1970, the new prime minister was Edward Heath (1916–   ), the very cabinet member who had negotiated with the EEC between 1961 and 1963 on Macmillan's behalf.

With President DeGaulle in retirement, Heath succeeded in fashioning a Treaty of Accession, and in February 1972 the House of Commons debated the European Communities Bill, a measure designed to give legislative force to the Treaty of Accession. As three excerpts from that debate suggest, the issue of British membership in the European Community remained a matter of considerable controversy within Britain itself. Peter Shore (1924–   ), the spokesman on European affairs for the Opposition Labour Party, was one objector. Enoch Powell (1912–   ), a former Conservative cabinet member, was another. (Powell had broken with his party's leadership a few years earlier when he proposed that nonwhite immigrants to Britain from the West Indies and Asia be encouraged to return to the lands of their birth and that no new such immigrants be allowed.) On what grounds of principle and procedure do Shore and Powell oppose British membership in the EC? On what grounds of principle, practicality, and procedure does Prime Minister Heath defend both the measure and British membership?

Heath won approval for the European Communities Bill by a narrow margin in 1972, and on January 1, 1973, Britain (along with Ireland and Denmark) formally joined the now nine-nation European Community. The government led by Heath's successor as prime minister, Harold Wilson of the Labour Party, did authorize a national referendum on British membership in 1975. The public approved by a margin of more than two to one, with the opposition headed by a handful of far-right Conservatives and a larger minority of far-left Labourites. As the relative political and judicial authority of the EC grew, the precise terms of British membership remained a matter of occasional political controversy throughout the 1980s, but by the early 1990s it had become clear that no British government would take Britain out of the European Community. By then Greece, Spain, and Portugal had joined as had East Germany (as part of a reunified German republic), and numerous other European countries were clamoring for admission as well.

CLEMENT ATTLEE The End of British Rule in India (1947)

On February 20, 1947, the head of the postwar Labour government, Prime Minister Clement Attlee, announces that the British government intends to withdraw all military forces and government officials from India.

I desire to make a statement on Indian policy.

It has long been the policy of successive British governments to work toward the realization of self-government in India. In pursuance of this policy an increasing measure of responsibility has been devolved on Indians and today the civil administration and the Indian Armed Forces rely to a very large extent on Indian civilians and officers. In the constitutional field the Acts of 1919 and 1935 passed by the British Parliament each represented a substantial transfer of political power. In 1940 the Coalition Government recognized the principle that Indians should themselves frame a new constitution for a fully autonomous India, and in the offer of 1942 they invited them to set up a Constituent Assembly for this purpose as soon as the war was over.

His Majesty's government believe this policy to have been right and in accordance with sound democratic principles. Since they came into office, they have done their utmost to carry it forward to its fulfillment. The declaration of the prime minister of 15th March last, which met with general approval in Parliament and the country, made it clear that it was for the Indian people themselves to choose their future status and constitution and that in the opinion of His Majesty's government the time had come for responsibility for the government of India to pass into Indian hands. . . .

It is with great regret that His Majesty's government find that there are still differences among Indian parties which are preventing the Constituent Assembly from functioning as it was intended that it should. It is of the essence of the plan that the Assembly should be fully representative.

His Majesty's government desire to hand over their responsibility to authorities established by a constitution approved by all parties in India in accordance with the Cabinet Mission's plan, but unfortunately there is at present no clear prospect that such a constitution and such authorities will emerge. The present state of uncertainty is fraught with danger and cannot be indefinitely prolonged. His Majesty's government wish to make it clear that it is their definite intention to take the necessary steps to effect the transference of power into responsible Indian hands by a date not later than June, 1948.

This great sub-continent now containing over 400 million people has for the last century enjoyed peace and security as a part of the British Commonwealth and Empire. Continued peace and security are more than ever necessary today if the full possi-

SOURCE: From *Hansard's Parliamentary Debates* (House of Commons), 5th Series, Vol. 433, cols. 1395–1398.

bilities of economic development are to be realized and a higher standard of life attained by the Indian people.

His Majesty's government are anxious to hand over their responsibilities to a government which, resting on the sure foundation of the support of the people, is capable of maintaining peace and administering India with justice and efficiency. It is therefore essential that all parties should sink their differences in order that they may be ready to shoulder the great responsibilities which will come upon them next year. . . .

His Majesty's government believe that British commercial and industrial interests in India can look forward to a fair field for their enterprise under the new conditions. The commercial connection between India and the United Kingdom has been long and friendly, and will continue to be to their mutual advantage.

His Majesty's government cannot conclude this statement without expressing on behalf of the people of this country their goodwill and good wishes toward the people of India as they go forward to this final stage in their achievement of self-government. It will be the wish of everyone in these islands that, notwithstanding constitutional changes, the association of the British and Indian peoples should not be brought to an end; and they will wish to continue to do all that is in their power to further the well-being of India.

This concludes the statement on policy.

WINSTON S. CHURCHILL **A Protest Against Britain's "Shameful Flight" from India (1947)**

Two weeks later, on March 6, 1947, the leader of the Conservative Opposition strongly condemns the policy of the Labour government toward India.

When great parties in this country have for many years pursued a combined and united policy on some large issue, and when, for what seemed to them to be good reasons, they decided to separate, not only in debate but by division, it is desirable and even necessary that the causes of such separation and the limitations of the differences which exist should be placed on record. This afternoon we begin a new chapter in our relations across the floor of the House in regard to the Indian problem. We on this side of the House have, for some time, made it clear that the sole responsibility for the control of India's affairs rests, of course, with His Majesty's government. We have criticized their action in various ways but this is the first time we have felt it our duty as the official Opposition to express our dissent difference by a formal vote.

Let us first place on record the measure of agreement which lies between us, and separate that from the differences that now lead us into opposite lobbies. Both sides of the House are bound by the declaration made at the time of the British mission to India in March, 1942. It is not true to suggest, as was done lately, that this decision marked a decisive change in the policy of the British Parliament toward India. There was a long story before we got to that. Great Britain had for many years been committed to handing over responsibility for the government of India to the representatives of the Indian people. There was the promise of dominion status implicit in the declaration of August, 1917. There was the expansion and definition of dominion status by the Statute of Westminster. There was the Simon Commission Report of 1930, followed by the Hoare-Linlithgow Reforms of 1935. There was the Linlithgow offer of 1940, for which, as head of the government in those days, I took my share of responsibility. By

SOURCE: From *Hansard's Parliamentary Debates* (House of Commons), 5th Series, Vol. 434, cols. 663–678.

this, the viceroy undertook that, as soon as possible after the war, Indians themselves should frame a fully self-governing constitution. All this constituted the preliminary basis on which the proposals of the Cripps Mission of 1942 were set. The proposals of this mission were not, in fact, a departure in principle from what had long been growing up, but they constituted a definite, decisive and urgent project for action. Let us consider the circumstances in which this offer was made.

The violent irruption of Japan upon east Asia, the withdrawal of the United States fleet to the American coast, the sinking of the *Prince of Wales* and the *Repulse*, the loss of Malaya and the surrender of Singapore, and many other circumstances of that time left us for the moment without any assured means of defending India from invasion by Japan. We had lost the command of the Bay of Bengal, and, indeed, to a large extent, of the Indian Ocean. Whether the provinces of Madras and Bengal would be pillaged and ravaged by the Japanese at that time seemed to hang in the balance, and the question naturally arose with poignant force how best to rally all Indian elements to the defense of their native land.

The offer of the Cripps Mission, I would remind the House, was substantially this: His Majesty's government undertook to accept and implement an agreed constitution for an Indian Union, which should be a dominion, framed by an elected Constituent Assembly and affording representation to the princes. This undertaking was subject only to the right of nonacceding provinces to receive separate treatment, and to the conclusion of a treaty guaranteeing the protection of religious and racial minorities. The offer of the Cripps Mission was not accepted by the political classes in India who alone are vocal and to whom it was addressed. On the contrary, the Congress, led by Mr. Gandhi and Mr. Nehru, did their utmost to make a revolt intended to paralyze the perilous communications of our army in Burma and to help the fortunes of Japan. Therefore, the National Coalition Govern-

ment of those days made a large series of mass arrests of Indian Congress leaders, and the bulk were kept in prison until the end of the war. I was not myself present in the cabinet when these decisions were taken. I was at Cairo preparing for the operations which opened at Alamein, but I highly approved of the action which was taken in my absence by the then deputy prime minister, the present prime minister, who sits opposite, and which I think was the only one possible on that occasion.

Therefore, it is quite clear that, whatever was the offer of the Cripps Mission, it was not accepted. On the contrary, it was repudiated by the parties to whom it was addressed. . . .

. . . Both sides of this House are bound by this offer, and bound by all of it, and it is on the basis of this offer being an agreed matter between the parties, and on that basis alone, that our present and future controversies arise. If I am bound by the offer of dominion status and all that it implies, the prime minister is equally bound, or was equally bound, to the conditions about agreement between the principal communities, about the proper discharge of our pledges about the protection of minorities and the like. The right hon. Gentleman has a perfect right to change his mind. He may cast away all these stipulations which we jointly made, and proceed only with the positive side of the offer. He has the right to claim the support of his parliamentary majority for any action he takes, but he has no right to claim our support beyond the limits to which we are engaged by the Cripps declaration. . . . I am only trying to lay down the basis on which we can agree to differ—the basis of 1942 and the present time. Before this latest pronouncement of theirs, His majesty's government had already departed from the Cripps Mission declaration of 1942, and they had departed from it in three major aspects. First, they had eliminated the stage of dominion status. The Cripps Mission expressly said that the objective was the creation of a new Indian Union which would constitute a dominion associated with the United

Kingdom and the other dominions by common allegiance to the crown, but equal to them in every respect, in no way subordinated in any aspect of domestic or external affairs. . . .

. . . If the dominion status procedure had been involved, in my view, the new Indian Dominion would have been perfectly free to leave the Commonwealth if it chose, but full opportunity would have been given for all the dangers and disadvantages to be surveyed by responsible Indian ministers beforehand, and also for the wishes of the great mass of the Indian people to be expressed, as they cannot be expressed now. It would have been possible to insert in the dominion constitution the necessary safeguards for minorities, and for the fulfillment of the British pledges to the various elements of Indian life, notably the depressed classes. This would have been a part of the agreement between the Indian Union and Great Britain, and would have been embodied in the necessary British legislation on the lines of the British North America Act, to which the great free Dominion of Canada has always attached importance, and still does. So the second departure from the Cripps Mission declaration was the total abandonment by His Majesty's government of all responsibility for carrying out its pledges to minorities and the depressed classes, as well as for fulfilling their treaties with the Indian states. All these are to be left to fend for themselves, or to fight for themselves as best they can. That is a grave major departure.

The third departure was no less grave. The essence of the Cripps Mission declaration was that there should be agreement between the principal Indian communities, namely, in fact, the Muslims and the Hindus. That, also, has been thrown overboard. . . .

I do not think that the 14–months' time limit gives the new viceroy a fair chance. We do not know what directives have been given to him. No explanation of that has been provided. Indeed, we are told very little. Looking on this Indian problem and having to address the House upon it, I am

surprised how many great gaps there are in information which should be in the full possession of the House. We are told very little. What is the policy and purpose for which he is to be sent out, and how is he to employ these 14 months? Is he to make a new effort to restore the situation, or is it merely Operation Scuttle on which he and other distinguished officers have been despatched? . . .

Everyone knows that the 14–months' time limit is fatal to any orderly transference of power, and I am bound to say that the whole thing wears the aspect of an attempt by the government to make use of brilliant war figures in order to cover up a melancholy and disastrous transaction. One thing seems to me absolutely certain. The government, by their 14–months' time limit, have put an end to all prospect of Indian unity. I myself have never believed that that could be preserved after the departure of the British Raj, but the last chance has been extinguished by the government's action. How can one suppose that the thousand-year gulf which yawns between Muslims and Hindus will be bridged in 14 months? Here are these people, in many cases, of the same race, charming people, lightly clad, crowded together in all the streets and bazaars and so forth, and yet there is no intermarriage. It is astounding. Religion has raised a bar which not even the strongest impulses of nature can overleap. It is an astounding thing. Yet the government expect in 14 months that there will be an agreement on these subjects between these races. . . .

Let the House remember this. The Indian political parties and political classes do not represent the Indian masses. It is a delusion to believe that they do. I wish they did. They are not as representative of them as the movements in Britain represent the surges and impulses of the British nation. This has been proved in the war, and I can show the House how it was proved. The Congress Party declared noncooperation with Great Britain and the Allies. The other great political party, to whom all main power is to be given, the Muslim League, sought to make a bargain about it, but no bargain was made. So both great political parties in India, the only forces that have been dealt with so far, stood aside. Nevertheless, the only great volunteer army in the world that fought on either side in that struggle was formed in India. More than three and a half million men came forward to support the king-emperor and the cause of Britain; they came forward not by conscription or compulsion, but out of their loyalty to Britain and to all that Britain stood for in their lives. In handing over the government of India to these so-called political classes we are handing over to men of straw, of whom, in a few years, no trace will remain. . . .

We are told that we cannot walk out of Palestine because we should leave behind us a war between 600,000 Jews and 200,000 Arabs. How, then, can we walk out of India in 14 months and leave behind us a war between 90 million Muslims and 200 million caste Hindus, and all the other tribulations which will fall upon the helpless population of 400 million? Will it not be a terrible disgrace to our name and record if, after our 14–months' time limit, we allow one-fifth of the population of the globe, occupying a region nearly as large as Europe, to fall into chaos and into carnage? Would it not be a world crime that we should be committing, a crime that would stain—not merely strip us, as we are being stripped, in the material position—but would stain our good name for ever?

Yesterday, the president of the Board of Trade and other speakers brought into great prominence our physical and military weakness. How can we keep a large army in India for 15 or 20 years? He and other speakers stressed that point; and, certainly, it is a very grave point. But he might as well have urged that in our present forlorn condition we have, not only not the physical strength, but not the moral strength and will power. If we, through lack of physical and moral strength, cannot wind up our affairs in a responsible and humane and honorable fashion, ought we not to consider invoking the aid or, at least, the advice of the world international organization, which is now clothed with reality, and on which so many of us, in all parts of the House, base our hopes for the peaceful progress, freedom and, indeed, the salvation of all mankind? . . .

I thank the House for listening so long and so attentively to what I have said. I have spoken with a lifetime of thought and contact with these topics. It is with deep grief I watch the clattering down of the British Empire, with all its glories and all the services it has rendered to mankind. I am sure that in the hour of our victory, now not so long ago, we had the power, or could have had the power, to make a solution of our difficulties which would have been honorable and lasting. Many have defended Britain against her foes. None can defend her against herself. We must face the evils that are coming upon us, and that we are powerless to avert. We must do our best in all these circumstances, and not exclude any expedient that may help to mitigate the ruin and disaster that will follow the disappearance of Britain from the East. But, at least, let us not add—by shameful flight, by a premature, hurried scuttle—at least, let us not add, to the pangs of sorrow so many of us feel, the taint and smear of shame. . . .

HAROLD MACMILLAN　**The Wind of Change (1960)**

During a visit to the Union of South Africa early in 1960, Prime Minister Macmillan alerts white South Africans to the fact that "the wind of change" is sweeping across the continent of Africa.

SOURCE: Abridged from "Address by Harold Macmillan, Cape Town, 3 February 1960" interspersed between his personal comments (pp. 155–159) from *Pointing the Way 1959–1961* by Harold Macmillan. Copyright © 1972 by Thomson Newspapers Limited. Index copyright © 1972 by Macmillan London Ltd. Reprinted by permission of Harper & Row, Publishers, Inc.

The meeting took place in a historic building—the chamber of the old Cape Colony Parliament. The audience amounted to some two hundred and fifty, of which ninety were members of the Senate and the rest of the House of Commons. I sat on a platform with the prime minister, the Opposition leaders, the Speaker and one or two other officials. On entering the door there was a polite ripple of applause. Although I had given Dr. Verwoerd an indication of what I intended to say, it was clear that, having merely seen the main outlines, the full effect of the actual text and especially of certain phrases came to him as a surprise, and perhaps a shock. I began by speaking of the pleasure that my wife and I had had in our travels through Africa and of the privilege to be visiting South Africa in 1960, the year of "Golden Wedding of the Union."

In the fifty years of their nationhood the people of South Africa have built a strong economy founded upon healthy agriculture and thriving and resilient industries. . . . I have seen the great city of Durban, with its wonderful port and the skyscrapers of Johannesburg, standing where seventy years ago there was nothing but the open veldt.

I turned next to Britain's part in this development—nearly two-thirds of the overseas investment outstanding in the Union at the end of 1956 was British. Our economies were now largely interdependent, Britain supplying one-third of all South Africa's imports and buying one-third of all her exports. I spoke of the contribution that South Africa had made to our common cause during the war and of the technical assistance which she was offering to the less well-developed parts of Africa in time of peace.

I then broached the topic which has caused this speech to be regarded as something of a watershed in African affairs—the emergence of nationalism in the African continent.

Ever since the break-up of the Roman Empire one of the constant facts of political life in Europe has been the emergence of independent nations. They have come into existence over the centuries in different forms, with different kinds of government, but all have been inspired by a deep, keen feeling of nationalism, which has grown as the nations have grown.

In the twentieth century, and especially since the end of the war, the processes which gave birth to the nation states of Europe have been repeated all over the world. We have seen the awakening of national consciousness in peoples who have for centuries lived in dependence upon some other power. Fifteen years ago this movement spread through Asia. Many countries there of different races and civilizations pressed their claim to an independent national life. Today the same thing is happening in Africa, and the most striking of all the impressions I have formed since I left London a month ago is of the strength of this African national consciousness. In different places it takes different forms, but it is happening everywhere. The wind of change is blowing through this continent, and, whether we like it or not, this growth of national consciousness is a political fact. We must all accept it as a fact, and our national policies must take account of it.

With what some of the critics regarded as a malicious deftness but which was really intended to soften the impact I continued:

Of course, you understand this better than anyone. You are sprung from Europe, the home of nationalism, and here in Africa you have yourselves created a new nation. Indeed, in the history of our times yours will be recorded as the first of the African nationalisms, and this tide of national consciousness which is now rising in Africa is a fact for which you and we and the other nations of the Western World are ultimately responsible. For its causes are to be found in the achievements of Western civilization, in the pushing forward of the frontiers of knowledge, in the applying of science in the service of human needs, in the expanding of food production, in the speeding and multiplying of the means of communication, and perhaps, above all, the spread of education.

Where would these new emerging nations align themselves—with the West or with the Communist East? What guidance would they receive from the independent members of the Commonwealth?

It is a basic principle of our modern Commonwealth that we respect each other's sovereignty in matters of internal policy. At the same time we must recognize that in this shrinking world in which we live today the internal policies of one nation may have effects outside it. We may sometimes be tempted to say to each other "Mind your own business," but in these days I would myself expand the old saying so that it runs: "Mind your own business, but mind how it affects my business, too."

We realized, I told my audience, that what we in the United Kingdom did in the Commonwealth countries now reaching independence must inevitably have consequences for the Union. We would act with full knowledge of the responsibility we had to all our friends; but equally in our own areas we must each do what we thought right; and that must, in our view, include offering the opportunity for an increasing share in political power and responsibility.

I went on to discuss the special problems of countries inhabited by several different races, pointing out that this applied not only to Africa but also, for instance, to Malaya, inhabited by both Chinese and Malays. The United Kingdom's attitude, I said, was expressed by the foreign secretary, Selwyn Lloyd, when he spoke at the United Nations General Assembly on 17 September 1959.

These were his words: "In those territories where different races or tribes live side by side the task is to ensure that all the people may enjoy security and freedom and the chance to contribute as individuals to the progress and well being of these countries. We reject the idea of any inherent superiority of one race over another. Our policy therefore is nonracial. It offers a future in which Africans, Europeans, Asians, the peoples of the Pacific and others with whom we are concerned, will all play their full part as citizens in the countries where they live, and in which feelings of race will be submerged in loyalty to new nations."

I recognized that the members of the Union Parliament had to face problems very different from those which confronted the parliaments of countries with homogeneous populations but I added:

As a fellow member of the Commonwealth it is our earnest desire to give South Africa our support and encouragement, but I hope you won't mind my saying frankly that there are some aspects of your policies which make it impossible for us to do this without being false to our own deep convictions about the political destinies of free men to which in our own territories we are trying to give effect.

I went on to speak of the impossibility, whether for men or nations, of living in isolation.

What Dr. John Donne said of individual men three hundred years ago is true today of my country, your country, and all the countries of the world:
"Any man's death diminishes me, because I am involved in Mankind. And therefore never send to know for whom the bell tolls; it tolls for thee."

It was in this conviction of the interdependence of nations, I told my audience, that I had made my journey to Moscow in 1959. It was in this belief that I had encouraged contacts between individuals and contacts in trade between the Western and the Communist world. "I certainly do not believe," I said, "in refusing to trade with people because you may happen to dislike the way they manage their internal affairs at home." I went on to express my disapproval of the attempts being made in Britain to boycott South African goods. It could only have serious effects on Commonwealth relations.

The independent members of the Commonwealth do not always agree on every subject. It is not a condition of their association that they should do so. On the contrary, the strength of our Commonwealth lies largely in the fact that it is a free association of independent sovereign states, each responsible for ordering its own affairs but cooperating in the pursuit of common aims and purposes in world affairs. Moreover these differences may be transitory. In time they may be resolved. Our duty is to see them in perspective against the background of our long association. Of this at any rate I am certain—those of us who by grace of the electorate are temporarily in charge of affairs in your country and in mine, we fleeting transient phantoms on the great stage of history, we have no right to sweep aside on this account the friendship that exists between our countries, for that is the legacy of history.

And I ended:

Let us resolve to build, not to destroy, and let us remember always that weakness comes from division, strength from unity.

The speech lasted for nearly fifty minutes, and as soon as I sat down Dr. Verwoerd thought it necessary to include in an official vote of thanks an impromptu defense of his policies, putting the case, as he expressed it, "for justice for the white man." The first reactions, however, in the local press were much less hostile than I expected, and it was not until the news came of the reception of the speech in Britain and throughout the world that criticism combined with a good deal of self-pity and resentment began to develop.

BERNARD LEVIN **Run It Down the Flagpole (1970)**

During the 1960s, the British Union Jack was "run down the flagpole" in numerous former colonies in Asia, Africa, and the Caribbean. The phrase therefore impressed a British journalist as an appropriate title for a series of essays on British society in the 1960s. In the selection that follows, he comments on Britain's decline as a world power during those years.

Politics still existed in the sixties, and although by the end of the decade there had been a widespread rejection, active or passive, of many of the traditional processes of political participation, and an even more widespread growth of cynicism about its practitioners, nevertheless the sixties were dominated, even if only formally, by politics. Nor was this surprising, for political events exemplified again and again the dilemma of Britain, her two-headed stance, her agony as the opposite forces in the decade, in trying to pull her one way and the other, seemed likely to pull her apart, and by the end of the decade almost had.

Politics in turn was dominated by economics; there was hardly a moment during the decade when some government or other was not exhorting the nation to work harder, to save more, to be more efficient, to export more vigorously, to import more selectively, to defend the health and strength of the pound sterling.

The purpose of all this, it was explained, was to enable Britain to survive with her

greatness intact. But wherein lay her greatness? And how might it be saved? On these grave questions no two could agree; but in time, from the whirling mass of advice and argument, action and reaction, three planets coalesced from the spinning fragments and came to dominate the heavens over Britain in the sixties. The end, the means, and the men who would provide the latter to bring about the former—these were the three themes of politics and economics in the sixties, and in each of them could be discerned the temper of the times and its effect on Britain.

Economic efficiency was needed in order to establish, or reestablish, Britain's place in the world; what that place was, or should be, had to be decided; the politicians would announce what Britain's place was and organize the efficiency that could bring her into it.

But what was it? For some there could be no doubt. Britain's place in the world was what it always had been. For these the lion still kicked, though every time it did so

SOURCE: From *Run It Down the Flagpole: Britain in the Sixties* by Bernard Levin. Copyright © 1970 by Bernard Levin. Reprinted by permission of Atheneum Publishers.

another tuft of fur came out. And in no field did it kick more vigorously, or shed more fur, than in that of Britain's overseas responsibilities. Once the Royal Navy had commanded the seas, but those days had long since gone by. Now, throughout the decade, the debate reverberated: what place was there for a British presence beyond Britain's shores? As part of the multi-national forces deployed under the NATO treaty, the British Army of the Rhine had an unexceptionable role to play, but outside Europe the matter was by no means so simple. Presently a phrase with ominous echoes began to be heard, and soon the entire debate began to revolve around it. "East of Suez"—a quotation from the supremely unfashionable Kipling, who had demanded to be shipped there—were the words; and many a further word was expended on discussing their implications. Britain had obligations—self-imposed for the most part—in the Middle East, where there was a permanent garrison in Aden and treaty commitments to the sheikdoms round about, and in the Far East, where Singapore and Malaysia looked to Britain, with fluctuating degrees of confidence, for military help in the last resort, and where Hong Kong kept up the brave pretense that she could or would be defended if China, having long since got out of bed ("Let China sleep," said Napoleon; "when she wakes, the world will be sorry"), should put her foot down on the rug beside it.

Britain was still a world power, ran one argument, and must show the flag in all the old familiar places. Britain was a small European power, ran the other, and must learn to itch where she could scratch. The empire had vanished, other countries managed to obtain their oil supplies without having troops sitting on the wells, and it was time to go. That at any rate was the final decision, taken by the Labour government, and it was followed, with only little more reluctance, by a decision to "liquidate our presence," as the phrase went, in the Far East also. Some rash promises were hastily made by the Conservative Opposition about re-

versing the policy if they were elected, but it soon became noticeable that the promises were made less and less frequently, and more and more vaguely, as time went by.

And yet the lion must needs adjust its dress before leaving. Just before the departure from Aden [1967–68], fierce fighting broke out there, partly between rival groups seeking to fill the power vacuum that the departing British would leave, partly between some or several of the rival groups on the one hand and the British on the other. Such hours commonly produce appropriate men, and this hour was no exception, the man being Colonel Colin Campbell Mitchell, one of those men who, denied inches by a niggardly nature (though lavishly supplied with courage instead), have throughout history tried to make up for their lack of physical stature by imposing themselves on the situation around them. It worked for Colonel Mitchell, who, with such inspiring cries as "One move out of them and we'll blow their bloody heads off," forcibly occupied an area of Aden that higher policy had previously decided the British should keep out of. With a fantastic stroke of luck that he, and his more romantic supporters at home, energetically maintained was in fact the result of judgment, he got away with it, bloodshed being almost entirely averted.

Thus did the little colonel become a hero overnight, and his face began to stare out of newspapers and television screens more and more frequently, there being no particular reason to suppose that this was in any way unwelcome to him. Soon afterward the continuing rationalization of the British armed forces brought about the merging of his regiment, the Argyll and Sutherland Highlanders, with another, and a campaign to "Save the Argylls" was launched. The campaign having failed, Colonel Mitchell resigned his commission and began to be interested in a political career, like Napoleon before him. For some time he seemed unable to make up his mind whether he was a Scottish Nationalist or a Conservative, but he was presently offered a distinctly winnable seat by the Conservatives, and accepted; he won it.

But Britain neither saved the Argylls nor stayed in Aden. Soon there would be no military presence east of Suez, and not much of one east of the Rhine; nor were voices lacking in Britain to insist that she should have no troops east of Dover, or west of it for that matter. One of the most remarkable stories in the world's history was coming to an end; it was the story of a tiny island which had sent forth her sons to conquer the world; and seen them succeed to such an extent that those at home had come to believe that it must go on for ever, and ultimately that it not only *must* go on for ever, but *should*. But the flag that had once flown over so many lands was coming down now, as dusk fell; and—ultimate indignity—there was none to give it the ritual sundown salute. As late as the fifties it was possible to hear regrets, or even complaints, about the Attlee government for, as it was put, "giving India away"; by the sixties such voices were all stilled, and the shrinking dominions could no longer boast a Clive or a Rhodes, a Milner or a Lugard, an Elgin or a Curzon. Perhaps it was fitting, seeing in what haste and hugger-mugger it was happening, what bathos attended the last rites, that the last proconsul should be Colonel Mitchell, and that it should be he who helped, all unknowing, to destroy the last illusions of empire as, amid a skirl of pipes and a flurry of sand, Britain's troops left the Middle East, where so many of her sons had laid their bones, for ever. . . .

But fast as the illusions were falling, they were not falling fast enough. When, halfway through the decade, the government of Rhodesia declared that country independent, in order to avoid having ultimately to hand over political power to men with unacceptably black faces, and for that matter black behinds, powerful words were expressed by the government in Britain. To a considerable extent and for a considerable time these were echoed by the Conservative Opposition, until a skilfully organized campaign forced the leaders of the party, os-

tensibly as committed as Labour to the mystic principle of "one man, one vote," to abandon their bipartisan support for the government's policy of bringing the dissidents to heel by economic sanctions, and to accept the policy, more and more cheerfully expressed by such figures as Lord Salisbury and Mr. Patrick Wall, of sympathy for the rebels.

All of which was greatly deplored; nevertheless it was not easy to see how anything could be done about it, except for those whose solution had from the start of the whole imbroglio been to put down the rebellion by force, heedless of the military logistics involved.

In the sixties Britain had begun to last to cut her international coat according to her national cloth; but fiction in such matters dies hard, and there was no apparent disposition to recognize the grim facts of life about Rhodesia. Rather was there the continuous chanting of "Sanctions are beginning to bite," followed by an increasing acceptance of the view that whatever was inevitable was also right, and therefore that the rule of the white minority in Rhodesia was in many ways quite admirable, and that its rulers fully intended to share power with the black majority in the not too distant future. Thus, as so often, the riven sixties got the benefit neither of policy nor of principle.

Individuals, as well as whole peoples, felt the sting of Britain's inability to move the world to her ends, and the unwillingness of so many of her leaders even to try. As good an index of Britain's declining power as the annual counting of the number of capital ships possessed by the navy, or the number of square miles still marked red on the map, was provided by the fate of two British citizens who ventured into Communist lands and there suffered bitterly, while the government, back home, wrung its hands and declared, like Lear, that it would do such things, that what they were as yet it knew not, but that they should be the terror of the earth.

Gerald Brooke was a young and idealistic

lecturer at a London technical college who visited Russia as a tourist in 1964, his visit happening to coincide with an urgent wish on the part of the Russian authorities to effect an exchange for a pair of Russian spies serving long terms of imprisonment in Britain. There being no British spies at that time imprisoned in Russia, Brooke was arrested and charged with illegally bringing into Russia publications forbidden within her borders. These, it transpired, were leaflets that he had with him, some of which contained views indicative of a belief that free institutions were to be admired, and tyrannical ones deplored. Brooke was arrested, and subsequently sentenced to five years' imprisonment in a concentration camp. There, as reports which seeped out made clear, he was subjected to the harshest possible conditions, in the hope that the British government would agree to the release of the Russian spies in order to save him further torment. The government, apart from claiming from time to time that they had the situation under review, did nothing, the difficulty of thinking of anything to do being considerably enhanced by the fact that Mr. Wilson[1] had long nursed a desire to build, or even to be, a bridge between East and West, over which the warring factions would advance, meeting in the middle to exchange embraces, and perhaps glass beads as well.

Anyway, Brooke stayed in his camp until the Russians let it be known that on the expiry of his original sentence he would be charged with further offenses and sentenced to an even longer term of imprisonment. At this, Wilson gave in and allowed the exchange for the Russian spies, who were sent off from London airport with champagne and smiles.

There were those in Britain who defended the Russian treatment of Gerald Brooke, or who were willing to condemn him for what he had done, or at least to urge that nothing should be done to save him if it might upset his captors. This last argument was even to be heard in connection with the case of Anthony Grey, a British journalist acting as representative of Reuters in Peking. He was arrested in 1967, shortly after the trial and imprisonment of a number of Chinese rioters in Hong Kong; he was not put on trial but confined to one room of his house, where he was subjected to a variety of psychological torments, under the stress of which his mind began, inevitably, to suffer, so that nearly a year after his release he was still unable to meet old colleagues, or even relatives, without strain. But in Grey's case it might be counted as gain that, since Mao Tse-tung had never visited Britain, Mr. Wilson was unable to tell him, as he had told Kosygin,[2] that he was part of the British way of life, and since Mr. Wilson had never visited China, he was unable to boast of his friendship with any of Mao's henchmen, as he did in the case of Mikoyan,[3] whom he had met a few times many years earlier.

Mr. Wilson was by no means the only appeaser. For some reason television organizations had, during the sixties, an outstanding record in this respect. On the occasion, for instance, of the fiftieth anniversary of the Russian Revolution, both the B.B.C. and Granada Television mounted elaborate commemorative programs of which the chief quality was their lack of any serious criticism of anything that had resulted from it. Even more extraordinary was the way in which the B.B.C. bent to Russian pressure over a program they had devised dealing with the show-trial in Moscow of Andrei Sinyavsky and Yuri Daniel; a Russian representative visited the B.B.C. and threatened that Russian cooperation in

---

[1]*Harold Wilson:* prime minister (Labour) from 1964 to 1970 and from 1974 to 1976   [2]*Alexei Kosygin:* premier of the Soviet Union (1964–1980)   [3]*Anastas Mikoyan:* first deputy premier of the Soviet Union (1955–1957; 1958–1964) and chairman of the Presidium of the Supreme Soviet (head of state) from 1964 to 1965

B.B.C. enterprises would be ended unless the B.B.C. abandoned the program. The B.B.C. for a time looked likely to accept the ultimatum, announcing that the program had been postponed and refusing to give a date for its transmission, but it soon became apparent that a considerable outcry would result if the program were cancelled, and it eventually went out, though it was postponed sufficiently for it not to interfere with the celebrations attendant on the anniversary of the Revolution.

Most remarkable, however, was the case of the unique film record that was destroyed after transmission by Rediffusion, then holders of the London weekday commercial television franchise. This concerned a program on Russia in which John Morgan had held an interview at a secret rendezvous outside Moscow with three young opponents of their regime; what made the episode unique was that all three insisted on speaking directly to the camera, so that they could be, and undoubtedly were, identified when the program was shown. Morgan warned them of the possible consequences to them—a warning that was, of course, quite unnecessary, as they would have known much better than he about what would follow—but they insisted on going the full length of their courage, and the interview was subsequently shown, and its text published, in Britain. Shortly afterwards, after Russian representations to Rediffusion, and in circumstances that were obscure, the film was destroyed (though there have been reports that the technicians, appalled by the order, surreptitiously made an extra copy; if so, its whereabouts remain unknown), and when the news leaked out Rediffusion claimed that they had destroyed the film because storage facilities for film that had already been shown were limited, much as the curator of the Louvre might excuse his burning of the Mona Lisa on the grounds that wallspace was in very short supply.

It was not easy to guess at the deeper national reasons for an attitude that had so worked itself into the country's bones that it was capable of producing examples like that. Britain's decline as a world power and as an industrial and economic force had been gradual but continuous; along with it, of course, went an even greater and more rapid increase in the number and vehemence of the voices drawing attention to this decline. It is a well-known psychological fact that if a man already conscious of a number of psychological deformities in himself has his attention repeatedly drawn to them by bystanders who exaggerate the extent and nature of these weaknesses, and even claim to have discovered further ones that he does not know about and that may be wholly imaginary, he will eventually begin to take on the characteristics attributed to him, and to behave in fact as he is told he behaves in imagination. It may be that Britain had declined so far, and had been told so often that she had declined even further, that she eagerly adopted the role for which she had been cast, and, convinced that she was a weak and spineless creature who would truckle to the powerful and ruthless, began to *be* such a creature, and to truckle to anybody who would pause long enough to be truckled to. Since it was in the interests of the Russians to be truckled to by Britain, their leaders were always willing to stop for a truckle, and since there seemed no likelihood that the due tribute of truckle would ever be denied, the process continued, and even increased, reaching its nadir at the time of the invasion of Czechoslovakia in 1968 by troops from Russia and her colonies, when Mr. Wilson condemned the invasion in the most forthright terms but declined to take any action whatever, however diplomatic, possibly on the grounds that if Britain would not take action to save her own citizens from wrongful arrest and false imprisonment, she could hardly be expected to do so on behalf of a far-off country of which we knew nothing. It is true that no member of the government attended the annual Revolution Day party at the Russian embassy in 1968, but they were back the following year, and it is not even certain that the Russians had noticed their brief fit of the sulks.

PETER SHORE, ENOCH POWELL, **Debate on Whether Britain Should Join**
and EDWARD HEATH   **the European Economic Community (1972)**

In the aftermath of signing a Treaty of Accession (1971) with the then six-nation European Economy Community (EEC or Common Market), the House of Commons debates the European Communities Bill. Introduced by the Conservative government headed by Prime Minister Edward Heath, the measure would give formal parliamentary sanction to Britain's membership as of January 1, 1973. Peter Shore is spokesman for the Labour Party in Opposition; Enoch Powell speaks for the independent Conservatives.

Peter Shore:

[The Conservative government has] now had over 18 months of very serious, in their case obviously most devoted, effort to enter the Common Market, yet they have only now begun seriously to consider this most important of all the issues which in the end are involved—the effect upon the Parliament and democracy of this country. . . .

What we are talking about is a bill which will so greatly change many of the matters which affect the lives of people in this country and the prospects for our nation. It will certainly affect the prosperity of the nation. It will affect our living standards, our chances of employment, as well as the future of great industries and many regions of this country. It will also affect, as we have just heard, the democracy of the country, the extent to which we continue to rule ourselves, and our freedom to use the state power for those purposes that we think right.

Last, and by no means least—I am speaking, as one inevitably must on a bill of this kind, in broad terms—it will affect our relationships with other countries, in particular whether we should forge a new and special relationship—that is what it is: a community—with the neighbouring countries of Western Europe, rather than maintain the relationships and associations in the Commonwealth, E.F.T.A. [European Free Trade Association] and elsewhere which we have enjoyed for so long and which we enjoy today.

These are all matters, very big matters. . . . First, the bill is about accession not just to the Treaty of Rome,[4] the Treaty of Paris, the Euratom Treaty—the major founding treaties of the Communities. [Second], I believe that we are acceding to the 10 volumes of additional treaties and subtreaties which were published last week, along with the original listed treaties.

The extent, the manner, the timetable, of our accession to these treaties is, of course, set out in the two volumes of the Treaty of Accession. Here, among other things, will be found the terms which the right hon. and learned Gentleman and his government have negotiated. These matters, which the government would wish us not to see or speak of, are to be found there—buried in a kind of shallow grave of protocols and annexes, but for all that, one can discover them there.

Part of our task in this debate and others will be to disinter these bodies and bring them before the gaze of the House. . . . There is no mention in the treaties of the very large contribution which this country will have to make in the form of its "membership fee." The only mention of sums of money is in the bill itself, in the financial

SOURCE: *Parliamentary Debates* (House of Commons), 5th Series, Vol. 831, cols. 287–301, 698–707, 743–752.

[4]*Treaty of Rome (1957):* served as the constitution of the original six-nation (France, West Germany, Italy, Netherlands, Belgium, Luxembourg) European Economic Community

memorandum, where, of course, the figures stop discreetly at the net £200 million in 1977. The most serious matters of all, in a sense—they are very serious—the assessment and the judgment about how all this would affect our future prosperity, are not mentioned. . . .

What inevitably will follow from the new systems of taxation which are being proposed and what will happen as a result of the very large and additional burdens on our balance of payments is that we shall endanger the possibilities of our continuing growth and prosperity in the years ahead. It will also have very retrograde effects upon the distribution of income in this country, particularly as it affects people with small incomes or below average earnings.

There is serious and genuine concern. Heavens!—there should be, with one million unemployed today and with the British economy, in comparison with the economies of the six, having shown a considerable difficulty in achieving a satisfactory rate of growth now over a number of years. There is real worry that in relation to this large and more dynamic market in Western Europe Britain could become as Northern Ireland has been to the United Kingdom. . . .

We pump large sums of money into the weaker areas [like Northern Ireland]. But in relation to the Common Market, what is being proposed is the very opposite. It is that we who are in relation to the six, I regret to say, economically weak, certainly in terms of our growth, should make a substantial contribution across the balance of payments to their economies, without limit in time or in amount under the formulae of the Communities' taxation that have been agreed. So one cannot help but have the most serious worry and concern about this. . . .

It has been an important part of the government's case that they have a fall-back position, that we need not worry too much about a particular set of inadequate terms in the negotiations because when and if we become a member and when particular matters needed to be renegotiated we should be able to get our way by insisting that the matter in question was of vital national interest to us and the other members would then have to accept our view. . . .

But there is no joy for us in this, for while the Common Market agricultural policy and its financing impose disastrous burdens on us, and cannot be vetoed by us—the policy can be changed only by unanimous agreement or by heavily qualified majority voting—the only hope of mitigation of these burdens for us lies in the development of common industrial and regional policies which would reverse the cash flow in our favor. Yet it is precisely on those policies that the president of France will be free to exercise his veto. It is of great concern and potential damage to this country that there is no British veto of what has been agreed, and for the past 13 years what has been agreed in the Community is basically the self-interest of France. . . .

Another important matter is involved in the loss of decision-making by this Parliament, or in the extent to which our decision-making processes will be curtailed in relation to the Community. The proposal before us—I say this perhaps more to some of my hon. Friends than to hon. Gentlemen opposite—is not to transfer power from our Parliament and democracy—operating, as it must, on the national level—to a new Parliament and democracy of equal weight or stature in Europe.

There is surely one thing about which we can agree: namely, that of all the institutions of the Community, the weakest is the European Assembly. It has no power, it is not directly elected, it seldom meets and it is only a talking shop[5]. . . . The transfer of power that is being contemplated is not to

[5]*European Assembly . . . shop:* The European Economic Community was to change its constitution a few years later, and in 1979 the first direct elections to the European Parliament were held.

this talking shop—how could it be a transfer to such a body?—but to the non-elected institutions of the Community; the Brussels Commission, the Council of Ministers and that most important body, the Committee of Permanent Representatives, which the Rome Treaty does not even mention. . . . Thus, what is involved is not merely a transfer of sovereignty from London to Brussels or from Britain to Europe, but a serious loss of democratic decision-making for this country. That is what is greatly in danger now.

I come to what I consider to be the gravest of all objections to the bill. For the massive changes which the bill involves, the government have not obtained the full-hearted consent of either the British Parliament or the British people. There have been many occasions in the past when measures have lacked public support, but the public have always known that such legislation could be, and often was, changed or amended by successor governments. It is the clear intention of this government—it is also the hope of the six—that joining the Community should be for Britain a permanent commitment. . . .

All countries have recognized that when major changes are to be made in their constitutions there has to be some special test of the nation's will. Other applicant countries—Norway, Ireland and Denmark—all have written constitutions, and it is part of their constitution that changes of the kind proposed should be subject to special procedures. As many of my hon. Friends will know, Norway requires a five-sixths' majority in Parliament, Denmark needs a two-thirds' majority. In addition, all three countries will operate a referendum to make sure that the people understand, and if they so will it they consent to what is proposed.

We have no written constitution in Britain, but we have practices and conventions which are no less important. . . .

I cannot emphasize too much how important I believe this matter of consent to be. . . . So we must give notice now to the government, to this nation and to the six that we shall fight this measure and we have high hopes and every intention of defeating it. But should the government somehow get their way and should they succeed in placing this measure on the statute book, then we warn them now that we intend to renegotiate and re-legislate. The argument will not end. No decision that they make can have more than an interim character until the people of this country have been able to vote upon it and themselves decide their own future.

Enoch Powell:

We are approaching this question for the first time as a practical one. Never till now has the House of Commons had placed before it proposed legislation on which it must take a definitive view and on which it must envisage as a practical issue what it will mean for this country if we accede to the Community.

The bill, whatever its defects, does manifest some of the major consequences. It shows first that it is an inherent consequence of accession to the Treaty of Rome that this House and Parliament will lose their legislative supremacy. It will no longer be true that law in this country is made only by or with the authority of Parliament—which in practice means the authority of this House. The legislative omnicompetence of this House, its legislative sovereignty, has to be given up.

The second consequence, which is equally manifest upon the face of the bill, is that this House loses its exclusive control—upon which its power and authority have been built over the centuries—over taxation and expenditure. In future, if we become part of the Community, moneys received in taxation from the citizens of this country will be spent otherwise than upon a vote of this House and without the opportunity, necessarily preceding such a vote, to debate grievance and to call for an account of the way in which those moneys are to be spent. For the first time for centuries it will be true to say that the people of this country are not taxed only upon the authority of the House of Commons.

The third consequence . . . is that the judicial independence of this country has to be given up. In future, if we join the Community, the citizens of this country will not only be subject to laws made elsewhere but the applicability of those laws to them will be adjudicated upon elsewhere; and the law made elsewhere and the adjudication elsewhere will override the law which is made here and the decisions of the courts of this realm.

Those three facts, those essential sacrifices of sovereignty, are evident upon the face of the bill; and they are not disputed, although they are sought to be qualified, and I will come presently to the qualifications. There is, however, a fourth consequence which, though not manifest, is inherent and implicit. That is the progressive strengthening of the executive as compared with this House, or, to put it the other way, the continuing diminution of the power of this House to influence and control the executive, as I will presently prove.

Let me come first to the two grounds on which the propositions I have stated are—not disputed; they cannot be, they are in the bill—but upon which it is sought to palliate them and render them palatable. The first is the *de minimis* argument—"Don't worry; it's not very important, because it will not refer to many subjects or very important matters." The second is the remonstrance "Don't worry, because, at any rate in future, we"—whoever "we" is—"will be participating in whatever decisions result in the overriding authority of the Community being exercised in this country."

I will take those two arguments in order. First, the *de minimis* argument. Of course, it is true that at present the great majority of Community law which will become part of our law . . . refers to two subjects. It refers to the common tariff and what is implicit in that; and it refers to the common agricultural policy, in the broadest sense of the term. Although these are important matters—many of us would consider that

they are far-reaching in their consequences—they are still relatively narrow compared with the whole sweep of administration and legislation.

But this is intended to be only a start. . . . The ground, on which British membership of the Community has been eloquently argued by . . . the prime minister and all its greatest advocates is not that the effect will be minimal but that this is intended to lead progressively to the political unification of this country with the countries of Western Europe. That has been said candidly, frankly, over and over again. So, although this surrender begins as minimal, it is intended to become maximal; and that intention is implicit in the policy and declarations of the government.

Then they say, passing to the other defense, "Ah, yes; but then, as this develops, as we go from the minimal to the maximal, at each stage—in the making of each new regulation, in the entry of the Community into each new area—we, the United Kingdom, will be a party to the decision; and since the government are sitting in this House, since the government will still be responsible to this House, it will be this House which will, in effect, still control the elaboration of Community law and Community powers and the progress of political unification at each stage." . . .

No, the clear fact is that at no stage will the House of Commons be able to take a decision with binding effect, neither before consideration in the Council of Ministers nor after a Community decision. Not only can this House in those circumstances take no binding decision, but neither it nor any future House can reverse that decision. And here we come to one of the most fundamental truths of this whole debate, that the power of this House depends, in the last resort, upon its power, humanly speaking, to reverse previous decisions; and not only the power of this House, but the power of those whose servants we are—the electorate. . . .

So it is implicit and inherent in the nature of the Community that the control of this House over the executive is progressively diminished, and consequently that the self-government of the electorate is diminished. . . .

It follows that for such a course to be taken it is indispensably necessary that it should be seen to be willed, and heartily willed, by the overwhelming majority of the people. . . .

That condition does not exist. I will take it in its two parts—the people first. I do not think that any hon. Member would be bold enough to say that he believed he could claim the full-hearted consent, the strong positive will, of the people of this country to give up all the things we know we have to give up in order to join the European Community. Let me put it more personally to my hon. and right hon. Friends here. Most of us in this chamber, not myself, did not happen to mention the European Community in their election addresses—

However, it is said, "Let it be Parliament that decides. Let us wrap it up, so that what we are talking about is the full-hearted consent of the House of Commons." There was a debate in October—a debate which did not deal with a precise proposition such as this—when the House decided affirmatively by a vote of seven-twelfths in favor. In no country with a written constitution, in none of the other countries which are participating in this operation with the United Kingdom, would such a proportion justify the major step which is involved in joining the Community. . . .

For this House, lacking the necessary authority either out-of-doors or indoors, legislatively to give away the independence and sovereignty of this House now and for the future is an unthinkable act. . . .

Edward Heath:

We are following the normal constitutional practice in relation to the conclusion of international treaties by British governments. We have followed, step by step, the statement which I outlined to the House last June in response to a request from the leader of the Opposition—a statement which was then warmly welcomed.

In October, we had a decisive vote from both Houses in favor of the principle of entry. We signed the Treaty of Accession on 22nd January. We are now asking the House to make the changes in our domestic law which are necessary to implement that treaty. By doing this, we fulfil the obligations which we accepted in that treaty; and we are then enabled to exercise the rights of our membership in full. This is a logical and clear consequence of events, consistent with our intention stated last June and consistent with the normal procedures of the House.

The vote last October came after more than a decade of negotiations; after a long period during which hon. Members had reflected on the matter and had discussed this thoroughly with all the various interests involved. When the time came for the vote, there was a free vote on this side of the House—[*Hon. Members: "No."*]—Yes, there was; and there was, in effect, a free vote on the benches opposite. Now we have moved to the next stage in the proceedings. . . . Overwhelmingly, the desire now, the decision of principle having been taken—[*Hon. Members: "No."*]—is for us now to take the opportunities which are open for ourselves and for Europe. . . .

The last thing the people of this country and the business community want is a continuation of uncertainty. The same is true of our friends abroad, and in particular those countries which will have special relationships with the Community. I believe, therefore, that this House—we are discussing the duties and responsibilities of the House of Commons—has a duty to show that it is clear and consistent in the decisions which it takes.

There has been a great deal of discussion of the nature and construction of this bill, and rightly so, because it is concerned, as the hon. Gentlemen said, with the rights of this House and how these can be safeguarded in the context of our being a member of the Community. We naturally attach great importance to that, but, as to the bill, there seems to be genuine misunderstanding of the constitutional position. . . . In fact the constitutional position has not changed in any single respect since the negotiations of 1961 when it was very fully discussed in this House time and again. It has not changed since the last government's[6] White Paper of 1967. The hon. Gentleman could have read his own government's White Paper and discussed it with them.

It has always been known that a certain amount of Community law, after discussion in the Community, after the Council of Ministers has decided, will become automatically applicable. It has always been known—and it was set out clearly in 1961 in the debate in the Lords and again in the White Paper. What we have done in this bill, in clause 2(1), is to make that effective. . . .

I believe we have now to look to the future. We have already been able to collaborate closely with the Community countries in seeking to resolve the world monetary and trade crisis which was precipitated by the United States measures last August. The crisis has been contained. It has certainly not been permanently resolved. The joint action between the Community and ourselves has played a considerable part, but we all recognize the need to go further, to move on to secure a fundamental reform of the international monetary system. By working closely with our partners in the enlarged Community we shall be able to exert a powerful influence in international discussion on proposals for reform.

Similarly, there will be further negotiations next year covering the whole future of international trading arrangements. The enlarged Community will have a dominant position in world trade; nearly 40 per cent. of world trade will be with the Community, the largest trade bloc which the world has ever seen and which no other trade blocs together can equal. So with this dominant position it will be strongly placed to secure agreement with the United States and Japan on measures to carry further the liberalization of trade which has added so much to the growth of prosperity in this post-war world.

In the political field membership of the Community offers us fresh opportunities. Those who have read of the meetings between the president of France and the chancellor of Germany will have seen the development which have been discussed there for closer consultation and collaboration in the wider questions of foreign affairs; and it has been agreed that we should take part with the existing members on the same basis in meetings of ministers and officials. It is true that in most essentials the countries of Western Europe share the same vital national interests, but in recent years they have failed to bring their proper united influence to bear on world events.

Looking to the future, the enlarged Community must aim at making its full contribution to resolving the problems of East-West relations, the problems of China's growing stature in the world, and the needs of the developing world. . . .

We shall take our part in helping the Community in its role in world affairs. Of course it has also been the ambition of the Community to move on from a customs union to an economic union. When they were in power, the Labour government found that an exciting prospect, and that is what it is. . . . Anything which the future offers to us would be put at risk and destroyed if the opponents of the bill had their way. Yet what alternative can they offer? They can offer only the negative proposition that Britain, which had turned its back on Europe, could still be secure and prosperous in its own right. Have they considered what the effect of turning back would be? The negotiations have succeeded, the Treaty of Accession has been signed and every government in the world now expects us to ratify it. . . .

I believe that our friends would find it incomprehensible if we were to tear up the agreement—the very agreement we have struggled for more than a decade to achieve. For years to come they would understand-

---

[6]*the last government:* the Labour government headed by Prime Minister Harold Wilson

400 The Past Speaks

ably ask whether any trust could be placed in Britain's role in any future international agreements. Our influence in world monetary and trade discussions would be destroyed. These questions would be settled by the United States, the European Community and Japan. The Community would not be broken up if we were to defect. It would suffer a bitter shock but it would survive and go on. But Britain would not benefit from the progress it was making.

I have dealt with many of the major issues raised in the debate. I will deal now in particular with one matter. As the House knows, I have always believed that our prosperity and our influence in the world would benefit from membership. I believed until recently that we could carry on fairly well outside, but I believe now that with developments in world affairs, and the speed at which they are moving, it will become more and more difficult for Britain alone. Faced with this prospect of change, I do not believe that any prime minister could come to this House and say, "We have secured the chance to join the European Community; we have signed the Treaty of Accession; we have the opportunity of full membership; but I now advise this House to

throw them away." I do not believe that any prime minister could say that, and it follows from what I have said that this bill is not a luxury which we can dispense with if need be.

It has been a central policy of three successive governments, irrespective of party, and of all three main parties in this House that Britain should join the European Community if suitable arrangements could be negotiated. By a large majority this House decided in principle last October that Britain should join the Community on the basis of the arrangements negotiated by my right hon. and learned Friend the chancellor of the duchy. Any government which thereafter failed to give legislative effect to that clear decision of this House would be abdicating its responsibilities. . . .

[By a vote of 309 to 301, the House of Commons approved the European Communities Bill. Three years later, in 1975, a Labour government headed by Harold Wilson authorized a national referendum on the issue. By a ratio of two to one the British people voted to have Britain remain a member state of the European Community.]

18

British Socialism in the 1960s and 1970s: The Road to Prosperity or to Stagnation?

British society during the 1960s and early 1970s was characterized by two apparently contradictory tendencies. One of these soon came to be known as the "Permissive Society." It involved the scrapping of decades-old or century-old laws and customs as to what might legally be printed in books or newspapers and as to what might legally be shown on the theater stage or on motion picture screens. It also meant the legalization of abortion and of homosexual conduct among consenting adults, and the easing of earlier barriers against divorce. It meant a flowering of "the cult of youth," and the lowering of the voting age from 21 to 18. Concomitantly it meant an increasing number of marriage break-downs, a growth in the use of addictive drugs, and a rise in the number of burglaries and robberies reported to the police.

The government that coincided with the flowering of the "Permissive Society" was the Labour government, headed from 1964 to 1970 and again (after a three-and-a-half-year interval of Conservative rule) from 1974 to 1976 by Harold Wilson. In 1976 Wilson gave way to Prime Minister James Callaghan, who presided over three more years of Labour government until the party was defeated in the watershed general election of 1979.

Even as successive Labour governments presided over, and in part encouraged, the relaxation of standards of custom and morality, they became paradoxically ever more rigorous in their efforts to regulate Britain's economy. Successive Labour governments nationalized additional private industries and spun an increasingly complex web of regulations designed to curb the powers of private employers and private landlords and to control both international trade and financial transactions. The second period of Labour rule took place in the aftermath of the quadrupling of world oil prices in 1973, an event that precipitated an economic downturn throughout much of Western Europe and North America. In Britain the affliction came to be known as "stagflation"—a combination of the fastest rate of inflation of wages and prices in all of British history (in 1975 almost 30 percent) and a downturn in production and employment. In 1976 the Callaghan government was compelled to seek the aid of the

Prime Minister Harold Wilson Conducts

"You can't expect the curtain to go up already—I've been playing the overture for only 609 dynamic days!"

International Monetary Fund in order to cope with a crisis in Britain's balance of international payments and a large deficit in its national budget. One consequence was a significant curb in the growth of "welfare state" spending within Britain. The four selections in this chapter throw light on both aspects of the era, the "Permissive Society" and the attempts by successive Labour governments to cope with economic difficulties.

Time Magazine's "Salute to 'Swinging London'" (1966) provides an upbeat assessment of the manner in which British society had liberated itself from old restraints and taboos. Why do the authors of the article describe London as "the city of the decade"? To what aspects of societal change and vitality do they call attention?

Not all Britons were as delighted as was *Time* with all the implications of popular permissiveness. Thus Lord Longford, a Labour peer, became convinced by the end of the decade that the pendulum had swung too far and that the "Permissive Society" had become the insensitive and the uncivilized society. In 1971 he introduced into Parliament a resolution contending that "pornography . . . has increased, is increasing, and ought to be diminished." Lord Longford's initiative was welcomed by Viscount Eccles (1904–   ), the member of Edward Heath's Conservative government (1970–1974) with prime responsibility for the arts. In "The Menace of Pornography," Eccles seeks to place its widespread diffusion in a broader context. How does he connect it with "the pattern of the last decade"? What other phenomena and what underlying questions of principle does he relate to the spread of pornography? How does Eccles assess the power of pictorial images in earlier ages and his own?

The other two selections in the chapter appraise the Labour Party's ability to manage Britain's government and economy during the greater part of the 1964–1979 era. Were the party's policies largely responsible for the economic stagnation combined with rapid inflation that became increasingly characteristic of Britain during the later 1960s and even more so during the mid-1970s? Or conversely, ought the Labour Party to be credited with preserving the welfare state that it had established between 1945 and 1951? Ought it to be credited also with using its powers of taxation and its authority over education to increase the degree of social equality in British life?

In "Anglo-Communism?" Robert Moss (1946–   ), the Australian-born foreign report editor of the influential British weekly *The Economist* and columnist for the London *Daily Telegraph,* observes how far in the direction of socialism (or "communism," as defined by Karl Marx and Friedrich Engels) Britain had moved by 1977. To what extent does Moss see Britain as a largely state-directed society? How does he explain the fact that a nation that had elected so few Communists to public office could fall so significantly under communist influence? In what ways does Moss see British democracy threatened by those members of the Labour Party who called themselves "democratic socialists"?

A far more complacent and favorable approach to the problems faced by Britain during the later 1970s was provided in *Britain: A Future That Works* (1978) by Bernard D. Nossiter (1926–1992), an American who had been serving since 1971 as London correspondent of the *Washington Post*. In addition to writing about Britain, Nossiter had written about American economics and politics in *The Mythmakers* (1964) and about India in *Soft State* (1970). How does Nossiter deal with Moss's concerns? In what context does he place the admitted facts that since the end of World War II the British economy had grown more slowly than had the economies of Britain's major continental neighbors and had experienced a high level of "stagflation" during the 1970s? What virtues does he find in the Britain of that decade? In what way does he see Britain as "a model for others in the postindustrial age"?

TIME MAGAZINE A Salute to "Swinging London" (1966)

A Britain shedding the responsibilities of world power abroad appeared to be shedding old restraints and inhibitions at home as well—in music, in the arts, in clothing, in mores. For jet-setters and less wealthy visitors, London became "the city of the decade"; according to Time's *headline, "You Can Walk Across It on the Grass."*

In this century, every decade has had its city. The *fin de siècle*[1] belonged to the dreamlike round of Vienna, capital of the in-bred Habsburgs and the waltz. In the chang-

---

SOURCE: "You Can Walk Across It on the Grass," from *Time* (April 15, 1966), pp. 30–34. Copyright Time Inc. 1966. Reprinted by permission.

[1]*fin de siècle:* end of the century

ing '20s Paris provided a moveable feast for Hemingway, Picasso, Fitzgerald and Joyce, while in the chaos after the Great Crash, Berlin briefly erupted with the savage iconoclasm of Brecht and the Bauhaus. During the shell-shocked 1940s, thrusting New York led the way, and in the uneasy 1950s it was the easy Rome of *la dolce vita*.[2] Today, it is London, a city steeped in tradition, seized by change, liberated by affluence, graced by daffodils and anemones, so green with parks and squares that, as the saying goes, you can walk across it on the grass. In a decade dominated by youth, London has burst into bloom. It swings; it is the scene.

This spring, as never before in modern times, London is switched on. Ancient elegance and new opulence are all tangled up in a dazzling blur of op and pop. The city is alive with birds (girls) and beatles, buzzing with minicars and telly stars, pulsing with half a dozen separate veins of excitement. The guards now change at Buckingham Palace to a Lennon and McCartney tune, and Prince Charles is firmly in the long-hair set. In Harold Wilson, Downing Street sports a Yorkshire accent, a working-class attitude and a tolerance toward the young that includes Pop Singer "Screaming" Lord Sutch, who ran against him on the Teen-Age Party ticket in the last election. Mary Quant, who designs those clothes, Vidal Sassoon, the man with the magic comb, and the Rolling Stones, whose music is most In right now, reign as a new breed of royalty. Disks by the thousands spin in a widening orbit of discothèques, and elegant saloons have become gambling parlors. In a once sedate world of faded splendor, everything new, uninhibited and kinky is blooming at the top of London life.

London is not keeping the good news to itself. From Carnaby Street, the new, way-out fashion in young men's clothes is spreading around the globe, and so are the hairdos, the hairdon'ts and the sound of beat; in Czechoslovakia alone, there are 500 beat groups, all with English names. London is exporting its plays, its films, its fads, its styles, its people. It is also the place to go. It has become the latest mecca for Parisians who are tired of Paris, where the stern and newly puritanical domain of Charles de Gaulle holds sway. From the jets that land at its doors pour a swelling cargo of the international set, businessmen, tourists—and just plain scene-makers.

Ingenuity of Indulgence

The new vitality of the city amazes both its visitors and inhabitants. "The planet which was England," confided Paris' *Candide* recently, "has given birth to a new art of living—eccentric, bohemian, simple and gay." Says Robert Fraser, owner of London's most pioneering art gallery: "Right now, London has something that New York used to have: everybody wants to be there. There's no place else. Paris is calcified. There's an indefinable thing about London that makes people want to go there."

Not everyone looks upon London's new swing as a blessing. For many who treasure an older, quieter London, the haystack hair, the suspiciously brilliant clothes, the chatter about sex and the cheery vulgarity strike an ugly contrast with the stately London that still persists in the quieter squares of Belgravia or in such peaceful suburbs as Richmond. They argue that credulity and immorality, together with a sophisticated taste for the primitive, are symptoms of decadence. The *Daily Telegraph*'s Anthony Lejeune two weeks ago decried "aspects of the contemporary British scene which have not merely surprised the outside world but which increasingly provoke its contempt and derision. To call them symptoms of decadence may be facile as an explanation, but it has a disturbing ring of truth." Tradition-loving Londoners like to cite John Ruskin's eloquent description of 16th and 17th century Venice, another aging empire built on maritime power: "In the ingenuity of indulgence, in the varieties of vanity,

---

[2]*la dolce vita:* the sweet life (also the title of a famous Italian film of the decade)

Venice surpassed the cities of Christendom, as of old she had surpassed them in fortitude and devotion."

The comparison is fair, if not perfectly apt. Britain has lost an empire and lightened a pound. In the process it has also recovered a lightness of heart lost during the weighty centuries of world leadership. Much of the world still thinks of Britain as the land of Victorianism, but Victorianism was only a temporary aberration in the British character, which is basically less inhibited than most. London today is in many ways like the cheerful, violent, lusty town of William Shakespeare, one of whose happiest songs is about a "lover and his lass, that o'er the green cornfield did pass." It is no coincidence that critics describe London's vibrant theatre as being in the midst of a second Elizabethan era, that one number on the Rolling Stones' newest LP is a mock-Elizabethan ballad with a harpsichord and dulcimer for accompaniment or that Italian novelist Alberto Moravia describes the British cinema today as "undergoing a renaissance."

Bloodless Revolution

Today, Britain is in the midst of a bloodless revolution. This time, those who are giving way are the old Tory-Liberal Establishment that ruled the empire from the clubs along Pall Mall and St. James's, the still-powerful financial City of London, the Church and Oxbridge. In their stead is rising a new and surprising leadership community; economists, professors, actors, photographers, singers, admen, TV executives and writers—a swinging meritocracy. What they have in common is that they are mostly under 40 (Harold Wilson, at 50 the youngest P.M. of the century, is referred to as "good old 'arold") and come from the ranks of the British lower middle and working class, which never before could find room at the top. Says sociologist Richard Hoggart, 47, himself a shy orphan from industrial Leeds: "A new group of people is emerging from society, creating a kind of

classlessness and a verve which has not been seen before."

. . . Even the physical city seems to shift and change under the impetus of the new activity. Throughout London, wreckers and city planners are at work. Once a horizontal city with a skyline dominated by Mary Poppins' chimney pots, London is now shot through with skyscrapers, including the 30-story London Hilton and the 620-ft. London post office tower. Westminster Abbey's statues and memorials have been newly cleaned and painted, and the dome of St. Paul's Cathedral is undergoing a $420,000 polishing that will return it to the splendor envisioned by Sir Christopher Wren—and, hopefully, keep it that way, since electric-shock pigeon deterrents are being added. London Bridge is falling down, and plans have been drawn for a $6,700,000 replacement.

More important than all the other changes is the fact that the center, the heart of London, has gravitated slowly westward to the haunts of the city's new elite, just as it did in centuries gone by. The ancient Tower, built by the Norman Plantagenets, gave way to the thriving guildhalls of the medieval City of London just up the Thames. The city yielded to neighboring Westminster and ultimately to the symbol of Victoria's empire, Buckingham Palace. After its latest shift, London's heart has come to rest somewhere in Mayfair, between the green fields and the orators of Hyde Park and the impish statue of Eros in Picadilly Circus.

A large slice of London's 2,400,000 young adults and working teen-agers live in Chelsea, Earl's Court and South Kensington, the residential district roughly comparable to Manhattan's upper East side. While the models and ad agency execs can afford quaint private houses, with black-painted doors and tidy flower boxes, the lesser lights pack themselves into shared flats (three or four to an apartment) that cost a minimum of $30 a month, or nest in "bed-sitters" (furnished rooms, $10 a week). "Youth has become emancipated," says

Mick Jagger, "and the girls have become as emancipated as the boys."

Dirty Dick's

No other city offers a wider variety of ways in which to pass the time, and Londoners pursue their pleasures as relentlessly as people anywhere in the world. London has hundreds of pleasant pubs with such charming names as the Bricklayers' Arms, Coal Hole, Crown and Two Chairmen, Dandy Roll and Dirty Dick's, but the two current favorites among the In set are the Cross-Keys and the King's Head and Eight Bells. Dozens of nightclubs offer totally uninhibited striptease, including Raymond's Revue Bar, sizzling in Soho, where the current attraction is an Australian blonde named Rita Elen, who does her exotic dancing with a full-grown live cheetah named Ginni.

The three reigning discothèques are close to Piccadilly; besides Dolly's and its rival The Scotch, Annabel's seems daintily restrained, but for that reason may be the most elegant of all; it has a series of wine-cellar rooms and a softly tuned stereo that alternates Sinatra and Ella with the native Animals and Stones. At these and dozens of other discothèques, beautiful gals with long blonde hair and slimly handsome men go gracefully through their explosive, hedonistic, totally individual dances, surrounded by mirrors so that they can see what a good time they're having.

Londoners are among the world's sportiest gamblers, willing to wager on everything from the greyhounds to whether or not the sun will shine (a hazardous bet, since the daily mean is only 4.16 hours of sunshine in the city). The Clermont Club, Crockford's and the Curzon House Club are the kings of the $3 billion-a-year fever, reigning over tables at which men and women do not gamble because they are on holiday, as they might at Deauville or Baden, but as part of their casual daily entertainment. It is not exceptional to see players win or lose $50,000 or so of an evening. Since gambling was legalized in 1960,

it has been taken up by just about everyone. Little old ladies now venture their shillings in flourishing bingo halls like the Burnt Oak off Edgware Road, and Britons placed $7,000,000 worth of bets on the March 31 election.

The city that once had the worst dining out in the western world now has a variety and a class of restaurants that rival New York or even Paris. . . .

Fear in Manhattan

Perhaps nothing illustrates the new swinging London better than narrow, three-block-long Carnaby Street, which is crammed with a cluster of the "gear" boutiques where the girls and boys buy each other clothing. Nine of the shops for boys on Carnaby Street are owned by Designer John Stephen, 29, who last week took his tatersall shirts, Dutch boy caps, form-fitting pants and vinyl vests to Manhattan to put the fear of God into parents there. As for the girls, the most In shop for gear is Biba's boutique in Kensington, which is a must scene for the switched-on dolly-bird at least twice a week. Designer Barbara Hulanicki, owner of Biba's, estimates that a typical secretary or shop girl, earning $31 a week, will spend at least $17 of it on clothing, which leaves her with a cup of coffee for lunch—but happy. . . .

The latest In look for girls is the very skinny look, striped jersey dresses, a lot of yellow, trench coats, berets (especially knitted ones), granny shoes (mostly yellow, please) and big earrings. Just as the '30s look is already returning for men (wider ties, big lapels, black-and-white shoes), some fashion designers believe that it is on its way for women and will force their hemlines down again.

Dirty, Filthy, Healthy

The same experimentation, the same passion for change, permeates London's theater, which is currently the best anywhere in the world. The theater is one of the strongest cultural contributors to the liveliness of

London today, brimming with new ideas and with new young people who are nonetheless working within a long and powerful creative tradition. Says Peter Hall of the Royal Shakespeare Company: "We are in a theater that is front-page news. We are denounced as subversive, immoral, filthy—it's all terribly healthy." John Osborne is one of the world's richest playwrights, though still as acid as ever: his latest, *A Patriot for Me*, is all about homosexuality in decadent Vienna.

There are as many as 40 or 50 plays on the London stage in any given week, and it costs little more to see one than to go to a movie. However, says Peter Hall, "we've got rid of that stuffy middle-aged lot that go to the theater as a sop for their prejudices. We're getting a younger audience who are looking for experiences and will take them from the latest pop record or *Hamlet*." The In Hamlet this year is David Warner, 24, who plays the Dane with Beatle haircut and a Carnaby Street slouch.

This spring, film makers from all over the world have been attracted to London by its swinging film industry. . . .

Greenness & Greyness

For all its virtues, which are many, and its faults, which are considerable, London has a large measure of that special quality that was once the hallmark of great cities: civility in the broadest sense. It takes away less of a person's individuality than most big cities, and gives the individual and his rights more tolerance than any. In texture, it has developed into a soft, pleasant place in which to live and work, a city increasing its talents for organizing a modern society without losing the simple humanity that so many urban complexes lack.

Melvin J. Lasky, a London-based co-editor of *Encounter*, believes that "London is the only European metropolis that has managed to maintain a combination of greenness and greyness, vitality and yet a certain gentleness. Paris hasn't got it. Rome is oppressive. Berlin is a special case. And all the others are villages." London's pressures are less than in many big cities, and it manages to maintain an ease, a coziness and a mixture of its different social circles that totally eludes New York. The results, as Manhattan-born Richard Adler, editor of London's *Town Magazine*, puts it, is that London is "far more accessible than anywhere else. In New York, Paris and Rome, actors, writers and so on each have their own little groups, their little street packs. If you put your toe in the wrong square, you get stepped on. In London, everyone parties with everyone."

That is a quality that Londoners themselves appreciate, for, while it existed 30 years ago in the world of the old Establishment—where the dukes, politicians, prelates, publishing lords, financiers and industrialists all knew one another—it is still truer today in the new society. The London that has emerged is swinging, but in a far more profound sense than the colorful and ebullient pop culture by itself would suggest. London has shed much of its smugness, much of the arrogance that often went with the stamp of privilege, much of its false pride—the kind that long kept it shabby and shopworn in physical fact and spirit. It is a refreshing change, and making the scene is the Londoner's way of celebrating it.

VISCOUNT ECCLES The Menace of Pornography (1971)

A member of the Conservative government of 1970–1974 assesses the underside of "The Swinging Sixties."

My Lords, the government are grateful to the noble earl, Lord Longford, and we admire his courage in raising the menace of pornography—a subject from which, as he

SOURCE: From *The Parliamentary Debates (House of Lords)*, 5th Series, Vol. 317, cols. 654–662.

himself said, many of us would like to run away. The whole topic is very hard to place with accuracy. Who among us is not baffled, even dismayed, at the contradictions of the last 25 years? So much has been done to improve our society and yet, in many ways, we are behaving worse. Public education, the social services and the distribution of increasing wealth have all been advanced as never before. We have given generous help to emerging nations in Asia and Africa. How disappointing that, at the same time, our society has developed weaknesses and faults which, taken together, have diminished the enterprise and now threaten the growth of the whole.

We should not consider the spread of pornography as an isolated phenomenon of mysterious origin. We ought to see it as part of the pattern of the last decade. We are not dealing with a new fashion in entertainment, like bingo. Here is one striking illustration of a major change in the moral climate of Great Britain. Living ourselves in the middle of this change, we cannot apprehend its implications at all clearly. This debate, therefore, should be very useful, because your Lordships can take a calm and experienced view of a subject overlaid with emotions and prejudices—much calmer, I think, than if we had to look for votes. . . .

Pornography is the ugly child of the permissive society, of which the rapid rise was predictable. All industrialized nations are now reacting to a technological revolution that has failed to match the growing power of the machines with constructive outlets for human energies. When a community like ours loses the secret of healthy growth, it is sure to demonstrate its distress in various ways. Consider how easily the British, of all sensible people, are now being flouted, held-up and hijacked by individuals and tiny groups who are not afraid to use force. The very size and interdependence of modern organizations—the motor car industry, for example—make it more difficult and much more expensive than ever before in history to resist the guerrilla warfare of the militants. Hijacking is now a characteristic operation of the 1970s. The pilot is forced at pistol-point to take his passengers to a place where they did not want to go, and the passengers are cowed into allowing it to happen. Kidnapping has begun here: universities are disrupted by quite small numbers of their students; many thousands of work-people go out on strike against their better judgment; security guards are shot-up in daylight; and sections of the arts are polluted by a few pornographers.

All these things happen at once because of their common origin. We can see, therefore, that to explore every kind of personal sensation is one way to participate in a general trend toward protest against the isolation of the individual and the emptiness of the age. In this sense the spread of pornography is natural. But it is also nasty, and we shall not stop it effectively unless we remove the causes of its popularity. It is not primarily the law which needs to be changed, but certain attitudes of mind that spring from the whole social, economic and political situation. The exploiters of the permissive society are, of course, bullies. Their game is to keep the passengers quiet while they force the pilot to take the aircraft to wherever they have an itch to go. These are the tactics of the pornographers. They are aided by those who insist that, as it cannot be proved that pornography has done, or will do, harm to any particular person, no one has any right to stop it.

One must expect abuse—I have had it myself—if one raises the question whether easy access to certain kinds of books, pictures, plays and films is likely to throw a significant number of people—especially young people—off their balance and make it harder for them to live reasonable, constructive and unselfish lives. Your Lordships will recognize this argument against doing anything to stem the flood of pornography. It is exactly the same that is used against warning the public that cigarette-smoking may lead to lung-cancer. We shall never know whether a particular smoker will contract the disease, but it does not follow that we should refuse to listen to the best medical authorities. . . .

Our evidence cannot be so scientific,

since we are dealing not with measurable phenomena, but with value-judgments and morals. Nevertheless, the belief that some thoughts are evil, that some thoughts can poison the mind and corrupt the character, has been central to the teaching of the world's greatest religions and philosophies. Can it really make sense to throw away the wisdom of the ages just because modern science can show us more clearly the causes of sexual deviations and of the urge to violence? Psychoanalysis has helped to remove the pruderies and hypocrisies that mutilated sex in the 19th century. Chemistry, physics and biology have made much plain that was hidden before. We are all glad of that, but no branch of science can tell us how to behave in a particular situation. Justice and mercy never will be concocted in a test tube or measured in mathematical terms. We certainly know more than our fathers, but we easily do worse. This is because scientific knowledge is not lost but always accumulates, whereas each child has to start again and make his or her own discoveries about the difference between good and evil.

What is the influence of pornography in this continually renewed struggle to behave well? Some people will be immune to images of lust and violence, just as others are immune to cigarette-smoking. As the noble and learned Lord who sits on the Woolsack[3] recently told us in his felicitous terms (mine are not quite the same), society has always been composed of a tiny handful of saints, a rather larger handful of villains and nine out of ten in the middle who, with a bit of luck and good friends, manage to behave well most of the time. Now history demonstrates that the example of the saints and the villains was crucial to how the majority made out. . . .

Saints and villains apart, we are concerned with the general run of mankind. They often act in one way rather than in another because of what they have seen and read. The noble Lord, Lord Snow, in our debate on the mass media, made a notable speech in which he pointed out that very large sums of money were spent on advertising precisely because salesmen know that pictures make customers. In this intensely professional business the advertisers have learned certain rules and techniques. One is that repetition pays off. The customer is captured if he sees or hears over and over again that Guinness or a pint of milk is good for him. Why should it be any different if he sees and hears over and over again that sex has nothing to do with love and that violence is a normal way of getting what you want? Those who say that everybody soon tires of pornography have a lot to explain. They may know very little about mass advertising, or they may know a great deal and want to persuade the rest of us to keep quiet while the dirty work is done.

My Lords, in the Middle Ages, when hardly anyone could read or write, the Christian clergy relied on the power of visual images. On entering a church the two dominating images—the Madonna and Child and the Crucifixion—analyzed and summed up for the illiterate congregation the very best and the very worst that men can do to each other. But the Church did not leave the laity to draw their own conclusions about the meaning of the images. The cruelty of the Passion and the death of martyrs were portrayed not to entertain but to instruct. Indeed, the instruction was the declared purpose of the architecture, the paintings and the sculpture.

In a significant sense the twentieth century resembles the twelfth century. Once again the general run of mankind are absorbing a large part of their experience through visual images. In this country, 19 million television sets and I do not know how many radios and transistor sets are switched on for hours every day. It is too early to know what these moving pictures and organized noise are doing to us. But there is a world of difference between representations of, let us say, cruelty offered for entertainment, with no instructions given, no moral drawn, and the use to which the Church

---

[3]*Lord . . . Woolsack:* the Lord Chancellor, Lord Hailsham

put art in the Middle Ages. In those days the quality of art was admired because it drove home the lesson. In our times we have completely changed the emphasis. Now the subject matter is of no importance; only the quality counts.

Recently I heard this esthetic dogma called in aid to justify pornography. When I was having a "set-to" with some students, one of them, thinking to clinch the argument, said, "Pornography is just another art form. The subject is not relevant. All that matters is that the picture should be the work of a genuine artist." . . . What this student was saying makes nonsense of a world devoted to reality. Every day we have to act, as well as to feel; and if we are concerned only with the manner in which things are done, and not with their content and meaning, we shall lose the power to tell the difference between good and evil. Conscience will be replaced by some kind of esthetic taste.

My Lords, I have gone into that in some detail because it is a change of this nature in moral standards which sets the stage for pornography. If one experience can be distinguished from another only by the sensation which it arouses, then we might as well try everything, however heartless, disgusting and cruel the action might be, however much it outraged our neighbors or damaged our own family life. So if we dislike pornography we must attack these ideas which alone give it scope to flourish. In short, we shall reduce the sale of dirty books, pictures, films and plays not by showing that they are bad art but because, regardless of time and place, they advertise behavior which mocks at love and tenderness and at the respect for other people. But then it will be asked: how do you know that love and respect for others are better than their opposites? And, if you really do believe this, how do you keep these values alive in our drifting generation? My Lords, science cannot answer questions like these, and for that very reason the pornographers are quick to declare that these questions should not be asked at all.

This is the heart of the matter. Either we believe that there are values and virtues like kindness and honesty, and institutions like the family, good and true in themselves, and essential if our society is to be held together, or we take our stand on the proposition that everything is permissible because no-one can tell in advance whether any experience would do a man more harm than good. Those are irreconcilable attitudes to life. When we as politicians decide between them, a minor and a major consideration should weigh with us. In the first place, we must pay attention to what people have up to now held to be the difference between right and wrong. It is faintly possible that in time the inhabitants of Westminster might get used to copulating in the street like dogs or pigeons; but, my Lords, not tomorrow morning. Judged, therefore, by its effect on holding together the community in which we are now living, it would be disastrous to let the permissive society go to any lengths. We should demoralize ourselves as surely as contact with European manners and Scotch whiskey demoralized certain South Sea Islanders.

Your Lordships would not expect me to argue the case against pornography solely from the present state of society. Much needs to be changed. I am sure that democracies will disappear if they cannot find peaceful ways to change in response to new knowledge and new leadership. But if the methods of change are not to be dictated by the hijackers we must hold on to certain basic values, and of these I would have thought that serious attention to the needs of others was the foremost. The reality of the human condition is that we must live in a community of which the vigor, spirit and cohesion can be sustained only by both positive action and also well-understood restraint. Pornography denies this concept of the human condition. It flourishes most when society is falling apart. In place of a concern for others it offers us a diet of nightmares. It holds that legal restraints upon the gratification of desire are the contemptible vestiges of a reactionary past. So too is a man's conscience which puts him on notice that there is a difference between good and evil. . . .

Our situation to-day may be exceptional because the pendulum has swung so violently toward total permissiveness. Will it return to center of its own accord? This really is the great question. I do not think so, because hijacking is now so easy in our apathetic and vulnerable society. On the other hand, I should be sorry if those who think as the noble earl and I do did not try

much harder to arouse the conscience of the public before they asked us to resort to new forms of statutory censorship. It may be that they would be surprised by the number of allies they would find. . . .

What a difference it would make if those who campaign so vigorously against inhumanity overseas—in South Africa, for instance, 6,000 miles away—were to campaign with equal vigor against the inhuman pornography on their doorstep! . . .

ROBERT MOSS Anglo-Communism? (1977)

Three decades after the post-1945 Labour government instituted Britain's welfare state, another Labour government was in power. In this essay, Robert Moss ponders how far toward the political left Britain has moved, either deliberately or simply by drifting.

I am sad to confess that every time I fly back to London from any other major western capital, my heart sinks. This may have something to do with the squalor of Heathrow airport, a dismal but perhaps fitting introduction to the new Britain for innocents from abroad. A few months ago, having touched down at Heathrow, I found myself swaying in the aisle with the other passengers for over half an hour, waiting for the steps to be rolled up to the plane so we could get off. The cabin crew were good enough to explain that "the ground crew have not finished their tea-break."

But the squalor stretches beyond the airport, with its chaos of ugly hoardings and perennial notices couched in Newspeak, apologizing for "temporary inconvenience" due to "improvements" that are being carried out. The more I compare Britain with the countries that it still regards as its peers, the more I succumb to the uneasy feeling that Britain is becoming a third world country. This is, of course, a subjective impression. But consider the following "third world" symptoms:

The Mañana Complex

For many British firms, "immediate delivery" means delivery in six weeks. The average working day in the steel industry, according to a recent survey, is five hours, when time is deducted for lunch-breaks, tea-breaks, and so on.

The State-Pensioner Mentality

The belief that Big Daddy will provide is devastatingly widespread, and is not altogether irrational. It is more profitable for some people in the British welfare state to stay at home and breed children than to go out to work. A man with a wife and four children, for example, can claim as much as the net income (after tax) of a man earning £85 a week. Recent investigations of the welfare system have produced the case of one man who was given the money to buy a new set of tires for his Jaguar by the Department of Health and Social Security—on the grounds that he needed the car to look for a job—and of another who was given the cash to buy a color television set with fitted doors, which could be officially classified as "furniture."

Animism

This kind of popular superstition is paid lip-service by many leading figures in the new British establishment, which is (contrary to what may be imagined by those reared on P. G. Wodehouse and Evelyn Waugh) a socialist establishment. Its credo is in fact a not-particularly-sophisticated form of animism, based on the idea that "society" is a kind of great disembodied being that can be held responsible for everything that goes on within it. Hence the myth of "social justice," which holds that all differences of wealth, education, or opportunity are "unjust," and that "society" must act to eliminate them. This myth has been used to justify punitive taxes on higher incomes—which led to a record flight of professionals to other countries in 1975—as well as the effort to abolish private medicine and choice in schooling, and to impose a wealth tax.

Cargo Cults

Like Solomon Islanders, the men who misspend public money keep watch for the ghostly ships that will bring miraculous "cargo"—oil from the North Sea. What is rarely mentioned is the fact that unless it mends its ways, Britain (with a forecast borrowing requirement in excess of £8.5 billion in 1977, even *after* the cuts made by Chancellor of the Exchequer Denis Healey last December) will have mortgaged its oil revenues in advance. The slogan of the Scottish Nationalists, "It's Scotland's oil," has begun, however, to give some people uneasy nights.

Resistance to Technology, or Inability to Use It

You might have thought that automatic ticket-collecting machines at subway stations were not exactly a breathtaking scientific innovation. Maybe not. But at London subway stations, where they were installed several years ago, they still do not function. Passengers emerging from the subway still have their tickets collected by hand. Something similar has occurred with postal zip codes. When these were first introduced, there was a great publicity campaign to persuade people to put the full zip code on their letters. It later became known that—due to unspecified backroom difficulties—the computers could only handle *six* zip codes out of thousands. Evil rumor has it that, in both these cases, trade unions intervened to save jobs that might have been lost if the new technology had been allowed to function.

Currency Fiddling and Tax Evasion

I do not know how much money is smuggled out of Britain each year, although our left-wing tribunes vie with each other in offering huger and huger guesstimates. But the police-state powers that have been given to tax inspectors in Britain (who are now authorized to enter a man's home at any hour of the day or night, confiscate documents, and interrogate his family), are signs both of the totalitarian drift in government and of the decline of that sense of civic duty that had long made the self-employed Briton a scrupulous unpaid tax collector. Tax accountants have coined the word "evoision" to describe that twilight zone between tax "avoidance" (which is legal) and "evasion" (which is not). Old ladies are arrested at Heathrow with their life savings in a suitcase; the chairman of a well-known finance house says in private that he is ready to move his entire operation abroad "within seven hours," and Bank of England officials are up on charges of currency fiddling.

Separatism and Tribalism

The loss of confidence in central government, and of belief in a world role for Britain, has produced a mood of introversion and the substitution of regional (or tribal) self-identification for a sense of national identity. Hence the rise of Scottish nationalism—in spite of the fact that there are as many Scotsmen living in England as in Scotland—and the sharpening of the race conflict that stemmed from resistance to non-white immigration.

Economic Dependence and Begging-Bowl Politics

Britain still maintains a Ministry of Overseas Development, and can still indulge in gestures like giving cheap loans to the Marxist rulers of Mozambique—or the credits, worth almost £1 billion, that Harold Wilson offered the Russians, at a rate of interest that was only half what a housing mortgage costs in London. But Britain's place among the major industrial nations is now that of the man with the begging bowl. The country goes on spending more than it earns, and goes on hoping that the International Monetary Fund will always be there with another loan. I am convinced that if the Labour government continues in office, it will be trying to touch the IMF for yet another emergency credit by mid-1977. The IMF, quite properly, insists that the British should set their economic house in order—but has achieved little more than the shifting around of the living-room furniture and squawks from our "Third World" economic nationalists who would like to set up a siege economy and send the capitalists packing.

The Revival of Feudalism

Every foreign visitor seems obliged to mention the "class problem" in Britain, as evidenced by Ascot, the House of Lords, and the fact that some of the natives still seem to be able to afford to drive a Rolls-Royce. Viewed from a different aspect, it is arguable that there are now only two classes that count: the people who belong to trade unions, and those who do not. A background paper recently produced by a certain John Hughes of the Trade Union Research Unit at Ruskin College, Oxford, contains the confident assertion that the British

Medical Association is the *only* organized body outside the Trades Union Congress (TUC) that has any significant "social bargaining power." This is a polite way of saying that no one else has the muscle to defend his interests, which indeed appears to be the case. The Labour government meets with the TUC in a special liaison committee. It *negotiates* with the TUC; it merely *consults* with the Confederation of British Industry. British trade-union leaders—most of whom are elected by fewer than 10 per cent of their members, some of whom are elected for life, and many of whom are openly committed to the overthrow of the mixed economy—enjoy a privileged social status and legal immunities that are not shared by any other social group. Hence the nickname that was recently conferred on them: the "new barons."

I could go on with my list of "Third World" symptoms. Any recent visitor to Britain will have examples of his own to contribute. Britain is fast becoming an offshore industrial slum, where most executives earn less than a good secretary in Washington, D.C., and where the good things of life, although increasingly beyond the reach of an overtaxed, underpaid middle class, are so cheap that Frenchmen and Germans come over on organized shopping sprees. The British have not as yet developed a "gringo" complex, but maybe that, too, is coming: the Arabs, who look different, talk different, and spend sterling as if it were confetti, may turn out to be Britain's gringos.

One of the more depressing aspects of this transformation of Britain is the decline of civility in everyday life: service is a rarity in shops and restaurants, wholly unknown in state-run industries, and something that affluent foreigners too frequently encounter only as a pimpish determination to fleece them.

The most sinister aspect, however, is the spread of political violence from the embattled province of Northern Ireland (where it continues to be financed by misguided Irish Americans) to the metropolis itself. The murder of Ross McWhirter, a man who believed that the responsible citizen should take action when government fail to do their duty, and who therefore set up a private reward scheme for information leading to the arrest and conviction of terrorist bombers, marked an important stage in Britain's national decline. He was shot at his own doorstep by IRA gunmen on November 7, 1975.

What is wrong with Britain? Where will the process end? These are urgent questions, and they deserve a serious and detailed answer. Perhaps even now it is not fully understood by Britain's allies that its internal condition poses perhaps the single most serious threat to the Atlantic Alliance—although that may have become a little clearer when, in mid-December, the Chancellor of the Exchequer announced that further cuts in the defense budget (totaling £300 million) would be made over the next two years. Britain's armed forces, when fully mobilized, were already smaller than those of neutral Sweden, Switzerland, and even Finland.

But if Britain is acquiring some of the social and economic characteristics of a Third World country, the most critical question of all is: will it end up with a Third World political setup as well—with a politburo or a junta?

In trying to answer this question, let me begin with a proposition that may appear absurd, or at any rate exaggerated, to most American readers. It is that Britain has traveled more than two-thirds of the way toward becoming a fully communist society, and that it is increasingly probable that it will either complete the journey or have to endure the most shattering social and constitutional crisis the country has known since the seventeenth century.

Note that I am using the word communism with a small c, in the exact sense that it is used in the original text: the 1848 *Manifesto of the Communist Party*, by Marx and Engels. Remember that the authors of that pamphlet suggested that communist theory could be summed up in a single sentence, as "abolition of private property." They also suggested ten measures that

might be employed to achieve communism in more advanced countries. Two years ago, Lord Chalfont examined the list (in a television program for which the Left will never forgive him) and concluded that about half the measures proposed had already been applied in Britain. Reexamining the list, I put the proportion rather higher; and the measures that have not been applied so far are part of the program of the Labour party and the Trades Union Congress.

It may be helpful to run quickly through the list.

Item 1 is the "abolition of property in land." Well, it is not yet *illegal* to own a private estate in Britain, but increased taxation has made it ruinous to maintain one.

Item 2 is "a heavy progressive or graduated income tax." There is no doubt on that score; tax levels in Britain rise to a maximum of 83 per cent on earned income and 98 per cent on what is officially classified as "unearned" income. There are plans afoot for a wealth tax as well. The Labour government, with a precarious majority of one in the House of Commons and plenty to worry about on other fronts, decided to shelve that proposal last December, but was firmly recalled to its socialist duty by the TUC, which compelled it to set up an official working party.

Item 3 is the "abolition of all right of inheritance." This has been three-quarters achieved through death duties and taxation, and will no doubt be fully achieved if present trends continue.

Item 4 is the "confiscation of the property of all emigrants and rebels." You are still allowed to take *something* with you if you decide to flee England's shores, but the maximum amount that a permanent emigrant can take out initially is not enough to support a family for a year. Another run on sterling and a further mass emigration of professionals (some 65,000 left in 1975) might bring that ceiling down even lower.

Item 5 is the "centralization of credit in the hands of the state, by means of a national bank with state capital and an exclusive monopoly." Through the Bank of England, the British government enjoys far-reaching powers to control credit and monetary expansion. But of course Marx and Engels were calling for more than that. So is the official Labour-party program, approved by 5,883,000 votes (to a pitiful 122,000 against) at the annual conference in Blackpool last year. This document calls, *inter alia*, for the nationalization of the major clearing banks and insurance companies. So we might say that Item 5 is coming up on the agenda.

Item 6: "Centralization of the means of communication and transport in the hands of the state." This was achieved long ago in Britain, with the creation of state monopolies in these areas— including the post-office monopoly whose performance induced a Labour M.P., Arthur Lewis, to say that it will soon be quicker to drop your letters in the gutter and hope that some altruistic passer-by will deliver them for you than to rely on the post office.

Item 7: "Extension of factories and instruments of production owned by the state." No doubt about that one, either. The state takeover of private firms is proceeding apace, and the sheer weight of government intervention in the British economy can be grasped at once from a simple statistic: public spending represents 63 per cent of the gross national product. To put it more crudely, out of every £100 that are spent in Britain, £63 are spent by the government sector. I can find no other example of a noncommunist society where government intervention has gone so far. John Maynard Keynes himself once said that the maximum desirable level of public spending was 25 per cent of the GNP. Beyond that, a society must begin to tremble for its freedom. Yet the appetite for still more government intrusion and intervention has not been slaked. Late last year, the chairman of the general purposes committee of the Labour-controlled Greater London Council circulated a study paper which proposed that professional football teams should be placed under the control of local councils, on the grounds that this would be a good way to get rid of "reactionary" managers and "democratize" the sport. Now that so many industries have been brought under state control, perhaps it is not entirely astonishing that the nationalizers have turned their attention to leisure.

But let us consider the last three items in the decalogue of the *Communist Manifesto.*

Item 8: "Equal liability of all to labor; establishment of industrial armies." The power of the leaders of organized labor in Britain today—and their power to conscript new recruits under recent closed-shop legislation—leaves me in no doubt that Marx's "industrial armies" already exist. Britain has not succeeded in making everyone work for a living. On the contrary, the excesses of the welfare state have encouraged widespread parasitism. But back in 1848, Marx and Engels were no doubt thinking about squeezing out the capitalist and the *rentier,*[4] and both species certainly seem to be heading for extinction in Britain.

Item 9 reads rather strangely today: "Combination of agriculture with manufacturing industries; gradual abolition of the distinction between town and country." This can surely be said to have come about, but can hardly be said to have been decisive for Marx's broader design except in one sense: the dwindling of the farming community (now only 4 per cent of the British work force) has added to the power of industrial and public-service unions. The voice of the farmer is barely heard in British life, and so one of the elements that is crucial to a system of social checks and balances in other societies is missing here.

The tenth and last item in the communist decalogue: "Free education for all children in public schools." Well, of course. But British socialism has improved on the *Communist Manifesto.* The Labour government has set out to impose a uniform type of state school, the comprehensive. It is closing down grammar schools (what in America would be called public academic high schools)—although it has run up

---

[4]*rentier:* a person who lives on the income of (often inherited) investments

against determined last-ditch resistance from local parents—and intends to cut off all forms of state support for private schools of every kind. It even appears to have been won over to the notion that the cause of equality requires a "fair" distribution of intellect among schools, which is to be achieved by sharing out brighter students on a quota basis. This remarkable scheme, politely known as "banding," would amount to a British arrangement for busing—based on IQ instead of color.

Six of the ten conditions for achieving communism that were laid down by Marx and Engels thus appear to be in the bag in Britain (Items 2, 6, 7, 8, 9, and 10). The remaining four conditions can hardly be said to be remote. One (the nationalization of credit) is part of the program of the ruling party. Another two (1 and 3) will be as good as fulfilled if current proposals for a radical wealth tax are allowed to proceed. And the confiscation of their property is perhaps one of the last things that "rebels" would need to worry about (Item 4) if any were so rash as to rear their heads after the other foundations for communism have been securely laid.

If, then, we accept that what Marx and Engels published in 1848 provides a workable definition of "communism," we are compelled to conclude that Britain has already acquired some of the definitive characteristics of a communist society—*despite the fact that there is not a single overt member of the Communist Party sitting in the House of Commons.* This brings me at once to the distinction only hinted at so far: between communism with a small c and Communism with a capital C.

In Britain, many people who have been laboring to bring about communism with a small c for many decades do not regard themselves as communists or even Marxists and do not belong to avowedly Marxist organizations. Suckled by Harold Laski and R. H. Tawney, they honestly believe that they are working in the cause of social justice, equality, or (quite simply) the "labor movement," and that history is laid out before them as a single linear progression toward more and more public ownership and the abolition of class differences through the redistribution of incomes and opportunities. They may be only dimly aware, if at all, that theirs is a quest which will lead, if successful, to the death of personal freedom and the abolition of the individual's right to use his talents for his own purposes.

This mentality is now predominant within the British Labour party. It is symptomatic that the "moderate" lobby within the party is known as the Manifesto Group. The manifesto on which the party was elected in 1974 ends with the following commitment: "Our objective is to bring about a fundamental and irreversible shift in the balance of wealth and power in favor of working people and their families." It may be that for the "moderates," the manifesto is the *limit* of their commitment to socialism. But for others in the party, it seems to be no more than the starting point.

Left-wing spokesmen within the party have recently taken to calling themselves "democratic socialists" as distinguished from "social democrats." This apparently arbitrary play on words is actually quite revealing. A "democratic socialist" is a socialist first and a democrat second; whereas with a "social democrat," it is the other way around. In a savage little article in *Tribune* (the paper of the Labour Left) Hugh Jenkins, M.P., recently heaped ridicule on "social-democrat" colleagues who acted as if "Parliament is the end, not the means" and as if "parliamentary government is good in itself, irrespective of what it does or does not do." Mr. Jenkins, of course, has a point. Parliamentary institutions *are* means, not ends. The purpose of political institutions should be to safeguard the freedom of the individual and the family within a secure, orderly, and just society. But that, I fear, was not what he meant. Mr. Jenkins's end is a form of "socialism" indistinguishable from the system outlined in Marx and Engels's *Communist Manifesto*—a system that would make democracy obsolete since, once established, it is intended to be irreplaceable. From this perspective, democracy is regarded as useful and desirable only so long as it provides the means to bring about a British version of communism. Once that is achieved, you can forget about democracy.

Now it is true that someone like Hugh Jenkins does not speak for the majority of his colleagues in the parliamentary Labour party, and still less for the bulk of his party's supporters in the country (who in turn represented only 29 per cent of those entitled to vote and 39 per cent of those who did vote at the last election). But as they never tire of pointing out, the "democratic socialists" are now the dominant voice within the "Labour movement"—which means the party's annual conference, its most important subcommittee, and, above all, the commanding heights of the trade-union movement. They have also profited from the attitude of *pas d'ennemis à gauche* ("no enemies to the Left") which has been adopted by most of their more moderate colleagues. . . .

[There is a] widespread refusal in the Labour ranks to draw an absolute distinction between social democracy and totalitarian Communism. . . ."There have always been Reds in the Labour party. I can't understand what all the fuss is about." That is how Sid Bidwell, past chairman of the Tribune Group and formerly active in a Trotskyist organization, described such goings-on in a recent exchange with the young Winston Churchill (spokesman on defense for the Tories). A member of the present government, the energy secretary, Tony Benn, provided a more reasoned defense of the same viewpoint. . . .

Benn argues that it is an "indisputable historical fact" that "Marxism has, from the earliest days, always been openly accepted as one of many sources of inspiration within our movement." While the Labour party has refused to admit members of other "socialist" parties who run candidates against the official Labour candidates in elections, "never since the earliest days of the Labour movement has Marxism itself been regarded as a disqualification for party membership." In a curious peroration Benn concludes that "the influences that lead individuals to embrace democratic socialism have always been left to the individual conscience, and there are no inquisitions to root out Marxism any more than there are to root out Catholics, atheists, or followers of Adam Smith, Sigmund Freud, Leon Trotsky, or Milton Friedman." I have yet to discover a rising star in the British Labour party who is a disciple of Smith or Friedman, and I doubt whether Benn seriously believes that they have anything to contribute to the cause of "democratic socialism."

Benn's defense of the *carrière ouverte aux idéologies*[5] is singularly revealing. He is so little interested in the argument that there is a line to be drawn between those who are willing to work within the limits of a parliamentary democracy and those who wish to overthrow it that he does not even refer to it. He jeers at the Conservative editorialist who suggested that the appointment of a Trotskyist to the Labour-party headquarters is comparable to what would have been the case if a Nazi had been appointed to the Tory central office in the 1930's, but then gives the game away by quoting Andy Bevan's description of himself and the faction linked with the radical weekly *Militant*. "We proudly describe ourselves as Marxists," Bevan declares, "and what we mean by that is that we stand on the traditions of Marx and Engels, Lenin and Trotsky."[6]

Now it may or may not have been forgotten by Benn, but Lenin was the man who closed down an infant parliamentary democracy in Russia, and Trotsky was the man who helped him to impose a new form of serfdom on the country by force of arms. For a leading official of the British Labour party (since confirmed in his appointment, despite objections from the party's professional staff) to say that he stands "on the tradition" of the Bolshevik revolution really *is* rather like a comparable Conserv-

---

[5]*carrière . . . idéologies:* career open to ideologies the Labour Party's national youth organizer.   [6]*Bevan:* Bevan had just been appointed as

ative figure proudly announcing that he "stands on the tradition" of the March on Rome.

Perhaps this example is enough to demonstrate the extent to which British socialism has succumbed to what Jean-François Revel has called the "totalitarian temptation." But the case of Andy Bevan is more than an example of the assimilation of a revolutionary communist ideology. It shows, clear as a warning flare, the growing influence of revolutionary *organizations* within a mass party whose remaining social democrats have, at best, been flaccid in the defense of their own beliefs. Dr. Stephen Haseler, a Labour member of the Greater London Council and one of the founders of the Social Democrat Alliance, describes his fellow social democrats as "men with the stuffing knocked out of them." . . .

The Labour party has not been organized to resist this kind of infiltration, although warnings have been issued by its national agent, Reg Underhill, and, very late in the day, by its former leader, Sir Harold Wilson. It has been clear all along to any intelligent revolutionary in Britain that the road to power lies through the penetration of the labor movement, since the openly Marxist parties have always been contemptuously rejected by the electorate; the Communist party counts itself lucky if it can pull in 0.3 per cent of the votes in a general election. Even more than the Labour party, the trade unions have been the prime target. Today, the TUC overshadows the British Parliament and might, indeed, be regarded as the *de facto* upper house. No major decision is made by the government without consulting the TUC.

Indeed, the most powerful man in Britain is not an elected Member of Parliament, not even the prime minister. It is Jack Jones, the leader of Britain's biggest labor union, the Transport and General Workers' Union. Although, by contrast with some of his rowdier colleagues, Jones appears to be regarded by many people in Britain as a relative "moderate," he made his own aspiration rather plain in June last year, when he vis-

ited East Germany and told a press conference that he felt "at home" in East Berlin. Jones is certainly not a crusader for the mixed economy, and anyone who lives in Britain must feel green with envy at the contrast between a union federation which promotes "fraternal" contacts with the state labor managers and factory policemen of Eastern Europe, and the AFL-CIO which provides platforms for Solzhenitsyn. Jack Jones is due to retire in 1977, but it seems probable that his successor will be a man from the same mold.

Trade-union power is *the* problem in Britain today, and it is exceedingly doubtful whether any other major problem can be solved until a solution is found for this one. The TUC has been praised, inside as well as outside Britain, for accepting voluntary wage curbs under the "social contract." But the price that has been paid for wage restraint has been an unprecedented expansion of the powers of the union leadership to dictate the government's overall economic policy and to bring the non-unionized sections of the work force under its control.

Although the various schemes for accomplishing these objectives are often described as proposals for extending "workers' participation" and "industrial democracy," it must be borne in mind that in Britain the union leaders who are most voluble in the use of such terms are no shining examples of democracy at work. Most of them owe their jobs to a singularly undemocratic process which presents enormous opportunities for tiny groups of radical left-wingers to win disproportionate influence. This can be gauged immediately from the political affiliations of the 345 members of the executives of Britain's thirteen biggest unions. About fifty are open Communist-party supporters. Most of the others, except for a few Trotskyists and Maoists, are nominal Labour-party supporters—in many cases on the Marxist side of the party. None is a Conservative. Yet a Gallup poll taken in June 1975, when support for the two major parties was evenly matched in the country as a whole, revealed that while 49 per cent of union members intended to vote Labour, no fewer than 25 per cent intended to vote Conservative, and 10 per cent Liberal. The proportion who planned to vote Communist was a derisory 0.1 per cent.

Against this background, the constitutional threat that is posed by trade-union power in Britain can be seen in its true light. The most powerful union leaders in Britain are men who are openly bent on the destruction of "capitalism"—although the word is, to put it mildly, an unsatisfactory description of a mixed economy in which the role of the state looms larger than that of the private sector. Their self-confidence was greatly enhanced by the events of February 1974, when the Heath government, in an effort to break the miners' strike, called an election on the issue of "who governs the country?"—and lost. The toppling of the Heath government produced a continuing mood of defeatism among politicians and the business community, many of whom concluded that it is now impossible to govern Britain against the wishes of the men who control the TUC....

BERNARD D. NOSSITER **Britain: A Future That Works (1978)**

The London correspondent of the Washington Post *surveys the same Britain discussed by Robert Moss and reaches a far more favorable verdict. The following summary of his book was published under the title, "The Leisurely British."*

Have professors and journalists misled us about the causes of Britain's illness? Is it possible that the whole episode is a case of hypochondria? Is it conceivable that the country has not been declining since the end of the war but, in fact, enjoying robust health—at least as far as social and economic indicators can measure such things?

This, indeed, is so. In the first thirty years after the Second World War, Britain enjoyed the fastest rate of economic growth in its recorded history and it has transformed the living standards of ordinary people.

When the queen celebrated her Jubilee in 1977, each of her subjects on average enjoyed incomes commanding almost four-fifths more in goods and services than their parents. At the start of her reign, the queen's statisticians still counted seven dwellings in every 100 without a toilet; by the Silver Jubilee, only one in 100 was so deprived. More than a third lacked a bath in 1952; twenty-five years later, 91 in 100 boasted their own bath.

Other gains were equally striking. Two secondary school graduates in 100 went on to university in 1952; twenty-five years later, the number had risen to 6. One in eight had a telephone; by 1977, more than one in two.

People with higher incomes enjoyed better diets. Each Briton consumed 29 ounces of meat weekly at the start of the reign, 36 ounces at the Jubilee. Health improved dramatically, thanks in part to a 46 per cent increase in the number of doctors for each thousand people. Men could expect to live to 69, three years more than their fathers; women to 75, four years more than their mothers. In 1952, 276 babies of each ten thousand born died in their first year; a generation later, infant mortality had been cut in half to 139.

Britain had become a cleaner, sunnier, brighter place in which to live. Thanks to greater output, the nation could afford to spend resources, cleaning up rivers, lakes and the air. It did so, and the famous pea-soup fog that had once been a London hallmark disappeared. In 1952, the sun peered through London's winter smog for only 70 minutes each day; twenty-five years later, Londoners enjoyed 107 minutes of sunshine daily between December and March.

A wealthier Britain could and did afford to spend more on the arts and take longer holidays. When the reign began, subsidies for opera, theater, concerts and other forms of expression and creation were £887,213; by 1977, this figure had jumped to £41.7 million. Only three in 100 Britons took more than two weeks' holiday in 1952. By 1977, two in three were enjoying holidays of three weeks or more each year.

It is true that the air had become more sulphurous (emissions of sulphur dioxide rose from 4.74 tons a years to 5.11). But this was another, if costly, sign of increased affluence; the emissions came from the exhausts of cars. Their numbers had swollen from one in every six households to three in every four.

To be sure, this more or less uninterrupted spurt in post-war prosperity was rudely halted in the last three years of Elizabeth's quarter century. From 1974 to 1977, national output was either stagnant or fell a little. . . . The average Briton's command over goods and services . . . [fell] 5.7 per cent. It was the first marked fall in living standards since the war and provided some color of substance to the gloomy diagnosis of the conventional interpreters.

Yet for most of the industrial west, the period 1974–7 marked a sharp break with the post-war experiences of ever-rising incomes. Every western nation suffered much higher price increases and unemployment than it had known for more than a generation; growth rates were sluggish. The phenomenon was called stagflation, an awkward mating of stagnation with inflation. Britain simply became a heavily publicized example. . . .

By the end of 1977, the OECD's experts were forecasting, along with others, that Britain's time of travail was over, that inflation was coming down and production was going up. A resumption of the rise in living standards, the familiar post-war experience, again appeared likely.

The single most important cause of the change in Britain's fortunes was a geological accident, North Sea oil. Instead of paying out £3 billion in foreign exchange to import oil—the cost in 1975—Britain was moving rapidly towards self-sufficiency by 1979 or 1980. In the 1980s the country will produce all the oil it burns and sell a surplus abroad, perhaps at the very inflated prices that had done so much damage to Britain and other western nations.

A treasury study in the summer of 1976 concluded that the oil would add £1,050 million to Britain's balance of payments in 1977, £5.4 billion by 1980 and £15.9 billion in 1985. This would be more than enough to pay off the debts Britain had contracted during its hardest times, wipe out any deficit in the trade accounts with other nations and leave Britain with a handsome surplus in its balance of payments during the 1980s at least.

The oil-created surplus in the payments balance will have two happy consequences for a lucky Britain: governments in London will no longer be bound by the balance of payments constraint, by fear that the pursuit of policies to mop up unused resources of men and plants will create an alarming deficit in the foreign accounts and thus come to an abrupt stop. Governments of all complexions will be much freer to adopt expansionary tax and spending programs to put Britain back on its post-war growth path. At the same time, the pound will tend to rise against other currencies and the import sector of Britain's cost of living—about one-fourth of all goods and services—should thus be falling throughout the 1980s.

The central point is clear: Britain has, in terms of its own past, enjoyed unprecedented prosperity in the post-war era. As in the rest of the industrial world, good times were rudely shattered after the 1973 oil price increase. Indeed, owing to some home-grown folly, Britain suffered more than most. But by the end of 1977, thanks largely to union wage restraints and geological chance, the prospects for resumed prosperity were better in Britain than in most other advanced countries.

What then have the pathologists been talking about? Are they writing in a world totally divorced from reality? If Britain is so well off, why do so many voices—in the U.S., *CBS, Time* magazine, the *New York Times*, Harvard scholars, a Nobel laureate; in Britain, an ambassador to Washington, editors of *The Times* and *Sunday Telegraph*, certified intellectuals of the left, right and center—all sound like mourners at a wake. The answer is far from clear. But a combination of herd instinct and ideological blinkers—tinted red or blue—can lead the most distinguished flocks astray.

If the Cassandras are talking about anything at all, it is that slippery concept of *relative* growth and prosperity, not *absolute* levels.

In these splendid twenty-five years of Elizabeth's reign, when Britain was expanding its output by 2.6 per cent a year, the Italians were growing by 4.6, the Germans by 4.8 and the French by 4.7. Britons got richer; their neighbors got richer faster.

Why some nations grew faster than others—even when they are at roughly similar levels of culture and industrial development—is one of the most discussed and least understood questions in economics. Perhaps the most careful attempt to measure the economic causes of economic growth was made by Edward Denison for the Brookings Institution in 1967. "The distinctive feature of the growth experience of the United Kingdom," Denison wrote, "was the small size relative to other European countries, of gains from economies of scale."

Translated into less formidable terms, Britain did not grow as fast as others because it had fewer farmers to put into car plants and its one-man shop owners were unwilling to trade the joy of being their own boss for the higher incomes of steel mills. Both these factors in turn meant that Britain's home market did not grow as fast as its neighbors. The domestic demand for steel, cars, chemicals and the rest did not jump by leaps and bounds but at a more sedate pace. That meant Britain's steel, car and chemical plants did not enjoy the same

economies of scale, the same gains in efficiency and output, as the more rapidly expanding Germans, French and Italians.

It now appears—at least according to Denison—that much of the post-war miracle in Germany, France, Italy (and also, Japan) rested on a very simple historical fact. Britain had been undergoing a revolution in agriculture since the seventeenth century. Over the centuries, men and women had slowly drifted from countryside to urban areas. . . .

Britain long ago used up the productive slack in its farm population. Inefficient farmers had gone to the towns. But for most of the post-war period and even today, France, Germany and Italy could and do tap a reservoir of under-used resources, moving farm workers to city plants.

But Denison was still not satisfied. He suspected that even when the last possible continental farmer and shopkeeper had moved into more "productive" factories, Britain would still grow more slowly. Somehow, its men and plants are less efficient.

Here his statistical inquiries ran into a dead end. He was reduced to explaining the slower British growth rate by "unaggressive management, labor resistance to change, and restrictive practices." All this, said Denison, "suggests that it must be a condition of long standing."

British industry, it is said, has been caught and overtaken by the American, German, French and even Italian, because British businessmen will not put enough money into new tools and factories. On the Right, it is argued, that British entrepreneurs and corporations are victimized by those familiar demons—lavish welfare spending, onerous taxes, radical and strike-mad unions. The executives lack both the cash and the incentive to build modern plants. On the Left, the demonology is simpler: grasping capitalists salt away huge profits in yachts, girls, jewels and villas at exotic tax havens. They invest abroad but not at home.

Once again, however, the statistics puncture the popular wisdom. The fact is that present levels of investment are three times what they were in the late nineteenth and early twentieth century, and twice those of the pre-war period.

Lack of investment, then, will not explain why Britain has fallen behind the *pace* of others; the country has ploughed back an ever-increasing share of its growing income into new plants and machines.

A subtler and more plausible explanation may lie in the *quality*, rather than the quantity of British investment. One clue to that quality can be gleaned from seeing how much extra production is generated from an extra slice of investment. The Confederation of British Industry has produced a useful comparison. For 1963–73 any German or U.S. outlay yielded nearly three times as much production as the same British investment. This suggests that the British outlays were mismanaged.

The famous CBS television image of British industry, a mill built in 1870, is entertaining but inaccurate. John Kenneth Galbraith's portrait in The Age of Uncertainty, of a headless corporation making heedless decisions, is much nearer the mark.

British Leyland, for example, is plagued by walkouts, low productivity and defective workmanship. One Leyland official complains anonymously in print, "The inertia at the top manifests itself in a lack of decision and a lack of direction." The press and composing rooms of Fleet Street provide another sterling example of obstinate labor relations and obsolete work performance; newspaper proprietors have typically been amateur businessmen, as much interested in power and prestige as in profits.

If British workers as a whole, then, are not very energetic, it is likely that British managers are not either. . . .

However intensely they may or may not work, British managers are drawn from society's less equipped members. The best and brightest British graduates rarely go to industry. They flock to the law, investment banking, the BBC and Independent television, *The Sunday Times* and *The Financial*

Times, the theatre, book publishing, the treasury and the Foreign Office. A 1977 study of the Foreign Office by the prime minister's "think tank," the Central Policy Review Staff, actually complained that "the work is being done to an unjustifiably high standard" and recommended "that the service should recruit a smaller proportion of the ablest candidates."

The reason for this is disputable. It is usually attributed to a snobbish disdain for grubby money-making. But the striking change in the class composition of British universities since the war, the rising share drawn especially from middle-class and, to a lesser extent, working-class homes, shakes this idea. Moreover, a substantial number of Oxbridge graduates do enter the law and merchant or investment banking. This strongly suggests that even products of the ancient institutions are not immune to the lure of money.

A more refined version of the snob theory holds that educated Britons prefer making money to things, that merchant banking has status but engineers barely rank above plumbers. . . .

In Britain, . . . industry lives by the adage that competition is the life of trade and the death of business, a sentiment nurtured by the captive colonial market of the past. The plain and seldom-noticed fact is that British manufacturers and their executives are uniquely free from competitive pressure and probably enjoy the most highly concentrated markets in the developed world. . . .

A Common Market survey limited to six major industries concludes that only France is as monopolized as Britain. In both countries, the four biggest concerns in each industry account for no less than 79 per cent of all the business. . . .

For executives, such concentration offers a secure existence. It would be unfair, no doubt, to call it a well-paid and extended tea break. But it is reasonable to assume that this life will persuade the brighter, more ambitious graduates of Oxford and Cambridge to continue avoiding industry in large numbers; it is also reasonable to assume that industrial workers will seek some of the cosy security enjoyed by their protected bosses.

The notion that the work styles of Britain's blue collar force are modelled on those of their bosses may bring outraged cries in London boardrooms. . . . It may even be true that British workers need no model. At any rate, the incontrovertible fact is that British factory workers are far less productive than those elsewhere in the industrial world.

This consistently low productivity is both measurable and indisputable. Perhaps the most dramatic illustration of the nation's easy work style came when [Prime Minister Edward] Heath ordered industry on to a three-day week [in 1973]. To the surprise of some, this made barely a dent in total production. During the three months of reduced hours of work, output from factories fell only 6 per cent. If these factories had been working at an efficient pace before Heath's order, production would have fallen two-fifths or 40 per cent. It was nothing like that, a remarkable demonstration that Britain's plants normally do three days work in five.

Why do British workers push themselves less than their counterparts in Europe and the U.S.? Why do they insist on tending a machine with three workers when two will do the job? Why do assembly lines move more slowly and machines run fewer hours?

At best, we can make a tentative guess, based on daily observation. Britons, to the dismay of the textbook writers, appear to be *satisficing* rather than *optimizing*. Workers and managers do not seek the greatest possible income; they seek instead an adequate or satisfactory level of income. They prefer tea breaks and long executive lunches, slower assembly lines and longer weekends to strenuous effort for higher incomes.

This, to be sure, is a sweeping generalization that obviously does not apply to all Britons. It does not embrace stock market speculators like Jim Slater who quickly made (and almost as quickly lost) a fortune.

It does not include Sir Freddie Laker, a working-class boy who made a small fortune buying and selling war surplus materials, a larger fortune with one private airline and is well on his way to a third with still another. It does not speak for the occasional worker disciplined by his union for trying to speed up the pace of work.

Above all, it does not describe countless craftsmen and artists, professionals and artisans who enjoy their work. It cannot account for writers, makers of television or cinema films, doctors, scholars, those who work in the theater, paint pictures, design buildings or jewelry, toil in laboratories, make cabinets or leather goods, attend the House of Commons after midnight, direct great departments or their own private enterprises—those for whom work is a joyful, creating form of expression, for whom pecuniary reward is a necessary but less than all-consuming motive. The preference for leisure over goods applies chiefly to those toiling in mines or on assembly lines, laboring at routine tasks in huge white-collar bureaucracies, public and private. Their work does not, cannot enlarge personality; quite the contrary. It diminishes it. They work because they must, to earn enough to support themselves and their families. It is these workers who have decided that there are limits to how long and hard they will labor for extra goods. This conclusion is supported by everyday experience as well as the indirect statistical evidence.

Britons, in short, appear to be the first citizens of the post-industrial age who are choosing leisure over goods on a large scale. Of course almost everyone everywhere all the time would welcome extra income, command over more goods and services. Britons have not renounced material things. But many appear to have arrived at a level of income at which they regard the extra effort to obtain extra income as not worthwhile. In economic terms, many have reached the point where the marginal cost of extra effort just equals the marginal return in the form of more income. This is a point of equilibrium. . . .

Why this preference should appear in Britain before any other industrial country is not clear. It may prove as hard to answer as that perennial exam question, "Why did the Industrial Revolution first come to Britain?" Perhaps the two are related.

Most foreign observers are struck with (and sometimes irritated by) the generally relaxed manner of Britons. Ralf Dahrendorf, the German sociologist and director of the London School of Economics, who likes it, traces it firstly to "the fact that Britain is essentially at one with its history."

The country has never been torn apart by prolonged, bloody class revolution; its rulers have accommodated themselves to change and reform. It has not suffered the shame of invasion since 1066. After discrimination against Catholics ended early in the nineteenth century, neither the state nor society as a whole has openly persecuted a minority group. Britain has a conscious, quietly confident sense of identity. Most of its people seem to feel less need than others to demonstrate superiority in the production of cars, missiles, steel ingots, widgets.

British justice can be as arbitrary and mean-spirited as anywhere else; judges are fallible and typically come from a class that better understands businessmen than workers. But British society, perhaps because it has been led so often by intelligent conservatives, values fair play and justice to a remarkable degree. The welfare state is one expression of a sense of justice. Britain is still a long way from equalizing either opportunity or income. But it has pioneered the belief that society has a responsibility for its more helpless members. This too retards productivity rates in manufacturing but appears to make life more tolerable.

Indeed, Britain is a very stable society; it has left and right fringes, but they play only insignificant roles. Britain is a society more or less at peace with itself, generally orderly, generally tolerant, more or less humane. If people worked harder would these qualities be threatened?

The preference for leisure over goods can be measured in several ways. Cleaning the air and rivers imposes a cost on society, one that is borne either by manufacturers who must invest in new anti-pollution devices or by citizens who pay taxes to subsidize their introduction. No marketable goods are produced from this outlay. But the quality of leisure has been enhanced.

Similarly the British have chosen to spend more and more on the arts. The results have been astonishing—a new Elizabethan age, at least in the theater. Tom Stoppard and Harold Pinter are not Shakespeare and Marlowe. Nevertheless, the heavily subsidized National Theatre which frequently presents their work is the envy of the Western world. Along with the state-supported Royal Shakespeare Company, it gives a lead to the commercial theater. Taken as a whole, London is the acknowledged world capital for drama.

More of society's income has been drawn from electronics or coal mines to encourage music. London alone boasts five world-class symphony orchestras, all receiving state funds. There are two or more concerts in London on any given night for each one in Vienna. The Covent Garden Opera receives state funds; so too does the National Portrait Gallery, the Tate Gallery, the Victoria and Albert and other museums. The money could have been invested to increase productivity in chemicals or ship building; British society, through the budgets adopted by elected governments, has chosen otherwise.

Indeed, there may even be some indirect economic benefits from the collective decision for leisure over goods. Apart from oil, the fastest growing component in Britain's balance of payments is tourism. There were an estimated 11.4 million tourists in 1977. Their outlays probably reached £3 billion. That pays for a lot of imported food and raw materials.

The tourists were drawn, of course, by many things, most notably an under-valued pound. But it would be surprising if they were not also drawn, at least in part, by British civility, sense of fair play and unhurried style, as well as the splendid music, theater and galleries.

By almost any indicator Britain is a solid, healthy society, bursting with creative vigor. Its lack-lustre performance in what Blake called "these dark, Satanic mills" is less a symptom of sickness than of health. Even in a difficult year like 1974, a government census found that 84.8 per cent of all men workers pronounced themselves as "satisfied" with their jobs; for women, the rate was 89.4 per cent. This is not the response of a sullen, class-ridden, divided nation. . . .

Britain is hardly the New Jerusalem. Neither is it the sinking, chaotic, miserable swamp depicted by the more imaginative journalists and professors. When and if stagflation is overcome throughout the West, Britain's preference for leisure over goods may yet serve as a model for others in the post-industrial age.

19

The "Thatcher Revolution" of the 1980s: A Change in Style or a Change in Substance?

There is general consensus, in retrospect, that the British general election of 1979 proved to be one of the most significant of the twentieth century. Voters returned the Conservative party to power for the longest uninterrupted period of government in post–1832 British history. It also brought to the prime ministership Margaret Thatcher, who was to hold the office for eleven and a half continuous years—also a post–1832 record—before she was deposed in November 1990 not by the electorate but by a rebellion within her own party.

As Britain's first woman prime minister and as both a forceful leader and an articulate public speaker, Margaret Thatcher became the first British head of government since Winston Churchill to become a household name throughout the world. Within her own country, she became not only well known and highly respected but also little loved and often intensely controversial. Her long personal tenure in power and that of her party were to a significant degree the consequence of a sharp division among her opponents. In the elections of 1979, 1983, 1987, and—for that matter—1992, Conservative party candidates received only between 42 and 43 percent of the total popular vote. The reason the party gained an overall parliamentary majority on each occasion was that the opposition was divided between a weakened Labour party, the largest Opposition party, and a temporarily revived Liberal party (allied with break-away Labourites) that in 1983 won as much as 25 percent of the total popular vote.

Whatever the contributing factors, until late 1990 Margaret Thatcher remained prime minister. Was she, as her more ardent supporters contended, a modern Joan of Arc saving her fellow Britons from a widespread sense of defeatism and the deadening hand of a form of state socialism that was extinguishing the remnants of private enterprise and personal initiative? Alternatively, as many of her opponents insisted, was she "Attila the Hen," leading her fellow Britons on the road toward a parochial, selfish, and greedy materialism, ready to tear holes into the "safety net" of welfare services still required by Britain's poorer citizens, including the

427

The cartoonist provides a mock-heroic celebration of the completion of the tenth year of Margaret Thatcher's eleven-and-a-half year "reign" as prime minister. The head on the platter is that of General Galtieri, the leader of Argentina who was defeated in the Falkland Islands War (1982). *(Mick Brownfield,* Sunday Times, *9 April 1989.* © *Times Newspapers Ltd.)*

ethnic and racial minorities that had come to constitute part of the United Kingdom?

The selections in this chapter throw light on both questions. The first selection provides the reader with an opportunity to sample the words both of Margaret Thatcher (1925–   ) and of Neil Kinnock (1942–   ), the leader of the Opposition Labour Party from 1983 until 1992. The year was 1987 and the occasion was the annual debate on the queen's Speech from the Throne (the custom on which the annual State of the Union address by American presidents is modeled). Parliament had just reassembled after the Conservative Party's third successive general election victory, and the debate provided both Kinnock and Thatcher with an opportunity to look to the past as well as to the future. On what grounds does Kinnock challenge the Thatcher record and her program of prospective legislation? In which of her accomplishments does Margaret Thatcher appear to take the greatest pride?

The other reading in the chapter is a lengthy excerpt from Peter Riddell's *The Thatcher Era And Its Legacy* (1991). Riddell is a political columnist and commentator for *The Times* of London; he also served for a number of years as U.S. editor of *The Financial Times* (London), and he is the author of two other books. The first portion of that excerpt was written in 1989, when Margaret Thatcher was still prime minister. The second was written within a year after her resignation, several months before Margaret Thatcher's successor as prime minister, John Major, astonished public opinion pollsters in April 1992 by leading his party to a fourth successive general-election victory. Does Riddell see Margaret Thatcher as the advocate of a completely consistent set of economic and political principles or is Thatcherism to him a compound of trial and error? To what degree, according to Riddell, did Margaret Thatcher accomplish the goals she set forth? Which of the changes that she helped set into motion appear most likely to last into the later 1990s and beyond?

NEIL KINNOCK and MARGARET THATCHER   **Debate on the Thatcher Government: Its Record and Promise (1987)**

In the aftermath of the Conservative Party's third successive general election victory, Neil Kinnock, the leader of the Labour Opposition, attacks and Margaret Thatcher, the prime minister, defends her government's past record and its future program as outlined a few days before in the queen's annual Speech from the Throne.

Mr. Neil Kinnock:

The question is how [the government will use its power]. Will it be used . . . with "circumspection," or will it be used ruthlessly to increase the theft of powers from local democracy? Will it be used contemptuously to ignore the overwhelming votes and indisputable views of the people of Scotland? Will it be used sensitively to unify, or savagely to deprive and to divide? All the signs are that this government, like the one before it, will use power malevolently—to decontrol rents and leave private tenants to the mercies of unscrupulous landlords; to conscript youngsters into training schemes regardless of the utility or suitability of those schemes; to break up the Inner London education authority. . . .

The government's way [is] to ensure that education, health care and so many other essentials of opportunity and security, are rationed by charges. They will make the offer of provision to everyone and then say that if one wants it, one will have to pay for it. Today they say, "Pay for field trips, music, sport, cookery and art"—so-called extras in the curriculum; tomorrow they will say, "Pay for books"—indeed, they are doing it already; and the day after they will say, "Pay for teachers." . . .

This government know the price of everything and the value of absolutely nothing. Not content with charging for health care or education, they will, with their poll tax, make people pay to vote. That is what the poll tax means. Apart from the fact that millions will be unable to pay the tax or will have immense difficulty in paying it because of their poverty, that there will be extra costs for business in many parts of the country, that there will

SOURCE: *Parliamentary Debates (House of Commons)*, 6th Series, Vol. 118, cols. 45–62.

be a massive increase in bureaucracy and the bills that go with that and that there will be a great increase in centralization by a government who always say that they want to roll back the state but always roll on the state over anything that stands in their way, the poll tax will mean that the people of this democracy of Britain will have to pay for their vote. . . .

In all of this the government turn the basic democratic rule of no taxation without representation on its head. With the poll tax, they are saying: no representation without taxation. . . .

In the United States, whose tax system the prime minister is said to admire very much, the 24th amendment to the constitution lays down that no poll tax should be allowed "to deny or abridge the right of citizens to vote."

That amendment was resisted by only one group in the whole of the United States during the early 1960s—the clique that controlled the state of Mississippi. Here in 1987, in the state of Missis Thatcher, we have a government who are insisting on imposing a poll tax and everything that goes with it—abridging the right to vote in a way that is forbidden under the Constitution of our sister democracy and should be forbidden by any decent government in this democratic country.

Even with all that, the prime minister still tells us that she wants more power to the people. She cannot want that and a poll tax, for the two are incompatible. Indeed, the prime minister does not appear to want a free society as we understand it. She appears to want a fee-paying society. Those who support her, those who support payment for schooling, those who support payment for health care and those who support the decontrolling of rents, the privatization of water and the conscription of the young unemployed should ask themselves one question: why was every single one of those ideas jettisoned 40, 50, 60 or 70 years ago by Liberal governments, Labour governments and by Conservative governments, too? Indeed, many of the acts abandoning the brutal and miserable system that this

government wants to reintroduce were instigated by previous Conservative governments whose memory this government disgrace. . . . No. The Conservative Party is exhuming the dead past. We are trying to keep it in the past; they are trying to make a tomorrow of all those yesterdays.

Are we getting independence for the householder who must buy water from a private monopoly? Are we getting independence for the pensioners and others who will be hit by further cuts in housing benefit? Where is the independence in all that?

Where is the choice? Where is the choice for the parents who are compelled to pay for the schooling of their children or take the risk that their education will be sacrificed? That is not choice; it is forced charges.

Where is the choice in a system that requires people to beg or borrow the price of an operation or to wait interminably in pain? Where is the choice for the widow whose entitlement to state earnings-related pension has been cut in half by the government? Where is the choice in all that? It is obvious that under this government independence is a mockery and that such choice is a taunt for those who do not have the money to buy education and health care, the opportunity and the essential services, at the time, on the day and in the place that they need them.

In every part of the government's program there are counterfeit offers of advance in choice and independence. The Government's inner city proposals are a prime example. . . .

We can wish the urban development corporations the very best of luck. We can hope that they will be new centers of employment, but, as we do, we know that continually over the past seven years the government have cut the rate support grant. They have chopped housing support by 60 per cent., reduced industrial development aid and abolished investment allowances. They do not have the desire or the will to commit the means necessary to deal with the corrosion of life in the inner cities and in many other areas of devastation. . . .

It is for all those reasons that the government inevitably decrease opportunities, increase poverty, multiply division and diminish democracy.... The maxim of modern Conservatism is that if one cannot pay, one should stay away; if one cannot afford the fee, one cannot be really free. That system was buried by history and need and by the decent consensus of all parties decades ago. It will be buried again.

The Prime Minister:

I listened carefully to what the right hon. Member for Islwyn (Mr. Kinnock) said. He seemed long on words but short on content and I began to understand why he lost the general election in such a decisive way. He seemed to address many of his remarks to some of the shibboleths of the 1930s. Those have no appeal whatsoever to the population of our country, which is becoming home-owning, share-owning, and savings-owning and having an independence it would never otherwise have got. Those class shibboleths have no relevance to our modern society. People know full well that they have a higher standard of living than they have ever had before, stemming from a government who, in a partnership with the people, have brought about economic strength and a standard of health care and social security that we have never had before....

At the heart of the Gracious Speech is the section referring to the economy, and at the heart of Britain's economic strength are the continuing policies of sound financial management. They are designed to reduce inflation further, to keep firm control of public expenditure, and to increase enterprise and employment by incentives and training. It takes time to establish a reputation for prudent economic policies of the kind enjoyed by Germany and Switzerland, with all the benefits that they bring, but Britain is now succeeding. Control of inflation through sound financial policies is and will remain our top priority.

It has been the habit in the past two terms of office and will be the same habit in the next for the government to set the financial and legal framework. However, the wealth of a country is the effort of its people and the way in which they respond to that framework. They have responded and that has brought a very high standard of living. However, effort depends upon incentives. That is frequently forgotten by those who make easy election promises, but, as the result of the last election showed, people were not taken in by those promises in any way....

The news since the dissolution [of the last Parliament] is good news, and of course Opposition Members do not want to hear such news. There have been good balance of payments figures.... There have been encouraging business surveys from the Confederation of British Industry and the chambers of commerce. There are lower mortgage rates and lower gas prices, and record British Telecom profits are helping to finance a record £2 billion investment program. In addition, the OECD forecasts that Britain this year will have the fastest growth of all the major industrial countries....

There will be guaranteed places on the youth training scheme, which is an excellent scheme, for school leavers under the age of 18 who do not go into employment or further education.

Legislation will be introduced to enable benefits to be withheld from young people who deliberately choose to remain unemployed, and quite rightly so....

Job opportunities are growing steadily— 1,100,000 more since March 1983. Our task is to help to ensure that those who are seeking work have the right training to fill those opportunities and the help to start a business on their own if they so wish.

I refer now to something that I referred to in reply to the leader of the Opposition. The spreading ownership of housing, shares, pensions and savings has been one of the great achievements of the past eight years. That is one reason—the bringing of independence and power to the people—why the right hon. Gentleman's party did so badly in the election. People do not want the songs and policies of collectivism. They want the capacity, ability and opportunity to own their own houses, shares, pensions and many other matters besides.

The Labour Party favors what it now calls social ownership, which is nationalization in sheep's clothing. The effect would be to concentrate power in Whitehall and to deprive millions of ordinary people of their shareholding in industry. By contrast, we shall continue our program of privatization, thus freeing businesses to respond to the needs of the customer and increasing the opportunities for share ownership.

Now we have a new task. Just as we took power from trade union bosses and restored it to their members, so we must now extend to the people new freedoms and responsibilities in housing, education and local authority finance. These will be the subject of three major bills that have been signalled in the Gracious Speech. It is our purpose to bring new opportunities into the inner cities in particular and to make town halls more accountable, for nowhere are the damaging effects of dependence and socialism seen more clearly than in some of our inner cities.

We shall abolish the domestic rates—a grossly unfair tax—and replace them with a community charge.[1] . . . Subject to proper protection for those in need, it is right that we should all pay something toward the cost of the local services from which we all benefit. The new unified business rate will protect businesses and jobs in inner cities from the councils which obstruct wealth and job creation by imposing very high rates.

We have made great strides toward a property-owning democracy. Some 1,000,000 council houses have been sold since 1979, and two-thirds of our people now own their own homes. . . . We will ensure that home ownership continues to spread by maintaining mortgage tax relief and the tenants' right to buy. . . .

Our new task must be to extend the benefits of greater choice and independence to those in rented accommodation. Rent controls have reduced the private sector to a mere 8 per cent of the housing market, with the result that there is almost a municipal monopoly in rented housing. Too many tenants are confined to large monolithic and sometimes badly kept council estates. It is high time for town hall monopoly to be replaced by individual choice in renting. We shall therefore introduce major housing reforms in this session. . . .

The reform of education is the third of the fundamental reforms to be introduced this session. Although in many of our local authorities children are receiving an excellent education, in others there is widespread dissatisfaction. In too many schools education does not match either what the parents want or what the children need. In this first session of the new Parliament we shall bring forward a major bill which will introduce a national curriculum with clear attainment targets and tests during the period of compulsory schooling; which will prevent local education authorities from putting artificial limits on numbers, so making it possible for popular schools to take in more pupils; which will enable maintained schools to opt out of local authority control where parents and governing bodies so wish and to be funded directly from the Department of Education and Science. The right hon. Member for Islwyn knew that when he made his mischievous statement from the dispatch box. He knows that no fees will be payable to those schools that opt out. . . .

Parents want schools that will provide their children with the knowledge, training and character to fit them for today's world.

---

[1]*Community charge:* the name that Margaret Thatcher gave to what Neil Kinnock had called a "poll tax." It was intended to replace the "rates" (local real-estate taxes) as the prime source of funding for local government authorities. It proved to be the most controversial of all the legislative measures of the Thatcher era; although enacted into law, it was replaced within a year after her resignation in November 1990.

They want them to be taught basic educational skills.

We shall enlarge the right of parents to choose those schools that will best meet the needs of their children. The legislation sets out to achieve the most far-reaching reform of education since the Education Act 1944.

Since 1979 we have transformed industrial relations by strengthening the rights of trade union members. In the coming session we shall take that a stage further by ensuring that all members of trade union governing bodies are elected by secret postal ballot at least once every five years; by limiting further the abuse of the closed shop; by protecting individual members if they refuse to join a strike they disagree with; and by establishing a new trade union commissioner with the power to help individual trade union members to enforce their fundamental rights. I believe that these steps, like those before them, will be widely welcomed by members of trade unions throughout the country. . . .

The Gracious Speech sets out the government's determination to keep Britain's defenses strong and to work for reductions in the overall numbers of nuclear weapons. . . . Britain has taken a lead in shaping the West's position in the negotiations on intermediate and shorter-range nuclear missiles in Europe. It is my belief that an agreement consistent with NATO's security can be reached by the end of this year.

Opposition Members have not learnt the simple lesson that a strong defense policy and a successful arms control policy are directly linked. . . . However, the British people have rejected totally the Opposition's defense policy.

Today, at the beginning of our third term, Britain's voice is heard with respect in Europe, in the Soviet Union and in the United States because we have made Britain strong again and because we have put freedom first. . . .

Indeed, trust in the people is at the heart of our policies. That is how we have, in the past eight years, transformed the climate for business, brought over-mighty trade unions within the rule of law and created a new confidence at home and abroad. That is why we were returned with such an excellent majority. The achievements of the past two terms of Conservative government show that that trust was well placed. Trust in the people will continue to be the foundation for the achievements for our third term.

PETER RIDDELL The Thatcher Legacy: A Provisional Assessment (1991)

A widely read journalist who has lived through the Thatcher years sums up the pros and cons of the political record of a remarkable prime minister.

The Nature of Thatcherism

There are dangers in consensus: it could be an attempt to satisfy people holding no particular views about anything. It seems more important to have a philosophy and policy which because they are good appeal to sufficient people to secure a majority. . . . No great party can survive except on the basis of firm beliefs about what it wants to do. It is not enough to have reluctant support. We want people's enthusiasm as well.

Margaret Thatcher
Chief Opposition Spokesman on Power
Conservative Political Centre Address
Blackpool, 10 October 1968

SOURCE: Peter Riddell, *The Thatcher Era and Its Legacy* (Oxford, UK, & Cambridge, Mass.: Blackwell, 1991), pp. 1–13, 218–222, 226–234, 242–245. Reprinted by permission of Peter Riddell, Political Editor and Principal Political Commentator of *The Times*, London.

It became the accepted wisdom, not merely that we were, as a nation, in a phase of relative decline which might soon become absolute, not to say terminal; but that our social cohesion, our political institutions, our very governability and even national integrity were in an advanced and probably irreversible state of decay. From Michael Shanks' The Stagnant Society, *in 1961, through the special 'Suicide of a Nation' issue of* Encounter *in 1963, all the way to Sir Nicholas Henderson's validictory despatch of 1979, the grimness of the diagnosis was unvarying. It was a theme which offered irresistible temptations both to the purveyors of gloom and the peddlers of glib solutions.*

Nigel Lawson, Energy Secretary
Patrick Hutber Memorial Lecture
London, 22 June 1982

The Conservative Political Centre lecture at each October's party conference is intended to be a prestige event. An invitation to deliver it confers the mantle of promise on the aspiring middle-ranking politician concerned. But that is all. No one then pays much attention to the platitudinous and safe comments generally uttered. October 1968 was no exception. The speaker was the most junior member of Edward Heath's Shadow Cabinet, and the lecture attracted almost no notice at the time. Yet the ten pages of the subsequently published pamphlet contain the essence of what has become known as Thatcherism.

With an ice maiden photograph of the author on the front, the pamphlet offers as clear a guide to Mrs. Thatcher's approach to politics as any she has subsequently given. More than 20 years later little has changed. Under the title of "What's wrong with politics?" she sets out her distrust of government: "What we need now is a far greater degree of personal responsibility and decision, far more independence from the government, and a comparative reduction in the role of government." There are passages urging greater concern with control of the money supply, with increasing personal re-

sponsibility for social provision, and with giving people a measure of independence from the state. There is the first appearance of her familiar argument that the Good Samaritan "had to have the money to help, otherwise he too would have had to pass on the other side." And, as the quotation at the beginning of this chapter shows, there is the dislike of consensus and a belief in firm and clear alternatives.

The pamphlet is interesting now not just as an illustration of the consistency of Mrs. Thatcher's views, but more to show that Thatcherism is a personal, highly distinctive, approach to politics rather than a coherent set of ideas. Mrs. Thatcher is not a great political thinker or theorist. Her inspiration is personal experience and a view of Britain. She is not a consistent free-market advocate, not an out-and-out libertarian opponent of the state—far from it. Mrs. Thatcher's attitudes and actions have often been contrary to free-market theories. In particular, she has always been sensitive to the interests of owner-occupiers in staunchly defending the retention of mortgage interest tax-relief against the views of the treasury and of most economists who believe the subsidy artificially distorts the housing market and inflates house prices. She has also taken a distinctly mercantilist view of industry and trade, championing British companies rather than adopting a purely free-market approach. Similarly, she has reacted to middle-class concerns over violence and pornography by balancing her support for the deregulation of broadcasting by also setting-up a body to monitor and supervise standards. The nanny state lives on.

As I have argued previously (1983), "Thatcherism is essentially an instinct, a series of moral values and an approach to leadership rather than an ideology. It is an expression of Mrs. Thatcher's upbringing in Grantham, her background of hard work and family responsibility, ambition and postponed satisfaction, duty and patriotism." In one of the characteristically frank insights which tend to come at the end of her television and press interviews, Mrs. Thatcher disclosed her underlying approach on the *Weekend World* program in January 1983. She extolled Victorian values:

I want to see one nation, as you go back to Victorian times, but I want everyone to have their own personal property stake. . . . I want them to have their own savings which retain their value, so they can pass things on to their children, so you get again a people, everyone strong and independent of government. Winston [Churchill] put it best. You want a ladder, upward, so anyone, no matter what their background, can climb, but a fundamental safety net below which no one can fall. That's the British character. . . . Of course, we have basic social services, we will continue to have those, but equally compassion depends on what you and I, as individuals, are prepared to do. I remember my father telling me that at a very early age. Compassion doesn't depend upon whether you get up and make a speech in the marketplace about what governments should do. It depends upon how you're prepared to conduct your own life, and how much you're prepared to give of what you have to others. . . .

Mrs. Thatcher stands for the values of the English suburban and provincial middle-class and aspiring skilled working-class. She is very much an English phenomenon, as shown by her lack of political appeal in Scotland and Wales. However, she is not a metropolitan establishment figure, partly because of her sex, but also because of her attitudes. Her style of conviction politics and self-conscious radicalism are uncomfortable for the established. Some of the greatest hostility to her has often come from representatives of traditional pillars of society like the universities, the Church of England, the Foreign Office and the professions. She is not a naturally clubbable person. Indeed, Mrs. Thatcher has been in equal parts patronized and disliked by the liberal intellectual establishment. This was brought out by several contributors to a vivid collection of views in the *Sunday Telegraph* in January 1988. Producer and writer Jonathan Miller talked of her "odious suburban gentility and sentimental saccharine patriotism, catering to the worst elements of commuter idiocy." Others complained of a bullying style, her materialism, and her hostility to the performing arts, education and research work. In response, novelist Kingsley Amis said Mrs. Thatcher brought out the latent snobbery in those no longer deferred to.

Her approach has revolved around a number of themes—a belief in Britain's greatness and the assertion of national interests, a prejudice against the public sector (at any rate in economic and industrial affairs), a backing for the police and the authorities in fighting terrorism and upholding law and order, a strong dislike of trade unions, a general commitment to the virtues of sound money, a preference for wealth creators over civil servants and commentators, and a support for the right of individuals to make their own provision for education and health. In a moment of stark self-revelation during the 1987 election campaign Thatcher said she used private health facilities because she wanted to go into hospital on the day "I want at the time I want and with the doctor I want. . . . I exercise my right as a free citizen to spend my own money in my own way."

Many commentators, notably though not exclusively on the left, have argued that this adds up to a coherent ideology—that Thatcherism represents the practical application of a set of theories, whose proponents are known as the New Right, which has swept to success on both sides of the Atlantic. . . . [But] hindsight often provides the coherence and clarity denied to contemporaries. . . . The new Marxists may be right to see the Thatcherism of the late 1980s as a deliberate attempt to replace the post-war social democratic consensus and to create an economic and political constituency for capitalist values and aspirations. But that has been very much a second and third-term phenomenon. That was not what the Conservatives were about in Opposition or in their first term, up to 1983. The radicalism of the late 1980s has developed on the basis of earlier political successes. Or, rather, many of the most important new policies have been the result of the failures of initial policies and in response to circumstances. Mrs. Thatcher's electoral and political dominance has given her the rare opportunity to remedy earlier setbacks and policy weaknesses.

There was no master plan. Mrs. Thatcher won the Conservative leadership in February 1975 in what amounted to a coup d'état against Edward Heath. It was based on the dissatisfaction felt by a majority of Conservative M.P.s after the party had suffered two electoral defeats in 1974. Some senior Tories, like her original mentor Lord (then Sir Keith) Joseph had become highly critical of the economic record of the Heath administration. But her victory represented no conscious ideological shift on the part of most Conservative M.P.s. . . .

Instead, the main concern of Mrs. Thatcher and her close allies was more general: the decline of Britain. As reflected in the quotation from Nigel Lawson at the beginning of this chapter, there was a growing feeling during the 1970s that the post-war settlement—Keynesian demand management of the economy, agreements with the trade unions and so on—was no longer delivering the goods. In a retrospective assessment in January 1988, Nigel Lawson saw the problem of the 1970s as the pursuit of equality, which, he argued, "led to growing discord and the exercise of big government led to the point where it was widely felt that Britain had become ungovernable":

> Yet it was not until the final stages of this process, in the mid-1970s, as the tensions that had been building up exploded in a holocaust of inflation, a disease as socially destructive as it is economically damaging, that the tide of ideas began to turn. Not until then did it come to be realized that the problem lay not in the inefficient management of the prevailing consensus, but in the consensus itself: that the use of state power to run the economy and to enforce equality lay at the very root of our national difficulties, and had to be abandoned.

Mr. Lawson talked of "a decade of self-doubt and relative decline." . . .

Mrs. Thatcher explicitly saw key political issues in terms of Britain's past greatness, recent decline and the possibility of recovery. Her vision was never purely economic. . . . Behind the election victory of May 1979, lay "the need for renewal of our traditional craftsmanship and civic spirit; renewal at every level, and in every profession, of our old vigor, and vitality." In the language almost of a prophet, she set out the government's objectives:

> The mission of this government is much more than the promotion of economic progress. It is to renew the spirit and solidarity of the nation. To ensure that these assertions lead to action, we need to inspire a new national mood, as much as to carry through legislation. At the heart of a new mood in the nation must be a recovery of our self-confidence and our self respect. Nothing is beyond us. Decline is not inevitable. But nor is progress a law of nature. The ground gained by one generation may be lost by the next. The foundation of this new confidence has to be individual responsibility.

After talking of the themes of opportunity, choice, strength and renewal, Thatcher revealingly drew an imperial parallel:

> It will not be given to this generation of our countrymen to create a great empire. But it is given to us to demand an end to decline and to make a stand against what Churchill described as the long dismal drawling tides of drift and surrender, of wrong measurements and feeble impulses.

This essentially moral vision was reflected in the Conservatives' 1979 election manifesto. The document itself was short on specific commitments and certainly did not represent the deliberate start of an ideological revolution, or rather that of a counter-revolution. The main influences on the manifesto and on the campaign were the events of the preceding few months, particularly the "winter of discontent" with its highly publicized trade union disruption. . . . The appeal was to the fears and aspirations of those disillusioned with Labour—skilled workers, especially those living in the suburbs, new towns and smaller cities of southern England and the Midlands. These were the people whose living standards had been squeezed during much of the 1970s, and many of whom were a ready market for one of the Tories' few specific pledges—to sell local authority owned homes to their occupiers. These people were also attracted by Mrs. Thatcher's emphasis on law and order and strong defense, and in some areas by her tough stand on further limits on immigration. . . .

Even the defeated prime minister James (now Lord) Callaghan was reported as acknowledging that "there are times, perhaps once every 30 years, when there is a sea change in politics. It then does not matter what you say or what you do. There is a shift in what the public wants and what it approves of. I suspect there is now such a sea change—and it is for Mrs. Thatcher." At the time, the sea change was seen as basically negative—against the collectivism of the 1960s and 1970s and the failures of the Callaghan administration rather than specifically in favor of a capitalist/individualist blueprint.

Once in office, Mrs. Thatcher's administration responded to Britain's problems by curbing the power of the trade unions, attempting to get on top of inflation via a tight monetary policy, seeking to cut public spending and taxes, rebuilding Britain's defense capacity and dealing with rising crime. In the social area there were some minor proposals—removing one tier of health authorities, cutting back on some social benefits and on education spending. After a couple of years few of these main goals were near achievement. Unemployment was soaring as output fell sharply, yet the money supply and public spending were rising substantially in excess of their targets. And there appeared to be little progress elsewhere, with serious inner city riots in the summer of 1981 and the Tories in electoral retreat in face of the newly formed Social Democratic Party and its Liberal allies. . . .

Yet 1981, for all its troubles, was the political turning point for the Thatcher government and for Thatcherism. In the March budget, Sir Geoffrey Howe, the chancellor—and one of the under-appreciated archi-

tects of the administration's policies—raised the tax burden in order to curb public sector borrowing, even though unemployment was still rising sharply. This turned on its head the conventional wisdom of post-war Keynesian demand management, under which fiscal policy should have been relaxed rather than tightened. This budget underlined not only what later became known as "the resolute approach," but also showed how the government was determined to change economic policy, for all the predictions of a U-turn. Secondly, that September, Mrs. Thatcher achieved dominance over her cabinet by the removal from it of some of her critics. . . . Her strong and successful leadership during the Falklands war in the following spring and early summer solidified public backing for her internal party dominance—and this was reinforced by the start of a recovery in living standards.

In domestic policy, Mrs. Thatcher's political victories in 1981–2 enabled her to regain the initiative in a number of areas where previous approaches had not worked. In particular, the failure to get to grips with the large deficits of the nationalized industries led to the development of the privatization program. As often during the Thatcher decade, what turned out to be a far-reaching initiative developed in an unexpected fashion in response to a particular problem, rather than as a result of some preordained plan. . . .

Even the most radical private thinking of the Conservatives in Opposition—let alone their cautious public commitments—had not envisaged the sale of the major monopoly utilities, as happened in the second half of the 1980s. The program which transformed the boundaries between the public and private sectors was in response to a policy crisis.

Similarly, in her second term from 1983–7, the proposals for the restructuring of the education system emerged as a result of a perceived crisis over standards in schools. This reflected concerns expressed during the lengthy teachers' pay dispute of 1984–6. Again, radicalism was the child of earlier failure. The government's checkered record on local authorities provides other examples. Each successive initiative—rate-capping, the abolition of the Greater London Council and the metropolitan counties, and the community charge or poll tax—was a response to earlier failures to establish Whitehall's control over mainly Labour controlled big city town halls. After Mrs. Thatcher's third election victory, the story was repeated when the chorus of protests over the funding of the health service during the winter of 1987–8 led to the announcement of a far-reaching review into the future of the National Health Service—contrary to the earlier intention to leave a fundamental review until a fourth term. On each occasion the government's response involved a similar approach—a dislike of public sector solutions, and particularly of local authorities, trade unions and the like. The instincts of Mrs. Thatcher and her allies have prevailed. In all this there can be detected a preference for individualism over collectivism—even though free-market economists have often despaired of some of the detailed proposals such as privatizing monopoly utilities without introducing sufficient competition. Yet the key point is that all these important policies have been a response to events rather than the execution of a clearly prepared and argued-out blueprint. . . .

Indeed, for all the setbacks and improvisations of the early 1980s, Thatcherism has become more coherent as the decade has advanced. After her second election victory in 1983, and more particularly after 1987, Mrs. Thatcher and her allies have deliberately attempted to defeat socialism and to challenge the traditional bases of Labour and the trade union movement in big city local authorities, council housing estates and nationalized industries. This has been aided by the divisions in the Opposition parties. . . .

The Thatcher Legacy

I have never been defeated by the people. I've never been defeated in an election. I've never been defeated in a vote of confidence in Parliament, so I don't know what that would be like. I'd still be there if I had my choice. I did not have my choice so I decided to do the best thing for my party for the future. . . . And I knew I'd still have a good bit of influence.

Mrs. Margaret Thatcher
Interview in *Vanity Fair*, June 1991

The Thatcher era ended dramatically and suddenly in November 1990, and British politics entered a more uncertain phase. The dynamic force had been pushed, reluctant and protesting, to the sidelines. But her influence over British politics and life had not ended. Mrs. Thatcher left a legacy, both in what her governments had achieved during the 1980s and in policies and attitudes which would continue to influence Britain during the 1990s. . . .

Mrs. Thatcher lost office because she had become a political and electoral liability in the eyes of a significant number of her cabinet and parliamentary colleagues. They believed it was necessary to modify some of the more unpopular aspects of Thatcherism. I see the events of November 1990 primarily as a change of personality and style, rather than of fundamental strategy. The Major government maintained the direction of Conservative economic and industrial policy (the poll tax apart), even though the pace and method of implementation may alter with his less ideological tone. . . .

I will not attempt to retell in detail the now familiar story of the dramas of those late autumn days at Westminster. There are both plenty of reasons for Mrs. Thatcher's departure—the poll tax, growing party divisions over Europe and the deteriorating economic outlook—and just one overarching one. She stayed on too long. . . .

The poll tax proved to be an even bigger political disaster than Chancellor of the Exchequer Nigel Lawson and his then deputy, Chief Secretary John Major, feared during the debates of 1987–8. Mrs. Thatcher herself once described the poll tax as her "flagship," which was strange since it was irrelevant to the thrust of her policies to revitalize the British economy or industry. Instead, all it showed was her hostility to local government and demonstrated those personal attributes which her colleagues and voters least liked about her—her determination to push through policies regardless of other views and her lack of concern for those adversely affected. . . . The public disobedience and occasional violence were reminiscent of the reaction in the American colonies in the 1760s to the Stamp Act.

A sizeable number of Conservative M.P.s concluded that, with Mrs. Thatcher still in Downing Street, the party's fortunes might not recover as they did after mid-term setbacks in 1981–2 and 1985–6. Her considerable virtues—courage, vision and the ability to appreciate and be decisive in face of key challenges—had by the end become overshadowed by her faults.

The events which precipitated her downfall—the devastating resignation speech of Sir Geoffrey Howe and the leadership challenge of Michael Heseltine—would not have proved fatal without that background and an accumulation of discontent and division. The cabinet, which she had for so long dominated, in the end turned against her in an exercise of its collective muscle. Never defeated by voters at a general election or in Parliament, she was deposed by her closest colleagues. "It's a funny old world," she remarked at her last, emotional cabinet meeting on 22 November 1990. . . .

Writing in *The Times* just after she resigned, Lord Blake, foremost Conservative historian, argued that "Margaret Thatcher's place in history is assured; the first woman to be prime minister, the first since Palmerston to win three successive general elections, the longest continuous holder of the office since Lord Liverpool. . . . She was on the British political scene a giant among pygmies. She was one of the two greatest Conservative prime ministers in the 20th century and one of the half dozen greatest prime ministers of all parties and all times." A more centrist commentator, Robert Skidelsky, wrote in the *Guardian* that "The historian will see the Thatcher premiership as a never-ending campaign, punctuated by set battles, sometimes broken off, but always resumed, against all those forces which, in her view, had brought, or were bringing, Britain low."

Skidelsky posed the central question of "whether the Thatcherite decade marks a new start for Britain or whether it is just the latest in a long series of failed attempts to reverse Britain's cumulative economic and political decline." There is no agreement about whether her policies had helped to check Britain's decline and how far they might persist; in short, had there been a Thatcher revolution, or had Thatcherism failed in its aims?

The word revolution tends to confuse. Britain in the late 1970s undoubtedly had severe economic and political problems. But it was not at the point of pre-revolutionary breakdown. Some of Mrs. Thatcher's more ideological supporters may have wanted a revolution. But that would have been alien to the essentially evolutionary character of British politics. That allows for periods of accelerated change, as in the 1906–11 period or the late 1940s, but not of wholesale alteration of attitudes. Yet the opposite reaction of many on the left that the Thatcher era was somehow a ghastly aberration—resulting in part from Labour's divisions—is equally mistaken. Important and lasting changes in British industry and society occurred during the 1980s. The fact that not everything changed does not mean that nothing changed.

What Britain required, and received, during the 1980s was a far-reaching, but not a revolutionary, change of approach. Mrs. Thatcher and her governments challenged many of the assumptions of the post-war era—Keynes in economic management and Herbert Morrison in nationalized industries—while leaving the Beveridge view of universal social provision intact in theory, if not always in practice. Mrs. Thatcher succeeded where she went with the grain of public attitudes and built on shifts already occurring in the late 1970s. . . . Mrs. Thatcher was less successful in trying to change the post-war welfare state; indeed, her efforts were mainly aimed at reforming rather than overturning it. . . .

The extent to which there was a revival of British industry and competitiveness remains open to debate. There are three basic questions. Has the behavior of workers and managers changed? Is there evidence of an underlying revival of entrepreneurship? Has Britain a leading role in sufficient industrial sectors? The verdict is mixed. On the first question, a survey of partners in accountancy firms carried out by Professors Brown and Sanford (1990) shows that nearly three-quarters of those questioned did not change their working hours between the last year when the top marginal income tax rate was 60 per cent and the first year when it was 40 per cent. The vast majority who said they worked longer hours said it was because of pressure of work and only a tiny number said it was because of the change in tax. Further down the income scale, David Guest (1990) maintained there was no reliable evidence that employees worked harder than before 1979. Links between increases in manufacturing productivity and increased worker effort are flimsy, and may reflect the shake-out of older and less capable workers and changes in industrial relations practices. "We cannot conclude that increased worker effort is a significant component explaining the increases in productivity. It would appear that on the shop floor this element of the Thatcherite revolution has failed."

There is evidence of an increase in entrepreneurship, . . . and the number of self-employed expanded by two-thirds. That alone might be sufficient to add a cutting edge to entrepreneurial behavior, even if such attitudes did not spread more widely in society.

The performance of much of British industry improved during the 1980s, as measured by its profitability and productivity. However, this was in many ways just narrowing the gap with Britain's main competitors. There was a long way to go. . . .

A balanced overall view of the industrial record of the Thatcher years has come from Professor Michael Porter of the Harvard Business School. In his mammoth study

(1990) of competitiveness, he acknowledged that there were some positive signs of renewal—in the chemical, oil, pharmaceutical, software, publishing, financial service and consumer goods sectors. There has been strength in retailing, while productivity growth and investment have improved. But, he warned, "Britain is far from assured of broad-based industrial success that might support a sustained increase in its standard of living." He noted that renewal was "fragile and spotty" and confined in manufacturing to one-off restructuring and cost-cutting. While the industries clustered around London and the south-east remain internationally competitive, these are not sufficient to generate sufficient employment. The problem in part has been an inadequate rate of new business formation, which in turn has reflected not only a lack of appropriate motivation and goals, active competition and access to capital, but also the level of skills and ideas.

The Conservatives set out in 1979 to defeat the political power of the trade unions and to reduce the disruptive impact of strikes—and they succeeded in both aims. Trade-union membership fell by more than a quarter over the decade and the number of officially recorded strikes was at a 55-year low in 1990, at less than a quarter of the level of the strike-prone 1970s. So the unions could no longer be portrayed as a threat to the British economy. The combination of the recession of the early 1980s and of the longer-term impact of a succession of trade-union laws helped shift the balance in favor of more assertive and self-confident managers, especially in the private sector.

Yet the economic problems posed by an inflexible labor market and a widespread framework of "going rate" collective bargaining persisted. . . . The IMF [International Monetary Fund] argued that to avoid a sharp rise in unemployment similar to that of the early to mid-1980s, additional measures were needed to increase the responsiveness of wages to market conditions and to promote labor mobility. In addition to reforms already put in place, the IMF suggested that further measures could include shortening the duration of unemployment benefits, increasing training programs and improving labor exchanges.

Equally significant have been rigidities in the labor market caused by inflexibilities in the provision of housing and inadequacies of training. John Muellbauer of Nuffield College, Oxford, who has specialized in the links between housing and economic performance, has noted that the mobility of manual workers in Britain is only about an eighth of the U.S. level, in part because of the absence of a large private rental market in the U.K. (now down to only 8 per cent of the total stock). He argued (1990) that the explosion of house prices in the south in the 1987–8 period prevented workers, particularly manual workers, from moving to areas with the largest labor shortages. This boom, encouraged by government monetary policies and financial deregulation, only intensified wage pressures. . . .

Privatization was probably the most far-reaching achievement of the Thatcher era. In the last two years of her premiership the program was extended to include not only water authorities but also the electricity distribution and generating companies. Both were highly controversial. . . .

Mrs. Thatcher herself would list restoring Britain's place in the world as among her main achievements. She certainly banished the half-heartedness and implicit defeatism of much of British foreign policy in the 1970s. The voice of Britain, and Mrs. Thatcher, was heard around the world. Her unabashed Atlanticism and hostility to closer European integration served her well politically for most of her premiership. In the first half of the 1980s her stand for Britain's money in the European Community outflanked Labour, which was eventually forced to come to terms with membership. But in time she lost touch both with changes in the community itself and with opinion inside her own cabinet. The European ideal enjoyed a renaissance in the second half of the 1980s, associated with the presidency of Mr. Jacques Delors and the program to complete the internal community market in 1992. . . . In the face of the movement toward greater integration, Mrs. Thatcher, with the backing of a substantial number of Conservative M.P.s, stood for a Europe of sovereign nations, co-operating in a movement towards free trade, rather than pooling their sovereignty in some federal enterprise of political and monetary union.

A reluctant Mrs. Thatcher was persuaded to accept sterling's membership of the ERM [Exchange Rate Mechanism]. But she remained opposed to proposals from Mr. Delors for monetary union, including the creation of a European central bank and a single currency. She equated this with a surrender of sovereignty by the British Parliament. . . .

Mrs. Thatcher's approach, while striking nationalistic chords among many Conservative M.P.s and voters, increasingly appeared to leave Britain isolated. The alternative of an Atlantic relationship was an illusion, as was underlined by the arrival of President George Bush in the White House and by the rapid pace of change in Europe from spring 1989 onwards. While U.S.–British relations remained friendly under Mr. Bush, there was not the personal warmth which Mrs. Thatcher had enjoyed with President Reagan. . . . The U.S. has always regarded Britain as a close, reliable and loyal ally on defense and intelligence matters, especially those outside the European theater. There is an unusually close working relationship between diplomats and armed service officers of the two countries. But on broader economic and social issues there is not such closeness and the U.S. sees Britain as one among several medium-ranking European powers. . . .

In detail, the main points of Mrs. Thatcher's record are:

1. By the time of her resignation the annual rate of retail price inflation was, at 10.9 percent, fractionally higher than the level when she entered office, though it did fall sharply back into single figures in the first half of 1991.
2. Adult unemployment fell for 44

consecutive months until April 1990 when it reached a low of 1.6 million, roughly half its mid-1980s peak. The total then rose by nearly half a million over the following 12 months to well over 2 million. Manufacturing employment dropped by more than 2 million between 1979 and early 1991 to less than 5 million, or from 31 to 23 per cent of the total workforce. Employment in services expanded from 58 to 70 percent.

3. Real Gross Domestic Product (GDP) rose by 27 percent over the Thatcher years. In 1990 it grew by just 0.5 percent compared with 1989 (after the rapid expansion of the late 1980s) and was headed for a 2 percent decline in 1991 according to the treasury.

4. The current account of the balance of payments had moved over the decade from a series of large surpluses (reflecting North Sea oil revenue) back into deficit by 1986–7. The deficit peaked at £19.6 billion in 1989, before falling gradually in 1990 and 1991 thanks to the recession. But Britain was still expected to have a sizeable deficit in 1992.

5. The public sector had moved into surplus in 1987 in response to buoyant revenue produced by the strong economy. But this disappeared in 1990–1 as the recession deepened, and by the March 1991 budget the treasury was forecasting a borrowing requirement of £8 billion for 1991–2.

6. Public spending rose by 16 percent in real terms but its share of GDP declined from 44 to 39 percent.

7. The number of individual shareholders rose from 7 to over 21 percent of the adult population, or roughly 11 million people, of whom 60 percent owned just one share. But the percentage of listed U.K. equities owned by individuals continued to decline, from 28 percent to roughly 20 percent over the decade.

8. The number of owner-occupiers rose from around 52/53 percent of all households to 66 percent. Three-quarters of homes had central heating by the end of the 1980s, compared with roughly 50 percent at the end of the 1970s.

9. The proportion of the population living on or below the social assistance level rose from 6 to 19 percent between 1979 and 1987. The number of children being raised on social assistance rose from 923,000 to more than 2 million. The number of households accepted as homeless increased from 68,000 to 163,000.

10. Living standards increased by just 1 percent between 1979 and 1987 for the poorest fifth of the population, compared with a gain of 30 percent for the richest fifth. Of the £27 billion in income tax cuts since 1979, some 21 percent went to those earning £70,000 or more a year, who represent just 0.1 percent of all taxpayers. But the 11 percent of taxpayers earning £5,000 or less a year received just 2 percent of the tax cuts.

11. The proportion of babies born outside marriage more than doubled to cover a quarter of all births.

12. Notifiable crime recorded by police rose by 60 percent.

This assessment of what can easily be measured in Mrs. Thatcher's record is obviously mixed—a nation generally better-off, but more unequal.

Even though her administrations increased spending on health, social security and education in real (inflation adjusted) terms, the Conservatives received little credit. It was partly Mrs. Thatcher's style. She appeared uncaring. Mrs. Thatcher might repeatedly state her belief in the National Health Service ("safe with us"), more money might be spent on such "community" services and her governments might reject more radical proposals for encouraging private provision, but the public remained suspicious of the genuineness of her commitment. The extra money appeared to be given half-heartedly and it was never quite enough. . . .

Mrs. Thatcher personified, and to some

extent led, a world-wide shift in thinking away from centralism and collectivism and toward free markets. All industrial countries faced common problems of inflation, rising demands for social spending and complaints over a rising tax burden in the late 1970s. While the solutions varied—and few European countries went as far as Britain in redirecting policy—the previous rate of growth of public spending was checked throughout the Organization for Economic Cooperation and Development (OECD). Mrs. Thatcher can only claim a small direct part in the events which led to the roll back of communism, though she was regarded as an inspiration and example by many in the new democracies of central and eastern Europe. She undoubtedly pioneered privatization, which was eagerly taken up by the new market economies of both eastern Europe and Latin America (notably Mexico and Argentina).

The extent of the change in views from the 1960s and 1970s is sometimes hard to appreciate, but is most clearly seen in the shift in attitudes in the opposition parties. Mrs. Thatcher had always set as one of her aims the destruction of socialism. Insofar as her definition of socialism meant the type of trade-union-led interventionism of the 1960s and 1970s Mrs. Thatcher may have succeeded. As Lord Joseph, her original mentor, wrote in the *Independent* in November 1990, "For monuments to her, look around you. The trade unions and the Labour party no longer breathe fire, but compete with the Liberal Democrats in presenting a reasonable, post-socialist face."

Apart from a change of image, Labour altered its policies, particularly after its third defeat in 1987. The transformation of Labour into a social democratic party along European lines was in large part a response to Mrs. Thatcher's success. . . .

Mrs. Thatcher wanted to do much more than force Labour to change its policies—she wanted to change British attitudes and hence behavior. Her encouragement of property ownership and challenge to monopoly public provision has further undermined the foundations of the Labour and trade-union movement. But, as Professor

Ivor Crewe of Essex University has argued (*The Times*, 4 January 1991), both the enterprise and the dependency communities have grown. The number of self-employed people rose from 1.9 million to 3.1 million during the 1980s, but the number reliant on income support and one-parent benefits increased over the decade from 3.4 million to more than 5.5 million. The self-employed were still only 12 per cent of the workforce. . . .

A whole series of surveys have indicated that the British public remains attached to non-Thatcherite values. The annual British Social Attitudes reports (1983–90) have shown that the British public is "obstinately resistant to the lure of the enterprise culture." The key finding is the rise from 33 to 56 per cent in the proportion favoring higher taxes to pay for better welfare. An analysis of a wide range of survey evidence by Professor Crewe (1990) also showed strong backing for public services, a reduction in support for privatization and a dislike of Thatcherite ideals. Consequently, he argued that "after 10 years of Thatcherism the public remains wedded to the collectivist, welfare ethic of social democracy." That does not mean that people are about to vote for Labour. . . .

Mrs. Thatcher said, shortly after entering Downing Street, that the mission of her government was "much more than the promotion of economic progress. It is to renew the spirit and solidarity of the nation." She succeeded, for a time, in helping to lift the national self-confidence of many.

However, Britain also became more divided, economically, socially, racially and regionally. Thatcherism was primarily a phenomenon of those in work in southern England and the Midlands, and there were only outposts of beneficiaries in northern England, Wales and Scotland. As if in reaction John Major consciously copied President George Bush in talking of a "kinder, gentler" Britain.

Mrs. Thatcher's premiership also posed questions about the role of the state. As she decried the power of government over economic decisions, she centralized power over local government and other bodies which had stood between Whitehall and the individual. She strengthened the power of the state to an extent not seen before. Some of her alleged centralism—the way she ran her Cabinet and Whitehall—disappeared with her and was only a memory within months of her resignation. But other aspects—the gradual erosion of the role of local authorities and the accretion of power in Whitehall—remained.

Mrs. Thatcher's record inevitably appears flawed both because of the forced manner of her departure and because of the serious economic problems at the time. Apart from her loyal band of followers, Mrs. Thatcher may now become an unfashionable figure. . . . A balanced assessment of the Thatcher era will take at least a decade. For the moment, she stands as one of Britain's most remarkable prime ministers. She helped to shift the political debate in Britain. If she did not halt Britain's decline—and no one could do that—she did what a politician could do. She challenged and shook up British industry and society with effects which will last well into the 1990s.